D1561094

University Textbook Series

December, 1991

Especially Designed for Collateral Reading

HARRY W. JONES
Directing Editor
Professor of Law, Columbia University

ADMINISTRATIVE LAW AND PROCESS (1985)
Richard J. Pierce, Jr., Dean and Professor of Law, University of Pittsburgh.
Sidney A. Shapiro, Professor of Law, University of Kansas.
Paul R. Verkuil, President and Professor of Law, College of William and Mary.

ADMIRALTY, Second Edition (1975)
Grant Gilmore, Professor of Law, Yale University.
Charles L. Black, Jr., Professor of Law, Yale University.

AGENCY (1975)
W. Edward Sell, Dean of the School of Law, University of Pittsburgh.

BANKRUPTCY, THE ELEMENTS OF (1992)
Douglas G. Baird, Professor of Law, University of Chicago.

BUSINESS ORGANIZATION AND FINANCE, Fourth Edition (1990)
William A. Klein, Professor of Law, University of California, Los Angeles.
John C. Coffee, Jr., Professor of Law, Columbia University.

CIVIL PROCEDURE, BASIC, Second Edition (1979)
Milton D. Green, Professor of Law Emeritus, University of California, Hastings College of the Law.

COMMERCIAL TRANSACTIONS, INTRODUCTION TO (1977)
Hon. Robert Braucher, Associate Justice, Supreme Judicial Court of Massachusetts.
Robert A. Riegert, Professor of Law, Cumberland School of Law.

CONFLICT OF LAWS, COMMENTARY ON THE, Third Edition (1986) with 1991 Supplement
Russell J. Weintraub, Professor of Law, University of Texas.

CONSTITUTIONAL LAW, AMERICAN, Second Edition (A TREATISE ON) (1988)
Laurence H. Tribe, Professor of Law, Harvard University.

CONTRACT LAW, THE CAPABILITY PROBLEM IN (1978)
Richard Danzig.

CONTRACTS, CONCEPTS AND CASE ANALYSIS IN THE LAW OF (1990)
Marvin A. Chirelstein, Professor of Law, Columbia University.

CORPORATE TAXATION, FEDERAL, Second Edition (1990)
Howard E. Abrams, Professor of Law, Emory University.
Richard L. Doernberg, Professor of Law, Emory University.

CORPORATIONS, Second Edition (1971)
Norman D. Lattin, Professor of Law, University of California, Hastings College of the Law.

CORPORATIONS IN PERSPECTIVE (1976)
Alfred F. Conard, Professor of Law, University of Michigan.

PRINCIPLES

OF THE

LAW OF PROPERTY

By

JOHN E. CRIBBET
Dean, Chancellor and Corman Professor of Law Emeritus
Urbana-Champaign Campus, University of Illinois

CORWIN W. JOHNSON
Edward Clark Centennial Professor Emeritus in Law
University of Texas at Austin

THIRD EDITION

Westbury, New York
THE FOUNDATION PRESS, INC.
1989

Library of Congress Cataloging-in-Publication Data

Cribbet, John E.
    Principles of the law of property / by John E. Cribbet and Corwin
W. Johnson. — 3rd ed.
        p.   cm. — (University textbook series)
    Includes index.
    ISBN 0–88277–718–1
    1. Real property—United States. I. Johnson, Corwin Waggoner.
II. Title. III. Series.
KF570.C7   1989
346.7304'3—dc19
[347.30643]   89–1374
                                                        CIP

    C. & J.Prin.Law of Prop. 3d Ed. UTB
    3rd Reprint–1996

"In civilized society men must be able to assume that they may control, for purposes beneficial to themselves, what they have discovered and appropriated to their own use, what they have created by their own labor and what they have acquired under the existing social and economic order. This is a jural postulate of civilized society as we know it. The law of property in the widest sense, including incorporeal property and the growing doctrines as to protection of economically advantageous relations, gives effect to the social want or demand formulated in this postulate."—**Pound, An Introduction to the Philosophy of Law 192 (1922).**

*

PREFACE TO THE THIRD EDITION

The first edition of Principles of the Law of Property was published in 1962, the second edition in 1975. We have reprinted the prefaces to those two editions, partly for historical reasons (and we "property types" are forever interested in history), but also because they contain the premises on which all three editions have been based. Note particularly the "big picture" story about General Patton and his dog, Willie, which was a true episode, witnessed by one of the authors, then Major John E. Cribbet. (See page xi).

The first two editions of Principles were the work of Professor Cribbet alone. At about the same time, however, Professors William Fritz and Corwin Johnson were collaborating with Professor Cribbet on Cases and Materials on Property. After the untimely death of Professor Fritz, Professors Cribbet and Johnson continued to work together and Cases and Materials on Property is now in its fifth edition. A sixth edition is in preparation and Professors Roger Findley and Ernest Smith will be joining Cribbet and Johnson as editors of the new casebook edition.

Obviously, a third edition of Principles was overdue since even property law has changed considerably in the last decade and a half, especially in the areas of landlord and tenant and land use. Trends that were already apparent in the mid-seventies have continued and new directions have emerged in the public regulation of land use and what is now becoming known as the "jurisprudence of taking." Since these subjects had been handled in the casebook by Professor Johnson it seemed reasonable to make Principles too a collaborative effort. Thus, this third edition emerges as a combined product with the two areas just mentioned (Parts Four and Six) having been totally rewritten by Professor Johnson. There are also major changes, as well as the usual updating, in the remainder of the book and Professor Cribbet has assumed the responsibility for those portions of the materials.

The purpose of Principles remains what it was in 1962. It is not a hornbook and it contains no black letter law in the usual sense. It is not a companion volume to the casebook although it does have essentially the same coverage and is designed to give the student the "big picture" of property law so that he or she will understand its basic principles. It has sacrificed depth for breadth and for brevity. It is not a book for the legal researcher and there are no long compilations of cases and statutes providing ready access to the law in fifty-one jurisdictions. These tools are readily available and there is no need to duplicate them.

In short, Principles is a teaching tool, designed primarily for students and we hope this third edition will be helpful to them as they are introduced, for the first time, into the intricacies of the Anglo-American law of property. We also hope that the book will raise questions about our property system and will cause the students to think about ways in which it can be modernized and improved. For more than four decades we have labored in this particular vineyard and found it exciting and challenging as well as intellectually stimulating. We have tried to communicate some of that enthusiasm, both in the casebook and in this text on Principles of the Law of Property. Whether we have succeeded only you, the students, can judge. In any case, we dedicate this third edition to the thousands of law students who have studied property law with us, primarily at the Universities of Illinois and Texas but also across the nation in colleges of law where we have been visiting professors or where our materials have been the basis of instruction. Anglo-American property law represents a rich lode and we wish you all good mining not only as law students but in your entire professional careers!

JOHN E. CRIBBET
CORWIN W. JOHNSON

Champaign, Illinois
Austin, Texas
January, 1989

PREFACE TO THE SECOND EDITION

The first edition of Principles of the Law of Property was published more than a decade ago in 1962. I still agree with most of what I stated in the preface to that edition, especially about the importance of the "big picture" for the student of land law. There is a plethora of detail available in the multi-volumed treatises, the law review articles, and the reported cases, but the sheer bulk of this material is more likely to confuse than to enlighten the student. If our property law has a rational base, disclosed in the principles enunciated by the courts and legislatures (and I believe it does), then an overview of those principles will be helpful as a partial chart through the maze. This is particularly true in a period of unprecedented change and in the light of a developing fragmentation in the property curricula of the law schools.

Prior to World War II, property law was typically taught in a series of more or less related courses which left the student with a disjointed view of the common thread which united all property law. In the decades since 1945, the casebook editors have consolidated these courses into two principal packages—the "live" area (estates, landlord-tenant, titles, vendor-purchaser, and land use) and the "dead" area (trusts, wills, and future interests) plus related courses, such as land financing, natural resources, etc. By 1970, these packages had begun to unravel under the pressure of social change and a drive for a kind of limited "specialization", even in law school. I view this new fragmentation as unwise and believe that the integrity of the two basic packages should be maintained in the first two years of law school leaving the third year for specialized seminars, problem courses, and the more technical subject matter areas. Every student should be introduced to the basic principles and then encouraged to go further into those areas which appeal to him. This, incidentally, is the approach being followed by the multi-state bar examination and this textbook has the same scope as the outline for the subject of property on that examination, plus a treatment of the land-use area, without which an understanding of the modern law of land is impossible.

Much of the second edition parallels the first. Some principles have altered very little and the historical background, so important in our tradition-centered institution of private property, has been retained. Errors have been corrected, new cases and statutes have been cited, and the book has been updated to 1975. Large portions of the book are new, however, and it is these portions, reflecting the rapidly changing land law, which required a second edition, lest the student be misled in relying on the first. The landlord-tenant materials have been rewritten in light of the shift toward tenant's (consumer's) rights; similar changes have been made in the sale of land, disclosing the fall of *caveat emptor*; materials on condominium and environmental controls have been added; and the public control of land-use segments have been expanded appreciably to acquaint the student with developments in this most volatile of all property areas.

While it would be presumptuous to call this a book on the jurisprudence of property, I have tried to infiltrate some philosophy into the prosaic fodder and I hope it will be sufficient to help the student form his own judgments as to the relative roles of private volition and public interest. I am convinced that property law is not dull, grubby stuff and I have tried to enliven the text with enough humor to make even the Statute of Uses readable. If attempted levity reduces the level of scholarship, I am apologetic but not contrite.

Finally, I am indebted to the University of Illinois for granting me an administrative leave from my decanal duties so that I could complete this edition in London, while refreshing my knowledge of the English common law which supplied the consistent thread on which the American law of land is based. This edition is dedicated * to my wife, Betty, who encouraged me to persevere despite the siren call of day-to-day administrative and teaching duties.

JOHN E. CRIBBET

Champaign, Illinois
December, 1974

---

* Not to be confused with a common-law or statutory dedication, carrying with it the profits à prendre, if any.

PREFACE TO THE FIRST EDITION

Property, which once dominated the law school curriculum by occupying from one-fourth to one-third of the total class time, is now being reduced to a more modest role in most American colleges of law. The shrink in quantity does not necessarily mean a decline in quality; it does herald a less leisurely approach to this significant segment of the law. The modern first year property course now encompasses no less than six traditional favorites—personal property, estates in land, landlord and tenant, vendor and purchaser, titles (conveyancing), and rights in land (land use). Although property books are legion, ranging from excellent multi-volumed treatises to concise outlines of the subject, none of the textbooks are tailored to the "new look" in the law school curriculum. This volume has been prepared with that gap in mind.

Principles of the Law of Property has two primary objectives: (1) to give the reader the "big picture" of "basic" property law, both in depth (history) and in breadth (scope of the subject); (2) to make the student aware of the changing nature of property law and the need for critical, responsible reform in what is all too often conceived as a static field of jurisprudence.

A true episode will illustrate the first objective. During the closing days of World War II, the author was aide de camp to Lt. General Troy Middleton, senior corps commander in General George Patton's Third United States Army. Patton's headquarters was in Luxembourg City and, following his return from SHAEF in Paris and a conference with General Eisenhower's chief of staff, General Smith, the colorful Patton told his assembled staff of his frustrations. While arguing for a swift, rapier-like thrust into the heart of Germany to end the war, Patton had been rebuffed and General Smith, after explaining that supplies must be diverted to General Montgomery in the north, had patted him patronizingly on the back, saying, "The trouble with you is, Georgie, you just don't understand the big picture!" As Patton told the story, his English bulldog, Willie, lay at his feet. Now Willie, when bored, was apt to yawn and when yawning it looked suspiciously as if he were smiling. He chose this moment to yawn and Patton, launching a kick which nearly carried him off his feet, yelled, "Laugh you little S.O.B., laugh, you don't know the big picture either!" As events have turned out, I doubt if Willie did know the big picture, it seems likely that General Patton did not, and most days I wonder if anyone did. I am convinced, however, that it is necessary for lawyers to know the "big picture" of property and to discern how its complex principles interact to form a coherent institution.

Obviously, a mass of detail is necessary before the lawyer can handle concrete situations but there are excellent volumes available for that purpose. The real danger is that the student will bog down in the narrow technicalities of property law and fail to *understand* the role of property as an institution and the law as a molder of that institution. Viewing the various strands of property law in a rather brief compass should offset that danger and give new insight into our property system.

As to the second objective, it is ironic that just as curricular time is contracting the law of property is expanding. On top of the always-important traditional areas of property has been piled the exciting new subject of land use with its heady infusions of public policy. The subject has not even been carefully defined as yet but it clearly includes zoning, planning, subdivision controls, water problems, public development of land, etc. While these matters must be left principally to senior seminars or advanced courses of a specialized sort, their impact is felt in the basic course and some coverage is essential so that the student will early be aware of the social, as well as the private, side of property rights. Some elementary understanding of zoning, for example, will do more to show the changing nature of property law than any amount of abstract discussion about how "law must grow or it will die."

Basically, this is a book on the law of land and personal property is treated only incidentally to illuminate certain property principles, such as the nature of gifts and the importance of possession. This approach has been followed for two reasons: (1) the most important aspect of personal property—commercial transfer—is the subject matter of specialized courses in the curriculum (Sales or Commercial Law) and requires textual treatment of its own and (2) Professor Brown's one-volume text on Personal Property is so complete that any extended duplication of that subject matter is unwarranted. At appropriate points in the text citations have been made to the Brown volume and the serious student should incorporate the cited materials by reference in order to complete "the big picture" of the law of property.

Finally, any contemporary writer in so ancient and fundamental a field as that covered by this book owes virtually everything but the organization and the sentence structure (and parts of those too!) to others more able than himself. To single out any specific group for special mention would be unfair and, in any case, appropriate documentation throughout the book discloses this debt to the past.

JOHN E. CRIBBET

Urbana, Illinois
June, 1962

*

SUMMARY OF CONTENTS

PART FIVE. METHODS OF TITLE ASSURANCE

PART SIX. THE USE OF LAND

PART SEVEN. CONCLUSION

xiv

TABLE OF CONTENTS

PART SIX. THE USE OF LAND

*

PRINCIPLES

OF THE

LAW OF PROPERTY

*

Part One

INTRODUCTION TO THE CONCEPT OF PROPERTY

Chapter 1

WHO OWNS BLACKACRE?

Blackacre is the most celebrated tract of land in the world of the law—a world which you are now entering. Blackacre is wholly mythical, yet totally real. It is a concept, living in the realm of the mind and doubly valuable since much of the law of property has the same type of reality. The small farm at the edge of town, the big estate in the country, the apartment building, the skyscraper, your father's house, the squalid tenement, the majestic cathedral—they are all Blackacre and the law of property deals with the rights and duties of people in relation to the Blackacres of this planet. (At the present rate of scientific progress in space this statement may need enlarging.) How does one acquire Blackacre? What are his rights and duties while he owns it? What happens to it on his death? How can he give or sell it to others? How many of the decisions about land use are subject solely to private volition? How many of the decisions must be made by society, speaking through various levels of government? In the complex answers to these simple questions lie the law of property.

Who owns Blackacre? Surely the answer is simple enough: Henry Jones does; he inherited it from his father, John. It may be, but consider the following facts about Blackacre. When John Jones died the tract was mortgaged to *A* for half its value and the debt has not been paid. John had contracted in writing to sell the place to *B*, subject to the mortgage, but the sale has not been completed. John made a will in which he left one-half of Blackacre to his wife for her life, then to his son Henry in fee simple absolute. The will left one-quarter to *C* in trust for the benefit of John's alma mater and the remaining one-quarter to his daughters, *D* and *E*, not as tenants in common but as joint tenants with right of survivorship. It is rumored that the wife is dissatisfied with the will and plans to renounce it and seek either dower or her statutory share of the land. *F*, who owns an adjacent farm,

1

has for many years used a road across Jones' tract to reach the highway and claims to have a right to continue doing so in spite of Henry's protest. *F* also claims the right to remove stone from the northern part of Blackacre under an old oral agreement. *G* was in actual possession of the parcel at John's death and has a written five-year lease as a tenant farmer which antedates both the mortgage and the contract. *H,* an oil company, has come forward with a written lease of the mineral rights under the surface of Blackacre. This lease was not recorded in the county recorder's office at the date of John's death and there is some contention that it is invalid. Blackacre is still raw farm land but the county has zoning laws and, in the master plan for the area, the tract is zoned for future residential development only. *B,* the contract purchaser, had planned to use the premises for a chemical plant if he were able to acquire a good title to the land. The state and federal governments are concerned about the environment and any major change in land use may require the filing of an environmental impact statement with the appropriate body. *J* claimed . . .; but that's enough for purposes of illustration.

Who owns Blackacre? What does it mean to ask such a question in the light of the facts just given? Later, perhaps, you can answer these questions. Now, it is sufficient if you see why they are significant to an understanding of the law of property. The hypothetical case is most appropriate to a tract of land (real property), but you will recognize that many parts of it could also be applied to automobiles, animals, goods of various kinds, stocks and bonds (personal property or chattels). This gives you an insight into one of the basic aspects of property law—you must distinguish between the thing (*res*) and the estates, interests, or claims which people may own in the thing. As a layman you are accustomed to speak of the thing itself as property; as a lawyer you must come to realize that property is a concept, separate and apart from the thing. Property consists, in fact, of the legal relations among people in regard to a thing.[1]

If the concept of property as defined in the previous paragraph is correct, an intriguing question arises as to which individuals have standing to sue to protect their property rights. In Sierra Club v. Morton[2], the United States Supreme Court gave the traditional answer. An environmental group, like the Sierra Club, has standing, i.e., a property right, only if it or its members

1. "The term 'property' is one which is often abused and seldom defined or subjected to a careful analysis. It is generally used to denote a subject matter of a physical nature, such as a house, a car, or a cow. It is also used to denote a complex group of jural relations between the owner of a physical subject and all other individuals." Nelson v. La Tourrette, 132 Ind.App. 584, 178 N.E.2d 67, 68 (1961).

2. 405 U.S. 727, 92 S.Ct. 1361, 31 L.Ed.2d 636 (1972).

would be affected in a particular way by a development which would change the natural environment (in this case a Disney Enterprises ski resort in what had been a part of the Sequoia National Forest). Mere special interest in such environmental changes is not enough. Dissenting justices took a less restrictive view and the controversy is far from over but it is clear that individuals or organizations have standing only if they can, at least, show a special reason for suing to protect the *res*. It is true that Mr. Justice Douglas, in dissent, felt that the trees themselves should be able to sue, through a representative, thus giving a new definition to the term property, but that position is unlikely to prevail.[3] For the indefinite future it remains true that property, in a legal sense, consists of the legal relations among people in regard to a thing (*res*).

In a complex society the relations between individuals are certain to be complicated. It follows that property law will be complicated as well since it is the product of society, the rules designed to maintain order in the acquisition, transmission, and use of things. Of course, these things constitute wealth, power, status, security, and many more verbal images which can be conjured up by the simple term, property. In the pages which follow, an attempt has been made to state the basic principles which govern the Anglo–American law of property. Even when reduced to broad principles the *corpus* of the law is complex, but it should be more manageable than when viewed in a multi-volumed treatise or even in a single, large text. These principles should serve as a chart to guide the beginning law student so that he will not lose his way in the maze and as a refresher to the older lawyer to remind him of the rational basis of our property law.

3. See Stone, Should Trees Have Standing? Toward Legal Rights for Natural Objects, 45 So.Cal.L.Rev. 450 (1972) and Baude, Sierra Club v. Morton: Standing Trees in a Thicket of Justiciability, 48 Ind.L.J. 197 (1973).

Chapter 2

THE INSTITUTION OF PROPERTY

It could be argued, although not very plausibly, that even animals have an institution of property.[1] A dog certainly treats a choice T-bone, once in its possession, as if it were a species of private property. Other dogs are warned off with appropriate indicia of ownership and even the master will trespass with respect after the original gift has been made. Why then is the bone not the dog's property? Aside from man's conceit in refusing to extend human institutions to orders lower than himself, the dog loses out because its rights in the juicy morsel are not protected by law. They are protected solely by brute force and while that may be sufficient for animals it is not enough, or should not be enough, for man. Jeremy Bentham, the great English legal reformer, put it thus: "Property and law are born together, and die together. Before laws were made there was no property; take away laws and property ceases."[2] Note that the thing, land or chattel, would still be there even in a state of anarchy and that man could stand over it, growling like a dog, but we could no longer call it property. One of the best simple definitions of property was given by Professor Cohen: "That is property to which the following label can be attached. To the world: Keep off unless you have my permission, which I may grant or withhold. Signed. Private citizen. Endorsed: The state."[3]

Thus analyzed, it will be seen that property can exist in relation to an infinite number of things, real and personal, tangible and intangible. It is obvious enough that land, automobiles, and a cask of rare amontillado can be the subject of property.[4] It is just as true, but less obvious, that checks, promissory notes, debts due from one person to another, documents of title such as

1. See Ardrey, The Territorial Imperative 3, 4 (1966) and Freedman, Crowding and Behavior 26–32 (1975).

2. Bentham, Theory of Legislation, Principles of the Civil Code, Part I, 112, Dumont, ed., Hildreth Trans. (1864).

3. Cohen, Felix S., Dialogue on Private Property, 9 Rutgers L.Rev. 357 (1954).

4. See Reich, The New Property, 73 Yale L.J. 733 (1964). Professor Reich would expand considerably the possible objects of property. He lists among these "new" objects of property, created by an expanding state: income and benefits, jobs, occupational licenses, franchises, contracts, subsidies, use of public resources, and services. These objects of property are of prime importance in modern society but they are beyond the scope of this text which confines itself to the more traditional view of property and focusses primarily on the principles of the law of land.

4

bills of lading and warehouse receipts, stocks, bonds, shares, patents, trademarks, copyrights, and even good will can be brought within the ken of property. If a thing so intangible as good will can be classified as property, where does the long embrace end? Can an idea, the merest wisp of something that is to be, enter the fold? Perhaps, as the court in Belt v. Hamilton National Bank said: "The law now gives effect to a property right in an idea even though the idea may be neither patentable nor subject to copyright. Such a concept, however, in order to receive the protection of the law, must be more than a mere abstraction. It must be reduced to a concrete detailed form. It must, of course, be novel." [5]

Occasionally, in your reading of cases, you will find a court saying, "We cannot grant the relief requested by the plaintiff because no property interest is involved and in this class of cases the court acts only to protect property rights." Is not this reasoning in reverse? [6] If the court grants the protection, it has created a species of property, as in the Belt case. If it refuses the remedy then no property can be said to exist because "take away laws and property ceases." No particular harm is done by the legal formula set forth above so long as you realize that property is not a mystical entity established by some fiat outside the framework of the law.

To the Western mind, the term property automatically translates as *private* property. It is the individual's relationship to the *res* that comes to mind, not the state's. We are aware of a large amount of public ownership and of a growing quantity of public interest and control even in private ownership, but the fundamental concept remains individualized.[7] Not surprisingly, Anglo–

---

5. 108 F.Supp. 689, 691 (D.D.C.1952).

6. Many courts have believed that it is reasoning in reverse. Note how one state court analyzed the question of whether property had been taken, destroyed, or damaged.

"It should be pointed out initially that the Minnesota Constitution requires compensation where private property is taken, destroyed, or damaged. Any statement of what constitutes 'property' can only be nebulous at best. Not every economic, social, or other interest or advantage is a property right, the taking of which must be compensated. As the United States Supreme court pointed out in United States v. Willow River Power Co., 324 U.S. 499, 502, 65 S.Ct. 761, 764, 89 L.Ed. 1101, 1107 (1945), only those economic advantages which have the law back of them are property rights. Thus, to begin by arguing that compensation must be paid because a property right has been taken really merely raises the question that must be ultimately answered. Property is more than the physical thing—it involves the group of rights inhering in a citizen's relation to the physical thing. Traditionally, that group of rights has included the rights to possess, use, and dispose of property." Alevizos v. Metropolitan Airports Commission of Minneapolis and St. Paul, 298 Minn. 471, 216 N.W.2d 651 (1974).

7. For an exploration of the growing emphasis on the public side of private property see Cribbet, Concepts in Transition: The Search for a New Definition of Property, 1986 U. of I. L.Rev. 1.

American law reflects this view of property to a high degree. But we must not suppose that this craving for "*my* rights in a thing" is solely Western or is confined to the growth of the higher civilizations. In fact, it seems to be universal, both in time and space. Although at one time it was supposed that primitive man lived in a state of true communism and claimed nothing, save collectively with his brethren, the later writers [8] establish that private property of a rudimentary sort did exist even in very early times.

If primitive man had some notion of private property, what happens to the idea that law is the basis of property? Did law, with its courts and enforceable remedies, also exist in these early societies? Obviously not, but there was custom and taboo and a kind of "obedience to the unenforceable" which stood in the stead of the formal law to come. Some writers would call this law of sorts and would not stick to the narrower definition of law which requires an effective sanction before a rule can be classified as law.[9]

No modern society has ever been without some species of private property; it is the extent of private ownership, the quantum of rights that the individual has over the thing, not the fact of private ownership, that has varied. Even the Russian Communists did not abolish *all* private property; it was the means of production that Marx and Engels proposed to put in the hands of the proletariat.[10] In present day Russia, a large quantity of private property remains and the ownership of a house, for example, may not differ materially from that in the West.[11] Of course, a great chasm yawns between the property systems of the communist world and the free world, but common elements remain.

Although the right to private property is one of the pillars of Western faith, its moral justification has always posed a bit of a problem for the philosophers, economists, and all those who must rationalize the existence of institutions. The difficulty has been particularly great in the case of land, since it existed in a state of nature, apparently created by God for the use of all of His

8. See Lowie, Incorporeal Property in Primitive Society, 37 Yale L.J. 551–554 (1928).

9. For a lucid presentation of this point of view see Goodhart, English Law and the Moral Law 18–28 (1953). Professor Goodhart states that he borrowed his theory from Sir Frederick Pollock. "After pointing out that history shows that law precedes the organised society which we know as a State and that it can exist without a formal sanction, he concludes that: 'Law is enforced by the State because it is law: it is not law merely because the State enforces it.'" Goodhart calls this the obligation theory of law and adds: "I should therefore define law as any rule of human conduct which is recognised as being obligatory."

10. Marx and Engels, The Communist Manifesto.

11. Gunther, Inside Russia Today 374–375 (1958), and Maggs, The Security of Individually–Owned Property Under Soviet Law, 1961 Duke L.J. 537.

creatures. How did it happen that some individuals had rights over so much of it and some none at all? It was easier in the case of man-created things, for then you could say that the individual was entitled to the fruit of his labor. This whole subject is an intriguing one and you may want to explore it further,[12] but for the moment it will be sufficient to state that at least five theories have been propounded as the justification for private property—the occupation theory, the natural rights theory, the labor theory, the legal theory, and the social utility theory. The latter theory furnishes the most satisfying rationalization. "Thus we are finally driven to *the social utility theory.* This is really implied in the preceding theories and supplies the link that binds them all together. In ancient as in modern communities, the individual is helpless as against society, however much under modern democracy society may see fit to extend the bounds of individual freedom. If we allow the individual to seize upon unoccupied wealth, if we recognize the existence of certain rights in what are deemed to be the products of labor, if we throw the mantle of the law around the elements of private property—in every case society is speaking in no uncertain voice and permits these things because it is dimly conscious of the fact that they redound to the social welfare. Private property is an unmistakable index of social progress. It originated because of social reasons; it has grown under continual subjection to the social sanction. It is a natural right only in the broad sense that all social growth is natural." [13]

We would add two comments to the preceding analysis. First, the universality of private property is itself an argument for its continued existence. It appeals to all societies, at all stages of historical development. It is wise to harness that which has so deep an appeal to human nature and to concentrate on devising the best possible system of property which will serve the needs of both the individual and the public. A later portion of the book will deal with that problem in the modern world.[14] Second, the paramount argument for private property is that it best protects the rights of the individual. The old argument about property rights versus individual rights is passé; they are one and the same. Only as the individual has specific, and to a limited extent exclusive, rights over a thing, does he have that liberty of action which is vitally necessary to the preservation of a free society.[15] Absolute dominion by the individual is out of the question; absolute control by the state is unthinkable. The great problem of the law, and of those who develop and administer it, is to find the

---

12. For a brief discussion see Seligman, Principles of Economics 131–134 (1905).

13. Id. at 134.

14. See Part Six. The Use of Land.

15. Lippman, The Method of Freedom 100–102 (1934).

golden mean between the two extremes.   Professor Powell has said it perfectly, "So then, the test of goodness must be some mean between the concept of the complete dominance of the individual and the idea of the all-importance of the state.   It is an assumption of any society based on private property that it is good for the individuals to have liberty of a high order in the use of things they own.   It is a postulate of any society which hopes to survive that there be limits imposed on the absoluteness of property so as to assure rules which will be accepted as fair for the distribution of scarcities.   Whenever a change in the institution of property is being tested for its quality, the change is unadulteratedly bad if it restricts an individual and contributes nothing to the social welfare.   If, however, as is usually the case, it restricts the individual but contributes something to the social welfare the disadvantage and the advantage must be weighed against each other and such action taken as the tipping of the scales thus found may dictate. This falls far short of a clear chart to wisdom but it provides an approach which will force persons to face squarely questions of social values, while preserving the benefits of private property." [16]

Now, we must turn our attention from the consideration of property as an institution on a universal basis to the specifics of Anglo–American property law.   This is the system which you will be called upon to administer and, we hope, improve.   Let us, then, tackle the principles of our property law.

16.   1 Powell, The Law of Real Property 33, 34 (1949).

Part Two

THE SCHEME OF OWNERSHIP IN ANGLO–AMERICAN LAW

Chapter 1

SOME BASIC CONSIDERATIONS

The study of any technical subject is plagued by its terminology and by the wealth of detail that needs explaining before the broad outlines make much sense. Where do you begin? It's no good replying, "at the beginning," because this is an Alice in Wonderland world and the origins are lost behind the mirrors. Professor Llewellyn has suggested the "bramble bush" approach [1] but its appeal lies mainly in retrospect. This chapter is an attempt to solve the dilemma by weeding out a few basic problems before proceeding to the main body of the subject.

SECTION 1. REAL AND PERSONAL PROPERTY [2]

Our first basic consideration is the distinction between real and personal property. Real property relates to land and those things, such as houses, barns, and office buildings, which are more or less permanently attached to it. Personal property describes all other things which are subject to individual rights, whether they are tangible or intangible. This simple definition blurs at

1. The nature of this approach is suggested by the verse quoted in the introductory page of The Bramble Bush:

"There was a man in our town
And he was wondrous wise.
He jumped into a bramble-bush
And scratched out both his eyes—
And when he found that he was blind,
With all his might and main
He jumped into another one—
And scratched them in again."

This cold plunge technique has much to commend it but you, as a beginning student, doubtless prefer a more gradual immersion. Nonetheless, you should read all of Professor Llewellyn's classic lectures on law and its study.

2. Personal property will be covered only incidentally in this book which deals primarily with land law. See Brown on Personal Property (3d ed. by Raushenbush 1975) for an excellent text on personal property.

9

the edges and it is not always easy to tell whether a specific item is realty or personalty, e.g., what about growing timber, a pig pen on runners, household appliances that are attached to the plumbing, etc.? A body of decisions has developed to help you predict the correct category when the need arises.

The terminology used here makes no sematic sense because a car is just as "real" as a farm and the family mansion is more "personal" to the owner than shares of stock. The explanation lies, not in the history of property but of procedure. At early common law a real action (so called because it led to the return of the thing itself) was used when land was wrongfully detained by another but a personal action (which gave only a money claim against the wrongdoer) was proper where things other than land were involved. Thus, the *res* took the name of the action and we have, to this day, real property and personal property. The latter is also called a chattel, derived from cattle, the most frequent form of personal wealth in the early days.

This was not just a matter of terminology but a distinction of great importance. The law governing realty was quite different from that relating to personalty and many of these distinctions exist today, although their impact is gradually diminishing. Reference will be made to this bifurcation throughout the book and distinctions will be pointed out. It should not be supposed, however, that the classification is a wholly meaningless accident of history. There is a genuine difference in kind between these two categories of property and all systems of law take some notice of the cleavage. The distinction is really between movables, in the main created by man, and immovables, based on the raw earth which is our common heritage. Artificial distinctions which obfuscate the law and complicate its practice should be abolished but the real difference should never be lost to sight.

SECTION 2. ACQUISITION OF PROPERTY

A second basic consideration relates to the acquisition of property. How does a specific *res* become the subject of individual rights? The most obvious answer is by transfer from a prior owner, either by sale or by gift during the life of the donor or at his death. The rules governing these transfers comprise a large part of the law of property and are discussed in Part Three of this book. But this leaves the basic question unanswered. How was the property right acquired in the first instance? Here the personal versus real property distinction is significant.

Most personalty is created specifically for sale or use by the creator and clearly belongs to its producer. Thus, a new automobile is the property of the manufacturer, a new calf the property of the owner of the mother, and a new story, piece of music or design pattern, the property of the holder of the copyright or patent. There may be complications, of course, and the applicable law of patent or copyright must be carefully followed if ownership is to be fully protected. Moreover, there are special problems arising when the chattel is a wild animal never before subject to human dominion (it usually belongs to the first effective possessor of the animal *ferae naturae,* although this is complicated if the capture is made on the land of another); a lost article not reclaimed by the original owner (it typically belongs to the finder as against all but the "true" owner, although again the rights of the owner of the land where found [locus in quo] may give a bit of trouble); or a finished product, the result of materials belonging to one individual with labor furnished by another, without agreement between them, so that ownership is difficult to ascertain (the rules governing accession are applicable here). But in most cases, the issue of original ownership of chattels is easy to settle and does *not* become increasingly difficult with the passage of time. The life of most items of personal property is relatively short and they are consumed or pass into the rubbish heap without causing much of a legal tangle.

Land furnishes an interesting contrast to chattels. It is permanent, immovable, and, with minute exceptions, not produced by man. Moreover, it is the source from which most other property must come. He who controls the land does, in fact, control the destiny of man. This monopoly, which we call private property in land, must come by a grant from the sovereign. It would be possible to grant quantities of land to an individual for his life, or for so long as he could profitably use it, and then return it to the state for regrant to another. In practice, we have not followed this pattern and once the land has been granted it belongs to that individual to sell or give to another. The state may take it back for public purposes (eminent domain) or, if a man dies without a will and without heirs, it may revert to the state (escheat), but each of these events is the exception, not the rule. A major question should leap into your mind! How can you ever be sure that you are dealing with the true owner of land when the chain of title must go back many years to a government grant? This puzzler will be discussed in Part Five but you should note now that it is a factor in land law which is largely absent from the law of chattels.

In England, the acquisition of original title goes back for centuries (usually to 1066 and the Norman Conquest) and the pattern of distribution of the land will be treated in some detail in a succeeding chapter. In the United States, the origin of land titles is much more recent but also more diverse since the land came from various sources by conquest,[3] purchase, and cession. However, the fundamental principle remains constant: the ownership of land is initially acquired from the state and passes by an ever-lengthening chain of title to the succeeding generations.

SECTION 3. POSSESSION, SEISIN, TITLE, AND OWNERSHIP

Our third basic consideration lands us squarely in the middle of a semantic jungle. We must sort out, in a preliminary way, the meanings of several closely related words—possession, seisin, title, and ownership.

"Possession is nine points of the law." This old saw happens to be true and in many a legal controversy involving property rights the principal issue can be phrased, "Who had the prior possession of this thing?" The common-law forms of action which were used to recover a detained *res* or its value (trover, detinue, replevin, ejectment) were usually phrased in terms of possession or of a right to possession and while more complicated questions of title could be raised it was not always necessary to do so. Suppose *A* finds an antique silver plate and then *B* takes it from *A's* house. *A* can recover the plate in an action of replevin, based on his prior possession, even though he cannot be said to be the owner of it. *A* simply has a better right than *B*. Or suppose Blackacre belongs to *O*, who has moved away and apparently forgotten his land, but it is being farmed by *A* who recently moved into the vacant land without permission. If *B* should eject (dispossess) *A* without any

---

3. An intriguing question arises, how did the United States acquire title to the land originally possessed by the Indians? The answer to that question is an involved (and ongoing) saga but for some light on the issue see Johnson v. McIntosh, 21 U.S. (8 Wheat.) 543, 5 L.Ed. 681 (1823) where Chief Justice Marshall denied the validity of Indian land titles and said: "Conquest gives a title which the courts of the conqueror cannot deny, whatever the private and speculative opinions of individuals may be, respecting the original justice of the claim which has been successfully asserted." See also Tee–Hit–Ton Indians v. United States, 348 U.S. 272, 75 S.Ct. 313, 99 L.Ed. 314 (1955) and Note, Indian Title: The Rights of American Natives in Lands They Have Occupied Since Time Immemorial, 75 Col.L.Rev. 655 (1975). In Cohen, Original Indian Title, 32 Minn.L.Rev. 28 (1947) the author concluded that: "The notion that America was stolen from the Indians is one of the myths by which we Americans are prone to hide our real virtues and make our idealism look as hard-boiled as possible." Myth or not, the story of our treatment of the Indians is not a pleasant one but we cannot develop it in this book.

authority from *O,* then *A* can recover Blackacre by an action in ejectment.   Clearly, *A* does not own the land but he has a protected interest in it.   Of course, if *B* sets up the title of *O* and establishes that he is the agent or is acting with authority from *O,* then *A* will lose.   *O* was not in possession but he did have the right to possession, based on his ownership.   Suppose *B* simply asserts *O's* title but does not tie himself to it, i.e., suppose *B* says, "I do not own Blackacre but neither do you; *O* does?"   This is technically known as a plea in *jus tertii* (title in a third person) and there is some authority that it is a good defense to a possessory action.[4]   The more recent cases, however, reject such a defense and allow *A* to recover on his prior possession.[5]

Possession, then, is something different from title and ownership but it is an exceedingly valuable property right.   Indeed, if continued long enough and adverse to the interests of the owner, it can ripen into absolute ownership by operation of the statutes of limitation or the doctrine of prescription.   These matters will be discussed in Part Five of this book.

What is possession?   The watch on my wrist and the wallet in my pocket are clearly in my possession.   So is the farm which I am cultivating daily or the house in which I am living.   These are simple illustrations and mask the difficulty of the question.   Actually, possession is one of the most illusive concepts in the law and you will have to wrestle with it for a long time before you see the dimensions of the problem.   This is because possession, like many other words, has a lay meaning and a legal meaning and they are not identical.   The law may say that a man has possession of a thing when the man in the street would hoot at the notion.   Thus, if a master gives a watch to a servant to take to a friend, the watch is never out of the possession (legally) of the master.   The servant does not have possession of it, he has only custody and if he converts the watch to his own use he is guilty of larceny, which requires a taking from the possession of the owner.[6]   This example is illustrative of a host of similar situations in which the word possession becomes very slippery indeed.   As your study progresses you will see why this is so; lawyers and courts are using the term to express certain legal consequences and the word may be expanded or contracted to make it better serve its purpose.   This is confusing to the neophyte but essential to the sophisticated practitioner.

The difficulty is further confounded by the practice of speaking of *actual* possession and *constructive* possession.[7]   The former

4.   Doe ex dem. Jefferson v. Howell, 1 Houst. (Del.) 178 (1855).

5.   Bradshaw v. Ashley, 180 U.S. 59, 21 S.Ct. 297, 45 L.Ed. 423 (1901).

6.   State v. Schingen, 20 Wis. 74 (1865).

7.   In one classic case the court was forced to deal with three types of pos-

tends to correspond to the lay concept of the term while the latter is a fictional use of the word to cover situations where the law requires a certain result but the facts fail to fit actual possession. Thus, two people may have possession of the same *res* at the same time although the individuals are widely separated geographically. The classic example is the gratuitous bailment [8] of a chattel. *A* loans his car to *B* to use to go to a party. *A* retains the constructive possession (sometimes defined as the right to immediate possession) of the car; *B* has the actual possession of the vehicle. If it is stolen or damaged, either party can maintain a possessory action against the wrongdoer since each has the requisite possession. Compare this with the master-servant situation where the former has possession, the latter custody, and make some sense out of the distinction, if you can!

Note that if the bailment were for hire, i.e., if *B* paid *A* to let him use the car for one week, a different result would obtain. *B* would then have the actual possession of the automobile but *A* would no longer have constructive possession (no right to immediate possession). *A* would then have a reversionary interest which would entitle him to possession of the vehicle at the end of the bailment, but not before, unless there was a breach of its terms. Similarly, in a lease of land, the lessor would have the reversionary interest and the lessee the possessory interest.

Professor Lawson offers a definition of possession that is worth pondering: "In practice indeed possession is often said to be a social rather than a physical fact, in the sense that a person will be held to possess a thing if he has the sort and extent of control that society, considered as being represented by the ordinary reasonable man, would regard as appropriate to the kind of thing and the circumstances of the case." [9]

Seisin is an even more mystical concept than possession. Although it has been argued that seisin applied to chattels as well as to realty,[10] for most practical purposes we can confine the term to real property. Its importance is largely historical but no understanding of our real property system is possible without some grasp of its meaning. For reasons which will be clarified later, the early English landholder seldom was thought of as owning the land, rather he was seised of it. The protected interest

---

session—actual, constructive, and constructive actual. New York–Kentucky Oil & Gas v. Miller, 187 Ky. 742, 220 S.W. 535 (1920). This would seem to be carrying a good thing too far.

8. A bailment is a transfer of possession of personal property, without the transfer of ownership, for the accomplishment of a particular purpose.

Gratuitous means that no consideration was paid and the bailor can reclaim the chattel from the bailee at will.

9. Lawson, Introduction to the Law of Property 33 (1958).

10. Maitland, The Seisin of Chattels, 1 L.Q.Rev. 324 (1885).

of value to him was his seisin. When he transferred his interest he did so by "livery of seisin", accomplished by going on the land and physically transferring a clod of earth or a twig to the new holder of the land. If an intruder ousted him from the land, he was said to have been disseised and until he re-entered the land, either by self help or by the appropriate legal remedy, he had lost his seisin. This could be disastrous since, if the original holder of the land died without regaining his seisin, the land did not descend to his heirs, while on the death of the disseisor the seisin would go to the latter's heirs by "descent cast."

In other words, seisin carried with it many aspects of ownership and was a vital part of the early land law. Just how vital will become more apparent when we discuss the types of common-law estates. But what was seisin? Many learned articles [11] have tried to answer this question but we can "get by" if we treat it as possession plus a mystical something which described a man's claim to an estate of freehold in land. If this seems a bit sticky, we apologize and ask your indulgence until we clarify freehold and non-freehold estates in a subsequent chapter. Non-freehold estates correspond to what the layman thinks of as leasehold interests in land, and seisin, for historical reasons, had no application to them. The tenant had possession of the leased property but he was not seised. The landlord (owner) did not have possession but he did have seisin, for his was the freehold estate (a reversionary interest, it is true). The owner of a chattel who had it under his control was said to be in possession of it but the owner of Blackacre in a similar situation was said to be seised of the land.

Title is a term frequently used as synonymous with ownership. While this is not strictly accurate we must recognize that it is so used or we will be confused unnecessarily. It certainly means something more than mere possession, although frequently "proof of title" is made solely by establishing prior possession; but one can have title to a thing and never have been close to possession of it. We prefer the definition that: "Title is a shorthand term used to denote the facts which, if proved, will enable a plaintiff to recover possession or a defendant to retain possession of a thing." [12]

The following illustrations should illuminate the definition. (1) *A* disseises *B* and holds Blackacre for twenty years (the relevant statute of limitation) adversely to *B's* interests. After twenty years, *A* has a better title than *B*. (2) *A* finds a ring which *O* purchased from its manufacturer. *B* takes the ring from *A*. *A* has a better title to the ring than *B* (based on prior possession); *O*

11. For one of the best, see Maitland, The Mystery of Seisin, 2 L.Q. Rev. 481 (1886).

12. Lawson, Introduction to the Law of Property 35 (1958).

has a better title to the ring than *A* (based on *O's* ownership by purchase). (3) *A* lives in a house on Blackacre and has an abstract of title (history of the various deeds, mortgages, etc. relating to the land) going back to a patent deed from the United States. *B* has never been in possession of Blackacre but has a warranty deed to the land for which he paid a large sum of money to *C* in good faith, relying on documents which *C* showed to him. These documents were forged. *A* has a better title to Blackacre than *B*.

You will note that in each case one person was said to have had a better title than another person. Most titles are relative and all that is necessary in the particular case is to say that *A* has a better title than *B, C,* or *D*. Seldom does the law speak of absolute title in the sense that *A* has title as against the whole world. The layman frequently does so and the lawyer may do so as a matter of convenience, but he recognizes that title is relative even when he speaks as if it were absolute. This is perfectly illustrated in real estate transactions where the vendor of land must have a merchantable title in order to force the purchaser to take it. An absolute or perfect title is not required, just a title which meets the ordinary demands of the market place. It may have slight flaws in it, but so long as a reasonable man would not object to them that is all which the law requires. Absolute title to land has meaning only in the Torrens system of land registration where the title to Blackacre is in fact registered in a public office and guaranteed by the state. Only a small proportion of land titles in the United States are of this sort, although registered titles are common in England and the rest of the common-law world. The registered title to an automobile is an analogous example in the personal property field.

This brings us, finally, to ownership. The interesting fact is that we could talk about the law of property and never mention ownership if it weren't for the significant lay meaning of the term. Early in the introduction we asked, "Who owns Blackacre?" We rather quickly saw that this was a meaningless question except as interpreted to read, "Who owns various estates or interests in Blackacre?" Legally, it would be more correct to ask, "Who has title to these various estates, etc.?" Or, "Who has possession or the right to possession of various geographical parts of Black-acre?" Or even, "Who is seised of Blackacre?"

The simple truth is that Anglo–American law has not made much use of the term ownership in a technical sense. The Roman law has, and *dominium* in the civil-law countries means ownership in the absolute sense of that term. In the next chapter we will explore the matter a little further and show why ownership in the sense of *dominium* never became a vital concept in the English, and hence American, law.

This still leaves the basic question unanswered. What is the *usual* meaning of ownership when it appears in our law? Apparently, it is the general concept of absolute title or at least of merchantable title. It is that quantum of rights in a thing that cause most people to assume that the thing "belongs" to the individual. In the case of land it is an estate in fee simple absolute (to be explained in due course) and in the case of chattels it is the same concept *sans* name.

SECTION 4. LAW AND EQUITY

The fourth and final basic consideration deserts property law entirely for a brief excursion into the adjective law and a quick look at those engaging twins—common law and equity. One of the unique features of Anglo–American law is that during its period of gestation the embryo split into two parts and although an attempt was made to weave the two into one the seams still show. The common law developed in the royal courts of King's Bench, Common Pleas, and Exchequer and was administered through the rigid common-law forms of action which prescribed the relief to be given when certain facts were established. The common-law system of estates was worked out within this framework; the rights of property protected by these courts were called legal rights; and the recognized estates and interests were referred to as legal in character.

The rigidity of the common-law remedies, plus certain other factors,[13] led to the denial of justice in many instances and the

---

13. The rise of a separate court of equity was due to many factors but Professor Delmar Karlen points out four common-law inadequacies of major importance:

"1. **Remedies.** Substantially all the forms of action yielded only money judgments. The only important exception was the action of ejectment which could be used to recover the possession of real property. There was no practicable remedy for recovery of possession of a chattel, because replevin, as we have noted, was limited to cases of unlawful distress, and detinue allowed the defendant the option of returning the chattel or paying its value.

"The greatest deficiency in common law remedies was the lack of any machinery to prevent wrongs, or to force a defendant to perform a contract or other obligation.

"2. **Harsh Rules.** Some of the rules administered in the common law courts were harsh and contrary to common notions of fairness. There was a good deal of emphasis upon formalism and ritual, particularly in the field of contract and property law. The tendency was to insist upon a literal interpretation of anything in writing.

"3. **Jury Trials.** While trial by jury was a vastly better method of determining facts than the methods which it supplanted, it had the disadvantage that juries were sometimes incapable of understanding complicated transactions, and in the Middle Ages, frequently subject to corruption or intimidation by powerful men. Thus the character

litigants appealed to the king, the source of all English justice, for additional relief. Instead of referring the parties to the law courts which had already denied relief, the king entrusted these matters to his chancellor, who in those days was usually an ecclesiastic. Slowly, a separate body of law grew up which was supposed to represent the king's conscience and to be more equitable and just than the common law. At first it was erratic and followed no set precedents, indeed the decrees were said to vary with "the length of the chancellor's foot." Not surprisingly, the chancery eventually fell into the hands of lawyers and became more systematic and "legal" in its approach.

At this point of development it was apparent that there were two rival systems of "law" in England—one was the common law and the other was equity, administered by the court of chancery. An epic struggle ensued [14] and out of the conflict emerged a kind of truce which allowed the two systems to co-exist in the legal world. In case of direct clash, equity was supreme but in the course of time the gears came to mesh well and the two parts became a satisfactory whole which represented English law. In 1873, in the Supreme Court of Judicature Act, England finally combined the courts themselves into a single High Court of Justice but separate branches remained for law and equity. In general, the American states had followed the English pattern and either set up separate courts of law and equity or created two divisions of the same court to handle the subject matter falling into the two areas. Starting with the Field Code in New York in 1848, the American legal reformers tried to wipe out the procedural distinctions between law and equity and develop a unified system. This process of amalgamation of law and equity is still going on but the split has left deep marks which may never be fully eradicated.

This is not the forum to explore the various differences between law and equity, the former with its jury trial as a matter of right and its so-called judgments *in rem,* the latter with its judge (chancellor) and master in chancery in lieu of a jury and its decrees *in personam.* What is important, here, is that certain parts of property law came to be administered in equity rather

of prospective litigants in some cases determined the feasibility of resort to the common law courts.

"4. **Blind Spots.** Some institutions and areas of conduct were not covered by the common law at all. Conspicuous were trusts and the administration of estates of persons who had died." Karlen, Primer of Procedure 149 (1950).

14. This struggle came to a head in Courtney v. Glanvil, Cro.Jac. 344 (1615), when the Court of King's Bench re-leased, on a writ of habeas corpus, an individual who had been imprisoned for contempt of a decree of a court of equity. King James, desiring to assert his supremacy over all judges, appointed a committee of lawyers to look into the conflict. On the basis of their report, he decided in favor of chancery. Cases of outright conflict were few, however, and, in the main, equity complemented law rather than clashing with it.

than in the common-law courts and another difficulty to ready understanding of property terminology arose. The rights and interests recognized by chancery were called equitable and so we have legal title and equitable title, legal rights and equitable rights.

Two of the principal heads of equitable jurisdiction will illustrate the point. (1) All trusts are administered on the equity side of the court (the historical reason for this will be clarified later) and although the trustee is said to have the legal title to the property interest, i.e., the title to the land or chattel is transferred to him by a method recognized by the law courts, the equitable title to the *res* is said to be in the beneficiary. This means that equity will protect the interests of the beneficiary and force the trustee to deal fairly with him. (2) If either party to a written contract [15] for the sale of an interest in land fails to carry out his bargain, equity will grant a decree for specific performance, i.e., force the vendor to deed the land to the purchaser and the latter to pay the purchase price. The only remedy at law is money damages for breach of contract and, since that is felt to be inadequate for a *res* so unique as land, equity asserts its extraordinary jurisdiction. The result is that the vendor has legal title until the deed conveying the interest in land is delivered to the purchaser but the purchaser is said to have equitable title just as soon as an enforceable contract for the sale of land is executed. This result arises from a maxim of the court of chancery, "Equity regards as done that which ought to be done." Since the vendor ought to convey the interest in land on performance by the purchaser, equity will treat the matter as if he had done so and give the buyer equitable title to the land. This doctrine had but limited application to personal property since chattels were seldom treated as unique (one plow was just as good as another) and money damages at law were adequate.

Like the distinction between real and personal property, this division into law and equity makes some sense aside from history, because of the inherent difference in the procedural relief involved. But the separate courts of law and equity have, all too frequently, created a chasm where none needed to exist. Even

---

15. In general, an oral contract for the sale of land is unenforceable because of the Statute of Frauds, the original English version of which reads in part: ". . . no action shall be brought . . . upon any contract or sale of lands, tenements or hereditaments, or any interest in or concerning them . . . unless the agreement upon which such action shall be brought, or some memorandum or note thereof, shall be in writing, and signed by the party to be charged therewith, or some other person thereunto by him lawfully authorized." An Act for Prevention of Frauds and Perjuries, Statute 29 Charles II, Chapter 3 (1677). Under proper circumstances the doctrine of part performance may allow the equity court to grant specific performance of even an oral contract. See p. 160 infra.

merger of the two courts has not always bridged the chasm.[16] Keeping in mind essential differences, the legal reformer should strive to eliminate all of the non-essentials.

With some of these basic considerations out of the way, we are now ready to turn our attention to the English law's principal contribution to the institution of property—the doctrine of estates.

16. "The most important obstacle to complete procedural unification in the United States is the presence in the federal constitution and in most state constitutions of guarantees of trial by jury in civil cases at law. As it has been graphically put, this guarantee of jury trial 'is the sword in the bed that prevents the complete union of law and equity.'" Scott and Simpson, Cases and Other Materials on Civil Procedure 246 (1950).

Chapter 2

THE CONCEPT OF ESTATES IN PROPERTY

The peculiar Anglo–American doctrine of estates can only be appreciated in the light of history. Indeed, Mr. Justice Holmes' famous aphorism, "There are times when a page of history is worth a volume of logic", fits property like a glove. Furthermore, a detailed discussion of each permissible estate is required to give any real substance to this area of the law. Both of these techniques will be applied in succeeding chapters, but we must clarify the concept of an estate before we pick its bones. The doctrine of estates is sometimes treated as if it made no sense except as an accident of history. This can scarcely be true or the doctrine would not have survived through the centuries. The law and lawyers may be a conservative force in society but they are not so hidebound as to retain a thoroughly worthless system of property law out of blind veneration of the past. F.H. Lawson, Professor of Comparative Law in the University of Oxford, successfully disposes of this bugaboo in *The Rational Strength of English Law* and concludes that, following some basic simplification of the law in England in 1925, "it (property law) is not only one of the finest parts of our law, but . . . in its main principles and structure it is superior to all foreign laws dealing with this subject." [1]

Once the student has mastered the full panoply of estates and interests in land (for it is to real property that most of this relates) he is apt to feel that it is the only system of land ownership and to forget that Anglo–American law represents but one way of dealing with the problem. Before this attitude has a chance to develop, let your mind speculate on the wide range of possible ownership schemes. As a starter, consider the following. (1) The state could own all of the land within its borders and (a) lease to its citizens for a set period of time, (b) lease to them for life, or (c) lease to them for so long as they use it wisely and economically. (2) The state could transfer outright the ownership of all of the land to its citizens for a fixed price and then regulate the extent of the interests which the new owner might have in the land, e.g., (a) allow the citizen to use it for life but then require that it go to his eldest son, etc., or (b) allow the citizen to own it absolutely, to do

---

1. Lawson, The Rational Strength of English Law 76 (1951). Pages 75–106 of this book deal with property and are eminently worth reading.

with it as he sees fit. (3) The state could grant land to families rather than individuals and give every member of the family a collective share in ownership so long as he remains loyal to the group. (4) The state could adopt the view that the land belongs to the person in possession of it and that all rights depend on possession and use. Abandonment of possession would leave the land open to the first taker by peaceful means.

This should be enough to suggest the wide range of possibilities. Note that all of those listed start with the state doling out certain rights in the land. This is essential at some point of time, although it may be in the forgotten past and may be only a recognition of an existing situation, since our earlier discussion established that property exists only as a creature of law, which presumes an organized state. It is the scheme of ownership which the law allows, after the land is distributed by the state, which is the important point to us.

The two principal legal systems of the West are the common law and the civil law (derived from the Roman law and the basis of most continental European law). The former developed the doctrine of estates as the scheme of land ownership, the latter settled on *dominium,* which denoted a nearly absolute property right. "The owner had an absolute title, he had an absolute right to dispose of the thing he owned, and his right to use it was limited by so few restrictions of a public-law character that it, too, could almost be called absolute. The kinds of incumbrances with which it could be burdened were kept down to the lowest possible number, and where they existed they were carefully distinguished from the *dominium* over the thing, which was regarded as retaining its character of a general undifferentiated right over the thing capable of resuming its original plenitude by the mere disappearance of the incumbrance." [2] This does not mean that the Roman law failed to recognize any interests outside that of *dominium.* It allowed hiring (*locatio conductio*), similar to a lease for a term of years and *usufruct,* not unlike a life estate. But these interests were subservient to the *dominium,* the true ownership of the land. They existed as mere rights issuing out of the land of another and not as separate estates of temporary ownership. Even the *fideicommisa,* which looked like a trust for purposes of a family settlement and required the *heres* (heir) to transfer to a third person designated by will, was bound by the idea of absolute ownership because the *heres* took the entire *dominium.*[3]

2. Lawson, The Law of Property 87 (1958).

3. For a more elaborate discussion of this point see Hargreaves, An Introduc-

tion to the Principles of Land Law 44–57 (3d ed. 1952).

If the preceding paragraph sounds a bit muddy, it boils down to the fact that in the civil law a thing has one absolute owner and while other individuals may have claims arising out of the thing they are personal claims (rights *in personam*) and not separate estates with real claims of ownership (rights *in rem*). The contrast with the common-law system will be apparent in a moment.

The estate concept is the child of feudal notions of tenure. Feudalism is long dead and tenure has modern meaning only in the landlord-tenant relationship, but the child has reached a healthy maturity. When the English king granted land to a powerful noble in return for military service, and that noble in turn allowed a lesser noble to use it, and so on down the line, it was difficult to speak of any one individual as owning the land. There was a tenurial relationship between the parties but what was the relationship of the parties to the land? The king could be said to own it ultimately, but what did the first noble, the second noble, etc., down the line, own? Of course, you could have said that they each had a personal right issuing out of the land, but with the development of forms of action it came about that the land itself could be regained, if there had been improper disseisin, and thus each party seemed to have a real right in the land. Each person in the tenurial chain owned an estate in the land but not the land itself. This was the crude beginning for what has become a highly sophisticated concept.

The estate and the land are two separate things.

Blackacre, the land	*Some Possible Estates in Blackacre* 1. Life estate—owned by *A* 2. Contingent remainder—owned by *B* 3. Reversion—owned by *C*

The estate is purely conceptual, yet it is treated by the law as if it were a real thing with an identity of its own. The land is, of course, a physical thing that is permanent, immovable, and continues to exist regardless of the changing character of the estates that relate to it. Note that the term estate is *not* being used in the lay sense, "Mr. Henry Blythe White has a beautiful country estate." The layman equates estate with Blackacre; the lawyer sees it as a separate entity.

A brief look at some of the basic estates will be sufficient to clarify the concept. Later, after a dip into history, we will spend some time on a detailed analysis of the permissible estates. By far the most common estate is the fee simple absolute. This shorthand expression (its origin will be explained later) signifies that the owner of it has the full quantum of rights possible in Blackacre. A familiar illustration is to visualize each right as a stick and say that in the fee simple absolute (usually shortened to fee simple) the owner has the complete bundle of sticks. This estate comes closest to the Roman-law concept of *dominium* and to the lay concept of absolute ownership. Subject to the rights of the state, to zoning laws, and to the rights of adjoining landowners that no nuisance [4] be committed on the premises, it could be said, without too much inaccuracy, that he who owns a fee simple estate in Blackacre owns Blackacre. Of course, the fee simple owner may decide to mortgage his estate or incumber it in various ways and while he would still be said to have a fee simple its utility would be greatly reduced.

Assume that *O* has an estate in fee simple in Blackacre. He has a wife, *W*, and one son, *S*. *O* would like to leave the land to the son eventually but *S* is now a young boy and *O* wants to be sure that the mother is provided for during her lifetime. To accomplish both results,[5] *O* can carve his estate into two new estates, either by an *inter vivos* conveyance (a deed delivered during his lifetime) or by a testamentary disposition (a will which speaks at his death). He can give *W* an estate for her life, followed by an estate in fee simple to *S*. This latter estate would be called a remainder, i.e., it is what remains after the life estate in *W*.

Several important points must be made. The moment *O* dies, if a will has been employed, *O's* fee simple estate becomes two new estates, one in *W* for life, the other by way of remainder in *S*. But the land, Blackacre, is physically unchanged, it has not been carved into two parts nor will it be. Only the estates have changed and they exist apart from the land. Moreover, both estates are *presently* in existence even though one of them, the remainder, will not become possessory until a future date, the death of *W*. *W's* estate is a present, possessory estate of indeterminate duration. So long as she lives she is entitled to the possession of Blackacre, to its rents and its profits. Subject to the doctrine of waste,[6] she can treat it as her property but, of course, will have some difficulty in selling or mortgaging her estate

4. The law of nuisance is based on an old Latin maxim, *sic utere tuo ut alienum non laedas* (use your own property in such a manner as not to injure that of another). The maxim suggests the scope of the doctrine.

5. *O* could also use a trust and place the legal title in a trustee, directing him to pay the proceeds to *W* for life and then convey the land to *S* on *W's* death.

6. Waste is the legal doctrine which determines the obligations of the life tenant to a remainderman or reversioner. Thus, a life tenant cannot remove the top soil, tear down a building, or cut the growing timber without being called to account for "wasting" the estate.

because of its uncertain duration. Does she own Blackacre? Of course not, but she does own a life estate *in* Blackacre.

S also has a present estate in Blackacre but it is not now possessory. He must wait for his estate to "fall in" on the death of his mother before he can claim a right to rents and profits. *S's* estate is also called a future interest [7] to distinguish it from a possessory interest. Note that *S* did not receive his estate from *W* but from *O*. He will not inherit Blackacre from *W* on her death; it has been his in remainder since the death of his father. Since *S* has a present estate, he can sell it or mortgage it and on his death intestate it will pass to his heirs. Its present value is diminished only by the existence of *W's* life estate. In this case, *S's* remainder is in fee simple because *O* gave him all of the bundle of sticks except the life estate. The remainder could itself be a life estate, however, as when *O* devises to *W* for life, remainder to *S* for life, remainder to another son, *X*, in fee simple.

If *O*, in the illustration above had conveyed the land to *W* for life but made no further provision as to disposition of the land, it is apparent that a large part of the bundle of sticks would have remained in *O*. This transaction could be viewed in several ways. (1) *O*, who had the fee simple before, could be said to have it still, subject to a life estate in *W*. (2) *O* could be said to have converted his present, possessory interest in Blackacre into a future interest. (3) *O* could be said to have changed his fee simple absolute into two estates, a life estate in *W* and a reversion in himself. The estate in reversion which *O* now has will be seen to be quite similar to *S's* remainder in the previous example. If the interest following a particular estate (the life estate in *W*, so called because it is only a fragment—*particula*—of *O's* estate) is transferred to a third person it is called a remainder but if it is retained by *O*, either expressly or by implication (as where nothing is said about what is to happen to his estate after *W's* death) it is called a reversion. Technically, the estate doesn't revert to *O*, he had it all the time, but the right to possession does revert to him and hence the name of the estate. Whenever an owner fails to dispose of all of his estate in the land there will be a reversion in him or in his successor to the title.

While still dealing with the broad concept of estates, we should take a preliminary look at the difference between a vested and a contingent remainder. A remainder is vested when its owner would be entitled to take possession of Blackacre immedi-

Vested

7. This terminology, "future interest", can be quite misleading. Some courts say the remainder is a present estate but a future interest. Actually, it is a present interest as well; only the enjoyment by way of possession is postponed. But, since the usage is so common, you must be prepared to deal with it.

ately upon termination of the particular estate (usually by the death of the owner of the life estate). The first example above was of a vested remainder because *S* would take possession just as soon as *W* died. Both the person to take the estate and the quantum of the estate were known. No condition had to be fulfilled other than the death of the life tenant. In the second example, the reversion too was vested, since the identity of the reversioner was known and *O* was to take as soon as the particular estate came to an end. Technically, these estates are said to be vested *in interest;* they do not vest *in possession* until the life tenant's death.

Consider the following example. *O* conveys to *W* for life, remainder to the first son of *O* to reach the age of twenty-one. *O* and *W* are childless at the time. There is a remainder all right but in whom is it vested? If *S*, a son of *O,* aged one year were alive, in whom would it be vested? This is an illustration of a contingent remainder and there are two contingencies to be fulfilled: (1) a son must be born to *O* (although *W* would not necessarily need to be the mother) and (2) that son must live to be twenty-one years of age. When both conditions are met the remainder will vest in the son, but not until then. It is not enough for the particular estate to come to an end; the contingencies too must be fulfilled.

What would happen if the contingencies were not met? Then, the estate would revert to *O* or his successors in title. Thus, whenever you have a contingent remainder you always have a reversion which will be effective if the condition is not satisfied. However, the reversion itself is conditional since it will give the estate back to *O* only if the contingent remainder fails to vest. Despite this attribute, the interest in *O* is still called a reversion and *not* a contingent reversion. Note that a contingent remainder is not truly an estate at all, but only the "expectancy" of an estate if the proper events take place. Nonetheless, even this "expectancy" came to be alienable (transferable) if the proper form of deed was used and it is common to speak of the owner of a contingent remainder just as we do of a vested remainder.

In this chapter we have dealt with the estates concept in terms of real property and it is true that its full development took place in relation to land. At the time when estates were evolving most of the wealth was in the soil and there was no need for a complicated system for the few chattels of importance. There is no necessary block which prevents the application of the doctrine of estates to personalty today and to some extent the idea of a split between the *res* and the estate is to be found in the modern law of personalty. This is especially true in shares of stocks and bonds. But the essential distinction between realty and personalty remains and there will never be a need for an extensive system of estates in items so short lived as most chattels. It is, after all, the permanency of land which creates the desire to control its destiny far into the future and this is the *raison d'être* for much of the doctrine of estates.

It has been the purpose of this chapter to introduce you to the idea of estates, to show you how a split between the *res* and the estate in the *res* can lead to flexibility and to a diverse pattern of ownership. Before we turn our microscope on the individual estates, we shall take a broad look at the historical setting which gave rise to our present system.

Chapter 3

THE HISTORICAL BACKGROUND OF
ANGLO–AMERICAN PROPERTY LAW

Law is a child of its past; property law still suffers from its infantile repressions. Our law of property was born in feudalism and came to maturity as feudalism was dying. It is a tribute to the intellect of the early property lawyers that the system has so long survived the society that give it birth. Our task is to try to understand the origins of the law so that we may grasp its modern essence. Only then can we be sure of retaining that which is meaningful and rejecting that which has outlived its social usefulness. This is not the place for a detailed or profound historical study,[1] but the sketch which follows should carry us forward in our search for the principles of the law of property.

SECTION 1.   THE RISE OF FEUDALISM

Feudalism grew out of the chaos of the Dark Ages, the period from the fifth to the tenth centuries A.D. It is difficult for us to visualize the total collapse of Western civilization which followed the decline of the Roman Empire. It was not just the fall of a single state but the disintegration of all law and order. Even the habit of or feeling for a stable society gradually disappeared. It became once again, as in the dawn of history, a world of disorganized individuals who looked to their own might for the minimum essentials of life. Unfortunately, we can best visualize the scene by realizing that we live on the brink of a similar precipice. A total nuclear war could reduce modern society to the same horrendous condition that preceded the rise of feudalism.

The need for security and some sense of stability survived the collapse of the Roman peace. Since it could not be found in the state, the individual turned to the strongest of his fellows and put his fate in hands which appeared to be more capable than his own. Thus arose the practice of *commendation* by which a weaker man became the vassal of a stronger man, the lord, through a ceremony

1. For a more detailed coverage with citations to a number of leading sources see 1 Powell, Real Property 35–66 (1949). See also, Bergin and Haskell, Preface to Estates in Land and Future Interests 1–18 (2d ed. 1984).

of homage which promised mutual duties of support and protection. The vassal needed protection for more than just his family
and himself; he needed security for his property which consisted
almost solely of land. The land was his means of livelihood and if
he lost it to marauders he might as well lose life itself. Feudalism, from the start, was both a system of government and a
method of holding property. The lord was, in effect, given the
land which he must then protect. The vassal no longer owned
what had been his land, he "held" the land "of" the lord as if he
were a tenant. This method of landholding had little in common
with the modern law of landlord and tenant, except the name, and
should not be confused with it. The land which the vassal now
held was called his "fief", "feudum," or "feud" and has become the
"fee" of our modern law.

This system of feudal tenure did not end with a simple
relationship between one lord and one vassal but became, by the
process of "subinfeudation," a lengthening chain between the top
feudal lord and the actual possessor of the land. There was no
theoretical limit to subinfeudation and as many as five or six
mesne lords might be involved, each serving as a link between the
lord above and the vassal below. As the central state began to
reassert its strength, the king became the lord at the top of the
heap and the only one who was always a lord and never a vassal.
Even this last statement needs modification, for William the
Conqueror was himself a vassal of the King of France. The
pattern was much as follows:

King
|
Tenant in chief (*in capite*)
|
Mesne lords (both lord and vassal)
|
Tenant in demesne (the vassal in possession of
the land)

This feudalistic system was general over all of western Europe
but it never became the sole method of land ownership on the
Continent. There were isolated pockets that held out, where the
landowners did not become tenants of some powerful noble. This
land was called *allodial* [2] as opposed to tenurial and it was subject
to various fates. Some of it developed into petty kingdoms and
other tracts were linked to the kings of France or Germany by
non-feudal ties. In England, on the other hand, all of the land
was subjected to feudalistic tenure by William the Conqueror and

2. Allodial means free, not held of
any lord or superior.

allodial lands were eventually unknown. This point is significant because the universality of feudalism in England led to the consolidation of the law into a systematic whole, while no such result followed on the Continent since the "law of the feuds" could not be applied to the *allodial* land.

English land law begins, for all practical purposes, with 1066 and the Battle of Hastings. The Anglo–Saxon England which existed before the Norman conquest had its own system of law, undoubtedly influenced by the feudalism of the Continent, but within a generation it had been absorbed into the new Norman scheme. How this happened is a fascinating story in its own right, but the key factor is that one powerful noble, William the Bastard, stood at the top of the landholding pyramid and all of the land in England was "held" of him. This complete feudalisation of England is eloquently evidenced by the Domesday Book,[3] a register of landholders compiled by William for tax purposes. The pages of the book reveal the substitution of the formula, "*A* holds of *B; B* holds of the King," for any prior conception of land ownership.

What was this law of the feuds? How was the relationship of tenure controlled between the king, the lords, and the vassals? The first question requires a look at the incidents of feudal tenures; the second a survey of the courts and remedies of twelfth century England. Tenures must, at the outset, be classified as free and unfree. Feudalism was an aristocratic concept and you can be sure that no overlord would be found plowing in the field. He restricted himself to such gentlemanly pursuits as warfare, hawking, hunting, and the ravishing of lovely ladies. The free tenures stopped just short of the actual tillers of the soil, the *villeins* who were bound to the land by an unfree tenure. We will first discuss free tenures and then turn briefly to the unfree type, followed by a quick look at the court structure which enforced them both.

---

3. The Domesday (pronounced Doomsday) Book did not get its awesome title until 1179, though it was held in universal respect, bordering on terror, as a record solid enough with which to confront doomsday. In 1986, England celebrated the 900th anniversary of its most important single historical treasure—the Domesday Book. For an excellent, brief account of the Book and its importance see Arnold, The British Are Making Book on Great and Little Domesday, 17 Smithsonian 83–95 (1986). The article notes that the Book "stands alongside the Bible and the Koran as one of the world's three most famous books. . . . By the time the book was commissioned the upheaval of the Norman Conquest was developing into some kind of recognizable pattern, with most of the land having been taken away from its Saxon owners and given to William's Norman barons (or tenants-in-chief). After all, they had conquered England for him in the first place on the promise of getting land. There were 1400 of these tenants-in-chief who paid land tax to the king and they in turn leased land to subtenants, the cotters, sokemen (free peasants) and villeins of the piece."

SECTION 2. FREE TENURES

There were four types of free tenure, each of them designed to fulfill a particular need. The principal need was for *security* and the typical tenure therefore was *knight service.*[4] The name fairly well describes the tenure. In return for his feud (fee), the tenant agreed to furnish forty days of armed service to the lord per year. At first this probably was done by the tenant himself but later he hired men to serve in his stead and as the need for a private army diminished, with the growth of the central government, a money payment (scutage) was substituted for the original personal service.

A second need was for *splendor*, for the full panoply of pomp and circumstance which went with a medieval aristocracy. Since there was no money economy, the lord bought these things with land and *serjeantry* tenure was the result. Serjeantry was subdivided into grand and petty; the former being restricted to tenants in chief who performed ceremonial services for the king and the latter covering the less august types of service. Examples of serjeantry tenure included: butlers, cooks, sword bearers, suppliers of military transport and weapons, and such improbable duties as "holding the head of our Lord the King between Dover and Whitsand as often as he should happen to pass over sea between those ports."[5]

A third need was for things of the *spirit.* In those rough times the days on this earth were none too pleasant at best and even a bloodthirsty old lecher had hopes of life eternal. How better make sure of the joy to come than by giving lands for that express purpose? *Frankalmoin* tenure resulted and while it took many forms the tenant was always a priest or a religious body.

The fourth and final need of the times was for *subsistence,* for the crops and products of the soil without which life could not continue. Out of this great need arose *socage* tenure. Actually, it was a kind of residual tenure and Professor Hargreaves[6] suggests that the only accurate way of defining it is to say that it comprised any free tenure which did not fall within the other three types. However, it frequently included labor services on the demesne land of the lord and hence is thought of as the subsistence tenure. It should not, however, be confused with the unfree tenures which will be discussed later and which also related to tilling the soil.

---

4. Knight service and serjeantry tenure are sometimes classified together under the broader heading of military tenure.

5. Blount, Ancient Tenures 57 (2d ed. 1784).

6. Hargreaves, Introduction to Land Law 29 (3d ed. 1952).

Socage tenure was less aristocratic than the other three, in fact it had aspects of the non-feudal, and this had interesting consequences in the development of the law.

In each of the four free tenures certain characteristic services were due from the tenant to the lord, but there were also other rights and obligations involved called the incidents of tenure. These incidents fell into two general classes, first, those which arose during the lifetime of the parties and which involved the personal relationship of the lord and tenant and, second, those which arose on the death of the tenant and hence might be called feudal problems of inheritance. The first class included homage, fealty, and the aids. The second was composed of escheat, relief, wardship, and marriage.

Homage was the ceremony by which the tenant became the lord's man.[7] Fealty was the oath taken by the tenant in which he promised to be loyal to the lord. The duty of the tenant to supply financial support to the lord on specific occasions was called an aid and eventually there came, in England at least, to be three such aids. They were the ransoming of the lord, the knighting of his eldest son, and the marriage of his eldest daughter.

The second class of incidents requires a bit more discussion. What happened to the feud when the tenant died? If he died without an heir [8] there was no problem. The land was originally the lord's, "held" of him by the tenant. Remove the tenant by death without an heir and the land simply returned to him who "owned" it before. This incident was called escheat and is the name still given to the similar process by which the state succeeds to the property of a man who dies intestate without heirs.[9] In feudal times the land also would revert to the lord if the tenant

---

7. Littleton describes homage as follows: "For when the tenant shall make homage to his lord, he shall be ungirt, and his head uncovered, and his lord shall sit, and the tenant shall kneel before him on both his knees, and hold his hands jointly together between the hands of his lord, and shall say thus: 'I become your man from this day forward of life and limb and of earthly worship, and unto you shall be true and faithful, and bear to you faith for the tenements that I claim to hold of you, saving the faith that I owe unto your sovereign lord the king'; and then the lord, so sitting, shall kiss him." Littleton, Tenures, bk. II, c. 1, s. 85.

8. The heir at this date was the eldest son, under the doctrine of primogeniture. England followed this doctrine until 1925 using the Canons of Descent to determine heirship. For a discussion of the Canons see Atkinson, Wills 41–50 (2d ed. 1953).

9. Heirs today are determined by the statute of descent in force in the particular state. The pattern of distribution varies but if there is a surviving spouse and children the former typically takes one-third, the latter two-thirds. If there is no surviving spouse, the children take all. Issue of deceased children take by representation, i.e., they take the share of their deceased parent. The statutes then proceed to spell out a complete scheme of heirship, including collateral as well as lineal heirs and usually ending with a provision for escheat in default of known heirs. See p. 144 infra. For the modern role of escheat see In re O'Connor's Estate, 126 Neb. 182, 252 N.W. 826 (1934).

committed a felony. This *forfeiture* of the feud was said to occur because the felon's blood was attainted or corrupted.[10]

Suppose the tenant had an heir who had attained his majority and was ready and able to succeed to the feud? The tenurial relationship was a highly personal one and just because the lord was willing to be served by the father was no reason that he should have to accept the son. The lord might want the land back so that he could give it to an entirely different person as a tenant. It was finally settled, however, that the land should pass to the heir but that he must pay a sum of money, called a relief,[11] to his lord for this privilege. This may not have been the origin of the modern estate and inheritance taxes but at least it was a feudal incident that had the same effect as our "death duties."

Suppose the tenant died leaving an heir who had not yet attained his (21 years) or her (14 years) majority? This placed a heavy burden on the overlord since the infant could not be of immediate service. To compensate for this difficulty the lord was allowed the profitable right of wardship and marriage. Wardship bore no resemblance to the modern law of guardian and ward, in fact it was the antithesis of it. The lord was allowed full use of the land during the period of minority and was under no obligation to render an account of his stewardship. Even upon attaining majority, the ward had to sue for possession of the land and pay a half year's profits for the privilege of receiving it.

Marriage, the other incident attending minority, was also quite onerous to the infant. Blackstone described it as follows: "While the infant was in ward, the guardian had the power of tendering him or her a suitable match, without disparagement or inequality: which if the infants refused, they forfeited the value of the marriage to their guardian: that is, so much as a jury would assess, or anyone would *bona fide* give to the guardian for such an alliance: and if the infants married themselves without the guardian's consent, they forfeited double the value." [12]

Not all of the incidents, just described, applied to all four types of free tenure. For example, wardship and marriage, which were so prominent in knight service, did not apply to socage. In this latter tenure, the guardian was the nearest relative who was incapable of inheriting the land (a very wise requirement) and the

---

10. In one situation the feud was forfeited directly to the king and did not escheat to the lord. This was when a tenant committed high treason—usually the outcome of having guessed wrong in the frequent struggles for the crown.

11. When the relief was due to the king from the tenants *in capite* it was called primer seisin.

12. Blackstone, Vol. ii, p. 70.

guardian had to account for the profits at the end of his stewardship. Moreover, he could not give or sell the ward in marriage.

In addition to the usual tenures there were certain abnormal
patterns which existed in some districts of England, e.g., gavelkind, borough-English, and ancient demesne. Gavelkind was the
name given to socage tenure in the county of Kent and involved
several peculiarities, including the fact that on intestacy the land
descended to all the sons equally rather than passing by primogeniture and the land itself was devisable at a period when testamentary distribution was unknown for land generally. Borough–
English was the custom, found in some parts of the country, by
which the land descended to the youngest son to the exclusion of
the rest of the children.[13] Ancient demesne was land held by
freehold tenants which had belonged to the Crown in the time of
Edward the Confessor and William the Conqueror. The ancient
demesne tenants were subject to special restraints but also had
special immunities.

SECTION 3. UNFREE TENURES

In spite of these variations, all of the free tenures had much
in common and represented a generally coherent scheme of land
distribution—a scheme which served the needs of a feudal society
quite as efficiently as the present law serves our twentieth century
society. But the feudal pattern did not stop with the free tenures,
it included another important type of land holding—copyhold
tenure, which grew out of the old custom of villeinage. Copyhold
was an unfree tenure and was reserved for those who actually
tilled the soil. It can be understood best by a brief glance at the
medieval manor.

The manor was the basic unit on which English feudalism was
built. The typical manor consisted of: "(a) the land belonging to
the lord, which was called his demesne, (b) the land held of the
lord by free tenants whether in socage or knight service, (c) the
land held of the lord by persons called villein tenants, (d) rights of
jurisdiction exercisable by the lord over the free tenants in the
Court Baron, and over the villeins in the Court Customary, and (e)
waste land on which the tenants were entitled to pasture their

---

13. If the custom of *prima nox*, allowing the lord the privilege of the first
night with the tenant's bride, could be
definitely established as having existed
in England, as it did on the Continent,
then this method of inheritance would
make some sense. The youngest rather
than the eldest son would have the better chance of being his father's heir.

cattle." [14] As we have pointed out previously, the free tenures were essentially aristocratic (especially knight service, serjeantry, and frankalmoin) so it was left to the villeins to do the backbreaking work of medieval farming. They were not free men but serfs who belonged to the manor and thus to the lord. It is true that some socage tenants also farmed the land but they held their feud according to the established incidents and were free men.

The position of the villein was not quite so precarious as it might seem and he was entitled to certain protection in the customary court of the manor. But he did not have any access to the king's court because he was thought of as a creature of the lord over whom the king had no direct control. With the passage of the centuries, the role of the villein changed and he was freed from the soil by processes the discussion of which lie beyond the scope of this book.[15] Suffice it to say that the individual became a free man but that the tenure itself continued to be classified as unfree and the nomenclature changed from villeinage to copyhold tenure. The term copyhold arose as follows: "The copyhold tenant, like his predecessor the villein, held at the will of the lord, but yet at the same time he held on the conditions which had become fixed by the customs of his particular manor. The lord's will could not be exercised capriciously, but only in conformity with custom. He still held a court, and that court kept records of all transactions affecting the lands. These records were called the rolls of the court. When, for instance, a tenant sold his interest to a third party, the circumstances of the sale would be recorded, and the buyer would receive a copy of the court rolls in so far as they affected his holding. Inasmuch as he held his estate by copy of court roll, he came to be called a copyholder." [16]

SECTION 4. COURTS, LEGISLATION, AND THE DECLINE OF FEUDALISM

This, then, was the law of the feuds. Of course, it was not written down in the form of legislation and much of it was more accurately custom [17] than law. It was enforced, when need be, by the courts of the period and they worked out the details of the

---

14. Cheshire, Modern Real Property 23 (8th ed. 1958).

15. Many factors contributed to the villeins' new status, including the shortage of labor caused by the Black Death which made the individual's services more valuable.

16. Cheshire, op. cit. supra note 13, at 25.

17. Some of the customs were not only strange but downright hilarious. Consider for example: "The manors of East and West Enborne, in the county of Berks, have this custom, that if a

feudal structure. Originally, the local courts of the lord handled most of the problems of the manor and there was no law common to all of England. But the king too had a court and from the early days of the Conquest the tenants-in-chief had access to the jurisdiction of the Crown when their land was in dispute. The developing writ system [18] gave them a *praecipe in capite,* a species of the Writs of Right for the recovery of land. Since the writ was so ancient it was dilatory, cumbersome, and subject to the defect of trial by battle.[19] The evolution by which this archaic remedy was ultimately replaced by writs of entry and, finally, by the action of ejectment makes a complicated story. The history of these early forms of action is really the history of the law of land, for within the mystic language of the writs was worked out the full significance of possession, seisin, and the relativity of title.[20] Beginning in 1154, with the accession of the great lawgiver Henry II, the royal courts gradually took over most of the controversies involving the land held by free tenure and eventually even the copyhold tenant found justice in the king's court.

By the early years of the thirteenth century the feudalistic system of tenures was firmly rooted in England. The later history of tenures is a tale of steady disintegration under the inexorable pressures of a changing society. The first departure of major significance came in 1290 with the statute of *Quia Emptores,* one of the most important pieces of legislation in the history of land law. *Quia Emptores* is still on the statute books in England and is considered to be a part of the law of most American states.[21] Simply put, it abolished subinfeudation and provided that all

---

copyhold tenant die, the widow shall have her free-bench in all his copyhold lands whilst she continues sole and chaste (dum sola et casta fuerit); but if she commits incontinency, she forfeits her widow's estate; yet, after this, if she comes into the next court held for the manor, riding backward upon a black ram, with his tail in her hand, and says the words following, the steward is bound by the custom to readmit her to her free-bench:

'Here I am,
Riding upon a black ram,
Like a whore, as I am;
And for my crincum crancum,
Have lost my bincum bancum;
And for my tail's game,
Am brought to this wordly shame:
Therefore, good Mr. Steward, let me have my lands again.' "

Hazlitt, Tenures of Land and Customs of Manors (Blount) 109 (4th ed. 1874).

18. For a brief summary of the development of the forms of action (writs) see Shipman, Common–Law Pleading 54–65 (3d ed. 1923).

19. This method of trial was brought from Normandy by William and allowed the accuser to fight the accused, in the belief that heaven would give victory to the one in the right. The modern jury is a distinct advance over this more primitive type of warfare!

20. Since judgment would be awarded to the one who had a better or prior right to possession, it was not necessary to decide who was the "owner" of the land, only whether *P's* title was relatively better than *D's.*

21. In most states *Quia Emptores* is considered a common-law statute and is treated as a part of the law brought by the colonists to this country and incorporated into the common law of the state.

future alienations of land must be by substitution. For various reasons [22] it was to the interest of the great lords to prevent a further lengthening of the feudal chain and this could be done only by ending subinfeudation. As a result, when a mesne lord conveyed his feud to a stranger the latter stepped into the conveyor's shoes (was substituted for him) instead of becoming a tenant of the conveyor. Since 1290, it has been legally impossible to alienate a fee simple absolute [23] so that there shall be tenure between grantor and grantee; the grantee holds the land as tenant of the grantor's lord. It should be noted that *Quia Emptores* also provided that no more tenures in frankalmoin could be created.

It was impossible to devise land until 1540, with the passage of the Statute of Wills. This meant that prior to that time the land frequently escheated to the overlord for want of an heir. Treason was a common offense, since the landholder was likely to choose the wrong side in the continuous struggle with the king.[24] This meant forfeiture of the land because of the tainted blood. Both escheat and forfeiture gradually reduced the length of the feudal chain and, since *Quia Emptores* had put an end to further subinfeudation, more and more land came to be held directly of the king.

Other forces were also at work, reducing the significance of the various obligations of tenure. Even in the twelfth century the money payment of scutage had taken the place of military service and by the sixteenth century most of the services due in socage tenure had been commuted to a fixed money rent. With the inflation resulting from the discovery of the wealth of the New World these fixed rents ceased to be valuable and indeed were hardly worth the trouble of collecting.[25] Wardship and marriage continued to be important since they gave actual control of the land but they never applied to socage tenure and eventually came to be of value only to the king in knight service. In the seventeenth century even they were abolished and the king received an hereditary excise on beer, cider, and spirits in their stead. In

22. The principal reason was that each addition to the chain carried the overlord further from control, by wardship, of the land itself.

23. It must be noted that this applied only to a fee simple absolute. It was still possible to carve out estates less than a fee simple absolute, as we shall see in the next chapter.

24. Witness the effect of the War of the Roses on the land titles of England.

25. An occasional trace survives, even in the atomic age, as see *Time*, Sept. 15, 1947, p. 27: "The owner of the Red Rose Inn in West Grove, Pa., solemnly went through the yearly ceremony stipulated by a 216-year old deed, handed over one red rose to the heir of William Penn." This species of subinfeudation was possible even after *Quia Emptores* because the statute was held not to apply to the king or his immediate tenants, of which William Penn was one.

1660, the Statute of Tenures marked the end of the strictly feudal period of English land law. It turned knight service and serjeantry into socage tenure, destroying all incidents of value except escheat. The honorary services of grand serjeantry were retained but this had no real significance to land law. The aids were abolished and this ended the last burdensome incident of socage tenure. Frankalmoin was not affected by the Act of 1660 and, in theory, it may still exist if created prior to *Quia Emptores* (1290), but the tenure has no practical modern significance.

The Statute of Tenures applied only to freeholds; copyhold tenure continued in England until the twentieth century. However, the special incidents of copyhold, which included the rights of the lord to the mines and timber of the tenant, could be sold to the copyholder and the great proportion of copyhold land had become freehold by the end of the nineteenth century. The last vestiges of the old distinctions were finally swept away in England on January 1, 1926, when a series of acts, known collectively as "The Property Legislation of 1925," came into effect. All copyholds were automatically converted into socage tenure. Escheat was abolished, even for those cases where an intervening lord could be discovered, and when a tenant dies intestate without any heirs his estate now goes directly to the Crown as *bona vacantia* (property without an owner).

Professor Hargreaves sums up the present law of England: "It follows that for practical purposes all land is now held directly of the King by socage tenure, though the services and incidents have now disappeared, and that consequently the existence of tenure no longer has any direct effects. Its indirect effects, however, still remain, for they are the basis of the modern doctrine of estates. . . ." [26]

SECTION 5. TENURE IN THE UNITED STATES

This chapter has been devoted entirely to English history, for obvious reasons. Feudalism never existed in the United States and, but for its vital role in shaping modern land law, could be omitted from our study. Except for Louisiana, the common law of England is the basis for our legal institutions. "When the American colonies were first settled by our ancestors, it was held as well by the settlers, as by the judges and lawyers of England, that they brought hither as a birthright and inheritance, so much of the

---

26. Hargreaves, op. cit. supra note 5, at 36.

common law as was applicable to their local situation and change of circumstances." [27]   This reception of the English common law into the American stream is a complicated matter and it varies from state to state,[28] but it is clear enough that the broad framework of property law is English, with all of its strengths and weaknesses.

The American colonies recognized, to some extent, the law of tenure and some of the charters provided that the land was to be held in free and common socage. In several colonies attempts were made to set up a "quit rent" system—the reservation of an annual rent on the grant of a tract of land. Some manors were even established, following the English manorial system but apparently no form of military tenure was ever recognized. The American Revolution destroyed any tenurial relationship beween American landowners and the English king but left open the question of whether the state succeeded to the position of the king as an overlord. In theory, this did happen in some states and a tenurial relation continued; in other states, there was an indication that the land was to be considered as allodial and that tenure had ceased to exist, even in theory, after the Revolution. It is interesting to speculate on this distinction between theories of land holding and whether it makes any practical difference which view a particular state adopts, but for our purposes it seems best to conclude, with Chancellor Kent, that in the United States "every real vestige of tenure is annihilated." [29]

This discussion of the historical background of Anglo–American property law has omitted any mention of the Statute of Uses and its widespread influence on property concepts. This statute and the role of the chancery court in the development of the law will be the subject of a later chapter. First, we must make a more detailed analysis of the permissible common-law estates.

27. State v. Campbell, T.U.P.Charlton 166, 167 (Ga.1808).

28. See for example Ill.Rev.Stat. ch. 1, s. 801 (1985). Illinois became a state in 1818 and its law included the enactments of the Northwest Territory which embraced an act of 1795 receiving the English common law and statutes as of the fourth year of James I. The fourth year of James I covers the period beginning March 24, 1606, and ending March 23, 1607.

29. Kent Comm. *24. For an excellent short discussion of tenure in United States with references to the leading articles and books, see 1 American Law of Property 57–60 (Casner ed.1952).

Chapter 4

PERMISSIBLE ESTATES AT
COMMON LAW

Now that we know something about the concept of estates and the feudal society out of which that concept grew, we must turn our attention to the estates themselves. Here, we shall be concerned with the estates not only as they were but as they now are, and an attempt will be made to indicate the contemporary law in each instance. The term estate apparently referred originally to status, i.e., it described the position of the landholder in feudal society. Later the word lost its significance as to status but the terminology remained. Thus, our first major classification is between freehold estates and non-freehold estates. The first category includes the various types of fees simple, the fee simple conditional, the fee tail, and the life estate. The second grouping encompasses the estate for years, the estate from period to period, the estate at will, and the estate at sufferance. These were the only estates that were recognized by the courts of common law and hence they are referred to as legal estates. Eventually, the rise of a separate court of equity enlarged the scheme of permissible estates and we will discuss the enlarged pattern in due course. The common-law courts were quite rigid in their handling of estates and unless the grantor of land followed the prescribed formula the conveyance was likely to be void or to reach an unexpected result. The owner of land was not free to create new types of estates just because they happened to strike his fancy.

The non-freehold estates should not be confused with the unfree tenure of copyhold. The latter was a part of the feudal scheme and a tenant could have a freehold estate (a fee simple, for example) in an unfree tenure. The non-freehold estates, on the other hand, were outside the feudal pattern and historically were not considered to be real property at all. The tenant who leased land for a term of years could not recover his leasehold by a real action but had to resort to a personal action for money damages. Thus, the leasehold was treated as personal property and called by the ambiguous name of chattel real. This term, and some of the legal consequences, have stuck to the non-freehold estates to this day.

SECTION 1. THE FREEHOLD ESTATES

A. THE FEES SIMPLE

When we say fee simple, or even fee, we normally mean the fee simple absolute, the largest quantum of interest that a landowner can have in Anglo–American law. However, there are two other kinds of fees simple which are of some importance: the fee simple determinable and the fee simple subject to a condition subsequent. These latter two estates are covered by the generic term defeasible fees or determinable fees and are also frequently called base or qualified fees. We are now in an area where exact terminology is called for so you must be careful not to confuse terms which, on the surface, seem very close to each other.

---

(1) THE FEE SIMPLE ABSOLUTE

This estate has several attributes which distinguish it from all other estates in land. It is the most common of all the estates and corresponds most closely to what the layman means by ownership. It is freely alienable, i.e., the owner of a fee simple absolute has all of the "bundle of sticks" and can transfer them to anyone whom he may choose, either for value or gratuitously. It is freely devisable, i.e., the owner of this estate can leave it, by will, to any person of his own choosing since the estate is not subject to control by the owner's heirs. (Both of these last statements are modified by the marital rights of a spouse, a matter for subsequent discussion.) If the owner dies intestate, the fee simple will be inherited by his collateral heirs if there are no lineal heirs and no spouse, i.e., the estate can pass, not only to descendants of the owner, but also to uncles, aunts, nephews, nieces and cousins, depending on the statute of descent in the particular jurisdiction. Finally, the owner is entitled to the full protection of the law in safeguarding his estate. He does not have absolute and sole dominion over the land, but so long as he complies with the public law and does not commit a nuisance on the land he can expect the full help of the state in preserving his bundle of rights in Blackacre.

The sum of these attributes means that the fee simple absolute, as an estate, has a potentially infinite duration. The original owner may sell it, give it away, devise it, or die intestate, but the estate itself continues merrily on its way. It can end only if the owner dies intestate without heirs, in which case it escheats to the state or its designees. Of course, the state can also acquire all or a part of it by eminent domain but this is true of any estate or interest in land.

At common law, there was only one way to convey [1] a fee simple absolute. It had to be done by a conveyance "to A and his heirs." Language which varied from this formula would not suffice; thus a grant "to A ", "to A forever," or even "to A in fee simple absolute" would result in a life estate in A rather than a fee simple absolute. This bit of mysticism seems odd to us now and, indeed, the need for the phrase "and his heirs" has been rather universally abolished.[2] A grantor, who has a fee, can now convey it by any language which indicates an intention to transfer an absolute estate. It is significant that the key phrase never was necessary to *devise* a fee simple absolute. But then this latter method of land transfer was not possible until relatively late in legal development—1540, with the passage of the Statute of Wills.

In legal analysis, "and his heirs" were said to be words of limitation rather than words of purchase. "To A ", on the other hand, were words of purchase. This cryptic language meant that A took an estate by the terms of the conveyance itself. Purchase was not used to imply that A paid for or purchased the estate—it might in fact be a gift—but only that he took the land by conveyance or devise. A's heirs, however, took nothing by the terms of the grant (if they ever received the estate it would have to be by descent) so the phrase "and his heirs" described or limited the estate held by A, i.e., a fee simple absolute. Note that when we speak of words of limitation we are using limitation in the old sense of bounding or describing, rather than in the sense of cutting down or holding back. The grant, "to A and his heirs", describes the fact that A takes a fee simple absolute rather than creating a joint estate in A and A's heirs. Even today, a conveyance "to A and his heirs" creates a fee simple absolute in A although, as previously pointed out, the cumbersome formula is no longer necessary.

"And his heirs" were also said to be words of inheritance since they indicated an inheritable estate, as opposed to a life estate

---

1. Convey is a word of art which means to transfer an estate in land *inter vivos*. When an estate in land is transferred by will it is said to be devised.

2. The Illinois statute is typical. "Every estate in lands which shall be granted, conveyed or devised, although other words heretofore necessary to transfer an estate of inheritance be not added, shall be deemed a fee simple estate of inheritance, if a less estate be not limited by express words, or do not appear to have been granted, conveyed or devised by construction or operation of law." Ill.Rev.Stat. ch. 30, § 12 (1985).

which died with the life tenant. Moreover, they were words of
general inheritance in contrast to "and the heirs of his body"
which created a fee tail and were words of special inheritance,
limiting the estate to descendants of *A*. No one is quite sure of
the origin of this famous phrase, "and his heirs",[3] but you should
note that it accurately described the estate in the very early days.
At a time when *A* could neither alienate nor devise land, it had
either to revert to the overlord (if a life estate) or pass to the heir
(primogeniture was in effect) if one existed. So, the words described an estate which would pass on death to *A*'s heir, thence to
A's heir's heir, etc. The change in the nature of a fee in the
direction of free alienability and devisability made the words
meaningless in the original sense but their vitality carried on
until recent times.[4]

(2) The Defeasible or Determinable Fees

Assume *O* has an estate of fee simple absolute in Blackacre.
O is a crusading teetotaler and, while he wants to sell Blackacre to
A, he abhors the thought of a tavern on the old home place. *A* is
dry as a bone and could be counted on to keep out the demon rum,
but *A* will not live forever and moreover he might sell at any time.
Rather than sell *A* the full "bundle of sticks", *O's* lawyer advises
him to convey a defeasible fee. The conveyance reads: "To *A* and
his heirs *so long as* the premises are not used for the sale of
spirituous beverages." *A* now has a fee simple determinable or a
fee on common-law limitation.[5] It has all of the characteristics of
a fee simple absolute, except one—it is not of infinite duration
because it will terminate if the premises are used for the sale of
liquor. The grant says nothing about what will happen if the
forbidden act occurs, but the law will supply this omission. The
estate will go back to *O* (or his heirs), who will then own it in fee
simple absolute again. Perhaps liquor will never be sold on the
land, so *O* is not at all sure that he, or his heirs, will ever possess
Blackacre again; thus it is not possible to call *O's* retained interest
a reversion (as would be the case if *A* had been given a life estate).

---

3. For a good account of the historical background of this phrase see Bigelow, Introduction to the Law of Real
Property 21–23 (3d ed. 1945).

4. The words "and his heirs" may
still be necessary in some states. See
Cole v. Steinlauf, 144 Conn. 629, 136
A.2d 744 (1957). See also, Dennen v.
Searle, 149 Conn. 126, 176 A.2d 561

(1961) and Grainger v. Hamilton, 228
S.C. 318, 90 S.E.2d 209 (1955). In
McLaurin v. McLaurin, 265 S.C. 149,
217 S.E.2d 41 (1975) the court continued
to insist on "and his heirs" to create a
fee simple absolute.

5. First Universalist Society of
North Adams v. Boland, 155 Mass. 171,
29 N.E. 524 (1892).

O has a possibility of reverter, the technical name for the future interest which follows a fee simple determinable.

O could have accomplished the same result by a slightly different technique. He could have conveyed Blackacre "to *A* and his heirs *on the condition that* the land is never used for the sale of liquor and if it is then *O* and his heirs may *re-enter* and repossess the land." This would create a fee simple subject to a condition subsequent. This estate is also called a fee on condition subsequent. *O* would then be left with a future interest, called a right of entry for condition broken or a power of termination. Both of these terms are used but the latter seems to be the more modern terminology. The fee simple determinable and the fee simple subject to a condition subsequent are obviously twins [6] with a great deal in common, but there are times when it is necessary to make a sharp distinction between the two.[7] The former estate terminates automatically on the happening of the named event, whereas the latter requires the affirmative act of re-entry by *O* or his heirs before the estate can be said to be back in the grantor.

It is not always easy to distinguish between the two types of defeasible fees, and poor draftsmanship often confuses the issue even further.[8] As a general guide, however, the words "so long as", "until", etc., denote a fee simple determinable in *A;* the words "on the condition that", "on condition", or words setting up an affirmative right of re-entry in any fashion indicate a fee simple

---

6. See Dunham, Possibility of Reverter and Powers of Termination—Fraternal or Identical Twins?, 20 U.Chi. L.Rev. 215 (1953).

7. Oldfield v. Stoeco Homes, Inc., 26 N.J. 246, 139 A.2d 291 (1958). For a more extended discussion see Williams, Restrictions on the Use of Land: Conditions Subsequent and Determinable Fees, 27 Texas L.Rev. 158 (1948). See also Mahrenholz v. County Board of School Trustees, 93 Ill.App.3d 366, 48 Ill.Dec. 736, 417 N.E.2d 138 (1981).

8. Nor is it always easy to distinguish between the defeasible fees and a fee simple absolute. Frequently, the courts will construe language in the deed as descriptive of the purpose of the conveyance rather than as a limitation on use. For example in Scott County Board of Education v. Pepper, 311 S.W.2d 189 (Ky.1958) land was conveyed "for purposes of a common school house, and for no other purpose." The court held the deed conveyed a fee simple absolute. In City of Tempe v. Baseball Facilities, Inc., 23 Ariz.App. 557,

534 P.2d 1056 (1975) the conveyance read: "Subject to the restriction that the . . . real property shall be operated and maintained solely for park, recreational and public accommodation, and convenience purposes." The court noted that the deed did not provide for a right of re-entry. "Therefore, it does not appear that a fee simple subject to a condition subsequent was created. The language could be construed as merely precatory. . . ." As the court pointed out in Roberts v. Rhodes, 231 Kan. 74, 643 P.2d 116 (1982), "Forfeitures are not favored in the law. The general rule is well settled that the mere expression that property is to be used for a particular purpose will not in and of itself suffice to turn a fee simple into a determinable fee." If a grantor wishes to create a defeasible fee of some sort he should use very specific language (easy to do). If he wants to create a fee simple absolute he should avoid ambiguous language of purpose since it may cause costly litigation at a later date.

subject to a condition subsequent. Professor Gray [9] thought that the fee simple determinable should have been impossible after the statute of *Quia Emptores* because the estate involved a continuing relation of tenure between the grantor and the grantee, whereas the statute allowed only a conveyance by substitution. Whatever may be said for Gray's position,[10] it was not adopted by the courts and both of the estates are very much alive today.

The future interests which follow these estates, the possibility of reverter and the power of termination, have caused a great deal of difficulty in the law. The courts have held that they are not subject to the Rule Against Perpetuities [11] and hence they can continue to exist for an indefinite period of time. The problem is further confounded by the fact that in many states these particular future interests are held to be neither alienable nor devisable.[12] They can descend to the heirs at law according to the local statute of descent or be released to the holder of the defeasible fee, thus giving him a fee simple absolute by way of merger of the present and future estates. The title situation becomes clear when we refer to the previous illustrations. In either case, *O* could release his interest to *A* and settle the matter, but he is not likely to do so since it was he who established the defeasible fee in the first instance. Years pass, the sentiment against liquor drinking fades, and *X* wants to buy the land from *A's* heirs to use for a hotel which will include a bar. From whom must *X* get conveyances? Obviously, he wants a deed from the present holders of the defeasible fee but he must also extinguish the future interest or run into difficulty later. *O* is long since dead and so are his immediate heirs, but the lawyer must trace the pattern of descent to discover the present owners of the possibility of reverter or power of termination and then buy their interests in the land.

In order to eliminate some of these title problems, the various states have passed statutes of limitation which bar the future

9. Gray, The Rule Against Perpetuities §§ 31–32 (4th ed. 1942).

10. The adoption of Gray's position would have simplified the law of estates and prevented the clouding of many real estate titles. On the other hand, the estate must have some social utility since it has been so widely used in practice.

11. Leach, Perpetuities in Perspective: Ending the Rule's Reign of Terror, 65 Harv.L.Rev. 721, 739–740 (1952). For a brief discussion of the Rule Against Perpetuities see p. 82 infra.

12. See Ill.Rev.Stat. ch. 30, § 37b (1985). "No possibility of reverter or

right of re-entry for breach of a condition subsequent is alienable or devisable . . ." In other states the problem can be even more complex since a distinction is drawn between these two future interests and a power of termination is destroyed by an attempt to alienate (assign) it while a possibility of reverter is not so destroyed. Rice v. Boston and Worcester R.R. Corp., 12 Allen 141 (Mass.1866); Halpin v. Rural Agricultural School District No. 9, 224 Mich. 308, 194 N.W. 1005 (1923); contra, Jones v. Oklahoma City, 193 Okl. 637, 145 P.2d 971 (1943).

interest after a period of time.   Some of these statutes [13] put a time limit on the enforcement of a claim after the specific event has occurred, e.g., *O* or his heirs must re-enter the land or bring suit for possession within seven years after Blackacre is used for the sale of liquor.   Other statutes [14] provide that the possibility of reverter or power of termination will cease to be effective after a gross period (say, forty years) from the date of creation of the estate.   Note that these latter statutes have the effect of turning defeasible fees into fees simple absolute after the passage of a sufficient length of time.   They do not abolish defeasible fees but they lessen their impact considerably.

Two additional points should be mentioned before passing to the next estate.   First, defeasible estates are not confined to the fee simple category.   You can have a determinable life estate, i.e., an estate for the life of *A* or so long as he uses the premises for school purposes.   Similarly, you can have an estate for years subject to a power of termination in the lessor, e.g., "to *A* for ten years on condition that he pay the rent the first of every month and keep the premises in repair, if he does not the lessor to have the power to terminate the estate."   In these latter two situations, the possibility of reverter and the power of termination are incident to a reversion in the grantor and will pass to anyone who acquires the reversion.   Thus, if the lessor sells his reversion to another person, the purchaser will have the power to terminate *A's* estate for years for non-payment of rent.   This should be contrasted with the future interests following defeasible fees, which are not incident to any reversion and, in many states, can only descend to the heirs of the creator of the interests.

Second, there is a third type of defeasible fee which we have not discussed at this point—the fee simple subject to an executory limitation.   This estate was not permissible at common law and came into existence only after the Statute of Uses (1535).   It will be explained in a later chapter but one or two comments should be made here.   At common law, the only estates that were permissible after a fee simple were the possibility of reverter and the power of termination.   Neither of them could be created in a third party, i.e., they could exist only in the grantor.   If *O* tried to convey "to *A* and his heirs for so long as the land is used for school purposes, then to *B* and his heirs", the latter part of the conveyance was void.   This was an attempt to create a shifting interest, shifting the fee from *A* to *B* on the happening of a certain event. After the Statute of Uses this became a permissible estate and today *A* would have a fee simple subject to an executory limitation

---

13. Ill.Rev.Stat. ch. 110, §§ 13–102   **14.** Id., ch. 30, § 37e.
and 13–103 (1985).

and *B* would have an executory interest in the land, similar to a possibility of reverter.

B. THE FEE SIMPLE CONDITIONAL AND THE FEE TAIL

The temptation is great to spend a long time on the fascinating estate of fee tail but the impulse must be resisted because the estate does not have much significance for the twentieth-century lawyer. It cannot be safely ignored, however, because the grant "to *A* and the heirs of his body" or "to *A* and his issue" may still be encountered in title search and we must have a clear idea of what it means.

The entailed estate represents one stage in the long struggle to tie up the family land in such a way that it would never cease to be family land. Coupled with the rule of primogeniture and, at a later date, the strict settlement,[15] it led to the perpetuation of a landed aristocracy in England which never had a real counterpart in this country. The idea was basically simple. Since a grant "to *A* and his heirs" gave *A* the full estate in fee simple absolute with free alienability and devisability, *A* could easily run through the estate and leave nothing for the next generation. A formula was needed which, in effect, gave *A* a life estate, followed by a life estate in his eldest son, followed by a similar estate in his eldest son, and so on down through the generations. Then *A* could never sell, devise, or incumber more than the estate for his own life, his son would be similarly bound, etc. The attempted solution was for *O* to grant the land "to *A* and the heirs of his body", "to *A* and his bodily heirs", or "to *A* and his issue."

In the very early days of the common law (prior to 1285), this device was not wholly successful, for the courts held that this created a fee simple conditional, which had the following consequences: (1) if *A* had no issue (heirs of body) he could make no conveyance during his lifetime and *O*, who had a reversionary interest would take the property on *A's* death; (2) if issue were born alive to *A*, then he could convey a fee simple to a third party, thus cutting off the inheritance by his issue and also *O's* reversion; (3) if, after the birth of issue alive, *A* did not convey the estate it passed to the issue in fee simple conditional and the same conse-

---

15. The strict settlement was an English device by which land was limited to a parent for life, then to his first and other sons or children in tail, with trustees interposed to protect contingent remainders. For a good, short discussion see Casner and Leach, Cases and Text on Property 382–384 (1951).

quences followed in the hands of the new holder. This meant that the original purpose of the conveyance could be defeated and there was no assurance that the property would stay in the family line. To remedy this situation the Statute *De Donis Conditionalibus* was passed in 1285, resulting in the fee tail estate. Since *De Donis* is a part of the received law of most American states, the fee simple conditional never existed in most of the United States. However, in a few states the statute *De Donis Conditionalibus* was never adopted and the old fee simple conditional is still a possible estate.[16] You should be careful not to confuse this anachronistic estate with the fee simple determinable and the fee simple subject to a condition subsequent, both of which sound similar to it but are quite different creatures.

The name fee tail comes from the French *tailler* (to carve) and probably meant that the grantor was able to carve a fee to his exact prescription. This carving could be carried to great lengths and the land could be limited to male descendants generally—fee tail male general; to female issue—fee tail female; or to issue of a specific wife—fee tail special. In the latter case, if the specified wife died, the holder of the estate was said to have a fee tail with possibility of issue extinct—a type of life estate. Note, however, that the limiting language must mean successive generations of bodily heirs, not just the bodily heir or heirs determined at the death of the first taker. Thus, a grant "to A and his children" [17] did not create a fee tail at all since this was a particular group of bodily heirs rather than an indefinite line of succession.

Assume a grant by O "to A and the heirs of his body." A dies survived by three sons, the eldest of whom is X. Under primogeniture, X would inherit the fee tail estate, but what if he died later without issue? The estate would then pass to O or O's heirs, if he were dead. Every estate tail was followed by a reversion since it was always possible that a given holder of the estate tail would die without bodily heirs. However, the grantor could create a remainder after a fee tail instead of keeping the reversion himself. This was done by the following language: "To A and the heirs of his body, but if A dies without issue then to B and his heirs."

---

16. South Carolina is the most conspicuous example of this group. See Blume v. Pearcy, 204 S.C. 409, 29 S.E.2d 673 (1944) and 2 Powell, Real Property 67–70 (1950).

17. This language called for the application of the Rule in Wild's Case (Wild's Case, 6 Co.Rep. 16b [1599]). If A had children at the time of the conveyance or devise, A and the children shared equal concurrent estates. If A had no children, the original Rule called A's estate a fee tail if created by a devise, but gave A a life estate with a remainder to the children of A, if any were born, if created by deed. The modern tendency is to apply the latter rule to both devises and deeds. At least one court has given A a fee simple in the latter situation. See Herrick v. Lain, 375 Ill. 569, 32 N.E.2d 154 (1941).

Remember, however, that no remainders could be created following any fees simple.

For about two hundred years after the Statute *De Donis Conditionalibus* the fee tail was in its hey-day. Then the lawyers, with the cooperation of the courts, developed techniques for defeating the purpose of the grantor by allowing the tenant in tail to convey a fee simple absolute to a stranger. The stranger could then reconvey the fee simple to the former tenant in tail who would now own the land free of the entail. These disentailing devices were called the fine and the common recovery [18] and they represent the rankest fictions in the history of the common law. Nonetheless, they undoubtedly served a purpose in the period when the fee tail was outgrowing its usefulness and can be cited as another example of the common law's capacity for growth without the intervention of legislation. Although the fine and the common recovery crippled the effectiveness of the fee tail they did not make it the same estate as a fee simple. If the tenant in tail failed to make a disentailing conveyance the land could not pass under his will and it would descend only to his lineal, not his general, heirs or if there was a failure of issue it would pass to the reversioner or remainderman. Moreover, the disentailment could be made only by a tenant in possession and out of this requirement grew the English system of strict settlement which from about 1650 to 1925 was used to keep English land in the family line.

The American colonies did not take kindly to entailed estates or to primogeniture. These twin attributes of a landed aristocracy did not mesh with democratic ideals and the state constitutions and statutes were used to prohibit this part of the English common law. Thomas Jefferson led the way with his draft of the Virginia constitution.[19] Despite the ban on the fee tail estate, the language "to *A* and the heirs of his body" continued to creep into the deeds and wills in this country and even today the lawyer may be faced with this ghost from the remote past. When he encounters this apparition there is no excuse for palpitation of the heart, since he can consult the statute books and cases in his

18. See Williams, Cases and Materials on the Law of Property 163–166 (1954) for a short account of how these fictional law suits operated.

19. 1 Schachner, Thomas Jefferson 146 (1951): "On the day after he brought in his court bill, Jefferson launched the first of his major assaults on the ancient regime—a request for leave to bring in a bill 'to enable tenants in taille to convey their lands in fee simple.' And, as if this revolutionary attack on the fundamental base for an aristocracy were not sufficient for a day, he followed it immediately with a demand for complete and drastic revision of the laws of Virginia." Incidentally, Schachner uses an interesting description of the fee tail estate when he writes, "The real title was in the biological family and not in the temporary individual."

particular jurisdiction and usually find an answer to the legal effect of "to *A* and his issue."

Although there are many variations among the states, the present treatment of the fee tail can be generally classified under four heads. (1) Some states still retain the fee simple conditional.[20] (2) Some states (New York falls in this category) treat the language as creating a fee simple absolute.[21] This is probably the least complicated expedient. (3) Some states (e.g., Delaware) retain the fee tail but allow the tenant in tail to execute a simple disentailing conveyance. This is a streamlined version of the fine and common recovery.[22] (4) Still other states (the Illinois statute is of this type) attempt to give some meaning to the language by giving *A*, the first taker, a life estate followed by a remainder in fee simple in *A's* issue.

Once you depart from the common-law pattern it is easy to make property law hard. This aphorism is neatly illustrated by the judicial gloss put on the Illinois disentailment statute. The Act reads: "In cases where, by the common law, any person or persons might hereafter become seized, without applying the rule of property known as the rule in Shelley's Case, in fee tail, of any lands, tenements, or hereditaments, by virtue of any devise, gift, grant or other conveyance, hereafter to be made, or by any other means whatsoever, such person or persons, instead of being or becoming seized thereof in fee tail, shall be deemed and adjudged to be, and become seized thereof, for his or her natural life only, and the remainder shall pass in fee simple absolute, to the person or persons to whom the estate tail would, on the death of the first grantee, devisee or donee in tail first pass, according to the course of the common law, by virtue of such devise, gift, grant or conveyance." [23] The Illinois Supreme Court [24] has interpreted this to mean that, in a grant "to *A* and his bodily heirs," *A* will take a life estate and so long as *A* has no issue the grantor, *O*, will have

---

20. Iowa, Oregon, and South Carolina are usually listed in this category although the estate seems to be important only in the latter jurisdiction.

21. More than twenty states have a statute of this type. Even with such an act all is not beer and skittles, however. The New York statute reads: "Estates tail have been abolished; and every estate which would be adjudged a fee tail . . . shall be deemed a fee simple; and if no valid remainder be limited thereon, a fee simple absolute. Where a remainder in fee shall be limited on an estate which would be a fee tail . . . such remainder shall be valid, as a contingent limitation on a fee, and shall

vest in possession on the death of the first taker, without issue living at the time of such death." New York Consolidated Laws ch. 50, § 32. Try your hand at the interpretation of this statute.

22. See Caccamo v. Banning, 6 Terry (Del.) 394, 75 A.2d 222 (1950).

23. Ill.Rev.Stat. ch. 30, § 5 (1973). Some slight changes in language were made in 1983 but they did not change the substance of the statute. See Ill. Rev.Stat. ch. 30, § 5 (1985).

24. Danberg v. Langman, 318 Ill. 266, 149 N.E. 245 (1925); Stearns v. Curry, 306 Ill. 94, 137 N.E. 471 (1922).

the reversion. As soon as the first child is born to *A* the remainder vests in him subject to partial divestiture to let in after-born children. *O's* reversion is, of course, cut off by the birth of this first child. As successive children are born to *A* they each take their aliquot share of the remainder, thus cutting down on the share of the first child. Moreover, since the remainder vests in each child, as born, there is no requirement that he survive *A* in order to take his share. Death in the lifetime of *A* will cause the child's portion to pass to his heirs or devisees. This interpretation flies in the teeth of the general rule that a living person has no heirs and hence a child, not being a bodily heir until *A's* death, should have to survive *A* in order to take. Arkansas,[25] which has a statute similar to that in Illinois, has adopted the latter interpretation and holds that *A* takes a life estate, followed by contingent (conditioned on outliving *A* and hence being his heir of body) remainders in *A's* issue. In a given case, widely divergent results could be reached under statutes which read almost the same. This should warn you that the fee tail can still be a tricky business and should be treated with proper respect.

C. THE LIFE ESTATE

Apart from the fee simple absolute, the life estate is the most common and the most important of the freehold estates. Although its origin was commercial—it was granted in return for rent in the period when a term of years was not entitled to "real" protection from the law—at the present time it is used primarily as a part of a family settlement, either inter vivos or testamentary. In some areas of the United States it is still common for the husband to leave Blackacre to his wife for life, remainder to his children. It is a growing practice, however, to establish a trust in these circumstances and leave Blackacre to *X*, a trustee with power of sale, to hold for the benefit of the wife for life and then to distribute the land or the proceeds of a sale to the children. This gives the wife an equitable life estate rather than a legal one.

Life estates are divided broadly into two classes, legal and conventional. The former are those estates created by operation of law rather than by act of the parties. Under this heading come curtesy, dower, and some of the other marital interests in land.[26]

---

25. Ark.Stat.Ann. § 50–405 (1947).

26. At common law, during the joint lives of husband and wife, the husband was seised of his wife's freeholds *jure* *uxoris*. The fee tail after possibility of issue extinct was also a legal life estate. It arose in the case of a fee tail special (where the estate was limited to the

Logically, these legal life estates should be discussed at this point but functionally they represent an attempt by society to provide security for a spouse by giving him or her an interest in the real property of the other. Hence, all such interests will be treated later under an appropriate heading.[27]

Conventional life estates are themselves subdivided into two classes, ordinary life estates and estates *pur autre vie* (for the life of another). The former are by far the most frequent and, if the creating language is ambiguous, the presumption always favors the use of the grantee's life as the measuring stick. Typically, the estate is created by *O* granting or devising "to *A* for life," although it should be remembered that a grant "to *A* ", without the addition of the mystic words "and his heirs", created a life estate in *A* at common law. If no further limitation by way of remainder appears there is, of course, a reversion in *O.* The ordinary life estate is obviously not an estate of inheritance and must end with the death of the life tenant. It can end earlier by merger with the reversion or the remainder and, at common law, it could also be terminated by forfeiture. This point will be mentioned again when we discuss the destructibility of contingent remainders. During the lifetime of *A,* both the seisin and the right to possession are in *A.* This means that the life tenant has the right to receive the rents and profits and is treated for most purposes as the "owner" of Blackacre, subject to the law of waste.[28] It is always possible to run into difficult problems of construction of a testator's language,[29] but in the main the ordinary life estate is a rather simple creature.

bodily heirs of a named spouse). After the named spouse died, her husband had a fee tail with possibility of issue extinct. Do you see why this was a life estate?

27. See Chapter 6, Section 1, Marital Interests, 88, infra.

28. Of course, the life tenant is treated as "owner" only during his life; on his death the fee simple title will be in the reversioner or the remainderman, depending on the terms of the original grant or devise. During the life of A, the holder of the future interest can protect his rights by preventing A from wasting the estate, i.e., from destroying the value of the freehold by removing the top soil, tearing down buildings, etc. See the classic case of Melms v. Pabst Brewing Co., 104 Wis. 7, 79 N.W. 738 (1899) where the life tenant "improved" the property by razing a dwelling on the land and grading the surface down to street level so it would be more useful as part of a brewery. The court traced the historical development of the doctrine of waste and agreed that "any material change in the nature and character of the buildings made by a [life] tenant is waste although the value of the property should be enhanced by the alteration." Although the grading constituted waste, the court said it was meliorating (beneficial) waste and hence no damages were due to the holders of the future interest. Normally, waste can be prevented by an injunction in equity or money damages can be recovered at law. The doctrine also applies to non-freehold estates where the landlord can sue a tenant for wasting the estate. For an excellent discussion of the modern law of waste see Moore v. Phillips, 6 Kan.App.2d 94, 627 P.2d 831 (1981).

29. What estate does the following language create? "The remainder of my property to go to my wife Virginia

The estate *pur autre vie* can be created in two ways. *O* can convey Blackacre "to *A* for the life of *B*." *B*, whose life is thus used as a measuring stick, is called the *cestui que vie* and he takes nothing by the grant. Sometimes, several people's lives may be used as the measuring device and the courts usually interpret this to mean that the estate of *A* continues until the death of the last *cestui que vie*.[30] The estate can also come into existence when an ordinary life tenant conveys his interest to a third party. The life tenant clearly has an alienable interest but just as clearly he can grant no more than he possesses. Thus when *A*, a life tenant, grants to *B*, the latter has a life estate measured by the life of *A*.

The common law was much disturbed by the death of the holder of an estate *pur autre vie* during the life of the *cestui que vie*. Because it was a life estate it was not inheritable by the heirs of the tenant, the *cestui que vie* had no interest, and the estate of the reversioner or remainderman could not vest in possession because the measuring life had not ended. The dilemma was solved by treating the land as being without a tenant and allowing the first person to occupy it after the death of the tenant to claim the seisin as a "general occupant." This claimant was entitled to hold the estate until the death of the *cestui que vie*. If, however, the original grant was "to *A and his heirs* for the life of *B* ", the heir of *A* was allowed to occupy the land, not because he had inherited it, but as a "special occupant." Thus, it came about that the words "and his heirs" had some significance even in a life estate. This mumbo jumbo of special and general occupancy has now been altered by statute so that the unexpired estate descends like other estates in land.[31]

SECTION 2. THE NON–FREEHOLD ESTATES

The law of the non-freehold estates is the law of landlord and tenant. A more extended discussion of leaseholds will follow later

Simpson as long as she remains my widow. In the event of her marrying then said remainder of my property is to be equally divided between my sons . . . ." See Dickson v. Alexandria Hospital, Inc., 177 F.2d 876 (4th Cir.1949) holding that this language created a defeasible fee simple in Virginia Simpson, which became a fee simple absolute when she died without having remarried. There are cases holding that simi-

lar language creates a defeasible life estate.

See also, Lewis v. Searles, 452 S.W.2d 153 (Mo.1970); Kautz v. Kautz, 365 Pa. 450, 76 A.2d 398 (1950); and Chesnut v. Chesnut, 300 Pa. 146, 151 A. 339 (1930).

30. 2 Powell, Real Property 90 (1950).

31. Restatement, Property, § 151 (1936).

in the book,[32] but at this point we must see the relevance of the estates for years, from period to period, at will, and at sufferance to the "big picture" of the legal estates. Never a part of the feudal pattern, the estate for years, for example, grew out of an attempt to evade the usury laws. *O* would grant his land to *A* for a term of years in exchange for a sum of money, badly needed by *O.* The term would be sufficiently long so that the rents would repay not only the principal sum but a goodly profit as well. Because of its lowly origin, the estate was not well thought of by the courts and many of the consequences persist even in the twentieth century. The earlier real actions would not protect the leasehold tenant and the law treated him as having only possession of the premises while the seisin remained in the lessor. Moreover, the non-freehold estates were called by the ambiguous name chattels real and were treated as personal property for various purposes. Thus, on the death of the lessee the estate would pass to the executor or administrator as personal property rather than to the heir as real property. This latter characteristic still persists except that most statutes of descent now treat both classes of property in the same way.

A. THE ESTATE FOR YEARS

The estate for years is also referred to as a tenancy for a term and a tenancy for a period. Its principal characteristic is that it must have a fixed beginning and ending. While this is normally stated in express terms, e.g., "To *A* for five years" or "To *A* from January 1, 1955 to December 31, 1960", it is sufficient if a gross period can be determined by implication from the language used. So long as a gross period is stated it remains an estate for years even though subject to earlier termination. Thus, you may have a determinable estate for years or an estate for years subject to a condition subsequent. The latter is particularly common, since the lessor may wish to keep a power of termination for failure of the lessee to pay rent or to perform certain other covenants in the lease. This may even take such an extreme form as allowing the lessor to terminate the estate at any time upon an event within his own control.[33] This does not convert the tenancy into one at will, if a gross period is set out in the lease.

---

32. See Part Four—Landlord and Tenant.

33. Cleveland Wrecking Co. v. Aetna Oil Co., 287 Ky. 542, 154 S.W.2d 31, 137 A.L.R. 352 (1941).

Any lease for a fixed period is called an estate for years, regardless of the length of the period. "To *A* for one day", "To *A* for six months," and "To *A* for nine hundred ninety nine years" [34] are all examples of estates for years. The estate will expire automatically upon the termination of the stated period, and, in the absence of a provision in the lease, no notice of any kind need be given by either the landlord or the tenant.

The estate for years involves a continuing relationship between the parties and thus differs materially from the conveyance of a fee simple which normally severs all contacts between the vendor and purchaser after the deed is delivered. Because of the Statute of Frauds,[35] leases for a term in excess of a certain period, usually one year, must be in writing in order to be enforceable. Quite apart from the statute, it is apparent that all but the most simple leases should be reduced to writing in order to hold disputes between the parties to a minimum. The average lease bristles with covenants, dealing with all manner of things that may or may not be done for the duration of the estate for years. The lease thus falls into two major areas of the substantive law— property and contract. It is a conveyance of Blackacre for a fixed period of time and it is also a contract between the lessor and lessee regulating their respective rights for that same period. Much of the ambivalence of landlord and tenant law is explained by this simple fact.[36]

B. THE ESTATE FROM PERIOD TO PERIOD

Also referred to as a periodic tenancy, the estate from period to period is characterized chiefly by the element of continuity. Whereas the estate for years will terminate automatically, the periodic tenancy, once created, will continue on its way until

34. Restatement, Property, § 19 (1936).

35. The English Statute of Frauds, 29 Car. II, c. 3 (1677) required that any lease for more than three years had to be in writing or it would create an estate at will. Present statutes vary but a majority of the states have reduced the period to one year.

36. There are many examples of this property-contract dichotomy, one of the best being the mitigation of damages problem. In contract law the non-breaching party must make a reasona-ble effort to reduce damages or he cannot recover his full loss. Traditionally the landlord-tenant cases, however, required no such mitigation by the lessor and he could let the premises lie idle following an unjustified vacation by the lessee. Lawson v. Callaway, 131 Kan. 789, 293 P. 503 (1930). This mitigation doctrine has been subject to re-examina-tion in the various states and will be modified in the proper case, see Wohl v. Yelen, 22 Ill.App.2d 455, 161 N.E.2d 339 (1959).

proper steps are taken to put it to death. The notice which either party must give in order to terminate the estate is rather technical and the statutes of the particular jurisdiction must be carefully checked in each situation.[37] As a general guide, at common law a tenancy from year to year required six months' notice and a tenancy for a lesser period required a notice equal to the length of the period, e.g., a month-to-month tenancy required a month's notice, etc. Moreover, the notice had to be given so as to terminate the estate at the end of a period and not in the middle of it. Thus, in a month-to-month tenancy which began on January 1, 1959, the notice to terminate on May 1, 1959, would have to be given on April 1. A notice on April 15 to terminate on May 15 would have no effect.[38]

An estate from period to period can be created expressly, as "To A from month to month, beginning on January 1, 1960", but, in fact, many such tenancies arise by implication. This can come about in several different ways. We have already mentioned that some leases must be in writing in order to be enforceable. Suppose that O orally leases to A for eighteen months in a jurisdiction which has a Statute of Frauds requiring all leases in excess of one year to be in writing. If A enters the land under this voidable lease, he will not be a trespasser and so long as he pays no rent he will probably be treated as a tenant at will. If he tenders the first month's rent, however, and O accepts it this will *probably* convert the tenancy into one from month to month and A can continue until either party elects to terminate by proper notice.[39] Similarly, if O should lease to A, without any statement of the term of the lease, and then A should pay rent on a monthly basis, a tenancy from month to month would result.[40] Or suppose O leases to A for one year and A holds over at the expiration of the year. Then, if O accepts the monthly rental from A, the holdover tenant, it is probable that a tenancy from year to year has been created.[41]

---

37. For a collection of these statutes see Lesar, Landlord and Tenant, § 3.90 (1957).

38. May v. Rice, 108 Mass. 150 (1871).

39. Note the use of the word *probably*. In Maine and Massachusetts the Statute of Frauds provides that any oral lease creates only a tenancy at will and in other states, while a periodic tenancy of some sort results, it may be month to month or year to year depending on whether the unenforceable lease for a term reserved an annual rent or a

monthly one. See Lesar, Landlord and Tenant, § 3.27 (1957).

40. Williams v. Apothecaries Hall Co., 80 Conn. 503, 69 A. 12 (1908). Here again, the way the rent is paid or reserved determines the period. Indeed, in some cases the reservation of the rent without actual payment has been held sufficient and some statutes so provide. Ala.Code, tit. 31, § 4 (1940); Kan. Gen.Stat. § 67–503 (1935).

41. The tenancy usually is from year to year if the original lease was for a year or more; if for less than a year,

C. THE ESTATE AT WILL

As in the case of the periodic tenancy, the estate at will can be created by the express agreement of the parties. So long as no gross period is stated,[42] any lease "To *A* at the will of *O* " creates an estate at will. An estate at the will of *O,* the lessor, is automatically an estate at the will of *A,* the lessee. The converse of this statement is not universally true because some jurisdictions treat an estate at the will of the lessee as if it were a life estate rather than an estate at will.[43] This means that *A* can terminate the estate if he so desires but that *O* has no power to do so except for breach of some of the covenants of the lease.

Usually, however, the estate at will is created by implication and arises whenever *A* takes possession of *O's* land with the latter's implied consent. Thus, an unenforceable contract for the sale of land may result in a purchaser in possession being treated as a tenant at will. We have already mentioned how the Statute of Frauds may give rise to an estate at will, at least until such time as some of the rent is tendered and accepted.

It was a common-law characteristic of this estate that it could be terminated by either party without any notice whatever. The harshness of this rule has been mitigated in some states by statutes which require a notice equal to the rent-paying period.[44] The effect of such statutes is to turn the estate at will into something very like the estate from period to period. In addition to termination by either party, the estate will come to an end automatically if either party dies or attempts to convey his interest. It is apparent that the tenancy at will is a very frail interest, but nonetheless it falls under the majestic cloak of an estate in land.

D. THE ESTATE AT SUFFERANCE

The tenant at sufferance does not have any estate in land, but because some writers have listed an estate at sufferance as one of the non-freeholds we should mention it here to complete the

the period is based on the way the rent was reserved. See Note, 108 A.L.R. 1464 (1937).

42. If a gross period is stated then a determinable term of years is created. See p. 54, supra.

43. Gunnison v. Evans, 136 Kan. 791, 18 P.2d 191 (1933). For a contrary view see Foley v. Gamester, 271 Mass. 55, 170 N.E. 799 (1930).

44. Mass.Gen.Laws Ann. c. 186, § 12.

pattern. This wispy interest arises only in the case of a holdover tenant. If *O* leases to *A* for five years, *A* is supposed to vacate the premises at the termination of the period. If he does not do so, he would seem to be a mere trespasser and entitled to no more consideration than any other wrongdoer. However, this could, in some cases, work against the interests of *O*. The statute of limitations would begin to run immediately and if *A* stayed on the land a sufficient length of time he might get title by adverse possession. To prevent this unfortunate result, the courts have sometimes referred to *A* as a tenant at sufferance, not holding adversely to *O*. It is clear that *O* in these cases has an election and can either evict *A* by the proper proceedings, probably a suit in forcible entry and detainer, or treat him as a holdover tenant and bind him to an estate from period to period.[45]

SECTION 3. THE SURVIVAL OF SOME ANACHRONISTIC RULES

One of Mr. Justice Holmes' wisest utterances ran: "It is revolting to have no better reason for a rule of law than that so it was laid down in the time of Henry IV. It is still more revolting if the grounds upon which it was laid down have vanished long since, and the rule simply persists from blind imitation of the past."[46] Since law, by its very nature, is precedent bound, many rules do survive whose principal claim to fame lies in services that they have long ceased to render. The law of property is particularly susceptible since it must be fairly stable if it is to be useful. Men cannot order their affairs if the law changes every time some inventive judge has a bright idea. On the other hand, occasional revision is essential lest the whole system bog down under the accumulated weight of centuries. Much of the supertechnical aspect of property law has been abandoned or remodeled and we have tried to deal here only with those antiquities which have modern relevance. Only in a full scale history of the law of land could all of those intricate snarls be unravelled. However, some of the anachronisms we have with us still, or, if buried, they have sufficient vitality to be felt beyond the grave. The three most important of these survivals from a darker age are, the Rule in

45. The problems of the holdover tenant are discussed further at p. 246, infra.

46. Holmes, The Path of the Law in Collected Legal Papers 187 (1921).

Shelley's Case, the Doctrine of Worthier Title, and the destructibility of contingent remainders.[47]

A. THE RULE IN SHELLEY'S CASE

You will recall that in a grant "to A and his heirs" the last three words were treated as words of limitation rather than of purchase, thus giving A a fee simple absolute. What would be the result, at common law, of a conveyance "to A for life, remainder to his heirs"? Logically, it would seem to create a life estate in A, a contingent remainder in the heirs of A (contingent because a living person has no heirs), with a reversion in O, the grantor. This would also seem to square with the intent of the grantor (or the testator) since by varying the formula, "to A and his heirs" he must have had a different result in mind. Moreover, the very words "remainder to his heirs" or "remainder to the heirs of A " would seem to indicate that the heirs were to take by "purchase." Similarly, a grant or devise "to A for life, remainder to the heirs of his body" seems to call for a life estate in A, contingent remainder in the bodily heirs of A, and a reversion in O. But, by the rule laid down in the famous (notorious might be a better word) Shelley's Case [48] the first grant would result in a fee simple absolute in A, the second in a fee tail in A.

47. In addition to the waning relevance of these three anachronistic rules, there are two reasons for including them in this text. First, they form a part of the legal culture and nearly every law student encounters them in some guise in his study of property law and you do not want to be culturally illiterate. (Moreover you must master some esoteric doctrine so that you can confuse the engineers.) Second, they are excellent tools for legal analysis and even an elementary understanding of the unholy trio will add to your mastery of estates doctrine.

48. 1 Co.Rep. 93b (1581). Actually, the Rule goes back to Abel's Case, Y.B. 18 Edw. II, 577 (1324). The Rule in Shelley's Case lives on in some American jurisdictions. For a particularly good example, see Jones v. Stone, 52 N.C.App. 502, 279 S.E.2d 13 (1981) where the court observed: "This year marks the 400th anniversary of the formal pronouncement of the rule in Shelley's Case. The rule is a vestige of feudal law and takes its name from an old English case, Wolfe v. Shelley, 1 Co. Rep. 93(b), 76th Eng.Rep. 206 (CB 1581) . . . Although the original objective of the Rule became outdated when feudal tenures were abolished in the seventeenth century, the rule enjoyed prominence until the twentieth century. The Rule was abolished in England in 1925; it has never been repealed in North Carolina, however. Indeed, one year after the Rule was abolished in England, the North Carolina Supreme Court said: 'Today, the rule serves quite a different purpose, in that it prevents the tying up of real estate during the life of the first taker, facilitates its alienation a generation earlier, and at the same time, subjects it to the payment of the debts of the ancestor.'" The decision provides a scholarly analysis of the Rule and its application but the Court decided it did not apply in the case at hand because the words "heirs at law" were not used in a technical sense.

Property experts differ as to the exact reason for this peculiar rule,[49] but since Shelley's Case dates from 1581 it has long been accepted as a part of the common law and applied without much analysis of the forces that called it into being. It applied to both deeds and wills and acquired such a sacrosanct character that it overrode even a clear indication of contrary intent,[50] i.e., it was treated as a rule of law and not merely as a rule of construction. Although some fantastic results have flowed from tortured application of this ancient rule, it has had at least one beneficent influence. Its application has led to freer alienability by giving a fee simple to *A* instead of creating a life estate followed by contingent remainders; but this has been an incidental effect and scarcely explains the hardy survival of the Rule.

Stripped of its legal jargon,[51] the Rule provides that where in the same instrument a freehold estate is limited to *A* with a purported remainder to the heirs of *A* (or the heirs of his body) and the estates are of the same quality (both legal or both equitable) then the purported remainder becomes a fee simple (or fee tail) in *A*. It is important to note that the Rule spends its force by changing the remainder in the heirs to a remainder in *A*, thus giving *A* a life estate followed by a remainder in fee simple (or fee tail) in *A*. This results in a fee simple in *A* because, by the doctrine of merger, the life estate and the remainder, being lodged in the same person, unite (or merge) to form the greater estate in fee. This may strike you as a minor analytical point but observe its consequences in the following devise. *O* devises to *A* for life, to *B* for life, remainder to the heirs of *A*. What result? Does *A* have a fee simple and, if so, what happens to *B's* life estate? *A* will have a life estate, followed by a life estate in *B*, followed by a remainder in fee simple in *A*. But so long as *B* lives, *A* will not have a present fee simple because *B's* life estate separates *A's* two estates and prevents merger. Of course, if *B* dies in the lifetime of *A* then merger can occur. You should analyze the various pos-

49. Perhaps the most likely explanation is that it prevented landowners from avoiding their feudal obligations since the estate had to pass to the heirs by inheritance rather than being given to them by the terms of the original grant.

50. Perrin v. Blake, 1 W.L. 672 (1769); Havely v. Comerford, 343 Ill. 90, 174 N.E. 830 (1931).

51. A classic statement of the rule appears in Hancock v. Butler, 21 Tex. 804, 808 (1858): " ' . . . when a person takes an estate of freehold, legally, or equitably, under a deed, will, or other writing, and in the same instrument, there is a limitation, by way of remainder, either with or without the interposition of another estate, of an interest of the same legal or equitable quality, to his heirs or heirs of his body, as a class of persons, to take in succession, from generation to generation, the limitation to the heirs entitles the ancestor to the whole estate.' 4 Kent 215. This result would follow, although the deed might express that the first taker should have a life estate only. It is founded on the use of the technical words, 'heirs' or 'heirs of his body,' in the deed or the will."

sibilities inherent in this situation and see why a precise understanding of the Rule is essential.

Broken into its component parts the elements of the Rule are:

(1) The estates must be created by one and the same instrument, i.e., by the same deed or the same will.

(2) The instrument must give *A* a freehold estate; a term of years in *A* will not invoke the Rule. "To *A* for five years, remainder to his heirs", means just what it says. Usually, the estate in *A* will be a life estate but it could be a fee tail.

(3) The estate in the heirs must be a remainder. At early common law the only future interest possible in a stranger was a remainder but, as you will see later, the Statute of Uses (1536) permitted certain other future interests (springing and shifting uses). However, the Rule never had any application to these "new" interests.

(4) The Rule applies only when the remainder is limited to *A's* heirs or the heirs of *A's* body. A grant "to *A* for life, remainder to *A's* children" does not give *A* a fee simple. It might well be that *A's* children will in fact turn out to be his heirs but that makes no difference. The word heirs has to be used in its technical sense. But what is the technical sense of "heirs"? This question was one of the greatest litigation producers in the application of the Rule. The refinements are too involved for an elementary text, but the puzzle can be illustrated by the following grant, "to *A* for life, remainder to those persons who, according to the statutes of Illinois, would take *A's* real estate if he should die intestate." [52] Does the Rule apply, thus giving to *A* a fee simple absolute? It does, if those persons who will take *A's* real estate when he dies intestate are the same as "heirs," used in a technical sense. It does not, if the word "heirs" must mean "heirs taking in succession in infinite generations" as opposed to heirs taking at the death of *A*. This "how-many-angels-can-dance-on-the-head-of-a-pin" argument must have delighted the property expert of another generation and the English courts followed the latter view thus refusing to apply the Rule. The American courts, however, tended to ignore this esoteric distinction and applied the Rule as if "heirs" meant those individuals who would take *A's* real estate immediately on his death.

(5) The Rule applies even though the freehold estate in *A* is separated from the remainder in the heirs by an intervening estate. This was illustrated earlier by the devise "to *A* for life, to *B* for life, remainder to the heirs of *A*."

52. People v. Emery, 314 Ill. 220, 145 N.E. 349 (1924).

(6) The Rule applies to future interests as well as to present possessory estates. Thus, in a grant "to *A* for life, to *B* for life, remainder to the heirs of *B*," *A* will take a life estate followed by a remainder in fee simple in *B*.

(7) The Rule applies only when the freehold estate and the remainder are both of the same quality, i.e., are both legal or both equitable. Assume a grant "To *A* for the life of *B*, in trust to collect the rents and profits and pay them to *B*, remainder to the heirs of *B*." The Rule does not apply to give *B* a fee simple. *B's* life estate is equitable since *A* holds the land in trust for him to pay out the proceeds, but the remainder in the heirs of *B* is legal since they will take the estate in fee simple on *B's* death. Had the grant provided that *A*, as trustee, was to hold the remainder in trust for *B's* heirs also, then the Rule would have governed because both estates would have been equitable.

This brief analysis does not exhaust the infinite possibilities of the Rule, but it should suffice to put you on notice and enable you to spot the situations in which the Rule may be involved. Indeed, for many students the Rule in Shelley's Case is not unlike a communist and is often seen hiding under every bed. At the present time the Rule has been abolished in most American jurisdictions [53] but it still has full force in a few. Even when abolished it may continue to be important in title examination since the statutes are not retroactive and in many instances have been passed quite recently. Abolition of the Rule was designed to allow the courts to follow the intent of the grantor or testator so that a conveyance, "To *A* for life, remainder to his heirs," will now result in the logical estates mentioned at the outset of this section. It should be mentioned in closing that the Rule in Shelley's Case does not generally apply to personal property since its whole excuse for being grew out of feudal land concepts.[54]

53. 2 Powell, Real Property 24 (1950). For an interesting case applying the Rule see Sybert v. Sybert, 152 Tex. 106, 254 S.W.2d 999 (1953). Later Texas abolished the Rule, see Tex.Civ. Stat.Ann., Art. 1291a (1964). Illinois had a particularly rich development of the Rule and it resulted in a large amount of litigation. See Young, The Rule in Shelley's Case in Illinois: A New Analysis and Suggestion for Repeal, 45 Ill.L.Rev. 173 (1950). Illinois did abolish the Rule in 1953 (Ill.Rev. Stat. ch. 30, ss. 186, 187 (1985)) but typically it had no retroactive effect. As a result, litigation continues, arising out of deeds or wills that became effective prior to 1953. That the Rule, in fact, continues to govern from the grave see Evans v. Giles, 80 Ill.App.3d 270, 35 Ill.Dec. 598, 399 N.E.2d 664 (1980).

54. 1 Simes and Smith, The Law of Future Interests § 367 (2d ed. 1956). For a case to the contrary see Fowler v. Lanpher, 193 Wash. 308, 75 P.2d 132 (1938) commented on in 15 Wash.L.Rev. 99 (1940).

B. THE DOCTRINE OF WORTHIER TITLE

Somewhat akin to (and frequently confused with) the Rule in Shelley's Case is the Doctrine of Worthier Title. Actually, it is a completely separate rule and should be treated as such. Its name comes from the maxim that a title by descent is worthier than one by grant or devise. This is errant nonsense except to the lord in a feudalistic society. He might think it worthier because if the title to land passed by descent to the heirs the lord would be entitled to a relief and, if the heirs were infants, to wardship and marriage. If the title passed to the heirs by devise the lord would get none of these feudal incidents. This fact probably explains the origin of the Doctrine; nothing adequately accounts for its hardy survival.

The Doctrine consists of two separate rules, the first of which has little modern significance. It runs: If a will purports to give a freehold estate to an individual and that estate is of the same quality and quantity which he would have received by the statutes of descent if the testator had died intestate, then the estate passes by descent rather than by devise. Thus, if *O* devises Blackacre "to *A* in fee simple absolute" and *A* turns out to be *O's* only son and heir then *A* will take Blackacre by descent rather than by the terms of the will. In modern times this will make no difference to *A*—he gets Blackacre in fee simple in either event—and this part of the Doctrine has been largely forgotten.[55]

The second rule still has teeth in it. If a fee simple owner of Blackacre purports to grant a life estate or an estate tail to *A*, with a remainder to the grantor's heirs, the latter take nothing by the grant but must take, if at all, by descent from the grantor, i.e., the remainder is void and the grantor is left with a reversion.[56] Note that this is like the Rule in Shelley's Case in that it turns an express grant to the heirs of an individual into an estate in the individual himself. An illustration is required to make much sense out of this Doctrine.

O grants "to *A* for life, remainder to *my* heirs." This would seem to give *A* a life estate, with contingent remainder in the heirs of *O*. But the Doctrine says, in effect, it is worthier for *O's* heirs to take the estate by descent from *O* when he dies intestate than to take it by grant in this present conveyance, therefore *O's* heirs get nothing and *O* still has the reversion. But, of course, if *O* still has the reversion his heirs may never get anything at all. Why?

---

55. Unfortunately, it has occasionally been resurrected and given unwarranted effect. See Leach, Cases on Future Interests 13–19 (2d ed. 1940).

56. For a detailed discussion in a modern case, see Braswell v. Braswell, 195 Va. 971, 81 S.E.2d 560 (1954).

Because *O* now has a future interest, a reversion in fee simple following the life estate in *A*, and he may sell it during his lifetime, creditors may levy on it in satisfaction of *O's* debts, or *O* may devise it to someone other than his heirs when it comes time for him to die. Only if *O*, in fact, dies intestate, still owning Blackacre, will it pass to his heirs. Note that this aspect of the rule applies only to a grant (an inter vivos transfer) by *O* and not to a devise by him. If he devises "to *A* for life, remainder to *my* heirs," it will make no difference since the heirs will take in either case.

The Doctrine has been abolished in a few states but it remains in full effect in many others.[57] It has even been unnecessarily extended to personal property by treating it as a principle of construction rather than as a technical rule of law.[58] In states where the Doctrine has been abolished, a grant by *O* "to *A* for life, remainder to *my* heirs" has the following result. *A* takes a life estate, followed by a contingent remainder in the heirs of *O*. If *O* dies in the lifetime of *A*, the remainder immediately vests in the heirs of *O*. If *O* is still alive when *A* dies, the estate reverts to *O* but is subject to an executory limitation in the heirs of *O*, i.e., as soon as *O* does die the estate will shift to the heirs in fee simple absolute. This latter type of estate is one made possible by the Statute of Uses and will be discussed in more detail in the next chapter.

C. THE DESTRUCTIBILITY OF CONTINGENT REMAINDERS

The third anachronism was the rule that under certain circumstances a contingent remainder could be destroyed so that the

57. It was abolished in England in 1833. Stats. 3 and 4 Wm.IV, c. 106, § 3 (1833). Illinois followed this trail-blazing lead in 1955! Ill.Rev.Stat. ch. 30, §§ 188, 189 (1985). The only modern justification for the rule is that normally a person making an inter vivos transfer does not intend to create irrevocable interests in his eventual heirs.

For a more extended discussion of the Doctrine, see Cunningham, Stoebuck, and Whitman, The Law of Property 126–132 (1984) and Johanson, Reversions, Remainders, and The Doctrine of Worthier Title, 45 Tex.L.Rev. 1 (1966).

58. Doctor v. Hughes, 225 N.Y. 305, 122 N.E. 221 (1919). Occasionally, the Doctrine is applied, or at least referred to, in fact situations which have nothing to do with the doctrine. See All Persons v. Buie, 386 So.2d 1109 (Miss. 1980) where the Supreme Court of Mississippi created confusion by invoking the doctrine even though there was no express limitation to the grantor's heirs. Despite the confusion the court did reach the right result in the case.

See also Harris Trust and Sav. Bank v. Beach, 145 Ill.App.3d 673, 99 Ill.Dec. 435, 495 N.E.2d 1170 (1 Dist.1986) where an Illinois Appellate Court applied the doctrine to a trust created prior to abolition of the doctrine. The Court held that the doctrine (prior to its abolition) was a rule of law not of Construction.

holder of the expectant estate would never come into enjoyment. Bluntly stated, a contingent remainder is destroyed unless it vests at or before the termination of the preceding freehold estate. *O* grants Blackacre "to *A* for life, remainder to the first child of *A* who attains the age of twenty-one." If *S*, a son of *A*, attains his majority during *A's* lifetime the remainder vests in *S* and all is well. Even if *S* dies the day after his twenty-first birthday, it does not affect the estate. *S* died owning a vested remainder and it will descend as such, if *S* died intestate, or pass by his will. If, however, *A* dies while *S* is only twenty years old, the contingent remainder is destroyed and Blackacre reverts to *O*. Even if *S* now lives to be twenty-one it makes no difference, the contingent remainder has been destroyed and cannot be revived.

This doctrine originated in the feudal rule that there could be no abeyance of seisin and, since the contingency had not occurred at the end of the particular estate, *S* could not be seised of the land. Blackacre could have reverted to *O*, however, thus giving him the seisin until *S* satisfied the condition by reaching twenty-one and then the land could have been automatically transferred to *S* who would then have had the seisin. This would have solved the abeyance problem but it ran smack into another difficulty—the common-law rule against springing and shifting interests. This rule held (1) that a freehold could not be created to commence in the future and (2) that a condition could not be reserved in a stranger. Stripped of a lot of verbiage, this meant that once a freehold estate had been created in one person it could not be cut short by the happening of a condition and shifted over to someone else. Applied to the present situation, it meant that once the estate reverted to *O* he had it in fee simple absolute and it could not spring[59] out of him to *S* when the latter reached the age of twenty-one. Oddly enough, even when the Statute of Uses allowed the creation of springing and shifting interests this had no effect on the doctrine of destructibility and *S's* estate would still be lost for failure to vest in the lifetime of *A*.

The situation was even more complicated than this initial analysis would indicate because a life estate could end in other ways than by the death of the life tenant. It could cease by forfeiture or by merger and frequently these methods were used to destroy the contingent remainder and bring the reversion into immediate enjoyment. Forfeiture (usually by renunciation of fealty or by a tortious conveyance, purporting to convey a fee when only a life estate was owned) has little modern significance, but

59. Technically, this would be called a springing interest because it would have to "spring out" of the estate of *O*, the original grantor; a shifting interest was one which would cut short an estate in a prior grantee and shift it over to a new one.

merger is quite another matter. We have already noted that if both the life estate and the remainder came into the ownership of the same individual the two estates would merge to form a fee simple absolute. It is this principle which clever lawyers used to destroy the contingent remainder.

Assume that O grants "to A for life, remainder to the first child of A who attains the age of twenty-one." If A wants to destroy the contingent remainder, and if O is willing, A can buy the reversion from O and the life estate will merge into the reversion, thus ending the contingent remainder. The life estate has ceased to exist and since no child of A is yet twenty-one the contingent remainder is lost. The same result would be reached if O had purchased the life estate from A. You can see that there are numerous possibilities if careful use is made of the doctrine of merger.[60]

There is one situation, however, in which the doctrine of merger does not automatically apply. If the life estate and the next vested estate (usually it will be a reversion) are created in the same person simultaneously, they will not merge to destroy the contingent remainder. Assume that O devises Blackacre "to A for life, remainder to A's first child in fee." A, in fact, has no child at the time of O's death so the remainder is contingent. A turns out to be O's sole heir and therefore he takes the reversion by the statute of descent. Despite the fact that A now owns both the life estate and the reversion there will be no merger; the two estates were created in the same person simultaneously. (Of course, if A now has a child the estate will vest in him, cutting off A's reversion.) But even in the simultaneous creation situation, A can easily destroy the contingent remainder if he so desires. This is true, because if the two estates unite in a third party merger will take place. Thus, if A conveys his life estate and his reversion to X, the latter will have the fee simple and the contingent remainder will vanish. Since X can be a straw party who will reconvey Blackacre to A, purged of the contingent remainder, you can see how easy it is for A to accomplish his purpose.

Like the Rule in Shelley's Case, this anachronistic doctrine has at least one merit, it promotes a freer alienability of land by allowing a fee simple to be conveyed without waiting for all of the possible contingencies to occur. On the other hand, it thwarts the apparent desires of the grantor or testator and deprives the parties who "own" the contingent remainder of their natural expectancy. Because this has not seemed fair to the modern mind, nearly all states have abolished the doctrine entirely and

60. See, for example, Stoller v. Doyle, 257 Ill. 369, 100 N.E. 959 (1913).

the judicial decisions have whittled away at its common-law rigidity in those states where it has not been totally rescinded.[61]   But, like its fellow survivors from the past, it can still be a vicious trap for the unwary in a few states.

Since the vested remainder could not be destroyed it was often necessary to distinguish between types of remainders. There were other reasons for making the distinction as well, e.g., vested remainders could be freely alienated whereas contingent remainders were subject to more restrictive rules and in case of involuntary transfers (attachment by creditors, bankruptcy, etc.) might be totally inalienable.[62]   Today, most courts allow both types of remainders to be transferred by deed or by will and to be subject to claims of creditors so the reasons for making this distinction are fading.   Nonetheless, you must be aware of the classification since it may be important in the state where you practice and it is frequently involved in the Rule against Perpetuities,[63] a common-law development designed to prevent remoteness of vesting and thus the tying up of property over too long a period of time.

It may be helpful to point out a more complete classification of remainders to illustrate how complicated the distinctions could be.   Thus, a remainder could be (1) indefeasibly vested (to *A* for life, remainder to *B* and his heirs); (2) vested subject to open, also called vested subject to partial divestiture (to *A* for life, remainder to the children of *B* and their heirs—*B*, having at the time of transfer one or more children with the possibility of further issue); (3) vested subject to total divestiture, also called vested subject to a condition subsequent (to *A* for life, then to *B* and his heirs, but if *B* fails to survive *A*, then to *C* and his heirs)—*C* has a shifting or executory interest, not possible until after the Statute of Uses; or (4) contingent, also called subject to a condition precedent (to *A* for life, then to *B* and his heirs if *B* survives *A*, but if *B* does not do so, then to *C* and his heirs)—*B* and *C* have alternative contingent remainders, sometimes called contingent remainders with a double aspect.   It is apparent that there is little difference between (3)

---

61. For the current state of the law, see Cunningham, Stoebuck and Whitman, The Law of Property 114–116 (1984) and Restatement, Property, s. 240 (1936).   See also Abo Petroleum Corporation v. Amstutz, 93 N.M. 332, 600 P.2d 278 (1979) where the court held the destructibility of contingent remainders was not a part of the received common law of New Mexico.   Said the court: "The only tenable argument in support of the doctrine is that it promotes the alienability of land.   It does so, however, only arbitrarily, and often times by defeating the intent of the

grantor.   Land often carries burdens with it, but courts do not arbitrarily cut off those burdens merely in order to make land more alienable.   Because the doctrine of destructibility is but a relic of the feudal past, which has no justification or support in modern society, we decline to apply it in New Mexico."

62. Kost v. Foster, 406 Ill. 565, 94 N.E.2d 302 (1950).   See also 1 American Law of Property, §§ 4.65, 4.66 (Casner ed. 1952).

63. See pp. 82 to 85, infra.

and (4) above, but so long as legal consequences flow from the vested-contingent classification, property rights may depend on just such semantic fine points.[64]

64. For a more detailed analysis of the various types of remainders, see Bergin and Haskell, Preface to Estates in Land and Future Interests 62–80 (2 ed. 1984).

Chapter 5

THE ROLE OF EQUITY

Writing about the Anglo–American law of property subjects one to a peculiar handicap, not unlike boxing with one arm in a sling. The writer, as he slugs it out with the common-law estates, must constantly be alert for the equitable estates but he cannot pause to take them on at the same time. Hence, he makes veiled references to chancery and statements that such and such is true except in equity. It is almost with a sigh of relief that he finally turns to the role of equity in shaping the modern law of property. It is chronologically proper to take up equity at this point since the chancery court did not appear on the scene until the basic common-law doctrine of estates was well established.

The law of the feuds was ideally adapted to serve the society that produced it, but by the time that law had matured feudalism was already dying as a *political* system. The strong central government, under the king, was now able to maintain the peace and the various feudal incidents lived on as burdens to the landowner without much benefit in return. Unable to destroy the burdens directly by legislation, since the rudimentary parliament was under the domination of the king who was the principal recipient of the incidents, the landowners turned to legal subterfuge. They adapted to their needs an ancient device, the conveyance to uses.

SECTION 1. THE RISE OF THE USE

The use was essentially a simple tool and not even a new one. For various purposes, the fee simple owner of land might convey it to another person to hold for certain specified uses. For example, the Franciscans, having taken a vow of poverty, could not own land, so religious followers would convey the necessary dwelling to some trusted individual to hold "for the use of" the friars. A similar transaction might be utilized to set up an estate for minor children while the father was on a crusade. The feudal lawyers were apparently as alert as contemporary ones and they hit upon the scheme of transferring Blackacre to two or more joint tenants

69

to hold "for the use of" the grantor or such persons as he might specify. The transferee was called the "feoffee to uses" and the person for whose benefit he was to hold was called the *cestui que use*. Note that the feoffee to uses had the legal title, i.e., he was seised of the fee simple estate recognized by the courts while the *cestui que use* had only a beneficial interest, in reality a claim that the feoffee hold the proceeds of the estate for him.

Now comes the beauty of the scheme. The feudal incidents attached only to the legal estate, not to the beneficial interest which the law did not even recognize. Thus, if the *cestui que use* died no incidents were due and the feoffee to uses simply held Blackacre for the person or persons designated by the original grantor. Since wills were not permitted at this time,[1] probably because the king wanted all land to descend to the heir so he could have the feudal dues, the feoffment to uses also served as a method for passing the land at death to someone other than the heir at law. But suppose the feoffee to uses died, wouldn't he have to ante up the incidents since he had the legal title? He clearly would have had to do so but since two or more persons were used as joint tenants the land was held by the survivor and the feudal dues were defeated. Moreover, as soon as one joint tenant died a new one was introduced into the picture so that seldom would any obligations be incurred.

This conveyance to uses had one weak spot. If the feoffee to uses were dishonest or unfaithful to his "trust" the *cestui que use* was left without a remedy. The courts recognized that the feoffee was seised of Blackacre since a fee simple estate had been transferred to him and so they would not interfere to make him perform his promise. When the device was infrequently used this caused but little difficulty, but with its rapid growth in the fourteenth century the frauds began to multiply. A solution had to be found or the use abandoned.

In this dilemma the *cestui que uses* turned to the king who was the source of all justice in the realm. Most justice was dispensed by the common-law courts but the king retained a residue of power which he exercised through the chancellor and which could be utilized in extraordinary cases where there was no relief at the common law. Why the king should have intervened to help landowners who were engaged in depriving him of the cherished feudal incidents is not clear, but at any rate the chancellor did order the feoffee to uses to carry out the "trust" or be held in contempt of the royal prerogative. This is not the place to trace the rise of the court of chancery as a rival to the common-

---

1. It was not until 1540 that the Statute of Wills, 32 Hen. 8, c. 1, made land generally devisable in England.

law courts [2] but a few comments must be made to clarify the operation of the feoffment to uses.

At first, the chancellor acted solely at his discretion and was not bound by any rules of precedent but eventually the chancery accumulated its own principles and equity became a separate system of "law" administered by an independent tribunal.[3] However, the chancery did not come into direct conflict with the common-law courts and did not attempt to interfere with the common-law estates. In fact, it adopted the same scheme of ownership so that you could have an equitable fee simple, fee tail, or life estate with the same consequences that we have already discussed. Equity went even further in permitting the creation of new interests in land and, since chancery was not bound by some of the more technical rules of the common law, it was possible to have springing and shifting uses as well as the more usual estates. Equity acted solely *in personam* by ordering the feoffee to uses to do certain things and then fining or imprisoning him for failure to do so. Thus, if *O* granted "to *A* and his heirs, to hold for the use of *B* for life, remainder for the use of *C* and his heirs", *A* had a legal fee simple while *B* had an equitable life estate followed by an equitable vested remainder in *C*. Equity recognized *A's* fee simple but if *A* refused to give the rents and profits to *B* during his lifetime or tried to sell Blackacre as his own, the chancellor, on request by *B*, would step in and see that the use was properly carried out. This power of the equity court extended to successors in interest of *A* and therefore an heir or devisee of *A* would take Blackacre subject to the use as would any purchaser from *A* who had notice (i.e., knew or should have known) of the use. The only person who could take free of the use would be a bona fide purchaser for value without notice (b.f.p.). Even in this last case, the *cestui que use* would have an action against the feoffee to uses for breach of confidence.

By the sixteenth century the use was a highly-developed device and vast quantities of English land were held to uses. Equitable titles were almost as common as legal ones and, since in each case the king was being deprived of his feudal incidents, it is not surprising to find an attempt being made to end the whole system.

---

2. For a brief account of the role of equity in Anglo–American law see de Funiak, Handbook of Modern Equity 1–26 (2d ed. 1956).

3. Equity has been defined as "that portion of remedial justice which is ex- clusively administered by courts of equity, as distinguished from courts of common law." Malone v. Meres, 91 Fla. 709, 109 So. 677 (1926).

SECTION 2. THE STATUTE OF USES

It was that multi-wived monarch, Henry VIII, who finally
forced the issue. He seems to have been perpetually pressed for
funds and a survey of the assets of the kingdom disclosed how the
feudal incidents were slipping through the royal fingers. In 1535,
he forced the Statute of Uses upon a reluctant parliament. It is a
peculiar statute since it attacked the use only indirectly; it did not
abolish the device or prohibit conveyances to uses but, rather,
executed the use. It accomplished this by providing that the
seisin, and therefore the legal estate, should be vested in the *cestui
que use,* passing right on through the feoffee to uses. Thus, the
feudal incidents would become due to the lord of the fee as soon as
the *cestue que use* died. The statute reads: "Where any person or
persons stand or be seised . . . to the use, confidence or trust of
any other person or persons or to any body politic . . . that in
every such case all and every such person or persons and bodies
politic that have . . . any such use in fee simple, fee tail, for
term of life or for years . . . or in remainder or reverter shall
stand and be seised . . . in lawful seisin estate, and possession of
the same . . . lands . . . to all intents of and in such like
estates as they had or shall have in the use." [4]

The theory of the Statute was simple. Suppose *O* granted
Blackacre "to *A* and his heirs for the use of *B* and his heirs." The
statute executed the use and *B* received a *legal* estate in fee simple
absolute. *A* did not receive anything but merely served as a
conduit through which the legal title flowed from *O* to *B*. Moreover, the *cestui que use* received a legal estate of exactly the same
type as the equitable one which he would have had before the
passage of the Statute. Thus, if *O* grants "to *A* and his heirs to
hold for the use of *B* for life, remainder for the use of *C* and his
heirs", *A* takes nothing, *B* receives a legal life estate in possession
and *C* a vested remainder in fee simple absolute (legal).

The immediate result of the Statute of Uses was to restore the
feudal incidents to the overlord and nullify the point of a feoffment to uses. It had a side effect—destruction of the use as a
method of devising property on death, the pre–1535 equivalent of a
will. The latter effect seems to have caused the most immediate
reaction because the habit of devising land to individuals other
than, or in addition to, the heir was widespread. Henry VIII was
forced to compromise on this issue and five years after the Statute
of Uses, in 1540, the Statute of Wills was passed. It did not allow
complete testation but it was adequate for the purpose and met

4. 27 Hen. 8, c. 10 (1535).

the demands of the landowners. The Statute of Wills did not require the intervention of the use but allowed the testator to execute a document, under proper safeguards, which passed the legal title directly to the named devisees.

SECTION 3. THE MODERN SIGNIFICANCE OF THE STATUTE OF USES

The Statute of Uses has been called the most important single piece of legislation in the Anglo–American law of property. It is still on the statute books of many American states and is considered as a part of the adopted common law of England [5] in many more. Why should an essentially revenue-raising act of Henry VIII have had so profound an influence on property law? Paradoxically, it is because (1) the Statute was not successful in its primary aim and (2) the Statute had some totally unforeseen consequences. It is a perfect example of the unplanned growth of English law. The Statute's lack of success gave rise to the modern law of trusts, and the unforeseen consequences led to new methods of conveying real property and to the possibility of new estates in land. Let us look at each of these points in turn.

A. THE MODERN TRUST

It must have occurred to you that the ancient use bore many similarities to what we now call a trust. The feoffee to uses was the trustee, the *cestui que use* was the beneficiary, and the grantor of Blackacre was the settlor or trustor. In the modern trust, the trustee takes the legal title but must hold it for the benefit (use) of the beneficiary who thus has equitable title. In our modern courts, with their merger of law and equity, the trust is still the creature of equity and is handled on the chancery side of the

---

5. The Statute of Uses was repealed in England as a part of the property reform legislation of 1925. Speaking of the abolition of the Statute, the Lord Chancellor said: "I am told that there is one most respected practitioner, grown grey in the practice of the Chancery Law, sixty years of whose successful and brilliant life has been spent in the exposition, not unremunerative exposition, of the Statute of Uses, who, when he heard, not from my lips but from lips perhaps less sympathetic, that at last the Statute of Uses was abolished, definitely and irrevocably announced his intention not to survive it, and that he resigned his practice at once."

court.[6] It is obvious that none of this could have come about if the Statute of Uses had been successful, for its avowed purpose was to destroy the split between legal and equitable ownership and return to the earlier concept of legal estates only.   In fact, the Statute probably had this effect for nearly a century, but eventually loopholes were discovered in the legislation and through them crawled the equitable jurisdiction of chancery to fashion the modern trust.   These loopholes were three in number: (1) the Statute did not apply to a use on a use; (2) it did not apply to personal property; and (3) it did not apply to active, as distinguished from passive, uses.

---

(1) USE ON A USE

Suppose *O* granted Blackacre "to *A* and his heirs for the use of *B* and his heirs for the use of *C* and his heirs."   Prior to the Statute of Uses, *A* would take the legal title and *B* would have the equitable one.   *C* would take nothing, since *O* had exhausted his estate in the grant to *B* and the further limitation to *C* would be repugnant to it.   After the Statute, you would normally assume that the legal title would pass to *C* since Blackacre was to be held to his ultimate use.   The Statute should execute the two uses and *A* and *B* should both become mere conduits for the legal title. However, the chancellors finally decided that the Statute would operate only once and then, with its force spent, would retire from the scene.   The state of the title would then be as follows: the Statute would execute the first use, so *A* would take nothing and *B* would have the legal fee, but the Statute would not execute the second use, so *B* would hold Blackacre in trust for *C*, who now had the beneficial interest.   By this bit of hocus pocus, equity was able to reassert its jurisdiction and in 1738 Lord Chancellor Hardwicke could claim that the Statute "has had no other effect than to add at most three words to a conveyance."   If all of this seems, as the English say, "a bit much", you should remember that in 1660 the Statute of Tenures had finally ended the feudal incidents and the crown no longer cared whether the Statute of Uses was thwarted. Of course, the Statute could have been repealed, but why bother when the desirable results of a trust could be attained by the simple device of a use on a use?

The use *on* a use should be distinguished from the use *after* a use, for in the latter case the Statute was fully operational.

---

6. See Karlen, Primer of Procedure 165–172 (1950) for a brief discussion of the fusion of law and equity in the modern judicial system.

Suppose *O* grants Blackacre "to *A* and his heirs for the use of *B* for life, remainder to the use of *C* and his heirs." This is a use *after* a use, first a use to *B* for life, followed by a use to *C* in remainder. As we have already pointed out, the Statute will operate to give *B* the legal life estate and *C* the legal vested remainder. Contrast this with the result in the previous paragraph where a use *on* a use was involved.

(2) Uses of Personal Property

The Statute of Uses was not concerned with personalty for no feudal incidents were involved. The Statute applied only where one person was *seised* to the use of another and seisin had no application outside of the freehold estates. If *O* gave a herd of cattle to *A* to hold for the use of *B*, you had a split between the legal and the equitable ownership and chancery would enforce the "trust" in favor of *B*, after, as well as before, the Statute. Suppose *O* granted Blackacre "to *A* for ninety-nine years, to hold for the use of *B* and his heirs." Would the Statute apply? It would not, because *A* was not *seised* to the use of *B*. *A* had only a non-freehold estate and, as we have already discussed, that was a species of personal property, a chattel real. Thus, *A* would be the trustee and *B* would have an equitable interest for the ninety-nine years, at the end of which time the land would revert to *O* or his heirs. Here, again, equity could retain its jurisdiction and while personal property did not bulk large in the seventeenth-century scheme of things, it makes up a large proportion of modern trust property. The most common ingredient of the contemporary trust *res* is likely to be stocks and bonds.

(3) Active Uses

Prior to the Statute of Uses, the feoffee to uses seldom had any duties to perform. After all, the use was only a scheme to evade the feudal incidents and perhaps to have the benefits of a will. The feoffee was in reality a straw man, holding a naked legal title for the true owner. Because of this fact, the common-law courts came to the conclusion that the Statute did not apply if, in fact, the feoffee was given some active duties to perform. It was reasoned that in such a case he was more than a straw man and must have the legal title if he were to successfully perform those duties. Moreover, the duties did not have to be very extensive before the court would say that the Statute had no application. Thus, if *O* granted Blackacre "to *A* and his heirs upon trust to collect the rents and profits and pay them to *B* ", the legal title remained in *A,* for how else could he justify his collection of the rents? Similarly, a trust for sale of the land by *A* was beyond the reach of the Statute, since *A* would have to hold the legal title in order to sell the estate. It was still possible to have a dry or passive trust where no duties were involved, but this became progressively less likely to happen. The typical, modern trust literally bristles with all sorts of duties for the trustee.

It should be clear that in these three areas where the Statute of Uses did not operate, there was sufficient room for the gigantic edifice which is the modern trust. Although the law of trusts is obviously a part of the law of property in the broad sense, it has become so specialized a subject that we will not spend further time on it in a book on the basic principles of property law. We will now turn our attention to two areas in which the Statute of Uses did operate, but with unforeseen consequences.

B. NEW METHODS OF CONVEYANCING

There were a number of methods of conveyancing at common law[7] but all of them were cumbersome and subject to various disadvantages. The most frequently used, the feoffment, involved the formal ceremony of livery of seisin and required the parties to be physically present on the land so that the clod of dirt or twig could be handed over to symbolize the transfer of seisin. Although a charter of feoffment was later given to memorialize the conveyance, the livery of seisin was the operative part of the feoffment. This bit of pageantry was undoubtedly appealing to the medieval mind but it was hardly the method on which to build the commercial use of land. Eventually, some simpler scheme for conveying real property was bound to be developed and the Statute of Uses happened to be the catalyst which called forth the modern deed. Like most brief descriptions of legal phenomena, this is an over-simplification of what actually happened but it should clarify the importance of the Statute in the field of convey-

---

7. Among those in normal use were the feoffment, the fine and common recovery, the lease, the grant, the lease and release, and the surrender. For a good, short discussion see Tiffany, Real Property 654–666 (New Abridged Edition, 1940).

ancing. The two new methods of transferring title were the bargain and sale and the covenant to stand seised.

Before the passage of the Statute, the feoffment to uses had become so common that a presumption existed that any conveyance was for the use of the grantor unless there was evidence to the contrary. Thus, if *O* enfeoffed *A*, nothing more appearing, *A* received the legal title but he held it for the use of *O*. This was called a resulting use, since the use came back or resulted to *O*. It was a justifiable conclusion, since *O* was probably trying to put the legal title in *A* to avoid the feudal incidents. Of course, this presumption could be rebutted by showing that *A* paid value (consideration) to *O* or that there was an express declaration of use, such as "to *A* and his heirs for the use of *A* and his heirs" or "to *A* and his heirs for the use of *B* and his heirs." There was a corollary to this presumption in the case of the feoffment. Suppose *O* "bargained and sold Blackacre to *A* and his heirs", i.e., suppose *A* paid value to *O* for the land but did not take a common-law conveyance. This bargain and sale might be oral or it might be evidenced by a written contract, but in any case no formal conveyance was made and so the legal title to the land remained in *O*. Since value had been paid, however, it was presumed that the parties had intended *A* to become the beneficial owner and equity would treat *O* as holding to the use of *A*. What was the result after the passage of the Statute of Uses? The Statute executed the use, since *O* was seised to the use of *A*, and the legal as well as the beneficial interest passed to *A*.

The way had now been cleared for a simple, efficient method of land transfer. After the Statute, the parties could gather in the lawyer's office, he could draft a "deed" of bargain and sale, the purchaser could pay the money to the vendor, the Statute would automatically execute the use, and the purchaser could walk out of the office as the new owner of Blackacre. The bargain-and-sale form of deed is still much used in the United States and while many states have a simplified form of statutory conveyance [8] others still rely on the Statute of Uses to give vitality to their land transfers.

The effectiveness of the bargain and sale depended upon the payment of consideration to raise the presumption of use in the payor. A parallel development gave rise to the covenant to stand seised where no "valuable" consideration (money or money's worth) was involved but where "good" consideration (a legal relationship based on blood or marriage) was found to exist. If *O* covenanted to stand seised—promised under seal to hold Black-

---

8. 3 American Law of Property 221–224 (Casner ed. 1952).

acre—to the use of *A*, and *A* was a stranger, the covenant had no legal consequence. There had been no legal conveyance to *A* and since value had not been paid there was no basis for a presumption of a use in *A*. But suppose *A* was the wife or son of *O*. Equity would now presume that, because of the close ties between *O* and *A*,[9] the equitable title was in *A* while *O* continued to hold the legal title for the former's use. After the Statute, the use would, of course, be executed and the full legal title would be in *A* although no common-law conveyance of the land had been made.

Henry VIII and his advisors had never intended to affect the common-law conveyancing structure of England; the Statute was designed to be a reactionary, not a liberal reform, measure. But, due to the accidents of history and the adaptability of the common-law lawyers, a modern system of land transfer was born.

C. THE CREATION OF NEW ESTATES IN LAND

In Chapter 4,[10] we discussed the permissible estates at common law and found them to be divided into two categories—freehold and non-freehold. The latter group was unaffected by the Statute of Uses but the freehold estates were expanded by the admission of certain types of future interests which had been impossible at common law. You will recall that the fees simple, the fee tail, and the life estate were the permissible freehold estates and the chancery court recognized equitable equivalents of each of them. The freehold estates could be further divided into present (possessory) estates and future interests. The future interests were also present estates but their owners were not entitled to possession until the preceding estate had ended, i.e., they were vested in interest but not in possession. These common-law future interests were the reversion, the vested remainder, the possibility of reverter, the right of entry for condition broken (power of termination), and the contingent remainder. Our prior discussion of these future interests pointed out that the first two were true estates in land, i.e., they represented interests that were certain to accrue to the holder or his heirs once the preceding possessory estate ended.[11] The latter three, however, were subject to further

9. Just how close these ties must be is an open question. See Dawley v. Dawley's Estate, 60 Colo. 73, 152 P. 1171 (1915), where the court decided an agreement to hold property to the use of an *adopted* son was a good covenant to stand seised.

10. P. 40, supra.

11. This is not strictly accurate since a reversion could be subject to a condition precedent, e.g., any reversion following a life estate and a contingent remainder. However, most reversions

conditions and might, in fact, never become true estates. More accurately, they should be called expectancies but long usage has led to their classification generally as species of future interests.

In recognizing these future interests the common law was typically rigid and required a strict following of the rules. In Section 3 of Chapter 4 [12] some of these anachronistic rules—the Rule in Shelley's Case, the Doctrine of Worthier Title, and the destructibility of contingent remainders—were explored and it was pointed out that they have survived into modern times. The Statute of Uses should have affected some of these rules [13] but it did not do so and they were adopted by the chancery, apparently as a part of the maxim that equity follows the law. But there were some further technical rules of the common-law courts that were not blindly followed in equity. These rules had to do mainly with seisin and the common-law insistence that seisin always be lodged in a specific person to whom the overlord could look for the feudal incidents. These rules were: (1) no freehold could be limited to begin *in futuro;* (2) no remainder could be limited after the grant of a fee simple; (3) no remainder could be limited so as to vest in possession prior to the normal ending of the preceding estate; and (4) no power of appointment could be used to vest in a third party an interest greater than that owned by the donee of the power.[14] It is necessary to look at each of these, in turn, and see the change wrought by the Statute of Uses.

(1) No freehold could be limited to begin *in futuro. O,* on January 1, grants "to *A* and his heirs from September 1." There might be many reasons why *O* would desire to do this, e.g., September 1 might be the marriage date of *A,* and *O,* going on a long journey, might want to make a present gift of Blackacre. At common law such a grant would be void because it must be made by a livery of seisin and once that was done *A* would be the owner. There could be no abeyance of seisin. (Of course, you realize that *O* could grant to *X* for eight months, then to *A,* but that was interpreted as a present grant to *A,* subject to an estate for years in *X*). This problem was easily solved by a use. *O* granted "to *X* and his heirs for the use of *A* and his heirs from September 1." The seisin passed to *X* immediately, thus no abeyance, and equity would enforce *A's* rights after September 1. Prior to that time, there would be a resulting use in *O* since *X* had given nothing of value and the language of grant was silent as to the intervening months. With the passage of the Statute of Uses, these equitable

are of the vested type, i.e., following a life estate or an estate for years.

12. P. 58, supra.

13. It clearly should have ended the destructibility of contingent remainders doctrine. Do you see why?

14. Hargreaves, Introduction to Land Law 105–106 (3d ed. 1952).

interests became legal ones and, in effect, *O* kept the legal estate until September 1 when the legal estate passed automatically to *A*. Thus, it was possible, after the Statute, to limit a freehold to begin *in futuro*. A new type of future interest had been added to the closed categories of the common law.

(2) No remainder could be limited after the grant of a fee simple. *O* could create a fee simple determinable or a fee simple subject to a condition subsequent and, if he did so, he would retain, respectively, a possibility of reverter or a power of termination. No other future interest was possible following a fee simple. Assume *O* granted "to *A* and his heirs, but if *A* shall marry a tradesman's daughter, then to *B* and his heirs." At common law, the limitation to *B* was void since it would result in shifting the seisin from *A* to *B* and would offend the rule under discussion. However, *O* could grant "to *X* and his heirs for the use of *A* and his heirs, but if *A* shall marry a tradesman's daughter, then to *B* and his heirs." Prior to the Statute, *X* would hold first for *A*, then if the condition occurred, he would hold for *B*. After the Statute, the use would be executed and both interests would be legal, the shift occurring automatically upon the happening of the contingency. Note, however, that *B* would not have a contingent remainder but a shifting use or interest, called an executory devise if it appeared in a will. *A's* estate would be a defeasible fee, technically referred to as a fee simple subject to an executory limitation.[15]

To be accurate, it should be explained that the term executory interest (or executory limitation) is generic and includes the shifting use (interest) and the springing use (interest). The former has just been illustrated and arises whenever the happening of the

15. If you have been following this discussion closely, you will now see why the Statute of Uses should have ended the destructibility doctrine. Suppose, after 1536, *O* bargains and sells "to *A* for life, remainder to *A's* first son who shall reach twenty-one." *A* dies, survived by a minor son. The court should say that the land reverts to *O* in fee simple subject to an executory limitation and the minor son will take the land by a springing use when he reaches twenty-one. Such interests are now possible because of the Statute of Uses. Instead, in Purefoy v. Rogers, 2 Wms.Saund. 380 (1670) the court announced the rule: "No limitation capable of taking effect as a contingent remainder shall, if created inter vivos, be held to be a springing use under the Statute of Uses, or, if, created by will, be held to be an executory devise under the Statute of Wills." The quote is from White v. Summers, L.R. [1908] 2 Ch. 256 but it is known as the Rule of Purefoy v. Rogers. As you know from the previous discussion, the doctrine of destructibility has now been changed by statute in most states. For a case where the distinction between contingent remainders and executory interests determined the outcome see Stoller v. Doyle, 257 Ill. 369, 100 N.E. 959 (1913). Since executory interests were nondestructible it became possible, after the Statute of Uses, to tie up property for an indefinite period and deadhand control became a distinct reality. This gave rise to the Rule against Perpetuities as a common-law policy opposed to remoteness of vesting.

condition destroys a legal estate vested in a grantee and shifts that estate over to another party. The latter term refers to an estate which springs out of the original grantor, i.e., where the happening of the condition destroys the original estate of the grantor. Thus, the estate in the immediately preceding subsection (1) is a springing use since it will spring into existence on September 1 and destroy the estate of *O*, the grantor. Similarly, *O* might grant "to *X* and his heirs for the use of *A* and his heirs when *A* shall attain the age of twenty-one." After the Statute, such a grant would leave *O* with a fee simple subject to an executory limitation and would give *A* a springing use.

(3) No remainder could be limited so as to vest in possession prior to the normal ending of the preceding estate. This rule is similar to the preceding one and, indeed, is another way of explaining why there could be no springing or shifting interests at common law. It is included here because it is a broader statement of the proposition and illustrates that any interest following a common-law estate had to wait for the natural end of its predecessor—"after you, my dear Alphonso!." Thus, if *O* granted "to *A* for life, but if he marries a tradesman's daughter, then to *B* for life", the grant to *B* was void since it might destroy *A*'s estate prior to its normal termination on *A*'s death. Again, it is apparent that this result could have been reached by a use and would now be possible because of the Statute of Uses.

(4) No power of appointment could be used to vest in a third party an interest greater than that owned by the donee of the power. Among the most flexible of the modern methods for the disposition of property is the power of appointment. By this device, a power can be given to a trusted friend or a bank to designate a person or persons who will ultimately take the property, without the donee of the power having any interest in the property himself. This could not be done at common law. A grant "to *A* for life, remainder to such children of *A* as *X* shall appoint" would give *A* a life estate but the power would be void and *O* would have a reversion. But *O* could grant "to *X* and his heirs for the use of *A* for life then for the use of such children of *A* as *X* (or someone else) shall appoint." Equity would enforce such a use and after the Statute the interests were held to be legal, thus allowing the powers of appointment to be added to the arsenal of the property lawyer. These powers may be either general or special. The former allows the appointment to be exercised in favor of any one, including the donee of the power, while the latter restricts the exercise to members of a specified class.[16]

16. A full discussion of powers of appointment is beyond the scope of this text. For a brief discussion see Powell on Real Property 479–525. (Abridged Ed. Powell and Rohan (1968).)

At the present time, all of these "new" estates in land are so well recognized that it is not necessary to follow the old formula, "to *X* and his heirs for the use of, etc.", in order to take advantage of the greater flexibility of equity. It is fair to say that the four rules just discussed no longer exist and that, in addition to the permissible common-law estates, executory interests and powers of appointment must be included in the list of estates in land.[17]

SECTION 4. THE RULE AGAINST PERPETUITIES AND RESTRAINTS ON ALIENATION

As the preceding section demonstrates, the Statute of Uses led to the creation of new estates in land. The distinction between contingent remainders and executory interests was a narrow one, based on the logic of history, but it had some significant consequences. Contingent remainders could be destroyed at common law but executory interests could not and hence they might vest at some indefinite (and remote) period in the future, thus tying up property interests in perpetuity. Since much of English law had been concerned with the free alienability of land, the courts viewed this prospect with alarm and set about (with all deliberate speed) the task of restraining too much "dead hand" control. The result was the Rule against Perpetuities—a deceptively stated Rule that has led to fantastic amounts of litigation and volumes of learned exegesis, expounding (and complicating) the application of the Rule. A little learning is a dangerous thing and no attempt will be made here to explain the full ramifications of the Rule, although you should be aware of its existence and should study it in detail in the advanced course in Future Interests or Trusts and Estates. If you wish a short explanation at this time, you should read the justly popular article, "Perpetuities in a Nutshell" by the late Professor Leach of Harvard.[18] It will show something of the complex character of the Rule.

17. While executory interests, both springing and shifting, have full legal recognition today, they cannot be used to reach a result that is contrary to public policy. Thus, in Capitol Federal Savings & Loan Ass'n v. Smith, 136 Colo. 265, 316 P.2d 252 (1957) the court refused to enforce a shifting interest which would have prevented the sale of land to black persons.

18. Leach, Perpetuities in a Nutshell, 51 Harv.L.Rev. 638 (1938). Note

Professor Leach's own *caveat.* "If this paper fails of its purpose it has, at least, eminent company. Lord Thurlow undertook to put the Rule in Shelley's Case in a nutshell. 'But,' said Lord Macnaghten, 'it is one thing to put a case like Shelley's in a nutshell and another to keep it there.' Van Grutten v. Foxwell, [1897] A.C. 658, 671." See also Bergin and Haskell, Preface To Estates in Land and Future Interests 178–229 (2d ed. 1984).

Professor Gray's classic statement of the Rule was as follows: "No interest is good unless it must vest, if at all, not later than twenty-one years after some life in being at the creation of the interest." It was a rule against remoteness of vesting and so long as the estate was vested in interest, even though not in possession, the Rule was not violated. After all, a fee simple absolute had a potentially infinite duration and that was no obstacle since someone had the power to alienate the land. The vice lay in tying up the land with non-destructible contingent interests in perpetuity. The Rule was designed to allow suspension of vesting for the lifetime or lifetimes of individuals living at the effective date of the deed, will, or trust plus the minority (hence twenty-one years) of someone not yet in being. (Later the twenty-one years was extended to include a period of gestation, twenty-one years plus nine months.) If the estate *might* vest in interest at a period more remote than that it was void for remoteness, being viewed as a perpetuity. The rest of the grant or devise was valid but the "gift over" failed and the intent of the grantor or testator was thwarted. Obviously, a devise to a living person for life, followed by a contingent interest in his issue (vesting on the death of the life tenant or within twenty-one years plus a period of gestation thereafter) was all right but attempts to keep the interest contingent through succeeding generations of the family would raise the spectre of the Rule.

One illustration, with which you are already acquainted, will demonstrate the complexities of the Rule. O devises Blackacre "to A and his heirs for so long as no liquor is sold on the premises." A has a fee simple determinable and O has a possibility of reverter. The Rule does not apply because a possibility of reverter, in common-law theory, is vested in interest (being a reversionary interest) and if liquor is ever sold on the premises (regardless of how long in the future, absent some special statute on the matter [19]) O or his heirs will get the land, which will then vest in possession. If, however, O devised Blackacre "to A and his heirs for so long as no liquor is sold on the premises but if liquor shall ever be sold on the premises then to B and his heirs", the interest given to B is void as violating the Rule Against Perpetuities. A had a fee simple subject to an executory limitation and B had an executory interest of the shifting type, which does *not* vest in interest until liquor is, in fact, sold on the premises. Since this *might* be at a time more remote than lives in being plus twenty-one years it is void *ab initio*. A would still have his defeasible fee which he could lose if liquor is ever sold on the premises, but the future interest would be in O or his heirs not in B.[20] Of course, O

19. See p. 46, supra.

20. First Universalist Society of North Adams v. Boland, 155 Mass. 171, 29 N.E. 524 (1892). See also The City of Klamath Falls v. Bell, 7 Or.App. 330, 490 P.2d 515 (1971). In the latter case,

could have saved the "gift over" to B by stipulating that if liquor is sold during the lifetime of A or twenty-one years thereafter then the land is to pass to B and his heirs.

Similarly, if O devised Blackacre "to A and his heirs at such time as liquor shall be sold on the premises", the interest in A would be void for violating the Rule. A would have had an executory interest of the springing type (springing out of O's heirs if liquor is ever sold on the premises) but, since the interest cannot vest until liquor is in fact sold, that *might* occur at a time more remote than allowed by the Rule and it must fail. O's heirs (or devisees) would take Blackacre freed of the executory interest in A.

This brief look at an intricate Rule should be sufficient to demonstrate why lawyers engaged in the property practice, especially in the drafting of wills and trusts, should have a thorough understanding of the subject. There is no reason why the client's interest cannot be adequately protected at the drafting stage (preventive law) but once the Rule has been violated it may require expensive litigation to settle the rights of the parties.

Somewhat related to the problems covered by the Rule Against Perpetuities are the numerous attempts to place restraints on the alienation of land. True, the Rule is concerned solely with the remoteness of vesting but its objective is to allow freer alienability and prevent the accumulation of large interests which no one can transfer. Having been astute to frustrate the landowner's desire to tie up his property in perpetuity by creating non-destructible future interests, the courts could scarcely be expected to allow more direct restraints on alienation which would have the same effect. Thus, a conveyance "to A and his heirs, provided he never sells, mortgages, or otherwise transfers the land" is a direct restraint on alienation and hence void. The basic principle is clear enough but its application can be difficult. If the restraint is a reasonable one, e.g., prohibiting transfer to a small group or for a limited purpose, but leaving a wide range of volition in the grantee, it will be enforceable. The key issue is: what is reasonable? [21] Like the Rule, the range of problems caused by

land was conveyed to a city so long as the site was used for a library then over to certain individuals. The city ceased to so use the land but claimed it now owned it in fee simple absolute because the gift over violated the Rule Against Perpetuities. The court held that the Rule was violated and the gift over was void since the executory interest might not vest within the period of the Rule. However, the city did not have a fee simple absolute because of the language "so long as" which created a defeasible fee in the city. This left a possibility of reverter in the original grantors or their heirs and assigns and the grantors being dead the land passed to their heirs.

21. For some light on this question, see Michalski v. Michalski, 50 N.J. Super. 454, 142 A.2d 645 (1958). The case involved a restraint on the inherent right to partition a tenancy in com-

attempted restraints is beyond the scope of this text and must be left to the student's initiative by a perusal of the excellent material on the subject [22] or to later courses in the property field.

SECTION 5. OTHER ASPECTS OF EQUITY

Equity's principal impact on the law of property came through the ancient use, modified into the modern trust. It must not be supposed, however, that this was equity's sole contribution to property law. Chancery's jurisdiction depended, in the main, on the inadequacy of the remedy at law. Thus, you could expect that the chancellor would range across the whole field of the common law and that eventually equity would come to permeate most areas of contract, tort, and property. So extensive was this infiltration that today, following the merger of law and equity, it is often difficult to tell whether a particular rule was legal or equitable in origin. If it really makes a difference which it is, as in cases where the right to a jury trial is in dispute, the lawyer may have to undertake a sizable piece of historical research.

Aside from trusts, the principal areas of equitable concern in property matters are: (1) the specific performance of real estate contracts; (2) the cancellation and rescission of contracts and deeds for fraud, mistake, duress, undue influence, and lack of capacity to contract (insanity, infancy, etc.); (3) the enforcement of covenants relating to land under the doctrine of equitable servitudes; and (4) the equity of redemption and certain other features of the law of mortgages. Some of these areas are beyond the scope of this book and will be dealt with only inferentially; others, such · as specific performance of real estate contracts and equitable servitudes, will be covered in some detail in later chapters.

mon. The restraint was for a period that did not violate the Rule Against Perpetuities (it did not extend beyond lives in being) and it was otherwise reasonable. However, the court refused to enforce the restraint because the changed circumstances of the cotenants made it inequitable to do so.

22. See, for example, Schnebly, Restraints Upon the Alienation of Legal Interests, 44 Yale L.J. 961, 1186, 1380 (1935).

Chapter 6

MULTIPLE OWNERSHIP

The study of law, and indeed the practice of it, involves a process of continual classification. We must call our concepts by name in order to talk about them, to deal with them, and to find out what others have said or done about them. Is a certain interest real or personal, present or future, vested or contingent? Once the classification has been made the problem is *not* solved; it has only been given a handle so we can start solving it. Moreover, the classifications are often vague and overlapping and frequently cause as much harm to our thinking as they do good. Consider for a moment the matter of multiple interests in the same *res*.

If the law recognized only one estate, the fee simple absolute, and if Blackacre could be owned by only one person at a time who could do nothing with it but possess and farm it, the law of property would be simple, but the social utility of Blackacre would be quite limited. Instead, the law, in order to increase the social utility, is complex and recognizes many interests in the same *res*. We cannot catalogue them all but it will be useful to direct our thinking to a number of the principal categories.

First, in the field of personal property, we encounter:

(a) *The finder and the "true" owner.* The former has possession and, in general, a claim that is good against the whole world except the "true" owner. The latter, unless he abandons the property, has ownership plus the right to possession if he can locate the finder.

(b) *The bailor and the bailee.* There are many forms of bailment—constructive, involuntary, gratuitous, for hire, etc.—but all of them involve multiple interests in the same piece of personal property. The basic idea is the transfer of the possession of personal property, without the transfer of ownership, for the accomplishment of a particular purpose. Thus, the bailor remains the owner of a pair of trousers left with a cleaner; the bailee has the right to their possession until they have been properly cleaned and pressed.

(c) *The pledgor and the pledgee.* The pledge is really a specialized form of bailment in which a chattel is bailed to a creditor as security for a debt. When the debt is paid the goods are to be returned but, in the meantime, the ownership remains in the pledgor and the pledgee has the right to retain possession only. Today, most pledges involve stocks and bonds and the pledgee is usually a bank.

(d) *The lienor and the lienee.* The lien is similar to the pledge since the lienor has the right to possession of the chattel but no ownership of it. However, the right to the lien arises out of improvements made on the chattel by a repairman or some artisan and the property is simply being retained until the bill is paid. The common law was very strict in its regulation of the rights of the lienor and if he surrendered possession of the chattel he surrendered his lien as well. There have, of course, been many statutory changes.

(e) *The chattel mortgagor and the mortgagee.* The owner of an automobile wishes to borrow $750, using his car as collateral. He signs a personal note for the $750 plus interest and gives a chattel mortgage on his car to secure the payment. The mortgagor still "owns" the car but the lending bank has a security interest in the same vehicle and can foreclose the mortgage if the debt is not paid.

(f) *The conditional seller and the buyer.* Using the previous illustration, if the seller of the car wished to employ the conditional sale device he would keep the "title" to the automobile himself but transfer the possession to the buyer. The latter would not own the car until he completed all of the payments plus the finance charges. If he did not meet the payments, the seller would "repossess" the vehicle.

In all of the above situations at least two people have a legal interest in the same *res.* As you would expect, many areas for dispute exist and the law has developed a series of rules and principles to adjust these difficulties. The common law covered most of the problems but it was too inflexible and the demands of a commercial society have required many statutory changes. Moreover, many of the relationships are regulated by special contracts and by the customs of the groups involved in commercial credit.[1]

Second, in the field of real property, we find all sorts of multiple interests in the same piece of land, e.g., the present interest and the future interest (life estate plus remainder), the landlord and the tenant, the vendor and the purchaser, the mortgagor and the mortgagee, the holder of the fee simple absolute and the owner of the non-possessory interest in that same land (easement, profit, restrictive covenant), and the trustee and the benefi-

---

1. For a full treatment of these areas see Brown, The Law of Personal Property (3d ed. by Professor Raushenbush 1975) and the course in Sales or Commercial Law.

ciary (the trust device applies to personal property as well). Most of these interests in land are within the scope of this book; some of them, e.g., trusts and mortgages, are too specialized to be covered extensively here.

Third, there are still other types of multiple interests in the same property and they form the principal subject matter of this chapter. These are marital interests and concurrent estates. While these interests are most important in the law of real property some of them have application to personal property as well. The concurrent estates are particularly intriguing since they involve present interests of the same quality in a single *res.* Moreover, these interests may exist in a whole series of individuals.

SECTION 1.   MARITAL INTERESTS

In a traditional classification of property interests the materials of this section, except for community property which is *sui generis,* are usually found under the heading "legal life estates", because in the main they tend to be estates for life and because they are created by operation of law rather than by act of the parties through a deed or will. However, with but few exceptions,[2] these legal life estates were created for the protection and use of either the husband or the wife and it is more realistic to look at them in this light. These marital interests were a kind of social security and they gave some assurance that the spouse of a man (or woman) of property would not be left entirely destitute. The interests created have many other effects, however, such as interfering with the rights of creditors, causing added difficulties in the sale of land, etc. Since the interests themselves grew out of the social conditions of the past you should ask the always pertinent legal question, "Have these particular property interests outlived their social usefulness?"

In this section we shall discuss the estate of *jure uxoris,* curtesy, dower, homestead rights, and the doctrine of community property. Since the first three have roots deep in the soil of the common law we shall try to get the feel of these interests by a brief excursion into the past. You should know, in advance, that

2. Tenancy in special tail with possibility of issue extinct was a legal life estate created incidentally to a specific type of estate in land; in some states (see Ark.Stat. § 61–110, 1947) a life estate may be given to a parent by operation of the statutes of descent; and homestead may protect the children as well as the surviving spouse.

the estate of *jure uxoris* has little modern significance, that curtesy is now merged with dower in many states and that either spouse is then entitled to dower, and that dower itself has been changed by statute in all states so that you are never safe without consulting the latest pronouncement of the legislature.

A. JURE UXORIS, CURTESY, AND DOWER

The common law regarded the husband and wife as one and the husband as the one. The married woman's lack of status was reflected in the law of property. When *H* married *W*, who was seised of an estate of freehold, *H* was entitled to the use, occupancy and profits of the land for the duration of the marriage. The English law, until comparatively recently, did not recognize absolute divorce without a special act of Parliament, so the estate of *jure uxoris* (by right of the wife) in effect gave *H* a right to the land for the joint lives of the spouses. He could sell or mortgage his interest to a third party and the estate was liable for his debts.[3] He could also sue for any injury to his interest. Nonetheless, his estate was only for life and on the death of either spouse, or upon absolute divorce, *H's* interest terminated, and *W*, if *H* died, or *W's* heirs, if she died, became entitled to the land, unaffected by a prior conveyance or incumbrance by *H*. If issue were born of the marriage, the estate *jure uxoris* merged into *H's* estate by curtesy. At an early date, equity interfered to protect the wife's interest in some situations and this reduced the harshness of the common-law rules. Land could be conveyed or devised to trustees for the benefit of a married woman and thus freed of the control of the husband. Eventually, it became possible to convey directly to *W*, "for her sole and separate use," and equity would still protect this "equitable separate estate." Today, the estate *jure uxoris* has been abolished by statutes, either directly or indirectly, and the married woman has full control over her own property, subject to a possible curtesy or dower interest in some states.[4]

3. Mattocks v. Stearns, 9 Vt. 326 (1837).

4. See, for example, G.L.Ann. (Mass.) ch. 209, § 1. "The real and personal property of a woman shall upon her marriage remain her separate property, and a married woman may receive, receipt for, hold, manage and dispose of property, real and personal, in the same manner as if she were sole. But no conveyance by a married woman of real estate shall, except as otherwise provided in this chapter, extinguish or impair her husband's tenancy by the curtesy by statute . . . unless he joins in the conveyance or otherwise releases the same."

"Tenant by the curtesy of England, is where a man marries a woman seised of an estate of inheritance, that is, of lands and tenements in fee simple or fee tail; and has by her issue, born alive, which was capable of inheriting her estate. In this case he shall, on the death of his wife, hold the lands for his life, as tenant by the curtesy of England." [5] Immediately on birth of issue the estate *jure uxoris* was changed to curtesy initiate which in turn became curtesy consummate upon the death of the wife. This distinction between *jure uxoris* and curtesy explains the eagerness with which the first heir was awaited, even by men with few of the normal fatherly characteristics. Blackstone demonstrates the learning on the subject. "The issue must be born alive. Some have had a notion that it must be heard to cry; but that is a mistake. Crying indeed is the strongest evidence of its being born alive; but it is not the only evidence. The issue also must be born during the life of the mother: for if the mother dies in labour, and the Caesarean operation is performed, the husband in this case shall not be tenant by the curtesy; because at the instant of the mother's death he was not clearly entitled, as having had no issue born, but the land descended to the child while he was yet in his mother's womb; and the estate being once vested shall not afterwards be taken from him." [6] Curtesy initiate has been generally abolished by statute so that the husband would have to survive the wife to receive an actual estate in the land. Curtesy consummate has likewise been generally abolished or modified by statute and you should consult the law of the jurisdiction in question.[7]

"Tenant in dower is where the husband of a woman is seised of an estate of inheritance, and dies; in this case, the wife shall have the third part of all the lands and tenements whereof he was seised at any time during the coverture, to hold to herself for the term of her natural life".[8] Note that dower for the wife bore some similarity to curtesy for the husband, but the former did not depend on birth of issue and was a life estate in only one-third of the husband's estate whereas curtesy extended to all of the wife's estate. Moreover, there was no dower initiate, i.e., the wife had no estate in the husband's land until his death. During his lifetime her interest was inchoate and amounted to no more than an expectancy based on her survival.[9]

5. Blackstone Com. 126 et seq.

6. Id.

7. See, for example, Ill.Rev.Stat. ch. 3, § 18 (1961) "A surviving spouse, whether husband or wife, may become endowed of a third part of all real estate of which the decedent was seized of an estate of inheritance at any time during the marriage by electing to take dower. . . . There is no estate of curtesy." In 1972, Illinois also abolished dower. Ill.Rev.Stat. ch. 110½, § 2–9 (1985).

8. 2 Blackstone Com. 126 et seq.

9. Flynn v. Flynn, 171 Mass. 312, 50 N.E. 650 (1898). The wife claimed a part of a condemnation award for her inchoate dower but was refused because

Even inchoate dower has some substance, however, because it attaches to all freehold estates of inheritance owned by the husband during marriage and once attached it can be barred only by the death of the wife in the lifetime of the husband, by release by the wife, or by divorce for the fault of the wife.[10] The usual way to release inchoate dower is for the wife to join in a deed or mortgage of the land but if she fails to do so her interest is unaffected and on the death of the husband she can elect to take dower even though Blackacre is now owned by a third party. By refusing to join her husband in a conveyance of land, a stubborn wife can exert a powerful "blackmail" influence and if the parties inadvertently fail to secure her signature on a deed or mortgage serious problems can arise affecting the merchantability of title.

The husband cannot use fraudulent devices to defeat the wife's dower and where H abstained from paying a mortgage in which W had joined, in order to force a foreclosure, and the property was purchased at the foreclosure sale with money advanced by H, W's dower interest was not destroyed.[11] This case is typical of many in which the courts have given substantial protection to inchoate dower. Moreover, the right of dower will be sustained against the claims of creditors of the deceased husband, if the claims originated after marriage.[12]

After the death of the husband, inchoate dower becomes consummate and an assignment of the dower property must be made if the widow so elects. In the early days, many large English estates had a Dower House on the premises and this was set aside for the widow when the son and heir moved on up to the manor house. The widow would then be entitled to one-third of the rents and profits of the estate for her own life. Today, the Dower House has disappeared and the interest itself survives as a kind of relic of a social security system of the past.[13] Modern legislation typically gives two rights to the widow (and in many cases to the husband as well) which did not exist at common law: (1) if H dies intestate, W is an heir and is usually given one-half of

she did not own any estate or interest in land. Of course, dower consummate is protected fully in eminent domain proceedings. Borough of York v. Welsh, 117 Pa. 174, 11 A. 390 (1887). For a good discussion of the nature of inchoate dower see Opinion of the Justices, 337 Mass. 786, 151 N.E.2d 475 (1958), which upheld the constitutionality of a statute abolishing inchoate dower, and hence all dower in Massachusetts, except where it was already a vested estate (consummate).

10. Divorce for the husband's fault leaves dower intact unless it is disposed of by the divorce decree or by a voluntary divorce settlement. At common law, absolute divorce would prevent the assignment of dower regardless of fault but statutes have rather generally reached the result just stated. 2 Tiffany, Real Property, § 531 (3d ed. 1939).

11. Stokes v. Stokes, 119 Misc. 168, 196 N.Y.S. 184 (1922).

12. 2 Tiffany, Real Property, § 487 (3d ed. 1939).

13. Comment, Does Dower Pay Its Way in Illinois?, 1956 U.Ill.L.F. 487.

the estate if there is no issue, one-third if there is issue; (2) if *H* dies testate, *W* may renounce the will (whether or not she is named in it) and take a statutory share of *H's* estate (this share will usually be the same as her intestate share). Such legislation makes dower of much less importance than it was at common law when the widow could not claim any of the real property as an heir and had no power to renounce the will of her husband. Some statutes expressly provide that the statutory share of a surviving spouse is in lieu of dower.[14] It should be noted, however, that the statutory share is a more tenuous interest than dower because it attaches only to the property which the husband owns at the time of his death. Thus, he can defeat the claim of the wife by an inter vivos conveyance of the property without her consent.[15]

Dower has survived the passage of time better than curtesy, but even so it has been abolished in most states and has been materially altered in the others.[16]

B. HOMESTEAD [17]

The homestead exemption did not grow out of the common law and hence it lacks the thread of consistency that binds *jure uxoris,* curtesy, and dower into some sort of package, untidy though it may be. Texas passed the first homestead statute in 1839 [18] and many states, by constitutional or legislative provision, have followed suit. Homestead represents a policy decision designed to give protection to the family unit by granting a certain exemption to the head of a family against the claims of creditors.[19] The basic idea is simple enough. Many a householder, through circumstances beyond his control, falls on evil days and creditors, seeking to collect their due, strip him to the bone, taking the very roof from over the heads of his family. To prevent a disruption of

14. McKinney's N.Y.Consol.Laws, ch. 13, Decedent Estate Law, § 82.

15. Redman v. Churchill, 230 Mass. 415, 119 N.E. 953 (1918).

16. See 2 Powell, Real Property, § 213 (incl. 1982 Supp.) It would appear only a handful of states still recognize dower or curtesy even in modified form. They are: Alaska, Arkansas, Hawaii, Kentucky, Massachusetts, Minnesota, Ohio, Pennsylvania, Rhode Island, Virginia, and West Virginia.

17. Do not confuse the state homestead exemption with federal homestead legislation designed to allow an occupying claimant to acquire title to unappropriated public land. "Homesteading" the West is popular on the television screens but has nothing to do with our present subject.

18. See Marshall, Homestead Exemption—Oregon Law, 20 Ore.L.Rev. 328 (1941).

19. Waples, Homestead and Exemption, § 3 (1893).

the home, society grants him an exemption defined in money value, area, or both, and creditors can then reach only the value or area which is in excess of the exemption.[20] As with many another good idea, the execution has fallen short of the conception. Originally, the exemption was probably large enough to preserve the home intact, but much of the legislation has not kept pace with changing economic conditions and today the dollar amount is often too small to protect the home although large enough to cause title problems when land is conveyed without the proper release of the exemption. In Illinois, the amount was $1,000 until 1957 when it was increased to $2,500.[21] At today's prices this might save a garage roof, but little else.

"Few statutory enactments have met with such a variety of interpretations as has been accorded to the homestead exemption laws. Statutes containing identical language have led the courts to entirely different conclusions in their application, and even the courts of the same jurisdiction have felt free to deviate from and ignore former opinions without much concern about stare decisis. 'Fireside equity' has found a fertile field among the Homestead Acts, and this, coupled with frequent amendments, repeals, and reenactments has thrown the law of homestead into a state of conflict and confusion."[22] A few general principles can be discerned, however, and a brief statement will help clarify the modern role of homestead.

Strictly speaking, homestead is broader than a marital interest since it is available to the head of a family whether or not he is married. Thus, any person who has a legal or moral duty to support dependent persons living with him may be considered the head of a family.[23] In Minnesota, any resident of the state, whether or not he is head of a family, may claim the exemption.[24] Some states allow the acquisition of homestead by the mere occupancy of real property as a home; others require a declaration filed of record in order to make the claim;[25] and at least one state (Texas) provides the exemption for land occupied for business purposes.[26] In spite of these variations, the usual situation involves a husband or wife who claims the privilege as protection for the family unit.

20. Burby, Real Property 365 (2d ed. 1954).

21. Ill.Rev.Stat. ch. 52, § 1 (1961). By 1985, Illinois had increased the exemption to $7500, thus saving the roof and the foundations. Ill.Rev.Stat. ch. 110, § 12–901 (1985).

22. Note, The Illinois Homestead Exemption, 1950 U.Ill.L.F. 99.

23. Webster v. McGauvran, 8 N.D. 274, 78 N.W. 80 (1899).

24. Note, Homesteads—Application of Minnesota Statutes, 25 Minn.L.Rev. 66 (1940).

25. 2 Thompson, Real Property, § 987 (1939).

26. Tex. Const. art. XVI, § 51.

What exactly is homestead? Most writers contend that it is no more than an exemption from debts and does not rise to the dignity of an estate. Tiffany, for example, says that it is difficult to see how the right of an owner to hold land exempt from liability for debts can be an estate and that even where a statute expressly declares it to be an estate, a new meaning must be given to that term.[27] But there is no reason why a legislature may not create a new estate unknown at common law, and the fact that a rise or decline in value of land set off as homestead does not change its boundaries shows that we may be dealing with an interest that is more than an exemption and may, indeed, be called an estate. The Illinois act speaks of an estate of homestead and the Illinois courts have reluctantly called it that.[28] In fact, in Illinois, "if a conveyance of real estate is made without waiving homestead, then at the death of the homesteader, the title to the homestead estate descends to his heirs at law or passes to the devisees under his will as in the case of other real estate. Thus, where the householder conveys homestead property worth in excess of [$7500] and fails to waive homestead, he retains the title to [$7500] worth of the property. Upon his death this [$7500] worth of the homestead property, if not conveyed by the householder before his death, passes to his heirs or devisees." [29]

Regardless of the jurisdiction, it is apparent that purchasers or mortgagees must be careful to see that homestead is waived at the time of the sale or mortgage so that they will not be plagued by the interest at a future date. The statutes prescribe how this must be done and, as a general rule, they require certain formalities, such as an acknowledgment by the grantors and the signatures of both spouses on the deed or mortgage.[30] Since dower also requires joinder in the conveyance by the wife (or husband in some states) both of these marital interests may be extinguished by the same act.[31]

C. COMMUNITY PROPERTY

Homestead makes a statutory break with the common-law tradition of marital interests; community property springs from a

27. 5 Tiffany, Real Property, § 1332 (3d ed. 1939).

28. Browning v. Harris, 99 Ill. 456 (1881).

29. Fitch, Real Estate Titles in Illinois 380 (1948).

30. 2 Thompson, Real Property, § 1005 (1939).

31. Acknowledgment, i.e., attestation before the proper official, usually a notary public, is typically required to release homestead but not dower.

completely separate tradition and is borrowed from the civil law of Spain and France. The eight jurisdictions [32] where the doctrine of community property now exists do not have curtesy or dower although they do have the homestead exemption. Except in Louisiana, the basic principles of the common law, including the concept of estates and interests in land, have full play in these states but the special rules of community property must also be considered in giving sound legal advice. Since the system is a creature of statute there are wide variations among the states and no attempt will be made to do more than sketch the general outline of the doctrine.[33]

It is the theory of community property that the husband and wife should share *equally* that property acquired by their joint efforts during marriage. The marriage itself is a "community" to which both partners contribute and it makes no difference whether the husband or the wife is the actual breadwinner. This one-half-to-the-husband, one-half-to-the-wife approach seems to be the ultimate in marital interests. It makes a startling contrast with the old common-law estate *jure uxoris*!

Where the doctrine prevails, the first big problem is to distinguish between community property and separate property because not everything a spouse owns falls under the community veil. Property acquired by the earnings of either husband or wife during marriage, income from community property, and property acquired by the sale of community property, must be shared equally. On the other hand, property owned by either spouse before marriage, acquired by gift, inheritance, or devise after marriage, and income from such property is considered to be separate and subject to control by the spouse concerned. Thus, a husband (or wife) has the power to transfer inter vivos any separate property he may own and can devise it freely, subject only to the possible right of the other spouse to renounce the will and take a statutory forced share. It is true that community-property jurisdictions typically give a surviving spouse a larger share on intestacy than is normal in the other states. It should be

---

32. Arizona, California, Idaho, Louisiana, Nevada, New Mexico, Texas, and Washington. Note that the Spanish background of Louisiana and Mexico accounts for five of these states having adopted community property. Idaho, Nevada, and Washington were converted in the early stages of their settlement.

33. For a short discussion of community property see Cunningham, Stoebuck and Whitman, The Law of Property 240–252 (1984). For a more

detailed treatment see de Funiak and Vaughn, Principles of Community Property (2d ed. 1971). For a useful survey of the comparative aspects of community property and the common law system see Greene, Comparison of the Property Aspects of the Community Property and Common–Law Marital Property Systems and Their Compatibility with the Current View of the Marriage Relationship and the Rights of Women, 13 Creighton L.Rev. 71 (1979).

noted that a presumption exists that all property of a married couple is community property and so careful records as to source of acquisition should be kept in order to rebut the presumption.

The earlier community-property doctrine paralleled the common law and gave the husband full control but this has now been changed by statute and transfers of such property do not affect the wife's interest, unless she joins in the deed or mortgage. At death, either party can devise one-half of the community property but, of course, the other half remains vested in the surviving spouse. If the death is intestate, the statutes vary considerably but in some instances they give all to the survivor. If the marriage tie is severed by divorce, the community property is divided equally but the court has the power to reach the separate property of the husband, or even his one-half of the community property, if the circumstances require it.

Does the community-property doctrine have sufficient social value to commend it to the forty-two states that have remained loyal to the common law? Professor Powell does not think so. "When adopted at the beginning of a society's existence, community property may be as good as its proponents claim. Any attempt to shift from the customs, practices and rules of a state having the common law traditions to the community property system involves changes in so many aspects of society that it is a shift not lightly to be undertaken. There is at present no apparent likelihood that the system will spread in continental United States to more than the eight states which have grown up in its practices." [34]

Prior to 1948, there was a swing toward community property because of the great tax advantage arising from the fact that one-half of the husband's earnings was his income and one-half was his wife's income. Michigan, Nebraska, Oklahoma, Oregon, Pennsylvania, and Hawaii passed community-property legislation, designed to secure for their citizens the tax reduction enjoyed by the "old" community-property states.[35] The Revenue Act of 1948 eliminated this inequity by extending to all married couples the opportunity to split income, thus reaching about the same result as that prevailing in community-property states. Interest in community-property doctrine receded apace and five of the jurisdictions repealed their acts. The sixth, Pennsylvania, solved the problem more neatly when the Supreme Court of Pennsylvania held its statute unconstitutional.[36] In the five states where the legislatures repealed the acts, there will be haunting problems for

34. 4 Powell, Real Property 675, 676 (1954).

35. de Funiak, The Community Property Trend, 23 Notre Dame Law. 293 (1948).

36. Willcox v. Penn Mutual Life Ins. Co., 357 Pa. 581, 55 A.2d 521 (1947).

years to come since the doctrine was in force from the date of passage to the date of repeal and could affect titles during that period.   In Pennsylvania, the court's action means that the statute was void *ab initio* and property rights are unaffected by this venture into "alien principles."

D.   THE MARITAL PROPERTY ACT

The discussion in this section discloses an inexorable trend toward greater recognition of the rights of the wife in the property of her husband.   Society has moved a long way from *jure uxoris* and the concept that the husband and wife are one and that the husband is the one.   This change has come about largely through legislation, starting with the Married Women's Property Acts of the post-Civil War period and extending through the various uniform acts promulgated by the National Conference of Commissioners on Uniform State Laws, such as the Uniform Probate Code.   Community property, as it exists in the eight states listed in the previous sub-section, has not spread beyond its original borders but the *concept* of *shared* property and a community of interests in that property which is the product of a marriage has had considerable influence on the developing law, including tax policy.   In recent years, this trend toward greater protection for the rights of the wife has been given impetus by the women's rights movement and considerable effort has been expended on removing past inequities in the law.

The latest development in marital estates is the Uniform Marital Property Act, adopted by the National Conference of Commissioners on Uniform State Laws in 1983.   So far the Act has been adopted in only one state, Wisconsin,[37] and it is too early to predict how influential this particular Uniform Act will be, but it probably reflects the direction in which the law is moving.   Its widespread adoption would not make obsolete the basic principles of multiple ownership with which this chapter deals but it would introduce a changed concept of marital interests and would have numerous practical consequences.   The changed concept is *sharing* —the equal sharing by husband and wife of the benefits and liabilities of the marriage partnership.   Note that the doctrine which has most nearly embodied this concept is community property, not the common law system.

37.   Wis.Stat.Ann. 766.001 to 766.97 (1986).

The Uniform Marital Property Act, together with the Prefatory Note and Comments, is a forty page document [38] and is too complex to discuss in detail here. Moreover, if the Act is widely adopted there will undoubtedly be various amendments by the state legislatures which will require careful analysis. It will be sufficient for our present purposes to outline the principal "running gears" of the Act so that you can see which way the winds of doctrine are blowing. The following summary is a portion of a short article by Professor Mary Moers Wenig on the Marital Property Act. [39]

"Rather than the terms *community* and *separate* property, used by the eight community property states, the act uses the terms *marital property* and *individual property.* Use of this terminology is not intended to belittle the community property roots. But the term *marital property* evokes the property distribution provisions of the Uniform Marriage and Divorce Act and of comparable provisions for equitable distribution on marriage dissolution, now adopted by all but two of the common law states. In addition, the terms *marital property* and *individual property* are employed in recognition that the Marital Property Act attempts to meld concepts from both community property and common law.

"The act provides that property acquired during marriage is marital property. Both husband and wife have a present undivided one-half interest in their marital property. Individual property includes property owned before marriage, or acquired at any time by gift or inheritance, and appreciation of individual property not resulting from substantial personal effort of the other spouse. Presumptions aid in the identification of marital property and simple rules, based on a time continuum, are provided for the sorting out of marital and individual property components of life insurance, pension and other deferred employee benefits which straddle the date of marriage.

"The act applies prospectively only, affecting interests acquired after the act's effective date by married couples within the adopting state.

"While title no longer governs the ownership of property acquired after the act's effective date, title bestows rights of management and control. Title can be in the name of one spouse or the other or both. If title is in the name of husband *and* wife,

38. The document can be obtained from the National Conference of Commissioners on Uniform State Laws, 645 North Michigan Ave., Suite 510, Chicago, Illinois 60611.

39. Wenig, The Marital Property Act, 12 Probate and Property 9 (1983).

Professor Wenig was Co–Chair, Probate and Trust Division Committee H–5 on Marital Property and ABA Advisor to the National Conference's Uniform State Laws Marital Property Act Drafting Committee.

there is joint management and control; if in the name of husband *or* wife, either can manage and control. Third persons who rely on title are protected in their dealings with a spouse but gifts to third persons in excess of a certain annual amount or in excess of the standard of giving set by the spouses can be set aside by the nondonor spouse who acts promptly. If necessary, a spouse may obtain judicial aid to add his or her name to the title of marital property (except for partnership interests or assets of an unincorporated business of the other spouse). Other judicial remedies, if sought promptly, may protect the interest of either spouse in marital property.

"Claims of third persons arising during an obligee's marriage can be satisfied from the obligee's individual property or from marital property; claims which antedate the marriage can be satisfied from the obligee's individual property and from his or her earnings during marriage. Broad scope is granted to husbands and wives to enter into marital property agreements which may vary the effect of the act. Marital property can be held in survivorship form or transferred to trust without losing its marital property characteristics if this is what the spouses want.

"The act is a property act, not a divorce act. Therefore, to use Reporter Cantwell's metaphor, in the event of divorce the act takes the couple up to the steps of the courthouse, each with his or her undivided one-half interest in marital property in hand, and leaves them there. The divorce law, and whatever power of equitable distribution the state has given to the court, then takes over. Because the act is a property act, at death of either spouse, that spouse has power of testamentary disposition over his or her undivided one-half interest in the couple's marital property.

"Because of the act's prospective application, couples who are married before the effective date of the act or married couples who move into an adopting state from a state which has not adopted the act may have considerable individual property, possibly all or substantially all owned by only one of the spouses. To protect the nonowning spouse on divorce, or to protect a surviving spouse, a deferred interest is given to that spouse in the other spouse's property which would have been marital property under the act's definition but for the fact that the property was acquired during the couple's marriage before the adoption of the act or before their move to the adopting state.

. . .

"The act may sound unfamiliar to lawyers accustomed to common law. But almost one-fourth of the population of the United States now lives in the eight community property states— Arizona, California, Idaho, Louisiana, New Mexico, Nevada, Texas and Washington. Married couples travel; their domiciles change as their jobs move or as their retirement plans direct. While the population of many of the community property states is growing, couples in these states also move. Should their rights in marital property turn on the accident of their choice of residence?

"The variegated marital property regimes of the common law states have been moving in many ways in the past two decades toward community property. 'Creeping community property' is reflected in piecemeal judicial decisions or legislation providing for equitable distribution on divorce; protection against disinheritance on death, increases in intestate shares of surviving spouses; presumptions classifying household effects and other family assets as joint and survivor property; recognition of husband-and-wife partnerships in family businesses and family farms; imposition of constructive trusts to aid one spouse's claim of interest in property held in the name of the other spouse; increasing validation of marital contracts; and the growing trend of the states, both before and after the federal adoption in 1981 of the unlimited marital deduction, toward tax-free interspousal transfers. In addition, federal law pertaining to public and private pensions has in recent years reinforced state law in giving increasing recognition to the necessity of permitting one spouse to share in the benefits earned by the other spouse.

"Justified by the trend exemplified by the many illustrations of creeping community property, the Marital Property Act would bring order and symmetry to the law of marital property. By looking at the length of the marriage and assuming that husband and wife are economic partners and that they have been acting as such during the course of the marriage, unless they agree that they have not, the act gives equal weight to the contributions of both spouses. The act smooths the jagged edges of laws that in one state may give a larger share to the surviving spouse of a decedent who dies intestate than to the surviving spouse of a decedent who dies with a will and that, in a neighboring state, may do the reverse. The act deals with nonprobate assets that are such a large part of wealth today, in a manner that neither the intestate nor elective share laws can provide. The act differentiates between marriages of short duration and longer marriages, not only upon divorce but in the course of the marriage and upon death of one of the spouses." [40]

---

40. As the ten paragraphs just quoted reveal, Professor Wenig is a proponent of the Act. (Not all commentators will be as enthusiastic, either because they find the concept faulty or because they are concerned about the new legal tangles which may result from the passage of the Act.) Professor Wenig indicates the Act is "the correct culmination and embodiment of a demand that

SECTION 2. CONCURRENT ESTATES

Most of the multiple interests in the same *res* are successive in character, e.g., a life estate followed by a remainder, or are different in quality, e.g., a mortgage (security interest) on a fee simple estate. In this section, we develop the concept of concurrent ownership where the parties, at one and the same time, have the same quality of rights in one and the same *res*. These co-owners have simultaneous interests in every portion of the thing, but no separate interest in any particular portion of it. They have a claim, determined by the extent of their share, to every part of the whole. Thus, if *O* dies intestate, survived only by three sons, they will take his property as tenants in common, owning no specific part in severalty but each having an undivided one-third of the whole. The relevant estates developed early in English history, during the fifteenth century, and have survived, with varying degrees of modification, to the present day. These concurrent estates are: coparcenary, tenancy by the entirety, joint tenancy, and tenancy in common. Although the interests originated as estates in land, they find modern application to personalty as well, in such interests as joint bank accounts, jointly payable government savings bonds, etc. Moreover, there are certain modern developments, such as partnership property, cooperative apartments, and condominiums which could be classified under the broad umbrella of concurrent estates.

A. COPARCENARY

This form of co-ownership is virtually extinct in United States and deserves space primarily to show the historical development of the law. It arose as a corollary to primogeniture and applied when there were no sons so that the daughters had to share equally as heir. (It applied by special custom in some English

the law recognize that marital property is not 'his' or 'hers' but 'ours.'" She believes that, "Another proponent may have been revealed by a wedding that occurred in [1981]. The Church of England marriage ceremony contains the traditional vow, 'with my worldly goods I thee endow.' The old English separate property regime grant of the limited right of dower is thus embodied in the marriage ritual. But those who watched the televised wedding of Prince Charles and Princess Diana . . . heard Prince Charles speak not that traditional vow but instead the words: 'All my goods, with thee I *share.*'" It should be noted that Prince Andrew reverted to the traditional vow for his wedding ceremony!

localities, where the land descended to two or more males.) The coparceners [41] took but a single estate and were viewed collectively as a single heir. Note that this idea was consistent with the feudal policy against dividing the ownership of the land among numerous heirs. Nevertheless, the estate in coparcenary was like the tenancy in common, in that no right of survivorship prevailed among the parceners and the share of each would go to that parcener's heir who would then hold in coparcenary with the survivors. Only if there was a partition would the land again be held in severalty. The term is still used occasionally, but today the individuals who share an inheritance are usually called tenants in common.

B. TENANCY BY THE ENTIRETY

Reference has been made previously to the common law's view of the husband and wife as one, giving rise to the husband's estate of *jure uxoris* in the wife's land. That estate has passed into limbo but the idea behind it survives, in many jurisdictions, in the tenancy by the entirety. That estate came into being when real property was transferred to husband and wife; since they were one they received but a single estate, an entirety. So strong was this presumption that, if land was conveyed to a man and his wife and a third person, the spouses took a one-half interest by the entirety and the third person took a one-half interest which he held as a joint tenant or tenant in common (depending on the presumption) with the spouses.[42] It follows that the estate could be created only where the legal unity of husband and wife existed, and a conveyance to two unmarried persons "as tenants by the entirety" resulted in a tenancy in common.[43] If the marriage bond were severed by an absolute divorce it severed the estate as well, since the unity was gone and a tenancy in common would result.[44]

The tenancy by the entirety's nearest relative was the joint tenancy since both carried the important right of survivorship which did not attach to the tenancy in common or to coparcenary. Indeed, the estate by the entirety so resembles a joint tenancy that

41. "The name parcener is derived from the fact that, apart from statute, such a tenant had the right to compel partition at a time when joint tenants and tenants in common had no such right." Moynihan, Preliminary Survey of the Law of Real Property 135 (1940).

42. Dennis v. Dennis, 152 Ark. 187, 238 S.W. 15 (1922).

43. Perrin v. Harrington, 146 App. Div. 292, 130 N.Y.S. 944 (1911).

44. Andrews v. Andrews, 155 Fla. 654, 21 So.2d 205 (1945).

it has been called a joint tenancy "modified by the common law doctrine that husband and wife are one person." [45] Despite the similarities, however, the two estates are different both conceptually and practically. To lapse into the mystical Latin of the property lawyer, tenants by the entirety were seised *per tout et non per my,* joint tenants were seised *per my et per tout.* This is shorthand for saying that the former own the whole interest collectively but not any individual share whereas the latter own both the whole interest and a share. This mysticism is clarified by the practical consequences: the estate by the entireties could not be partitioned except by the voluntary act of *both* parties or by divorce, nor could the estate be defeated by an act on the part of a single spouse, i.e., by voluntary conveyance of his or her interest or by a sale on execution to reach their assets; the joint tenancy could be partitioned and was, in fact, severed by a voluntary or involuntary conveyance by a single party.

The modern role of the tenancy by the entirety varies widely from state to state. In Massachusetts, it long retained most of its common-law glory and seemed unaffected by the emancipation of women.[46] In all but twenty states, however, the tenancy has no modern significance and a conveyance to husband and wife will give rise to a joint tenancy or a tenancy in common, depending on the language used.[47] This result has been reached for a variety of reasons, the most common being the Married Women's Property Acts which were held to destroy the spousal unity. Some states have simply rejected this type of property ownership as "repugnant to our institutions and to the American sense of justice to the

---

45. Pray v. Stebbins, 141 Mass. 219, 221, 4 N.E. 824, 825 (1886).

46. Licker v. Gluskin, 265 Mass. 403, 164 N.E. 613 (1929); Hoag v. Hoag, 213 Mass. 50, 99 N.E. 521 (1912). As recently as 1979, it was held that the husband's continued control over property in Massachusetts, held in tenancy by the entirety, did not violate the 14th Amendment's equal protection clause. D'Ercole v. D'Ercole, 407 F.Supp. 1377 (D.Mass.1976). The court pointed out that, while the presumption in Massachusetts was for a tenancy by the entirety in a conveyance to husband and wife, the parties had an option to take as joint tenants or tenants in common (this option was not available to the husband and wife at common law). Said the court: "This court is sympathetic with plaintiff's concern that the tenancy by the entirety is to some degree a legal artifact, formerly justified by the presumed incompetence of women to manage property. But this decision is not based on such an archaic and patently invalid stereotype. Rather, the fact is that, regardless of its roots, the tenancy by the entirety exists today as one of several options open to married persons seeking to purchase real estate. Its existence constitutes a matter of choice not discrimination." The husband's control over the property was eliminated later in Massachusetts by the adoption of the Equal Rights Amendment to the Massachusetts Constitution. See West v. First Agricultural Bank, 382 Mass. 534, 419 N.E.2d 262 (1981), holding that the ERA was not retroactive.

47. See Cunningham, Stoebuck and Whitman, The Law of Property 211 (1984) where the states are listed.

heirs and therefore not the common law."[48] Between the extremes, other states have retained the common-law concept while modifying its practical consequences,[49] usually by giving the parties equal rights in the control and enjoyment of the land rather than vesting these rights in the husband alone. Aside from the divorce problem, there has been little litigation between the spouses themselves and most of the cases arise when a creditor seeks to reach the interest of one of the parties.[50]

Prior to Massachusetts' adoption of the Equal Rights Amendment, which eliminated the husband's control over the property held in tenancy by the entirety,[51] that state was a prime example of the common law view of the rights of creditors to reach the asset represented by a tenancy by the entirety. Thus, a Massachusetts creditor would find that he could not do with the interest of a tenant by the entirety that which the tenant could not do. Since the wife could not sell the land alone, her creditor could not sell it by resort to attachment and levy on an execution in an action at law.[52] All the wife had, in effect, was a right of survivorship and this apparently was not assignable either voluntarily or involuntarily.[53] It followed that the husband's interest could be reached for his life at least, but would be defeated if the wife survived. In the jurisdictions where the tenancy is extinct, the creditor has the right to reach the respective shares of either

48. For a complete discussion of ownership by the entireties with reference to specific states see 4 Powell, Real Property 653–671 (1954) plus continuing supplements.

49. Despite the attacks on the tenancy by the entirety, it is a hardy survivor in many states. For example, the Court of Appeals of Maryland has recently stated that: "Maryland retains the estate of tenancy by the entirety in its traditional form." Beall v. Beall, 291 Md. 224, 434 A.2d 1015 (1981). The court then proceeded, in what it called a case of first impression in the United States and Great Britain, to hold that an option to purchase land given by a husband and wife, as tenants by the entirety, lapsed upon the death of one tenant and thereafter could not be accepted by the offeree. The court reasoned that the offer was made by the tenants by the entirety as a team rather than as two individuals. The continuation of the offer depended upon the continuous assent of both members of the team. There was a dissent by two judges who obviously thought that the estate should be abolished rather than

extended and that the offer survived the death of the husband and hence the widow should have been bound.

50. Ohio provides another good example of the hardihood of the tenancy. Ohio had no common law tenancy by the entirety but in 1972 the estate was authorized by statute. In Donvito v. Criswell, 1 Ohio App.3d 53, 439 N.E.2d 467 (1982), the court construed the statute to prevent the creditor of only one spouse from attaching or levying upon any interest of that spouse in property held by tenancy by the entirety. Apparently, a significant number of married couples are taking title to real estate in Ohio as tenants by the entirety.

51. Note 46 supra.

52. Note 46 supra.

53. This latter point seems inconsistent with the Massachusetts rule that "a contingent interest is assignable if the chance of the contingency happening is not so uncertain as to make it a mere speculative possibility." Newhall, Future Interests in Massachusetts, s. 13 (1938).

spouse and this same result is reached in those states which retain the tenancy but allow the spouses to share the beneficial ownership equally. A third position is taken by a number of states which hold that the creditors of neither spouse can reach the land, since to allow such involuntary transfer would be too great an interference with the other spouse's use and enjoyment.[54] This last position is particularly undesirable since it allows a married couple to render a large portion of their estate inaccessible to creditors and this can be especially inequitable in a jurisdiction which allows the tenancy to exist in personal property as well. In 1944, a committee of the American Bar Association recommended that the tenancy by the entirety be abolished in all states and it seems high time for this vestige of an older day to join *jure uxoris* and coparcenary in the real property museum.

Until such time as tenancy by the entirety is abolished in all states it will continue to cause some interesting litigation. Suppose, for example, a house held by the entirety is destroyed by fire. Will the insurance proceeds be impressed with the tenancy or should they be paid equally to H and W? In Hawthorne v. Hawthorne,[55] the Court of Appeals of New York held that W was entitled to one-half of the insurance proceeds. "Since personalty cannot be held by the entirety this ends the question as far as a legal estate or title is concerned unless equity demands exact equivalence in both quantity and quality of ownership in all cases resembling 'involuntary conversion'." In a case involving a condemnation award, the New York court [56] had held that the survivorship right continued into the substituted *res* but that was a true case of "involuntary conversion" and, moreover, the issue of severability was not raised, only the right to the proceeds as survivor. Since there was no question of survivorship in the insurance case (both H and W were alive) the insurance proceeds (being personal property) were severable and the wife was entitled to her share. This seems to be the correct result if tenancy by the entirety is restricted to land, as in New York, but the problem would be different in states allowing such tenancies in personalty.[57]

---

54. Fairclaw v. Forrest, 130 F.2d 829 (D.C.Cir.1942); Ward Terry and Co. v. Hensen, 75 Wyo. 444, 297 P.2d 213 (1956) (this case contains an excellent analysis of the various American views).

55. 13 N.Y.2d 82, 242 N.Y.S.2d 50, 192 N.E.2d 20 (1963).

56. In re Jamaica Bay, 252 App.Div. 103, 297 N.Y.S. 415 (1937).

57. In many jurisdictions, a tenancy by the entirety can now be created in personal property if the parties indicate their intention to do so. Dodson v. National Title Insurance Co., 159 Fla. 371, 31 So.2d 402 (1947) and Carlisle v. Parker, 38 Del. 83, 188 A. 67 (1936).

An even more intriguing problem was presented in Benson v. United States.[58]   H and W had owned land as tenants by the entirety but were later divorced.   In all jurisdictions except the District of Columbia the divorce would have ended the entirety and H and W would have become tenants in common.   A special statute in the District allowed the tenancy by the entirety to continue even after divorce, if there was a valid antenuptial or postnuptial agreement in relation to its continuance.   Since the entirety still continued in this case, the property was not subject to a federal tax lien against the husband alone.   The tax lien could not attach until H survived W; if W survived H it would not attach at all.   Of course, if the tax lien had been against both H and W it would have attached to the property.

While the two previous examples are, admittedly, unusual cases they do illustrate the complex problems caused by the continued existence of an outmoded concurrent estate.   Incidentally, it should be pointed out that, while a tenancy by the entirety was non-severable by the unilateral act of either H or W, both could join in a conveyance of the full fee in severalty (or otherwise) to a third party.   Similarly, either spouse could convey his or her interest to the other.   Indeed, in Union Planters National Bank v. United States[59] H conveyed his interest in a tenancy by the entirety to W as a completed gift, without reserving any legal title, right, or interest therein to himself, and even though he continued to live with his wife in the home until his death, the value of the residence was not included in his taxable estate for federal estate tax purposes.   The court did point out that, "in some situations this may prove to be an unfortunate test of one's partner's judgment of the security of the marriage."

C.   JOINT TENANCY

The outstanding feature of the joint tenancy is the right of survivorship which is inherent in it.   When one joint tenant dies the other is the sole owner; if there are several joint tenants, the deceased's share is owned by the survivors jointly.   The deceased's share does not "pass to" the survivor, as in a testate or intestate succession, since each joint tenant is conceived as owning the whole, subject to the equal rights of the other or others.   Thus, when one dies the estate of the survivor is simply freed from the former's rights in the property.   This can have some interesting

58. 143 U.S.App.D.C. 197, 442 F.2d   **59.** 361 F.2d 662 (6th Cir.1966).
1221 (1971).

consequences, as when one joint tenant murders another [60] or when joint tenants die simultaneously.[61]

The common-law presumption favored the creation of a joint tenancy over a tenancy in common when the exact nature of the concurrent estate was not specified. This was consistent with the doctrines of primogeniture and coparcenary since it carried out the feudal desire to keep the land in a single ownership, if possible. There is no modern justification for the survivorship principle, unless the parties expressly wish this feature to apply, and it can be dangerous since the surviving tenant will exclude the heirs and devisees of the decedent, frequently contrary to the intent of the parties. Consequently, the common-law presumption has been universally reversed and many states have statutes which provide that there shall be no joint tenancy unless the right of survivorship is expressly provided for in the creating instrument.[62] A few states do not permit joint tenancies in land at all. Usually, an exception is made for fiduciaries (trustees, executors, etc.) since the survivorship principle aids them in the performance of their duties. The exact language necessary to rebut the presumption of a tenancy in common is far from clear. Since it depends on the intent of the parties, as shown by the creating instrument, you may be sure that the cases are not consistent. If the grantor desires to create a joint tenancy, he should make this wish crystal clear by some such language as, "to *A* and *B*, not in tenancy in common, but in joint tenancy, with right of survivorship." [63] The worst possible language is, "to *A* and *B* jointly",

60. In Welsh v. James, 408 Ill. 18, 95 N.E.2d 872 (1950), Comment, 1951 U.Ill. L.F. 172, the right of survivorship was held to take its customary course, but this case was overruled in Bradley v. Fox, 7 Ill.2d 106, 129 N.E.2d 699 (1955). See also Duncan v. Vassaur, 550 P.2d 929 (Okl.1976) for a good discussion of the options available where one joint tenant murders another. The court concluded "that the most equitable solution . . . is to hold that by the murder, the joint tenancy is separated and terminated and one-half of the property should go to the heirs of the deceased husband (murdered person) and the other one-half to the murderer, wife, or to her heirs, when deceased. By such holding the joint tenancy is changed to a tenancy in common."

61. The Uniform Simultaneous Death Act, § 3 provides: "Where there is no sufficient evidence that two joint tenants or tenants by the entirety have died otherwise than simultaneously the property so held shall be distributed one half as if one had survived and one half as if the other had survived. If there are more than two joint tenants and all of them have so died the property then distributed shall be in the proportion that one bears to the whole number of joint tenants." This statute, which has the effect of treating the parties as having died as tenants in common, has been adopted in some forty states.

62. The New York Real Property Law, § 66 is typical. "Every estate granted or devised to two or more persons in their own right shall be a tenancy in common, unless expressly declared to be in joint tenancy; but every estate, vested in executors or trustees as such, shall be held by them in joint tenancy."

63. See Ill.Rev.Stat. ch. 76, § 1 (1985).

since this conjures up images of both types of estates and is thoroughly ambiguous. It would seem that the courts should treat this language as not sufficiently rebutting the presumption and thus creating a tenancy in common.[64]

There is no way to prevent people from using language outside the legal norm and when this occurs litigation may be the only recourse for clearing the title. In these cases, the court's role will be to ascertain the intent of the parties as disclosed by the deed or will. Sometimes, the parties are attempting to create a non-severable estate with a right of survivorship and this can be done if the correct language is used. A grant to "*A* and *B* for their joint lives with the remainder vesting in the survivor of them" would seem to do the job. This does not create a joint tenancy, although it is similar to such an estate in many ways. While both *A* and *B* are alive they have life estates measured by their joint lives with a contingent remainder in the survivor, vesting in one on the death of the other. There would be no way to sever this estate other than by the joint action of *A* and *B*. [Note that a true joint tenancy could be severed by either party acting alone.]

Similarly, a grant to "*A* and *B* and their heirs, and to the survivor of them" could be construed as conveying to *B* a life estate as a tenant in common, plus a remainder in fee (or executory interest) if he survives *A* or it could be held that the deed creates a tenancy in common in fee plus a somewhat anomalous "right of survivorship".[65] Either construction would seem to create a non-destructible right of survivorship.

If the language is ambiguous, the court will have to choose between a construction which creates a somewhat anomalous estate in the land and a more conventional joint tenancy with its inherent right of severance. For two interesting cases where the court wrestled with this problem. See Bernhard v. Bernhard [66] and Palmer v. Flint.[67] In the former, the Alabama Court seems to have been led astray by the statute abolishing joint tenancies as they existed at common law; in the latter the trial court was led astray but the Supreme Court of Maine returned to basic principles and decided the parties had intended to create a joint tenancy, despite the ambiguous language.

According to common-law dogma, a joint tenancy could be created only where the four unities of time, title, interest, and

64. Taylor v. Taylor, 310 Mich. 541, 17 N.W.2d 745, 157 A.L.R. 559 (1945).

65. Runions v. Runions, 186 Tenn. 25, 207 S.W.2d 1016, 1 A.L.R.2d 242 (1948) and Anson v. Murphy, 149 Neb. 716, 32 N.W.2d 271 (1948).

66. 278 Ala. 240, 177 So.2d 565 (1965), overruled in Nunn v. Keith, 289 Ala. 518, 268 So.2d 792 (1972).

67. 156 Me. 103, 161 A.2d 837 (1960).

possession were present. It followed that any severance of these four unities would also end the joint tenancy. A brief analysis of each of these unities is called for: *time* meant that the interests of the joint tenants must vest at the same time; *title* meant that the parties must take their interests by the same instrument—deed, will, etc.; *interest* meant that they must have estates of the same type and duration; and *possession* meant that the joint tenants must have undivided interests in the whole, not divided interests in the several parts. This legal formula was fully expounded by Blackstone [68] and found its way into American law where it has shown surprising vitality. As a general proposition it is harmless enough and, indeed, can be viewed as little more than descriptive of the nature of the estate, but it, like many a common-law rule, has caused a few real hangovers. Suppose *A* owns Blackacre in fee simple absolute and decides he would like to convey it to himself and his new bride, *B*, as joint tenants, so she will have a right of survivorship and thus avoid the necessity of making a will. If he makes a deed directly to "*A* and *B*, as joint tenants" he will fail in his purpose and will create only a tenancy in common because two of the four unities—time and title—are missing. At common law a party could not convey to himself, that would be a nullity, so the wife received her interest at a different time and by a different instrument than the husband. The intent to create a joint tenancy was clear but, because of this "pitfall for the unwary," *A* failed to accomplish his purpose. To avoid this result the device of a straw man was used; *A* conveyed to *X*, who in turn reconveyed to "*A* and *B* as joint tenants." Now the four unities were present and, *voila*, a joint tenancy resulted. For an interesting Maine case involving this bit of legal sleight of hand see Strout v. Burgess.[69] To avoid this weird result and do away with the necessity for a straw party, several states have passed legislation which allows the creation of a joint tenancy by direct conveyance.[70] The spirit behind these statutes was urged on the court in the Maine case but the judge wrote, as is so frequent in the property field, "If the law with relation to the creation of joint tenancies or with relation to survivorship between co-owners is to be further modified it should be accomplished by the Legislature and not by the Court."

Once a joint tenancy has been created it is easy to destroy it—a simple conveyance by one of the joint tenants will do the job. If *A* and *B* hold as joint tenants and *B*, with or without the permission of *A*, conveys to *C* the severance is complete since the unities are no more. The result is that *A* and *C* now hold as tenants in common. Of course, *B* could not convey more than he owned and

---

68. 2 Blackstone Com. 180 et seq.

69. 144 Me. 263, 68 A.2d 241 (1949).

70. See, for example, Ill.Rev.Stat. ch. 76, ss. 1 b. and 2.1 (1985).

in the hypothetical case that was an undivided one-half interest. If *A, B,* and *C* are joint tenants and *C* conveys to *D,* then *A* and *B* continue as joint tenants in an undivided two-thirds of the estate and *D* has an undivided one-third as a tenant in common with *A* and *B.*[71] While it is clear that a conveyance of the fee by one joint tenant will work a severance, there is some dispute as to the effect of a mortgage, a lease, a contract of sale, etc. Since these transfers, although of limited interests, can be said to destroy the essential unities the tendency is to hold that they, too, cause a severance.[72] It follows that a sale of a joint tenant's interest under execution severs a joint tenancy just as a voluntary convey-ance does.[73]

Unlike the tenancy by the entirety, the joint tenancy has considerable social utility so long as it is clear that this is the estate which was intended to be created. Since the estate is severable, it does not serve as a bastion from which to repel the attacks of creditors and the survivorship feature allows it to serve as a "poor man's probate." According to *property* theory, the survivor's share would not be subject to death taxes since the deceased's estate did not pass to the survivor at death but was his from the inception. You may be sure, however, that *tax* theory (whatever that may be) plugged this loophole at an early date and the hopes for tax savings proved to be illusory. The same result was reached as to the tenancy by the entirety.[74] It is fair to say that the problems of joint ownership can be considerable, both taxwise and otherwise, and that the lawyer should tread this area of property law with great care.[75]

---

71. For an interesting example of this point see Jackson v. O'Connell, 23 Ill.2d 52, 177 N.E.2d 194 (1961).

72. For a more extended discussion see 2 American Law of Property, § 6.2 (Casner ed. 1952).

The issue of severance in these cases will depend on the legal effect of the mortgage, or other legal instrument in the particular jurisdiction. Thus, in People v. Nogarr, 164 Cal.App.2d 591, 330 P.2d 858, 67 A.L.R.2d 992 (1958) a mortgage by H alone did not sever a joint tenancy and the surviving W took the property free of H's mortgage. This was because California followed a lien theory of mortgages; if they had fol-lowed a title theory the court admitted a severance would have occurred. See also Brant v. Hargrove, 129 Ariz. 475, 632 P.2d 978 (1981) where the court followed the Nogarr decision and said:

"We do not believe that dogged adher-ence to the requirements of the four unities in the context of severance is required by our case law. Here there were no facts to indicate an intention to sever the relationship."

73. Albright v. Creel, 236 Ala. 286, 182 So. 10 (1938); Young v. Hessler, 72 Cal.App.2d 67, 164 P.2d 65 (1945).

74. U.S. v. Jacobs, 306 U.S. 363, 59 S.Ct. 551, 83 L.Ed. 763 (1939) rejected any differences between the two estates as "shadowy and intricate distinctions of common law property concepts and ancient fictions."

75. To get a further idea of the com-plexities of these rather simple-appear-ing estates, see a symposium of five articles on the Problems of Joint Own-ership, 1959 U.Ill.L.F. 883–1040. See also Severing Joint Property Interests,

D. TENANCY IN COMMON [76]

By this time, the tenancy in common has been identified by a process of elimination. It is that concurrent estate which results if none of the estates in Sections A, B, and C are created. Today, it is the most common of all concurrent estates and is favored by a statutory presumption which must be rebutted by the expressed intent of the parties. The unity of possession is the only essential unity involved in a tenancy in common and Blackstone wrote, "For indeed tenancies in common differ in nothing from sole estates but merely in the blending and unity of possession." [77] There is no right of survivorship between tenants in common and it is accurate to say that the share of each tenant is several and distinct from that of his cotenant, except that it is an undivided interest so that he cannot lay claim to any specific portion of the whole until there is a partition in kind. Tenants in common may receive their respective interests by different instruments of conveyance, at different times, and their interests need not be equal either in size of share or in quantum of estate. Thus *O*, owning Blackacre in fee simple absolute, may convey a one-quarter interest to his wife, *W*, by warranty deed and then die testate, devising an interest in one-eighth of the land to two of his children and a one-half interest to a third child. A tenancy, in common would ultimately result, with *W* owning an undivided one-quarter, two children an undivided one-eighth each, and one child an undivided one-half. It follows that each tenant can transfer his own interest as he sees fit (further subdividing the tenancy perhaps) and that his creditors can reach the estate just as if he owned it in severalty.[78]

The basic distinction between a joint tenancy and a tenancy in common is illustrated by the marital rights of a spouse in each case. Assume *A* and *B* are brothers, owning Blackacre as joint tenants, and both are married. The wife of neither can be said to have an inchoate dower in Blackacre because neither is seised of

---

16 Real Property, Probate and Trust Journal 435 (1981).

76. Note the tenant in common was seized *per my et non per tout i.e.* by the share or moiety but not by the whole.

77. 2 Blackstone Com. 180.

78. While a tenant in common (or joint tenant, for that matter) can transfer his *undivided* interest to another he cannot convey a *specific* interest, as by a metes and bounds description, since this would amount to partition by self help. See Kean v. Dench, 413 F.2d 1 (3d Cir.1969) where the court said: "While some of the earlier authorities hold such a conveyance is void, we think that the better rule, which is followed by a majority of the states and which was applied by the district court in this case, is that such a conveyance is voidable only and as between the parties is valid and is to be given full effect if it can be done without prejudice or injury to the non-conveying cotenant."

an estate of inheritance. If *A* dies first, *B* has the whole estate
and *A's* wife has no claim, although at this point *B's* wife acquires
an inchoate dower. On the other hand, if *A* and *B* own as tenants
in common, the wife of each has an inchoate dower in the
undivided share of her husband since he has an estate of inheritance. Of course, if dower has been abolished in the particular
jurisdiction, this illustration would have no application but the
same principle would apply to statutory rights of descent. On the
death of a joint tenant or a tenant by the entirety, the surviving
tenant owns the property whereas the interest of a tenant in
common descends to his heirs or passes under his will.

There are some problems that are inherent in concurrent
estates and which arise regardless of the specific tenancy involved.
These difficulties cluster around the concept of unity of possession
and the legal relationship among co-owners of the same *res*. By
definition, each tenant is entitled to possession of the entire parcel
of land yet he cannot exercise that possession without coming into
conflict with the reciprocal right of his cotenant. So long as one
tenant occupies the whole without objection from his fellows no
particular problem ensures since the law treats the possession of
one cotenant as the possession of all, but disputes can easily arise
and joint possession can be difficult.[79] As one court colorfully
remarked, "Two men cannot plow the same furrow."[80] If one
tenant excludes his cotenants from the whole or any part of the
land, he is guilty of an ouster and ejectment will lie at the option
of the dispossessed tenant. One tenant can get title to the whole
estate by adverse possession if he ousts his co-tenant and then
occupies himself for the requisite statutory period. In these cases,
however, the ouster must be clear-cut and the claimant must
"hoist his flag high and keep it flying." Some states even hold
"that in order to start the running of the Statute of Limitations
against a cotenant, it must be shown that the tenant in possession
gave *actual* notice to the tenant out of possession that he was
claiming adversely, or that the tenant out of possession had
received notice of such claim of the tenant in possession by some
act which would amount to an ouster or disseizin."[81] This is
clearly a higher standard than required for adverse possession
generally; and it should be, because of the close legal relationship
between the parties.[82]

79. Note this is true even of joint
occupants, like two lessees of an apartment, who do not have a technical concurrent estate in the sense used in this
Section. See Tompkins v. Superior
Court of San Francisco, 59 Cal.2d 65, 27
Cal.Rptr. 889, 378 P.2d 113 (1963).

80. Mastbaum v. Mastbaum, 126
N.J.Eq. 366, 372, 9 A.2d 51, 55 (1939).

81. Mercer v. Wayman, 9 Ill.2d 441,
445, 137 N.E.2d 815, 818 (1956).

82. Goergen v. Maar, 2 A.D.2d 276,
153 N.Y.S.2d 826 (1956) called it "a
quasi trust relationship" and held that

The nature of this legal relationship between cotenants is difficult to define but it can be described. In Andrews v. Andrews,[83] the Florida Supreme Court pointed out that each tenant by the entirety owes the other the highest degree of confidence and trust and proceeded to hold that one tenant could not eliminate the interest of the other by purchasing at a tax sale in his own name, after a default in payment of taxes. If one tenant purchases the joint property at a tax sale, his act benefits all the cotenants and discharges the lien. Of course, the confidential relationship is higher in the entireties' situation because of the marriage but the same principle applies to other cotenancies and to mortgage redemptions as well as tax sales.[84] The cotenant who made the expenditure is entitled to contribution from his fellows and although he may have difficulty in a direct suit for reimbursement he can adjust his rights in a suit for partition.[85] Similarly, adjustments can usually be made for improvements, repairs, insurance, etc., which have been paid for by one cotenant in excess of his aliquot portion of the estate. The principal difficulty will be one of finding the proper remedy, since many states will not allow a direct suit for these items alone and will require an accounting only on partition.

A particularly troublesome problem can arise as to the duty of one cotenant to account to his fellows for rents and profits derived from the common land. At common law, there was such a duty if one tenant agreed to act as bailiff or manager, if the land was rented to a third party who paid all or a disproportionate share to one tenant, or if one tenant excluded his fellows from possession. But if a cotenant entered the land, not excluding or interfering with his cotenants, he was not liable for the profits of his occupancy.[86] This view still prevails in some states but others have repudiated it. "No practical or reasonable argument can be

in an accounting for profits the statute of limitations on the accounting does not ordinarily begin to run until the termination of the relationship of the cotenants, by a sale of the property.

83. 155 Fla. 654, 21 So.2d 205 (1945). See also Stoltz v. Maloney, 129 Ariz. 264, 630 P.2d 560 (1981) where the court noted: "We recognize the general rule that there exists a fiduciary relationship between tenants in common. . . . It is the general rule that tenants in common cannot buy the common property at a tax sale except for the benefit of all. . . . An exception to this general rule arises where the land has been assessed upon the tax books in the names of the owners of the undivided interests separately, and

where the owner of each undivided interest could have paid his own tax unaffected by the fact of the joint interest." On this last point see also Jennings v. Bradfield, 169 Colo. 146, 454 P.2d 81 (1969).

84. Knesek v. Muzny, 191 Okl. 332, 129 P.2d 853 (1942).

85. Kirsch v. Scandia American Bank, 160 Minn. 269, 199 N.W. 881 (1924).

86. Pico v. Columbet, 12 Cal. 414 (1859).

For a detailed analysis of this point see Baird v. Moore, 50 N.J.Super. 156, 141 A.2d 324 (1958), and Burby on Real Property 228–232 (3d. ed. 1965).

advanced for allowing one in possession to reap a financial benefit by occupying property owned in common without paying for his personal use of that part of the property owned by his cotenants. The fairest method in cases in which the cotenant occupies and uses common property, instead of renting it out, is to charge him with its reasonable rental value." [87]

The ultimate destiny of many a concurrent estate is the chancery side of a court of general jurisdiction and a suit in partition. Here the chancellor will endeavor to do what the cotenants presumably have failed to do—reach an equitable severance of the interests and make the parties owners in severalty at last. Today, this usually means a sale with an apportionment of the proceeds rather than partition in kind.[88] The proceeding will probably be regulated by statute and discussion of it is beyond the scope of this book but a good review of its history and theory can be found in the Michigan case of Henkel v. Henkel.[89] It should be noted that while partition is normally an absolute right of any cotenant (other than a tenant by the entireties) the courts will enforce an explicit agreement between the parties not to partition, at least so long as the agreement does not bind the parties for an unreasonable time and run afoul of the Rule Against Perpetuities or become an unreasonable restraint on alienation.[90]

E. CONCURRENT ESTATES IN PERSONALTY

The concurrent estates discussed in the preceding sections can exist in personal property as well as in land, except that a tenancy by the entirety may be restricted to real property in some states. Indeed, in modern society, the joint bank account (checking or savings), the jointly owned government bonds, the joint ownership of the family automobile, etc., may be the most striking manifestations of these property concepts. It is the survivorship feature that has the most appeal and the popularity of the joint bank account is due, in part at least, to the fact that a testamentary disposition can be made without the expense of drafting a will or

87. McKnight v. Basilides, 19 Wash. 2d 391, 407, 143 P.2d 307, 315 (1943). See also Ill.Rev.Stat., ch. 76, § 5 (1985) and Clarke v. Clarke, 349 Ill. 642, 183 N.E. 13 (1932).

88. For two interesting cases involving the issue of partition in kind versus partition by sale see Johnson v. Hendrickson, 71 S.D. 392, 24 N.W.2d 914 (1946) and White v. Smyth, 147 Tex. 272, 214 S.W.2d 967, 5 A.L.R.2d 1348 (1948).

89. 282 Mich. 473, 276 N.W. 522 (1937). See also Cunningham, Stoebuck and Whitman, The Law of Property 230–239 (1984) for a more extended discussion of partition.

90. Michalski v. Michalski, 50 N.J. Super. 454, 142 A.2d 645 (1958).

the delay of probate proceedings. Despite the deceptive simplicity of these joint interests, they can be real sources of trouble, as attested by the volume of litigation involving ownership of joint bank accounts.[91]

The basic difficulty is that the courts have not agreed on the theory to be used to sustain such joint interests. At least four theories, with varying results, have been utilized: the gift theory,[92] the trust theory,[93] the contract theory[94] and the joint tenancy theory.[95] Oddly enough, none of the theories fit exactly, e.g., the joint bank account cannot be a true joint tenancy because the four common-law unities—time, title, interest and possession—are lacking and the trust theory is so "far-fetched" that only Maryland follows it today. Oregon has faced the issue squarely saying, "It is not important that the interest created has no well-settled legal name. . . . It is enough that it was intended to be created, and that it violates no rule of statute or common law. . . . Out of the practice, now extensively engaged in, of keeping money in joint bank accounts, there has grown up a considerable body of law, reflecting the view held by a majority of courts that such arrangements, when entered into in good faith, are not opposed to any policy of the state, and that the purposes which are sought to be accomplished by them should not be set at naught by employing in too narrow and technical a spirit the legal principles which are found to be involved."[96]

The joint account is typically created by a deposit agreement, signed by both parties and reading: "As joint tenants, with right of survivorship and not as tenants in common." The bank is usually protected by statute and can pay either of the parties without fear of a later claim by the other.[97] Because the creating instrument gives either party the power to withdraw all the funds during his lifetime, the issue of ownership generally does not arise until after the death of one of the depositors and the contending parties are then the estate of the deceased and the surviving "joint tenant." The following hypothetical problem illustrates the point.

91. For a brief discussion of the point see Comment, The Joint and Survivorship Bank Account, 1957 U.Ill.L.F. 655.

92. Estate of Schneider, 6 Ill.2d 180, 127 N.E.2d 445 (1955).

93. Kornmann v. Safe Deposit Co., 180 Md. 270, 23 A.2d 692 (1942).

94. Castle v. Wightman, 303 Mass. 74, 20 N.E.2d 436 (1939).

95. Tacoma Sav. and Loan Ass'n v. Nadham, 14 Wash.2d 576, 128 P.2d 982 (1942).

96. Beach v. Holland, 172 Or. 396, 417, 418, 142 P.2d 990, 998, 149 A.L.R. 866 (1943).

For a good analysis of the entire problem see Miller v. Riegler, 243 Ark. 251, 419 S.W.2d 599 (1967).

97. Ill.Rev.Stat. ch. 76, § 2(a) (1985); Mass.Gen.Laws Ann., c. 334, § 1 (1953); Tenn.Code Ann. § 45–412.

H, a businessman, has his wife, *W*, working as his secretary and for convenience in his operations he deposits all funds in a joint checking account with his wife, using the form quoted in the previous paragraph. *H* and *W* have three grown children and, becoming estranged from his wife maritally although continuing to find her an excellent secretary, *H* leaves the bulk of his estate to the children by will. *H* dies, a major asset of his estate is the business cash, and *W* claims it all as surviving joint tenant while the executor claims it for the children. If the jurisdiction follows a strict contract theory, the wife takes it all under the terms of the agreement. Similarly, she is the winner if a joint tenancy was created.[98] But, if the basis of the joint account is the gift theory, then the wife can succeed only if there was donative intent on the part of *H*. Since such intent can be rebutted by the facts of the case (business convenience, not the desire to make a gift to the wife, was the reason for the joint account) the children have an excellent chance of reaching the joint funds.[99] As so frequently happens in the law, two basic policies conflict here—certainty and fairness. To refuse to go behind the joint-account mask frequently may be unfair to the parties; to do so introduces a flexibility in the concurrent estate concept which may destroy much of its utility. At the present time, these varying policies have not been wholly reconciled, so even the innocent-appearing joint bank account may have booby-trap tendencies.

Brief mention should be made of the Totten trust, christened for the case which popularized the device—Matter of Totten,[1] because it is closely related to the joint bank account, although sustained on another theory. "Typically, it involves a deposit of his own money by *A* to the account of '*A*, in trust for *B*.' After careful consideration, the New York court concluded that such a deposit should be deemed the declaration of a 'tentative trust'— one which the donor-depositor may revoke by withdrawing the fund or by changing the form of the account. The transfer of

98. It is, perhaps, misleading to say W wins. She takes the legal title as the survivor under the contract and joint tenancy theories but that does not end the matter. Equity may impress the proceeds with a constructive trust and order the survivor to hold them as a part of the deceased's estate, if it can be clearly and satisfactorily proved that the joint account was for convenience only. There is, in effect, a rebuttable presumption that the donor depositor intended a right of survivorship in the cotenant. In re Estate of Michaels, 26 Wis.2d 382, 132 N.W.2d 557 (1965). Note this same device, the constructive trust, has been used to reach a just result in a case where one co-owner of a joint bank account has allegedly murdered the other. See Vesey v. Vesey, 237 Minn. 295, 54 N.W.2d 385, 32 A.L.R.2d 1090 (1952).

99. Imirie v. Imirie, 246 F.2d 652 (D.C.Cir.1957); Estate of Schneider, 6 Ill.2d 180, 127 N.E.2d 445 (1955).

As the discussion in the previous footnote points out, the final result *may* be the same under any of the theories but the process of legal reasoning is different and indicates the continuing confusion of legal thought about joint accounts.

1. 179 N.Y. 112, 71 N.E. 748 (1904).

ownership becomes complete only upon the depositor's death; thereafter the donee may effectively claim any amount credited to the account, but he has no enforceable claim during the depositor's lifetime, nor may he recover any sum which the depositor has withdrawn from the account. Occasionally a court is candid enough to recognize such a device as the Totten trust or the joint bank account with right of survivorship as 'the poor man's will.' " [2]

2. Cribbet and Johnson, Cases and Materials on Property 215 (5th ed. 1984).

For a discussion of both the Totten Trust and joint bank accounts see Brown on Personal Property 174–188 (3d ed. by Raushenbush 1975).

Chapter 7

CONDOMINIUM

The preceding chapter on Multiple Ownership provided some insight into the wide variety of legal interests which the law recognizes in a single *res*. Some of these interests have been recognized since time immemorial and are steeped in arcane lore; others, like the marital interests created by the Marital Property Act, are of recent origin. The chapter does not cover all of the multiple interests but does touch base with the most important ones. Even a text on basic principles would be incomplete, however, without some discussion of the old-new concept of condominium as a form of multiple ownership. The concept cuts across a number of property areas, including leases, sales, covenants running with the land, etc., but it is appropriate to include it at this point by way of contrast with the other multiple interests in land. Moreover, since adequate housing plays so vital a role in any society, this separate chapter will provide the opportunity to take a brief look at a relatively new concept which has had considerable influence on the developing law.

There is a rich lode of legal material on condominiums [1] and the student of the subject can delve as deeply into the literature as he desires, but some elementary treatment is called for to complete the "big picture" of the modern law of property. The present chapter is designed to explain the importance of condominiums as a tool for dealing with housing (and to some extent, commercial) problems. It uses a comparative, historical approach, discusses the basic principles involved and ends with an analysis of the advantages and disadvantages of condominium as a method of land ownership. [2]

1. See for example, Rohan and Reskin, Condominium Law and Practice (1973).

2. The material in this chapter is based on an article by Professor Cribbet in the Michigan Law Review. See Cribbet, Condominium—Home Ownership for Megalopolis? 61 Mich.L.Rev. 1207 (1963).

"Some two thousand years before the first European settlers landed on the shores of the James River, Massachusetts Bay, and Manhattan Island, a group of ancient people, planning a new city-state in the Peloponnesus in Greece, called it *Megalopolis*, for they dreamed of a great future for it and hoped it would become the largest of the Greek cities. Their hopes did not materialize. Megalopolis still appears on modern maps of the Peloponnesus but it is just a small town nestling in a small river basin. Through the centuries the word *Megalopolis* has been used in many senses by various people, and it has even found its way into Webster's dictionary, which defines it as 'a very large city.' Its use, however, has not

118

The past decades have witnessed no real let up in the intense competition between East and West, despite sporadic efforts for detente. In the race for the conquest of space, in the battle of national rates of economic growth, in the propaganda struggle to fix the responsibility for nuclear testing, in the earlier trial of strength over Cuba, in the more recent confrontation elsewhere in the world, and in countless other areas, each bloc leader has continued to measure achievement against the rival's successes or defeats. The cold war is a deadly business and produces little to warm the cockles of a man's heart, but, if only the threat of nuclear destruction *could* be averted, there is something of fascination and, indeed, high-spirited adventure in this clash between powerful societies founded on different economic, political, social, and religious theories. To the lawyer (or layman for that matter) interested in the institution of property, the struggle for superiority has an added fillip—the opportunity to see basic principle tested in times of great stress and change. The worldwide population explosion, the mass migration to urban and suburban areas, and the accelerating rate of technical advance call for a legal response to the needs of the new society without abandoning the heritage of the past. This broad generality becomes concrete when we look at the specific problem of home ownership in the United States of America and in the Union of the Soviet Socialist Republics. Here is a facet of the domestic economy that touches the quick of every individual. A society [3] which fails to provide satisfactory housing for its citizens has stubbed its toe at the threshold of the good life.

Until August 1962, the prime example of private property in Russia was the individual home. It resisted collectivization and flourished, even under Stalin, primarily because of the acute housing shortage. By 1960, thirty-one percent of all living space in Soviet cities was privately owned, although built on land rented from the state.[4] Many of these homes were built by factory managers and government officials with construction loans obtained from the state bank. Due to shortage of building materials, to embezzling public servants who invested hoarded rubles in private houses, and to Chairman Khrushchev's propaganda that the imminent shift from socialism to communism would make

become so common that it could not be applied in a new sense, as a geographical place name for the unique cluster of metropolitan areas of the Northeastern seaboard of the United States. There, if anywhere in our times, the dream of those ancient Greeks has come true." Gottmann, Megalopolis 4 (1961).

3. I am not using "society" as synonymous with "government," although the latter must play a role if the normal functions of the economic system leave large numbers of people beyond the pale of decent housing.

4. Time, Aug. 17, 1962, p. 21, col. 3. For an interesting statement of how the Soviet Government views its own housing position vis-á-vis the West, see Sosnovy, Book Review, 22 Slavic Review 169 (1963).

privately-owned houses unnecessary, the August decree [5] banned all future private construction while allowing the existing private houses to continue as before. The new thrust was to be toward cooperatives, similar to the big apartment houses that already dot the Moscow landscape. Kruschev's decree ran so counter to basic human drives for "my own home" that it is doubtful that it had the desired impact on Russian housing policy. Nonetheless, it demonstrated an approach quite different from that in the West.

It is clear, however, that the Western yearning to have an individual castle for everyman's home is running into a barrier that is just as real, though stemming from a different source. American presidents have issued no decree against private home building, but choice construction sites have all but disappeared in megalopolis, and suburban sprawl has added to the cost and inconvenience of the traditional house and lot. Unless there is a major reversal in present trends, people are likely to be "forced" back into the central city or into the close-lying peripheral areas, at an accelerating rate, in order to avoid prohibitive commuting distances and to reduce the cost of dwelling units.[6] This inevitably means apartment living of some sort, which has traditionally required the head of the family to be a tenant rather than a homeowner. Even in a cooperative apartment he is not technically the owner, although he has many of the indicia of ownership. This tenant half of the landlord-tenant relationship, whatever its considerable advantages, runs counter to a deep strain in the American psyche. Long ago, Mr. Justice Story commented on this trait as it related to agricultural life in America: "One of the most remarkable circumstances in our colonial history is the almost total absence of leasehold estates. . . . The philosophical mind can scarcely fail to trace the intimate connexion which naturally subsists between the general equality of the apportionment of property among the mass of a nation, and the popular form of its

5. State and Law, Current Digest of the Soviet Press No. 41, Nov. 7, 1962, p. 23. Actually, the words "August decree" are misleading. Rather, a series of decrees passed in several of the republics culminated in the stated ban on private construction.

6. The alternative is increased decentralization of the city so that the job moves to the man and so that manageable-sized dwelling areas can grow up around the smaller core. I do not propose to debate the desirability or inevitability of these alternatives, since both of them will probably occur at the same time. The current trend toward apartment dwelling is quite apparent, however. "More and more American families

are moving into apartment houses, and the dramatic shift in their mode of living is having a profound effect in construction and real estate. . . . Realty men attending the annual convention of the National Association of Real Estate Boards discussed today the growing public preference for apartment living. . . . The foremost reason for the increase in apartment living, the realty men agreed, was the high cost of land in and around the nation's large cities. This has made the cost of buying land and creating single-family homes prohibitive to builders in many areas." N.Y. Times, Nov. 14, 1962, p. 63, col. 5.

government." [7] Admittedly, this drive for individual ownership is less in the city than in the rural areas, and less in the atomic age than in the colonial era, but millions of American renters still regard their fate as a temporary one and long for the full benefits of ownership *cum* mortgage.

If the preceding analysis is correct, it would seem that the law should provide some format that would allow private ownership of the individual unit involved in communal living. In fact, this format is now available under the esoteric heading of condominium, *i.e.*, "individual ownership in fee simple of a one-family unit in a multifamily structure coupled with ownership of an undivided interest in the land and in all other parts of the structure held in common with all of the other owners of one-family units." [8]

SECTION 1. THE HISTORY OF CONDOMINIUM

It is tempting to remark that while the Russians have moved away from what little private property their system provides, the Americans have developed a legal technique which allows private ownership in the midst of mass living, and then add, "It could only happen in America." [9] That it could happen anywhere, however, is evidenced by the fact that condominium had its genesis in Europe during the Middle Ages, has had a marked renaissance there since World War II, has flourished in Puerto Rico in recent years, and has belatedly burst upon the scene in the United States, following the Housing Act of 1961 which extended FHA mortgage insurance to condominium projects. [10] Some writers seem to think that the concept found its origin in ancient Rome, [11] but this seems doubtful since classical Roman law followed the

7. 1 Story, Commentaries on the Constitution of the United States 159, 166 (1833).

8. Ramsey, Condominium: The New Look in Co-ops 3 (pamphlet published by Chicago Title & Trust Co., 1961). For a more scholarly definition which should be sufficient to confuse the engineers, see Black, Law Dictionary 391 (3d ed. 1933): "In the civil law. Co-ownerships or limited ownerships, such as *emphyteusis, superficies, pignus, hypotheca, ususfructus, usus,* and *habitatio.* These were more than mere *jura in re alienā,* being portion of the *dominium* itself, although they are commonly distinguished from the *dominium* strictly so called."

9. This recalls the two women in New York City who watched the parade for Lord Mayor Robert Briscoe, the Jewish mayor of Dublin, and then commented, "It could only happen in America."

10. Housing Act of 1961, 75 Stat. 160, 12 U.S.C.A. § 1715y (Supp. III, 1961).

11. "[T]he concept of property ownership to which it pertains is literally as old as the hills—the hills of ancient Rome where it is said to have had its beginning." Ramsey, op. cit. supra note 8, at 3.

principle *superficies solo credit* —whatever is attached to the land forms part of it—and did not visualize separate ownership of floors in a dwelling. During the Middle Ages, however, the ownership of floors of houses, and even separate rooms, appears to have been common in various parts of Europe. There is recorded history of such ownership (*Geschosseigentum* or *Stockwerkseigentum*) back to the twelfth century in German cities, and similar evidence exists as to the late Middle Ages in France and Switzerland.[12]

Apparently, the splitting up of ownership of housing units became excessive, and, since there were no clear rules as to repair and maintenance of the structure, disputes became common. These difficulties, plus the reception of Roman law principles, so jeopardized the whole concept that some of the codifications by German states either failed to recognize this form of ownership or even prohibited outright the ownership of parts of buildings. The Code Napoleon, however, recognized the separate ownership of floors of a building, in line with established customary law, as a special type of co-ownership of an immovable. Through the years it became common to define the rights of the various floor or flat owners by special agreement, the *réglement de copropriété,* which prevented some of the earlier disputes. However, doubtful points remained, including the fact that the special agreement did not bind successors in title. Legislation in 1938, amended in 1939 and 1943, cured most of the defects.[13] The purpose of the legislation, as described by a French property lawyer, was three-fold:

> "First, it was to clarify the rights and obligations of the owners of flats with regard to the common parts of the buildings.

> "Second, it was to create an organization of the various flat owners in a building by (a) giving binding force to the *réglements de copropriété,* and (b) giving a majority of flat owners the right to make decisions binding on all.

> "Third, it was to provide for the appointment of a person (the syndic) authorized to represent the flat owners and to contract on their behalf." [14]

West Germany now allows ownership of individual flats in a building, as do most other European countries. Switzerland is one

---

12. For a detailed treatment of the historical background, see Leyser, The Ownership of Flats—A Comparative Study, 7 Int'l & Comp.L.Q. 31, 33–37 (1958). For a presentation of the French law on fee ownership of apartments and an explanation of why this is blocked in Louisiana, see Comment, Individual Ownership of Apartments in Louisiana, 19 La.L.Rev. 668 (1959).

13. Law of June 28, 1938, [1938] Collection des Lois 654, as amended by order (Décret Loi) of Nov. 29, 1939, [1939] Collection des Lois 1408, and Law of Feb. 4, 1943, [1943] Collection des Lois 70 (Fr.).

14. Planiol & Ripert, 3 Traité Pratique de Droit Civil Français 314 (Picard 2d ed. 1952).

of the few continental states which has no legislation enabling an individual to own a flat, and changes in the law are contemplated even there.

> "Although the creation of ownership rights in individual flats has thus now been made possible in most Continental countries, the legislation is by no means uniform. Not only are there differences in the concept of the right itself, but there are interesting variations in other aspects, such as the organisation and representation of the community of flat owners in a building, the binding force of statutory provisions, and the role of the courts in the administration of flat ownership schemes." [15]

In contrast to the Roman law, the common law developed no aversion to separate floor or room ownership, and hence no special legislation is required to allow the creation of condominiums in countries whose legal system is based on English law. At first blush this seems odd, since the concept comes from the continent of Europe, but it is another example of the flexibility and capacity for growth inherent in the common law. Ownership rights in a portion of a building are mentioned in *Coke on Littleton,* and such "superimposed freeholds" have existed in England for a long period of time.[16] Many of the American states have long recognized the legality of conveying a freehold estate in a portion of a building.[17] The difficulty is that the interest created in the grantee may be a defeasible fee simple which will determine with the destruction of the building, the title reverting to the owner of the soil.[18] This falls short of the requirements desired by the purchaser of a home. Although the common law is broad enough to allow separate ownership of individual units in a building, it is only relatively recently that much interest has developed in the condominium concept as a large-scale solution to housing shortages. The immediate impetus in this country has come, not from Europe, but from Puerto Rico, where *condominios,* as the buildings themselves are called, enjoy a wide popularity.

15. Leyser, supra note 13, at 37.

16. Buckland & McNair, Roman Law and Common Law 78 (1936). The authors mention specifically New Square, Lincoln's Inn, where the houses consist of layers of freehold sold as such centuries ago.

17. Thompson v. McKay, 41 Cal. 221 (1871); McConnel v. Kibbe, 43 Ill. 12 (1867); Townes v. Cox, 162 Tenn. 624, 39 S.W.2d 749 (1931). See also Ball, Division into Horizontal Strata of the Landscape Above the Surface, 39 Yale L.J. 616 (1930).

18. Weaver v. Osborne, 154 Iowa 10, 134 N.W. 103 (1912); Hahn v. Baker Lodge, No. 47, 21 Or. 30, 27 P. 166 (1891); Bell, Air Rights, 23 Ill.L.Rev. 251, 257 (1928). For a contrary English view, see George, The Sale of Flats 29 (2d ed. 1959); Watts, The Conveyance of a Flat—The Question of Defeasibility, 1 Austl.L.J. 363 (1928).

Three factors were apparent in the Puerto Rican picture. First, the island was faced with a major housing shortage that appeared in a particularly acute form because of the expanding population and the lack of good building sites. Second, the average Puerto Rican had a great desire for home ownership which was certain to be thwarted if he had to wait for an individual house and lot. Third, the cost of construction and the monthly payments on a mortgage had proved to be less in a cooperative venture of the condominium type than in any other form of comparable housing. The legality of this plan of ownership was first established in 1951,[19] and the present "Horizontal Property Act" was approved June 25, 1958.[20] The latter act includes virtually all of the provisions of the former, but it goes into much greater detail and has become the model for much of the current legislation being enacted in the various states. Several aspects of the act will be discussed later in connection with current legislation, but it should be mentioned here that its provisions apply only to those buildings where the parties expressly declare by a public deed, recorded in the Registry of Property, that they intend to submit the structure to the "Horizontal Property Regime." [21] Thus, while it may be possible to have split-unit ownership outside the act, a deliberate decision is required in order to receive the advantages provided by legislation. This is significant because, in discussion of the relative advantages of condominium and cooperative apartments, or other legal devices, it will be demonstrated that the former has problems all of its own. Even though this new tool is not a panacea, there seems to be no reason not to make the benefits available by statute for those who elect to follow it.

This brief historical sketch brings us to the present and the surge of American interest in condominium.[22] The same factors that accounted for its Puerto Rican popularity are undoubtedly at work in the states. Modern megalopolis has caused a land shortage formerly found only in small countries, and American states no less than Puerto Rico, need new legal devices to satisfy old human needs. The current interest was sparked, however, by the Housing Act of 1961, which promised to provide the necessary financing, and by the willingness of title companies to insure the title, so long as correct procedures are followed in setting up the

---

19. P.R.Laws Ann. tit. 31, §§ 1275–93k (1955 & Supp.1962).

20. P.R.Laws Ann. tit. 31, § 1291 (Supp.1962).

21. For a detailed analysis of the Puerto Rican Act, see Ramsey, op. cit. supra note 8, at 8–13.

22. By 1987, all fifty states had enacted some form of condominium stat-

ute. The first statutes were based on the Federal Housing Administration's "Model Statute for the Creation of Apartment Ownership" promulgated in 1961. More recently, the Commissioners on Uniform State Laws have developed two new model acts for guidance of the various states. See 7 Uniform Laws Annotated 101–231 (Master ed. 1978) and 1983 Supplement 61.110.

condominium. The role of the title insurance companies was particularly interesting since they devoted considerable space in their house organs to the new device, and the members of their legal staffs wrote articles and made speeches on the subject. For example, an issue of Lawyers Title News had a handsome picture of the leaning tower of Pisa on the cover with the following marginal comment:

> "A Way–Out Example—If the leaning tower of Pisa in Italy bordering the Gulf of Genoa had been built as a condominium, its famed 'leaning' would now be the world's most extreme example of encroachment on adjoining air rights. All buildings settle and constantly shift; yet, the space lot conveyed to condominium purchasers theoretically never changes. To cure the problem of possible encroachments and to preserve marketability of title . . . [the] author . . . suggests that the deeds contain reciprocal easements to exist as long as the building stands." [23]

This brief statement not only illustrates a typical problem in condominium, and a possible solution, but it shows the growing role of title insurance companies in shaping the American law of property.[24]

Before proceeding to an analysis of the practical advantages and disadvantages of condominium, cooperative apartments, etc., it may be well to take a further look at the classical property concepts involved in this type of ownership.

---

23. Lawyers Title News, Sept. 1962. See also the August 1961 issue of the same publication, which is referred to as the "Condominium Issue." Reference has already been made in note 8 supra to the pamphlet by Mr. Ramsey, a title officer for the Chicago Title and Trust Company.

24. Some commentators feel that the role of title insurance is already too great and is crowding the lawyer out of his traditional position in the real estate practice. See Payne, In Search of Title (pts. 1–2), 14 Ala.L.Rev. 11, 278 (1962). "The basic issue before conveyancers today is whether title insurance will spread and become the dominant form of conveyancing or whether the system of direct records examination can be restored. . . . The economic stakes involved are enormous, and the professional interests of the bar deeply involved. In this struggle the title insurance companies have the marked advantage, in that if they can simply block any action, the movement toward title insurance will undoubtedly continue. The bar, on the other hand, must take decisive action if the present trend is to be reversed. Whether the bar is capable of mobilizing its forces so as to achieve such a result will determine the course of future events."

SECTION 2. THE CONCEPT OF CONDOMINIUM

The common law has long recognized multiple interests in a single *res*. Indeed, much of the law of property deals with the complex rules and principles developed to regulate the relationships among the owners of these multifarious interests. Ranging from the relatively simple problems of bailment in personal property to the intricate snarls of the Rule Against Perpetuities in future interests, the law has struggled, more or less successfully, with the concept of a *single* thing subject to *multiple* rights. The nearest approach to condominium, aside from the sub-surface, surface, and air rights cases, has been in one form or another of cotenancy. But whether coparcenary, tenancy by the entirety, joint tenancy, or tenancy in common, the legal concept has always called for unity of possession. The shares of each owner need not be equal, e.g., tenancy in common, but the possession of one is the possession of all, and, in legal theory if not in fact, each owner has a claim to every square inch of Blackacre subject only to correlative claims by the other cotenants. Only on partition, whether by voluntary action or suit in equity, does the individual owner have a claim to his specific share of the res. At that point the ownership ceases to be joint and becomes several. A concept of ownership which is joint, i.e., in common, as to part of the res, but several as to another part, goes beyond the ordinary theory of cotenancy. It means, in effect, that the owner of one unit in the structure has a fee simple absolute as to that unit, accompanied by the broad right to exclude others, which is of the essence of a fee, plus a tenancy in common with others as to the land and certain common elements of the building.

Although, as suggested in the previous section, the common law recognized the rights of ownership in separate floors, rooms, etc., it did not, prior to the development of condominium, work out a theory of several plus joint rights which could be fixed in space and would survive even the destruction of a building. Nothing in the common law would prevent this from being done by special agreement among the parties,[25] but it scarcely stands alone as a separate type of property ownership like joint tenancy or tenancy in common. This may be significant in deciding whether a statute is needed in a particular jurisdiction to serve as a kind of enabling

25. It has been pointed out that, in England, vesting of the common parts of the premises in the ownership of freehold titles to flats as tenants in common is impossible due to the Law of Property Act of 1925 [15 & 16 Geo. 5, c. 20, §§ 1(6), 34(2)]. See Leyser, supra note 12, at 51. However, this is due solely to legislation which itself modified the common law, and no such barrier exists in this country.

act for this form of multiple ownership. If the concept were well recognized in the legal system, it might be best to let it develop without legislative interference, but, where the concept itself is new, a more specific charter seems required.

One illustration should be sufficient to illuminate the conceptual difficulty. The typical cotenancies carry with them the right to partition, and lawyers are accustomed to thinking of this right as one of the "sticks in the bundle." This right, transferred to condominium, could wreck a project since the land plus certain common elements must remain unsevered, although attached to the ownership of the individual air space represented by an apartment, office, or store. These common elements must pass, like easements appurtenant, to the successive owners of the individual unit. Interestingly enough, the right to partition has not always been an incident of co-ownership and, in the early common law, the joint tenancy had to remain joint in order to maintain the socially desirable unity of title. Indeed, coparcenary's very name was derived from the fact that, without benefit of a statute, the parceners could compel partition at a time when joint tenants and tenants in common enjoyed no such right.[26] In many states, the tenancy by the entirety is still non-severable, except on divorce, just as it was at early common law.[27] Thus, although the common law is flexible enough to deny partition of the common elements, the issue may be confused since condominium does not yet have sufficient status to stand alone as a type of new estate in the law. The concept will have to be delineated in a case-by-case approach, after the method of the common law, or clarified by specific statutory authority.

SECTION 3. THE COMMON–LAW APPROACH TO CONDOMINIUM

Apart from the specific concept of condominium, cooperative ownership of apartments is old hat in this country.[28] The familiar

26. Moynihan, Introduction to the Law of Real Property 235 (1962).

27. Licker v. Gluskin, 265 Mass. 403, 164 N.E. 613 (1929); Hoag v. Hoag, 213 Mass. 50, 99 N.E. 521 (1912). But see p. 103 supra.

28. The earliest reported case in this country involving a cooperative apartment is Barrington Apartment Ass'n v. Watson, 38 Hun 545 (N.Y.Sup.Ct.1886). Among the many excellent discussions of cooperative ownership, see Hennessey, Co-operative Apartments and Town Houses, 1956 U.Ill.L.F. 22; Yourman, Some Legal Aspects of Cooperative Housing, 12 Law & Contemp. Prob. 126 (1947); Note, 61 Harv.L.Rev. 1407 (1948). See also, Hoeflich and Malloy, The Shattered Dream of American Housing Policy—The Need for Reform, 26 Boston Coll.L.Rev. 655 (1985).

pattern is to vest the title to both building and land in a corporation or trust. The tenant-owner holds stock in the corporation or a certificate of beneficial interest in the trust plus a proprietary lease of a particular apartment in the building. The rights and duties of the tenant-owners are covered in great detail in the lease, charter, bylaws, or trust agreement. This type of cooperative ownership is easily accomplished without the necessity for statutory authorization. The relative advantages and disadvantages of this legal device vis-á-vis condominium will be discussed later, though a detailed analysis is beyond the scope of this text.

As suggested earlier, the common law recognized the separate ownership of rooms or floors in a building, and, since air rights could be conveyed apart from the fee in the land,[29] it has long been possible to have condominium-type developments *sans* the esoteric name. Indeed, a 1947 example in New York City is discussed in some detail by Mr. Ramsey in his pamphlet, Condominium: The New Look in Co-ops.[30] This project involved a six-story building, containing twelve apartments, and conveyances of each unit were made separately by the legal description of a cube of space.

Similarly, the California "Own Your Own Apartment" plan functioned without a statute on condominium and was attractive to both purchasers and lenders in that boom state.

"Under this method a purchaser receives a deed which conveys an undivided fractional interest in the land and building, subject, however, to the reservation by a grantor of the exclusive use and right to occupy all the apartments in the building as shown on a plat attached to and made a part of the deed, excepting from such reservation such rights of occupancy and use as are thereinafter granted to the grantee. A subsequent clause then grants to the grantee the exclusive right to occupy a particular apartment identified by number on the above mentioned plat."[31]

The California experience, plus an analysis of the problems that may arise in any jurisdiction, is thoroughly discussed in an excellent note in the California Law Review.[32] Most of the common-law precedents are mentioned, and the authors make it apparent that condominium can function effectively without the interposition of a legislative enabling act. Nonetheless, there are strong reasons for preferring the legislative approach, and some

29. See Note, 1960 U.Ill.L.F. 303. For a major example, note the forty-one story Prudential Building in Chicago, erected in air lots over the Illinois Central Railroad tracks.

30. Ramsey, op. cit. supra note 8, at 6–7.

31. Id. at 7.

32. See Note, Community Apartments: Condominium or Stock Co-operative?, 50 Calif.L.Rev. 299 (1962).

writers feel that legislation is a virtual necessity. Thus, Mr. J. Leonard Smith, Jr., a member of the Legislative Committee of the Real Property, Probate and Trust Law Section of the Pennsylvania Bar Association, in urging immediate adoption of a condominium act in Pennsylvania stated:

"The same problems have arisen in California where several condominium type projects have been built without the benefit of specific condominium legislation. One California developer stated flatly that although he was more than pleased with his condominium project and the acceptance of it, he would not be inclined to do another one until something was done to remove some of the legal and practical roadblocks." [33]

Whatever the common-law possibilities of condominium, the real future for projects of this sort lies with a sound enabling act, and attention is now turned to that phase of the problem.

SECTION 4. THE LEGISLATIVE APPROACH TO CONDOMINIUM

There are two principal reasons for preferring the legislative approach to condominium: (1) a carefully drafted statute can clarify many of the uncertainties which would otherwise have to wait for the answers to be produced by judicial decision, and (2) such an act will provide uniformity in the creation of projects and thus ease title and financing difficulties. Since the statutes are permissive, and therefore govern the condominium only if the owner or owners elect to follow the legislative plan, there seem to be no real arguments against the passage of enabling legislation. It is possible, however, that statutes will tend to freeze projects into a common mold and thus reduce valuable experimentation, but this seems a slight risk in view of the desirable features of a statute.

As pointed out earlier, Puerto Rico led the way with its 1951 act, followed in 1958 by the "Horizontal Property Act," a somewhat confusing name for a well thought out statute. Arkansas [34] and Hawaii [35] were the first states to take up the Puerto Rican challenge, and Arizona, Kentucky, South Carolina, and Virginia [36] quickly joined the parade. Over the past few decades the interest has been increasing at a rapid rate, and, by 1987, all states had

33. J.L. Smith, The Case for a Condominium Law in Pennsylvania, 33 Pa. B.A.Q. 513, 516 (1962).

34. Ark. Acts 1961, No. 60, § 2(a).

35. Hawaii Rev.Laws § 170A (Supp. 1961).

36. See 60 Mich.L.Rev. 527 (1962).

passed such legislation. The best way to illustrate the role of legislation would be to set forth an actual act and comment on its provisions. However, that approach is too detailed for a basic text and the interested student is referred to special works dealing solely with the subject of condominium.[37]

One provision of the various acts, should be mentioned—the right of first refusal. This provision gives to the unit owners the first right to purchase any unit when it is offered for sale. If they fail to purchase within a reasonable time,[38] the vendor can then accept the outside offer on the terms originally proposed. If the unit owner sells without giving the co-owners the option to buy, they have the right to redeem from the sale. This right of first refusal is thought to be necessary in a cooperative enterprise so that the unit owners will have a voice in the selection of their neighbors. Does it violate the doctrine of restraints on alienation of fee interests? Mr. Ramsey thinks that it does not, because "the purpose of such a provision is not to restrain an owner from selling, but rather to enable a particular person to buy." [39] However, the provision was purposely omitted from the Hawaiian act and does not appear in some of the other acts. It should be noted that the provision does not afford complete protection in all cases since it deals only with voluntary sale and does not cover transfer by gift, judicial sale, or devolution on death.

The omission of this provision from the particular legislation does not prevent the inclusion of a similar clause in the by-laws if the owners so desire. While the right of first refusal may be valid if attacked solely as an unreasonable restraint on alienation,[40] it could raise questions under the doctrine of Shelley v. Kraemer [41] if it becomes apparent that the provision is but a mask to conceal restrictions on racial or religious grounds.

---

37. For a discussion of American statutes generally see Rohan and Reskin, Condominium Law and Practice (1973) plus supplements.

38. The Puerto Rican act set the period at ten days, but this seems an unreasonably short time within which to expect the other unit owners to respond.

39. Ramsey, op. cit. supra note 8, at 21. See also Gale v. York Center Community Co-op, Inc., 21 Ill.2d 86, 171 N.E.2d 30 (1960) (upholding a comparable restraint).

40. It could also run afoul of the Rule against Perpetuities as an unlimited option to purchase, but for provisions in the acts. See Eastman Marble Co. v. Vermont Marble Co., 236 Mass. 138, 128 N.E. 177 (1920); Starcher Bros. v. Duty, 61 W.Va. 373, 56 S.E. 527 (1907).

41. 334 U.S. 1 (1948).

SECTION 5.   ADVANTAGES OF CONDOMINIUM

The advantages of all things are relative.[42] The advantages of condominium must be stated in relationship to ordinary apartment dwelling, to ordinary home ownership, and to other types of cooperative apartments. Moreover, as the advantages to the purchaser will be different from the advantages to developers, lenders, and brokers, they must be stated separately for each group. Finally, since some of the advantages will turn out to be illusory, and because certain disadvantages exist which will offset some of the rosy claims made for condominium, a group-by-group analysis of advantages must be followed by a realistic look at the other side of the coin.

A.   ADVANTAGES TO THE PURCHASER

1. *Compared to Ordinary Apartment Dwelling.* The advantages of condominium as compared to ordinary apartment dwelling are roughly those claimed for any form of cooperative ownership. It is possible to compile a list of fifteen to twenty specific advantages, depending on the zeal with which the advocate of cooperative dwelling approaches his task.[43] Basically, however, these advantages fall into two large categories: first, the improved financial situation of the owner vis-à-vis the tenant, and second, the added security and sense of status that accompanies ownership of a dwelling unit.

There is no denying that substantial savings can be realized in a well-run cooperative. The landlord's profit is eliminated, and all of the economies produced by mass purchase of supplies, fuel, public utilities, etc., can be passed on to the unit owners. Tax deductions for interest on the mortgage payments and real estate taxes should be most attractive to prospective purchasers. Since the owner is building an equity in his unit, which can later be sold, he is adding to the total of his estate rather than paying out rent which disappears with each passing day. It has even been noted that the homestead exemption laws would apply to the unit

42. This is best illustrated by an old canard. A man greeted his friend with, "Life is odd isn't it?" Came the reply, "Compared to what?"

43. For illustrations, see Teitelbaum, Representing the Purchaser of a

Co-operative Apartment, 45 Ill.B.J. 420 (1957); Wall St.J., March 8, 1962, p. 1, col. 1.

so that something might be salvaged if the owner fell on evil days. However, since lenders will invariably require a waiver of the homestead right, this is likely to be one of the illusory advantages.

The sense of ownership that goes with cooperatives in all forms, and which is strongest in condominium, may well be the principal advantage over a normal tenancy. The owner can sink his roots into his apartment with an assurance of tenure that would be lacking if he could be evicted by a landlord at the termination of any given period of the lease. He can make alterations, decorate his own unit to his individual taste, and have a voice in managing the entire structure in a way not possible except through cooperative ownership. It is true that he must share the management with others, but even this has its advantages since he may find a sense of purpose and fellowship in the united effort for maintenance and improvement of the building and grounds. The exclusiveness of this type of ownership is usually listed as an advantage—the ability to choose one's neighbors, in a way denied to the tenant, being heavily stressed. It is easy to overplay this point, however, since the initial subscribers may have no right to pass on other initial subscribers and the developer may dispose of the remaining units, in a slow-moving cooperative, without much thought of exclusivity. Later sales may also fall short of the ideal if the project runs into financial difficulties, and a situation may develop in which any solvent buyer begins to look better than the burden of extra assessments. Nonetheless, the cooperative in any form is likely to be more exclusive than ordinary apartment living, and the right of first refusal in the condominium has a distinct appeal to many purchasers.[44]

2. *Compared to Ordinary Home Ownership.* Many of the advantages just discussed are inherent in ordinary home ownership. The merit of the cooperative device is that it makes these advantages available in urban areas where land scarcity and high cost cause individual home ownership to be next to impossible. Cooperative units of all types tend to combine the values of separate home ownership with the economy and stability of a large-scale enterprise. It becomes possible to have landscaping, garden areas, swimming pools, and other luxuries infrequently found in the "cheesebox on a raft" type of large-scale, individual unit subdivisions. These can be financed at a lower cost per unit because of the "one basement, one roof, high rise" approach to urban dwelling. In short, the advantages of apartment living with the freedom from worry over the petty details of day-to-day maintenance and operation can be combined with the pride of ownership that strikes a common chord for most Americans.

44. See text supra at 130 for a discussion of this point.

These apartment-type advantages are likely to be particularly appealing to the older generation whose children are grown and away from home. Since the life expectancy tables disclose increasing prospects of longevity for the average American, this advantage of condominium may be of prime importance.

3. *Compared to Other Types of Cooperative Apartments.* An extensive brief could be prepared for condominium as opposed to other types of cooperative apartments currently in operation. However, most of the arguments can be reduced to a single claim, i.e., condominium combines the advantages of cooperative dwelling and separate home ownership. Thus, the unit owner's tenure is more akin to a fee simple title than would be the case under a proprietary lease with stock in a cooperative corporation. Granting that he is bound by the cooperative aspects of the declaration and bylaws, he comes as close as it is possible to get to "true ownership" of his apartment. This is important, not only psychologically, but in many, more tangible ways. The history of cooperative apartments, especially during recessions, has been an unfortunate one,[45] and the liability under a blanket mortgage is enough to scare away many interested purchasers. The unit owner is not quite so financially dependent upon the activities of his fellows. He negotiates his own mortgage and can make accelerated payments much as he could on a separate home. He pays his own taxes, and thus can avoid forfeiture and the ignominy of a tax sale. Although the condominium purchaser is not entirely free from the defaults of others (as will be seen in the later discussion of disadvantages), he probably avoids the worst hazards of the other types of cooperatives.[46]

The unit owner's greater degree of financial independence is illustrated in another way. He may sell his unit at market price and thus reap a capital gain, instead of being required to sell his shares to the corporation for the amount originally paid in, as is frequently the case in the ordinary cooperative. Even if the other owners have a right of first refusal, they must exercise it at the market level. This can be of major importance in an era of steadily rising real estate values. Moreover, the owner has assurance that his family will have a place to live on his death without undergoing scrutiny from other members of the cooperative as to popularity and financial resources. In other forms of cooperatives, leases frequently terminate on death, with a right of the family to remain for a limited period only.[47]

45. Postwar Co-ops, Architectural Forum 93 (June 1948).

46. For a good analysis of these hazards, see Note, 68 Yale L.J. 542 (1958).

47. Note 61 Harv.L.Rev. 1407, 1419 (1948).

It is well known that owning a home offers several significant income tax advantages over renting. These same benefits should be available to a unit owner in a condominium, although they may not accrue to the participant in a typical cooperative. Thus, the unit owner should be entitled to casualty loss deductions, to interest and property tax deductions, to deferred recognition of gains on sale of an old residence and to a depreciation allowance if he rents the unit to another.[48]

B. ADVANTAGES TO THE DEVELOPERS, LENDERS AND BROKERS

In essence, the advantages to the developers, lenders, and brokers arise from the advantages to the purchaser. If the consumer finds condominium to be an attractive investment, then the suppliers of housing are certain to fulfill the demand. The impetus toward condominium was furnished principally by the 1961 amendments to the federal housing laws, which recognized this concept of real property ownership and authorized the FHA to insure a first mortgage given to secure the unpaid purchase price on individual units.[49] As late as 1958, commentators noted that mortgage loans for ordinary cooperatives were "practically unobtainable," even with federal insurance, because the terms were too long and the maximum interest rate too low.[50] Condominium should alleviate this problem with its smaller individual mortgages, rather than a single blanket one, and with negotiated down payments that may well run higher than that possible for the entire structure. As with any cooperative, the builder or promoter can find equity capital from the potential purchasers, rather than being forced to provide his own. Moreover, smaller lending institutions may be able to participate in financing the individual units in situations where they could not have financed the entire project.

There may be less "red tape" in the sale of condominium units than in the handling of a stock cooperative. The latter must meet the requirements of the appropriate state blue sky laws, whereas condominium, since involving the sale of real property, should be regulated by the real estate laws of the several states.[51] However, since real property interests have on occasion been held to be

48. Note 32 supra at 332.

49. Housing Act of 1961, 7 Stat. 160, 12 U.S.C.A. § 1715y (Supp. III, 1961).

50. Note 46 supra at 569.

51. See Brothers v. McMahon, 351 Ill.App. 321, 115 N.E.2d 116 (1953).

securities, the developer will want to check carefully the law of his own jurisdiction.[52]

The advantages to the real estate broker are easy to visualize since each unit becomes a potential listing. One enthusiastic writer outlines five distinct advantages to the realtor and sums it up this way.

"The condominium subdivision is an answer to the land scarcity problem. The two-dimensional subdivision that passage of time and increase of land values has rendered obsolescent and uneconomic, is transformed by the condominium into a three-dimensional subdivision, section stacked vertically upon section. It restores the realtor's base of individually owned, single family units destroyed in land clearing operations, but in a new and different form."[53]

SECTION 6. DISADVANTAGES OF CONDOMINIUM

Ironically, the advantages of condominium carry the seeds of disadvantage. The more you strengthen individual unit ownership the more you weaken cooperative control by the group. It may be true "that condominium is simply another form of cooperative ownership of real property,"[54] but the very security of the fee simple title runs counter to the traditional view of a cooperative. This is but a legal affirmation of the truth in the saw, "you can't have your cake and eat it too." It is not an argument against condominium, as such, since all legal devices have weaknesses as well as strengths, but it does suggest caution in dealing with overly optimistic claims about the merits of this kind of project.

A. DISADVANTAGES TO THE PURCHASER

As in the case of advantages, a long list of claimed disadvantages of condominium to the purchaser could be compiled. The

52. Note 32 supra at 338.

53. Maki, Condominiums: New Prospects for Realtors, Lawyers Title News, Nov. 1962, p. 5.

54. Ramsey, Condominium, The New Look in Cooperative Building, in Proceedings of the American Bar Ass'n Section of Real Property, Probate and Trust Law, Part II, Real Property Law Division 4–5 (1962).

problem areas can be isolated under three heads, however: first, the cumbersomeness of this legal device, especially if unaccompanied by statutory authorization; second, the lack of control by the co-owners of the activity of a recalcitrant owner; and third, the legal problems peculiar to any new technique that has not been fully developed by the case law.[55]

The first point has been well stated by Professor Powell, writing before the current impetus for condominium and not mentioning the concept by name:

> "The legal patterns employed in creating cooperative apartments fall into four categories, of which two are extremely rare. . . . Under the second of the rare patterns, each tenant acquires the legal ownership of the cubic footage constituting his apartment but a joint tenancy or tenancy in common is established as to the areas used in common, such as halls, stairways and grounds.[56] Few persons have resorted to these cumbersome and unsuitable patterns for the creation of a cooperative apartment relation." [57]

In a footnote, Professor Powell adds:

> "The inconvenience of requiring the joinder of many persons in deeds, leases or mortgages, the complete absence of a simple method of forcing the individual participant to perform his financial obligations, and the risk of heavy individual personal liability, combine to prevent both of these devices from ever having popularity."

The previous discussion in this chapter indicates that some of these objections have been met by the Puerto Rican experience and by carefully drafted statutes and bylaws, but others remain, and the whole idea will undoubtedly strike many purchasers as too complicated for their tastes. Just as the sale of realty can never be made as simple as the transfer of personalty, neither can the sale of a condominium unit be reduced to the simplicity of the deed, mortgage, and closing statement to which individual home owners are accustomed. Moreover, the expense may be increased because of the separate fees and separate mortgages. The latter will require more servicing and may carry a higher interest rate than a blanket mortgage on the same project.[58]

55. The point can be illustrated by the true story of a lawyer who visited Minneapolis for the first time. On his way in from the airport, he spotted a mammoth building complex and asked the taxi driver, "What is that big building?" "Oh", said the cabby, "that's one of them new pandemoniums!"

56. See, e.g., Woods v. Petchell, 175 F.2d 202 (8th Cir.1949), where the result was found to be a cooperative apartment. [Footnote by Professor Powell.]

57. 4 Powell, Real Property 709–10 (1954).

58. See Note 46 supra, at 603.

Perhaps the financing problems of condominiums are no more complex than those of other large projects but

The appeal of individual ownership may also be lessened when the purchaser realizes the necessity for a long-term mortgage on which he will remain personally liable even after he leaves the project. In ordinary cooperatives the agreement usually has an "escape clause" which allows a member to get out after the payment of a fixed sum.

The second disadvantage comes down to this—it may be difficult to get rid of a "bad egg" if one owns a fee. The lessee can be evicted by summary proceedings, but the owner has a security of tenure which protects the undesirable participant as well as the desirable one. Remedies do exist, but lien foreclosures and breach of covenant suits can be costly and protracted if the built-in social pressures fail to resolve a dispute. Moreover, it may be difficult to insure, even through restrictive covenants in the deed and the binding force of the statute and bylaws, that future purchasers will be desirable and financially responsible.[59] The principal difficulty, however, lies with the owner who becomes *in*voluntarily undesirable, i.e., one who, for reasons beyond his control, cannot pay his share of the common expenses and taxes. These defaults are anticipated in the various statutes, and remedies are provided. They should work well when the defaults are few and the bulk of the owners are solvent, but what will happen in times of recession or of major depression? It was the latter which broke the back of the old-style stock cooperative, and no one knows how condominium would fare in such troubled times. The mortgages are several but the common expenses are joint.

The third area of disadvantage is the most difficult to handle. Condominium has a long history, but it is only now being tried in the crucible of twentieth-century America. An inventive mind can visualize numerous problems for which the solutions are not at hand. The more cautious investor may wish to let others provide the answers before casting his own lot with condominium. Central to this problem is the exact nature of the management association and its relationship to the unit owners. It has been suggested that the board of managers might be considered an "association" and taxable as a corporation.[60] This seems doubtful since there is no intent to carry on a business for joint profit;[61]

they can be staggering. For example, a businessman went to Florida to look over a huge hotel that was for sale. He called his partner, "I've got some good news and some bad news. The good news first. They only want $10,000,000 for a building worth $15,000,000. The bad news? Oh, they want a $1,000 down!"

59. See Comment, 13 Hastings L.J. 357 (1962).

60. See Int.Rev.Code of 1954, § 7701(a)(3). For a detailed discussion of the point, see Note 32 supra at 334.

61. Treas.Reg. § 301.7701–2(a)(2) (1960) states that "the absence of [either associates or an objective to carry on business for joint profit] will cause an arrangement among co-owners of property for the development of such property for the separate profit of each

but it would be possible to show a profit in a given year, and one is never too sure about tax matters. On the other hand, the management group is not incorporated and hence there is no limited liability either in contract or tort. This may not cause difficulty since the role of the board is carefully circumscribed; it deals principally with the common elements, and proper insurance coverage is mandatory. Nonetheless, one can foresee situations where the coverage would be inadequate, and the unit owner might find himself liable for a sizable judgment with no protecting corporate screen.[62] Similarly, on the insurance point, would a breach of warranty by one co-owner (say, in a fire insurance policy) void the policy for all? Can the management association sue a unit owner, or a third party, without joining all other owners? What if some refuse to join? What can be done to facilitate class actions by the association?

Other questions come readily to mind. In an eminent domain proceeding, is each unit owner entitled to a separate hearing on his fee or can the condemning authority proceed against the entire building? Many statutes of limitations read, "No person shall commence an action for the recovery of lands . . . unless within twenty years," etc. Is a unit land, and, if not, will the contract statute apply?[63] There is no point in continuing this list since the moral should now be clear. None of these objections are, in any sense, fatal, but collectively they must be treated as some of the disadvantages of a new legal tool like condominium.

B. DISADVANTAGES TO THE DEVELOPERS, LENDERS, AND BROKERS

The disadvantages to the developers, lenders, and brokers follow the same pattern as those to the purchaser. The principal objection is administrative complexity. At the outset, the developer must make two applications for FHA insurance, one for a blanket mortgage for the project, the other for individual mortgages for the unit owners. Each must comply with the FHA

[or for no profit] not to be classified as an association."

62. Note 32 supra at 312. The board of managers could be set up as a not-for-profit corporation to avoid some of these problems. This is being done in some condominiums. For a typical problem see Dutcher v. Owens, 647 S.W.2d 948 (Tex.1983).

63. For example, in Centex Homes Corp. v. Boag, 128 N.J.Super. 385, 320 A.2d 194 (1974) the court held a vendor could not get specific performance of a contract to sell a condominium unit since it was not unique and was more like personal property for the purpose of using the equitable remedy of specific performance.

regulations and the developer may run into delay while individuals arrange for FHA approval. If the developer is unable to sell all the units, he may have difficulty in discharging the original project mortgage, with the result that the entire venture could bog down.[64] Moreover, the lender may be restive under a security which is subject to rules and assessments imposed by a management group over which he has little or no control. This is particularly true if incompetent amateurs are in the position of running the show.

Prior discussion has indicated other administrative problems. In the absence of statute, the building may be taxed as a whole, and even with statutory authorization some assessors may be less than cooperative in carrying out their duties.[65] The developers may have to comply with subdivision regulations which would not be involved in ordinary apartment houses.[66] In short, the suppliers of condominiums will find that all is not beer and skittles, and that they, too, must deal with the cumbersomeness inherent in this type of multiple unit housing and with some of the uncertainties involved in the new and the different.

SECTION 7. THE FUTURE OF CONDOMINIUM

Will condominium help provide home ownership for megalopolis? The advantages and disadvantages to the purchaser, the developer, the lender, and the broker are relevant in answering that question, but the issue for society as a whole is how to provide more and better housing for a rapidly expanding urban population. On balance, condominium should be a useful legal tool because it appeals to the basic American urge for private ownership and provides a greater degree of independence from one's fellows than is normally available in the landlord-tenant relationship or in the traditional cooperative. While it is far from perfect and while some of its advocates may be overly optimistic in its praise,[67] condominium is more than an attractive gimmick de-

---

64. See Note 32 supra, at 330.

65. See Annot., 80 A.L.R. 867 (1932).

66. See Note, Community Apartments: Condominium or Stock Cooperative? 50 Calif.L.Rev. 299, 336 (1962).

67. "Think of a condominium as a high-rise apartment building, a garden-type housing development of detached and semi-detached units each consisting of one or more stories, a row of attrac-

tive town houses, an office building in which each occupier owns his own office space, a shopping center where each shopkeeper owns his own storeroom, an industrial complex where each industry owns its own plant or facilities, a warehouse or terminal with ownership of areas divided among the occupiers— think of a condominium as any conceivable type of project where it is desirable for the various occupiers to own their

signed to lure reluctant capital into the housing market. It has more to commend it than the availability of FHA insurance, and, if approached with the usual legal skepticism and caution, it should join its older cousins as a respectable member of the property family. Although not strictly required, condominium should be undergirded by a well-drafted statute, and the bar should watch its growth closely so that needed changes can be made as experience discloses the weak spots in the pioneer projects.

Finally, it should be noted that condominium is, in a sense, a new type of subdivision—vertical rather than horizontal—and it has much of the same potential for development that we have seen in subdivision growth generally since the end of World War II. It has the same vulnerability to exploitation that unregulated growth of traditional subdivisions has already disclosed but also the identical opportunity for decent housing if properly planned and controlled.[68] The discussion in this chapter should be compared with the later material on land use generally.[69]

respective areas and to have joint control of common areas or facilities. The possibilities are unlimited. Think, also, of the unlimited possibilities for land development and redevelopment and the possibilities for more and better housing, as well as urban renewal and rejuvenation. Do not overlook the possibilities for commercial and industrial expansion and all of the economic advantages that can accrue to our Commonwealth and its residents, *if* we are farsighted enough to provide the legislation and legal working tools so that condominium projects will be feasible in Pennsylvania." Smith, note 33 supra at 514. As Mr. Smith correctly points out, condominium is useful for many projects other than housing and, if it operates successfully in the apartment field, it will undoubtedly be used in a variety of commercial ventures.

68. See Krasnowiecki, Townhouse Condominiums Compared to Conventional Subdivisions With Homes Association, 1 Real Estate Law Journal 323 (1973).

69. See Part Six. The Use of Land.

Part Three

TRANSFER OF OWNERSHIP

In Part One, we discussed property as an institution and sought some insight as to the role of private property in modern society. In Part Two, we explored the scheme of ownership as developed in Anglo–American law with slight references to other systems of jurisprudence. Now, assuming you understand such esoteric matters as freehold versus non-freehold estates, seisin versus possession, etc., we turn our attention to the transfer of ownership from one party to another. There are various ways to categorize these transfers but the broad division is between voluntary and involuntary. The former are more important for our present purpose since they include the major commercial aspects of property law—sale, mortgage, and lease—but the latter will be discussed first in order to provide perspective.

While the lease is a voluntary transfer of ownership, i.e., the transfer of a non-freehold estate, just as much as an outright sale of the land, we will save the discussion of that material until Part Four—Landlord and Tenant. This seems desirable because of the many specialized legal problems involved in the leasing of land. None of these transfers of ownership are of maximum utility unless the title itself is merchantable, i.e., capable of being transferred profitably to others. Like landlord tenant law, however, the specialized problems of title assurance deserve a separate Part of the book and they will be covered in Part Five—Methods of Title Assurance.

Chapter 1

INVOLUNTARY TRANSFER

Although we tend to think first of a sale, a gift, or perhaps a lease, when we visualize transfers of ownership from one party to another, many changes in title take place against the express desires of the owner. Judgments may be obtained which will be liens against the property, resulting in levy of execution and sale;[1] involuntary bankruptcy proceedings may force the debtor to strip himself of his limited assets;[2] adverse possession by a rival claimant may ripen into a new title under the Statute of Limitations;[3] title to personal property may be changed due to doctrines of accession and confusion;[4] the boundary-changing propensities of rivers may take land from one riparian owner and give it to another;[5] etc. While all of these title changes may involve serious legal problems, they cannot be discussed in a short, elementary book. One type of involuntary transfer, however, does call for our attention—transfer at death.

Testate and intestate succession, i.e., transfer through a will or by operation of a statute of descent in absence of a will, are frequently classified as gratuitous transfers, operating as a type of gift. This is a useful concept since it separates these transfers from commercial transactions and highlights the donee aspect of the recipient. It may seem odd to call a testamentary disposition an involuntary transfer since the making of the will is clearly voluntary and may have been accompanied by estate planning of a high order. Still, it is doubtful if many testators voluntarily slip over the great divide so that the objects of their bounty may enjoy the material possessions left behind. If there were pockets in shrouds, no doubt the man of property would depart this life heavily laden. Hence, the title of this chapter seems appropriate.

---

1. See Brown, The Law of Personal Property 39–48 (3d ed. by Raushenbush 1975).

2. See generally MacLachlan, Handbook of the Law of Bankruptcy (1956).

3. Discussed herein as a method of title assurance at p. 333 infra.

4. Note 1 at 49–75.

5. 3 American Law of Property, § 12.113 (Casner ed. 1952).

SECTION 1.   INTESTATE SUCCESSION

————

It is difficult to separate intestate and testate succession for discussion, but it may clarify our thinking to see the distinct categories represented by the two methods of transfer. The former was the more ancient method and, so far as land was concerned, it was the middle of the sixteenth century in England [6] before fee simple estates were freely devisable. Here, again, the split between realty and personalty played a key role in the development of the law since personal property could be disposed of by will from very ancient times. It was, at one time, thought to be a religious duty to bequeath all of one's chattels and the church, through the ecclesiastical courts, exerted a powerful influence to see that no person of wealth died intestate. You may be sure that this religious interest was not wholly altruistic and the worldly position of the church was enhanced by the wealth acquired through carefully planned wills. One English historian writes that "this abandonment of jurisdiction [over personal property] to the ecclesiastical courts has tended, more than any other single cause, to accentuate the difference between real and personal property; for even when the ecclesiastical courts had ceased to exercise some parts of this jurisdiction, the law which they had created was exercised by their successors." [7]

Even if we grant the power to the individual to dispose of his property at death more or less as he sees fit, we are a long way from settling the issue. While it might seem that no aspect of private property is more basic than the power to choose the objects of one's bounty, many individuals will die without exercising this power even where it is available to them. The law must then decide how the deceased's estate shall be distributed. Of course, it could be argued that, due to the former owner's lack of personal concern, all of the property should pass to the state to be used for the general welfare, but this extreme position has not in fact been taken, except in the rare cases where there are no heirs at law or next of kin and the property escheats to the state. More than three hundred years ago Grotius said that the purpose of the intestate succession law was to provide that the property of a dead man would descend "to the person to whom it is especially probable that the dead man had wished that it should belong." Writers and courts have generally taken this position since that

---

6. The Statute of Wills was passed in 1540.

7. 1 Holdsworth, History of English Law 625 (7th ed. 1956).

time so that we seem to have a mandate to make our law conform to the probable wishes of the community.[8]

Any detailed historical analysis of intestate succession [9] is out of place in a book of basic principles but it would show the constant striving, inept at times and full of digressions, of the parliament in England and the state legislatures in this country to make the law conform to the social needs and the probable wishes of the community at any given time. Thus, in the modern law, primogeniture and the canons of descent have been confined to the ash heap and vigorous efforts have been made to remove the differences between real and personal property. This latter reform is not yet complete in all states but the distinctions are fast disappearing. The present law of intestate succession is wholly controlled by local statutes and the details vary from state to state, yet, not too surprisingly, the general "running gears" are pretty much the same throughout the United States and an understanding of one such statute makes it easy to work with others. The pattern of distribution is about the same with the "one-third to the spouse, two-thirds to the children" or "one-half to the spouse, one-half to the children" apparently representing the wishes of the community. A typical statute follows, together with comments, so that you may put some flesh on the skeleton just outlined.

Illinois Law of Descent [10]

2–1. Rules of descent and distribution

§ 2–1. Rules of descent and distribution. The intestate real and personal estate of a resident decedent and the intestate real estate in this State of a nonresident decedent, after all just claims against his estate are fully paid, descends and shall be distributed as follows:

(a) If there is a surviving spouse and also a descendant of the decedent: ½ of the entire estate to the surviving spouse and ½ to the decedent's descendants per stirpes.

(b) If there is no surviving spouse but a descendant of the decedent: the entire estate to the decedent's descendants per stirpes.

(c) If there is a surviving spouse but no descendant of the decedent: the entire estate to the surviving spouse.

---

8. For an excellent discussion of this point, including how we are supposed to discover the wishes of the community see Dunham, Social Science Research for Legislative Reform, 46 A.B.A.J. 1020 (1960).

9. See Atkinson, Wills 1–158 (2d ed. 1953).

10. Ill.Rev.Stat. ch. 110½, § 2–1 (1985).

(d) If there is no surviving spouse or descendant but a parent, brother, sister or descendant of a brother or sister of the decedent: the entire estate to the parents, brothers and sisters of the decedent in equal parts, allowing to the surviving parent if one is dead a double portion and to the descendants of a deceased brother or sister per stirpes the portion which the deceased brother or sister would have taken if living.

(e) If there is no surviving spouse, descendant, parent, brother, sister or descendant of a brother or sister of the decedent but a grandparent or descendant of a grandparent of the decedent: (1) $\frac{1}{2}$ of the entire estate to the decedent's maternal grandparents in equal parts or to the survivor of them, or if there is none surviving, to their descendants per stirpes, and (2) $\frac{1}{2}$ of the entire estate to the decedent's paternal grandparents in equal parts or to the survivor of them, or if there is none surviving, to their descendants per stirpes. If there is no surviving paternal grandparent or descendant of a paternal grandparent, but a maternal grandparent or descendant of a maternal grandparent of the decedent: the entire estate to the decedent's maternal grandparents in equal parts or to the survivor of them, or if there is none surviving, to their descendants per stirpes. If there is no surviving maternal grandparent or descendant of a maternal grandparent, but a paternal grandparent or descendant of a paternal grandparent of the decedent: the entire estate to the decedent's paternal grandparents in equal parts or to the survivor of them, or if there is none surviving, to their descendants per stirpes.

(f) If there is no surviving spouse, descendant, parent, brother, sister, descendant of a brother or sister or grandparent or descendant of a grandparent of the decedent: (1) $\frac{1}{2}$ of the entire estate to the decedent's maternal great-grandparents in equal parts or to the survivor of them, or if there is none surviving, to their descendants per stirpes, and (2) $\frac{1}{2}$ of the entire estate to the decedent's paternal great-grandparents in equal parts or to the survivor of them, or if there is none surviving, to their descendants per stirpes. If there is no surviving paternal great-grandparent or descendant of a paternal great-grandparent, but a maternal great-grandparent or descendant of a maternal great-grandparent of the decedent: the entire estate to the decedent's maternal great-grandparents in equal parts or to the survivor of them, or if there is none surviving, to their descendants per stirpes. If there is no surviving maternal great-grandparent or descendant of a maternal great-grandparent, but a paternal great-grandparent or descendant of a paternal great-grandparent of the decedent: the entire estate to the decedent's paternal great-grandparents in equal parts or to the survivor of them, or if there is none surviving, to their descendants per stirpes.

(g) If there is no surviving spouse, descendant, parent, brother, sister, descendant of a brother or sister, grandparent, descendant of a grandparent, great-grandparent or descendant of a great-grandparent of the decedent: the entire estate in equal parts to the nearest kindred of the decedent in equal degree (computing by the rules of the civil law) and without representation.

(h) If there is no surviving spouse and no known kindred of the decedent: the real estate escheats to the county in which it is located; the personal estate physically located within this State and the personal estate physically located or held outside this State which is the subject of ancillary administration of an estate being administered within this State escheats to the county of which the decedent was a resident, or, if the decedent was not a resident of this State, to the county in which it is located; all other personal property of the decedent of every class and character, wherever situate, or the proceeds thereof, shall escheat to this State and be delivered to the Director of Financial Institutions of the State pursuant to the Uniform Disposition of Unclaimed Property Act.

In no case is there any distinction between the kindred of the whole and the half blood.

Amended by P.A. 81–400, § 1, eff. Jan. 1, 1980.

The opening paragraph of the statute betrays the history of the subject. Reference is made to both real and personal estate—not just to property or to the estate—and it descends and shall be distributed. Real property was said to descend to the heirs at law on the instant of death (note this typically meant pass by descent to the eldest son—primogeniture) while personal property was collected by the administrator, the debts were paid, and then it was distributed to the next of kin, who might be different parties than the heirs. Note that this modern statute has abolished all distinctions between real and personal property so far as descent is concerned. This simplifies the problems and eliminates one area of potential litigation. Dower and curtesy which applied only to real property, have been abolished in Illinois.[11]

The statute uses the quaint language, *per stirpes,* to describe how the property shall pass to descendants. The Model Probate Code prepared by the American Bar Association substitutes the more meaningful phrase, "by representation", but they both come out at the same place. *Per stirpes,* Latin for by roots or stocks, is a term taken from the civil law and describes the method for dividing an intestate estate so that a group of distributees take the share that their deceased ancestor (root?) would have been entitled

11. Ill.Rev.Stat. ch. 110½, s. 2–9 (1985).

to take, i.e., they inherit by virtue of representing such ancestor rather than as so many individuals, *per capita*. Thus, in the first paragraph, if a father is survived by his wife, a son and two grandchildren, descendants of a deceased daughter, the wife will take one-half, the son one-fourth, and the two grandchildren will share the deceased daughter's one-fourth. If the son were deceased, leaving four children, they would take only his one-fourth, so that the deceased daughter's children would take twice as much as the deceased son's children because of the *per stirpes* doctrine. Contrast this with a *per capita* gift by will to all of the grandchildren where they would share equally. It follows that no descendant can take *per stirpes* while his root or stock is still alive, i.e., the grandchildren take nothing if their parent survives the intestate.

The statute is progressive in the sense that in applying it you move from paragraph to paragraph to determine the pattern of distribution. Paragraph seven (g), for example, has no application until you exhaust all of the preceding six paragraphs and find no relatives that fit the described categories. At that point you move to the rules of the civil law and determine the nearest collateral heirs according to the following formula.

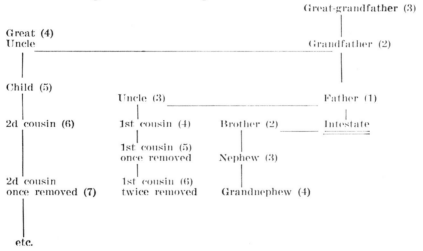

etc.

Ascertain the closest common ancestor of intestate and claimant. Count the steps from intestate to common ancestor and from common ancestor to claimant. The sum of the two figures represents the degree of relationship between claimant and intestate. The claimant who stands in smallest numerical degree of relationship to the intestate takes the property.

In addition to the civil-law rule for determining inheritance by collaterals there was a canon or common-law rule but it need not be considered as a part of the basic principles of intestate succession. There are serious policy questions as to whether distant collateral relatives should be allowed to participate in any case. Typically, these individuals are far removed from the deceased and do not have any real concern for him other than the windfall which has come their way, hence the highly appropriate term, "laughing heirs." [12] This point can be illustrated best by the famous *Wendel* case. "Ella V. von E. Wendel died on March 13, 1931, leaving an estate of about $40,000,000, including 143 parcels of real estate in New York County, bank deposits of $1,900,000 in New York, and securities of the value of $2,900,000. Her estate was long in the courts, and a total of 2303 claimants appeared to file claims. The court in 146 Misc. 260, 262 N.Y.S. 41 (1933) accepted the claims of 9 claimants of the fifth degree. It denied the claim of another that he was related to the deceased in the fourth degree and referred the matter to the District Attorney for prosecution. [He was sentenced to a three year term on conviction of conspiracy. Some of the fraud and conspiracy attempted in the litigation is summarized in Matter of Wendel, 159 Misc. 443, 287 N.Y.S. 893 (1936), wherein the Surrogate felt called upon to call to the attention of attorneys canons 30 and 31 of the American Bar Association.]" [13]

If all of the paragraphs (or rules) fail to produce a winner the eighth paragraph (h) governs and the property escheats. It has been argued that this listing of the state (or its designate, the county, state university, etc.) in the statute of descent makes it an heir, in effect, and thus subject to an inheritance tax. In re O'Connor's Estate [14] rejects this argument and holds that escheat is an incident of state sovereignty and the state's rights set forth in the last paragraph of the statute do not make it a beneficiary of the deceased.

The last sentence of the statute erases any distinction between kindred of the whole and half blood and subsequent sections go on to cover all possible problems, such as posthumous children (they can inherit as if born in the father's lifetime), adopted children (in general, they can inherit as if they were natural children), heir murdering an ancestor (he is cut out to prevent profit from a Kind–Hearts–and–Coronets [15] situation), and illegitimate children. At common law, the lot of a bastard was a hard one and he could not succeed to the property of his ancestors or collateral relatives,

12. Cavers, Change in the American Family and the "Laughing Heirs", 20 Iowa L.Rev. 203 (1935).

13. Williams, Cases and Materials on the Law of Property 108 (1954).

14. 126 Neb. 182, 252 N.W. 826 (1934).

15. The allusion is to an Alec Guiness movie where a remote heir slowly murdered his way to a dukedom and great wealth.

nor could the latter take from him on intestacy. His property went to the crown if he died without a wife or descendants. Today, the law is much kinder [16] and for quite some time it has been possible for an illegitimate child to inherit through the mother although most statutes still excluded the child from the father's estate unless the parents later intermarried and the father acknowledged the child. In 1977, the United States Supreme Court [17] declared such an Illinois provision invalid as a denial of equal protection of the law. The Court said that a classification based on illegitimacy was required to bear a rational relationship to a legitimate state purpose and that the provision could not be justified on the ground that it promoted legitimate family relationships. The difficulties involved in proving paternity in some situations did not justify total statutory disinheritance of children born out of wedlock and the fact that the father could have provided for the child by making a will did not save the provision from invalidity.[18]

At this point, it would be wise for you to conjure up several fact situations of your own and try your hand at solving them so that you will be sure to understand the operation of a statute of descent. A little speculation will reveal survival patterns which would distribute the estate in ways not likely to be foreseen by the deceased and clarify the reason for a will, even in small estates.

SECTION 2.   TESTATE SUCCESSION

Should a testator be permitted to dispose of his property by will according to his own unrestricted fancy and caprice, without regard to wife, children, kin or charities? Is the assertion so frequently made, that there is complete freedom of testation in England and America, justified by the facts? These are fascinating questions and the temptation to rest awhile and talk of jurisprudential matters is hard to resist. However, Professor Simes has already pre-empted the subject and I remand you to his Cooley Lectures.[19] Suffice it to say that most societies have put

---

16. This is due not only to a more civilized society but to the recognition that bastards have contributed much to their fellows. Bennett Cerf in his Trade Winds Column in The Saturday Review told of the professor who wanted to offer a course in the lives and talents of authors of illegitimate birth. He labelled the course, "Some Misconceptions in English Literature."

17. Trimble v. Gordon, 430 U.S. 762, 97 S.Ct. 1459, 52 L.Ed.2d 31 (1977).

18. For an excellent brief discussion of the legal problems of the illegitimate child see Krause, Family Law 148–162 (2d ed. 1986) (Nutshell Series).

19. Simes, Public Policy and the Dead Hand 3, 7 (The Thomas M. Cooley

restraints on testation but that the testamentary power has been freer in Anglo–American law than elsewhere. Thus, France restricts freedom of testation in favor of both descendants and ascendants and Germany protects descendants, parents, and surviving spouses. Even in England and United States, there are some curbs and while the testator can disinherit his children (even without the device of giving them one dollar and a pat on the head) he typically finds his spouse a protected party. Modern statutes tend to allow the surviving spouse (widow or widower) to renounce the will and take a stated statutory share of the estate.[20] The fee tail estate, with its line of descent restricted to lineal heirs, was, at one time, a limiting factor but with modern disentailing statutes [21] this restriction disappears. Dower, homestead, and community property, in the states utilizing these features of property law, all serve as fetters on testation. Tax policy, exerted through federal estate taxes and state inheritance taxes, also has an effect on free choice and some estate planning looks as if it were designed more to save taxes than to transfer property to the natural objects of one's bounty. One wag tells the story of the wealthy client who said, "I don't care who gets it so long as the government doesn't."

In the main, however, there is relative freedom of testation in the Anglo–American countries and a decedent can cut off his children while leaving his property to a blonde mistress or a cat and dog hospital. The will may be contested for fraud, duress, or undue influence or its admission to probate may be attacked for improper execution or forgery but that is another matter entirely.

Since the Statute of Wills in 1540, it has been possible for the decedent to transfer his property, both real and personal, to those persons whom he has properly designated. Some degree of formality was demanded even by the Statute of Wills—it required a written instrument but did not specify that the testator must himself write or sign the document—but reliable proof was first required by the Statute of Frauds in 1676. It directed that the will be signed by the testator or, at his direction, by a person in his presence, and that it be attested and subscribed, in his presence, by three or four credible witnesses. The modern requirements are based on these two old statutes but the details vary from state to state and the local law must always be consulted. There are also such things as nuncupative wills and holographic wills. The former is an oral will declared or dictated by the testator in his

Lectures, University of Michigan Law School, 1955).

20. See e.g., Ill.Rev.Stat. ch. 110½, s. 2–8 (1985), which gives the surviving spouse who renounces: "one-third of the entire estate if the testator leaves a descendant, or one-half of the entire estate if the testator leaves no descendant."

21. P. 49, supra.

last illness, before witnesses, and afterwards reduced to writing; the latter is a will entirely written, dated, and signed by the hand of the testator himself. Frequently, these latter types are not allowed by the language of the statute even though they clearly reveal the intent of the deceased. Of course, if the will fails, for any reason, the decedent dies intestate and the property is distributed according to the relevant statute of descent.

The great merit of a will over other types of testamentary disposition, some of which will be discussed in the next chapter, lies in its clarity and in its ambulatory character. Ambulatory (literally walking) means the instrument is revocable and lets the testator change his will whenever he feels the need, providing he uses the proper formalities. Since the will does not speak until the date of death this allows alterations to meet changing conditions and represents the reverse of the deed which becomes effective as soon as delivered. The fact that the will must be in writing, plus the simple formalities, usually means that the pattern of distribution is well thought out, rather than being a sudden whim of the testator.[22]

22. This sketchy discussion of testate succession is included to make the material which follows more understandable. For a good basic treatment of the subject see Atkinson's Hornbook on Wills (2d ed. 1953).

Chapter 2

VOLUNTARY TRANSFER BY GIFT

There are many forms of voluntary transfer of property but we shall restrict our discussion to gift, sale, and lease. This does not mean that other transfers are unimportant but only that they tend to be more specialized and hence beyond the purview of a book on basic principles. The transfer of property for security purposes, as in a mortgage, raises a host of legal problems and the creation of a trust,[1] involving a transfer of the legal title to a trustee to hold and utilize for the benefit of the original owner or a third party, obviously calls for a complex body of law. Fortunately, these more specialized forms of transfer are built on the basic property foundation and if you understand the principles of gift, sale, and lease you should be able to find your way around in the other types of transfer.

It would seem, at first blush, that an owner ought to be able to give his property away without any legal entanglements other than those arising from the ever-present tax collector. In one sense he can—so long as both parties, donor and donee, agree that a gift has in fact been made, there is no difficulty. This proves nothing, however, since it is rather like saying there are no legal problems unless a dispute arises and that is a difficult proposition to debate. The law of gifts develops principally around the issue of whether the owner ever intended to become a donor. The dispute can arise while the alleged donor is still alive, but more often it develops after his death when the heirs contend no gift was ever made and that the property passed to them either by testate or intestate succession. Thus, it will be seen that the voluntary transfer by gift bears a close relationship to the involuntary transfer by death.

---

1. For basic treatment of mortgages and trusts see, Nelson and Whitman's Hornbook on Real Estate Finance Law (2d ed. 1985) and Bogert's Hornbook on Trusts (5th ed. 1973).

SECTION 1. GIFTS OF PERSONALTY

Gifts of personal property have been analyzed so well by Professor Brown that no extended discussion is required here and the student is requested to incorporate by reference the Brown materials.[2] Traditionally, the gift of a chattel required intent, delivery, and acceptance; this was a sacred trinity, like offer, acceptance, and consideration for a contract. Intent could be proved by the facts as later disclosed by admissible evidence, delivery was conceived to be a manual tradition (handing over) of the object of gift, and acceptance could normally be presumed if the gift was a beneficial one. So long as the law was in a period of extreme formalism each element of a gift had to be carefully established and delivery became the touchstone. The *res* had to change possession and pass from the donor to the donee or the gift failed,[3] even though the intent to make a gift was clear. While it is still good doctrine that no parol gift of a chattel capable of manual tradition is valid without the requisite delivery, there are so many exceptions to the basic rule that it is impossible to make dogmatic statements on the subject.

The nature of the problem can be quickly illustrated by a partial catalogue of difficulties. How do you deliver one-fourth of a horse, if you wish to make a gift of this fractional interest in the animal?[4] Can you deliver the property to a third person to hold for the donee? Can you have a symbolic or constructive delivery, as of a key to a safety deposit box, when it is impossible or impractical to transfer possession of the thing itself? How can you make delivery of a chattel already in possession of the donee or in the common possession of the donor and the donee? The list could be extended indefinitely but since, in the proper case, the gift has been sustained in each of the above situations, it is apparent that delivery no longer means manual tradition from the donor to the donee but has become a fiction that is roughly equivalent to intent and may be viewed as one way of proving that the donor wanted to transfer ownership of his property. This is not to say that delivery, in its traditional sense, has no modern importance. It is clearly easier to sustain the gift if it is present, but the gift does not necessarily fail without it. Professor Mechem argued persuasively that the requirement should be retained by the courts because it (1) makes vivid and concrete to

2. Brown, Personal Property 76–188 (3d ed. by Raushenbush 1975).

4. Cochrane v. Moore, L.R. 25 Q.B.D. 57 (1890).

3. Irons v. Smallpiece, 3 B. and Ald. 551 (1819).

the donor the significance of his act, (2) the manual tradition is unequivocal to witnesses to the transaction, and (3) the delivery gives the donee *prima facie* evidence in favor of the gift.[5] On the other hand, the retention of so formal a requisite may cause many gifts to fail in cases where there is little doubt that the donor intended his property to pass to the donee. In Foster v. Reiss [6] the conflicting theories of gift collided in a spectacular fashion and a careful analysis of the majority and minority opinions in that case will add immeasurably to your understanding of the problem.

Since the policy of the law is crystal clear in this area—the protection of the owner from ill-founded and fraudulent claims of gift which rest only on oral statements, concerning which the evidence may be doubtful and open to controversy—it might seem reasonable to require that all gifts of chattels be accompanied by a written document, stating the reason for the gift and manifesting the donor's intent. A statute could even require that the document be witnessed after the manner of wills so that proof would be always forthcoming. In fact, a deed of gift (i.e., a sealed document) or other written instrument, in those states where the private seal has lost its significance, is a recognized method of making an effective gift. Usually, the instrument would need to be delivered to the donee, or to a third party in his behalf, but there would be no need for delivery of the chattel itself.[7] However, this has never been recognized as the exclusive method for making a gift for the very good reason that it is the custom of people generally to give away their property in a much more informal fashion and the law, to some extent at least, must deal with people as it finds them. It seems fair to conclude that most modern courts will sustain a gift of chattels on some theory,[8] so long as they are convinced that the

5. Mechem, The Requirement of Delivery in Gifts of Chattels, 21 Ill.L.Rev. 341, 342–352 (1926).

6. 18 N.J. 41, 112 A.2d 553, 48 A.L.R.2d 1391 (1955). Writing for the majority, Chief Justice Vanderbilt followed the traditional view and held a gift invalid because of the lack of delivery (manual tradition), which he saw as "the only safeguard imposed by law upon a transaction which would ordinarily fall within the statute of wills." (A gift *causa mortis* was involved.) The dissenting judges, including William J. Brennan, then on the Supreme Court of New Jersey, felt that delivery was an "artificial requirement" and since the intent of the donor was clear the gift should have been sustained. See also

Scherer v. Hyland, 75 N.J. 127, 380 A.2d 698 (1977) where the New Jersey Supreme Court, in effect, adopted the view of the dissenting judges in Foster v. Reiss, in a case where the intent of the donor was clear but there was no manual tradition because the donor committed suicide without delivering two handwritten notes and a check endorsed in blank to the donee.

7. Note 2 supra at p. 106.

8. The theory may be that of an oral trust which dispenses with delivery entirely since the donor can declare himself a trustee of the *res* for the benefit of the donee. See Smith's Estate, 144 Pa. 428, 22 A. 916 (1891).

parties intended that result and gave some objective manifestation of that intent.[9]

The motivation for a gift is not normally of any concern to the law. It may spring from the purest of sentiments, such as filial devotion, or it may arise from a less noble source, to wit the gratification of the whim of a mistress. A man's property is his own and the right to dispose of it as he sees fit should be protected. However, there is a situation in which motivation becomes crucial, i.e., the gift *causa mortis,* which is made in apprehension of imminent death. Most gifts are classified as *inter vivos,* i.e., transfers made between living persons where the donor has no particular expectation of approaching death.[10] The cases abound with statements that gifts *inter vivos* must be absolute, unconditional, and irrevocable if they are to be valid.[11] This general view requires a surrender of dominion and control over the chattel so that a present gift can be sustained. Like most general statements, this ban on conditional *inter vivos* gifts is subject to many exceptions and the courts frequently sustain donations which are, in fact, revocable. This is usually done on the theory that there has been the present transfer of a future interest [12] or that some present interest, such as a share of a joint bank account, has been transferred even though it may be revoked later by a withdrawal of the funds.[13] The fact remains that most *inter vivos* gifts are unconditional and that, if the condition is precedent to the vesting of present rights, the attempted transfer is one *in futuro* and hence void. By way of contrast, the gift *causa mortis* is, by its very nature, conditional and will not fail for that reason.

The conditional aspect of the gift in apprehension of death is well stated in Allen v. Hendrick [14]: "A gift *causa mortis* is made subject to three conditions implied by law, the occurrence of any one of which will defeat the gift: (1) the recovery of the donor from the sickness or his delivery from the peril; (2) revocation by the donor before his death; (3) death of the donee before the death of the donor." Aside from the conditional character of such gifts, the essential elements are the same as in *inter vivos* transfers, i.e., intention, delivery, and acceptance. However, the courts will

9. In re Cohn, 187 App.Div. 392, 176 N.Y.S. 225 (1919); Beach v. Holland, 172 Or. 396, 142 P.2d 990, 149 A.L.R. 866 (1943).

10. Presumably all individuals with the mental capacity to make a gift realize they will die eventually and it could be argued that they are now disposing of their estate due to that mournful fact.

11. Grignon v. Shope, 100 Or. 611, 197 P. 317 (1921).

12. Conlon v. Turley, 56 App.D.C. 95, 10 F.2d 890 (1926); Innes v. Potter, 130 Minn. 320, 153 N.W. 604, 3 A.L.R. 896 (1915).

13. In re Estate of Michaels, 26 Wis. 2d 382, 132 N.W.2d 557 (1965) and Malone v. Walsh, 315 Mass. 484, 53 N.E.2d 126 (1944).

14. 104 Or. 202, 219, 206 P. 733, 738 (1922).

scrutinize these gifts with even more care because of the greater opportunity for fraud inherent in a claim made against the estate of a now deceased person. Moreover, it is clear that such gifts are really testamentary in character, partaking of the nature of a nuncupative will. If the law will not allow a testator to dispose of his property other than by jealously guarded formalities, why should it sustain a clearly oral and frequently ambiguous donation? [15]

This last question continues to plague the courts and accounts for many of the irreconcilable decisions. Manual tradition becomes even more important here since it furnishes stronger proof of the purported gift. A major theoretical hurdle for the courts is erected out of the conditional aspect of the gift. If the condition is precedent, i.e., if the gift becomes absolute only when the donor dies of the apprehended peril then it is clearly testamentary, title passing at the instant of death. If the condition is subsequent, i.e., if the donee's title vests immediately on delivery, subject to revocation if the donor fails to die, then the gift is not testamentary and can be sustained. You can be sure that the majority of cases have accepted the condition subsequent theory in order to sustain such gifts.[16]

SECTION 2.   GIFTS OF REALTY

A watch may be physically handed to the donee but Blackacre resists such casual treatment and this makes the gift of realty a more formal affair. It is true that, in earlier times, the symbolic delivery of a clod or twig in the ceremony of livery of seisin came close to manual tradition, but since the passage of the Statute of Frauds a writing has been required for the conveyance of land and this applies to gratuitous transfers as well as to those for value. Occasionally, an oral gift of land will be sustained where the equities are exceptionally strong in favor of the donee, as where the possession has been transferred, valuable improvements have been made on the premises, and it would work substantial injustice or fraud to hold the gift void under the statute.[17] These situations are so rare, however, that we can assume the necessity for a deed in nearly all cases, thus approaching a greater degree of certainty than is possible in the gift of chattels. Assuming the

---

15. See Note 6 supra.

16. Note 2 supra, at p. 133–136.

17. Hayes v. Hayes, 126 Minn. 389, 148 N.W. 125 (1914).

deed is properly executed, along the lines discussed later,[18] the only serious problems are likely to arise in connection with delivery of the document and the always troublesome issue of a conveyance which is meant to be effective only at the donor's death. There is some dispute over the necessity for consideration in order to have a valid deed, but this is easily solved by the recital of "one dollar and other good and valuable consideration" even though no money is, in fact, paid. This minor quibble arises out of the theory under which modern deeds operate. If they are still bargain and sale deeds, functioning by virtue of the Statute of Uses, then consideration is essential. Even if they are covenants to stand seised under the Statute of Uses, they require a consideration of blood or marriage and this might be absent in some gifts. But if they operate under modern conveyancing acts, no consideration is required and the gift is complete on delivery of the deed. Since there is still doubt in some states as to the exact nature of a conveyance, it may be well for the careful draftsman to recite a consideration even in a deed of gift.[19]

The question of delivery of a deed to realty is essentially the same as that discussed in the previous section. It has never been stated better than in Kyle v. Kyle.[20] "That delivery is essential to the effectiveness of a deed to real estate is elementary, but just what amounts to a delivery is sometimes a question of doubt. Ordinarily it is the simple transfer of possession of the written instrument from the grantor to the grantee with intent on part of the grantor to convey and on part of the grantee to acquire title to the property described therein. But an actual manual transfer of the paper is not necessary. A delivery may be effected by acts without words, or by words without acts, or by both words and acts. Assuming the instrument to have been properly executed ready for delivery, acts and words evincing intent to part with it and relinquish the grantor's right over it is a sufficient delivery. . . . It may be made direct to the grantee or to a third person in his behalf. . . . In final analysis it may be said that delivery is a matter of intent, or any distinct act or word by the grantor with intent to pass the title to the grantee by transferring the deed to him or to another for his benefit is a delivery."

The terms *inter vivos* and *causa mortis* are not much used in relation to gifts of realty but the same kind of problem does exist. A gift of land must be unconditional and the donor's attempt to retain dominion and control over Blackacre will normally cause the gift to fail, but if the facts disclose that the donor kept only a

---

18. See p. 208, infra.

19. Hill v. Bowen, 8 Ill.2d 527, 134 N.E.2d 769 (1956). For a comment on the case see 1956 U.Ill.L.F. 513.

20. 175 Iowa 734, 737, 157 N.W. 248, 249 (1916).

life estate and that the remainder passed immediately to the donee then the gift can be sustained.[21] If the deed is delivered directly to the donee but with oral conditions that must be met before the conveyance is to be effective, the majority of cases treat the conveyance as presently valid and ignore the conditions precedent.[22] These statements of general doctrine set the stage for a type of testamentary disposition that does not comply with the Statute of Wills. The donor delivers a deed to a third person with directions to deliver it to the donee on the donor's death. When does the title pass to the donee? If it passes at death, the agency of the third party is revoked by death and the gift fails for lack of delivery in the lifetime of the donor. If, however, the deed is placed beyond the grantor's control, i.e., if he has reserved no right to get it back from the third party, then it is relatively easy to conclude that the donor has retained an estate for his own life and that a future interest by way of remainder passed to the donee with the delivery to the third party.[23] This arrangement is similar to escrow [24] since it involves delivery to a third person with further delivery to the donee on the happening of a condition. However, in this case the condition, death, is certain to occur sometime and in this sense the delivery to the third party is not conditional at all. At any rate, this method of making a gift has been sustained by the courts on so many occasions that it, like joint tenancy, can be said to operate as a will substitute, a poor man's probate.

21. Ferrell v. Stinson, 233 Iowa 1331, 11 N.W.2d 701 (1943).

22. Ivancovich v. Sullivan, 149 Cal. App.2d 160, 307 P.2d 989 (1957). But see Chillemi v. Chillemi, 197 Md. 257, 78 A.2d 750 (1951) where the equities in favor of the donor were too strong and the deed was set aside.

23. Milligan v. Milligan, 161 Neb. 499, 74 N.W.2d 74 (1955); Mann, Escrows—Their Use and Value, 1949 U.Ill.L.F. 398, 418.

24. Discussed at p. 213 infra.

Chapter 3

VOLUNTARY TRANSFER BY SALE

The commercial transfer of a property interest from one owner to another, while simple in theory, can be complex in actual operation. The law which has developed to protect the parties to a sale is a curious blend of common law, custom, and statute. As usual, the laws of personalty and realty have followed divergent paths, due both to historical accident and to inherent differences between movables and immovables. Much of the schism springs from questions of title to the *res*. In personalty, only a few complicated questions of ownership arise and the sale is readily consummated without a long delay while the title is being searched. Possession usually means ownership and, if the jeweler sells a watch he does not own, the remedy lies in a suit against him for the sale price. Realty is far more complex and, in Part Five, a discussion of the methods of title assurance will show the need for a gap between the signing of the contract and the delivery of the deed. Of course, some of the principles are the same regardless of the *res* being sold and the lawyer should be thoroughly familiar with both the similarities and the differences.

No attempt will be made here to cover the sale of goods. These transfers are governed largely by statute,[1] plus the inevitable judicial gloss, and appear in law school curricula as a part of the commercial law subjects under the usual title of Sales or Commercial Transactions. A good brief discussion of the elementary aspects of the sale of goods appears in Brown on Personal Property[2] and a perusal of that material will be most helpful before proceeding with the sale of realty.

The sale of land centers around two separate legal documents—the contract to sell and the deed which actually conveys the title. In addition, many commercial transfers involve the use of an escrow agreement and its role must be understood in order to visualize the operation of a sale. Therefore, this chapter will be developed under three headings—contract, deed, and escrow. A fourth document, the mortgage, is a vital partner in most transac-

---

1. The Uniform Sales Act and the Uniform Commercial Code.

2. Pages 189–208 (3d ed. by Raushenbush 1975).

tions but it will be discussed only incidentally since its complexities call for extended coverage in their own right.[3]

SECTION 1. THE CONTRACT

It would be possible to sell real estate without the use of a contract. A purchaser, walking down the street, could pick out a house he liked, as he would a melon in the supermarket, exclaim, "I'll take it," and accept a deed forthwith from a willing vendor. In practice, this will seldom happen, not only because of the title search, but also due to the financing details and the multifarious items that must be adjusted before a transfer. All of the law of contracts is applicable at this juncture and the well-drafted instrument covers a host of detail that has only inferential relationship to the law of property. Since the contract is the blueprint of the transaction it is the most important document in the sale and must be carefully handled. However, this is not a book on drafting[4] and we will concentrate here on some of the typical problems involved in all real estate contracts.

A. THE STATUTE OF FRAUDS

Our seventeenth-century friend, the Statute of Frauds, still applies to real estate contracts, even in England.[5] The entire, detailed agreement need not be reduced to writing since the Statute itself provides for a memorandum, but this is designed for the aberrational case and a lawyer would obviously cover the full terms in writing. The sufficiency of the memorandum has been challenged in countless cases, and from them it appears that an adequate memo must identify the parties to the contract, give a sufficient description of the property so that it can be identified,

---

3. A good brief treatment is found in Casner and Leach, Cases and Text on Property 673–688 (First Standard Ed. 1950).

4. There are many excellent articles on drafting a real estate contract. For a succinct treatment of the essential points see Friedman, Buying a Home: Representing the Purchaser, 47 A.B. A.J. 596 (1961) and Drafting of Real Estate Contracts, 35 Chi.Bar Record (1954). For a detailed practice book see Holtzschue, Real Estate Contracts (1985).

5. England has now repealed most of the Statute but the sections on land and suretyship remain. Act 1954, 2 and 3 Eliz. 2, c. 34.

state the terms and conditions of the agreement, and be signed by the party to be charged.[6]

These general principles are so flexible that the courts can decide many cases either way without doing violence to the stated law. What is a sufficient identification of the parties? They need not be mentioned by name and labelled as vendor and purchaser, providing their identity can be ascertained by words contained in the writing, which writing may include hasty notes, memoranda in books, papers, letters, or telegrams.[7] However, the failure to disclose in any way the vendor or the purchaser is fatal as a mere "offer lanced into the void." [8]

What is an adequate description of the property? It need not be a fully accurate legal description in metes and bounds or by governmental survey, but it must point out a specific piece of real property with such particularity that only one tract is identified. A building described by street number is sufficient if the city, county, and state are mentioned. Less than this may cause real difficulty.[9] Property referred to as "my house or building" (meaning the vendor's) is satisfactory if the seller owns only one such piece, but is ambiguous and fatal if he owns more than one tract fitting the description.[10] If the language is restricted to "a frame residence" rather than "my", it may be fatal even if the vendor owns only one such house since it could refer to property he does not yet own but plans to buy.[11]

When are the terms and conditions sufficient? Clearly, they need not be set out with the specificity of a mature contract, but the "key" points must be included if they have been agreed upon. Thus, if special financing has been set up, failure to include it in

6. Kohlbrecher v. Guettermann, 329 Ill. 246, 160 N.E. 142 (1928). See also Ward v. Mattuschek, 134 Mont. 307, 330 P.2d 971 (1958).

7. In A.B.C. Auto Parts, Inc. v. Moran, 359 Mass. 327, 268 N.E.2d 844 (1971) a check with a somewhat detailed endorsement was held to be sufficient. See also Bennett v. Moring, 33 Colo.App. 390, 522 P.2d 741 (1974) where the court noted: "Where more than one writing is used to satisfy the requirements of the statute of frauds, some nexus between the writings must be shown."

8. This is Mr. Justice Cardozo's language in Irvmor Corporation v. Rodewald, 253 N.Y. 472, 171 N.E. 747, 70 A.L.R. 192 (1930).

9. Some courts are very strict about the description. Martin v. Seigel, 35 Wash.2d 223, 212 P.2d 107 (1949) re-

quired the lot number, block, addition, city, county, and state. See 27 Wash.L. Rev. 166 (1952) for a comment on the case. Similarly, Wilson v. Wilson, 134 Ind.App. 655, 190 N.E.2d 667 (1963) invalidated a description which would have been sufficient in many states. Said the court: "Though the recent trend is for American courts to liberally interpret the Statute of Frauds, we believe that a decision to the contrary would completely abrogate a statute of our legislative branch. . . ."

10. Corrado v. Montuori, 49 R.I. 78, 139 A. 791 (1928).

11. Draper v. Hoops, 135 Ill.App. 389 (1907). See also Hertel v. Woodard, 183 Or. 99, 191 P.2d 400 (1948) where the court refused to imply "my farm" or "my property" to save a deficient memo.

the memo may wreck the transaction, whereas if no such agreement has been reached the law can imply that the sale is for cash.[12] Even failure to include the price of the land may be overlooked if no agreement was reached, since the court can insert a reasonable price. This doctrine can have interesting consequences, such as allowing a vendor to prove that, in fact, the parties agreed on a specific price per acre, but failed to put it in the memo and hence made the contract unenforceable because of the Statute of Frauds.[13]

Who must sign the memorandum in order for it to be enforceable? The English statute, and most of the American ones which used it for a model, required only that the memo be signed by the party to be charged. This translates, "by the party being sued." Thus, if the vendor signs he can be sued by the purchaser but he cannot sue in return unless the purchaser signed. The reverse is obviously true. This leads to the anomaly that frequently one party has a remedy, the other none, and seems to fly in the teeth of the so-called mutuality of remedy rule.[14]

Occasionally, the memo will contain the necessary elements but some of them will be in error. If this is due to a mutual mistake of fact on the part of the vendor and the purchaser, i.e., if they both meant Blackacre but the typist inserted Whiteacre and they signed without realizing it, then a court of equity can reform the memo to correct the error. Reformation is not available, however, to fill in missing elements since this would allow the complainant to hoist himself by his own bootstraps and reform nothing into something.[15]

Most of the memo problems arise when the parties seek no outside advice but rely on their native skill and put something into writing because they vaguely recall that oral land contracts

12. Much of the difficulty concerning terms relates to financing provisions. Some courts are quite strict while others are very liberal in their requirements. Contrast Montanaro v. Pandolfini, 148 Conn. 153, 168 A.2d 550 (1961) (contract unenforceable for failure to specify when the monthly payments are to commence or the amount of each payment in a purchase money mortgage) with Monaco v. Levy, 12 A.D. 2d 790, 209 N.Y.S.2d 555 (1961) (contract on its face satisfied the Statute of Frauds, despite its silence as to the mortgage maturity date and the mortgage interest rate).

13. Hanlon v. Hayes, 404 Ill. 362, 89 N.E.2d 51 (1949). Comment, 1950 U.Ill. L.F. 309.

14. See, for example, Cottom v. Kennedy, 140 Ill.App.3d 290, 94 Ill.Dec. 683, 488 N.E.2d 682 (1986) where the vendor did not sign but was allowed to sue the purchaser who did sign. Said the court: "It is no defense . . . that such a contract lacks mutuality of obligation in that it is not enforceable against the other, non-signing party. Rather, by bringing suit on the contract to enforce it, the non-signing party has bound himself and thereby rendered the contract mutual."

15. For some insight into the remedy of reformation see Laycock, Cases and Materials on Modern American Remedies 451–457 (1985).

are ineffective. However, the real estate broker [16] causes his share of the difficulties when he uses an informal memo as a receipt or binder on the assumption that a formal contract will be drafted and signed later. Too often the binder stands in lieu of the contract and the parties never get professional legal advice at all.[17]

Even if the contract is entirely oral, all is not necessarily lost. The law courts tend to follow the exact language of the statute and, while not treating the contract as void, refuse to enforce the parol agreement. If the contract is wholly executory there is probably no hope, but if sufficient acts of part performance have taken place, equity may grant specific performance in order to prevent the Statute from working a fraud.[18] The exact reason behind the doctrine of part performance is not too clear but it usually operates on one of two theories—unequivocal referability or equitable fraud. The former phrase was enunciated best by Mr. Justice Cardozo in Burns v. McCormick [19] and means that the acts done must unequivocally refer to the existence of a contract before that contract can be enforced. "The theory of part performance rests on the fact that one sees from the acts of a man that he has title to or some interest in the property or he would not be doing those things.[20] Thus, the purchaser would not have paid money down, gone into possession, and made improvements on the land unless he had a contract to purchase. This view of the doctrine is based on adequacy of proof and the court of equity is allowing the contract to be proved by parol, if the acts of part performance point sufficiently to a contract. The equitable fraud theory holds that, "The foundation of the doctrine is fraud; not necessarily an antecedent fraud, consciously intended by the party making the

16. In most states the Statute of Frauds applies to real estate brokerage contracts and many of the same problems covered in this section on the real estate contract arise in the broker's agreement. For example, the adequacy of the description or designation of the property is often in issue. See Owen v. Hendricks, 433 S.W.2d 164, 30 A.L.R.3d 929 (Tex.1968). In some states, the Statute does not apply to real estate brokerage contracts and the broker's agreement may be oral although the contract between the vendor and purchaser remains subject to the provisions of the Statute.

17. For the problems that can arise when the informal memo meets the required minimum but contains the phrase, "Formal contract to be signed on or before September 1, 19__", see

C. & J. Prin.Law of Prop. 3d Ed. UTB—7

Levine v. Lafayette Building Corp., 103 N.J.Eq. 121, 142 A. 441 (1928) reversed by the Court of Errors and Appeals 105 N.J.L. 532, 148 A. 772 (1930). See also King v. Wenger, 219 Kan. 668, 549 P.2d 986 (1976). The court noted: "But where the intent of the parties is clear that they are negotiating with an understanding that the terms of the contract are not fully agreed upon and a written formal agreement is contemplated a binding contract does not come into existence in the absence of execution of the formal document."

18. Shaughnessy v. Eidsmo, 222 Minn. 141, 23 N.W.2d 362 (1946).

19. 233 N.Y. 230, 135 N.E. 273 (1922).

20. Neverman v. Neverman, 254 N.Y. 496, 501, 173 N.E. 838, 839 (1930).

contract, but a fraud inhering in the consequence of thus setting up the statute." [21] This view is sometimes referred to as estoppel, the court saying the offending party is estopped to deny the existence of a contract because of the acts of the other party. It does not depend so much on proof as it does on the hardship [22] which would result if the defendant were allowed to plead the Statute of Frauds successfully.

While the equitable fraud theory and estoppel are closely related they are not necessarily the same doctrine. Thus, in Hickey v. Green [23] the vendor orally agreed to sell a lot to the purchaser who gave a deposit check to the vendor. The check was not an adequate memo because, among other things, it was not signed by the vendor who turned out to be the party to be charged. There was no transfer of possession and no improvements were made on the lot. However, the vendor was told that the purchaser intended to sell his present home and build on the new lot. The purchaser did promptly sell his present home and then the vendor refused to complete the oral contract because she had decided to sell to a third party for a higher price. The court held specific performance would be available to the purchaser on the theory of equitable estoppel because the purchaser had so changed his position in reasonable reliance on the oral contract that injustice could be avoided only by specific enforcement.[24] Of course, the key to the case was the fact that the vendor had been told of the purchaser's plans and knew that the latter was relying on the oral contract by selling his own home. Absent that fact, it is difficult to see how the oral contract could have been enforced since there was no adequate memo and the usual legally significant acts of part performance were not present. It would be a "fraud" on the purchaser to deny him relief in a case of this sort but the estoppel doctrine of Hickey v. Green goes a step beyond the traditional theories of unequivocal referability and equitable fraud.

The theories of unequivocal referability and equitable fraud are not mutually exclusive, even though they proceed on different premises, and both depend on the same legally significant acts—

21. Pomeroy, Specific Performance, § 104 (3d ed. 1926).

22. "Hardship alone, according to the Supreme Court of California, may remove an oral contract from the Statute of Frauds by estoppel. . . . California courts have been clearly progressing toward abrogation of the Statute of Frauds." Note, 3 Stan.L.Rev. 281 (1951).

23. 14 Mass.App.Ct. 671, 442 N.E.2d 37 (1982).

24. The court relied heavily on the Restatement (Second) of Contracts, s. 129 (1981). "A contract for the transfer of an interest in land may be specifically enforced notwithstanding failure to comply with the Statute of Frauds if it is established that the party seeking enforcement, in reasonable reliance on the contract and on the continuing assent of the party against whom enforcement is sought, has so changed his position that injustice can be avoided only by specific enforcement."

payment, change of possession, and improvements. There may be other acts of part performance as well but most cases follow the stated pattern. There seem to be at least five different views in this country as to what acts are necessary and each view has substantial adherents. (1) Possession alone is sufficient. (2) Possession accompanied by payment is sufficient. (3) Possession accompanied by the making of valuable and lasting improvements is sufficient. (4) There must be both possession and such a change of position by the purchaser that irreparable injury will result unless the oral contract is enforced. (5) No acts of part performance will be recognized to take an oral real estate contract out of the Statute of Frauds.[25] In none of the states is payment alone sufficient because the purchaser can always maintain an action at law for the return of his money, plus interest. This makes the remedy at law adequate and does not call for the intervention of chancery. In most states, if all three acts appear, in combination, the chance of enforcement is very good. It should be noted that it makes no difference what has been done in part performance of an alleged contract to sell land unless it can be clearly shown that such a contract exists, i.e., the agreement must be proved by oral testimony like any other parol contract, in addition to showing the acts of part performance.[26] These acts, while they may themselves go to the question of proof, are principally significant because they provide a peg on which the chancellor can hang his jurisdictional hat.

If the acts of part performance are done by the purchaser, can the vendor use them to enforce the contract for his own benefit? At first glance, the answer would appear to be no since the vendor has done nothing to entitle himself to specific performance if the purchaser wants out of the contract. This result follows under the equitable fraud theory since it is no fraud on the purchaser if he wants out of the contract.[27] However, under the unequivocal referability theory the acts of the purchaser tend to prove the existence of a contract regardless of which party relies on them and the contract should be enforced even at the suit of the vendor.[28]

Even though a lawyer drafts a satisfactory contract, the client may scuttle it with an attempted oral modification. The weight of American authority holds that a total oral rescission of a written contract for the sale of land is permissible on the theory that the Statute applies only to enforcement of the contract, not to release

25. Chafee and Re, Cases and Materials on Equity 609 (4th ed. of Chafee and Simpson's Cases on Equity, 1958).

26. Wright v. Raftree, 181 Ill. 464, 54 N.E. 998 (1899).

27. Palumbo v. James, 266 Mass. 1, 164 N.E. 466 (1929).

28. Pearson v. Gardner, 202 Mich. 360, 168 N.W. 485 (1918).

of the rights under it by the parties.[29] On the other hand, a parol modification of some of its terms would be ineffective because you cannot enforce a land contract which is partly written and partly parol.[30] The original contract stands, as written, and the changes fail unless it is possible to enforce them on a theory of estoppel. This latter situation can arise when the vendor agrees to a change in the manner of performance and then on the day for the final payment and delivery of the deed, after the purchaser has relied on the oral change, tries to go back to the written agreement. He may be estopped to deny the change or at least required to give the buyer additional time in which to comply with the written contract.[31]

So much litigation has arisen because of the Statute of Frauds and so many exceptions have been engrafted upon the original, simple prohibition against the enforcement of any oral contract for the sale of land that it may be that the Statute itself should be repealed so far as it relates to contracts and retained only for deeds.[32] At any rate, the moral for the lawyer is clear: put your land contracts in writing when you are involved at the drafting stage and search hard for a precedent allowing specific performance in equity if you come in at the litigation phase of an oral contract.

B. TIME STIPULATIONS

A real estate contract typically remains in the executory stage for three to five weeks and, in installment land contracts, may continue to incubate for years. The day set for final performance,

---

29. Niernberg v. Feld, 131 Colo. 508, 283 P.2d 640 (1955). See Comment, 28 Rocky Mt.L.Rev. 268 (1956).

30. Malken v. Hemming Bros., 82 Conn. 293, 73 A. 752 (1909).

31. Imperator Realty Co., Inc. v. Tull, 228 N.Y. 447, 127 N.E. 263 (1920). See also Catoe v. Knox, 709 P.2d 964 (Colo.App.1985). The court noted: "The Statute of Frauds does not prevent enforcement of oral modifications to a contract for the sale of land where reinstatement of the original contract terms would be unjust in view of material change of position in reliance on the subsequent agreement."

32. See Annual Survey of New York Law, 25 N.Y.U.L.Rev. 1201 (1950).

"The quantity of litigation required to construe a seventeenth-century statute recalls Chancellor Kent's statement more than a century ago that the cost of explaining the statute has been a million dollars or more. And the decisions themselves lend support to the Lord Chancellor's Committee proposal in 1937 that the statute be repealed." Of course, it is impossible to determine how much litigation has been prevented because people know that land contracts must be in writing. In any case, the Statute of Frauds appears to be hale, hardy and ready for the next century, at least.

when the remainder of the purchase money is to be paid and the deed delivered, is called law day. Suppose law day is set for June 1, 1989, but one party cannot perform exactly on that date. What is the result of this failure to meet the contract date? The law courts took the position that time was of the essence in all contracts for the sale of land, unless the document provided otherwise by express or implied agreement.[33] This meant the non-breaching party was excused from performance, provided he was ready, willing, and able to perform and made a proper tender. Law thus treated performance by a day certain as a condition precedent to further rights under the contract. Of course, it followed that the non-breacher also had a cause of action for damages against the party unable to perform on the set day.

This rigid position led to many hardships, particularly when coupled with a forfeiture clause which might cause the purchaser to lose substantial payments which he had already made. Moreover, the breach was frequently nominal and the party who failed on law day would have had the money in hand, or the title defects cured, a few days later. Accordingly, equity took a more flexible view of the time for performance and treated the time stipulation as a promise rather than as a condition.[34] This allowed the non-breaching party nominal damages (or more if real injury resulted) but did not excuse performance. The contract remained enforceable so long as it could be carried out within a reasonable period. This tended to square with the probable intention of the parties who usually would not attach importance to a specific day. However, time can be made of the essence even in equity due to the nature of the property, surrounding circumstances, or the express stipulation of the parties.[35]

If both vendor and purchaser know that a professor wants a home to live in at the opening of school, September 15, and the contract sets that date as law day, this circumstance may be sufficient to cause time to be of the essence, even in equity. Similarly, if the real property interest being sold is a relatively short term lease that will soon expire or if it is a sale on

33. Sugden, Law of Vendors and Purchasers 352 (5th ed. 1818).

34. King v. Connors, 222 Mass. 261, 110 N.E. 289 (1915); Kasten Construction Co. v. Maple Ridge Construction Co., 245 Md. 373, 226 A.2d 341 (1967).

35. Edgerton v. Peckham, 11 Paige (N.Y.) 352 (1844). See also Kaiman Realty, Inc. v. Carmichael, 2 Hawaii App. 499, 634 P.2d 603 (1981) where the court said: "Time may be made of the essence of the contract by express stipulations, or even without an express stipulation to that effect where such intention is clearly manifested from the agreement as a whole, construed in the light of surrounding facts." In Kossler v. Palm Springs Developments, Ltd., 101 Cal.App.3d 88, 161 Cal.Rptr. 423 (1980), the court quoted Professor Pomeroy to the effect that: "The general rule in equity is that time is not of the essence unless it has been made so by . . . express terms or is necessarily so from the nature of the contract."

speculation in times of rapidly fluctuating prices, this may cause chancery to follow the rule at law. The most common situation, however, is where the contract expressly states, "time is of the essence of this agreement." When so specifically drafted that the court feels the meaning is clear to both parties the delay of even half an hour in producing the purchase money has been held to excuse performance by the vendor.[36] Although time is not made of the essence when the contract is first drafted, it can be made so by notice of either party, provided it is given a reasonable length of time before law day.[37] This sounds suspiciously like a unilateral change in the terms of a contract and the view has been criticized by legal writers.[38]

Because time of the essence clauses are frequently inserted (or left in a standard, printed form) without any real appreciation of their effect, courts naturally struggle to relieve a defaulting, but good faith, vendor or purchaser. The most common relief mechanism is waiver. Thus, repeated acceptance of late payments by a vendor, followed by a sudden decision to cut off the purchaser's rights for one specific delinquency, can lead to a successful plea of waiver by the purchaser. Even here, however, the vendor can rely on the legal effectiveness of the clause by giving proper notice. "The vendor who has, by a practice of accepting later payment, permitted the purchaser to rely on this course of conduct, need only give reasonable notice that thereafter he will insist on strict performance of the contract. Further defaults would entitle him to his foreclosure remedy." [39]

Because time is not normally of the essence in equity, a court may, in the proper circumstances, allow specific performance long after the stated law day. For example, in Hochard v. Deiter [40] the court allowed the remedy after three and one-half years. Time had not been made of the essence and the facts did not indicate that it was a material factor. The contract price was $11,200 and there was testimony that the fair market value of the property was $32,500 at the time of suit but the court held this change in value was not a sufficient reason for denying specific performance.

36. Doctorman v. Schroeder, 92 N.J. Eq. 676, 114 A. 810 (1921).

37. Schmidt v. Reed, 132 N.Y. 108, 30 N.E. 373 (1892).

38. Walsh, Equity 361–377 (1930).

Despite Professor Walsh's attack on "unilateral modification" many cases seem to allow it. See Shullo Construction Co. v. Miller, 2 Ohio App.2d 177, 207 N.E.2d 393 (1965).

39. Stinemeyer v. Wesco Farms, Inc., 260 Or. 109, 487 P.2d 65 (1971).

See also, Fisher v. Tiffin, 275 Or. 437, 551 P.2d 1061 (1976) holding that a non-waiver provision in a contract could itself be waived by the vendor's action in accepting late payments. For further discussion of the waiver doctrine see Hart v. Lyons, 106 Ill.App.3d 803, 62 Ill. Dec. 697, 436 N.E.2d 723 (1982).

40. 219 Kan. 738, 549 P.2d 970 (1976).

Apparently, an inflationary (or deflationary) economy over a course of time was not enough to make time of the essence by implication where the parties had not done so expressly.

Cases like Hochard v. Deiter illustrate why the parties should consider the importance of time stipulations at the drafting stage and cover the matter expressly one way or the other. Most printed forms do make time of the essence (frequently as a throwaway line in small type) but the parties often sign without any understanding of the legal significance of the phrase. It is for this reason that the Uniform Land Transactions Act in Section 2–302 [Time of Performance; Time of Essence] states: "The phrase 'time is of the essence' or other similar language does not of itself provide explicitly that failure to perform at the time specified discharges the duties of the other party." Unfortunately, the Act has not been widely adopted and courts continue to give considerable weight to the phrase in deciding specific cases. Lawyers should be aware of its significance and help their clients to understand this possible pitfall for the unwary.[41]

C. FINANCING ARRANGEMENTS—MORTGAGES AND INSTALLMENT LAND CONTRACTS

Real estate financing involves a host of practical and legal problems and only the general "running gears" can be discussed in a basic text.[42] Since few people pay cash for real property, the financing arrangements tend to be the heart of the matter. Frequently, the purchaser signs a contract without being certain as to how he will pay for the property. In order to protect himself, he typically wishes to insert a clause making the contract contingent on his obtaining the proper financing. Unless this clause is carefully drafted, the result may be an ambiguous agreement which will cause litigation. In Gerruth Realty Co. v. Pire[43] the real estate broker inserted the following clause in the offer: "This offer to purchase is further contingent upon the purchaser obtaining the proper amount of financing." The purchaser was in such financial condition that he could not get a conventional

---

41. While in Hochard v. Deiter it was the vendor who would have been protected by such a phrase, it is frequently the purchaser who suffers by its presence, especially if he runs into financing difficulties and cannot come up with the purchase money on a day certain.

42. All law schools offer separate courses in Mortgages or Real Estate Financing which analyze these problems in depth.

43. 17 Wis.2d 89, 115 N.W.2d 557 (1962).

mortgage in the amount needed and he sought to escape from the contract and to cancel a $5000 promissory note he had given as a down payment. The Wisconsin Supreme Court felt the ambiguous clause came dangerously close to making the agreement an illusory or aleatory contract. While this difficulty might be cured by reading in a requirement that the purchaser make reasonable efforts to secure proper financing, the court felt the contract should fail for indefiniteness. The court apparently believed the real estate agent was more eager to earn a commission than to serve his client properly. "The real estate broker, presumably familiar with the difficulties, details and terms of financing, might have asked the defendant for more details, but was apparently content with putting something in writing and having it signed by the purchasers."

In Anaheim Co. v. Holcombe,[44] the parties were somewhat more specific: "This offer is contingent on obtaining a loan of $25,000." The Oregon Supreme Court held that there was an implied condition that the purchaser use reasonable diligence in procuring a loan. The question of reasonable diligence was for the trial court to decide and the purchaser failed to sustain the burden and could not recover his $5,000 earnest money payment.

These cases illustrate the perils involved for both vendor and purchaser, but the necessity for some such clause remains since the purchaser may locate the property he wishes to buy before he can fully investigate available financing. In these situations, the clause should specify the exact amount of money needed, the kind of financing sought, including the acceptable terms for repayment, interest rates, etc.[45]

Some of the worst financing problems stem from the use of forfeiture clauses, usually coupled with a time of the essence provision. Here, we must digress briefly to clarify the elementary aspects of real estate financing. Seldom does the buyer find himself in that happy state of liquidity which would allow him to pay cash for the property, so he will finance through a purchase money mortgage, a mortgage (or trust deed) to a third party (bank, insurance company, or savings and loan association), or an installment land contract. Using the first method, he pays the vendor what he can afford, receives a deed to the land, and gives a mortgage (in lieu of the rest of the purchase money) back to the seller. By the second method, he pays the vendor what he can afford, takes a deed to the land, mortgages the property to a third

44. 246 Or. 541, 426 P.2d 743 (1967). See also Osten v. Shah, 104 Ill.App.3d 784, 60 Ill.Dec. 497, 433 N.E.2d 294 (1982) and Billman v. Hensel, 181 Ind. App. 272, 391 N.E.2d 671 (1979).

45. For a discussion of the various issues see Raushenbush, Problems and Practices with Financing Conditions in Real Estate Purchase Contracts, 1963 Wis.L.Rev. 566.

party and pays the proceeds of the mortgage loan to the seller who bows out of the transaction. In the third method, he pays the vendor what he can afford, the vendor keeps title to the land, the purchaser goes into possession and pays installments to the vendor over so long a period as necessary to complete the purchase price. When the purchaser makes the last payment he receives a deed. In all three situations, the buyer is, in effect, borrowing money and must repay it in installments plus interest, but in the first two methods he receives legal title to the land subject to a mortgage, in the latter he does not receive legal title until all payments are made.

The fundamental difference occurs on default. If the buyer fails to pay in the first two cases the mortgage must be foreclosed, accompanied by all of the safeguards that the legislatures and courts have established to protect the mortgagor. Usually, this means judicial foreclosure with an equity of redemption in the buyer-mortgagor. In theory, although sometimes not in practice, it means the property will be sold to the highest bidder, the mortgage loan plus interest, costs, etc., paid to the mortgagee, and the surplus returned to the mortgagor. By contrast, the contract-buyer may find that he forfeits all of his payments to date, if he fails to perform, and is left without his money, land, or even an equity of redemption.[46]

Since the purchaser has less legal protection in an installment land contract, why would he choose this method of financing? He does not choose it, exactly; he is forced into it by lack of capital.[47] When we indicated that the buyer paid down what he could afford and gave a mortgage for the rest, the oversimplification should have been apparent. If he can afford too little—the amount varies but typically one-third to one-fourth of the purchase price is required—mortgage money is not available and his only recourse is to buy "on contract." Naturally, the vendor wants maximum protection for his investment in the property since the buyer has

46. Pease v. Baxter, 12 Wash. 567, 41 P. 899 (1895).

For a good, brief discussion of the difference between mortgages, with their equity of redemption, and installment land contracts see Kratovil, Real Estate Law 203–212, 220 (5th ed. 1969).

47. Not surprisingly, the burden falls more heavily on minority groups and others in the lower income brackets than on the public generally. This was recognized in Rosewood Corp. v. Fisher, 46 Ill.2d 249, 263 N.E.2d 833 (1970) where the contract buyers league (a group of Chicago blacks) sought relief from the harsh terms of installment land contracts. The Illinois Supreme Court allowed the purchasers to raise equitable defenses to a vendor's suit in Forcible Entry and Detainer (summary action for possession for non-payment of installments due), a defense not previously available in Illinois. For the intriguing story of the contract buyers league see McPherson, "In My Father's House There Are Many Mansions—And I'm Going to Get Me Some of Them Too," 229 Atlantic Monthly 51–82 (April, 1972).

put up very little; the forfeiture on default results. This device is not always as harsh as it sounds since the purchaser has possession, the payments may be roughly the equivalent of rent, and the amount forfeited may therefore square rather well with the actual damages on breach.[48] On the other hand, the contrast with mortgage financing is striking and on occasion the inequity can be substantial. In these hardship cases, courts of equity, which "abhor a forfeiture", struggle to find some way to allow the defaulting vendee to continue the contract. Dean Pound has suggested that, "Strict doctrines as to forfeiture inevitably produce loose doctrines as to waiver", and the cases bear out the truth of the aphorism. The vendor may lose his right to rely on forfeiture by prior acceptance of late payments or other acts and one court has gone so far as to distinguish between notice of intent to declare a forfeiture and *declaration* of a forfeiture. Since the contract called for the former and the vendor relied on the latter, the purchaser had not lost his rights.[49]

Modern courts have freely stated their "abhorrence of odious forfeitures" and have given relief to defaulting purchasers under a wide variety of circumstances. Thus, in State v. Superior Court for King County,[50] a purchaser who had been in default for a year was allowed to complete the contract, which contained both time of the essence and forfeiture clauses, upon payment of the full balance plus interest and all expenses incurred by the vendor. In Land Development, Inc. v. Padgett,[51] the court allowed similar relief by ordering forfeiture only if the purchasers failed to pay the accrued interest within one week and the principal balance within three months. This last approach is very much like strict foreclosure of a mortgage and, indeed, that technique now seems fairly common. See Nelson v. Robinson,[52] where the court treated a $48,000 contract, based on a crop payment plan, as an equitable mortgage, setting a six to eighteen month redemption period and Henry Uihlein Realty Co. v. Downtown Develop. Corp.,[53] where strict foreclosure was ordered but the purchaser's demand for restitution to prevent unjust enrichment was denied. This last point remains a tough problem. Assuming the purchaser can pay at a later date the courts can act to prevent unfairness but if he is hopelessly insolvent does he have to lose all his payments and improvements or can he seek salvation through further recourse to mortgage doctrine? It should be clear, in any case, that the

48. Bishop v. Beecher, 67 N.M. 339, 355 P.2d 277 (1960).

49. Zeta Bldg. Corporation v. Garst, 408 Ill. 519, 97 N.E.2d 331 (1951).

50. 57 Wash.2d 571, 358 P.2d 550 (1961).

51. 369 P.2d 888 (Alaska 1962).

52. 184 Kan. 340, 336 P.2d 415 (1959).

53. 9 Wis.2d 620, 101 N.W.2d 775 (1960).

courts will not always allow redemption and will usually enforce the contract as written if it involves no real hardship for the purchaser.[54]

The purchaser who relies on the conscience of a court of equity puts his faith in a variable standard, however, and in many situations the buyer cannot continue the contract, even if allowed to do so, because he is insolvent. In these cases he wants restitution for the money he has paid in excess of actual damage, i.e., he would like the favored position of a mortgagor on default. His chances of such treatment are slight unless there has been some statutory or judicial change which entitles him to equitable relief.[55] It should be noted that the vendor has problems too. If the installment land contract is recorded, this puts a cloud on the merchantability of title and even when the buyer defaults it may be difficult to clear that title. It is always possible that equity may aid the purchaser and subsequent buyers, having notice of the prior contract, may be unwilling to take that chance.

As the preceding paragraphs indicate, there is a trend toward greater protection for the purchaser in installment land contracts if it appears that the buyer will suffer a substantial loss. This trend is based on the realization that the installment land contract is merely another form of real estate financing and, if it is being used as a security device, the purchaser should have many of the same remedies granted to the mortgagor, of which the contract purchaser is an analogue. Skendzel v. Marshall [56] is a good example of this trend. In that case, the Indiana Supreme Court used the mortgage analogy to grant relief to a purchaser and noted that: "In fact, the Commissioners on Uniform State Laws have recognized the transparency of any such distinctions. Section 3–102 of the Uniform Land Transactions Code (working draft of first tentative draft) reads as follows: 'This Article applies to security interests created

---

54. Dorman v. Fisher, 52 N.J.Super. 70, 144 A.2d 805 (1958).

55. Union Bond and Trust Co. v. Blue Creek Redwood Co., 128 F.Supp. 709 (D.C.Cal.1955) illustrates how the California statute rescues the buyer. See also Petersen v. Hartell, 40 Cal.3d 102, 219 Cal.Rptr. 170, 707 P.2d 232 (1985).

An interesting Florida statute, which provides in effect that a contract may be deemed a mortgage where the purpose or intent is to secure the payment of money, was involved in Mid–State Investment Corp. v. O'Steen, 133 So.2d 455, 457 (Fla.1961). Said the court: "In our opinion the contract before us was clearly intended to secure the payment

of money and must be deemed and held to be mortgage, subject to the same rules of foreclosure and to the same regulations, restraints and forms as are prescribed in relation to mortgages, to use the words of the statute."

The general problem is thoroughly discussed in Corbin, Right of a Defaulting Vendee to the Restitution of Installments Paid, 40 Yale L.J. 1013 (1931) and some of the legislation is analyzed in a Note, 52 Harv.L.Rev. 129 (1938).

See also Kratovil, Forfeiture of Installment Contracts in Illinois, 53 Ill. Bar J. 188 (1964).

56. 261 Ind. 226, 301 N.E.2d 641 (1973).

by contract, including mortgage . . . land sales contract . . . and any other lien or title retention contract intended as security. *We believe this position is entirely consistent with evolving case law in the area."* [Emphasis added.] [57]

In a concurring opinion, Justice Prentice expressed concern that the decision might be viewed by some as indicating an attitude of indifference towards the rights of contract vendors and stated: "Because the installment sales contract with forfeiture provisions, is a widely employed and generally accepted method of commerce in real estate in this state, it is appropriate that a vendee seeking to avoid the forfeiture, to which he agreed, be required to make a clear showing of the inequity of enforcement." [58]

Some of the difficulties with the installment land contract stem from a failure to distinguish the purposes for which the contract is employed. To paraphrase Gertrude Stein, the courts tend to say "a contract is a contract is a contract. . . ." Professor Hetland [59] makes this point clear: "A 'land contract' often is a security device in lieu of a mortgage or deed of trust. To the extent this is the meaning of 'land contract', security remedies may be appropriate; perhaps the judicial sale, redemption period and deficiency judgment prohibition should replace the traditional action for specific performance or for damages. But a 'land contract' also is an earnest money contract, or a deposit receipt, or occasionally mutual escrow instructions; in other words, it is often the basic buy-sell agreement rather than a security device. And if this is what 'land contract' means, the security debtor's protections should not interfere with the vendor's action for damages, his retention of liquidated damages, or his action for specific performance." [60]

D. MERCHANTABLE TITLE

What does a purchaser expect to get for his money when he signs a contract of sale? Obviously, he wants physical possession

57. Id. at 237 and 648.

58. Id. at 243 and 651. See also Ebersold v. Wise, 412 N.E.2d 802 (Ind. App.1980) where the court said: "Under the doctrine of Skendzel v. Marshall . . . forfeiture is inappropriate when the vendee has acquired a substantial interest in the property and a forfeiture would result in substantial injustice.

In certain cases, forfeiture is still permitted." [Emphasis added.]

59. Hetland, The California Land Contract, 48 Calif.L.Rev. 729 (1960).

60. See also Note, Forfeiture and the Iowa Installment Land Contract, 46 Iowa L.Rev. 786 (1961).

of Blackacre, but this will do him little good if the vendor's interest turns out to be a life estate or a fee simple determinable. At a minimum, a non-defeasible fee simple is required. Even this may not be enough, since the fee could be subject to various liens, charges, covenants running with the land, etc. The courts have developed the concept of a merchantable title to cover the situation. The words roll off the tongue but their meaning is hazy. The judicial definitions add little. "A merchantable title is a title not subject to such reasonable doubt as would create a just apprehension of its validity in the mind of a reasonable, prudent and intelligent person; one that persons of reasonable prudence and intelligence, guided by competent legal advice, would be willing to take and pay the fair value of the land for." [61] In the last analysis, a merchantable title is one that a court of equity will force an unwilling purchaser to accept in a suit for specific performance. This still begs the question but it makes it perfectly clear that the standard is laid down by the chancellor. Any number of defects, e.g., a break in a chain of record title, an outstanding mortgage, dower, taxes, special assessment, etc., may destroy merchantability and it is clear that equity will not force a man to buy a lawsuit. The full impact of merchantability will be clarified in Part Five when we discuss the recording system and the various methods of title assurance.

The contracting parties can handle the title question in any way they see fit. They may contract for something less than a merchantable title, e.g., a defensible title (one that could be defended against a suit in ejectment) or such interest as the vendor may have; or they may require something more, such as title satisfactory to a third party or even to the purchaser himself; or they may demand something that is simply different, to wit, an insurable title. Suppose the contract is silent on the point and calls only for a conveyance of the premises or of the property? Then the courts will imply that a merchantable title is called for: "Although the writing does not say so, the law says so, and the law is part of the writing." [62] This implication will be made even though the contract calls for conveyance by a quitclaim rather than a warranty deed.[63]

Merchantability does not require a perfect title, indeed it is doubtful if many perfect titles exist, but it is not necessary to prove that a title is wholly "bad" in order to destroy its

61. Eggers v. Busch, 154 Ill. 604, 607, 39 N.E. 619, 620 (1895).

62. Wallach v. Riverside Bank, 206 N.Y. 434, 437, 100 N.E. 50, 51 (1912).

63. Id. See also Tymon v. Linoki, 16 N.Y.2d 293, 266 N.Y.S.2d 357, 213 N.E.2d 661 (1965) where the court distinguishes between the *title* to be conveyed and the *kind of deed* to be used for the conveyance.

merchantability. It is sufficient if there is enough doubt or uncertainty to form a reasonable basis for litigation.[64] The purchaser cannot wait until law day and then suddenly reject the title as unmerchantable and slip out of the bargain. He must examine the title and notify the vendor of the defects within a reasonable time so that they can be removed by the time set for performance. Failure to do this will simply extend the law day, even when time is of the essence, so that the defects can be cured, unless, of course, such defects are irreparable.[65]

In the typical real estate contract the parties expect the title to be merchantable by law day. How does this principle apply to installment land contracts? Here too, in the absence of a special provision, the vendor satisfies his part of the bargain if the title is merchantable on the date set for delivery of the deed. This means that the purchaser may have to make payments over many years with no real assurance that he will eventually get a merchantable title to the land.[66] If it appears that the vendor is insolvent, so that he could not respond in money damages if the title fails, or if the title is subject to an incurable defect, equity may grant relief to the purchaser by allowing him to rescind before law day or by requiring the vendor to clear his title at an earlier date.[67] The purchaser should not rely on this "chancy" proposition, however, but should insert a provision in installment land contracts that the vendor must produce a merchantable title by a set date in the reasonably near future or the purchaser is entitled to his money back and is excused from further performance.

Traditionally, titles based on the annual tax sale deed, where the original owner was in default for non-payment of taxes, have not been viewed as merchantable by the courts. This was because the tax deeds were usually issued by administrative officials, such as a county clerk, and any defects in the proceedings were viewed as jurisdictional, thus opening the title to collateral attack at any time by the original owner. In recent years, many states have made the issuance of tax deeds a judicial matter with the result that they are usually subject only to direct attack and, after the time for appeal has gone by, such deeds may be the basis of a merchantable title.[68]

64. Bartos v. Czerwinski, 323 Mich. 87, 34 N.W.2d 566 (1948).

65. Easton v. Montgomery, 90 Cal. 307, 27 P. 280 (1891).

66. Luette v. Bank of Italy Nat. Trust & Savings Ass'n, 42 F.2d 9 (1930). See also Horn v. Wright, 157 Ga.App. 408, 278 S.E.2d 66 (1981) and Tolbird v. Howard, 101 Ill.App.2d 236, 242 N.E.2d 468 (1968).

67. Marlowe Investment Corp. v. Radmall, 26 Utah 2d 124, 485 P.2d 1402 (1971); Leavitt v. Blohm, 11 Utah 2d 220, 357 P.2d 190 (1960).

68. Cherin v. R. & C. Co., 11 Ill.2d 447, 143 N.E.2d 235 (1957). See also Young, The Tax Deed—Modern Movement Towards Respectability, 34 Rocky Mt.L.Rev. 181 (1962). The courts continue to have problems with the merchantability of tax titles, however,

A merchantable title must be a paper title, i.e., one that is disclosed from the records based on the connected chain of deeds, mortgages, probate proceedings, etc. While a title based on the statute of limitations may be good in fact, it is too uncertain to be called merchantable.[69] The only way to make a title gained by adverse possession merchantable is by a suit in equity to quiet title. This is also the way to cure other serious defects in title, if in fact they can be proved to be invalid clouds on the owner's claim to the land.[70]

E. TENDER [71]

Tender calls for brief mention because of its relationship to time stipulations and merchantability of title. Even if time is made of the essence, performance may be extended beyond law day simply because neither party puts the other in default by tendering his own performance. For the purchaser, this means proving that he is ready, willing, and able to perform by offering to pay the rest of the purchase money or to deliver a properly executed purchase money mortgage; for the vendor, it means offering to deliver a properly executed deed, sufficient to convey a merchantable title. The tender need not be absolute since the other party could then accept it with a brief, "thanks", but still remain in default. Conditional tender—offer to perform if the other party will do so—is sufficient since the principal purpose of this requirement is to fulfill the condition precedent to the right to sue for breach.[72]

Under proper circumstances, tender may be excused if it is clear that the other party would not perform in any case. The law does not require a person to do a useless act and if the

as see Potomac Building Corp. v. Karkenny, 364 A.2d 809 (D.C.App.1976) where one of two required notices of a tax sale was not published due to a newspaper error. The trial court held there had been substantial compliance with the statute and that was sufficient. The appellate court reversed, holding that substantial compliance was not enough for a valid sale.

It has long been recognized, however, that even an invalid tax deed may constitute color of title and that if the purchaser takes possession and pays taxes for the requisite period he will obtain title under a short term statute of limitations. See Quality Plastics, Inc. v. Moore, 131 Ariz. 238, 640 P.2d 169 (1981).

69. Escher v. Bender, 338 Mich. 1, 61 N.W.2d 143 (1953).

70. Note, Enhancing the Marketability of Land: The Suit to Quiet Title, 68 Yale L.J. 1245 (1959).

71. For the modern view of tender see Uniform Land Transactions Act, Section 2–301 (1978).

72. Pelletier v. Dwyer, 334 A.2d 867 (Me.1975).

purchaser has already repudiated the contract (anticipatory breach) the vendor need not tender, or vice versa.[73]

While it is clear that tender is a prerequisite to suit on the contract, i.e., a suit for specific performance in equity or for money damages at law, less clarity surrounds a suit for rescission of the contract and a return of the purchase money plus interest. If tender is required before there is a breach, then it is necessary in both cases but if it is only a condition precedent to suit for the benefits under the contract then it is superfluous in rescission. In Christopher v. West,[74] an Illinois appellate court took the former position but it was reversed on appeal, the Supreme Court saying, "The only question for us here to decide is whether the law imposed upon Christopher, as a necessary condition precedent to the maintenance of this suit to recover back the earnest money paid, the duty of tendering performance to West in order to acquire the right of restitution. The party who insists upon performance by the other party must show performance on his part, while he who desires to rescind the contract need only show nonperformance or inability to perform by the other. Inability to perform is sufficient excuse on the part of the purchaser for not tendering performance, for, in this event, a tender would be devoid of meaning. . . . If any claimed defect was such as to affect the merchantability of the title and one which was not cured or curable within a reasonable time as provided in the contract, no tender of the full purchase price was necessary." [75]

At the moment of breach, the future plaintiff does not know what remedy he will ultimately seek and the voice of caution should counsel him to make his tender whether it is strictly necessary or not. The place of tender can also be confusing since some cases put it at the vendor's place of business, others at the purchaser's. This matter should be covered in the contract by stating precisely where the settlement is to occur.

F. ASSIGNMENT

The mystic rites of assignment are better left to texts on contract law, but some reference is required here to complete the picture of the real estate sale. Many contracts for the sale of land

73. Cohen v. Kranz, 12 N.Y.2d 242, 238 N.Y.S.2d 928, 189 N.E.2d 473 (1963).

74. 340 Ill.App. 225, 91 N.E.2d 613 (1950).

75. Christopher v. West, 409 Ill. 131, 136, 98 N.E.2d 722, 725 (1951).

end with this boilerplate: "It is mutually agreed by and between the parties hereunto, that the covenants and agreements herein contained shall extend to and be obligatory upon the heirs, executors, administrators, and assigns of the respective parties." This language adds little to the contract since it simply makes explicit what is implicit anyway. It may focus the attention of the parties on the free assignability of the contract and, in effect, warn them to place some prohibition on assignment if they desire to deal only with the original parties.

The vendor can assign his contract rights by selling the fee, subject to the contract, and the purchaser can transfer his interest by the usual assignment process. Of course, neither one can rid himself of obligations incurred in the contract, unless released by the other party, and the assignor will remain secondarily liable, as in contracts generally. A prohibition on assignment may not be very effective, even if coupled with a forfeiture, since equity still abhors a forfeiture and may find that no harm has occurred to the vendor when all that remains to be done is to pay the purchase money and receive the deed.[76] The law has traditionally favored the free alienability of land and since the purchaser has equitable title after signing the contract, as we shall see in the next section, the courts dislike clauses which hamper his power to transfer that title, unless there is some clear-cut reason for it.

G. REMEDIES

If a lawyer handles the real estate transaction there is less likelihood of litigation than in the do-it-yourself approach, since the attorney will foresee the danger spots and cover them in the contract.[77] However, even the most carefully drafted document

---

76. Handzel v. Bassi, 343 Ill.App. 281, 99 N.E.2d 23 (1951).

The judicial attitude toward prohibition on assignment of a real estate contract should be contrasted with the approach to identical clauses in landlord-tenant law. See pp. 271–276, infra. The difference lies in the continuing relationship between the parties in the lease situation and the early termination of such relationship in the sale.

Some courts do enforce non-assignment clauses in contracts as rigidly as they enforce such clauses in leases. See Rother–Gallagher v. Montana Power Co., 164 Mont. 360, 522 P.2d 1226 (1974)

but this is rare. More frequently the courts take a lenient attitude even in the presence of a clause against assignment as see Cheney v. Jemmett, 107 Idaho 829, 693 P.2d 1031 (1984) where the court held that a prohibition on assignment must be reasonable and Paperchase Partnership v. Bruckner, 102 N.M. 221, 693 P.2d 587 (1985) where the court held a subcontract was not an assignment and hence did not breach a non-assignability clause.

77. For an illustration of the lawyer's role in draftsmanship note the next section and the relationship of insurance to risk of loss.

cannot avoid occasional controversy and the client's remedy may have to be a judicial one. The property lawyer has a choice from a varied arsenal of weapons when he finds it necessary to engage in combat by trial. His basic choice will lie between an equity action for specific performance or a suit at law for money damages but other options may be possible, depending on the nature of the dispute.

If the purchaser refuses to perform because the title is unmerchantable due to minor but colorable defects, the vendor may be forced to bring a suit to remove cloud on title so that he can make a proper tender to the buyer.[78] If the purchaser is in breach but refuses to vacate the land, actions for the recovery of possession, either ejectment or forcible entry and detainer, may be in order. At times, the best remedy is to seek rescission of the contract and a restoration of the status quo. In this latter situation, the enforcement of a vendor's or a vendee's lien may be required in order to give priority over assignees with notice of the contract.[79]

Land has long been considered unique, "for the peculiar locality, soil, vicinage, advantage or markets and the like conveniences of an estate contracted for, cannot be replaced by other land of equal value." [80] It follows that the remedy at law is inadequate since it can give only money damages at best and the purchaser is entitled to specific performance in equity in nearly all cases. He need not prove the uniqueness of the *res* in each case, as he would have to do with personal property, but need only establish a valid contract that is certain enough to support the decree. Since the purchaser is entitled to equitable relief, the vendor has the same right in order to give mutuality of remedy and also because "he may not wish the lands, even with the damages, but may prefer to have them off his hands, and he has a right to require that the vendee shall take them and pay the stipulated price." [81]

Some doubt has been cast on the automatic availability of specific performance at the behest of the vendor, at least in condominium cases. In Centex Homes Corp. v. Boag[82] a New Jersey court refused to allow the developer-vendor of a large condominium (3600 units) to force the title to a single unit on an unwilling purchaser who had been transferred to a distant city. The court felt that for purposes of specific performance the sale

78. Holland v. Challen, 110 U.S. 15, 3 S.Ct. 495, 28 L.Ed. 52 (1884).

79. For a detailed coverage of remedies for breach of contract see Cunningham, Stoebuck and Whitman, The Law of Property 640–669 (1984).

80. Losee v. Morey and Cramer, 57 Barb. (N.Y.) 561, 565 (1865).

81. Id. at 566.

82. 128 N.J.Super. 385, 320 A.2d 194 (1974).

was more like personal property and that a single unit could not be viewed as any more unique than mass produced chattels. For most purposes a condominium is treated as real property but not when the vendor wishes specific performance of the contract. The court said: "[M]utuality of remedy is not an appropriate basis for granting or denying specific performance. . . . The test is whether the obligations of the contract are mutual and not whether each is entitled to precisely the same remedy in the event of breach." Eliminating the mutuality of remedy argument, the vendor did not need equitable relief since the remedy at law was adequate in this case.[83]

While it would be unwise to read too much into the Centex case because of its peculiar facts, there does appear to be a trend against automatically giving the vendor specific performance of real estate contracts. Thus, the Uniform Land Transactions Act, sect. 2–506(b), gives the vendor the right to the purchase price "only if the seller is unable after a reasonable effort to resell it at a reasonable price or the circumstances reasonably indicate the effort will be unavailing." It remains to be seen how influential this uniform act will be in the face of equitable doctrine that is centuries old.

The draftsman must be careful not to barter away this most valuable of remedies by too much zeal for liquidated damages. For example, in Davis v. Isenstein [84] the contract read, in part: "The willful neglect or failure by either of the parties hereto to perform his or their respective parts of the undertakings hereunder is to subject such party to the payment of the sum of $1500 fixed and liquidated damages to the party injured, and upon such payment thereof this contract is to become null and void." The court held that this created an option to perform or pay the stipulated damages. Since the buyer was prepared to do the latter, the suit was dismissed for want of equity.[85] There is serious doubt about the correctness of this view since the primary objective of contracts is performance rather than non-performance, and the liquidated damages provision should be interpreted as cumulative, or as added security, rather than as creating an option.[86] However, this is clearly a pitfall to be avoided by the alert lawyer.

---

83. On the other hand, in Giannini v. First National Bank of Des Plaines, 136 Ill.App.3d 971, 91 Ill.Dec. 438, 483 N.E.2d 924 (1 Dist.1985), the court granted specific performance to a purchaser for a condominium unit *not yet built* despite the fact that exactly the same units were available in other buildings.

84. 257 Ill. 260, 261, 100 N.E. 940, 941 (1913).

85. See also Duckwall v. Rees, 119 Ind.App. 474, 86 N.E.2d 460 (1949).

86. Nolan v. Kirchner, 98 N.J.Eq. 452, 131 A. 104 (1925).

Sometimes, the vendor is in a position where he can perform in major part but not fully. He may be quite willing to convey the land but an outstanding dower interest, an easement across one corner, a deficiency in quantity, etc., may place him in breach. In these situations the purchaser, still desiring the property but not wanting to pay the full price, may seek specific performance with compensation for the deficiency.[87] This can create very difficult questions of fact in trying to arrive at the amount of compensation, and in some cases the remedy is denied for that very reason.[88] The situation differs considerably if the vendor seeks specific performance with compensation against the purchaser and the courts will rarely grant such relief since to do so would force the purchaser to accept something he did not bargain for on the theory that it is just as good as what he expected to receive.[89]

Specific performance is not always available, as where the vendor has sold the land to a third party bona fide purchaser for value without notice, and sometimes the parties prefer money damages to equitable relief. In these cases, the usual action at law for breach of contract will be chosen. The principal difficulty here relates to the amount of damages. The rule in personal property cases is straightforward and easy to state. It is aimed at giving the non-breaching party the benefit of his bargain. This is determined by the difference between the contract price of the property and the market price at the time and place when the contract should have been performed. Thus, if the contract price was $50,000 and the market rises to $60,000, the buyer has suffered a $10,000 loss if the seller refuses to perform. If the market falls, the buyer suffers only nominal damages. Conversely, if the market falls to $40,000 and the purchaser refuses to buy, the seller has suffered a $10,000 loss. About half of the American states use this same rule for real property.[90]

As early as 1776, the English courts, in Flureau v. Thornhill,[91] recognized that the personal property cases were not necessarily analogous to the real property ones. Once again, title was the crux. A chattel owner nearly always knows the state of his title and, if he is unable to perform, the breach is usually wilful. The real property owner may have only the vaguest idea of whether

87. For a brief treatment see de Funiak, Handbook of Modern Equity 195–198 (2d ed. 1956). See also Rosenthal v. Sandusky, 35 Colo.App. 220, 533 P.2d 523 (1975) and Note, Specific Performance With Abatement, 24 Okla.L. Rev. 495 (1971).

88. Horack, Specific Performance and Dower Rights, 11 Iowa L.Rev. 97 (1926).

89. Van Blarcom v. Hopkins, 63 N.J. Eq. 466, 52 A. 147 (1902).

90. Smith v. Warr, 564 P.2d 771 (Utah 1977) and Doherty v. Dolan, 65 Me. 87, 20 Am.Rep. 677 (1876). See also McCormick, Damages 680–700 (1935).

91. 2 W.Bl. 1078, 96 Eng.Rep. 635 (1776).

his title is merchantable and his failure to convey a satisfactory title may spring from no real fault of his own. To tax him with huge damages for a non-wilful default may be unfair. This is particularly true in times of widely oscillating land values or where the discovery of minerals, unknown at the time of the contract, may cause the damages to skyrocket. The "English" rule, therefore, limited the purchaser, except where the vendor had acted in bad faith, to the money paid down by the purchaser, plus interest and expenses connected with examination of the title.[92] You will note that this is the amount generally recoverable on rescission of the contract. The "English" rule made good sense to many American courts and it has been adopted in about half the states.[93] The biggest difficulty with the "English" rule is the determination of bad faith on the part of the vendor. The English cases have expanded the original idea by holding that if the seller fails to "do his best" to remove a title defect he becomes liable for the value of the bargain. This is fair enough, but it introduces an additional uncertainty. What is meant by "do his best"? This is another example of the age-old conflict between certainty and flexibility in the law.

As the previous paragraph discloses, the "English" rule restricts the purchaser to rescission of the contract if the vendor has been guilty of a "good faith" breach. Regardless of the nature of the breach, the purchaser may prefer to rescind the contract, following breach by the vendor, rather than seek specific performance or money damages, i.e., he may no longer wish to buy the property and wants out of what he now views as a bad bargain. The remedy of rescission will not always be available, however. For example, in Northwest Kansas Area Vocational-Technical School v. Wolf,[94] a purchaser contracted to buy a solar-heated house built as part of a school curriculum. A malfunctioning valve caused 750 to 900 gallons of water to escape, damaging the ceiling, floors and walls of the house. Most of the damage was covered by insurance but the vendor refused to correct a design defect which cost $500 out of a $93,000 purchase price. The court denied rescission, saying: "It is not every breach which gives rise to the right to rescind a contract. In order to warrant rescission of a contract the breach must be material and the failure to perform so substantial as to defeat the object of the parties in making the agreement." The court granted specific performance

92. Bain v. Fothergill, L.R. 7 H.L. (E. and I. App.) 158 (1874).

93. For a good statement of the reasons behind the "English" rule see Crenshaw v. Williams, 191 Ky. 559, 567,

231 S.W. 45, 49, 48 A.L.R. 5 (1921). See also, Kramer v. Mobley, 309 Ky. 143, 216 S.W.2d 930 (1949).

94. 6 Kan.App.2d 817, 635 P.2d 1268 (1981).

of the contract but allowed the purchaser $500 for the cost of the design defect.

One common, and troublesome, damages question relates to the nature of the down payment (earnest money). In event of breach, the purchaser will naturally wish its return but he may well fail if it is viewed as liquidated damages and he is in default. Moreover, the liquidated damage clause may be for a larger amount than the down payment and still be sustained. See, for example, Chaffin v. Ramsey,[95] where the court allowed a ten percent ($13,000) liquidated damage clause ($1,000 was paid down) as against a claim that it was a penalty. Said the court: "The trial court's finding has the effect of categorizing the agreement to pay ten percent of the sale price in case of breach as a provision for 'a penalty' rather than as a provision for 'liquidated damages.' In order for such a clause to be construed as one for liquidated damages, the sum provided, at the time of the making of the contract, must seem to bear a reasonable relationship to anticipated damages and the actual damages must be difficult or impossible to ascertain." The court held that the provision in question met both tests and reversed the trial court. There was a vigorous dissent.

In some instances, the purchaser may desire to have the down payment treated as liquidated damages so that he will have no further liability for compensatory damages. But in Frank v. Jansen[96] the court refused to treat a $2,000 down payment as liquidated damages and held the purchaser liable for a larger amount. In the syllabus by the court it was noted: "Whether a provision in a contract for the sale of real property calling for the forfeiture of the buyer's earnest money in the event of breach constitutes a liquidated damage clause and limits the buyer's liability to the amount of the earnest money must be gleaned from the language of the contract and the evidence as to the intention of the parties, and where the evidence did not support a finding that the parties intended the stipulated amount to be in lieu of compensatory damages, the trial court's finding of a liquidated damages agreement could not stand."

In Gryb v. Benson,[97] the court held the vendors were entitled to recover their actual damages even though the contract contained an optional liquidated damages provision allowing the vendors to retain the earnest money in event of breach by the purchasers. The vendors chose not to exercise that option. The

95. 276 Or. 429, 555 P.2d 459 (1976). See also Gomez v. Pagaduan, 1 Hawaii App. 70, 613 P.2d 658 (1980).

96. 303 Minn. 86, 226 N.W.2d 739 (1975).

97. 84 Ill.App.3d 710, 40 Ill.Dec. 423, 406 N.E.2d 124 (1980).

vendors were entitled to recover the difference between the contract price and the resale price but other losses, which arose from their attempts to finance the purchase of a second house upon learning that the expected proceeds from sale of the first house would not be forthcoming, were remote rather than proximate and reasonably foreseeable, and thus were not recoverable.

Of course, the parties can make their intent clear in the original contract by stipulating that forfeiture of the earnest money either is or is not in lieu of other remedies (specific performance and suit for compensatory damages). If this is not done, the actual intent may be difficult to determine.

Even a careful stipulation in the contract of the remedies available in event of breach will not necessarily avoid litigation. Thus in S.E.S. Importers, Inc. v. Pappalardo,[98] the purchaser's remedies were clearly stated in the event that the vendor, for any reason, not his fault, could not convey title in accordance with the terms of the contract. Specific performance was not included, nonetheless the Court of Appeals granted specific performance in a situation where the title was defective, due to outstanding leases, at the time for performance but where the defect was resolved by the time the litigation began. The majority of the court believed that the contract provision related only to procedural remedies and not to substantive rights. "Thus, nothing therein operated to deprive this buyer of its right to go to court for a judicial resolution of the critical substantive issue—whether the seller could give good title—and in that action to seek specific performance by way of remedy should the court conclude that the seller could do so." There was a vigorous dissent on the theory that the court was re-writing the contract for the parties. Noted the dissent: "It is elementary that equity enforces contracts; it neither reviews nor rewrites them."

SECTION 2.   THE CONTRACT AND EQUITABLE CONVERSION [99]

Nowhere does the peculiar nature of the real estate contract appear in such bold relief as in the doctrine of equitable conver-

---

98. 53 N.Y.2d 455, 442 N.Y.S.2d 453, 425 N.E.2d 841 (1981).

99. The insurance material in this section is based on a speech by Professor Cribbet to the Real Property, Probate and Trust Law Section of the American Bar Association, delivered at an annual meeting of the American Bar Association. The full text of the speech appears in Proceedings, Real Property Probate and Trust Law Section, A.B.A. 3–12 (1961). The material has been updated and numerous non-insurance as-

sion.[1] In one sense, the relationship between vendor and purchaser is wholly *personal,* with the right of either to sue the other in event of breach. In another sense, the contract creates a status of vendor-purchaser and the latter acquires *real* rights in the property due to the possibility of specific performance. Equity, by treating as done those things which should be done, looks upon the purchaser as having equitable title to the land even though the legal title remains in the vendor. The concept of equitable conversion cannot be carried to its logical extreme in all cases and it presents inconsistencies, as do most legal concepts, but it has had a profound influence on the development of the law.[2] Note, however, that although the purchaser is said to have equitable title, after an enforceable contract has been made, he does not have the right of possession, unless the contract expressly or impliedly gives it to him, until the delivery of the deed. Possession, in other words, follows the legal title. Moreover, even if the purchaser is entitled to possession, he is not free to treat the land in such a fashion that the vendor's security for the remainder of the purchaser price is threatened. A court of equity may even enjoin the cutting of timber, the removal of minerals, etc., by using the mortgagor-mortgagee analogy. In any long-term contract involving land which must be denuded in order to be useful, it is essential that rather exact limits be set for activities by the purchaser.

If this way of looking at the status of vendor-purchaser under an enforceable executory contract were a matter of academic theory only, we could dismiss it with an explanatory wave of the pen, but the doctrine of equitable conversion has had practical consequences in several areas of property law. The most important areas are: creditors' rights,[3] the devolution of property inter-

pects of equitable conversion have been added.

1. Even when the doctrine is not applied it has a pervasive effect. See Clay v. Landreth, 187 Va. 169, 45 S.E.2d 875, 175 A.L.R. 1047 (1948), where there were zoning changes after the contract was signed so that the purchaser could not use the land for the purpose for which both parties knew he was buying it. The vendor claimed the risk was on the purchaser under the doctrine but the court refused to apply an equitable doctrine inequitably and denied specific performance to the vendor.

2. When real estate is under a valid contract of sale, a question frequently arises as to who is the "owner" for a wide variety of legal purposes. See, for example, Committee of Protesting Citi-

zens, etc. v. Val Vue Sewer District, 14 Wn.App. 838, 545 P.2d 42 (1976), where, applying the logic of equitable conversion, the court held that the purchaser, not the vendor, was "owner" for the purpose of protesting the formation of a local improvement district under a Washington statute.

3. The doctrine is often invoked where creditors are trying to reach the assets of either the vendor or the purchaser. While the doctrine makes considerable difference in legal theory, in practice the creditor usually reaches the available assets of either, provided he uses the correct remedy for the particular jurisdiction. See First Security Bank of Idaho, National Ass'n v. Rogers, 91 Idaho 654, 429 P.2d 386 (1967). See also Simpson, Legislative Changes

ests on the death of either the vendor or the purchaser while the contract is still executory, and the issue of which party has the risk of loss for property damaged or destroyed during the contract stage.

In a book of principles, the authors usually are forced to sketch in broad outlines, but occasionally a portrait in some detail is called for to illustrate the nature of the problem. Rather than a few general statements about each of the three important areas, we will give a greater emphasis to the risk of loss problem and tie in creditors' rights and devolution on death at the appropriate points. More extended knowledge of these latter two areas can be obtained by perusal of the appropriate footnotes references. This will make possible a treatment of the relationship of insurance to the real estate contract, without which an understanding of risk of loss is impossible. Furthermore, since this is a book on principles, this will provide an excellent vehicle to point out a principle gone wrong—a segment of the law which is caught in the toils of its own fictional logic and which needs to re-examine its major premise.

The accurately descriptive, but dull-sounding, title of this section conceals a fascinating controversy which has been raging in Anglo–American law since 1801.[4] While it will never compete in the public press with civil rights or space law, particularly in this age when our earthly antics become more and more lunar, it does have its appeal for those who like to inspect a microcosm of the law and draw conclusions about the macrocosm from it. Moreover, judging from the large quantity of appellate litigation over the years, there is a practical flavor to the problem which should interest our always pragmatic profession.

Before proceeding to an analysis of the law on this subject, let the late Judge Goodrich of the United States Court of Appeals for the Third Circuit, set the stage for a little playlet, Vogel v. Northern Assurance Co.[5] The judge, a former law teacher and dean, briefs his own case so well that we shall quote rather than paraphrase. "The undisputed facts present a question with all of the tantalizing niceties of the type which examiners pose to law students. Indeed, the problem of the case can be posed in the form of a hypothetical examination question. Here it is:

"*S*, a seller of real property (in the actual case a man named Shank) agrees to sell the land to *V*, the vendee, for

in the Law of Equitable Conversion by Contract: I, 44 Yale L.J. 559, 575 (1935) and Annot., 1 A.L.R.2d 727 (1948).

4. In that year Paine v. Meller, 6 Ves.Jr. 349, 31 Eng. Reprint 1088 (1801), decided that the risk of loss in

an executory contract for the sale of real property was on the purchaser.

5. 219 F.2d 409 (3d Cir.1955). The case was decided according to Pennsylvania law.

$15,000. (The vendee's real name in this case is Vogel, so the initials fit happily.) *S* then takes out fire insurance on the property in the amount of $6,000; *V* does likewise but in the amount of $9,000. Before *S* conveys the property to *V*, a fire occurs, damaging the house on the land to the extent of $12,000. *V* goes ahead and completes his part of the purchase agreement and receives a deed from *S*. Following this, *S* assigns to *V* all of his rights against the insurance company under the policy. *V* then sues both *S's* insurer (Northern Assurance Company, Ltd.) and his own insurer (Mount Joy Mutual Insurance Company). Was the district court correct in giving judgment against each company even though the total recovery exceeds the stipulated loss by $3,000?"

We pause, to see how many students can pass the test. The final paragraph of the opinion gives the answer.

"This brings us out to an affirmance of a judgment for $15,000, $3,000 more than the loss. This, it is true, seems incongruous in view of the often stated generalization that fire insurance is indemnity insurance. Vance on Insurance, § 14 (3d ed. 1951); 1 Richards on Insurance 3. The incongruity, if there is one, reaches clear back to 1853 in the settled rule in Pennsylvania that the seller can recover fully against the insurance company for a loss occurring between the time of the agreement and final settlement even though the buyer has taken title according to the terms of the contract. We have no doubt that the ingenuity of insurance counsel will draft a provision whereby total recovery can be limited to actual loss if that is an object to be desired. And if this Court has failed in its examination of Pennsylvania law on the subject, it will be compelled to take the course over."

For the reasoning between the two quoted paragraphs we remand you to Judge Goodrich's opinion, with the sole comment that it has something to do with the fact that both the vendor and the purchaser have an insurable interest in the property. It would be unfair to claim that the judge flunked his examination on *existing* Pennsylvania law, but it should be pointed out that the following year the Supreme Court of Pennsylvania, while citing the *Vogel* case with apparent approval, seemed to reverse its field on the issue of indemnity, stating, ". . . the liability of the two insurance companies will properly be limited to the amount of the damage occasioned by the fire, . . . and they will prorate their respective liabilities therefor in accordance with the terms of the policies." [6] The recovery in excess of loss represented by the *Vogel*

6. Insurance Company of North America v. Alberstadt, 383 Pa. 556, 119 A.2d 83 (1956).

case is thoroughly explored by Professor William F. Young, Jr., in an article, "Some 'Windfall Coverages' in Property and Liability Insurance",[7] in the Columbia Law Review; suffice it for the moment to agree with Mr. Justice Schaefer of the Illinois Supreme Court. "When insured property is in a single ownership, it is not hard to hold to the orthodox concept of an insurance contract as a personal contract of indemnity. But there are inherent difficulties when there are multiple interests in the property. Those inherent difficulties are augmented because the effect given to an executory contract to sell realty, and to the doctrine of equitable conversion, differs significantly from one jurisdiction to another. The result is that neither courts nor commentators are agreed upon proper solutions for the many variations on the vendor-vendee-insurer theme."[8]

Now that the stage has been set, let us proceed to the critic's role in the developing drama.

A. WHO HAS THE RISK OF LOSS?[9]

The executory contract for the sale of real estate is a peculiar beast. It is a creature of equity, enforceable in proper circumstances by a decree of specific performance, and hence caught up in the odd Anglo–American bifurcation of law and equity. In an action at law the risk was traditionally stated to be on the vendor,[10] whereas in a suit in equity the majority of courts would place it on the purchaser.[11] This ancient distinction has nothing

7. 60 Col.L.Rev. 1063, 1066–1072 (1960).

8. First National Bank v. Boston Insurance Company, 17 Ill.2d 147, 150, 160 N.E.2d 802, 804 (1959).

9. The material in this sub-section deals primarily with the risk of loss but also includes some discussion of the effect of equitable conversion on the devolution of the property when either the vendor or purchaser dies while the contract is still executory. Note that the basic principle is the same in each situation, i.e., the property may be converted from realty into personalty by the logic of equitable conversion.

10. "If a contract be made for the purchase and sale of land which has buildings on it, and, after the making of the contract, but before the conveyance of the land, the buildings be casually destroyed by fire, upon whom will the loss fall? At law it will clearly fall upon the vendor in all cases." Langdell, A Brief Survey of Equity Jurisdiction 58 (2d ed. 1908). Not surprisingly, the decisions on the point are considerably less clear than the Langdell statement would indicate. See, e.g., Handler, Cases and Materials on Vendor and Purchaser, ftn. 27, p. 369 (1933).

11. Cases on the risk of loss are collected in Annot., 27 A.L.R.2d 44 (1953).

See Bleckley v. Langston, 112 Ga. App. 63, 143 S.E.2d 671 (1965), where the court placed the risk of loss on the purchaser after an ice storm had damaged all of the pecan trees on the real property contracted to be sold. Since the purchaser bears the burdens he also gets the benefits, e.g., he is entitled to the award when the property is taken

but the logic of historical accident to commend it and is of less importance today because of the continuing merger of law and equity. Even if the action begins at law, an equitable counterclaim will doubtless take precedence and the rule in chancery will prevail. Do not cheer too soon, however, for all is not beer and skittles on the equity side and even the chancellor suffers from the infantile repressions of an undersized boot,[12] the particular boot being the fiction of equitable conversion.

This hoary chestnut has undoubted utility due to the gap between the signing of the contract and the delivery of the deed. During this interval, while the title is being checked [13] and other incidental messes are being tidied, many interesting events can occur. One or both parties may die, become insane, descend into hopeless bankruptcy, be rigorously attacked by determined creditors, or the property itself may be damaged due to fire, flood, earthquake, or governmental action through eminent domain. Who owns what during the gap? The chancellors answered this simple query with a maxim, "Equity regards as done that which ought to be done." This stated a conclusion rather than giving a reason, but after sufficient repetition it acquired the ring of truth. Since the parties obviously intended that the contract should be performed, the equitable title was said to pass to the purchaser as soon as a valid, enforceable contract for the sale of realty was signed. "The vendee is looked upon and treated as *the owner of the land;* an equitable estate has vested in him commensurate with that provided for by the contract, whether in fee, for life, or for years; although the vendor remains owner of the legal estate he holds it as a trustee for the vendee, to whom all the beneficial interest has passed, having a lien on the land, even if in possession of the vendee, as security for an unpaid portion of the purchase-money." [14]

Equitable conversion thus treats the parties as having changed positions, the original estate of each having been converted—that of the purchaser from personal into real property, and that of the vendor from real into personal property. Various legal consequences flow from the application of this fiction, including a change in the devolution of property on death. If the vendor dies, the "personalty" (in the form of the money still due under the contract) descends to the takers of the personal property (although

by eminent domain. See Arko Enterprises, Inc. v. Wood, 185 So.2d 734 (Fla. App.1966). In the last case, there was a vigorous dissent on the grounds that the contract was not capable of specific performance at the time the land was condemned.

12. You may recall that discretion in equity was said to be measured by the length of the Chancellor's foot.

13. For a discussion of the mystic rites of modern conveyancing see p. 340, infra.

14. 2 Pomeroy, Equity Jurisprudence 21 (5th ed. 1941).

the naked legal title to the land will descend to the takers of the realty, who hold it in trust as the vendor did) whereas, if the purchaser dies, the "realty" will descend to the takers of his real property even though the remaining purchase money must come from the share going to the takers of the personalty.[15] This aspect of equitable conversion has little present-day effect in an intestate succession since the statutes of descent typically treat real and personal property alike, but it may have some unforeseen consequences where either party dies testate.[16] The death cases will not be discussed in detail here, but they do show the pervasiveness of the doctrine and point out that basically it is designed to carry out the supposed intent of the parties. Thus, the making of a contract to sell land previously devised has the same effect in equity as the conveyance of such land would have at law. On the other hand, if the devise is subsequent to the contract and is specific it has been regarded as being, in effect, a bequest of the purchase money due on the contract.[17] In brief, equitable conversion, like all legal theories, should be applied to reach a just result, consistent with the probable intent of the parties. It should *not* be lifted mechanically from its embalmment in black letter text and vigorously applied in all land contract cases.

Viewed in this perspective, it is clear that the risk of loss should not pass automatically to the purchaser the instant he signs an enforceable contract.[18] In the typical situation the ven-

---

15. For interesting cases involving devolution on death see Eddington v. Turner, 27 Del.Ch. 411, 38 A.2d 738, 155 A.L.R. 562 (1944) and Clapp v. Tower, 11 N.D. 556, 93 N.W. 862 (1903).

The former case involved an option to purchase where the vendor died before the option was exercised. While the purchaser could still exercise the option after the vendor's death, the court refused to apply the doctrine of relation back (as some English cases had done) and so invoke equitable conversion. Thus, the vendor died owning realty, not personalty, and the proceeds of the sale were treated as realty in his estate and passed to the takers of the real property. In the latter case, the doctrine was applied even though the contract was forfeited by the personal representative of the vendor after his death, thus the land was treated as personalty, not realty. The cases are consistent since in each situation it was a question of whether there was a valid, subsisting contract, capable of being enforced in equity, at the instant of the vendor's death. In the former there

was not—only an option which might or might not ripen into a contract; in the latter there was even though it was subsequently forfeited.

16. Of course, if realty and personalty descend differently in a particular jurisdiction then the doctrine could have legal significance. Shay v. Penrose, 25 Ill.2d 447, 185 N.E.2d 218 (1962). The doctrine may also affect survivorship rights in concurrent estates although it is doubtful if it should do so. Panushka v. Panushka, 221 Or. 145, 349 P.2d 450 (1960) and Watson v. Watson, 5 Ill.2d 526, 126 N.E.2d 220 (1955).

17. For a good, brief discussion of this whole matter see Chafee, Simpson, Maloney, Cases on Equity 516–522 (1951).

See also Father Flanagan's Boys' Home v. Graybill, 178 Neb. 79, 132 N.W.2d 304 (1964).

18. Note the constant emphasis on *enforceable* contract. If neither party has signed a memorandum sufficient to satisfy the Statute of Frauds or if the

dor remains in possession; he already has his interest insured; and it would never occur to either party that the purchaser assumes the risk prior to the transfer of legal title or possession. Without belaboring the point, it should be noted that the case on which the doctrine is based, Paine v. Meller,[19] did not require such a result and most legal commentators have criticized the unwarranted expansion of *dicta* in the case into different fact situations. The maxim, "equity regards as done that which should have been done," stems from cases in which the vendor and purchaser were ready to perform the necessary acts and the time had arrived for them to do so, but because of mistake, delay, accident, concession to convenience, or some wrongful neglect on the part of the one against whom the maxim was invoked, actual performance had not occurred.　Law could not aid the parties, so equity treated the situation as if the transaction had been executed.

It is precisely because the present majority rule runs counter to the normal intent of the parties and to the logic of the maxim itself, that so many variations on the theme have developed.　No less than five different theories have been advanced: (1) the risk of loss should be on the vendor until legal title is conveyed; (2) the risk should be on the vendor until the time agreed upon for the conveyance of the legal title, and thereafter on the purchaser, unless the vendor is then in such default as to be unable specifically to enforce the contract; (3) the risk should be on the party in possession, whether vendor or purchaser; (4) the risk should be on the vendor unless there is something in the contract or the relations of the parties from which the court can infer a different intention; and (5) the risk should be on the purchaser from the time the vendor-purchaser relation arises.[20]

Ten states [21] have settled the issue by legislation, adopting the Uniform Vendor and Purchaser Risk Act which leaves the casualty risk on the vendor, as long as the contract is executory and the purchaser has not gone into possession.　In the other forty states the courts still decide the matter, with results ranging from the majority view, following the *dicta* of Paine v. Meller, to the minority view of Massachusetts in Libman v. Levenson [22] where the court said: "It is now settled . . . that the contract is to be construed as subject to the implied condition that it no longer

---

title is clearly unmerchantable, equitable conversion does not take place and the risk remains on the vendor.　Sanford v. Breidenbach, 111 Ohio App. 474, 173 N.E.2d 702 (1960); Amundson v. Severson, 41 S.D. 377, 170 N.W. 633 (1919).

19. Note 4 supra.

20. Note 17 at 556–557.

21. California, Hawaii, Illinois, Michigan, New York, North Carolina, Oklahoma, Oregon, South Dakota, and Wisconsin.

22. 236 Mass. 221, 224, 128 N.E. 13, 14 (1920).　See also Anderson v. Yaworski, 120 Conn. 390, 181 A. 205, 101 A.L.R. 1232 (1935) for a good statement of this view.

shall be binding if, before the time for the conveyance to be made, the buildings are destroyed by fire. The loss by the fire falls upon the vendor, the owner; and if he has not protected himself by insurance, he can have no reimbursement of this loss; but the contract is no longer binding upon either party. If the purchaser has advanced any part of the price, he can recover it back."

Other states take positions somewhere between the two extremes and hold that the purchaser is the equitable owner only in cases in which he has fulfilled all conditions and become absolutely entitled to a conveyance. In what was long the leading Illinois case, Budelman v. American Insurance Company,[23] the Court put it succinctly: "The law is well settled in this State that an executory contract of sale does not convey title to the vendee. The vendor retains the legal title and the vendee does not even take an equitable title. . . . When the vendee performs all acts necessary to entitle him to a deed, then, and not until then, he has an equitable title and may compel a conveyance."[24]

The moral of the preceding discussion is clear; there is no uniform answer to the question "who has the risk of loss?" The real estate lawyer must determine who bears the risk in a particular jurisdiction and then draft the contract (or build the lawsuit) on the basis of that determination. But even in those jurisdictions which purport to place the risk on the purchaser with the signing of the contract, it may be possible to get the court to revert to first principles and overrule (or distinguish) cases which mechanically apply the doctrine of equitable conversion. The Uniform Vendor and Purchase Risk Act represents the best answer to the question by placing the emphasis on the issue of possession or delivery of the deed and should be widely adopted. This view is shared by many of the writers who have struggled with the issue.[25]

---

23. 297 Ill. 222, 225, 130 N.E. 513, 514 (1921). See also Newman v. Mountain Park Land Co., 85 Ark. 208, 107 S.W. 391 (1908) and Good v. Jarrard, 93 S.C. 229, 76 S.E. 698 (1912).

24. Interestingly enough, the Illinois law is *not* well settled that an executory contract conveys no equitable title to the purchaser. Indeed, in Shay v. Penrose, 25 Ill.2d 447, 185 N.E.2d 218 (1962), the Illinois Supreme Court specifically applied the doctrine, even in an installment land contract, and, in effect, repudiated the basis of the *Budelman* case. For a good discussion of the Illinois law of equitable conversion see Note, The Doctrine of Equitable Conversion in Illinois, 1955 U.Ill. L.F. 743.

25. But see Pound, The Progress of the Law, Equity, 33 Harv.L.Rev. 813, 826 (1920). Dean Pound disagreed with Professor Williston's argument for possession at the time of the loss as the proper criterion. Williston's view was adopted by the Uniform Act.

B. FIXING THE RISK BY CONTRACT

In any jurisdiction, it is unwise to leave the risk of loss issue to the operation of law. The contract is the blueprint of the transaction and it should cover all of those contingencies which might arise but which we hope will not. A poorly drafted contract, or even none at all, will serve quite well so long as everything goes smoothly. The test of any legal document is how it stands up in a crisis.

The parties clearly have the right to handle the risk of loss in any way they see fit.[26] Just as clearly, there is no set formula which will fit all situations. A common clause provides: "The risk of loss or damage to said premises by fire is assumed by the vendor until the delivery of the deed." At first blush this appears clear enough, but doubts soon creep in. Loss may occur from windstorm, vandalism, boiler destruction, hurricane, erosion, subsidence and collapse of a retaining wall, etc., and this clause covers only loss by fire. It is obviously too narrow. Moreover, how is the risk of loss to be handled, granting it falls on the vendor? Does this clause merely entitle the purchaser to rescind the contract and receive his down payment or does it allow him to seek specific performance of the contract with substantial abatement from the purchase price? There is authority for both positions.[27] Finally, this clause is silent as to possession and would not be helpful in installment land contracts or other situations calling for a transfer of possession prior to delivery of the deed. Brevity has its own virtue but it can be a false god. More detail and more precision is needed here.

Mr. Milton R. Friedman of the New York Bar, in an article on real estate contracts in the American Bar Association Journal,[28] lists résumés of three possible clauses:

"A. In case of injury, seller has the option to restore. If seller fails to restore purchaser may: (1) terminate the contract; or (2) accept a deed, without abatement, but with seller's rights to insurance.

"B. (1) If the injury is less than 10 per cent of the purchase price purchaser shall complete the contract; and (2) if the injury is

26. Coolidge and Sickler, Inc. v. Regn, 7 N.J. 93, 80 A.2d 554, 27 A.L.R.2d 437 (1951).

27. See Lampesis v. The Travelers Insurance Company, 101 N.H. 323, 143 A.2d 104 (1958). In this case the risk of loss being on the vendor apparently

gave him the option of repairing the property and enforcing the contract or treating the contract as at an end.

28. Friedman, Buying a Home: Representing the Purchaser, 47 A.B.A.J. 596, 602 (1961).

greater than 10 per cent purchaser has the option of completing or terminating the contract. If in either case the contract is completed purchaser is entitled to an abatement commensurate with the damage.

"C. (1) If the injury does not exceed a stated amount purchaser shall accept the premises as damaged, with seller's right to insurance; and (2) if the injury exceeds the sum mentioned purchaser has the option of either completing the contract, and receiving seller's right to insurance, or terminating the contract."

All of these stipulations provide that if the contract is terminated because of the injury the vendor will repay any advance on the purchase price. Each of these clauses has merit, but a little reflection will reveal aspects that will not be entirely satisfactory to both parties. They are sufficient, however, to suggest solutions to the drafting problems and each contract must be approached in light of the peculiar fact situation involved.[29]

Without attempting to reconcile the conflicting theories as to risk of loss, and even without settling the issue by contract, the parties can substantially avoid loss through insurance. There is agreement that both the vendor and purchaser have insurable interests; hence both can be insured. A "contract of sale" endorsement can be added to the existing insurance policy, after first ascertaining that there is sufficient coverage to take care of any loss. This last point is essential since in these days of unending inflation many properties are woefully under-insured at the time the contract is signed. The "contract of sale" clause recites that a contract has been executed between the insured and the named purchaser, and that any loss shall be adjusted with the insured and paid to him and the purchaser as their respective interests may appear. An alternative is to cause the policy to be amended, constituting the purchaser an additional insured, or the latter may secure a separate policy. As an insured he would have the right to participate in the settlement of any controversy as to the amount of the claim, whereas under the "contract of sale" endorsement his only right is to share in the proceeds when paid.[30]

---

29. For a discussion of the fire clause with a detailed analysis of the problems which can arise even with well-drafted contracts see Drafting of Real Estate Sales Contracts, 35 Chicago Bar Record 247, 260 (1954). This article was prepared by the Committee on Real Property Law of the Chicago Bar Association.

30. Although see Dubin Paper Co. v. Insurance Co. of North America, 361 Pa. 68, 63 A.2d 85 (1949) which apparently would allow the purchaser to sue on the vendor's policy.

C. WHO RECEIVES THE INSURANCE PROCEEDS?

If the transaction is handled by a lawyer who is familiar with the preceding material (or at least the last few paragraphs of it) all but the most stubborn problems will disappear. Not all vendors and purchasers of real estate are so circumspect as to seek legal assistance, however, and even in this enlightened age some complicated messes can result. It is interesting to note that as long ago as Paine v. Meller the insurance issue reared its head. The vendor had allowed the insurance on the premises to lapse shortly before the fire and the purchaser claimed this was a significant factor in determining the risk of loss. Said Lord Eldon: ". . . For I do not see how I can allow it, unless I say, this Court warrants to every buyer of a house, that the house is insured, and not only insured, but to the full extent of the value. The house is bought, not the benefit of any existing policy. However general the practice of insuring from fire, it is not universal; and it is yet less general that houses are insured to their full value, or near it. The question, whether insured or not, is with the vendor solely, not with the vendee; unless he proposes something upon that; and makes it matter of contract with the vendor, that the vendee shall buy according to that fact, that the house is insured." [31]

This remains good law and the vendor's failure to insure adequately, or indeed at all, puts no added burden upon him unless he had contracted to so protect the premises. Suppose, however, the vendor has insurance, the purchaser has none, the contract is silent, and the jurisdiction puts the risk of loss on the purchaser—what then? The inexorable logic of the law grinds out the following answer. Both parties have an insurable interest; the vendor protected his interest; the purchaser, like the foolish virgins, did not; insurance is a personal contract, payable only to the insured; the purchaser "has had it." [32] But surely such logic would result in a major windfall to the vendor, since he would have the insurance proceeds to cover his loss plus the right to sue the purchaser for specific performance and receive the full purchase price of the land. The English court had the courage of its misplaced convictions, holding that the vendor, having collected both the insurance and the purchase money, held the latter in trust for the insurer on the principle that the latter was entitled to subrogation against the purchaser. [33] This judicial logic was too

31. Note 4 supra.

32. Rayner v. Preston, 18 Ch.Div. 1 (1881); Brownell v. Board of Education, 239 N.Y. 369, 146 N.E. 630, 37 A.L.R. 1319 (1925).

33. Castellain v. Preston, 11 Q.B.D. 380 (1883).

much for Parliament and the English rule was changed by statute to provide that the purchaser might claim the insurance money received by the vendor, subject, however, to any stipulation to the contrary.[34]

No such statutory changes have been made in this country and a minority of American jurisdictions still echo the old English view which denies the purchaser any access to the vendor's insurance proceeds.[35] These cases follow the *dictum* of Judge Pound in Brownell v. Board of Education: [36] "These reasons [for holding for the purchaser] may savor of layman's ideas of equity, but they are not law. . . . Insurance is a mere personal contract to pay a sum of money by way of indemnity to protect the interest of the insured. . . . In common parlance the buildings are insured but every one who stops to consider the nature of the insurance contract understands that they are not. Both in the forum and the market place it is known that the insurance runs to the individual insured and not with the land. The vendor has a beneficial interest to protect, i.e., his own. The vendee has an insurable interest and may protect himself. The trustee as such has no insurable interest and can only act for the *cestui que trust*. Plaintiff may not have the insurance money collected by defendant. It is not a part of the *res* bargained for and no trust relation exists in regard to it."

The amazing vitality of the old Brownell case was demonstrated in Raplee v. Piper.[37] The contract of sale required the purchaser to keep the property insured against fire in the name of the vendor. A loss occurred while the purchaser was in possession and the company paid the vendor $4,650. The purchaser insisted that, while the risk of loss was his under the Uniform Act, the insurance money should be credited on the balance of the purchase price. The vendor refused on the theory that the insurance was his even though the purchaser paid the premiums. The Court of Appeals of New York held for the purchaser, distinguishing the Brownell case, although stating it was still the law of New York, because there the vendor had obtained the insurance at his own cost, for his own protection, and not because of any agreement.

Surely this corollary to the Brownell doctrine is reasonable but there was a vigorous dissent by three judges who felt that even here the purchaser was entitled to no part of the insurance proceeds because of the settled law of New York. Said Judge Burke: "In light of these circumstances we think that this court

34. 15 Geo. V, c. 20, § 47 (1925).

35. Cases on the rights of vendor and purchaser, as between themselves, in insurance proceeds are collected in Annot., 64 A.L.R.2d 1397 (1959).

36. 239 N.Y. 369, 374, 146 N.E. 630, 632 (1925).

37. 3 N.Y.2d 179, 143 N.E.2d 919, 64 A.L.R.2d 1397 (1957).

should adhere to the rule established by the Brownell case. Such adherence, it seems to us, is imperative, not only because this is a well-recognized rule which the legislature has not undertaken to change, but also because many businessmen and their lawyers may have entered into contracts in reliance upon it." [38] It is far from clear, however, that the purchaser, businessman or no, intended to pay the vendor's premiums and receive nothing in return but the opportunity to pay the full purchase price for a damaged building. Fortunately, the majority of the court reached a just result but the litigation itself could have been avoided by a properly drafted contract or even by a more sensible rule of law than that represented by the Brownell case.[39]

The "inexorable logic of the law," which led to the older English rule and the Brownell case, proved too much for most American courts. Said the court in a leading New Jersey case: "As purchaser under a valid contract of purchase vendee became the equitable owner of the property; in equity the property is regarded as belonging to him, the vendor retaining the legal title simply as trustee and as security for the unpaid purchase money. By reason of this equitable relation of the parties to a contract of sale of land, it has been determined by the great weight of American authority that money accruing on a policy of insurance, where the loss has occurred subsequent to the execution of the contract, will in equity inure to the benefit of the vendee; the vendor still retaining his character as trustee, and the insurance money in his hands representing the property that has been destroyed." [40] The court was correct in calling this view the great weight of American authority, as decisions in at least fifteen states attest.[41] The ever-useful remedy of constructive trust has proved flexible enough to reach a just result and what once savored of a "layman's ideas of equity" has now become the law in most states. Professor Vance suggested, long ago, that in the business world

---

38. Id. at 184 and 922. Since the law of the Brownell case was judge-made (or was it only judge-discovered?) it would seem that it could be judge-altered if shown to be erroneous. For a fascinating analysis of the modern English attitude toward the judge's role see Davis, The Future of Judge–Made Public Law in England: A Problem of Practical Jurisprudence, 61 Col.L.Rev. 201, 210 (1961). "What is now the orthodox English attitude was stated several centuries ago by Francis Bacon: 'Judges ought to remember that their office is . . . to interpret law, and not to make law, or give law.' My assertion is largely the opposite: Judges ought to remember that the easier part of their office is to discover and to apply previously-existing law to the problems that come before them, but the most important and most difficult task they perform is the molding of a body of case law that will satisfactorily serve the needs of society."

39. See Kindred v. Boalbey, 73 Ill. App.3d 37, 29 Ill.Dec. 77, 391 N.E.2d 236 (1979). The Illinois Court cited Raplee v. Piper and said: "Equity demands that the plaintiff (vendor) not be unjustly enriched by receiving a double recovery in this instance."

40. Millville Aerie v. Weatherby, 82 N.J.Eq. 455, 457, 88 A. 847, 848 (1913).

41. Note 35 supra.

the insurance runs with the land and that the courts should give effect to that understanding.[42] That view should soon prevail generally in this country. One state adopting this position was Alabama,[43] in 1958, and the court proceeded to do complete equity by decreeing that the purchaser should reimburse the vendor for the amount of the premiums paid by him.

Even this enlightened view will not solve all problems since the vendor may not be willing to sue the insurance company to collect on the policy and the purchaser, not being a party to it, may be hard up for a remedy. The Dubin case [44] in Pennsylvania comes closest to suggesting an answer here. The fire occurred before the date of settlement under the contract, the purchaser performed his part, and the vendor received checks from his insurance companies to cover the loss but returned them to the companies. (Now why would a vendor behave in that fashion?) The purchaser sued in equity to compel the companies to pay the proceeds to the vendor and asked the court to declare that the vendor held the proceeds as trustee for the plaintiff. The court concluded that the action was well brought and the purchaser was entitled to relief. This, too, may savor of "barnyard equity" but it makes good sense.

Although there is dispute as to the purchaser's rights to the insurance proceeds in the situations discussed in the preceding paragraphs, it seems clear that where the vendor agrees to keep the premises insured for the benefit of the purchaser, or when the vendor assigns his rights under the policy to the purchaser, either before or after the loss, the insurance proceeds belong to the purchaser.[45]

Since the constructive trust theory has been applied to allow the purchaser to reach the insurance proceeds in the hands of the vendor it might seem to follow, in the interest of symmetry if nothing else, that the purchaser too could be held as a constructive trustee for the benefit of the vendor. The equities are not really parallel, however, since the vendor, having been owner all along and being the apparent bearer of the risk of loss, might be expected to carry insurance for the benefit of all interested parties. The purchaser, on the other hand, is a "Johnny-come-lately" to the property and if he insures at all will probably do so solely to protect his own interests. This analysis seems to be reflected in the judicial attitude and, in the absence of a provision in the

42. Vance, Vendee's Claim to Insurance Money Received by Vendor, 34 Yale L.J. 87 (1924).

43. Alabama Farm Bureau Mutual Insurance Service, Inc. v. Nixon, 268 Ala. 271, 105 So.2d 643 (1958).

44. Note 30 supra.

45. Vierneisel v. Rhode Island Ins. Co., 77 Cal.App.2d 229, 175 P.2d 63 (1946); Allyn v. Allyn, 154 Mass. 570, 28 N.E. 779 (1891).

contract requiring the purchaser to insure for the benefit of the vendor or the presence of some special equities, the purchaser will not be compelled to account for any part of the proceeds paid on a policy taken out to protect his own interests.[46]

Obviously, the words "special equities" in the previous sentence can cover a lot of ground and you can visualize situations in which the vendor might have a claim to the purchaser's insurance. For example, in Cetkowski v. Knutson [47] the vendor had the right to rescind a contract of sale because he was induced to enter it by the purchaser's fraud. The court made the purchaser a trustee of the insurance proceeds for the benefit of the vendor, even though the policy was maintained in the purchaser's name and for his benefit.

D. A TYPICAL PROBLEM

We began this discussion with a quiz based on a Pennsylvania case, and we daresay most of you flunked it. We conclude this section with a question from an Illinois decision [48] to see whether you have shown sufficient improvement to remain in class. The vendor, holding title as trustee under a land trust, insured a building with four companies, aggregating $46,750.[49] Each of the policies indemnified the insured "to the extent of the actual cash value of the property at the time of loss, but not exceeding the amount which it would cost to repair or replace the property with material of like kind and quality within a reasonable time after such loss . . . nor in any event for more than the interest of the insured, against all direct loss by fire." The vendor then entered into a contract to sell the property to the purchaser for $19,000 of

46. Deming Investment Co. v. Dickerman, 63 Kan. 728, 66 P. 1029 (1901).

47. 163 Minn. 492, 204 N.W. 528, 40 A.L.R. 599 (1925).

48. Note 8 supra.

49. When an owner insures a building with more than one company and a loss occurs, the coverages of the two or more policies are added together and the loss is apportioned in accordance with the ratio which each policy bears to the total loss. In Sanford v. Breidenbach, 111 Ohio App. 474, 173 N.E.2d 702 (1960), the trial court used this method where both the vendor and the purchaser had their own policies. The case was reversed on appeal because the court held that the risk of loss was on the vendor, not the purchaser, and hence the latter's insurer was not liable at all and the vendor could recover only on his own policy. The risk was on the vendor because at the time the loss occurred there were unfulfilled conditions in the contract (certain septic tank easements had not been obtained by the vendor) which would have prevented specific performance. Absent the right to that remedy, equitable conversion had not occurred. Incidentally, the vendor was still in possession but the court apparently did not deem that fact to be relevant in reaching its decision.

which $3,000 was paid down. The form contract provided that premiums were to be prorated as of the date of the delivery of the deed and the policies would then be assigned to the buyers. It also provided, "If, prior to delivery of deed hereunder, the improvements on said premises shall be destroyed or materially damaged by fire or other casualty, this contract shall, at the option of the buyer, become null and void."

The building was totally destroyed by fire before law day and appraisals secured by the insurance adjusters showed reproduction costs in excess of $230,000. The companies conceded that the building's value was in excess of the $46,750 coverage but refused to pay more than $16,000 to the insured vendor. Why? Said the companies, the "interest of the insured" under the doctrine of equitable conversion is $16,000, the amount unpaid on the purchase price. How would you decide this case?

Mr. Justice Schaefer, admitting that the problem presented by the case was not an easy one, held against the companies, pointing out that equitable conversion had evolved as a fiction to carry out the intent of the parties to the contract and should have no effect upon the rights of others. Had the fire occurred prior to the signing of the contract or had the contract been performed before the fire took place and the policies been assigned to the purchaser, there would have been a recovery for the face amount of the policies. Legal realism required brushing aside the fiction of equitable conversion and allowing full recovery. The case represents the "old school try" by insurance counsel in a lost cause. Incidentally, during oral argument and in response to questions from the bench, counsel for the insured vendor stated that the insured was obligated to account to the purchasers for the proceeds. This caused a flurry of excitement and led to the filing of supplemental briefs since the companies' counsel complained this fact had not been previously revealed. However, the court held this was immaterial, pointing out that the purchasers had the option to cancel the contract in event of fire and could have left the property entirely in the ownership of the vendor. Concluded the court: "That contingency [the fire] occurred, and we do not see how the way in which the contracting parties have dealt with the resulting situation can be a matter of concern to the insurers." This point scarcely puts Illinois in the company of those who make the vendor a trustee of the insurance for the purchaser but it does indicate which way the winds of doctrine are blowing.

We can agree with Professor Young, who stated in the Columbia Law Review article [50] cited earlier: "Enough has been said to suggest that the state of the law in a particular jurisdiction

50. Note 7 supra at 1070.

depends largely on the order in which the issues arise for appellate consideration. . . . The doubt and disagreement existing about these relationships cannot be overlooked. This should not be charged naively to judicial ineptitude. Rather, it may be supposed that 'proper solutions' cannot be found easily for the issues involved, which are so diverse yet so interrelated, in the fashion of courts, case by case." Once again the common law may need the helping hand of beneficent legislation.

SECTION 3. THE DEED

Compared to the contract or the lease, the deed is a simple document. The first two instruments must govern the relationship of the parties over a period of time; the deed, in a sense, ends the relationship since its very purpose is to transfer legal title from the grantor to the grantee. So strong is this terminal character of a deed that, under the doctrine of merger, many of the contract rights of a purchaser are extinguished when he accepts a deed. Thus, a purchaser who was entitled to a warranty deed conveying merchantable title but who accepted a quitclaim deed found himself without recourse when the premises turned out to be subject to a mortgage.[51]

The doctrine of merger is an old but misleading concept. Briefly stated, it means that any covenants in the contract merge into the deed on the execution of the contract and are no longer enforceable. Actually, the contract covenants are terminated rather than merged and the parties must then look to the deed for any cause of action. It is basically a titles doctrine designed to prevent the grantee from going behind the deed to earlier promises. There are many exceptions to the doctrine when title is not directly involved and when the covenant is collateral to the promise to convey land. See, for example, Re v. Magness Construction Co.,[52] where the suit was for breach of a construction contract due to the defendant's failure to build in accordance with

---

51. Whittemore v. Farrington, 76 N.Y. 452 (1879). The court noted: "If the grantor and grantee had both intended that the deed should contain covenants, and supposed at the time of its delivery that it did contain them, but through a mistake of the scrivener they had been omitted, the Court might insert them. But no such case is made out here." See also Secor v. Knight, 716 P.2d 790 (Utah 1986) for a discussion of the merger doctrine as it relates to title matters (recorded restrictive covenants) not collateral to the contract. The court said: "Therefore, in such a case, the deed is the final agreement and all prior terms, whether written or verbal, are extinguished and unenforceable."

52. 49 Del. 377, 10 Terry 377, 117 A.2d 78 (1955).

written plans and specifications. The deed to the property had been accepted although the work was not completed and was improperly done. The court allowed recovery saying, "Clearly the agreement calls for the performance of two separate acts, the conveyance of land improved by a dwelling and the building of a house in accordance with certain plans and specifications. This contract falls within the exception to the rule. There is no merger." [53] Even in title situations there is some chipping away at the doctrine and in Mayer v. Sumergrade,[54] the court allowed a purchaser to sue on a covenant against special tax assessments in the contract after delivery of the deed. There was a vigorous dissent, however, and the case represents a minority position on the title issue.

The merger doctrine continues to be discussed in the recent cases but it seldom prevails to defeat a suit by the purchaser. In Mallin v. Good,[55] the court said: "While no Illinois reviewing court has considered the specific question of whether a vendor's covenant to make repairs will be merged into the subsequent deed, the weight of authority in other jurisdictions is that such agreements are collateral to the deed and are not merged into it. . . . In our view, an examination of the analogous authority in this state leads to a similar conclusion." On the other hand, in Bakken v. Price,[56] the court held that a covenant to provide title insurance was merged into the deed and that after conveyance the deed controlled the rights of the parties. Note, however, that this was a title matter not collateral to the deed. The court held that the purchaser's remedy for the vendor's breach was in damages for breach of warranty rather than rescission. The Uniform Land Transactions Act would abolish the doctrine of merger entirely.[57]

The essential simplicity of the deed is illustrated by the statutory short form warranty deed in use in Illinois.[58]

53. See also Rhenish v. Deunk, 193 N.E.2d 295, 26 O.O.2d 416 (1963) and Richmond Homes, Inc. v. Lee-Mar, Inc., 20 Ohio App.2d 27, 251 N.E.2d 637 (1969).

54. 111 Ohio App. 237, 167 N.E.2d 516 (1960).

55. 93 Ill.App.3d 843, 49 Ill.Dec. 168, 417 N.E.2d 858 (1981).

56. 613 P.2d 1222 (Wyo.1980).

57. Section 1–309. [Effect of Acceptance of Deed on Contract Obligations].

Acceptance by a buyer or a secured party of a deed or other instrument of conveyance is not of itself a waiver or renunciation of any of his rights under the contract under which the deed or other instrument of conveyance is given and does not of itself relieve any party of the duty to perform all his obligations under the contract.

58. For the exact statutory language for warranty deeds, quitclaim deeds, and mortgages see Ill.Rev.Stat., ch. 30, ss. 8, 9, and 10 (1985). Other states have similar statutes providing for statutory short form deeds.

WARRANTY DEED   DOCUMENT NO. _____

For Recorder's
Certificate Only

THE GRANTOR__, _____

_____

of the _____, in the County of _____,
and State of _____ for and in consideration of _____ DOLLARS in hand
paid, CONVEY__ and WARRANT__ to

_____

of the _____, County of _____, and
State of _____, the following described
Real Estate:

situated in the County of Champaign, in the State of Illinois,
hereby releasing and waiving all rights under and by virtue of the
Homestead Exemption Laws of the State of Illinois.

Dated this _____ day of _____, A.D. 19__.

_____ [Seal]
_____ [Seal]
_____ [Seal]
_____ [Seal]

STATE OF ILLINOIS, ⎱
Champaign County, ⎰ ss

[Seal]

I, the undersigned, a Notary Public in
and for said County and State aforesaid,
DO HEREBY CERTIFY, that _____

_____

personally known to me to be the same
person__ whose name__ _____ subscribed
to the foregoing instrument appeared before me this day in person and acknowledged that __he__ signed, sealed and delivered the said instrument as _____ free
and voluntary act, for the uses and purposes therein set forth, including the release and waiver of the right of homestead.

Given under my hand and Notarial
Seal, this _____ day of _____, A.D. 19__.

My Commission expires _____, A.D. 19__.

Notary Public

The simplicity of the deed should not lead you to underrate its importance, however. Since it is the operative instrument of conveyance, questions of title turn on its validity and adequacy. The conveyance of land has had a fascinating history, starting as a physical act dramatized by the livery of seisin, accompanied by the words "I give" (Latin, "do") "to him and his heirs" or "to him and the heirs of his body." [59] The Statute of Frauds required a writing and the private seal added the touch that made the modern deed. The role of the Statute of Uses, with its new methods of conveyancing—the bargain and sale and the covenant to stand seised to uses—has already been explained.[60] Modern conveyancing acts tend to operate independently of the Statute of Uses and the statute of the particular jurisdiction should be carefully followed. However, the earlier methods often survive and, while not regularly used today, they may be invoked to save a conveyance that would otherwise fail.[61]

A. TYPES AND ELEMENTS OF THE MODERN DEED

While no one form of deed is in universal use, the modern deed does follow a general pattern. There are two basic types— warranty and quitclaim. Either type is sufficient to transfer such interest as a grantor *presently* [62] has, but the former includes personal covenants by the grantor that his title is good. If the deed contains all of the usual covenants, it is classified as a general warranty deed; if it contains only a few or creates some new promises, it is called a special warranty deed. Since these covenants are a type of title assurance they will be discussed in Part Five. The warranty deed is typically used where the grantor purports to convey an indefeasible fee simple, while the quitclaim (sometimes called a release deed) is used to surrender such interest as the grantor may happen to have. Thus, if title examination discloses that there is an outstanding dower interest in some prior owner's widow that claim would probably be released by a quitclaim deed from her. Of course, there are various types of deeds which are used for a special purpose, such as mortgage deeds, trust deeds, deeds in trust, etc. These may be either warranty or quitclaim in form. Another classification you may encounter is the indenture versus the deed poll. The former is executed by all

59. 1 Patton, Titles 3–8 (2d ed. 1957).

60. P. 76, supra.

61. French v. French, 3 N.H. 234 (1825).

62. The warranty deed will also pass after-acquired title, whereas the quitclaim will not do so unless there are added representations as to the grantor's title. See p. 304, infra.

parties to it (usually the grantor and the grantee); the latter is executed by the grantor only.[63] Today, virtually all deeds to real property are deeds poll, being signed only by the grantor and spouse or the proper corporate officials. The grantee need not sign since by his acceptance of the deed he becomes bound by its terms.

Traditionally, the deed was divided into four parts—the premises, the habendum, the execution clause, and the acknowledgement. The premises consisted of the names of the grantor and grantee, any recitals of fact explanatory of the transaction, the operative words of conveyance, the consideration, and the legal description of the land. The habendum,[64] sometimes called the "to have and to hold" clause because it was introduced by those words, described the estate to be taken by the grantee (fee simple, life estate, etc.), contained the declaration of trust, if any, set forth any conditions or powers affecting the grant, and included the covenants of title when it was necessary to state them *in haec verba.*[65] The execution clause contained the date, the signatures of the grantor and spouse, the seal (if still required) and, in some states, the signatures of witnesses. The acknowledgment—attestation by a public officer—completed the instrument. The acknowledgement might not be necessary to the passage of title, but it was frequently a prerequisite to recording and was required as a condition to the admission of the deed into evidence without further proof of execution. Its role was to add to the authenticity of the document and cut down on the likelihood of fraud or forgery. The modern deed usually contains these traditional parts, but a conveyance may be sustained even though it consists only of the names of the parties, the consideration, the words of conveyance, and the description of the land.[66]

As always in the law, there is a considerable gulf between what competent draftsmanship requires and what a court may be induced to sustain under proper circumstances.[67] For example,

63. These odd names derive from the fact that originally the deed poll was on paper that was *polled* or cut in a straight line, whereas the indenture was indented or cut in a wavy line across the top. The indenting practice originated from cutting the deed through the middle of a word and giving each party part of the document.

64. If there was a conflict between the granting clause and the habendum clause, thus creating an ambiguity in the deed, the traditional view was that the granting clause prevailed. This view was rejected in Grayson v. Holloway, 203 Tenn. 464, 313 S.W.2d 555

(1958). "The technical rules of the common law as to the division of deeds into formal parts have long since been disregarded in this state, and the rule now is that all parts shall be examined to ascertain the intention."

65. Modern statutes allow the use of a single word, such as *warrant,* to stand for the usual covenants. See p. 292, infra.

66. For a more detailed analysis, see Tiffany, Real Property 670–681 (New Abridged Edition, 1940).

67. See, for example, the discussion in Hinchliffe v. Fischer, 198 Kan. 365,

the general rule of law is that a deed is a nullity until the name of the grantee is lawfully inserted therein.[68]   Yet in Womack v. Stegner,[69] a Texas court stated: "It appears to be well settled in Texas that when a deed with the name of the grantee in blank is delivered by the grantor with the intention that the title shall rest in the person to whom the deed is delivered, and that person is expressly authorized at the time of delivery to insert his own or any other name as grantee, title passes with the delivery."   In that case, the court used the concept of equitable title, which passed at the time of the delivery, and even the subsequent death of the grantor, before the authority was exercised and the blank filled, was immaterial.   Similarly, the law clearly requires operative words of conveyance, i.e., words like convey, grant, bargain and sell, which show the grantor's intent to transfer an interest to the grantee.   So strong was this requirement that words of reservation or exception in a deed were traditionally insufficient to create a new interest in a *third party;* they could only retain an interest in the grantor out of the estate conveyed.   Thus a reservation or exception in a stranger to the deed would fail despite the intention of the parties to create such an interest.[70]   This view is gradually changing as the courts look more to the intent of the parties and are less concerned about the technical doctrine.   Thus, in a South Carolina case, the court held that a husband could "reserve" a life estate in his wife, even though she had no previous interest in the premises, other than inchoate dower.[71]   The court said that while this might not be strictly logical, "pure logic for its own sake, should not be allowed to frustrate the clearly ascertained intention of a grantor which does not violate an established rule of construction of law."   More importantly, the Supreme Court of California effectively overruled prior doctrine in that state and allowed the reservation of an easement in a total stranger to the title where the grantor's intent to give a church a parking easement was clear.[72]   Nonetheless, the old doctrine dies hard and it is always wiser to use operative words of conveyance

424 P.2d 581 (1967) and Cribbet and Johnson, Cases and Materials on Property 1313 (5th ed. 1984), where a valid deed in the form of a poem is reproduced. See also First National Bank of Oregon v. Townsend, 27 Or.App. 103, 555 P.2d 477 (1976) where the court held that an ambiguous document entitled Warranty Timber and Mineral Deed passed a full fee simple interest.

68. Hedding v. Schauble, 146 Minn. 95, 177 N.W. 1019 (1920).

69. 293 S.W.2d 124 (1956).   See Comment, 35 Tex.L.Rev. 435 (1957).

70. Leidig v. Hoopes, 288 P.2d 402 (Okl.1955).

71. Glasgow v. Glasgow, 221 S.C. 322, 70 S.E.2d 432 (1952).

72. Willard v. First Church of Christ Scientist, 7 Cal.3d 473, 102 Cal.Rptr. 739, 498 P.2d 987 (1972).   See also Johnson v. Republic Steel Corp., 262 F.2d 108 (6th Cir.1958) and Simpson v. Kistler Inv. Co., 713 P.2d 751 (Wyo. 1986). In the latter case, the court held that mineral interests were properly reserved by deed to all partners, not just the title holder to the land.

that make a direct grant to the third party rather than risk the indirect reservation or exception route.

B. EXECUTION OF THE DEED

Aside from the type of deed used and the elements it must contain, there are certain acts which must be done before the document becomes anything more than a piece of paper. This execution of the deed is summed up in the old saw, "signed, sealed, and delivered." As we have already seen it may have to be attested and acknowledged as well. Some states require the affixing of documentary tax stamps but fortunately the conveyance is valid even though the stamps are omitted. All of these matters of execution are mechanical and require little discussion except for the subject of delivery. Delivery is the final operative act and without it the whole transaction fails. We have already discussed this requirement under gifts and since the same principles control in commercial transfers we will not repeat that material.[73] The most important additional aspect of delivery arises from the use of the escrow agreement and that will be covered in some detail in the next section.

Acceptance should also be considered as a part of execution. Seldom does it raise any real difficulties, since if the conveyance is beneficial it will be presumed and if, in fact, acceptance does not occur until much later because the grantee did not know of the conveyance, then it will be held to relate back to the delivery of the deed. Occasionally, intricate problems can arise and it has been determined that the fiction of relation back will not be used to cut off the intervening rights of a third party, usually a bona fide purchaser for value without notice.[74]

---

73. Page 157 supra. For a case which further illustrates the importance of intent as the key to delivery see Lenhart v. Desmond, 705 P.2d 338 (Wyo.1985). The grantor had placed a warranty deed in his safety deposit box and had given the grantee access to the box. The grantee obtained possession of the deed and recorded it. The court held there was no delivery in view of the grantor's testimony that he did not intend to divest himself irretrievably of his property but rather intended the grantee to have the property at his death.

74. Although in Green v. Skinner, 185 Cal. 435, 197 P. 60 (1921) the court refused to relate the acceptance back to cut off the interest of a surviving joint tenant.

C. DESCRIPTION OF THE LAND

It is difficult to overestimate the importance of an accurate legal description of the land conveyed. Unless the land can be accurately located, the deed is void and a sloppy description may make the title unmerchantable, even though it can ultimately be sustained in court. The improvements on the land need not be identified since they are included in the legal description of the real estate. Conveyancing customs vary in different sections of the country and no attempt will be made to give a technical account of this phase of the law. Most descriptions are based on a survey of the land and, in the final analysis, a new survey may be called for to determine the exact boundaries of a plat of land. The governmental or rectangular survey system controls in vast areas of the nation and the familiar "Southeast one quarter of the southwest one quarter of Section 6 in Township 4 North, Range 4 East of the Third Principal Meridian in _____ County, State of _____" will be the formula for much agricultural acreage.[75] In the East, the metes and bounds description is much more common and this requires a careful drafting of the calls and distances, related to the established monuments which furnish the points of departure. Urban descriptions will usually be based on a subdivision plat which has been recorded and which leads to: "Lot 1 in Block 10 of the McAdams Addition to the City of Pleasantville in the State of Ohio."

The legal standard involved in description is simple—so describe the land that only one possible tract can be identified by the language used. But suppose this simple standard is not met, does the deed fail? Since courts exist to settle disputes, you may be sure that some of these problems will land in the judge's lap. The court has one basic principle to guide it—the intent of the parties, as gathered from the four corners of the deed. All so-called rules of construction are simply guides for ascertaining the intent. There is a strong tendency for the courts to sustain the deed if at all possible, since it is apparent that the parties intended for something to be conveyed or they would never have been involved in the transaction. It is this underlying assumption which accounts for some of the weird descriptions which are upheld.

75. See generally, Cunningham, Stoebuck and Whitman, The Law of Property 723–731 (1984). See also Maley and Thuma, Legal Descriptions of Land (Pamphlet published by Chicago Title and Trust Co., 1955) and Ward, Illinois Law of Title Examination 69–74 (2d ed. 1952).

The cases on legal description are legion but a "feel" for the judicial construction problem may be obtained by a look at ten canons of construction. They are as follows.

1. The construction prevails which is most favorable to the grantee, i.e., the language of the deed is construed against the grantor. If the deed contains two descriptions, the grantee can select that which is most favorable to him. This canon is based on the presumption that the grantor drafted the deed and, if an ambiguity has resulted, he has only himself to blame. As in insurance law, where the policy is typically construed against the insurer, this canon is frequently the unstated premise in a case otherwise inexplicable.[76]

2. If the deed contains two descriptions, one ambiguous and the other unambiguous, the latter prevails in order to sustain the deed. This is not so likely to happen with modern, short form deeds but with the old, prolix instruments it was not uncommon.

3. Extrinsic evidence will be allowed to explain a latent ambiguity but a patent ambiguity must be resolved within the four corners of the deed.[77] This old chestnut has lost much of its validity but it still must be reckoned with. It was based on the idea that if the defect was latent (not apparent to the parties when the deed was drafted) evidence of surrounding circumstances should be admitted to clarify intent, but if it was patent (apparent on the face of the document) the parties must have been aware of it when the deed was executed and no extrinsic evidence is necessary. It has long been clear that this canon is easily controlled by the determination of what is latent or patent and many writers have called for abolition of the distinction.[78]

4. Monuments control distances and courses; courses control distances; and quantity is the least reliable guide of all.[79] In a metes and bounds description, it is relatively easy to start with a

76. See Hall v. Eaton, 139 Mass. 217, 29 N.E. 660 (1885) which makes little sense on any other basis.

77. Walters v. Tucker, 281 S.W.2d 843 (Mo.1955).

78. McBaine, The Rule Against Disturbing Plain Meaning of Writings, 31 Cal.L.Rev. 145 (1943). In a footnote it is pointed out that the distinction "is gradually disappearing" and the hope is expressed that the time will soon come "when it will be of interest only to students engaged in tracing the history of law through periods of formalism to a period of realism."

79. Pritchard v. Rebori, 135 Tenn. 328, 186 S.W. 121 (1916). Not all commentators would agree that courses should control distances in cases of conflict. See 1 Fitch, Abstracts and Titles to Real Property 304 (1954). "The weight of authority appears to be that no rule governs for preference of one over the other where courses and distances conflict, and that the whole description must be considered for the purpose of determining the intention of the parties. However, there are several cases holding that in conflict between the two, courses control distances." See also Application of Sing Chong Co. Limited, 1 Hawaii App. 236, 617 P.2d 578 (1980).

known monument (the side of a road, a stream, a rock, etc.), move in a stated direction or course for a set distance, and end up with an impossible description because one of these elements is in error. This canon tries to set up a priority of reliability, based on presumed intent of the parties. Most monuments would be difficult to mistake so they are probably identified correctly. A course, "northerly at a 90° angle", is more certain than a distance, "thence eighty feet," since most people cannot measure distances with any degree of accuracy with the naked eye. Quantity, which is always hard to estimate, logically brings up the end of the list.

5. Useless or contradictory words may be disregarded as mere surplusage. The difficulty with this canon is patent. Which are the useless or contradictory words? Nonetheless, it states a useful truth since many prolix, confusing descriptions can be pared down to meaningful size to sustain a deed.

6. Particular descriptions control over general descriptions, although a false particular may be disregarded to give effect to a true general description. Any more questions?

7. A description, insufficient in itself, may be made certain through incorporation by reference. This is a particularly useful canon since it enables shorthand reference to be made to involved descriptions in other documents. It can create major merchantability problems, however, if the instrument referred to is not recorded and hence not available for title search.

8. If an exception in a deed is erroneously described, the conveyance is good for the whole tract and title to all of the land passes. Frequently, the grantor will convey Blackacre "except for" a described area. If the description of the exception is faulty, it could be argued that the entire deed should fail but this canon would sustain the larger grant at the expense of the grantor who made the error.

9. When a tract of land is bound by a monument which has width, such as a highway or a stream, the boundary line extends to the center, provided the grantor owns that far, unless the deed manifests an intention to the contrary.[80] The converse of this canon would lead to undesirable policy results. Suppose *A,* who owns to the center of a highway, conveys to *B,* but the description uses the edge of the road as one boundary. Years pass and the highway is vacated so that the easement of public use is removed. At this point, the narrow strip of land becomes valuable due to the

---

80. Bowers v. Atchison, T. and S.F. Ry. Co., 119 Kan. 202, 237 P. 913, 42 A.L.R. 228 (1925).

For an excellent recent discussion of this canon and the exceptions to it see City of Albany v. State of New York, 28 N.Y.2d 352, 321 N.Y.S.2d 877, 270 N.E.2d 705 (1971). See also Roeder Co. v. Burlington Northern, Inc., 105 Wash. 2d 567, 716 P.2d 855 (1986) and Parr v. Worley, 93 N.M. 229, 599 P.2d 382 (1979).

discovery of oil or a change in the direction of urban growth. Who owns the strip? If the parties thought of it at all, they probably intended to transfer whatever land the grantor owned since the retention of a strip under an existing highway would be unreasonable. To prevent endless litigation over narrow strips and gores of land, the courts, in general, have followed the rule stated above.

10. A description in a deed includes the appurtenances to the tract even though they are not specifically mentioned in the deed.[81] Normally, only that portion of the land passes to the grantee which is specifically described in the deed. However, there are interests in the land which are appurtenant to the described tract in such a way that they have no existence apart from their parasitical attachment to the host premises. Thus, if *A* owns Blackacre and has an access road across Whiteacre to the highway, a conveyance of Blackacre to *B* will include the appurtenant easement even though not described in the conveyance.[82]

A study of the canons will reveal that they overlap in their statements of law and that some of them are contradictory. Moreover, it should be clear that any one of them will yield to a clear manifestation of intent, which is always the courts' major guideline. Even so, they serve a useful purpose, if only as a point of departure, and do give some degree of predictability in an uncertain area of the law.

Two additional points should be brought to your attention. Even though the description in the deed is unambiguous it may no longer state the true boundaries of the land. The parties may have orally agreed to a new fence line, built the fence, and treated it as the boundary for a long period of time. Thus, the doctrine of acquiescence may have settled a boundary that is, in fact, different from that shown by the records.[83] Only a physical inspection of the premises and, perhaps, a survey can clarify this situation. The Statute of Limitations may affect the case also since title to land not described in the deed may have been acquired by adverse possession.[84]

Occasionally, the description is so general that a look at the deed tells you little, yet the intent of the parties is clear. Thus, a conveyance of "all lands and real estate belonging to the said party of the first part, wherever the same may be situated," has been sustained.[85] A more difficult problem is the conveyance of a stated number of acres out of a much larger tract, without indicat-

81. Stockdale v. Yerden, 220 Mich. 444, 190 N.W. 225 (1922).

82. For further treatment of easements see p. 368, infra.

83. Provonsha v. Pitman, 6 Utah 2d 26, 305 P.2d 486 (1957).

84. Gregory v. Thorrez, 227 Mich. 197, 269 N.W. 142 (1936).

85. Pettigrew v. Dobbelaar, 63 Cal. 396 (1883).

ing where the land is located in the larger area. This little gem has received a variety of judicial reactions, ranging from a determination that the conveyance was void because too indefinite and uncertain.[86] to a finding that an undivided interest in the whole was transferred, making the grantor and the grantee tenants in common of the land.[87] An interesting mid-point was reached where the description called for "one acre and a half in the northwest *corner* of section five." This was held to mean a square of that quantity in the corner since the governmental survey laid out the state in rectangular forms.[88]

Even this brief discussion should be sufficient to establish the truth of the earlier statement that the courts struggle to uphold the validity of a deed where at all possible. The lawyer, as draftsman and property planner, should strive for accuracy and certainty, but the lawyer as litigator must realize that he can build a successful case on precious little, if the intent can be established.

SECTION 4. THE ESCROW AGREEMENT

The sale of real property can be conducted without the use of an escrow agreement. In rural areas and in smaller communities it is not usually involved because the parties know and trust each other and the title questions tend to be less complex. In big metropolitan centers it is much more likely to be a part of the transaction and frequently is as common as the contract and the deed. Also, an understanding of escrow will throw considerable light on the always troublesome issue of delivery. For these reasons, plus the fact that escrow usually receives scant treatment in basic property texts, an extended discussion is included here.[89]

For at least five centuries, the escrow has served as a convenient mechanism for closing real estate transactions.[90] The use of

86. Harris v. Woodard, 130 N.C. 580, 41 S.E. 790 (1902).

87. Morehead v. Hall, 126 N.C. 213, 35 S.E. 428 (1900).

88. Bybee v. Hageman, 66 Ill. 519 (1873).

89. The rest of the material on escrow is taken, in edited form, from an article, "Escrows—Their Use and Value," by John Mann, formerly associate general counsel of the Chicago Title and Trust Company. This article was first published in 1949 University of Illinois Law Forum 398 as a part of a symposium on real estate transactions. At that time Professor Cribbet was faculty editor of the Law Forum. The article states so clearly the principles called for at this point that it seemed wiser to use it, with the author's permission, than to draft a new statement. Certain changes have been made in the text and many of the copious footnotes have been omitted.

90. The practice of depositing deeds as escrows was recognized by the Eng-

this familiar device involves the deposit of a deed or other document with a third party to be held by the latter pending performance of certain conditions. When those conditions have been performed, the third party is authorized to deliver the deed or other document to the person then entitled thereto.

Perhaps the simplest illustration of such an escrow transaction is the deposit by the vendor of his deed with a third party to be delivered over to the purchaser upon payment of the purchase price. Thus a nonresident vendor of an Illinois farm may forward his deed to an Illinois bank or trust company in the city where the purchaser resides with instructions to deliver the deed to the purchaser if and when the purchase money has been duly deposited for the vendor's account. In this way the vendor can guard against delivery of the deed without concurrent receipt of the purchase price. Or a vendee who has entered into a contract for the purchase of a home where the purchase price is to be paid in monthly installments over a period of years may insist that the vendor deposit his deed with a bank or trust company to be delivered if and when the purchase price has eventually been paid in full. The deed will thus be available for delivery when the last installment is paid some years later, even though the vendor may have died in the interim.

Generally this basic type of escrow transaction between vendor and purchaser, sometimes referred to as a "Deed and Money Escrow," involves conditions relating to title. Thus it may be provided that the third party is to deliver the deed to the purchaser and turn over the purchase money to the vendor only if and when the abstract of title has been examined and approved by the purchaser's attorney. In Cook County, where the great volume of instruments continuously passing through the recorder's office makes it impossible to check the status of a title as of any current date, the third party is frequently authorized to record the vendor's deed as soon as the purchase money has been deposited by the purchaser and before any investigation has been made with respect to title. In addition to the purchase money, the purchaser also deposits with the third party a quitclaim deed back to the vendor. After the vendor's deed has been recorded, a title examination is made up to and including the recording of that deed, and if the title is ready to be guaranteed in the purchaser or is otherwise approved, the third party disburses the purchase money to the vendor and returns the quitclaim deed to the purchaser. If

---

lish common law courts at least as early as the first half of the fifteenth century. 4 Tiffany, The Law of Real Property, § 1052 (3rd ed. 1939). The general subject of escrows is dealt with by early law commentators. Coke, Commentary Upon Littleton 36a (1628); Sheppard's Touchstone *58–59 (7th ed. by Hilliard 1820).

the title cannot be guaranteed or is not found good in the purchaser, the third party records the latter's quitclaim deed in order to put the vendor back in status quo and returns the purchase money to the purchaser.

There may, of course, be many variations in the form of a "Deed and Money Escrow," depending upon the facts of the particular case. For example, the third party is frequently authorized to use a part of the purchase money in discharging liens and encumbrances on the property so that the purchaser will receive an unencumbered title, as agreed.

Another common type of escrow transaction is that known as a "Money Lender's Escrow." In general this involves deposit of the proceeds of a mortgage loan with a third party to be disbursed as directed when satisfactory evidence has been furnished showing the mortgage to be a valid first lien. This type of escrow transaction not only provides the mortgagee with a convenient method of protecting its interests, but it may also be used to advantage by an owner who has made a mortgage loan for the purpose of refunding an existing mortgage or of paying accumulated taxes and special assessments, judgments, mechanic's liens, or other encumbrances on the property. . . .[91]

The foregoing illustrate only a few of the varied forms which escrow transactions may assume.[92] In essence, however, they involve as their basic framework the deposit of deeds and other documents with a third party to be delivered upon the performance of specified conditions.

It is well settled, of course, that the use of escrows is not restricted to real estate transactions. Instruments other than deeds for the conveyance of real estate may legally be deposited as escrows.[93] Indeed, the Illinois Supreme Court has said that "the term 'escrow,' though usually applied to deeds, is equally applicable to all written instruments."[94] This section, however, is limited to a discussion of "escrows" in relation to real estate transactions. It deals entirely with the escrow as a device for the closing

---

91. An extended discussion of a "Deed and Money, Proceeds–of–Loan Escrow" is omitted.

92. A very common type of transaction used in Cook County in closing sales of real estate is that known as the "Joint Order Escrow." Here the contract for the sale of real estate and the earnest money are deposited with a bank or trust company, subject to the joint direction of the parties in interest. The vendor is thus assured that in event the transaction fails, the contract will not be recorded, clouding his title,

and the purchaser is assured that in event the deal fails, the earnest money will be available for repayment to him.

93. The term has been applied, although technically somewhat inaptly, it is said, to money deposited to be held until the performance of a condition. Nash v. Normandy State Bank, 201 S.W.2d 299 (Mo.Sup.Ct.1947). Compare American Service Co. v. Henderson, 120 F.2d 525 (4th Cir.1941).

94. Main v. Pratt, 276 Ill. 218, 224, 114 N.E. 576, 578 (1916).

of sales of real estate and the transfer of title between vendors and purchasers.

A. TERMINOLOGY

An "escrow" has been defined to be "any written instrument which by its terms imposes a legal obligation, and which is deposited by the grantor, promisor or obligor, or his agent, with a stranger or third party, to be kept by the depositary until the performance of a condition or the happening of a certain event and then to be delivered over to the grantee, promisee or obligee."[95] It thus appears that the term "escrow" in its strict technical sense characterizes the instrument while it is being held by the third party awaiting performance of the condition upon which it is to be delivered. An instrument for the conveyance of real estate while so held on deposit is not accurately speaking a deed because it has not been completely delivered. It is, on the contrary, an "escrow." Thus it has been said that an escrow differs from a deed only in respect to its delivery.[96]

Present-day usage, however, would seem to justify some enlargement of this technically correct terminology. Both judges and lawyers alike so commonly refer to "deeds" being deposited as escrows that this convenient form of expression would now seem to have the sanction of common usage. Furthermore, the term "escrow" is often used in a broad sense to describe the general arrangement under which an instrument is deposited with a third person to be delivered upon the performance of a condition. Thus instead of speaking of an instrument being deposited "as an escrow," it is often said today that it is deposited "in escrow." It has likewise become common usage to refer to the parties as "creating an escrow" for the purpose of closing a real estate transaction. There would appear to be no reason why this modern and enlarged use of the term "escrow" should lead to any confusion or misunderstanding.

95. Johnson v. Wallden, 342 Ill. 201, 206, 173 N.E. 790, 792 (1930).

96. Fitch v. Bunch, 30 Cal. 208, 212 (1866). In his Commentaries, Blackstone said: "A delivery may be either absolute, that is, to the party or grantee himself; or to a third person, to hold till some conditions be performed on the part of the grantee; in which last case it is not delivered as a *deed*, but as an *escrow;* that is, as a scroll or writing, which is not to take effect as a deed till the conditions be performed; and then it is a deed to all intents and purposes." 2 Bl.Comm. 307 (1765).

The third-party depositary is sometimes called the "escrow agent" or "escrowee." [97] The directions to the depositary are frequently characterized as the "escrow agreement." [98]

B. WHY ESCROWS ARE USED

Inasmuch as the escrow has been so long used as a convenient device for closing sales of real estate between vendors and purchasers, it is obvious that it possesses certain practical advantages. Some of these may be enumerated as follows:

1. The use of an escrow renders the transaction less likely to "fall through." The sale in its material aspects is very largely executed by one or both of the parties at the time the contract is signed or shortly afterwards. Only mechanical details are left to be carried out through the instrumentality of the third-party escrowee.

2. Where an escrow is not employed, death of the vendor after the contract of sale has been executed but before the transaction has been finally closed often raises complications with respect to the subsequent execution of a proper deed. A judicial proceeding may even be necessary in such a case.[99] However, where the vendor has executed a deed and deposited it as an escrow during his lifetime, the escrowee may, notwithstanding the grantor's death, properly deliver the deed upon performance of the conditions, and a deed so delivered will operate as a valid conveyance to the purchaser.[1]

3. If an escrow is used, the concurrent acts involved in a sale of real estate can ordinarily be performed in such a manner as to protect more adequately the interests of both vendor and purchaser. Thus where a sale is closed without an escrow and the vendor delivers a deed to the purchaser and receives the latter's check

---

97. The term "escrowee" is probably to be preferred over "escrow agent" inasmuch as there seems to be a growing tendency to regard the third-party depositary as being in effect a trustee. Dodson v. National Title Ins. Co., 159 Fla. 371, 31 So.2d 402 (1947); Tomasello, Jr., Rec'r v. Murphy, 100 Fla. 132, 129 So. 328 (1930); Stark v. Chicago Title and Trust Co., 316 Ill.App. 353, 45 N.E.2d 81 (1st Dist.1942).

98. This terminology is used in Clodfelter v. Van Fossan, 394 Ill. 29, 37, 67 N.E.2d 182, 183 (1946). And see

Home Insurance Co. v. Wilson, 210 Ky. 237, 241, 275 S.W. 691, 692 (1925).

99. Ill.Rev.Stat. ch. 29, §§ 2–8 (1985).

1. The conveyance will in such a case be sustained as against a claim that the grantor's death terminated the escrowee's authority to make a valid delivery, on the theory that the deed relates back to and takes effect as of the time of its original deposit with the escrowee. The deed would also be sustained on like reasoning in.event of the grantor's subsequent incompetency.

(frequently large) in return, there is sometimes a lurking fear in the mind of the vendor, which he may hesitate to express, that the check may not clear. It is a simple matter, however, to provide at the outset in an escrow agreement that the purchaser's check be cashed by the escrowee and the deed delivered only when the check has cleared. The utility of the escrow where problems of concurrent performance are involved can also be illustrated by the situation which arises where current property taxes are to be prorated between the parties but the amount of the tax bill has not been ascertained at the time the sale is closed. If a final adjustment is made on the basis of the known taxes for the preceding year, one party will actually lose if the current tax bill when later rendered should differ from that of the preceding year. There generally is a variance, and where a large transaction is involved, the loss could be substantial. The parties may be required, however, under the terms of an escrow agreement to leave a sufficient amount on deposit with the escrowee to cover the current tax bill when it comes out. The bill can then be paid by the escrowee, and the excess remaining in its hands can be so distributed as to adjust the rights of the parties exactly.

4. Particularly is the escrow convenient in closing complex real estate transactions involving the interests of a number of different parties. For example, an escrow may be used by a purchaser as a convenient means of borrowing money on the security of property he is about to acquire and of using the proceeds of the loan as a part of the purchase price.[2] It may, as already indicated, be used to consummate a four-party transaction whereby an existing mortgage is replaced by a new mortgage concurrently with the completion of the sale between vendor and purchaser. It may be used to advantage in closing a transaction looking to the consolidation of numerous titles into one ownership. In general the escrow is a particularly convenient closing device in that type of case where a clearing house is needed for involved real estate transactions.[3]

5. The use of the escrow often proves of advantage to the real estate broker by relieving him of mechanical details, which he

---

2. In such a situation the seller is willing to convey, provided he receives the purchase money. The mortgage lender, who is supplying a substantial part of the purchase money, is willing to pay out the proceeds of the loan, provided he receives a valid title. Use of the escrow assures each party he will receive that which his particular interest in the transaction requires.

3. In fact it would seem that the lawyer might well give consideration to the use of an escrow when planning the mechanical procedure for closing any complicated transaction, whether one involving real estate or not, particularly where a number of interests are involved. Thus the escrow has often been used to advantage in working out complex compromises of pending litigation where the concurrent adjustment of various adverse interests is required.

might otherwise be expected to perform. Where an escrow is used, the earnest money, which would ordinarily be held by the broker, can be deposited with the escrowee; and at the same time, provision can be made in the escrow agreement under which the broker will still be authorized in effect to look to the earnest money for the payment of his commission. The broker is thus relieved of the responsibility and clerical detail of maintaining the earnest money as a separate trust account.

6. In a large county such as Cook, where the volume of daily transactions in the recorder's office is so great that it is physically impossible to ascertain the actual state of a title at any precise current moment, the use of an escrow may be required in order to make certain that the purchaser's interests are protected. In a smaller county it is often possible for the parties to meet at the courthouse, check the records in the recorder's office and in the offices of the clerks of the circuit and county courts from the date of the last abstract continuation down to the current moment so as to make certain that nothing recent has occurred to affect the vendor's title, and thereupon close the transaction forthwith and record the deed to the purchaser. Under such circumstances the purchaser can be reasonably sure, in most instances, that his interests have been protected against any last minute changes in title. In Cook County, however, the volume of daily business at the county courthouse is so great that it is impossible to ascertain from the records the status of a title as of any current point of time. There, as previously indicated, this situation is frequently met by use of the escrow, the escrowee being authorized to record the deed to the purchaser as soon as the purchase money is in its hands but before it is disbursed to the grantor. The title can then be later checked to include the actual recording of the deed, and when title is ready to be guaranteed in the purchaser or is otherwise approved, the escrowee is authorized to disburse the purchase money to the vendor. A quitclaim deed from the purchaser back to the vendor is customarily deposited with the escrowee to be recorded in event the title should not be found good in the purchaser. In the absence of such an arrangement, a purchaser who pays the purchase money to the vendor and receives the vendor's deed in concurrent transactions must necessarily be without positive knowledge at the time of such payment as to the condition of the record title during the highly important interval of time immediately preceding the completion of the sale.

C. SELECTION OF THE DEPOSITARY

One of the first questions presented to a vendor and a purchaser who desire to close the sale by means of an escrow is the selection of an escrowee. In general it would seem clear that the escrowee selected should be a third party who is a stranger to the transaction.

The Illinois Supreme Court has said that the "rule is established in this State that a deed cannot be delivered to the grantee as an escrow, to take effect upon a condition not appearing upon the face of the deed, but such deed becomes absolute at law unless delivery is made to a stranger." [4] In the early case of Price v. Pittsburg, Ft. Wayne and Chicago R.R. Co.,[5] it was contended that deeds to a railroad company had been deposited as escrows with an attorney for the company to be delivered only upon the performance of certain conditions. The Illinois Court held, however, that since the deposit had not been made with a stranger but with the grantee's attorney, the deeds took effect immediately. This holding does not appear to have been overruled or modified by subsequent decisions.[6]

It is true that the modern tendency seems to be to relax in some measure the rigidity of the "third-party stranger" rule,[7] and delivery of a deed as an escrow to the attorney who advised the grantor and drew the deed for him has in some cases been sustained.[8] In order to eliminate any possible question, however, it would appear to be the prudent course for the parties to select a disinterested third party as escrowee who is neither the agent nor attorney for either vendor or purchaser.

D. REQUIREMENTS AS TO WRITINGS

Another important preliminary problem which may arise where a sale of real estate is to be closed by means of an escrow

---

4. Szymczak v. Szymczak, 306 Ill. 541, 546, 138 N.E. 218, 220 (1923). For a discussion of the legal difficulties involved in the attempt to deliver a deed "in escrow" (i.e. subject to conditions not appearing on the face of the deed) see p. 158 supra. See also State, By Pai v. Thom, 58 Hawaii 8, 563 P.2d 982 (1977).

5. 34 Ill. 13 (1864).

6. See Clark v. Harper, 215 Ill. 24, 74 N.E. 61 (1905).

7. Gronewold v. Gronewold, 304 Ill. 11, 136 N.E. 489 (1922). And see Levin v. Nedelman, 141 N.J.Eq. 23, 55 A.2d 826 (1947); 19 Am.Jur., Escrow, § 15 (1939); Note, 11 A.L.R. 1174 (1921).

8. Van Epps v. Arbuckle, 332 Ill. 551, 164 N.E. 1 (1928).

relates to the nature and extent of the writings or memoranda necessary in order to meet the requirements of the Statute of Frauds.[9]

The Illinois rule is that a binding and irrevocable escrow between a vendor and purchaser must be based on a contract of sale between those parties which is enforceable under the Statute of Frauds. The Illinois Supreme Court has held that in the absence of such a contract, a deposit by the vendor with a third party of a deed in ordinary form for the conveyance of the real estate to be delivered to the purchaser upon payment of the purchase price constitutes a mere revocable transaction only, and the vendor may, under such circumstances, cancel the instructions to the third party and recall the undelivered deed at any time before there has been a performance by the vendee sufficient to take the case out of the Statute.[10] Some commentators have criticized this view on principle,[11] but it, nevertheless, appears to be in accord with the weight of authority from other jurisdictions.[12]

It has also been held that a deed in ordinary form does not in and of itself supply the necessary written memorandum.[13]

9. For a general discussion of the Statute of Frauds see pp. 160 to 166 supra.

10. Johnson v. Wallden, 342 Ill. 201, 173 N.E. 790 (1930); Main v. Pratt, 276 Ill. 218, 114 N.E. 576 (1916); Kopp v. Reiter, 146 Ill. 437, 34 N.E. 942 (1893). See also Mode v. Whitley, 30 F.Supp. 129 (D.C.Ill.1939). It is indicated by the language in Main v. Pratt, supra, and Johnson v. Wallden, supra, that this principle would not apply to the situation where a deed is delivered to a third person with instructions to deliver it to the grantee therein named upon the happening of an event certain to occur, such as the death of the grantor. In the latter type of case, the decisive issue of whether the grantor did or did not intend to reserve control over the deed at the time it was delivered to the third person may be shown by what the grantor said and did at the time. McReynolds v. Miller, 372 Ill. 151, 22 N.E.2d 951 (1939); Johnson v. Fleming, 301 Ill. 139, 133 N.E. 667 (1922).

11. Aigler, Is a Contract Necessary to Create an Effective Escrow?, 16 Mich.L.Rev. 569 (1918); Comment, Aigler, Necessity of Valid Contract to Support Escrow, 15 Mich.L.Rev. 579 (1917). Compare, however, Bigelow, Conditional Deliveries of Deeds of Land, 26 Harv. L.Rev. 565, 567–75, 578 (1913). See, in general, Ballantine, Nature of Escrows and Conditional Delivery, 3 Ill.L.Bull. 3, 14–18 (1920); Ballantine, Delivery in Escrow and the Parol Evidence Rule, 29 Yale L.J. 826, 830–32 (1920); Note, 17 Minn.L.Rev. 817 (1933).

12. Ballantine, Nature of Escrows and Conditional Delivery, 3 Ill.L.Bull. 3, 14–18 (1920). In this article (pp. 15, 16), Dean Ballantine observed: "Tiffany says that the view that a contract is necessary to a conditional delivery 'has no considerations of policy or convenience in its favor. No doubt the courts have been influenced in their present tendency to require a contract to uphold escrows by an instinctive hostility to this method of evading the statute of frauds and the parol evidence rule. There is a strong policy against having contracts and conveyances of land rest any more than is necessary in parol, or having title depend upon the performance of unwritten conditions.' "

13. Cases cited under note 10 supra.

A further question, however, still remains. Is it essential in such a case that the instructions to the third-party escrowee also be reduced to writing and signed by the latter?

While this question does not appear to have been fully discussed in the Illinois decisions, yet in Osby v. Reynolds [14] the Illinois Supreme Court pointed out that it was "well settled that the conditions upon which a deed is delivered in escrow may be proved by parol evidence." That statement is not, it would seem, inconsistent with the Illinois holdings previously mentioned [15] to the effect that an enforceable escrow for the closing of a sale of real estate must rest on a contract between the vendor and purchaser enforceable under the Statute of Frauds. [16] The agreement between the vendor and purchaser which fixes the basic rights of those contracting parties may be distinguished, it seems, from the escrow arrangement which merely provides the mechanics by which those basic rights are to be carried out.

This distinction was long ago pointed out by Mr. Chief Justice Ryan of the Wisconsin Supreme Court in the following apt language:

> "I have no doubt that an *escrow* may be proved by parol. The difficulty here is not in the proof of the alleged *escrow*, but in the proof of the contract of sale and purchase itself. When there is a valid contract under the statute, the papers constituting it, or executed in compliance with it, may be delivered in *escrow*, and the *escrow* may be proved by parol. But the validity of the *escrow* rests on the validity of the contract; and the validity of the contract rests on the statute." [17]

It would seem, therefore, that in view of the above-mentioned principle a vendor and a purchaser should be able to create by parol a valid and binding escrow agreement with a third-party escrowee, under which a deed deposited by the vendor as an escrow is to be delivered to the purchaser upon the performance of certain conditions—provided, of course, that the rights of the vendor and purchaser have been definitely fixed by a written agreement between themselves sufficient to meet the requirements of the Statute of Frauds.

14. 260 Ill. 576, 583, 103 N.E. 556, 559 (1913) citing 1 Devlin, The Law of Real Property and Deeds, § 312a (3d ed. 1911).

15. Note 10 supra.

16. Stanton v. Miller, 58 N.Y. 192 (1874); Akers v. Brooks, 103 Okl. 98, 229 P. 544 (1924); McLain v. Healy, 98 Wash. 489, 168 P. 1 (1917); Nichols v. Oppermann, 6 Wash. 618, 34 P. 162 (1893); Jozefowicz v. Leickem, 174 Wis. 475, 182 N.W. 729 (1921); Campbell v. Thomas, 42 Wis. 437, 24 Am.Rep. 427 (1877).

17. Campbell v. Thomas, supra note 16.

There appear to be strong practical considerations, however, why the directions to the escrowee should be reduced to writing.

In the first place, it is doubtful whether a responsible escrowee would consent to act unless its duties were clearly and specifically defined by written instructions. The sound view undoubtedly is that aside from the proposition that an enforceable escrow agreement may rest in parol, nevertheless, where such an agreement has been reduced to writing and is neither ambiguous nor uncertain, parol evidence is inadmissible to modify or vary its terms.[18] Hence where the instructions to the escrowee have been reduced to writing, the latter is in a position to rely on such written instructions as specifically defining and limiting its duties and responsibilities. Without instructions in writing, misunderstanding and uncertainty with respect to the escrowee's duties might well result, and a responsible escrowee would doubtless insist upon obviating such possible difficulties.

In the second place, this effect of written directions to obviate possible misunderstanding and uncertainty with respect to the escrowee's duties likewise operates to the benefit of the vendor and the purchaser. An escrowee, in reasonable doubt as to the proper performance of its duties, is not required to decide close questions at its own risk.[19] It is accordingly to the interests of both vendor and purchaser to have the duties of the escrowee clearly and certainly defined in writing since that will tend to eliminate the possibility of delay and expense which would likely ensue if a controversy over the exact terms of the directions to the escrowee should make it necessary for the latter to resort to a judicial proceeding for a determination of its rights and duties.

Finally, written instructions to the escrowee tend to minimize any risk that the vendor and the purchaser may inadvertently run afoul of the Statute of Frauds. It is easy enough in theory to differentiate between the contract of sale, which must be evidenced by writing to satisfy the Statute, and the incidental instructions to the escrowee, which may rest in parol. In actual practice, however, there is always the lurking danger that the two may through inadvertence not be kept separate and distinct. A

---

18. Clodfelter v. Van Fossan, 394 Ill. 29, 67 N.E.2d 182 (1946); Note, 49 A.L.R. 1529 (1927). In Colorado Title & Trust Co. v. Roberts, 80 Colo. 258, 259, 250 P. 641 (1926), the court said: "Defendant claims that the rule against the variation of written contracts by parol does not apply to escrow instructions. It would seem that in reason the rule ought to be especially beneficial there. How can a bank holding perhaps scores of escrows be expected to remember oral instructions given in connection with written ones? We are not willing to assent to the claim of the defendant in error."

19. Stark v. Chicago Title and Trust Co., 316 Ill.App. 353, 45 N.E.2d 81 (1st Dist.1942). And see Note, 60 A.L.R. 638 (1929).

note of warning is sounded in Jozefowicz v. Leickem,[20] wherein the Supreme Court of Wisconsin says:

> "To constitute a true escrow the contract of sale must be fully executed and nothing left but the transfer of title when the terms of the escrow are complied with. Those terms, however, cannot embody a substantive part of the contract of sale, resting in parol, though the fact of escrow may be shown by parol."

E. SPECIFIC DIRECTIONS TO ESCROWEE

Regardless of whether the directions to the escrowee are made a part of the contract of sale between the vendor and vendee or whether they are set forth in a separate escrow agreement, it is important that the draftsman should see to it that they are complete, detailed, and specific.

The need for particularity is well illustrated by Ortman v. Kane.[21] The directions to the escrowee were, in that case, incorporated in the basic contract between the vendor and purchaser. This contract, after setting forth the terms and provisions of sale between the vendor and purchaser, recited that a deed had been executed by the vendor and delivered to the third-party escrowee (naming him) together with a copy of the contract. It was provided that the deed should be held by the escrowee in escrow and delivered to the purchaser upon his full compliance with the provisions of this contract. Except for a stipulation that upon default of the purchaser the escrowee was to surrender all papers, including the deed, to the vendor, nothing further was said with respect to any steps to be taken by the escrowee.

The Court pointed out that under these facts, the escrowee was not authorized "to accept the balance of the purchase money or to do anything else in connection with the transaction except deliver the deed after the contract had been complied with" by the purchaser. "The depositary of an escrow," said the Court, "is a special and not a general agent. His powers are limited to the conditions of the deposit."

Ordinarily an important object of an escrow transaction is to authorize the depositary to receive the balance of the purchase money in order that the vendor may be sure that the purchase money has actually come into its hands for his account before the

20. 174 Wis. 475, 478–79, 182 N.W. 729, 730 (1921).

21. 389 Ill. 613, 621, 60 N.E.2d 93, 97 (1945).

deed is delivered over to the purchaser. The Ortman case makes it clear, however, that in order to effectuate that purpose, express authority must be conferred upon the escrowee to receive such payment. The same principle would apply, it seems, to other steps to be taken by the escrowee, such as proration of taxes and similar items, return of the deed and other papers to the vendor in certain eventualities, and even the affixing of proper revenue stamps to the deed before it is finally delivered to the purchaser. Each step to be taken by the escrowee should be covered with certainty and particularity.

F. WHEN DEED TAKES EFFECT

Where a sale of real estate between vendor and purchaser is to be closed by means of an escrow, with final delivery of the deed by the escrowee dependent upon the performance of some uncertain future condition, the general rule is that the escrow will have no effect as a conveyance, and no estate will pass until the event has happened and the second delivery has been made, or at least until the grantee has become absolutely entitled to such a delivery.[22]

This general rule is, however, subject to the important qualification that where the condition has been fully performed, and the deed delivered by the escrowee, it will under certain circumstances be treated as relating back to and taking effect at the time of its original deposit as an escrow.[23] Thus the Illinois Supreme Court

22. Fitch v. Miller, 200 Ill. 170, 65 N.E. 650 (1902); Skinner v. Baker, 79 Ill. 496 (1875). The sound view appears to be that upon full performance of the condition, title will be regarded as having vested in the grantee notwithstanding a want of formal delivery of the deed by the escrowee. Park Avenue Church v. Park Avenue Colored Church, 244 Ill.App. 148 (1st Dist.1927); 19 Am.Jur., Escrow, § 25 (1939).

23. In general the doctrine of "relation back" does not come into play unless the condition upon which the instrument was deposited as an escrow has been fully performed. County of Calhoun v. American Emigrant Company, 93 U.S. (3 Otto) 124, 23 L.Ed. 826 (1876). Thus where both parties abandon the escrow agreement, a subsequent delivery of the deed will not relate back. Whitney v. Sherman, 178

Cal. 435, 173 P. 931 (1918). And where the grantee wrongfully obtains possession of the instrument held as an escrow, the doctrine of "relation back" will not be applied even though the grantor afterward ratifies the delivery. Mosley v. Magnolia Petroleum Co., 45 N.M. 230, 114 P.2d 740 (1941); Carlisle v. National Oil & Development Co., 108 Okl. 18, 234 P. 629 (1924). And see Illinois Central R.R. Co. v. McCullough, 59 Ill. 166 (1871). However, in Meyers v. Manufacturers & Traders Nat. Bank, 332 Pa. 180, 2 A.2d 768 (1938), where a deed to the purchaser at a tax sale was deposited by county commissioners as an escrow, to be delivered to the purchaser (who had also deposited the purchase money) when title had been adjudged good, it was held the grantee could, in view of the doctrine of "rela-

has said that "the instrument will be treated as relating back to and taking effect at the time of its original deposit in escrow, where a resort to this fiction is necessary to give the deed effect to prevent injustice, or to effectuate the intention of the parties." [24]

G. INSTANCES OF "RELATION BACK"

The operation of this doctrine of "relation back" can be illustrated best by reference to certain concrete situations.

Death of grantor. Where the grantor dies before the condition is performed, his death would, if the doctrine of "relation back" were not employed, operate as a revocation of the escrowee's authority to make a valid delivery to the grantee upon subsequent performance. Accordingly in such a case, the rule is universal that the transaction will be effectuated by holding the conveyance operative as of the time when the deed was originally deposited as an escrow, and the grantee's title will for such purpose relate back to that date.[25]

Dower of grantor's widow. Likewise, where the grantor dies before the condition is performed, the doctrine of "relation back" has been applied to protect the grantee against a claim of dower by the grantor's widow where such a claim could not have been properly asserted had the grantor's deed been unconditionally delivered at the time it was deposited as an escrow.[26]

Incompetency of grantor. The doctrine of "relation back" is also applied to effectuate the escrow transaction where the grantor becomes incompetent before the condition has been performed.[27]

Death of grantee. Where the grantee dies after the deed has been deposited as an escrow but before the condition has been performed, the doctrine of "relation back" will be applied to

tion back," maintain a suit to confirm title before final delivery of the deed.

24. Clodfelter v. Van Fossan, 394 Ill. 29, 37, 67 N.E.2d 182, 186 (1946).

25. The authorities generally are collected in a Note, 117 A.L.R. 69, 74–78 (1938). Some later cases are Ryckman v. Cooper, 291 Mich. 556, 289 N.W. 252 (1939); Anselman v. Oklahoma City University, 197 Okl. 529, 172 P.2d 782 (1946); Morris v. Clark, 100 Utah 252, 112 P.2d 153 (1941), cert. denied 314 U.S. 584, 62 S.Ct. 357 (1941).

26. Bucher v. Young, 94 Ind.App. 586, 158 N.E. 581 (1927); First Nat. Bank & Trust Co. v. Scott, 109 N.J.Eq. 244, 156 A. 836 (1931); Vorheis v. Kitch, 8 Phila. 554 (Pa.1871). Compare Tyler v. Tyler, 50 Mont. 65, 144 P. 1090 (1914), where the escrow agreement was in the form of an option to purchase real estate.

27. This is recognized in Price v. Pittsburg, Ft. Wayne and Chicago R.R. Co., 34 Ill. 13, 34 (1864). Authorities generally are collected in the Note, 117 A.L.R. 69, 80 (1938).

sustain the transaction, and the deed may, after the condition has been performed, be delivered by the escrowee to the grantee's heirs.[28]

Conveyance by grantor to a third party. Where the grantor has deposited his deed as an escrow but thereafter, pending performance of the condition, he conveys to a third-party purchaser with notice, it has been held that the doctrine of "relation back" will be applied to protect the title of the grantee under the deed previously deposited as an escrow.[29] However, it appears that the doctrine will not be so applied where the third party to whom the grantor conveys is a bona fide purchaser for value without notice of the escrow.[30]

.   .   .[31]

"Relation back" for one purpose and not others. The fact that the doctrine of "relation back" is applied for one purpose does not necessarily mean that it must be applied for all other purposes in the same transaction.[32]

The fiction of "relation back" would seem to afford an apt illustration of the flexibility of the common law in adapting itself to practical situations. The escrow has long been a convenient mechanism which serves a useful and practical end.[33] The doctrine of "relation back" is the method by which the common law has exempted that particular transaction from certain general rules governing delivery of instruments so that parties may avail themselves of the escrow as a useful, workable device.

H. UNAUTHORIZED DELIVERY AND BONA FIDE PURCHASERS

Where a deed has been deposited as an escrow, the general rule is that unauthorized delivery by the escrowee before the conditions have been complied with conveys no title.[34]

28. Authorities generally will be found in the Note, 117 A.L.R. 69, 79 (1938).

29. Leiter v. Pike, 127 Ill. 287, 20 N.E. 23 (1889); Emmons v. Harding, 162 Ind. 154, 70 N.E. 142 (1904).

30. Heffron v. Flanigan, 37 Mich. 274 (1877); Waldock v. Frisco Lumber Co., 71 Okl. 200, 176 P. 218 (1918).

31. The discussion of ten other instances of relation back is omitted since

they are simply further illustrations of the basic principle.

32. Stone v. Duvall, 77 Ill. 475, 480–81 (1875).

33. "An escrow fills a definite niche in the body of the law." Squire v. Branciforti, 131 Ohio St. 344, 353, 2 N.E.2d 878, 882 (1936).

34. Tucker v. Kanatzar, 373 Ill. 162, 166, 25 N.E.2d 823, 825 (1940).

Suppose, however, that the grantee in such a case records the deed, and thereafter the property passes into the hands of an innocent third party who purchases in good faith and for value in reliance on the public records. Is the latter protected notwithstanding the unauthorized delivery? This question is one upon which there is much conflict of authority.[35] There are strong considerations, it would seem, to support the view that the bona fide purchaser should be protected. One well-known commentator, after stating that this is the better view upon principle and the one supported by the weight of authority, advances the following persuasive reasons why the bona fide purchaser should be accorded protection.[36] The first is based on the familiar doctrine that when a loss has occurred which must fall on one of two innocent persons, it should be borne by him who is the occasion of the loss. A deed deposited as an escrow is ordinarily regular on its face and is capable of clothing the grantee with apparent title. Consequently when the maker of such an instrument has voluntarily parted with the possession of it and delivered it into the care and keeping of a person of his own selection, he should be responsible for the use that may in fact be made of it in a controversy subsequently arising between himself and a bona fide purchaser. Second, a contrary view would tend to render titles insecure. Many real estate transactions are today closed by means of escrows with nothing of record to indicate that fact. If a purchaser could acquire such a title only at his peril, the merchantability of real estate generally as an article of daily commerce would be impaired. These considerations should, it is believed, carry weight with the courts.[37]

Aside from the principle just considered, it is to be noted that a grantor may ratify an unauthorized delivery by the escrowee or estop himself by his conduct from questioning such delivery.[38]

See also Blakeney v. Home Owners' Loan Corp., 192 Okl. 158, 135 P.2d 339 (1943) and Clevenger v. Moore, 126 Okl. 246, 259 P. 219, 54 A.L.R. 1237 (1927).

35. Thompson, Commentaries on the Modern Law of Real Property, §§ 3953–3955 (1924).

36. Id. §§ 3954–55.

37. See Tutt v. Smith, 201 Iowa 107, 204 N.W. 294 (1925); Shurtz v. Colvin, 55 Ohio St. 274, 45 N.E. 527 (1896); Note, 16 Calif.L.Rev. 141–46 (1928).

38. 4 Thompson, op. cit. supra note 88, § 3959. And see Harris v. Geneva

Mill Co., 209 Ala. 538, 96 So. 622 (1923); Home Owners' Loan Corp. v. Ashford, 198 Okl. 481, 179 P.2d 905 (1946); Beck v. Harvey, 196 Okl. 270, 164 P.2d 399 (1944); Hansen v. Bellman, 161 Or. 373, 88 P.2d 295 (1939); Smith v. Goodrich, 167 Ill. 46, 47 N.E. 316 (1897); Illinois Central R.R. Co. v. McCullough, 59 Ill. 166 (1871); Eichlor v. Holroyd, 15 Ill. App. 657 (2d Dist.1885); Note, 48 A.L.R. 405, 424 (1927). Compare Chicago & Great Western Railroad Land Co. v. Peck, 112 Ill. 408, 443–44 (1885).

I. STANDARD OF CARE REQUIRED OF AN ESCROWEE

Most of the escrow work in real estate transactions is handled by corporations (title insurance companies, banks, etc.) which maintain escrow departments. Their service is usually professional and efficient but they do make mistakes. In Akin v. Business Title Corp.,[39] the escrowee recorded a mortgage in the wrong county. The corporation attempted to rely on an exculpatory clause intended to insulate it from its own ordinary negligence. The court held that the escrow agreement was a contract of adhesion, that the corporation was one suitable for public regulation, and that the transaction was one that "affects the public interest." The exculpatory clause was held to be invalid and the escrowee was liable for its negligence. "While the general rule still is that an exculpatory clause relieving individuals of liability from their own ordinary negligence does not contravene public policy, a contract entered into between two parties of unequal bargaining strength, expressed in the language of a standardized contract written by the more powerful bargainer to meet its own needs and offered to the weaker party on a 'take it or leave it' basis carries some consequences that extend beyond orthodox implications. When the public interest is affected the exculpatory clause will be held invalid." [40]

SECTION 5. THE ROLE OF THE REAL ESTATE BROKER [41]

It is impossible to deal extensively with the role of the real estate broker in a basic book on principles of property.[42] On the other hand, the student should have some understanding of the role played by this important member of the land-transfer team. Most real estate on the market today is listed with a broker. The

---

39. 264 Cal.App.2d 153, 70 Cal.Rptr. 287 (1968).

40. See also Miller v. Craig, 27 Ariz. App. 789, 558 P.2d 984 (1976). The court noted: "The law is well settled in this state that an escrow agent acts in a fiduciary capacity and must conduct the affairs with which he is entrusted with scrupulous honesty, skill and diligence."

41. A portion of this material is reprinted from Cribbet and Johnson, Cases and Materials on Property 1285–86 (5th ed. 1984).

42. For a general treatment of agency principles see Steffen's Agency—Partnership in a Nutshell (1977).

listing process involves a contract between the broker and the vendor which obligates the latter to pay a commission, typically a percentage of the sales price, if the broker is successful in selling the property. This contract may take a variety of forms and, of course, the listing can be tailor-made for the needs of the vendor, if he or she is astute enough to really negotiate a special contract. Typically, however, the listing is on a prepared form which gives the broker an exclusive right to sell the property. (In a non-exclusive listing, the broker may be only one of several people who are authorized to seek a buyer).

"Exclusive listing agreements are of two types. An 'exclusive agency' agreement is interpreted as prohibiting the owner from selling the property through the agency of another broker during the listing period, but the owner may sell the property through his own efforts. However, an 'exclusive right to sell' agreement (exclusive sales contract) prohibits the owner from selling both personally and through another broker without incurring liability for a commission to the original broker. In the event the owner breaches this type of agreement, he is liable for the commission which would have accrued if the broker had procured a purchaser during the period of listing. The broker need not show that he could have performed by tendering a satisfactory buyer or that he was the procuring cause of the sale. The owner may breach the agreement by negotiating a sale in violation of the agreement or by action which renders the broker's performance impossible.[43] Most listing agreements are of the second, "exclusive right to sell", type.

Today, many brokers participate in a local multiple listing service (MLS) which makes the listing available to all broker members of the service. MLS speeds up the marketing of real estate by giving maximum publicity to the availability of the listed property. Non-members of the MLS do not have access to the listing and, of course, non-brokers, such as the vendor himself, are excluded. There are anti-trust problems involved in MLS,[44] but those problems are reserved for the course in anti-trust law. Incidentally, it is possible for a broker to represent both buyer and seller but it is rarely done and carries with it an almost impossible duty to make full disclosure to both vendor and purchaser.[45]

Real estate brokers are often highly professional and frequently understand more about the sale of real property, particularly the financing aspects, than the lawyer who may be a non-specialist in real estate transactions. Usually, however, the broker will

43. Carlsen v. Zane, 261 Cal.App.2d 399, 67 Cal.Rptr. 747 (1968).

44. See, for example, McLain v. Real Estate Board of New Orleans, Inc., 444 U.S. 232, 100 S.Ct. 502, 62 L.Ed.2d 441 (1980).

45. See Wilson v. Lewis, 106 Cal. App.3d 802, 165 Cal.Rptr. 396 (1980).

know relatively little law outside the narrow confines of his expertise and title problems, for example, are not his responsibility. Breathes there a broker with soul so dead that he knows the intricacies of the Rule in Shelley's Case?

Are brokers, like lawyers, subject to licensure and to regulation by the state? In partial answer to this question, note the following comment by Professors Nelson and Whitman.[46] "In every state, brokers and their sales personnel are licensed by some state agency, usually a Real Estate Commission or the like. In most states there are two levels of licensure. The *salesperson*'s license requires (beyond proof of good character) only the passing of an examination which can usually be managed with a modest amount of rote memorization. Salespeople, however, cannot work on their own, but must be supervised by a licensed *broker*. To become a broker one must accrue some period of experience as a salesperson and pass a harder examination. Some states have added to the foregoing various educational requirements for obtaining or keeping one's license. In many states members of the bar are permitted to do everything a licensed real estate broker can do, except perhaps to employ others as salespeople.

"The regulation of brokers and salespeople in many states is not especially vigorous, but what the Real Estate Commissioner giveth, he may also take away."[47]

One of the trickiest questions involved in the broker-client relationship turns on when the broker earns his or her commission. Is the commission earned when the broker finds a ready, willing and able purchaser and a valid contract of sale is signed or when the sale is actually consummated and the transaction closed? Of course, this question can be resolved by the terms of the listing agreement but frequently those terms are ambiguous. Typically, the commission is not *paid* until the closing on law day when it is taken out of the purchase price but that does not resolve the issue of when the commission is *earned*. In Tristram's Landing, Inc. et al. v. Wait [48] the broker procured a purchaser who signed a valid contract and paid $10,500 in earnest money, representing a ten percent down payment. The purchaser did not appear for the closing and thereafter refused to go through with the contract. The vendor did not attempt to enforce the agreement or recover damages for the breach but did retain the down payment. The broker sued for his commission, five percent of the agreed sales price. The trial court held that the broker was

46. Nelson and Whitman, Real Estate Transfer, Finance and Development 11 (1981).

47. For an example of the last point see Hickam v. Colorado Real Estate Commission, 36 Colo.App. 76, 534 P.2d 1220 (1975).

48. 367 Mass. 622, 327 N.E.2d 727 (1975).

entitled to the full amount of the commission. The Supreme Court of Massachusetts reversed and gave judgment for the vendor.[49] The Court conceded that: "In the past, this rule has been construed to mean that once a customer is produced by the broker and accepted by the seller, the commission is earned, whether or not the sale is consummated. . . . Furthermore, execution of a purchase and sale agreement is usually seen as conclusive evidence of the seller's acceptance of the buyer. . . . We believe, however, that it is both appropriate and necessary at this time to clarify the law, and we now join a minority of states who have adopted the Rule of Ellsworth Dobbs, Inc. v. Johnson, 50 N.J. 528, 236 A. 843 (1967." [50]

The reason behind the newer rule was well stated by Lord Justice Denning in the English case of Dennis Reed, Ltd. v. Goody.[51] "When a house owner puts his house into the hands of an estate agent, the ordinary understanding is that the agent is only to receive his commission if he succeeds in effecting a sale . . . The common understanding of men is . . . that the agent's commission is payable out of the purchaser price. . . . The house-owner wants to find a man who will actually buy his house and pay for it. He does not want a man who will only make an offer or sign a contract. He wants a purchaser 'able to purchase and able to complete as well.' "

The Massachusetts Supreme Court recognized that this new rule could be circumvented easily by language to the contrary in agreements between vendors and brokers but the court added an important *caveat*. "Informal agreements fairly made between people of equal skill and understanding serve a useful purpose. But many sellers, unlike brokers, are involved in real estate transactions infrequently, perhaps only once in a lifetime, and are thus unfamiliar with their legal rights. In such cases agreements by the seller to pay a commission even though the purchaser defaults are to be scrutinized carefully. If not fairly made, such agreements may be unconscionable or against public policy."

This brief discussion of the role of the real estate broker in the sale of land is obviously only the tip of the iceberg but it should provide some insight into the myriad of problems involved in the

49. The court did not decide whether the broker was entitled to five percent of the retained earnest money since the count in *quantum meruit* was waived at the trial and the action proceeded on the written contract only.

50. That Rule holds that the commission is not earned until the sale is

actually consummated. Kansas and Oregon have adopted the Ellsworth rule in its entirety. See Winkelman v. Allen, 214 Kan. 22, 519 P.2d 1377 (1974) and Brown v. Grimm, 258 Or. 55, 481 P.2d 63 (1971). Other state courts have cited the Ellsworth case with approval.

51. 2 K.B. 277, 284–285 (1950).

modern real estate transaction.[52]   Most of these problems can be (and usually are) avoided or resolved by careful planning and draftsmanship and by cooperation among lawyers, brokers, mortgage lenders, title insurance companies and escrowees.   It is another area where preventive law (like preventive medicine) can serve the client best.   But when disputes arise that can be resolved only by litigation, it is vital that the courts follow legal principles that given maximum protection to the unwary public— a public that knows little of the Statute of Frauds, time of the essence and forfeiture clauses, risk of loss, the technicalities of delivery of deeds, when broker's commissions are earned, etc. Some of these principles may "savor of a layman's idea of equity" but that may be the very reason why they should be the law.[53]

---

52. For a glimpse further down the iceberg see Graff v. Billet, 64 N.Y.2d 899, 487 N.Y.S.2d 733, 477 N.E.2d 212 (1984) where the brokerage agreement provided that the commission was due when "title passes." The vendor's refusal to enter into a contract with the broker's prospective buyer did not entitle the broker to a commission. If there had been a valid contract of sale and then the vendor had wilfully breached, the commission would have been earned.

53. The allusion is to Brownell v. Board of Education, 239 N.Y. 369, 146 N.E. 630, 37 A.L.R. 1319 (1925), a risk of loss case, where the court said: "These reasons may savor of layman's ideas of equity, but they are not law."

*

Part Four

LANDLORD AND TENANT

The typical lease is a transfer (or carving out) by an owner of a freehold estate (usually a fee simple absolute) of a non-freehold estate (a leasehold) entitling the transferee (tenant) to exclusive possession of all or a described part of the transferor's (lessor's) land for a stated period of time.[1] But the modern lease is more than a conveyance; it has many contractual aspects. Unlike most modern deeds, leases are signed by both transferor and transferee and contain numerous covenants by each party. The complexities of commercial leases, particularly those for long terms, are responsible for their bulk. Even residential leases often extend for several pages. Attempts by the parties to anticipate and address satisfactorily all of the problems that may arise during the course of a lease term encounter difficult drafting problems. This book does not undertake to discuss such problems comprehensively.[2] The focus here is upon the most commonly used lease provisions, especially in residential leases, and upon legal principles that govern matters not expressly covered in the lease.

The dual nature of the lease as a conveyance and as a contract has had some unfortunate consequences. One might suppose that litigation concerning contractual aspects of leases would be resolved by application of the same principles applicable to contracts outside leases. However, in several important respects, contract law may be inconsistent with the lease as a conveyance of a leasehold estate. When such doctrinal conflicts occurred, the traditional judicial resolution was to prefer the view that the lease is a conveyance of an estate. Many, if not all, of the instances of refusal by courts to apply contract law to leases have produced results generally regarded, at least in modern times, as undesirable.[3] Courts and legislatures were slow to address this problem, but when they finally began to do so, during the second half of the twentieth century, they brought about sweeping reforms of landlord-tenant law within a relatively short period of time. This

1. The types of leasehold estates recognized as common law have been discussed earlier in this book. See p. 53.

2. A book that does so is Friedman on Leases (Practicing Law Institute, 1983).

3. See Hicks, The Contractual Nature of Real Property Leases, 24 Baylor L.Rev. 443 (1972).

process continues. In general, these reforms are bringing the law of leases more nearly in line with contract law. In the material that follows, the tension between contract and property, and efforts to relieve that tension, are recurring themes.

Much of modern landlord and tenant law is statutory. In part, this is due to failure of the courts to adapt this body of law to modern conditions. On the other hand, some legislation is a response to judicial reforms perceived by legislatures to require legislative implementation, limitation, or reversal. A significant legislative development within the past two decades was approval in 1972 of the Uniform Residential Landlord and Tenant Act by the National Conference of Commissioners on Uniform State Laws. Thirteen states have adopted it, with varying modifications. Although the great bulk of law concerning leaseholds is state law, acts of Congress also affect significantly some aspects of the legal relationship of landlord and tenant. The most important of these are civil rights legislation and housing programs. This book refers to representative or particularly noteworthy statutory landlord and tenant law, but does not attempt comprehensive coverage.

Chapter 1

CREATION OF THE MODERN LANDLORD AND TENANT RELATIONSHIP

SECTION 1. THE STATUTE OF FRAUDS

State statutes prescribing formalities for creation of lease-holds are not uniform, but in most states the Statute of Frauds allows leases for one year or less to be oral; leases for longer durations are required to be in writing and signed by the party to be charged.[4] Failure to comply with the typical statutory formalities does not necessarily bar creation of the landlord and tenant relationship. If the "tenant" enters into possession, a tenancy at will comes into existence; if rent is also tendered and accepted, the tenancy becomes a periodic tenancy.[5] Moreover, except for duration, the terms of the tenancy at will and the periodic tenancy are identical to those of the lease made void or unenforceable by the Statute of Frauds.[6] Even as to duration, the prevailing view is that the periodic tenancy will terminate without notice at the end of the void or unenforceable lease if the tenancy has not been terminated earlier.[7] In addition, a lease not complying with the Statute of Frauds may nevertheless be fully effective when circumstances satisfy the part performance or estoppel doctrines.[8]

In two instances, despite the Statute of Frauds exception for oral leases not exceeding one year, such leases may nevertheless be void or unenforceable. One instance is the oral lease for one year to commence on a date subsequent to the date of execution (a not uncommon occurrence). Some courts hold that a writing is required for such a lease because the duration should be measured

4. A survey of formalities required for leases in the various states appears in Restatement (Second) of Property, Landlord and Tenant § 2.1, Statutory Note (1977).

5. See p. 55, supra.

6. Darling Shops Delaware Corp. v. Baltimore Center Corp., 191 Md. 289, 60 A.2d 669 (1948).

7. See the discussion in Schoshinski, American Law of Landlord and Tenant § 2.225 (1980), concluding: "A more logical and consistent rule would seem to require the same notice to end a periodic tenancy in the last year of the agreed upon term as in any previous year." The Darling Shops case, supra note 5, supports Schoshinski's position. But this position appears to set a trap for the parties, who usually would assume that the lease is valid and requires no notice of termination.

8. See p. 160, infra, for general discussion of these doctrines.

"from the date of the making" of the lease.[9] Other courts disagree.[10] This divergence usually results from different judicial approaches to statutory construction rather than to differences in clearly manifested legislative policy. Persuasive arguments can be stated for each position. A practical consideration relied upon by some courts is the existence in many regions of a customary practice of entering into oral one-year leases, usually farm leases, to commence at a later date.[11]

Another instance of an oral lease for one year that may run afoul of the Statute of Frauds is the lease containing an option to renew. Some courts add the renewal period to the original term and treat the combined terms as violative of the Statute of Frauds.[12] A contrary approach invalidates only the option.[13] The latter has been criticized as giving effect to lease terms that the parties did not agree upon.[14]

SECTION 2. DELIVERY

The conveyance aspect of the lease suggests that delivery is essential to its validity. There is some authority to this effect,[15] but court opinions and treatises generally are silent on this matter. Despite its conceptual support, the requirement of delivery of leases is unsound. The common understanding of the parties to leases, especially negotiated leases, is that it is a contract. It would not occur to the parties that control of the lease document should pass from lessor to lessee. Each party typically retains an original or copy of the lease document. If the lease is oral, there is nothing to deliver.

Although the rigor of the delivery requirement as applied to deeds has been weakened almost to the point of extinction by judicial exegesis stressing intent that the deed be effective, rather than control over the deed,[16] it seems unnecessary and productive of confusion to require delivery of leases at all. It should suffice

9. Shaughnessy v. Eidsmo, 222 Minn. 141, 23 N.W.2d 362 (1946).

10. Bell v. Vaughn, 46 Ariz. 515, 53 P.2d 61 (1935).

11. "The legislature must be presumed to have understood the subjects upon which it legislated." Bateman v. Maddox, 86 Tex. 546, 26 S.W. 51, 53 (1894).

12. Anderson v. Frye & Bruhn, Inc., 69 Wash. 89, 124 P. 499 (1912).

13. Bateman v. Maddox, 86 Tex. 546, 26 S.W. 51 (1894).

14. Anderson v. Frye & Bruhn, Inc., 69 Wash. 89, 124 P. 499, 501 (1912).

15. 219 Broadway Corp. v. Alexander's, Inc., 46 N.Y.2d 506, 414 N.Y.S.2d 889, 387 N.E.2d 1205 (1979).

16. A striking example is Ferrell v. Stinson, 233 Iowa 1331, 11 N.W.2d 701 (1943).

to comply with the legal requirements for formation of contracts. This may be the unstated position of all courts, even if the parties have agreed during negotiation that delivery is required. A standard form provides that it is submitted for inspection only and becomes "effective as a lease upon execution and delivery both by Lessor and Lessee." One court has construed this language as requiring "execution of a formal document," but apparently nothing more.[17] The form's requirement of delivery by the lessee shows that the word "delivery" was not used by the parties as a requirement for transfer of an estate.

SECTION 3. ENTRY INTO POSSESSION

Another requirement sometimes asserted for creation of a leasehold is entry into possession by the lessee.[18] Until then, the legal relations between the parties are purely contractual; the lessee could be liable for breach of contract, but not for rent.[19] The lessee's interest in such instances has been labeled an "*interesse termini*, a right to enter."[20] Authoritative support for any such requirement is very weak and there appears to be no reason for it.[21] The supposed requirement of entry may have been confused with the status of parties who enter into a lease not intended to create the relation of landlord and tenant until the occurrence of some event, usually the arrival of a future date.[22] The American Law Institute views the relations of the parties during that interim as purely contractual, but it does not require entry, the occurrence of the event being sufficient to create the leasehold.[23]

17. Ebert v. Dr. Scholl's Foot Comfort Shops, Inc., 137 Ill.App.3d 550, 92 Ill.Dec. 323, 484 N.E.2d 1178 (1985).

18. See Arthur Treacher's Fish & Chips of Fairfax, Inc. v. Chillum Terrace Ltd. Partnership, 272 Md. 720, 327 A.2d 282, 287 (1974).

19. Id.

20. Id.

21. 1 Am.L.Prop. § 3.22 (Casner ed. 1952).

22. Examples of such apparent confusion are the Arthur Treacher's Fish & Chips case, supra note 17, and Byrd Companies, Inc. v. Birmingham Trust Nat. Bank, 482 So.2d 247 (Ala.1985).

23. Restatement (Second) of Property, Landlord and Tenant § 1.8 (1977).

SECTION 4. RIGHT TO EXCLUSIVE POSSESSION

One essential requirement for creation of the relationship of landlord and tenant is that the right to exclusive possession of a described area be transferred. It is not sufficient that the parties have labeled a document "lease." If the right to exclusive possession has not been created, the "lessee" probably has an easement or a license. In one case, a document bearing a "lease" label conferring "the exclusive right and privilege to maintain an advertising sign . . . on wall of building" was held to have conveyed an easement, not a leasehold, because the owner of the building retained the right to possess the wall.[24] Persons who engage hotel rooms usually are not lessees, but are guests or lodgers.[25] Such decisions have been influenced by the continuing control of the premises by the proprietor for maid service and other purposes. Arrangements for long-term occupancy in hotels are extremely difficult to classify.[26] Contracts for occupancy of a private dormitory by students during the academic year were held not to be leases, the court relying primarily upon reservation by the proprietor of the right to move occupants from one room to another.[27] However, the American Law Institute does not regard such reservation as inconsistent with creation of a leasehold.[28]

Suppose that a document satisfies all of the requirements for leases, including vesting the right of exclusive possession in the occupant, but contains a declaration that the parties do not intend to create a landlord and tenant relationship, but rather intend that their legal relations be governed exclusively by the document. Despite such expressed intent, a landlord and tenant relation would be created.[29] The terms of the document also would be effective, but only if they are consistent with aspects of the relationship of landlord and tenant that cannot be bargained away. For example, a statute mandating certain rules for security deposits not only could not be evaded by a lease provision for some security deposit rule contrary to the statutory rule, but also could not be evaded by a declaration in a lease that it is not a lease.[30]

---

24. Baseball Publishing Co. v. Bruton, 302 Mass. 54, 18 N.E.2d 362, 119 A.L.R. 1518 (1938).

25. These and other non-tenants are discussed in Restatement (Second) of Property, Landlord and Tenant § 1.2, Reporter's Note (1977).

26. Consider Chawla v. Horch, 70 Misc.2d 290, 333 N.Y.S.2d 531 (1972).

27. Cook v. University Plaza, 100 Ill. App.3d 752, 56 Ill.Dec. 325, 427 N.E.2d 405 (1981).

28. Restatement (Second) of Property § 1.1, Comment a, Illustration (1977).

29. Cf. Cook v. University Plaza, supra note 27.

30. Id.

Chapter 2

SELECTION OF TENANTS

Unlike innkeepers,[1] landlords are allowed by the common law to exclude from occupancy any person for any or no reason, by refusing to enter into the relationship of landlord and tenant with that person.[2] But landlord discretion in this respect is now constrained significantly by acts of Congress, state legislation and municipal ordinances.[3]

SECTION 1. RACIAL DISCRIMINATION

Racial discrimination in leasing is banned by two acts of Congress and many state statutes.[4] The scope of these acts and remedies for their enforcement are not identical. One significant distinction is that the Civil Rights Act of 1866[5] applies to all residential and commercial leasing, while the Fair Housing Act of 1968[6] applies only to residential leases and exempts most single-family dwellings. Under these acts, landlord practices that are not overtly racially discriminatory, but have disparate effects upon racial groups, may be found by courts to come within the statutory prohibition. One case involved a challenge to a landlord's requirement that prospective tenants have incomes above a stated level.[7] The court upheld this practice, despite its racially discriminatory effect, because a racially discriminatory motive had not been established. However, the same court in a later case eased the burden of proof of racially discriminatory motive, at least in some instances, by holding that a prima facie showing of

1. By becoming innkeepers, such entrepreneurs were deemed to have undertaken to serve all persons without unreasonable discrimination. 40 Am. Jur.2d Hotels, Motels and Restaurants § 62 (1968).

2. Restatement (Second) of Property, Landlord and Tenant § 3.1, Introductory Note (1977); Schoshinski, American Law of Landlord and Tenant § 11.1 (1980).

3. Id.

4. This legislation is discussed briefly in Restatement (Second) of Property, Landlord and Tenant § 3.1, Comment (1977).

5. 42 U.S.C. § 1982.

6. 42 U.S.C. §§ 3601 et seq.

7. Boyd v. Lefrak Organization, 509 F.2d 1110 (2d Cir.1975), rehearing denied 517 F.2d 918 (2d Cir.1975), cert. denied 423 U.S. 896, 96 S.Ct. 197, 46 L.Ed.2d 129 (1975).

such motive is made by evidence "(1) that [the applicant] is Black;
that he applied for and was qualified to rent . . . the housing; (3)
that he was ejected; and (4) that the housing opportunity remained available." [8]

SECTION 2. OTHER DISCRIMINATION

The Fair Housing Act of 1968 also prohibits landlords from
rejecting tenants on the ground of religion, national origin and
sex. In some states, statutes and municipal ordinances prohibit
discrimination in leasing not only on those grounds, but also upon
grounds of age, marital status, physical handicaps, blindness,
children in household, illegitimate children in household, public
welfare status, military status and political affiliation.[9]

Discrimination against tenants with children has stirred up
controversy in recent years. The relevant policy issues have been
raised by legislative proposals to ban such discrimination and by
litigation alleging that a state civil rights statute couched in broad
terms should be construed as protecting persons denied tenancy
because they have a child or children.[10] The author of one careful
analysis concluded that it is only in regions having severe
shortages of housing for low-income families that one could justify
legislative interference with landlord efforts to obtain tenants
willing to pay relatively high rent for child-less environments.[11]

Expansive construction of a state civil rights act by the
Supreme Court of California [12] has been viewed as requiring landlords to show good cause for refusal to rent to anyone.[13] This, of
course, imposes upon landlords the same obligation placed upon
innkeepers by the common law. Lawyers and law students may
have a special interest in this development in view of the practice

8. Robinson v. 12 Lofts Realty, Inc., 610 F.2d 1032 (2d Cir.1979).

9. These statutes are identified and classified in Restatement (Second) of Property, Landlord and Tenant § 3.1, Comment (1977).

10. Marina Point, Ltd. v. Wolfson, 30 Cal.3d 721, 180 Cal.Rptr. 496, 640 P.2d 115 (1982), cert. denied 459 U.S. 858, 103 S.Ct. 129, 74 L.Ed.2d 111 (1982), construed statute as protecting such persons.

11. Comment, Why Johnny Can't Rent—An Examination of Laws Prohibiting Discrimination Against Families in Rental Housing, 94 Harv.L.Rev. 1829 (1981).

12. Marina Point, Ltd. v. Wolfson, supra note 40.

13. Rabin, The Revolution in Residential Landlord–Tenant Law: Causes and Consequences, 69 Corn.L.Rev. 517, 532 (1984).

of some landlords of refusing to rent to lawyers, who as a class are considered by such landlords to be troublemakers.[14]

14. Refusal to rent on this ground was upheld in Kramarsky v. Stahl Management, 92 Misc.2d 1030, 401 N.Y.S.2d 943 (Sup.Ct.1977).

Chapter 3

INTERFERENCE WITH TENANT'S POSSESSION

The leasehold is a possessory estate, entitling the tenant to exclusive possession, except as limited by the terms of the lease. The tenant has the usual remedies of owners of possessory estates against trespassers—damages and injunctive relief.

SECTION 1. ACTS BY LANDLORD AND OWNERS OF PARAMOUNT TITLE

If the trespass is by the landlord, and results in substantial interference with tenant's possession, the tenant also has the remedy of termination of the lease. This significant remedy stems from the covenant of quiet enjoyment, which is a contractual assurance by the landlord, implied (if not expressed) in leases in nearly all states, that the tenant's possession will not be disturbed by either the landlord or an owner of a title paramount to that of the landlord.[1] Protection of the tenant from defects in the landlord's title is a notable exception to the traditional rule that lessees, as purchasers of an estate, are subject to the doctrine of caveat emptor. The implication of this title covenant in leases also contrasts with the well established rule that no title covenants are implied in deeds. The courts obviously have long regarded tenants as particularly in need of judicial protection against title defects.

Eviction may be total or partial. If it is total, the leasehold estate is terminated. If eviction is partial and due to paramount title, such as an easement, the leasehold estate may remain in effect, the tenant's remedy being suit for damages. If, however, the eviction is partial and is due to an act of the landlord, such as

---

1. E.g., Cohen v. Hayden, 180 Iowa 232, 163 N.W. 238 (1917). New Jersey might be the sole exception. There, it appears, the covenant of quiet enjoyment will be implied in leases, if at all, only if the lease contains one of the following words: "demise," "let," or "lease." May v. Levy, 88 N.J.L. 351, 95 A. 999 (1915). Cf. Adrian v. Rabinowitz, 116 N.J.L. 586, 186 A. 29 (1936). Historical origins of implication of this covenant are discussed in 7 Holdsworth, History of English Law 251 et seq. (2d ed. 1937).

construction by the landlord of a building on an adjoining lot in a manner encroaching substantially on the leased lot, courts have held that the tenant may remain in possession and pay no rent so long as the encroachment continues.[2] This extraordinary remedy for "actual partial eviction" appears to be excessive. It is rejected by Restatement (Second) of Property, Landlord and Tenant (1977).[3] But the traditional rule may not be as harsh as it seems. After all, the landlord can revive the tenant's obligation to pay rent simply by removing the encroachment. Moreover, the tenant would be answerable in quasi-contract for benefits of occupancy during the period of rent suspension. Two eminent jurists—Holmes and Cardozo—endorsed the traditional rule.[4]

SECTION 2.   EMINENT DOMAIN

Eviction of a tenant by exercise of the power of eminent domain is not a breach of the covenant of quiet enjoyment. Such eviction does not result from a defect in the lessor's title, but is a consequence of lawful governmental power to condemn private property for a public purpose upon payment of just compensation. Accordingly, courts traditionally have held that condemnation of part of the leased premises does not affect the tenant's obligation to pay rent, at least where sufficient usable land remains.[5] The tenant's sole remedy is to share in the condemnation award for the taking of part of the tenant's leasehold. If, however, the condemnation embraces all interests in the entire leased premises, the leasehold estate is terminated, the usual explanation being that the estates of landlord and tenant have merged in the condemning authority.[6] If part of the premises is condemned and that part is not sufficient to enable the tenant to use them in the manner contemplated by the lease, the better position is that the lease is ended in this situation as well, in view of the frustration of its purpose, despite the inapplicability of the merger doctrine.[7]

2. Smith v. McEnany, 170 Mass. 26, 48 N.E. 781 (1897).

3. Section 6.1, Reporter's Note 6.

4. Holmes wrote the Court's opinion in Smith v. McEnany, supra note 46. Cardozo expressed his views in Fifth Avenue Building Co. v. Kernochan, 221 N.Y. 370, 117 N.E. 579, 580 (1917).

5. Elliott v. Joseph, 163 Tex. 71, 351 S.W.2d 879 (1961). Contra: Great Atlantic and Pacific Tea Co. v. State, 22 N.Y.2d 75, 291 N.Y.S.2d 299, 238 N.E.2d 705 (1968).

6. Corrigan v. City of Chicago, 144 Ill. 537, 33 N.E. 746 (1893).

7. Yellow Cab Co. v. Howard, 243 Ill. App. 263 (1927).

The traditional rule obligating a tenant to continue to pay full rent after partial condemnation that leaves usable land has been much criticized—not because this rule is unfair to the tenant, but because it may be unfair to the landlord.[8] The harm to the landlord is the lack of assurance that the tenant, after having received a substantial condemnation award, will actually pay rent as it comes due for the use of premises of diminished value. Coordination of landlord and tenant law with the law of eminent domain is essential. Such coordination should require partial abatement of rent for significant partial condemnation and reduce the tenant's share of the condemnation award accordingly.[9]

SECTION 3. UNLAWFUL POSSESSION BY ANOTHER AT BEGINNING OF TERM

Ordinarily, a landlord is not obligated to prevent or terminate interference by third persons with a tenant's possession of the premises. Remedies available to the tenant usually afford sufficient protection against such third persons. But there are exceptions to the general rule of non-responsibility by the landlord and the current trend of court decisions is to increase and broaden them. One exception, recognized long ago in England, is an implied duty of the landlord to remove a holdover tenant or anyone else in possession at the beginning of the term.[10] Surprisingly, some American courts have not deemed the landlord obligated to assure a tenant that the premises will be vacant at the beginning of the lease.[11] To courts taking this position, the so-called "American Rule", it is sufficient that a tenant has the legal right to enter and remedies to enforce that right. This view ignores the practical consideration that the landlord is in a better position to prevent the holding over. It is also contrary to the usual understanding of the parties, especially where the lease is for residential use or short-term commercial use. Recent decisions,[12] several state legislatures,[13] the American Law Institute,[14]

8. Restatement (Second) of Property, Landlord and Tenant § 8.1, Comment (1977); 1 Am.L.Prop. § 3.54 (Casner ed. 1952); 2 Powell, Real Property ¶ 247[2] (1986).

9. The Uniform Eminent Domain Code § 1013 does this.

10. Adrian v. Rabinowitz, 116 N.J.L. 586, 186 A. 29 (1936).

11. Hannan v. Dusch, 154 Va. 356, 153 S.E. 824 (1930).

12. See Weissenberger, The Landlord's Duty to Deliver Possession: The Overlooked Reform, 46 U.Cin.L.Rev. 937 (1977).

13. Listed in Restatement (Second) Property, Landlord and Tenant § 6.2, Statutory Note (1977).

14. Id.

and the Commissioners on Uniform State Laws [15] support putting the obligation on the landlord to deliver possession.

15. URLTA § 2.103.

Chapter 4

INTERFERENCE WITH TENANT'S USE: CONSTRUCTIVE EVICTION

Tenant's use of the leased premises may be interfered with by others without ousting tenant from possession of any part of the premises. In addition to remedies of damages and injunctive relief based upon the law of nuisance, a tenant may be able to terminate the lease when the landlord is responsible for the interference. In order to make this remedy available, courts found it necessary to resort to a fiction—"constructive" eviction. If the landlord's acts have been of such grave and permanent nature as to frustrate the tenant's use, the tenant may abandon the premises and will not be liable for rent that would have accrued thereafter.[1]

Termination of the lease for constructive eviction is an important tenant remedy, but it is fraught with difficulty. There is the possibility that a court or jury may decide that the circumstances did not justify abandonment.[2] A tenant may resolve this dilemma by bringing a declaratory judgment suit prior to vacating,[3] but this is time-consuming and expensive.

The typical constructive eviction results from some act by the landlord, such as excessive and persistent noise emanating from a unit occupied by the landlord. It also may be based upon failure by the landlord to perform a lease covenant substantially affecting use of the premises, such as a covenant to supply heat.[4] If courts had not extended the doctrine of constructive eviction to such instances of nonaction by the landlord, the tenant's remedies for breach of covenant by the landlord would have been extremely inadequate. The effective remedy of rent-withholding was denied tenants by the traditional judicial view that lease covenants are independent, a logical consequence of characterization of leases as conveyances. Fortunately, in recent cases, some courts have approved rent-withholding as a remedy in recent years.[5] In such

1. Thompson v. Poirier, 120 N.H. 584, 420 A.2d 297 (1980).

2. The Automobile Supply Co. v. Scene-In-Action Corp., 340 Ill. 196, 172 N.E. 35 (1930).

3. Charles E. Burt, Inc. v. Seven Grand Corp., 340 Mass. 124, 163 N.E.2d 4 (1959).

4. One court was willing to apply constructive eviction to this situation even in the absence of an express covenant to supply heat, there being circumstances justifying implication of such a covenant. Jackson v. Paterno, 58 Misc. 201, 108 N.Y.S. 1073 (1908).

5. See 251, infra.

jurisdictions, tenants might prefer in some instances to withhold rent rather than to terminate the lease.

Is a landlord impliedly obligated to abate unreasonable noise caused by other tenants of the landlord? The traditional negative judicial response has been rejected by recent court decisions and other authorities in situations where the landlord has the legal power to terminate the noise.[6] The source of such legal power may be a covenant in the lease of the offending tenant,[7] a statute,[8] or the landlord's control over common areas.[9] Even in the absence of legal power in the landlord to abate the noise, the covenant of quiet enjoyment may be breached if the disturbance is a consequence of leasing to neighboring tenants for uses likely to be incompatible, such as a residence and a cocktail lounge, respectively.[10]

6. Annot., 1 A.L.R. 4th 849 (1980); Restatement (Second) Property, Landlord and Tenant § 6.1, Comment d (1980).

7. Bocchini v. Gorn Management Co., 69 Md.App. 1, 515 A.2d 1179 (1986).

8. Gottdiener v. Mailhot, 179 N.J. Super. 286, 431 A.2d 851 (1981).

9. Phyfe v. Dale, 72 Misc. 383, 130 N.Y.S. 231 (Sup.Ct.1911).

10. Blackett v. Olanoff, 371 Mass. 714, 358 N.E.2d 817 (1977) (alternate holding).

Chapter 5

FITNESS OF THE PREMISES

Until the 1970's, traditional doctrine in most jurisdictions held that leases contain no implied assurance by the lessor that the premises are suitable for the contemplated uses or that they will remain suitable during the term.[1] This was another logical consequence of characterizing the lease as a conveyance. The lessee, as purchaser of an estate, was regarded as being in the same situation as the purchaser of a fee simple. It was the responsibility of each to inspect the premises and determine their suitability. Only if the vendor or lessor had committed fraud, as by making false representations of fact or by concealing serious defects not discoverable by reasonable inspection, would the law come to the aid of either purchaser or lessee. If the premises became unfit after transfer of title to purchaser or lessee, such as by deterioration for lack of repair or sudden destruction by fire or flood, neither was entitled to any relief against the vendor or lessor. Every owner was deemed to assume such risks. Indeed, the duty to repair was on the tenant, who might be liable for waste for the consequences of failure to repair.

A more realistic view of the lease, at least the modern residential lease, is that it essentially is a contractual exchange of use of the premises for rent. In the absence of a lease provision to the contrary, the usual understanding of parties to residential leases, and perhaps some short-term commercial leases also, surely is that the obligation to pay rent is conditioned upon fitness of the premises. But traditional doctrine not only rejected implication of a covenant of fitness by the lessor, but also usually treated even express covenants by the landlord as independent of the tenant's rent covenant.[2] This meant that even if the landlord were obligated to provide and maintain fit premises, the tenant could not withhold rent pending improvement of the premises. A tenant who attempted this could be evicted by the summary procedure commonly known as forcible entry and detainer, or FED. The tenant could not assert as a defense to such a suit that the lessor had breached a covenant of fitness rendering the premises unin-

---

1. 1 Am.L.Prop. §§ 3.45, 3.78 (Casner ed. 1952).

2. Restatement (Second) of Property, Landlord and Tenant § 5.1, Reporter's Note (1980). Compare judicial treatment of covenants in contracts other than leases. Corbin, Contracts Ch. 30 (1960).

habitable. The tenant could only bring a separate suit to recover damages for breach of the lessor's covenant or vacate the premises and hope that a court would hold that the lease had been terminated by constructive eviction. Neither of these was usually an adequate remedy.

Housing codes adopted by cities, especially in the 1960's, mandated that owners of housing, whether rental housing or not, observe certain health and safety standards. These codes were not enacted for the purpose of redressing the balance of landlord-tenant law as to responsibility for fitness, but rather were intended to preserve an adequate stock of decent housing, retard the spread of urban blight, and minimize the need for costly urban renewal programs. At least until the 1970's, they did not even expressly vest enforcement remedies in tenants, but relied for enforcement upon inspections by administrators authorized to seek court fines for violations. Nevertheless, housing codes would have benefited tenants enormously had the codes achieved their goals. But, alas, their effects upon housing quality were disappointing.[3]

SECTION 1. IMPLIED WARRANTY OF HABITABILITY

This terrible trio of doctrines—no implied covenant of fitness, no obligation by lessor to repair, and independence of lease covenants—were dealt a devastating blow by the 1970 opinion by Judge J. Skelly Wright of the United States Court of Appeals for the District of Columbia in Javins v. First National Realty Corp.[4] Scattered earlier court decisions had begun the assault,[5] but it was Judge Wright's opinion that attracted nationwide attention and precipitated a so-called "revolution" in the law of landlord and tenant. Within little more than a decade, the major aspects of Judge Wright's opinion had been endorsed by the courts or legislatures (or both) of at least forty states,[6] as well as by the American

3. Report of the National Commission on Urban Problems, Building the American City 273–295 (1968); Gribetz & Grad, Housing Code Enforcement: Sanctions and Remedies, 66 Colum.L. Rev. 1254 (1966).

4. 138 U.S.App.D.C. 369, 428 F.2d 1071 (1970), cert. denied 400 U.S. 925, 91 S.Ct. 186, 27 L.Ed.2d 185 (1970).

5. E.g., Pines v. Perssion, 14 Wis.2d 590, 111 N.W.2d 409 (1961).

6. Glendon, The Transformation of American Landlord–Tenant Law, 23 B.C.L.Rev. 503, 523 (1982). For other comprehensive reviews of statutes and decisions, see Cunningham, Stoebuck & Whitman, The Law of Property § 6.36 et seq. (1984); Restatement (Second) of Property, Landlord and Tenant, Statutory Note to Chapter 5 and Reporter's Note to Section 5.1 (1980); Cunningham, The New Implied and Statutory

Law Institute [7] and the Commissioners on Uniform State Laws.[8] *Javins* held that a tenant of a residence in the District of Columbia could defend a suit for eviction for nonpayment of rent by showing violations of the housing code affecting habitability and that the court or jury would determine the extent to which, if at all, the rent should be abated. This holding was based upon the court's conclusion that the housing code implied a warranty of habitability measured by the code's standards in all housing covered by the code. Although Judge Wright's opinion contains support for implication of a warranty of habitability based solely upon inferred intention of the parties, it relies upon the housing code. An important consequence of this grounding of the implied warranty of habitability was Judge Wright's assertion that the warranty cannot be waived in the lease.

Two years prior to *Javins,* the District of Columbia Court of Appeals had held that tenants could rely upon the doctrine of illegal contract as a defense to actions for rent when the premises at the beginning of the lease were not in compliance with the housing code requirement that they be safe and sanitary.[9] Both of these decisions went beyond the text of the housing code by implying remedies in addition to those specified in the code. The rationale for this broad construction in each case was that the legislative body's paramount purpose was that its mandate of decent rental housing should be carried out effectively, and therefore, the specified remedies were not intended to be exclusive. At least one critic of these decisions has questioned this reading of legislative purpose and has asserted that the more probable legislative purpose was to rely exclusively upon the discretion of administrative officials for enforcement.[10] Whatever the legislative purpose may have been earlier, recent legislation in most states leaves no doubt that enforcement of housing codes is no longer intended to be limited to administrative enforcement.

The defense of illegal contract may be helpful to tenants in some situations, but it offers no protection against defective conditions occurring after commencement of the lease. While it absolves the tenant of liability for rent, the tenant still may be required to pay the reasonable rental value of the actual occupancy,[11] which may be not much different from the rent. It also

Warranties of Habitability in Residential Leases: From Contract to Status, 16 Urb.L.Ann. 3 (1979). Some courts, however, steadfastly decline to join the trend. E.g., Young v. Morrisey, 285 S.C. 236, 329 S.E.2d 426 (1985).

7. Restatement (Second) of Property, Landlord and Tenant § 5.1 et seq. (1980).

8. URLTA §§ 2.104, 4.101–4.105.

9. Brown v. Southall Realty Co., 237 A.2d 834 (D.C.App.1968).

10. Meyers, The Covenant of Habitability and the American Law Institute, 27 Stan.L.Rev. 879, 901, 902 (1975).

11. William J. Davis, Inc. v. Slade, 271 A.2d 412 (D.C.App.1970).

seems that the tenant who asserts that the lease is illegal has no right to remain on the premises, though creative lawyering (and judging) enabled one tenant to stay on for over three years.[12] Tenants who can rely upon an implied warranty of habitability usually will prefer it to the defense of illegal contract.

Although a revolution in the law of landlord and tenant may have occurred, leaving traditional doctrines in shambles in most jurisdictions, the contours of the new law are not uniform in the various jurisdictions. The URLTA and the Restatement (Second) of Property have provided guidance for courts and legislatures, but nevertheless much diversity exists. To a much greater extent than during the pre-*Javins* era, the new law is statutory.[13] As is true of most legislation, statutes on the law of landlord and tenant bear the marks of lobbying by interest groups. In some states, gains won by tenants in court decisions recognizing a warranty of habitability have been cut back by legislatures.[14] In other states where courts had not taken that step, legislation on the subject of habitability of rental housing has been deemed to preempt the field, barring judicial fashioning of an implied warranty of habitability and associated doctrines.[15] Losses by tenants at the hands of some legislatures are not of such magnitude and pervasiveness as to constitute a counterrevolution, but they dampen the euphoria generated by *Javins* and its progeny.

State laws differ as to types of housing subject to the implied warranty of habitability. In many states, it has been extended to nearly all rental residences, including those not covered by a housing code.[16] The implied warranty of habitability has been applied by at least one court to cooperative housing.[17] Owners of condominium units have attempted, unsuccessfully to date, to claim its protection.[18] In some states, an implied warranty of fitness has been extended to commercial leases by statute[19] or court decision,[20] but other courts and legislatures have refused to

12. Robinson v. Diamond Housing Corporation, 150 U.S.App.D.C. 17, 463 F.2d 853 (1972).

13. One writer maintains that this has been the real revolution. Glendon, The Transformation of American Landlord–Tenant Law, 13 B.C.L.Rev. 503 (1982).

14. Compare Kamarath v. Bennett, 568 S.W.2d 658 (Tex.1978) with Tex. Prop.Code Ann. ch. 92 (Vernon 1984).

15. Worden v. Ordway, 105 Idaho 719, 672 P.2d 1049 (1983).

16. See e.g., the URLTA § 1.201. An example of judicial extension is

Glasoe v. Trinkle, 107 Ill.2d 1, 88 Ill. Dec. 895, 479 N.E.2d 915 (1985).

17. Suarez v. Rivercross Tenants' Corp., 107 Misc.2d 135, 438 N.Y.S.2d 164 (Sup.Ct.1981).

18. Kelley v. Astor Investors, Inc., 78 Ill.Dec. 877, 123 Ill.App.3d 593, 462 N.E.2d 996 (2d Dist.1984).

19. Wis.Stat.Ann. § 704.07 (West Supp.1985).

20. Houma Oil Co., Inc. v. McKey, 395 So.2d 828 (La.App.1981); Pylate v. Inabnet, 458 So.2d 1378 (La.App.1984); Reste Realty Corp. v. Cooper, 53 N.J. 444, 251 A.2d 268 (1969) (limited to la-

make this extension.[21] A court might plausibly refuse to imply a warranty of fitness in a commercial lease on the grounds that (1) housing codes are not applicable to commercial premises and (2) commercial tenants are more likely to enjoy equality of bargaining power with landlords than are residential tenants. Despite those considerations, however, a court might plausibly imply a warranty of fitness in a commercial lease on the ground that to do so gives effect to the probable intention of the parties. This argument would seem to be especially persuasive when applied to short-term leases of small units such as offices or shops, rather than large buildings, as lessees of such leases are not likely to inspect for latent defects or to have equality of bargaining power with the landlord.

The requisite standard of habitability varies among states—from the very detailed provisions of housing codes of local governments to broad generalities of court opinions and legislative mandates that premises be safe and healthful.[22] The Texas statute requires only that the landlord make a "diligent effort" to remedy a condition that "materially affects the physical health or safety of an ordinary tenant" and this is required only if the tenant has notified the landlord of the condition and if the tenant was not delinquent in the payment of rent at the time notice was given.[23]

A long list of tenant remedies for uninhabitability would include mandatory injunction, withholding of rent pending restoration of habitability and the concomitant defense of uninhabitability to landlord's suit to evict for non-payment of rent, repair by the tenant and deduction of costs of repair from the rent, judicial abatement of rent to the extent of the impairment of habitability, return of rent paid, compensatory and punitive damages, recovery of attorney's fees and court costs, requests for administrative and penal enforcement of housing codes, and termination of the lease. Not all of these remedies are available to the same extent in all jurisdictions that impose landlord responsibility for habitability. In some states, the tenant's arsenal of remedies bulges,[24] while in others it is almost empty.[25] The important remedy of rent withholding is not available everywhere. The

tent defects); Davidow v. Inwood North Professional Group, 747 S.W.2d 373 (Tex.1988).

21. J.B. Stein & Co. v. Sandberg, 95 Ill.App.3d 19, 50 Ill.Dec. 544, 419 N.E.2d 652 (2d Dist.1981); Knapp v. Simmons, 345 N.W.2d 118 (Iowa 1984) (agricultural lease); Buker v. National Management Corp., 16 Mass.App.Ct. 36, 448 N.E.2d 1299 (1983); Mobil Oil Credit Corp. v. DST Realty, Inc., 689 S.W.2d 658 (Mo.App.1985); Gehrke v. General Theatre Corp., 207 Neb. 301, 298 N.W.2d 773 (1980).

22. E.g., Hilder v. St. Peter, 144 Vt. 150, 478 A.2d 202 (1984) (judicial standard).

23. Tex.Prop.Code Ann. § 92.052(a) (Vernon 1984).

24. E.g., Hilder v. St. Peter, 144 Vt. 150, 478 A.2d 202 (1984).

25. E.g., Tex.Prop.Code Ann. Ch. 92 (Vernon 1984).

Texas statute not only denies this remedy, but also penalizes an attempt to exercise it by making the tenant liable to the landlord for one month's rent plus $100 and attorney's fees.[26] Tenants in some states must follow detailed procedural steps in asserting their remedies. The Idaho statutory requirement that tenants, before bringing suit, give the landlord three days' written notice to cure defects has been construed as requiring that such notice be given before tenant vacates the premises.[27] The Texas statutory requirement of two notices by tenant—one to establish landlord's duty to repair and the other as a prerequisite to termination of the lease or filing suit—has been criticized as a "procedural trap for the unwary tenant. . . ." [28]

Diversity among the states also exists as to whether, and under what circumstances, landlord and tenant are allowed to waive habitability obligations placed on landlords by modern statutes or court decisions, but the trend is to prohibit waiver.[29] The waiver issue raises important policy considerations. If the sole reason for implying a warranty of habitability is to give effect to the inferred intention of the parties, waiver should be allowed in the absence of such disparity of bargaining power that the lease should be deemed a contract of adhesion. Some tenants may willingly, even eagerly, enter into leases to occupy substandard premises for substandard rent, or agree to perform repairs in return for reduced rent. If, however, the basis for the landlord's habitability obligation is legislative or judicial policy that rented residences should satisfy minimum standards of safety and health, regardless of intention of the parties, it follows that persons should be forbidden to enter into "as is" leases.[30] The policy of mandatory habitability has been criticized on the ground that its practical effect is to make scarcer already scarce affordable housing, by imposing costs upon landlords that cannot be recovered from nonaffluent tenants.[31] The logic of this criticism seems

26. Id. §§ 92.052(a)(2), 92.058.

27. Worden v. Ordway, 105 Idaho 719, 672 P.2d 1049 (1983).

28. Comment, Recent Statutory Developments in Texas Landlord–Tenant Law: A Sword Without a Shield?, 35 Sw.L.J. 645 (1981).

29. Cunningham, Stoebuck & Whitman, The Law of Property § 6.40 (1984).

30. The Wisconsin legislature demonstrated an awareness of this distinction when, after placing a duty to repair upon all landlords, it allowed commercial landlords, but not residential landlords, to waive this duty by a writing signed by both parties. Wis. Stat.Ann. § 704.07 (West 1981 & 1985).

31. Meyers, The Covenant of Habitability and the American Law Institute, 27 Stan.L.Rev. 879 (1975). But compare: Ackerman, Regulating Slum Housing Markets on Behalf of the Poor: Of Housing Codes, Housing Subsidies and Income Distribution Policy, 80 Yale L.J. 1093 (1971); Ackerman, More on Slum Housing and Redistribution Policy: A Reply to Professor Komesar, 82 Yale L.J. 1194 (1973); Kennedy, The Effect of the Warranty of Habitability on Low Income Housing: "Milking" and Class Violence, 15 F.S.U.Law Review 485 (1987); Markovits, The Dis-

compelling, but empirical studies of the actual effects of mandatory habitability have been viewed as inconclusive, due to failure of such studies to exclude other factors influencing the supply of affordable housing.[32]

Even if mandatory habitability significantly reduces the supply of housing affordable by the poor, it would be more productive and more humane to address the problem of housing supply directly and to seek solutions other than compelling persons by economic necessity to occupy uninhabitable dwellings. Possibly mandatory habitability will constitute a helpful prod to devise effective measures addressing the complex and seemingly intractable problem of housing supply. Another consideration is that the assumed adverse effects of mandatory habitability upon housing supply may be outweighed by positive effects upon housing quality. It would seem to be axiomatic that unsafe and unhealthful dwellings produce personal injuries and ill health and that these in turn impose costs upon the community as well as upon persons affected directly.[33] Measuring such effects, however, is extremely difficult, if not impossible. It has even been doubted that such adverse effects actually occur to a significant extent.[34] In any event, despite the uncertain economic effects of mandatory habitability, the growing support for this policy indicates that our society is no more tolerant of unsafe housing than of unsafe working conditions, food, autos, and other consumer products.

SECTION 2. TORT LIABILITY

When defective condition of the premises results in injury to person or property, tort law may impose liability upon the landlord. A recent rapid expansion of such liability, matching the expansion of landlord responsibility outside the law of torts for habitability, and related to it, has occurred.

Traditionally, the landlord was generally immune to liability for injuries suffered by the tenant or the tenant's family or guests

tributive Impact, Allocative Efficiency, and Overall Desirability of Ideal Housing Codes: Some Theoretical Clarifications, 89 Harv.L.Rev. 1815 (1976).

32. Glendon, The Transformation of American Landlord–Tenant Law: 23 B.C.L.Rev. 503, 561 (1982); Rabin, The Revolution in Residential Landlord–Tenant Law: Causes and Consequences, 69 Corn.L.Rev. 517, 558 (1984). But see Judge Richard Posner's opinion in Chi-

cago Board of Realtors, Inc. v. City of Chicago, 819 F.2d 732, 742 (7th Cir. 1987). Theoretical studies of the economic effects of housing codes also have arrived at conflicting results.

33. But see Rabin, The Revolution in Residential Landlord–Tenant Law: Causes and Consequences, 69 Corn.L. Rev. 517, 570 (1984)

34. Id.

as a consequence of defective condition of the premises. Exceptions to landlord immunity were created and expanded by courts as this body of law developed. Chief Justice Kenison's opinion for the Supreme Court of New Hampshire in Sargent v. Ross summarized these exceptions: "(1) a hidden danger in the premises of which the landlord but not the tenant is aware, (2) premises leased for public use, (3) premises retained under the landlord's control, such as common stairways, or (4) premises negligently repaired by the landlord." [35] This opinion went on to discard that formalistic approach and substituted for it the case-by-case rule that "landlords as other persons must exercise reasonable care not to subject others to unreasonable risk of harm." [36]

According to the traditional law, even if the landlord promised to repair and breach of this covenant resulted in injury to the tenant, recovery was confined to the cost of repair. If the injured person was a member of the tenant's family or a guest, even this meager recovery was unavailable, as the injured person was not in contractual privity with the landlord. Some courts finally abandoned both of these severely restrictive rules and imposed liability upon landlords for personal injuries to tenants, their families, and guests resulting from negligent breach of a promise to repair.[37]

Breach of the implied warranty of habitability, whether consensual or mandated, should have the same consequences for tort liability as the modern position on breach of a promise to repair. That appears to be the trend, but it is not uniform. The divergent views are illustrated by two Ohio Supreme Court cases. In the 1980 case of Thrash v. Hill,[38] that court concluded that the expressed statutory remedies for unfitness of rented dwellings, which did not include tort actions, were exclusive. The following year, in Shroades v. Rental Homes, Inc.,[39] the same court, discovering that the legislature had impliedly authorized tort remedies, overruled *Thrash*. Violation of the statute, the court declared, constitutes "negligence *per se* " and the landlord would be liable for personal injuries proximately caused by a defective condition covered by the statute if the landlord had received notice of the defect.

---

35. 113 N.H. 388, 308 A.2d 528, 531 (1973). See generally Browder, The Taming of a Duty—The Tort Liability of Landlords, 81 Mich.L.Rev. 99 (1982); Davis & DeLaTorre, A Fresh Look at Premises Liability as Affected by the Warranty of Habitability, 59 Wash.L. Rev. 141 (1984).

36. Id., 308 A.2d at 534.

37. Faber v. Creswick, 31 N.J. 234, 156 A.2d 252 (1959).

38. 63 Ohio St.2d 178, 407 N.E.2d 495 (1980).

39. 68 Ohio St.2d 20, 427 N.E.2d 774 (1981). Accord: Horvath v. Burt, 98 Nev. 186, 643 P.2d 1229 (1982).

The Supreme Court of California has gone even further. It held, in Becker v. IRM Corp.,[40] that a landlord could be liable for personal injuries to a tenant due to a latent defect, even in the absence of concealment of a known danger or an expressed contractual or statutory duty to repair. The tenant's arm had been severely lacerated when he slipped and fell against a glass shower door that, unknown to the landlord (who had acquired the building more than a decade after its construction), was untempered. The court's reasoning drew upon the law of product liability: "Landlords are an integral part of the enterprise of producing and marketing rental housing"[41] and accordingly are liable on the same ground as manufacturers of defective products. The California landlord's strict liability as a marketer of rental housing clearly is broader than landlord responsibility for habitability of the *Javins* genre. The untempered glass shower door in *Becker* probably would not constitute a housing code violation and certainly would not be sufficiently substantial to justify rent withholding.

Indicative of the broad sweep of the revolution in landlord-tenant law, in recent years some tenants have recovered damages for emotional distress due to unfitness of dwellings, even if they have suffered no other associated personal injury. Despite the reluctance of courts to award damages for such claims,[42] verdicts for a tenant for $35,000 for "recklessly inflicted" emotional distress and $1,000 for breach of the covenant of habitability, based on repeated flooding of tenant's basement apartment with ankle-deep filthy water, were upheld by Massachusetts' highest court.[43] There was evidence that the flooding was caused by the landlord's failure to repair a porous wall and that the tenant had suffered severe emotional distress. In a subsequent case, however, the same court made it clear that such recoveries would not become routine. It upheld a finding that evidence was insufficient to show that a landlord's failure to prevent mice from entering an apartment was a reckless infliction of severe emotional distress.[44]

It should come as no surprise at this point to learn that landlords increasingly are being held liable for criminal attacks upon tenants attributable to failure of landlords to comply with the safety aspect of their habitability duty.[45] However, some

40. 38 Cal.3d 454, 213 Cal.Rptr. 213, 698 P.2d 116 (1985).

41. Id., 698 P.2d at 124.

42. Prosser & Keeton, The Law of Torts §§ 12, 54 (5th Ed.1984).

43. Simon v. Solomon, 385 Mass. 91, 431 N.E.2d 556 (1982). This and similar cases are discussed in Smith, Tenant Remedies for Breach of Habitability: Tort Dimensions of a Contract Concept, 35 Kan.L.Rev. 505 (1987).

44. Wolfberg v. Hunter, 385 Mass. 390, 432 N.E.2d 467 (1982).

45. Kline v. 1500 Massachusetts Ave. Apartment Corp., 439 F.2d 477 (D.C.Cir.1970); Flood v. Wisconsin Real Estate Investment Trust, 503 F.Supp. 1157 (D.Kan.1980); Samson v. Saginaw

courts have refused to impose such liability except in quite limited circumstances. The Supreme Court of Pennsylvania, in Feld v. Merriam, in 1984, declared that there is a "crucial distinction between the risk of injury from a physical defect in the property, and the risk from the criminal attack of a third person . . . [The latter] arises not from the conduct of the landlord but from the conduct of an unpredictable independent agent."[46] This view reflects the past, but surely not the future. It surely is predictable that criminals will enter doors with defective locks, lie in wait in unlighted halls, or prey upon tenants in unguarded parking lots. However, aside from the issue of foreseeability, it must be determined that the landlord had an obligation to provide the security in question. In some instances, the landlord may have failed to comply with a specific statutory mandate, such as equipping doors with effective locks, but in other instances the landlord's obligation must be found in general concepts of habitability or general statutory terms such as the URLTA duty to keep common areas in a "safe" condition.[47] One court has read these terms as restricted to "failures of the building," such as collapsing stairs, and therefore not providing a basis for landlord liability for criminal attacks upon tenants.[48] This is an exceedingly narrow and unrealistic construction.

Landlords have sought to protect themselves from tort liability by inserting in leases a clause declaring that they not be liable for any injury to the lessee or any other person entering the demised premises or the building and grounds of which the demised premises are a part. A few years ago, such exculpatory clauses were often upheld, but today they generally are invalidated by statute or court decision,[49] a reflection of the reality that tenant injuries would go unremedied in most instances if residential landlords could insulate themselves from tort liability by routinely inserting exculpatory clauses in form leases.

Professional Building Inc., 393 Mich. 393, 224 N.W.2d 843 (1975); Trentacost v. Brussel, 82 N.J. 214, 412 A.2d 436 (1980).

46. 506 Pa. 383, 485 A.2d 742 (1984).

47. URLTA § 2.104(3).

48. Deem v. Charles E. Smith Management, Inc., 799 F.2d 944 (4th Cir. 1986) (applying Virginia law).

49. Rabin, The Revolution in Residential Landlord and Tenant Law: Causes and Consequences, 69 Corn.L. Rev. 517, 530 (1984).

Chapter 6

RENT CONTROL

There are no common law restraints upon the discretion of landlords to charge any rents tenants are willing to pay. It is assumed that the market will regulate satisfactorily the price of rental housing. In some situations, however, legislative bodies have recognized that the market will not so function.[1] Congress enacted wartime rent controls to prevent landlords from taking unfair advantage of the drastically reduced supply of new housing during such periods. In response to rapid inflation, Congress also regulated rents in 1971 and 1972. Since the termination of national controls, many large cities have regulated residential rents, in response to continuing shortage of affordable housing. These regulations may not be temporary. In some states, this trend has been turned aside by statutes banning municipal rent control.

Rent control, except for temporary emergencies, is generally criticized by economists as counter-productive, as it discourages construction of new rental housing and maintenance of existing housing, and also induces landlords to attempt to convert rental housing to other uses, such as condominiums.[2] In addition to making these points, President Reagan's Commission on Housing concluded in 1982 that "rent control essentially yields an income distribution from landlords to tenants by implicitly taxing landlords for the benefit of tenants" and that this is "an inefficient and inequitable" tax.[3]

Despite such criticism, the central features of rent control ordinances have been upheld by the courts against challenges based upon constitutional and other grounds.[4] Nevertheless, some

1. The law of rent control is thoroughly covered in Schoshinski, American Law of Landlord and Tenant § 7.8 (1980). See also Hoeflich & Malloy, The Shattered Dream of American Housing Policy—The Need for Reform, 26 B.C.L. Rev. 655, 663 (1985).

2. Muth, Redistribution of Income Through Regulation in Housing, 32 Emory L.J. 691, 693 (1983).

3. The Report of the President's Commission on Housing 91 (1982). For another view, see Note, Reassessing

Rent Control: Its Economic Impact in a Gentrifying Housing Market, 101 Harv. L.Rev. 1835 (1988).

4. Fisher v. City of Berkeley, 475 U.S. 260, 106 S.Ct. 1045, 89 L.Ed.2d 206 (1986) (rent control ordinance not invalid as being pre-empted by Sherman Act); Woods v. Cloyd W. Miller Co., 333 U.S. 138, 68 S.Ct. 421, 92 L.Ed. 596 (1948); Birkenfeld v. City of Berkeley, 17 Cal.3d 129, 130 Cal.Reptr. 465, 550 P.2d 1001 (1976); Hutton Park Gardens

landlords may successfully challenge the particular application of rent control ordinances to them. The most likely allegation is that they have been deprived of a "reasonable" return in violation of the ordinance or constitutional due process. Also, specific aspects of some rent control programs may be legally vulnerable.[5] But tough measures intended to prevent landlords from circumventing regulation have been upheld. Among these are denial of rent increases for premises in substantial violation of housing codes,[6] denial of permission to convert rental units to condominiums,[7] and even denial of permission to demolish rental buildings.[8]

v. Town Council, 68 N.J. 543, 350 A.2d 1 (1975).

5. A provision entitling landlords to less rent from tenants with economic hardship than other tenants was upheld in Pennell v. City of San Jose, 108 S.Ct. 849, 99 L.Ed.2d 1 (1988).

6. Orange Taxpayers Council, Inc. v. City of Orange, 83 N.J. 246, 416 A.2d 353 (1980).

7. Flynn v. City of Cambridge, 383 Mass. 152, 418 N.E.2d 335 (1981).

8. Nash v. City of Santa Monica, 37 Cal.3d 97, 207 Cal.Rptr. 285, 688 P.2d 894 (1984).

Chapter 7

RIGHT TO EXTENDED OCCUPANCY (RETALIATORY EVICTION AND GOOD CAUSE EVICTION)

Traditional common law gave tenants no right to remain in possession after the end of their terms or termination by notice of periodic tenancies. Indeed, if they failed to vacate promptly, they were liable for damages and possibly for imposition of another term against their will. Today, in an increasing number of situations, tenants in many states are allowed to remain in possession after their terms or periodic tenancies have ended.

Motives of a landlord for declining to continue renting to a tenant are usually irrelevant. If, however, the motive is to punish a tenant for reporting housing code violations to a code official, the landlord's conduct undermines the code by deterring complaints that would be helpful, if not essential, to enforcement of the code. For this reason, Judge J. Skelly Wright, in another famous opinion, Edwards v. Habib,[1] concluded that a prohibition of such conduct was implied in the District of Columbia housing code. Other courts and legislatures quickly followed this lead.[2] In most states, eviction, as well as other landlord action, such as increasing rent or cutting off services, in retaliation for tenant assertion of rights to habitable dwellings, and even some rights not related to habitability, is forbidden. The scope of this prohibition varies significantly from state to state and continues to be an issue in litigation.

Definition and proof of retaliatory motive are difficult issues. Retaliatory motive may be inferred from the timing of an eviction notice shortly after complaint by a tenant. But when should it be inferred that the retaliatory motive has been dissipated? And what should be the effect of multiple motives, including one or more non-retaliatory motives such as a desire to get rid of a noisy tenant or to rent to a close friend? An issue of paramount importance is location of the burden of persuasion. Courts and legislatures have resolved these questions in different ways.[3] Perhaps the best solutions are to: (1) define as retaliatory motive one that is predominantly retaliatory; (2) shift the burden of persua-

---

1. 130 U.S.App.D.C. 126, 397 F.2d 687 (1968), cert. denied, 393 U.S. 1016, 89 S.Ct. 618, 21 L.Ed.2d 560 (1969).

2. Schoshinski, American Law of Landlord and Tenant ch. 12 (1980).

3. Id. §§ 12.5, 12.6.

sion to the landlord when eviction comes shortly after assertion of tenant rights; and (3) shift the burden of persuasion back to the tenant after lapse of a specific time, such as six months.

The retaliatory eviction doctrine is no longer limited to tenant acts to enforce habitability laws. A California landlord who served notice of termination seven days after the tenant complained to police that the landlord had sexually molested tenant's daughter was held barred by retaliatory motive from eviction.[4] This was based upon two grounds: (1) the common law defense of retaliatory eviction is available because "effective enforcement of this state's criminal law depends upon the willingness of victims and witnesses to report crime and participate in the criminal justice process"; and (2) a California statute expressly prohibits retaliation for exercise of "any rights under the law."[5] In the absence of such a statute, courts have been reluctant to rest the retaliatory eviction doctrine upon constitutional rights of expression and petition, due to the difficulty of finding state action.[6]

To a greater extent that most other courts, the California courts have expressed concern that recognizing retaliatory eviction as a defense to summary actions to recover possession (FED suits) is inconsistent with legislative policy that such proceedings be summary. Each judicial broadening of the defense increases the inconsistency, but the Supreme Court of California has continued to find that the policies supporting the extensions outweigh FED policies.[7]

Legal recognition of a right to extended occupancy has gone beyond retaliatory eviction. Concern about dislocation of tenants incident to conversion of residential rental units to condominiums has led to enactment of ordinances in some cities allowing tenants to remain in possession for varying periods of time.[8] Much more far-reaching are statutes and ordinances allowing some residential tenants to remain in possession so long as there is no "good cause" to evict. These apply to tenants in governmentally owned or subsidized housing,[9] to tenants in rent-controlled units (to prevent

---

4. Barela v. Superior Court of Orange County, 30 Cal.3d 244, 178 Cal. Rptr. 618, 636 P.2d 582 (1981).

5. Id., 636 P.2d at 585, 586.

6. Schoshinski, American Law of Landlord and Tenant § 12.2 (1980).

7. E.g., in addition to Barela, see S.P. Growers Ass'n v. Rodriguez, 17 Cal. 3d 719, 131 Cal.Rptr. 761, 552 P.2d 721 (1976).

8. Comment, Regulating Condominium Conversions: Do Municipal Ordi-

nances Adequately Protect Tenants' and Owners' Constitutional Rights?, 1985 Ariz.St.L.J. 935.

9. 24 C.F.R. §§ 247.3, 882.215, 996.4(1) (1984); Note, Are Applicants for Section 8 Housing Subsidies "Entitled" to the Benefits, 1985 Ill.L.Rev. 757; Sarshik, The Effect of Statutory Changes upon the Rights of Section 8 Tenants, 14 Urb.Law. 749 (1982).

evasion),[10] and, at least in New Jersey, to nearly all tenants.[11] Several identified causes are declared by the New Jersey statute to constitute good cause, but there is still room for judicial discretion. One specified good cause is refusal by a tenant to accept "reasonable" changes in the landlord's proposed terms of the extended tenancy.

Will other states, or should they, follow New Jersey's lead in enacting good cause statutes? The case for them is that it is unfair to require residential tenants to endure the expenses and difficulty of moving, especially in areas of severe housing shortage, in the absence of some good reason to evict. What is the harm to the landlord from this? The case against good cause eviction statutes is that they not only override the terms of the lease, but also expose landlords to the risk that the meaning given to the term "good cause" by legislatures and courts and the burden of persuasion placed on the landlord may make it extremely difficult for a landlord to establish good cause.[12]

10. Gruen v. Patterson, 55 N.Y.2d 631, 446 N.Y.S.2d 253, 430 N.E.2d 1306 (1981).

11. N.J.Stat.Ann. § 2.A: 18–61.1 (West Supp.1987).

12. Bell, Providing Security of Tenure for Residential Tenants: Good Faith as a Limitation on the Landlord's Right to Terminate, 19 Ga.L.Rev. 483 (1985) proposes that a better approach than good cause eviction statutes (which Bell thinks will not be widely adopted because perceived to be too radical) is judicial application to evictions of the "good faith" requirement implied in termination of employment contracts and franchises. The good faith standard is not as protective of tenants as is the good cause standard as the former puts the burden on the tenant to show that the landlord's motive was improper. The good cause standard requires that even a well motivated landlord show a good cause for eviction.

Chapter 8

RESTRICTION ON USE

Uses of the leased premises may be restricted by provisions of the lease and by certain legal doctrines. Courts have often declared that leases will be construed in favor of freedom of use, consistent with the venerable common law policy of opposition to restraints on alienation of land.[1] But courts have also declared the goals of construction of provisions claimed to restrict use should be to carry out the intent of the parties.[2] The latter statement appears to describe what courts actually do in such cases. A lease that states a use without expressly making it exclusive is construed as permissive, not impliedly restrictive, but only if admissible evidence fails to establish that the parties probably intended that the stated use be exclusive. Two cases illustrate the point. In one, a lease of a building to be used as a "real estate office" was construed as not impliedly forbidding use of the building as a grocery and dairy store.[3] In the other, however, a lease for the sale of "food and nonalcoholic beverages" was construed as impliedly prohibiting sale of alcoholic beverages.[4] Both results are explainable by reference to the probable intent of the parties, without resort to any constructional bias. In one instance, URLTA reverses the traditional constructional bias by prohibiting nonresidential use of dwelling units, in the absence of agreement to the contrary.[5] This is probably consistent with mutual intent in most instances.

Consider the following case. Premises leased "for the sale of gifts, novelties, etc." were used for an enterprise called the "Birds & Bees Adult Book Store." The lessor's other tenants and neighbors protested vigorously. Should the lease have been construed as impliedly forbidding a use that would harm relations between the lessor and other tenants and neighbors? This issue was never litigated in this case, because the court rescinded the lease on the ground that the lessor has been induced to enter into the lease by "half-truths and concealment of special knowledge."[6]

1. See Beck v. Giordano, 144 Colo. 372, 356 P.2d 264, 265 (1960).

2. See Bovin v. Galitzka, 250 N.Y. 228, 165 N.E. 273, 175 (1929).

3. Id.

4. Id.

5. URLTA § 3.104.

6. Stroup v. Conant, 268 Or. 292, 520 P.2d 337 (1974).

If the use restriction is a covenant, it may be enforced by suits for damages, injunction, or both. If the restriction is a condition, rather than a covenant, the lessor's remedy is forfeiture. In leases, as in other documents, courts are reluctant to construe restrictions as conditions, unless it is clear that the parties so intended, in view of the harshness of this remedy.[7]

SECTION 1. WASTE

The common law has long protected lessors against unauthorized acts by tenants that harm lessors' reversions. Such acts, termed "waste," may be enjoined, compensated by damages (double or treble damages by statute on many states) or entitle lessors (according to modern authority) to terminate the lease.

Waste may be voluntary or permissive. The former is an affirmative act, such as razing a building. Permissive waste is harm resulting from neglect, such as water damage to floors of a building due to failure to repair the roof. Recognition of the implied warranty of habitability in modern times, shifting the duty to repair dwellings to landlords, has greatly narrowed the ambit of permissive waste.

Acts by tenants that substantially change the physical nature of the premises have been deemed waste, even through the change enhanced the value of the land—meliorating waste.[8] An example is the razing of an old building and replacement of it with a new building. The lessor may have preferred the old building. The meliorating waste doctrine, however, is very harsh to a tenant (especially with a long unexpired term) who can make a beneficial use of the premises only by altering them substantially. A flexible approach that allows tenants to make "reasonably necessary" changes for their reasonable uses has some support.[9]

Tenants have been held liable for acts of third persons.[10] Of course, such tenants may have causes of action over against the culpable third persons. If the tenant has an option to purchase the property, however, the tenant's liability for waste will be

7. Shoshinski, American Law of Landlord and Tenant § 5.9 (1980).

8. Chicago Auditorium Ass'n v. Willing, 20 F.2d 837 (7th Cir.1927), rev'd on other grounds 277 U.S. 274, 48 S.Ct. 507, 72 L.Ed. 880 (1928).

9. Restatement of Property (Second) Landlord and Tenant § 12.2(1), Com-

ment d and Reporter's Note 1 (1977). Accord: Melms v. Pabst Brewing Co., 194 Wis. 7, 79 N.W. 738 (1899) (involving a life estate).

10. Consolidated Coal Co. v. Savitz, 57 Ill.App. 659 (4th Dist.1894).

suspended until it is known whether the option will be exercised.[11] Tenant liability for acts of third persons who are trespassers may have very little support today.[12] Tenant liability for destructive acts by sublessees and other persons on the premises with the tenant's permission seems extreme in instances where the tenant lacks effective control of such persons. Consider the case of Prevo v. Evarts,[13] involving a man who became a tenant of a dwelling for occupancy by the tenant's estranged wife and her sons, but not by the tenant himself, who was held liable for destructive acts by his wife's sons and their friends. It did not appear that the tenant had any notice that these destructive acts would occur.

SECTION 2. ILLEGAL USES

If a lease authorizes an illegal use, the lease usually is void or unenforceable.[14] If the lease neither authorizes nor prohibits an illegal use, the landlord and tenant relationship is unaffected by an illegal use by the tenant—according to the traditional judicial view.[15] A contrary position, adopted by the American Law Institute, impliedly incorporates the prohibitory law into the lease, allowing lessors to recover damages, obtain injunctions, or even terminate the lease in some instances.[16] This position recognizes that illegal uses may harm lessors in many respects, including impairment of relations between them and their tenants and neighbors, difficulty in obtaining future tenants or purchasers, and possibly harm to the reputation of lessors. In addition, the deliberate pace of public law enforcement may leave lessors unprotected for a period against continuing illegal use, in the absence of private law remedies.

A problem often arises as to the effect of a lease for lawful purposes, which subsequently become illegal. Where subsequent legislation is enacted prohibiting a certain business and a lease limits the use of the premises to that business, the tenant will be relieved from further liability to pay rent on the ground that performance has become impossible due to this legislation.[17] How-

---

11. Keogh v. Peck, 316 Ill. 318, 147 N.E. 266 (1925).

12. Restatement of Property (Second) Landlord and Tenant § 12.2(2), Comment g and Reporter's Note 7 (1977).

13. 146 Vt. 216, 500 A.2d 227 (1985).

14. Brown v. Southall Realty Co., 237 A.2d 834 (D.C.App.1968).

15. McKenzie v. Carte, 385 S.W.2d 520 (Tex.Civ.App.1964).

16. Restatement of Property (Second) Landlord and Tenant § 12.5 (1977).

17. Levy v. Johnston and Hunt, 224 Ill.App. 300 (1st Dist.1922).

ever, where a lease provides that the tenant might pursue multiple purposes and only some of these purposes subsequently become unlawful, the tenant is not excused from liability for the rent. As long as the tenant is authorized to perform any lawful acts under the lease, despite the fact that the value of the remaining lawful purposes is substantially diminished, the tenant is still required to pay the rent.

A related group of cases deals with the rights of the parties when the use of the premises is not made unlawful, but the business which the lessee is to transact is materially restricted. Under the general rule, if there is a total frustration of the purposes originally contemplated, the lessee will be excused. In the case of Deibler v. Bernard Bros., Inc.[18] an appellate court construed a lease as providing that the premises could be used as an automobile showroom and for no other purpose. Subsequent government restrictions made the sale of new automobiles difficult, if not impossible. It was held that the sale of automobiles was not prohibited, only restricted; therefore, the lessee was not relieved from obligations under the lease. The fact that business was not as good as usual would not alter the decision. This opinion would seem to commit the court to a very strict interpretation of the general rule. However, on appeal to the Supreme Court of Illinois, the case was affirmed on the ground, seemingly sound, that the lease contained no use restriction.[19]

SECTION 3. FIXTURES

If the lease does not authorize removal of things annexed to the premises by the tenant, the law of fixtures may preclude removal. To that extent, the law of fixtures indirectly restricts use of the leased premises. Fortunately for tenants, the once-rigid rule that chattels attached by tenants in such manner as to be fixtures become property of lessors has been greatly moderated. Courts long ago began to allow tenants to remove trade fixtures, in furtherance of commerce. They also began to attach more weight to the intention of the annexor at the time of annexation than to the other factors deemed relevant to the issue of whether a chattel has become a fixture—annexation and adaptation. It may be generalized that today most tenant fixtures are removable, if

---

18. 319 Ill.App. 504, 48 N.E.2d 422 (1st Dist.1943).

19. Deibler v. Bernard Bros., Inc., 385 Ill. 610, 53 N.E.2d 450 (1944).

removal can be accomplished without substantial damage to the premises and if it occurs before the tenant gives up possession.[20]

Difficulties may still be encountered by tenants in some jurisdictions. A court might feel committed to the old, now discredited, position that removal must occur before the end of the term, even though the tenant remains in possession under a new lease or otherwise.[21] Even the more modern version of the rule on timeliness of removal would not protect the tenant who seeks to remove within a reasonable time after surrender of possession. A better approach, favored by The American Law Institute,[22] is to allow removal during a reasonable time after surrender. Perhaps a still better approach is to allow removal of fixtures at any time, subject to liability for harm caused by delay in removal. After all, a tenant does not lose title to chattels by failing to remove them at any time.

Another possible problem for tenants is that the typical judicial statement conditioning removal upon absence of substantial damage to the premises does not make it clear that, in instances of substantial damage, the tenant could remove by providing adequate security for restoration. There seems to be no good reason for denying removal in such cases.[23]

Much of the litigation today concerning fixtures focuses upon construction of lease clauses.[24] There is an evident need for more careful drafting of such clauses.

SECTION 4. SECURITY DEPOSITS

Leases commonly require a tenant to deposit a sum of money at the outset to protect the landlord against tenant defaults. Security deposits are relied upon primarily by landlords to provide some reimbursement for physical damage to the premises.

Attempts by tenants, especially residential tenants, to obtain return of security deposits at the end of their terms often have been frustrated. If the landlord wrongfully refuses to return a deposit, the costs of litigation to recover it leave the tenant without an effective remedy in most instances. Lessors also have drafted security deposit agreements so as to minimize their obliga-

---

20. Handler v. Horns, 2 N.J. 18, 65 A.2d 523 (1949).

21. Discussed and rejected in Handler v. Horns, Id.

22. Restatement of Property (Second) Landlord and Tenant § 12.3 (1977).

23. Id. § 12.2(4).

24. Schoskinski, American Law of Landlord and Tenant § 5.27 (1980).

tion to return the deposit. If the landlord becomes insolvent, the tenant usually discovers that the security deposit agreement merely created a debt, with no priority over claims by other creditors.[25] If the landlord conveys the reversion, authority is conflicting as to whether the new landlord is obligated by the security deposit agreement.[26]

These and other problems have led to widespread adoption of statutes concerning residential security deposits. Unfortunately, the statutes are not uniform and have not eliminated all of the problems. A major accomplishment of these statutes is the establishment of procedures to be followed by each party and entitlement of tenants to double or treble damages and attorney's fees for noncompliance by landlords. Some statutes make this entitlement available only if the landlord's noncompliance was in bad faith. Whether the landlord acted in bad faith is likely to be a difficult fact issue. At least one court has held that the burden of persuasion on this issue is on the tenant.[27]

When the reversion is transferred, the tenant ought to be able to recover from either the new landlord or the old landlord and, if recovery is had against the original landlord, that one should be entitled to subrogation against the new one. URLTA so provides,[28] but some statutes do not. One of these relieves the old landlord of responsibility if the new one informs the tenant in writing that the obligation has been assumed by the new landlord.[29] This seems unfair to the tenant as it deprives the tenant of contractual benefits without consent. It has been argued that continued liability of the old landlord requires as a practical matter that that landlord negotiate a release from each tenant, which would pose a substantial impediment to sales of multi-unit projects.[30] Such negotiation might be avoided, however, by placing security deposits in a trust fund at the time of transfer.[31] Some statutes require creation of trust funds for security deposits when first received, and also payment of interest to the tenant.[32]

25. Young v. Cobbs, 83 So.2d 417 (Fla.1955).

26. Restatement of Property (Second) Landlord and Tenant § 16.1, Reporter's Note 3 (1977).

27. Roeder v. Nolan, 321 N.W.2d 1 (Iowa 1982).

28. URLTA §§ 2.101(e) & 2.105(a).

29. Tex.Prop.Code Ann. § 92.105(b) (Vernon 1984).

30. Strum, Proposed Uniform Residential Landlord and Tenant Act: A Departure from Traditional Concepts, 8 Real Prop., Probate & Trust J. 495 (1973).

31. Mixon, Tenant's Security Deposits: Liability of Former Landlord and New Owner After Sale of an Occupied Project, 15 Tex.Tech.L.Rev. 549, 590, 591 (1984).

32. A Chicago ordinance requiring deposit of residential security deposits in interest-bearing, federally insured accounts in Illinois financial institutions was involved in Chicago Board of Realtors, Inc. v. City of Chicago, 819 F.2d 732 (7th Cir.1987).

Chapter 9

TRANSFERS

SECTION 1. FORMALITIES

Landlords and tenants may convey their respective interests unless they have validly agreed to restrict transfers. They must, of course, comply with the Statute of Frauds and, to obtain protection against some third parties, comply with applicable recording acts.

A conveyance of the lessor's reversion (typically a fee simple) usually has the effect of substituting the grantee as lessor. Long ago, attornment—i.e., acceptance by the tenant of the grantee as landlord—was required, but this is now obsolete.[1]

SECTION 2. ASSIGNMENT AND SUBLEASE

A transferee of the leasehold, however, is substituted for the tenant only if the transfer is an assignment. If the transfer is a sublease, the transferor remains the tenant and the transferee is a subtenant, obligated in most respects only to the tenant. If the tenant transfers the leasehold for the entire term in all or a part of the leased premises, the transfer is an assignment. If, however, the tenant retains a reversion, the transfer is a sublease.

Courts have disagreed as to whether reservation by the tenant of a right of entry in the event of default by the transferee is to be treated as a reversion.[2] The traditional view of the right of entry is that it is a mere chose in action and not a reversion. Adherence to this view stamps the transfer as an assignment, despite reservation of a right of entry. Some courts depart from the traditional view and regard the reservation of a right of entry as a reversion, at least for the purpose of resolving the issue of classifying a

1. Compare Fisher v. Deering, 60 Ill. 114 (1871) with Barnes v. Northern Trust Co., 169 Ill. 112, 48 N.E. 31 (1897).

2. The conflicting cases are collected in Restatement of Property (Second) Landlord and Tenant § 15.1, Reporter's Note 8 (1977). This section supports those cases holding that a right of entry is a reversion for this purpose. See Comment i.

transfer as an assignment or sublease. In one case, a court adopted a flexible approach of relying primarily upon the intent of the parties in determining whether a transfer by a tenant reserving a right of entry is an assignment or a sublease.[3] In that case, a transfer clearly intended by the parties to be an assignment, but containing a right of entry, was treated as an assignment.

SECTION 3. EFFECT OF TRANSFERS UPON BURDENS AND BENEFITS

Grantees of the landlord and assignees of the tenant (but not sublessees) are bound and benefitted by most of the provisions of the prime lease so long as they own their respective estates. They are in privity of estate, but not privity of contract, with the owner of the other estate in the land. Thus, an assignee is liable to the landlord for rent that accrues during the period of the assignee's ownership of the leasehold estate, but is not liable for rent that accrues after the assignee has validly assigned the estate to another.[4]

Grantees and assignees will not be bound, however, by covenants in the prime lease that either were not intended to bind successors or that fail to "touch and concern" their respective estates.[5] The touch and concern requirement serves the policy against unreasonable restraints on alienation by freeing successors from covenants that are not substantially related to the landlord and tenant relationship. Courts and commentators have had little success in stating this requirement with sufficient precision to make it a reliable predictive test.[6] Perhaps most helpful is the simple statement that a lease covenant satisfies this requirement "to the extent its performance is not related to other

3. Jaber v. Miller, 219 Ark. 59, 239 S.W.2d 760 (1951). This rationale, however, may not have been essential to this court's decision.

4. A.D. Juilliard & Co. v. American Woolen Co., 69 R.I. 215, 32 A.2d 800 (1943).

5. These requirements were stated in Spencer's Case, 5 Co. Rep. 16A, 77 Eng.Rep. 72 (1583). That case required that intent be manifested by use of the word "assigns" if the covenant related to something not in existence—such as a covenant to repair a building not yet constructed. Fortunately, the *in esse*

rule, which is intent-defeating and unsupported by policy, is generally obsolete. Purvis v. Shuman, 273 Ill. 286, 112 N.E. 679 (1916). But it may be alive and well in some states. See Mercantile–Safe Deposit and Trust Co. v. Mayor and City Council of Baltimore, 308 Md. 627, 521 A.2d 734, 737, 738 (1987). The runability of covenants with the land also is important in contexts other than the landlord-tenant relation. See 380, infra.

6. For one attempt, see Bigelow, The Content of Covenants in Leases, 12 Mich.L.Rev. 639 (1914).

property and affects the use and enjoyment" of the burdened estate.[7]

One can imagine covenants that clearly would not touch and concern the estates of the parties, such as a covenant "by lessee and assigns to give weekly piano lessons to the lessor's children for reasonable compensation." Even though this covenant expressly binds assigns, and thus appears to satisfy the intention requirement, it has nothing to do with interests of either lessor or lessee in the premises. Unfortunately, some types of covenants that clearly do affect the use and enjoyment of the estate in issue have been held by some courts not to touch and concern, and therefore not to burden, that estate. The covenant by a landlord to return a security deposit is one of these.[8] Such decisions are manifestations of general hostility by some courts to the running of any obligation to pay money, whatever its purpose, except, of course, the covenant to pay rent.

A sublessee holds a new leasehold estate carved out by the tenant, therefore is not in privity of estate with the landlord, and accordingly is not liable to the landlord for rent or most other obligations in the lease. However, there are important exceptions. Provisions (promissory or otherwise) in leases that prohibit specified acts, such as bringing pets on the premises or transferring to a new occupant without the lessor's consent, bind even sublessees.[9] The basis for enforcing restrictions against sublessees is the equity doctrine that a transferee of any interest in land with notice of restrictions cannot in good conscience disregard them, and therefore will be restrained from doing so. Sublessees, as well as assignees, are deemed to have notice of provisions in the prime lease, as they claim under it.

Although assignees are liable by virtue of privity of estate for rent that accrues during their period of ownership of the leasehold estate, the original tenant also remains liable in the absence of a release by the landlord. One cannot unilaterally rid oneself of contractual obligations. Consent by the landlord to an assignment by the tenant is not viewed as an implied release of the tenant's obligations in the lease, as it would be unrealistic to infer such intent.[10] The landlord may sue either the original tenant or an assignee or both. The judgment against each may be for the full amount of rent owed, but the landlord is entitled to only one

7. Restatement of Property (Second) Landlord and Tenant § 16.1, Comment b (1977).

8. Joseph Fallert Brewing Co. v. Blass, 119 App.Div. 53, 103 N.Y.S. 865 (1907). Contra: Moskin v. Goldstein, 225 Mich. 389, 196 N.W. 415 (1923).

9. Cesar v. Virgin, 207 Ala. 148, 92 So. 406 (1921); Boston Properties v. Pirelli Tire Co., 134 Cal.App.3d 985, 185 Cal.Rptr. 56 (1982).

10. Cauble v. Hanson, 249 S.W. 175 (Tex.Com.App.1923).

satisfaction, i.e., as soon as the total unpaid rent is recovered on either judgment, by voluntary payment or by levy, both judgments are considered fully satisfied. As between the original tenant and the assignee, the latter is primarily liable; if the tenant is required to pay the landlord, the tenant is entitled to recover over against the assignee.

SECTION 4. LEASE RESTRICTIONS ON TRANSFERS BY TENANTS

Leases frequently contain a provision requiring prior written consent by the lessor to assignments or subleases. The reasons for such restrictions are fairly apparent. Lessors seek to avoid occupation of the premises by any party who is likely to engage in conduct harmful to the premises or who is not financially sound. This concern is particularly acute as to assignments by assignees of leases with long unexpired terms. Since assignees are not obligated to pay rent after they have in turn assigned, and since the original tenant of a long-term lease may be nonexistent or insolvent, the current assignee may be the sole party from whom the rent is collectible. It is thus of critical concern to the lessor that the current assignee be financially sound. As no common law requirement exists that assignments be made to financially responsible parties,[11] lessors must protect themselves by reserving the right to pass upon prospective assignees.[12]

Judicial construction of provisions requiring landlord consent to tenant transfers has been inconsistent. Some decisions construe such restrictions narrowly, in line with the policy opposed to restraints on alienation. Thus, it is generally held that a restriction referring only to assignments is not applicable to subleases.[13]

An extreme instance of judicial antipathy for restraints on alienation of leaseholds was the 1603 decision in Dumpor's Case [14] that consent by a landlord to an assignment was deemed to be consent to all future assignments. It is inconceivable that a landlord would have had such intent, either at the time of execu-

---

11. A.D. Juilliard & Co. v. American Woolen Co., 69 R.I. 215, 32 A.2d 800 (1943).

12. Statutes requiring lessor's consent to lessee's transfers exist in some states. E.g., Tex.Prop.Code Ann. § 91.005 (Vernon 1984).

13. De Baca v. Fidel, 61 N.M. 181, 297 P.2d 322 (1956). Similarly, a con-

sent requirement was held inapplicable to an assignment back to the original lessee. Fashions Four Corporation v. Fashion Place Associates, 681 P.2d 830 (Utah 1984).

14. 4 Coke 119b, 76 Eng.Rep. 1110 (1603).

tion of the lease or at the time of consenting to an assignment. The Rule in Dumpor's Case was abolished long ago in England,[15] but has been followed by some American courts.[16] Fortunately, where the rule is in force, it is easily avoided by drafting lease clauses that clearly state that consent to one assignment is not consent to any subsequent assignment. The rule also may be avoided by giving only a qualified consent, i.e., conditioned on no further assignments without consent. American courts recognizing Dumpor's Case have gone to great lengths to distinguish it. It is not applicable to subleases.[17] It is not applicable if the restriction purports to bind heirs and assigns.[18] In one case in which the restriction expressly bound the lessee by name—"R.D. Craver"— and referred to no one else, the court seized upon the word "assigns" in the habendum clause to find that the restriction bound assigns.[19] The time is long past for outright repudiation of Dumpor's Case.

On one constructional issue the traditional judicial position is at the opposite extreme from Dumpor's Case. Most courts have refused to find in restrictions requiring lessors' consent to transfers by tenants an implied limitation that consent not be unreasonably withheld.[20] This position allows lessors to condition their consent to transfers upon renegotiation of leases to obtain higher rents and other benefits for themselves. This seems difficult to justify. To allow lessors to withhold consent arbitrarily appears to be contrary to the policy opposed to restraints on alienation and also to the probable intention of parties to the lease. There is growing support, judicial and otherwise, for implying in consent clauses a limitation that refusal of consent must be reasonable.[21] However, even these authorities allow a lessor to withhold consent arbitrarily if the lease expressly so authorizes, at least if the provision was "freely negotiated."

This trend is opposed by one writer on two grounds: (1) a reasonableness standard generates uncertainty and litigation; and (2) if the trend will culminate in invalidation of lease clauses expressly allowing arbitrary withholding of consent, which is predicted, this will mean the "death of long-term leases as we know them."[22] The latter ground rests upon the rationale that

15. 22 & 23 Vict., ch. 35 (1959).

16. Aste v. Putnam's Hotel Co., 247 Mass. 147, 141 N.E. 666, 31 A.L.R. 149 (1923).

17. Zotalis v. Cannellos, 138 Minn. 179, 164 N.W. 807 (1917).

18. Childs v. Warner Bros. Southern Theatres, Inc., 200 Cal. 333, 156 S.E. 923 (1931).

19. Id.

20. B & R Oil Company, Inc. v. Ray's Mobile Homes, Inc., 139 Vt. 122, 422 A.2d 1267 (1980).

21. Kendall v. Ernest Pestana, Inc., 40 Cal.3d 488, 220 Cal.Rptr. 818, 709 P.2d 837 (1985); Restatement of Property (Second) Landlord and Tenant § 15.2(2) (1977).

22. Johnson, Correctly Interpreting Long–Term Leases Pursuant to Modern

long-term leases will not be entered into unless lessors can gain protection against inflation by requiring assignees to pay higher rents. It is argued that other devices for dealing with the risk of inflation, such as an escalation clause tied to a price index, would be rejected by prospective lessees whose business enterprises require predictable costs. These arguments opposing implication of a reasonable ground for disapproving assignments may be based upon unrealistic assumptions as to future behavior of courts and parties to leases.

What is the effect of a tenant's violation of a provision requiring the landlord's prior written consent to assignment or sublease? This depends upon the form of the provision and election of remedies by the landlord when alternative remedies are available. If the restriction on transfers is solely promissory, a transfer in violation of it is valid, but the transferor is liable for damages for breach. If, however, the landlord had reserved a right of entry for breach of this covenant, the transfer is voidable;[23] if voided, both the transfer and the lease are terminated.[24] If the provision against transfer without lessor's prior consent is simply a prohibition, it follows that an attempted transfer is void and the tenant who attempted the transfer remains the owner of the estate. However, even in this situation, the landlord could waive the restriction and let the transfer stand.[25]

Contract Law: Toward a Theory of Relational Leases, 74 Va.L.Rev. 751, 808 (1988).

23. People v. Klopstock, 24 Cal.2d 897, 151 P.2d 641 (1944).

24. Kew v. Trainor, 150 Ill. 150, 37 N.E. 223 (1894).

25. See the discussion of distinctions between forfeiture restraints, disabling restraints and promissory restraints in Restatement of Property (Second) Landlord and Tenant § 15.2, Comments b, c and d (1977).

Chapter 10

LANDLORD REMEDIES FOR TENANT ABANDONMENT

The remedies of landlords when tenants abandon the premises vary widely from state to state and are in transition in some states. Unsatisfactory consequences of the historic view of the lease primarily as a conveyance are largely responsible for this diversity and fluidity.

The traditional view is that landlords are not subject to the general duty to mitigate damages from breaches of contracts.[1] The tenant's obligation to pay rent is not a mere contract, but rather is an incident of the leasehold estate, obligating only its owner. Thus, landlords can, if they wish, do nothing when their tenants abandon the premises, and sue periodically for accrued rent.

It is apparent, however, that landlords would prefer solutions other than leaving the premises unoccupied and hoping for continuing solvency of the departed tenant. A landlord might wish to recover at once damages in full for anticipatory breach of covenants to pay rent in the future. But many courts, asserting that a tenant is not obligated to pay rent until rent day, withheld this remedy from the landlord.[2] However, there is growing recognition that anticipatory breach doctrines do apply to leases.[3] This is useful to the lessor when rental value of the premises is lower than the stipulated rent. The lessor can recover the difference between the agreed rent and the actual rental value, over a period of time, discounted to its present value. This result is highly speculative since the market oscillates over time and is probably one reason why many states stick to the older rule. The same result can be reached even in those jurisdictions, however, by the use of an acceleration clause in the lease. As a result of the high degree of speculation involved, courts are likely to limit recovery to prospective losses on long-term leases with many years to run to some shorter period. In one case, the court was unwilling to peer into the future further than ten years.[4]

1. Gruman v. Investors Diversified Services, 247 Minn. 502, 78 N.W.2d 377 (1956).

2. Cooper v. Casco Mercantile Trust Co., 134 Me. 372, 186 A. 885 (1936).

3. Hawkinson v. Johnston, 122 F.2d 724 (8th Cir.1941), cert. denied 314 U.S. 694, 62 S.Ct. 365, 86 L.Ed. 555 (1941).

4. Id.

Another solution to the abandonment problem that might appeal to the landlord is to relet to a new tenant and hold the original tenant for net loss. Unfortunately, reletting appears to be inconsistent with continuing existence of the original lease and therefore to constitute a surrender by operation of law. Abandonment is viewed as an offer by the tenant to surrender (i.e., transfer) the leasehold to the landlord. The surrender is completed, and the leasehold terminated by merger, when the landlord manifests intent to accept the offer or acts in a manner inconsistent with continued existence of the leasehold. The latter is surrender by operation of law, whatever may have been the landlord's intention.

It logically follows that rent could not accrue after termination of the leasehold and that the landlord could not hold the original tenant for net loss incurred in reletting for the balance of the original term.

That logic has had much influence, but many courts have struggled to escape it.[5] One view is that no surrender occurs if the landlord notifies the tenant in advance that the original lease will remain in effect and that reletting will be for the account of the original tenant. I.e., the landlord acts as the tenant's agent in assigning the leasehold. This is better than regarding every reletting as a surrender, but this view also has some difficulties. It is of no benefit to a landlord who clearly intends that reletting not release the original tenant but who fails to manifest that intent in a formal manner. It is also difficult to explain the origin of the authority of the landlord to act as the tenant's agent. Moreover, if the landlord must relet for a term extending beyond the expiration date of the original term, or with different provisions, or for premises larger than those covered by the original lease, a court is likely to conclude that the reletting is for the landlord's benefit rather than for the tenant's, resulting in surrender by operation of law.

A few courts, notably the highest courts of New Hampshire and Oregon, have taken the much bolder step of treating abandonment as governed entirely by contract doctrines, unfettered by the concept of surrender by operation of law.[6] These decisions require reasonable efforts by lessors to mitigate losses. They thus may require, not merely allow, lessors to relet the premises and continue to hold original tenants liable for net losses. The approach of these courts appears preferable to the alternative views, but even

---

5. See Schnebly, Operative Facts in Surrenders, 22 Ill.L.Rev. 117 (1927); Updegraff, The Element of Intent in Surrender by Operation of Law, 38 Harv.L.Rev. 64 (1924).

6. Novak v. Fontaine Furniture Co., 84 N.H. 93, 146 A. 525 (1929); United States National Bank of Oregon v. Homeland, Inc., 291 Or. 374, 631 P.2d 761 (1981).

it has some difficulties. Explaining how rent could accrue after the leasehold has ceased to exist is not easy. It is not entirely satisfactory to say, as these courts do, that this is similar to the continued contractual liability of a tenant after assignment, because an assignment does not terminate the leasehold. Another problem is that courts adhering exclusively to contract doctrines in the abandonment situation have not stated how they would deal with abandonment by an assignee who has not entered into a contract with the landlord.

The prospect that the New Hampshire–Oregon position may appeal to other courts has been dampened somewhat by the failure of the Commissioners on Uniform State Laws and the American Law Institute to embrace that position, at least in toto.

URLTA requires a landlord to make reasonable efforts to relet at a fair rental following abandonment by the tenant, but it also provides that, if reletting occurs, the original lease is terminated as of the date of the new tenancy.[7] This seems to preclude recovery of net loss from the original tenant, in the event that the new tenancy is for less rent or in the event of abandonment by the new tenant prior to the termination date of the original tenancy. The soundness of this limitation is doubtful.

Regrettably, the American Law Institute continues to adhere to the old rule relieving landlords from any duty to attempt to relet to mitigate the liability of tenants who have abandoned.[8] The rationale advanced for this position is that abandonment "is an invitation to vandalism, and the law should not encourage such conduct by putting a duty of mitigation of damages on the landlord." Is this sound? Is it really likely that tenants would be encouraged to abandon by a rule requiring landlords to mitigate losses? Tenants still would be liable for potentially large sums for rent. In addition, if vandalism attributable to abandonment occurs, tenants would be liable for this, too, as the Institute acknowledges.

The American Law Institute allows a landlord to relet following abandonment by a tenant and recover net loss from the original tenant only if the landlord notifies the tenant prior to reletting that the landlord does not accept surrender of the leasehold and will relet for the tenant's account. If the landlord relets without giving this notice, the leasehold is deemed to have been terminated by surrender, and the tenant is not liable for rent that would have accrued thereafter. The Institute does not adopt the view that liability for damages for failure to pay postsurrender

7. URLTA § 4.203(c).

8. Restatement of Property (Second) Landlord and Tenant § 12.1(3), Comment i (1977).

rent could be based upon privity of contract. The Institute would give effect to an agreement in the lease authorizing the landlord to relet and hold the tenant for net losses, but does not regard this as liability for "rent." One consequence of withholding the "rent" label here is the unavailability to the landlord of a lien for rent. Another is that the landlord in this instance is subject to the duty to mitigate damages. Great care must be exercised in drafting lease provisions on this subject, as some such provisions have been found inadequate when tested by litigation.[9]

Comparison of recent cases, particularly those in New Hampshire and Oregon, with URLTA and the Restatement of Property (Second) Landlord and Tenant indicates that the law on remedies of the landlord when the tenant abandons will continue to be marked by diversity for a long time.

9. Hermitage Co. v. Levine, 248 N.Y. 333, 162 N.E. 97 (1928); Flack v. Sarnosa Oil Corp., 293 S.W.2d 688 (Tex. Civ.App.1956).

Part Five

METHODS OF TITLE ASSURANCE

Much of the Anglo–American law of land is explicable only in the light of man's search for title security. No great problem with chattels, since possession normally indicates ownership and the buyer can sue the seller if title proves defective, assured ownership of the vendor of land still plagues the real property lawyer. In this chapter, we shall discuss the legal principles involved in the various methods of title assurance and then conclude with a critique of the present systems, plus some suggestions for conveyancing reform. This approach will involve sections on covenants for title, the recording system and the methods based on it—examination from the records (or an abstract) and title insurance—title registration (Torrens system), and Statutes of Limitation. Bear in mind that much which has gone before in this text is of no avail if the purchaser, lessee, or mortgagee cannot be assured of receiving a merchantable title.

Chapter 1

IMPLIED COVENANTS OF HABITABILITY (QUALITY)

Before proceeding to a discussion of the methods of title assurance, however, it is necessary to take a look at the dwindling role of *caveat emptor* in areas other than title to land. Of course, implied covenants of habitability have nothing to do with title to the land; one can have merchantable title to an uninhabitable dwelling. But, just as there were no implied covenants of title, traditionally there were no implied covenants of *any* kind in a deed. Therefore, it is logical to explore the rise of the implied covenant of habitability before analyzing the title issues.

As pointed out in a recent Illinois case: "The use of the term 'habitability' is perhaps unfortunate. Because of its imprecise meaning it is susceptible of misconstruction." [1] The covenant can

1. Petersen v. Hubschman Construction Co., Inc., 76 Ill.2d 31, 27 Ill.Dec. 746, 389 N.E.2d 1154 (1979). See also Evans v. J. Stiles, Inc., 689 S.W.2d 399 (Tex.1985) where the Court held that the implied covenant was broader than

be breached even though the house is habitable in the sense that it is sufficient to keep out the elements and is not unsafe to occupy. The Illinois court suggests language similar to that used in the Uniform Commercial Code—warranty of merchantability (although that too is ambiguous in land law where the term normally refers to *title* only) or warranty of fitness for a particular purpose. The Uniform Land Transactions Act in Section 2–309 calls it an implied warranty of quality. This appears to be the best term for a relatively new concept.

We have previously discussed the role of implied covenants of habitability in landlord-tenant law and have noted the dramatic change in the past few years.[2] A similar development has occurred in the freehold estates and for essentially the same reasons. As recently as 1961 an American court could say: "The great weight of authority does not support implied warranties in real estate transactions but requires any purported warranties to be in written contractual form. . . . No decision has come to our attention which permitted recovery by the vendee of a house upon the theory of implied warranty."[3] The Alabama decision was typical of the prevailing judicial attitude which put the full burden on the purchaser to inspect and discover defects before he accepted the deed. After delivery of the deed, it was too late to complain unless he had had the unusual foresight to include an express covenant or unless there was actual fraud on the part of the vendor. In the Alabama case the plumbing was not even connected to the sewer system and the waste was discharged under the house but, no matter, *caveat emptor* applied. There was an express covenant involved but it was for a limited period only and had expired.

It requires no extended discussion to see the full implications of such a rule in an era of tract housing, frequently shoddy workmanship, and an increasingly mobile population. Some cases and many legal commentators began to attack the inequity of this legal doctrine and by the late 'sixties *caveat emptor* was everywhere in full retreat. In Humber v. Morton[4], the Texas Supreme Court carefully analyzed the entire problem and correctly stated the modern rule that covenants of habitability can be implied. Said the court:

> "If at one time in Texas the rule of caveat emptor had application to the sale of a new house by a vendor-builder, that time is now past. The decisions and legal writings herein

inhabitability and extended to use of faulty brick on a house.

2. Pp. 251–256 supra.

3. Druid Homes, Inc. v. Cooper, 272 Ala. 415, 131 So.2d 884 (1961). By 1971, Alabama had reversed its position. See Cochran v. Keeton, 287 Ala. 439, 252 So.2d 313 (1971).

4. 426 S.W.2d 554, 25 A.L.R.3d 372 (Tex.1968).

referred to afford numerous examples and situations illustrating the harshness and injustice of the rule when applied to the sale of new houses by a builder-vendor,[5] and we need not repeat them here. Obviously, the ordinary purchaser is not in a position to ascertain when there is a defect in a chimney flue, or vent of a heating apparatus, or whether the plumbing work covered by a concrete slab foundation is faulty. It is also highly irrational to make a distinction between the liability of a vendor-builder who employs servants and one who uses independent contractors. Compare, Connor v. Conejo Valley Development Co., 61 Cal.Rptr. 333 (App.1967). The common law is not afflicted with the rigidity of the law of the Medes and the Persians 'which altereth not,' and as stated in Cardozo in 'The Nature of the Judicial Process,' pp. 150–151 (quoted in 415 P.2d 698):

> 'That court best serves the law which recognizes that the rules of law which grew up in a remote generation may, in the fullness of experience, be found to serve another generation badly, and which discards the old rule when it finds that another rule of law represents what should be according to the established and settled judgment of society, and no considerable property rights have become vested in reliance upon the old rule. . . .'

"The caveat emptor rule as applied to new houses is an anachronism patently out of harmony with modern home buying practices. It does a disservice not only to the ordinary prudent purchaser but to the industry itself by lending encouragement to the unscrupulous, fly-by-night operator and purveyor of shoddy work."

The shift from *caveat emptor* to implied covenants of quality (habitability) is not yet complete in all jurisdictions,[6] and, of

---

5. In the vendor-builder situation, Professor Roberts seems inclined to agree with Mr. Bumble's estimate of the law and points out that when caveat emptor is retained with regard to the sale of new houses, the law seemingly concerns itself little with a transaction which may and often does involve a purchaser's life savings, yet may afford relief by raising an implied warranty of fitness when one is swindled in the purchase of a two dollar fountain pen. Roberts, The Case of the Unwary Home Buyer: The Housing Merchant Did It, 52 Cornell L.Q. 835 (1967). Similarly, in Samuels, Warranties for New Houses, 111 The Solicitors' Journal 22 (1967) (London), it is pointed out that, "the purchaser buying a new house with legal assistance is often less well protected legally than the purchaser buying a chattel without legal assistance." It is further urged that, "The legal profession should have made it their business to insure proper protection for the purchaser without waiting for building societies to take the initiative" for their own protection since most builders "try to do a good job (but) the reputation of all may be injuriously affected by the low standards of a few."

6. See Bruce Farms, Inc. v. Coupe, 219 Va. 287, 247 S.E.2d 400 (1978) where the court preferred to wait for legislative action.

course, difficult problems of proof remain, but the purchaser, like the lessee, now has legal protection almost totally lacking a few decades ago. Typically, the implied covenant doctrine has been restricted to unfinished buildings and to new structures. It has had little application to older buildings and there the purchaser's eyes have remained his bargain, unless he can convince the vendor to include an express warranty. There are some situations in which even the purchaser of an old building may have legal recourse. This is particularly true in the case of termite infestation where purchasers have been allowed to recover on the basis of a representation that the buildings were "in good sound condition," although there was no express warranty against termites.[7] An American Law Reports comment noted: "In a few recent decisions, however, the courts have held that termite infestation can obviously become a serious and dangerous condition and, if known to the vendor, must in good faith be disclosed to the purchaser, since caveat emptor is no longer rigidly applied to the complete exclusion of any moral and legal obligation to disclose material facts not readily observable upon reasonable inspection by the purchaser, and that the object of the law is to impose on parties to the transaction a duty to speak whenever justice, equity and fair dealing demand it."[8]

Some of the more recent decisions are crossing this final barrier of used housing as well and successors in interest of the first purchaser are being given the right to sue on an implied covenant even though the structure is now "used" housing.[9] This raises the issue of privity [10] and the question of how long the

7. Maser v. Lind, 181 Neb. 365, 148 N.W.2d 831, 22 A.L.R.3d 965 (1967) and Halpert v. Rosenthal, 107 R.I. 406, 267 A.2d 730 (1970).

8. 22 A.L.R.3d 965, 975 (1967). For an especially interesting case, see Reed v. King, 145 Cal.App.3d 261, 193 Cal. Rptr. 130 (1983), where the Court held a cause of action for rescission or damages had been stated for failure to disclose that a murder had occurred in the house ten years earlier. Note that breach of an implied covenant of habitability may be grounds for rescission as well as for damages. See Finke v. Woodard, 122 Ill.App.3d 911, 78 Ill.Dec. 297, 78 Ill.Dec. 297, 462 N.E.2d 13 (1984).

9. Posner v. Davis, 76 Ill.App.3d 638, 32 Ill.Dec. 186, 395 N.E.2d 133 (1979) and Redarowicz v. Ohlendorf, 92 Ill.2d 171, 65 Ill.Dec. 411, 441 N.E.2d 324 (1982). See also Note, Builders' Liability for Latent Defects in Used Homes, 32 Stan.L.Rev. 607 (1980).

10. Strong v. Johnson, 53 N.C.App. 54, 280 S.E.2d 37 (1981), allowed a person inheriting from the initial purchaser to sue and Terlinde v. Neely, 275 S.C. 395, 271 S.E.2d 768 (1980) allowed a subsequent purchaser to sue, noting that the key inquiry is foreseeability *not* privity. By placing the house in the stream of commerce, the builder owes a duty of care to those who will use it and renders him accountable for negligent workmanship. In Minton v. Richards Group of Chicago, 116 Ill.App.3d 852, 72 Ill.Dec. 582, 452 N.E.2d 835 (1983) the implied covenant was extended to a subcontractor where the builder-vendor was insolvent. Lack of privity was held not to be a bar. See also, McMillan v. Brune–Harpenau–Torbeck Builders, Inc., 8 Ohio St.3d 3, 455 N.E.2d 1276 (1983) to the effect that privity of con-

covenant will continue to bind the vendor.[11] Some courts have specifically rejected the application of implied warranties in favor of subsequent owners [12] but in most states the issue is still an open one. The trend, however, is apparent and is consistent with the policy of providing more consumer protection for an unwary public. Both the language and the holdings of the courts point in this direction. For example, Illinois has held that an implied warranty can attach to the sale of a condominium and that such a warranty can extend to defects in the common elements.[13] Illinois has even extended the doctrine to cover vacant property where a developer had installed a septic system which was inadequate due to underlying soil conditions.[14] Texas held that the doctrine applied where a contractor built a townhouse on land owned by another.[15] The court said that a sale of realty was not a prerequisite, because to hold otherwise would deny recovery to a consumer who proved faulty workmanship and materials if the consumer owned his lot and hired a contractor, but would allow recovery under the same fact situation to a consumer who bought his lot and house in a package deal.

The trend, previously mentioned, will undoubtedly be given impetus by the Uniform Land Transactions Act, Section 2–309, which adopts the strongest position so far suggested for implied covenants. The Act refers to an implied warranty of quality and it appears to apply to all real estate, not merely housing. The warranty also arises in cases of used, as well as new, buildings or other improvements on real estate.[16] While the Act has not yet

tract is not a necessary element in a suit by a purchaser of real property against a builder-vendor.

11. Terlinde v. Neely, note 10 supra, said the vendor was bound for a reasonable period of time. Could a period less than the relevant statute of limitations be held unreasonable and thus release the vendor from liability? Probably so, since this is a difficult area and used housing does raise problems different in kind from new housing.

12. Oliver v. City Builders, Inc., 303 So.2d 466 (Miss.1974).

13. Herlihy v. Dunbar Builders Corp., 92 Ill.App.3d 310, 47 Ill.Dec. 911, 415 N.E.2d 1224 (1980).

14. Kramp v. Showcase Builders, 97 Ill.App.3d 17, 52 Ill.Dec. 749, 422 N.E.2d 958 (1981). Cf. Jackson v. River Pines, Inc., 276 S.C. 29, 274 S.E.2d 912 (1981) where the court denied recovery in a similar case, saying *caveat emptor* applied to the sale of unimproved land.

15. Young v. DeGuerin, 591 S.W.2d 296 (Tex.Civ.App.1979).

16. The Act reads in relevant parts:

Section 2–309. [Implied Warranty of Quality]

(a) Subject to the provisions on risk of loss (Section 2–406), a seller warrants that the real estate will be in at least as good condition at the earlier of the time of the conveyance or delivery of possession as it was at the time of contracting, reasonable wear and tear excepted.

(b) A seller, other than a lessor, in the business of selling real estate impliedly warrants that the real estate is suitable for the ordinary uses of real estate of its type and that any improvements made or contracted for by him will be:

(1) free from defective materials;

(2) constructed in accordance with applicable law, according to sound engineering and construction

been adopted in full by any state, it is already having an impact on the developing law. Thus, the Illinois Supreme Court [17] has said: "While the warranty of habitability has roots in the execution of the contract for sale . . . we emphasize that it exists independently . . . Privity of contract is not required." The Court further stated that safeguards which have evolved to help home owners should not be frustrated because of the short intervening ownership of the "first purchaser," and that the defects in a new house should be the responsibility of the builder or vendor who created the problems. Going beyond the analogy to the Uniform Commercial Code, the Court adopted the standard of the Uniform Land Transactions Act. "[W]e do not believe it logical to arbitrarily limit that protection to the first purchaser of a new house." Latent defects, which are noticed within a reasonable time of purchase, whether by an initial or a subsequent purchaser, can be the basis of an implied warranty of habitability.

The consumer's battle against *caveat emptor* has not been fully won and many skirmishes on the fringe lie ahead but the doctrine is everywhere in full retreat. Not surprisingly, the builders have launched a counter attack through the time-honored technique of disclaimer or waiver. Thus, in G–W–L, Inc. v. Robichaux,[18] the purchaser signed a contract which included the clause, "there being no oral agreements, representations, conditions, warranties, express or implied, in addition to said written instruments." The roof of the new house had a substantial sag in it and the purchaser sued, only to be met by the defense of the disclaimer. It was agreed that to be effective the disclaimer must be in "clear and unequivocal language." The majority of the court felt that it was and that: "The parties to a contract have an obligation to protect themselves by reading what they sign" hence the purchaser could not recover. Three judges, in a strong dissent, believed that public policy required more than a disclaimer

standards, and in a workmanlike manner.

(c) In addition, a seller in the business of selling real estate warrants to a protected party that an existing use, continuation of which is contemplated by the parties, does not violate applicable law at the earlier of the time of conveyance or delivery of possession.

(d) Warranties imposed by this section may be excluded or modified as specified in the provisions on exclusion or modification of warranties of quality (Section 2–311).

(e) For purposes of this section, improvements made or contracted for by a person related to the seller (Section 1–204) are made or contracted for by the seller.

(f) A person who extends credit secured by real estate and thereafter acquires the real estate by foreclosure, or in lieu of foreclosure, does not become a person in the business of selling real estate by reason of selling that estate.

17. Redarowicz v. Ohlendorf, 92 Ill. 2d 171, 65 Ill.Dec. 411, 441 N.E.2d 324 (1982).

18. 643 S.W.2d 392 (Tex.Sup.Ct. 1982).

buried in a long contract and not specifically called to the attention of the purchaser so that he knew what he was signing. "The better rule is the waiver must be in *clear and unequivocal* language specifically naming the warranty that is being disclaimed." An Illinois court [19] had taken a position more nearly in line with the Texas dissent and said that a disclaimer clause located near the end of a standard form contract in the same print size and type as other clauses, and which did not mention or refer to a warrant of habitability nor explain the consequences of disclaimer, was not necessarily a sufficiently valid disclaimer. The role of the disclaimer can be a critical issue in the future development of implied covenants and unless the courts are willing to strictly construe such clauses against the builder-vendor much of the consumer protection afforded by the covenants will be negated.

In response to the new doctrine of implied covenants of quality, many large homebuilding firms now offer some type of *express* warranty. For example, in 1974 the National Association of Home Builders instituted a Home Owners Warranty (HOW) program which provided for a ten-year express warranty, backed by an insurance policy to protect the buyer should the builder become insolvent.[20] A number of state legislatures have also gotten into the act and attempted to define the rights of purchasers of new houses, although some of these statutes are less protective than the HOW program.[21]

Many troublesome problems remain, such as the issue of when the statute of limitations begins to run. Does the cause of action arise when the defective construction occurs or when it is finally discovered, which may be many years in the future? If the defect is latent (which is typically the case) the builder may be sued years after the construction occurred.[22] Because of the possibility of this open-ended liability, more than forty states have passed special statutes of limitation which begin to run upon completion

19. Ftn. 13, supra.

20. For a good discussion of this development and related doctrine see Ellickson and Tarlock, Cases and Materials on Land Use Controls 456–465 (1981).

21. See, for example, Maryland Real Property Code s. 10–203 (Michie Supp. 1979) which essentially limits the warranties to one year so that the purchaser would be better off with a HOW policy.

22. See Bradler v. Craig, 274 Cal. App.2d 466, 79 Cal.Rptr. 401 (1969), where the plaintiff brought an *unsuc-* *cessful* action for soil failure that occurred in 1966 under a house built in 1948 and McAllister v. Stoeco Homes, Inc., 740 F.2d 957 (3d Cir.1984), where a latent defect claim was not actionable on an 18 year old home. (There was a ten year statute of limitations.) See also Gaito v. Auman, 70 N.C.App. 21, 318 S.E.2d 555 (1984) where a four year old house was considered "new" for implied warranty purposes. The court concluded that a home should be considered "new" throughout the duration of the maximum statute of limitations period of ten years.

of the project, irrespective of when the defect is discovered or gives rise to injury.[23]

The problems created by faulty construction are apparently as old as man's proclivity for dwelling in buildings more permanent than tents or caves. "The Code of Hammurabi, who ruled Babylonia during the 20th Century, B.C., provided in part: 229. If a builder has built a house for a man and his work is not strong, and if the house he has built falls in and kills the householder, that builder shall be slain. 230. If the child of the householder be killed, the child of that builder shall be slain. . . . 233. If a builder has built a house for a man, and his work is not done properly and a wall shifts, then that builder shall make that wall good with his own silver." [24]

The Code should have been effective although it seems a bit extreme for 20th Century, A.D. tastes! It took Anglo–American law a long time to recognize the seriousness of the problem, but in the period since Druid Homes, Inc. v. Cooper, in 1961,[25] the legal developments have at last put the builder's silver, if not his life, at risk. The rise of HOW programs, the statutory tinkering, etc., provide a prime example of how quickly the industry and society can respond to judicial changes in an evolving common law.

Obviously, the law is in transition as consumer rights come to the fore in real property as well as in personal property. It is impossible to predict how far the law will move in its reversed direction but there are many straws in the wind. For example, in a precedent-shattering California case, Connor v. Great Western Savings and Loan Association [26], the court allowed purchasers of tract housing to sue a savings and loan association which had financed the project and was heavily involved in various stages of the development. The purchasers' homes had suffered serious damage from cracking caused by poorly-designed foundations that could not withstand the expansion and contraction of the adobe soil. The case depended on its peculiar facts. "In undertaking these relationships, Great Western became much more than a lender content to lend money at interest on security of real property. It became an active participant in a home construction

23. The statutes differ in terminology and length of time, ranging from four to twenty years. The American Institute of Architects, National Society of Professional Engineers, and Associated General Contractors have adopted a Model Statute which has been enacted in many states, although a few state courts have invalidated statutes based on the model because it violates state constitutional provisions against special laws and granting special immunities to corporations. See Skinner v. Anderson, 38 Ill.2d 455, 231 N.E.2d 588 (1967). See also Collins, Limitation of Action Statutes for Architects and Builders, An Examination of Constitutionality, 29 Fed.Ins. Counsel Q. 1 (1978).

24. Ftn. 20, supra at 459.

25. Ftn. 3 supra.

26. 69 Cal.2d 850, 73 Cal.Rptr. 369, 447 P.2d 609 (1968).

enterprise." There were vigorous dissents, even given the special facts, and the court realized that the implications of its decision would end the traditional isolation of the financing institution from any liability for injury to the ultimate consumer. This is a major step since frequently the vendor-developer is insolvent and a suit against him for breach of an implied covenant of quality is a hollow victory. Carried to its logical conclusion this decision would place a responsibility on the lending institution which is now largely absent.[27]

The *Connor* case became one of the most widely noted and debated California civil cases of the sixties.[28]

In 1969, the California legislature passed the following statute: "Liability of lender financing design, manufacture, construction, repair, modification or improvement of real or personal property.

"A lender who makes a loan of money, the proceeds of which are used or may be used by the borrower to finance the design, manufacture, construction, repair, modification or improvement of real or personal property for sale or lease to others, shall not be held liable to third persons for any loss or damage occasioned by any defect in the real or personal property so designed, manufactured, constructed, repaired, modified or improved or for any loss or damage resulting from the failure of the borrower to use due care in the design, manufacture, construction, repair, modification or improvement of such real or personal property, unless such loss or damage is a result of an act of the lender outside the scope of the activities of a lender of money or unless the lender has been a party to misrepresentations with respect to such real or personal property. (Added by Stats.1969, c. 1584, p. 3222, § 1.)" [29]

The statute was designed to reverse the result of the *Connor* decision [30] and restrict the lender's liability to loss or damage caused by an act of the lender which lies outside the scope of activities of a lender of money or to cases in which the lender has

27. See also Bradler v. Craig, 274 Cal.App.2d 466, 79 Cal.Rptr. 401, (1969) where the purchasers sued the general contractor and the construction and purchase money lender to recover damages for alleged negligent construction of a house. The court cited the principal case with apparent approval but held that any legal duty to protect the purchasers had expired by lapse of time. The plaintiffs had purchased the house eighteen years after its construction.

28. See for example, Comment, "New Liability in Construction Lend-ing: Implications of Connor v. Great Western Savings and Loan," 42 S.Calif. L.Rev. 353 (1969) and Comment, "Liability of Institutional Lender for Structural Defects in New Housing," 35 U. of Chi.L.Rev. 739 (1968). The latter comment was prepared while the case was at the intermediate appellate level.

29. West's Ann.Cal.Civ.Code, § 3434.

30. See Lasher, Lending–Institution Liability for Defective Home Construction, 45 State Bar of Calif.J. 338 (1970).

been a party to misrepresentations with respect to the property. Nonetheless, the door has been opened and the issue is unlikely to disappear if the pressure for consumer protection continues to rise. Thus, a Michigan case [31] held that a lender was potentially liable because he was involved so closely with a fraudulent real estate broker. However, the *Connor* case has not been widely followed, usually because the courts have found that the lender was less closely involved with the builder-vendor than in the California situation.[32] It should be noted that the Uniform Land Transaction Act, Section 2–310, provides that a construction lender is *not* liable for defects "solely by reason of making the loan."

Some further light on the complicated legal relationships between the vendor, lender and purchaser is cast by United States Financial v. Sullivan.[33] There the court held that even if a developer was strictly liable in tort to a purchaser for a defective structure it did not follow that a mortgage lender could sue the developer for the impairment of his security interest. Said the court:

> "The doctrine of manufacturers' and suppliers' strict liability in tort was developed primarily to protect individual consumers. . . . A lender is not in such a vulnerable position. Without its money, the mass production of homes could not proceed. When it is called upon to lend its money, a lender is in a position to require of the developer not only plans and specifications but engineering reports of all sorts, including a soil test report. Thus, the historical reason for imposing strict liability is absent when sought by a lender whose resources are loaned to facilitate the mass construction of homes. . . . Unlike the consumer . . . the lender is itself a link in the marketing chain of mass-produced homes and residential lots and is itself in a position to spread the risks of harm resulting from a defective lot or home."

The key issue remains open for further exploration. Does (or should) the lender owe any duty to the purchaser beyond the obligation which he has assumed to lend the money to finance the sale? Traditional doctrine has said no and perhaps the *Connor* case and a few others depend on their peculiar facts but it will be interesting to watch the cases as lawyers for the purchasers continue their search for a "deep pocket." A full discussion of the fascinating problems involved in the merchandising of housing developments is beyond the scope of this text, but each student

31. Jeminson v. Montgomery Real Estate and Co., 396 Mich. 106, 240 N.W.2d 205 (1976).

32. See, for example, Butts v. Atlanta Federal Savings and Loan Association, 152 Ga.App. 40, 262 S.E.2d 230 (1979).

33. 37 Cal.App.3d 5, 112 Cal.Rptr. 18 (1974).

should be aware of the implications of such statutory devices as the Interstate Land Sales Full Disclosure Act [34] and related state legislation.

34. See, e.g., a letter from the Department of Housing and Urban Development, published in 19 Real Property Newsletter (I.S.B.A.) (1973).

"The purpose of this letter is to alert you to consequences which may ensue from your failure to understand fully the Interstate Land Sales Full Disclosure Act and its implementing regulations.

"The 1968 Interstate Land Sales Full Disclosure Act became effective April 28, 1969, and has now been operative for nearly four years. Although the Office of Interstate Land Sales Registration (OILSR) has processed thousands of registrations on both domestic and foreign subdivisions, it is nevertheless likely that an even larger number of subdivisions covered by this Act are still unregistered.

"Unless exempt, any developer having 50 or more lots or parcels of subdivided land who sells these lots by using the U.S. mails or any other instruments of interstate commerce, without first registering with OILSR and providing the purchaser in advance of sale with an approved property report, is in violation of the law and may be sentenced to a jail term of 5 years or a $5,000 fine, or both.

"In addition, all such contracts are voidable at the absolute and unconditional election of the purchaser. Besides refunding the purchase price of the lot, the developer may be re-quired to pay the reasonable costs of all improvements on the lot or lots. Once an unregistered developer is faced with the wholesale repurchasing of properties previously sold, many of which have already been improved, his bankruptcy is more than a remote possibility. All developers should be forewarned to reassess their positions on the need for registration before it is too late.

"Attorneys who have developers as clients have a professional responsibility to familiarize themselves with the provisions of the Interstate Land Sales Full Disclosure Act and its implementing regulations, and to advise their clients accordingly.

"In addition to the direct penalties that the developer may face, there may be serious derivative consequences for the accountants, bankers and title companies, and even the real estate brokers of unregistered developers under certain circumstances.

"We urge you to read and study the Interstate Land Sales Full Disclosure Act and the OILSR Regulations. We are ready at all times to answer any questions from concerned parties."

Sincerely,
George K. Berstein
Interstate Land Sales
  Administrator
Department of Housing and
  Urban Development
Washington, D.C. 20410

Chapter 2

COVENANTS FOR TITLE

The doctrine of *caveat emptor* finds its natural home in the law of titles. In the absence of express covenants for title the full risk of title failure falls on the purchaser. The common law did not allow covenants to be implied and so strong is that doctrine that even the promises made in the contract are merged or extinguished when the deed is accepted.[1] This means that any right to sue the grantor, for title failure, in absence of fraud, mistake, duress, etc., must be based on covenants for title in the deed. If these covenants are included they give the purchaser of land some of the same protection which the buyer of personal property would have but they do not establish that the vendor definitely owned the interest he purported to convey.

In feudal times the grantor of a fee was typically a lord with large estates at his disposal.[2] He owed protection to the grantee, his vassal, in return for homage and other feudal services. If the vassal happened to be ousted from possession the lord simply furnished another fief of equal value. This feudal warranty operated rather like specific performance of a contract in equity, but it was not based on contract at all; it arose out of the tenurial relationship between the lord and his vassal. The warranty could be enforced either by a real action against the disseisor, where the warrantor was impleaded and forced to defend the title, or by a writ of *warrantia chartae* brought by the grantee directly against the grantor. If the warrantor lost he was forced to give up land of equal value (the value of the original land at the time of the grant) or, if he did not possess sufficient land for this purpose, he was assessed damages to make up the difference. This feudal warranty had a complicated history and was subjected to many statutory modifications. It gradually became too cumbersome for modern times, fell into disuse, and finally was abolished in England in 1834. The feudal warranty, as such, was never a part of American law.

Modern covenants find their genesis in the feudal warranty, but they are quite different in scope and operation. The basic difference is that today's covenants are contractual in nature;

1. P. 202 supra.

2. The following thirteen paragraphs are reprinted from Cribbet and Johnson, Cases and Materials on Property 1382–1385 (4th ed. 1978).

hence they can be molded to fit the needs of the particular case. While this section will deal only with the traditional or so-called usual covenants, you should remember that the lawyer can draft any covenant which suits his purpose so long as it does not run counter to public policy. Legislation has played a major role in this area so that you must always check the statutes before attempting to draft a deed in an unfamiliar jurisdiction. Typically, the statutes provide for a short-form warranty deed, the usual covenants, or some of them, being implied from the use of such key words as "grant," "bargain and sell," or "warrant." This means that in present-day practice you may never run into the exact language of a covenant set forth in the deed itself. This may sound contrary to the earlier statement that "no covenants are implied in deeds." However, the implication is statutory and incorporates by reference, in warranty deeds, the covenants spelled out in the statute. There are no such covenants in quitclaim deeds.

In the present section we are concerned with the operation of these covenants and with the answers to several crucial questions. Why should there be more than one covenant? What is the meaning of each covenant? Do the covenants in fact overlap? Can the same act breach more than one covenant? Do they run with the land; i.e., do they protect successors in interest or only the original warrantee? How much protection do they actually give to a purchaser?

But first it is important that we try to define and classify the six usual covenants. They are as follows: (1) the covenant of seisin; (2) the covenant of right to convey; (3) the covenant against incumbrances; (4) the covenant for further assurance; (5) the covenant of quiet enjoyment; and (6) the covenant of warranty. Collectively they are called covenants for title to distinguish them from restrictive covenants of the type discussed in Part Six of this book. The first three are called present covenants because they are breached, if ever, as soon as the deed is delivered. The last three are referred to as future covenants because they may be breached at some future date when actual injury accrues to the warrantee. A word about each of them will be helpful before we proceed with our discussion.

Of Seisin. This covenant is so entwined with the mysteries of seisin that its usefulness tends to be reduced. Maupin, a leading writer on marketable titles, states: "A covenant for seisin is usually expressed by the formula 'that he, the said (vendor), is lawfully seised of the said premises,' but as a matter of prudence in some of the states, and of necessity in others, it is customary for the grantee to require a covenant that the grantor 'is seised of an absolute, perfect and indefeasible estate in fee simple.' This is to avoid the rule established by those cases which hold that a covenant that the grantor is 'lawfully seised' is satisfied by a mere seisin in fact, whether with or without right. . . . It is a rule of property in several of the states that a covenant that the grantor is 'lawfully seised' does not require that the grantor should have an indefeasible estate, and is satisfied by an actual though tortious seisin, provided it be under claim of title. The rule thus announced applies in but few of the states and has been distinctly repudiated in others." [3]

The covenant is broken by any lessening of the corpus or physical extent of the granted property, or by any diminution of the quantity of the estate; e.g., the conveyance of a life estate rather than a fee simple. On the other hand a mere incumbrance, such as an outstanding judgment, mortgage, lease, easement, dower, etc., does not amount to breach of the covenant, since none of these operates as a divestiture of the warrantor's technical seisin. The seisin passes to the warrantee but subject to the incumbrance.

An eviction is not necessary, as the mere existence of an outstanding paramount title is a breach of the covenant if it is properly worded. This raises some interesting questions regarding the statute of limitations and the amount of damages, but we shall discuss these points later.

Right to convey. This covenant usually is included with the covenant of seisin and is considered coextensive with it. Oddly enough this identity holds true even in those states where the covenant of seisin is satisfied by delivery of seisin in fact. Like its twin, the covenant operates *in praesenti,* and an outstanding paramount title at the time the deed is delivered amounts to breach. No eviction is essential.

Against incumbrances. To quote Maupin again: "The precise legal definition of the term *incumbrance* is a matter of some nicety. In a popular sense, it means a clog, load, hindrance, impediment, weight. Perhaps the best judicial definition of the term is that of Chief Justice Parson: 'Every right to or interest in the land granted, to the diminution of the value of the land, but consistent with the passing of the fee.' Hereunder all incumbrances may be classed as: (1) Pecuniary charges on the granted premises; (2) Estates or interests less than a fee in the premises; and (3) Easements or servitudes to which the premises are subject." [4]

3. Maupin, Marketable Title to Real Property 270, 272 (3d ed. 1921). See Note, Scope and Effect of a Covenant of Seisin in an Ohio Deed, 21 U.Cinc.L. Rev. 293 (1952).

4. Id. at 310.

Examples of the first class are mortgages, judgment liens, taxes, special assessments, and mechanics' liens; of the second, leaseholds, life estates, or dower rights; and of the third, restrictive covenants, affirmative obligations burdening the property, rights of way, and easements generally. This covenant, like the first two, operates *in praesenti* and is breached by existence of an incumbrance at the time of the conveyance. Again, eviction is not necessary.

Further assurance. This covenant is the least important of the six and is not much used in the United States, although it has more vitality in England. In essence it is a promise by the grantor that he will, in the future, make any conveyance necessary to vest in the grantee the title intended to be conveyed. The covenant may be specifically enforced in equity and bears some similarity to the old feudal warranty. Although there has not been much litigation over its effect, there is no apparent reason why a draftsman could not use it to good purpose.

Quiet enjoyment and warranty.[5] These two covenants are virtually the same and should be considered together. The covenant of warranty should not be confused with its feudal ancestor, since it does not require the warrantor to provide lands of equal value. The warrantor can, however, be held liable for damages resulting from eviction. The covenants may be either general, protecting the grantee against the claims of all persons; or they may be special, protecting him only against persons claiming through or under the covenantor.

The covenants are prospective, operating *in futuro,* and breach does not occur until eviction. They do not promise that the title is indefeasible—that is the role of the first two covenants—they do promise that the grantee will not be evicted by the holder of a paramount title. Note that while these covenants do not include the covenants of seisin and against incumbrances, a violation of these latter covenants, followed by an eviction, will result in a breach of quiet enjoyment and of warranty.

The classification of the six usual covenants and their respective roles, just discussed, is further clarified by a recent Illinois case, Brown v. Lober.[6] In that case, the grantor had used a statutory short-form warranty deed that included all of the usual covenants for title implied from the statute. There was an immediate breach of the covenant for seisin and probably of the covenant against incumbrances as well (although the court did not

---

5. For a detailed analysis of the broadest and most effective of the usual covenants for title see Comment, The Covenant of Warranty, 14 Baylor L.Rev. 77 (1962).

6. 75 Ill.2d 547, 27 Ill.Dec. 780, 389 N.E.2d 1188 (1979). See also Foley v. Smith, 14 Wash.App. 285, 539 P.2d 874 (1975).

decide that question since the law suit was not based on that covenant) due to the reservation of a recorded two-thirds interest in the coal rights by a former owner, a stranger to the law suit. However, the suit on the present covenants was barred by a ten-year statute of limitations which started to run when the deed was delivered and the plaintiff was forced to rely on the future covenants of quiet enjoyment and warranty which were not yet barred. Unfortunately for the plaintiff, the court held those future covenants had not yet been breached since the paramount title holder (former owner) had not ejected the plaintiff either actually or constructively. In fact, the former owner had done nothing, although he had a valid recorded claim to a two-thirds coal interest, and the plaintiff had to wait until the paramount title holder took action before he could successfully sue the warrantor. Note that, despite the presence of all six covenants, the grantee had no present cause of action and was left in a kind of legal limbo until such time as the former owner asserted his right. Of course, if the grantee had searched the title before accepting the warranty deed, he would have discovered the recorded reservation of a two-thirds mineral interest and could have resolved the issue or refused to accept a deed to the land. The *Brown v. Lober* case, and those like it, demonstrates one reason why covenants for title may be less than adequate to protect the purchaser's interests.

SECTION 1. RUNNING OF COVENANTS WITH THE LAND

You will recall our earlier discussion of this problem in connection with leases.[7] There the principal difficulty was "touch and concern", a matter of no great moment here since a promise relating to title clearly "touches and concerns" the land. But the basic question remains, how can a subsequent purchaser of the land sue on a promise never made to him? So far as the three present covenants were concerned the answer of the common law was clear—he could not! These covenants, being breached as soon as made, i.e., when the deed was delivered the grantor either was or wasn't seised, either did or didn't have a right to convey, and the land was either incumbered or it wasn't—became choses in action and hence unassignable at common law.[8] The original

7. P. 272 supra. See also p. 381, infra, for a discussion of the same issue as it relates to restrictive (protective) covenants.

8. Mitchell v. Warner, 5 Conn. 498 (1825).

grantee could sue for breach but when he sold the land his grantee's sole cause of action was against him, not the remote grantor. The non-assignability of choses in action has largely disappeared into the limbo it so richly deserves, but the bulk of American courts still follow the common-law doctrine. England and some American states, both by decision and by statute, have abandoned this "technical scruple" and allowed even the present covenants to run with the land.[9]

The future covenants do not raise this runability problem since they are not breached until an eviction occurs, which may be years and many grantees in the future. Granting, however, that the particular covenant runs with the land there must be privity of estate, i.e., the remote grantee must prove that he now owns the estate once conveyed from the remote grantor to the first grantee. If he fails to so prove or must rely on the Statute of Limitations to take the place of a missing link in his title chain, he cannot sue.[10] A more serious problem arises when there is a total failure of title from the start. If the grantor never owned an estate to convey to the grantee, how can the covenants attach to nothing and run with a non-existent estate? This may sound like another quibble, but it appealed to courts, not too happy with the "runability" of covenants anyway, and many of them held that this barred a suit

For a good analysis of California law, which is fairly typical, see Comment, Covenants of Title Running With the Land in California, 49 Calif.L.Rev. 931, 945 (1961). The writer concludes: "Present covenants cannot run with the land however, for the whole concept of present and future covenants precludes this. Nevertheless, there is no reason why virtually the same result could not be accomplished by holding that covenants of title are assigned by operation of deed. If this were done the only reason for distinguishing between present and future covenants would be to determine when the statute of limitations begins to run." See also Comment, Covenants for Title—Protection Afforded Buyer of Realty in Florida, 7 U.Miami L.Rev. 378 (1953).

9. Schofield v. The Iowa Homestead Co., 32 Iowa 317, 7 Am.Rep. 197 (1871).

Some states have solved the runability problem by a simple statute. See, for example, Colorado Revised Statutes, c. 118, art. 1–21 (1953): "Covenants of seisin, peaceable possession, freedom from incumbrances, and of warranty, contained in any conveyance of real estate, or of any interest therein, shall be held to run with the premises, and to inure to the benefit of all subsequent purchasers and incumbrancers."

Such a statute does not solve the problem of the time of breach and the resulting difficulty as to when the statute of limitations will bar a suit by the covenantee. See Bernklau v. Stevens, 150 Colo. 187, 189, 371 P.2d 765, 768, 95 A.L.R.2d 905 (1962). "The purpose of C.R.S. '53, 118–1–21, as to such covenants, is not to change the time of the accrual of the cause of action, but rather to extend the benefit of such covenants to subsequent purchasers and incumbrancers. Wheeler v. Roley, 105 Colo. 116, 118, 95 P.2d 2 (1939). Thus the accrual of a cause of action still depends upon the time of breach; and the time of breach varies with the particular covenant. Consequently whether defendants' counterclaim is barred by the statute of limitations depends upon the particular covenants alleged to have been breached." See also ftn. 6, supra, and the text discussion of *Brown v. Lober.*

10. Deason v. Findley, 145 Ala. 407, 40 So. 220 (1906).

by a remote grantee. If possession passed, although no title, the covenants could latch onto the possession, but if neither title nor possession was transferred the paradox was complete. Nevertheless, some courts were friendly to suits by the remote grantee even in these cases.[11] One court stated it this way: "We should be inclined rather to say, that although the covenant of warranty is attached to the land, and for that reason is said in the books, to pass to the assignee, yet this certainly does not mean that it is attached to the paramount title, nor does it mean that it is attached to an imperfect title, or to possession, and only passes with that, but it means simply, that it passes by virtue of the privity of estate, created by the successive deeds, each grantor being estopped by his own deed from denying that he has conveyed an estate to which the covenant would attach."[12]

Assuming that the particular covenant will run with the land, it is not essential that all of the deeds in the chain be warranty deeds. Thus, if *A* delivers a warranty deed to *B; B*, a quitclaim deed to *C; C*, a warranty deed to *D;* and the title is now in *E* by virtue of a sheriff's deed coming through a mortgage foreclosure against *D; E* may have the following choices, in event of a title failure which antedates *A's* conveyance. He may sue *C* or *A* on the covenants running with the land, but he cannot sue *B* or *D* who gave no covenants for title.

SECTION 2. BREACH OF COVENANT

Apart from the right of a remote grantee to sue when a covenant is breached, difficult questions arise as to the breach itself. There is general agreement that the present covenants are breached as soon as made, if ever, but this scarcely solves the matter. Although there is a technical breach of the covenant of seisin, for example, the grantee may be undisturbed in possession so that no actual damage accrues. The third party who, in fact, owns all or a portion of the estate may be unaware of it and may slumber on his rights until the grantee's title is perfected by adverse possession. To allow the grantee damages prior to ouster, or threat thereof, may thus be unfair. On the other hand, if the grantee is forced to wait, the relevant statute of limitations (typically five to ten years on a written contract) may run so that the grantee will lose his cause of action against the grantor. If he sues presently and recovers only nominal damages, he runs the

---

11. Solberg v. Robinson, 34 S.D. 55, 147 N.W. 87 (1914).

12. Wead v. Larkin, 54 Ill. 489, 499 (1870).

risk of a successful plea of *res judicata* when actual damage occurs because of ouster. This dilemma was faced squarely in the leading case of Bolinger v. Brake [13] and full damages were allowed to the grantee when he proved title failure, even though his possession was undisturbed. Other cases have ignored the dilemma and restricted the grantee to nominal damages until an eviction occurs.[14] This problem is non-existent with future covenants since they are not breached prior to eviction.

Future covenants, then, require eviction; present covenants, except for the one against incumbrances, *may* demand the same test. But what is eviction? Certainly, it must be by a person claiming under title paramount, for the covenants never promise freedom from interference by a stranger to the title. Actual ouster by self help, ejectment, etc., clearly qualifies as a breach of covenant. Constructive eviction, that ever-helpful legal fiction, may also qualify. Thus, if the grantee is faced with ouster under a decree in partition, foreclosure, etc., he need not wait until the sheriff places him in the street, but may pay the sum due to the paramount title holder to prevent such drastic results. If he relies on constructive eviction, however, he should notify his warrantor (grantor) of the pending suit and, preferably, request him to appear and defend.[15] Failure to do this will not be fatal to his cause, but in a second suit by the grantee against the grantor on the covenant he will have to prove that the payment was justified, whereas had the grantor been notified and requested to defend that issue would have been *res judicata*. It follows that any time the grantee pays a third party claimant without suit he does so at his peril since the warrantor may later deny the validity of the claim.

The covenant against incumbrances does not necessarily require eviction in order to prove breach. An outstanding easement or restrictive covenant may interfere with the grantee's possessory rights but still leave him in control of most of the premises. In these situations, all the warrantee has to prove is the existence of the outstanding incumbrance. One troublesome question arises when the grantee knows of the existence of an easement but accepts a covenant against it. May he later sue for breach if the easement is not extinguished? The classic answer is yes, since knowledge of the outstanding incumbrance may be the very reason for insisting on a covenant against it.[16] This yes must be

13. 57 Kan. 663, 47 P. 537 (1897).

14. For a collection of cases see Burby on Real Property 479, ftn. 35 (2d ed. 1954).

15. Morgan v. Haley, 107 Va. 331, 58 S.E. 564 (1907).

16. Jones v. Grow Investment and Mortgage Co., 11 Utah 2d 326, 358 P.2d 909 (1961); Lavey v. Graessle, 245 Mich. 681, 224 N.W. 436, 64 A.L.R. 1477 (1929).

qualified and tempered with reason, however, for sometimes it is clear that the parties did not intend to remove the incumbrance. "Some of the cases are decided upon the theory that, whenever the actual physical conditions of the property are apparent, and are in their nature permanent, and irremediable, such conditions are within the contemplation of the parties when contracting, and are therefore not included in a general covenant against encumbrances. These principles have led to a conflict among the authorities, especially in the cases where a public highway or railroad right of way existed upon the land conveyed." [17]

A recent Oregon case, Leach v. Gunnarson,[18] is particularly helpful on this latter point. The grantor had used a statutory short-form warranty deed with full covenants of title. A third party had a "license" to use water from a spring on the land conveyed. The grantee knew of the "license" but apparently had been told it could be revoked. Later it was held to be an "executed license" due to the expenditures by the licensee, i.e., in effect an easement. The grantor, despite the fact that he had warranted against incumbrances, denied liability because the use of the spring was open, notorious, and visible and the grantee was aware of the use. The court distinguished railroad and public utilities cases in Oregon where the grantor had been held not liable and said the grantee had stated a cause of action. However, the case was remanded to give the grantee an opportunity to show that the existence of the incumbrance diminished the value of his land. The moral of this and similar cases is clear. If the land is subject to an incumbrance and the grantee is willing to accept title in that condition, the warranty deed should contain an exception as to the specific incumbrance and not leave the issue to the vagaries of judicial interpretation.

Although an easement is clearly an incumbrance, it is not always easy to determine whether a particular interference with a purchaser's rights amounts to breach of the covenant against incumbrances. The mere existence of use restrictions by way of zoning or building codes does not constitute an incumbrance but violation of these restrictions prior to sale may be sufficient to cause a breach of the covenant in the warranty deed. Thus in Lohmeyer v. Bower,[19] the court decided that the location of a structure in violation of a zoning ordinance specifying a minimum distance from the rear lot line exposed the owner to the hazard of litigation and made the title doubtful and unmarketable. Similar-

17. 64 A.L.R. 1479, 1480 (1929). See also Merchandising Corp. v. Marine Nat. Exchange Bank, 12 Wis.2d 79, 106 N.W.2d 317 (1960).

18. 290 Or. 31, 619 P.2d 263 (1980).

19. 170 Kan. 442, 227 P.2d 102 (1951).

ly, in Brunke v. Pharo,[20] the court held that violation of a building code, prescribing standards of safety to be met by apartment buildings, constituted an incumbrance violative of the grantor's covenant, where the agency charged with enforcement of the code had begun official action before conveyance and such action was thus imminent when the deed was delivered.

On the other hand, in Fahmie v. Wulster,[21] a prior owner had constructed a culvert on the land which did not conform to government specifications. The plaintiff acquired title by a warranty deed which included a covenant against incumbrances. He was then notified by the state that the culvert was inadequate in size and would have to be replaced. The court held that while breach of a covenant against incumbrances can involve physical conditions concerning the property, such as a building encroachment, this concept would not be extended to the condition of a structure on the property which is in violation of some governmental law or regulation. The court cited Brunke v. Pharo but distinguished that case because the conveyance there was made after violations of the building code had been found and official action begun to compel compliance. The court then concluded: "The present situation is different and, in any event we are not inclined to follow the Wisconsin approach. To expand the concept of encumbrance as urged by the plaintiffs would create uncertainty and confusion in the law of conveyancing and title insurance. A title search would not have disclosed the violation, nor would a physical examination of the premises. The better way to deal with violations of governmental regulations, their nature and scope being as pervasive as they are, is by contract provision which can give the purchaser full protection in a situation such as here presented."

In Brewer v. Peatross,[22] the court allowed a suit based on an incumbrance created by a special improvement district. Wrote the court: "In regard to the defendant's argument that there was no encumbrance on the property because the assessment ordinance had not become effective nor created as a lien by the statute, it is appropriate to note that the term 'encumbrance' is more comprehensive than 'lien.' For instance, mortgages, tax liens, labor and materialmen's liens, are encumbrances but without expatiating thereon, there are some encumbrances upon property which are not liens. An encumbrance may be said to be any right that a third person holds in land which constitutes a burden or limitation upon the rights of the fee title holder." In the case, there was evidence that the purchaser had inquired as to whether

20. 3 Wis.2d 628, 89 N.W.2d 221 (1958).

21. 81 N.J. 391, 408 A.2d 789 (1979).

22. 595 P.2d 866 (Utah 1979).

the price of the lots included the improvements to be made by the special district and the vendor assured him that it did. This represents a situation where the parties should be especially careful and put their agreement in writing because it can be a prime source of litigation.

SECTION 3. DAMAGES

We are immediately confronted by another dilemma. If the title proves defective it may not be discovered for many years and, by this time, the land may have increased greatly in value and major improvements may have been added to the premises. Is the damage to be determined by the actual loss suffered at the future eviction or will it be restricted to the purchase money paid to the warrantor? A small minority of states (all in New England) have followed the former rule and thus given the warrantee the maximum protection under the future covenants.[23] The overwhelming majority of the states have felt this placed too great a burden on the warrantor, especially in a society where the trend of land values appears to be always upward, and have restricted recovery to the purchase price, or a proportionate share thereof for partial breach, plus interest.[24] Interest is usually allowed, however, only in the cases where the grantee has not had the benefit of the rents and profits from the land or has had to surrender them to the paramount title holder. As an additional sop, the grantee can usually recover the costs, including attorney's fees, for an unsuccessful defense of his title against a paramount owner.[25] In the case of an incumbrance, the warrantee can recover the reasonable cost of removal, not to exceed the purchase price paid to the warrantor, or if the claim cannot be extinguished, as in the case of an easement where the holder refuses to release it, the diminution in value of the estate due to the incumbrance.[26]

---

23. For a collection of cases and a more detailed discussion of the damage question see McCormick on Damages 700–709 (1935).

24. Id. For a good discussion of the reasons behind the majority rule see Davis v. Smith, 5 Ga. 274, 48 Am.Dec. 279 (1848).

25. Suppose the defense is successful? Since this proves the third party claim was unjustified, there has been no breach of covenant and, although the warrantee has had to bear substantial court costs and attorney's fees, he cannot recover them. Elliott v. Elliott, 252 Ark. 966, 482 S.W.2d 123 (1972). There may be some exceptions to this rule if the warrantor has "thrust" the warrantee into litigation with a third party. First Fiduciary Corp. v. Blanco, 276 N.W.2d 30 (Minn.1979). Contrast this result with title insurance where the insurer will bear the costs of even an unjustified claim against the title.

26. Notes 16 and 18, supra.

When the covenants run with the land all sorts of puzzles are possible. Try this one for size. *A* delivers a warranty deed to *B* for $10,000. *B* delivers a warranty deed to *C* for $8,000. *X*, a paramount title holder, ousts *C*. *C* can recover $8,000 from *B*, but since the covenants of warranty and quiet enjoyment run with the land he can also sue *A*. He is restricted, of course, to one satisfaction. How much can *C* recover from *A*? Brooks v. Black,[27] in a well-reasoned opinion, allowed *C* to recover $10,000, i.e., the court held the original warrantor liable for the full price received by him, even though the remote grantee paid less to his own grantor. Other courts have limited recovery to the amount paid by the plaintiff to his own grantor.[28]

The purchaser of land who makes improvements in good faith, relying on his supposed ownership, may nonetheless be ousted later by a stranger who in fact owns the property. If a warranty deed was used the grantee may be able to recover a portion of his loss, but it will probably fall short of his real damages. Can he recoup any portion of this loss from the stranger-owner? At common law, the innocent improver was considered to be an interloper without legal remedy and since the buildings were annexed to the soil they became the property of the true owner.

This rigid rule of the common law was manifestly unfair in many cases. Assume that an innocent improver, thinking that he has good title to the land, builds a substantial structure on "his" property only to discover that a paramount title holder has priority of claim to the land. If the latter is entitled to possession of the land plus building, he will receive a windfall and will be unjustly enriched by the amount that the structure has enhanced the value of the land. To prevent this result and reverse the harsh rule of the common law, statutes and judicial decisions have mitigated the doctrines relating to mistaken improvements.[29] The statutes, typically referred to as "betterment acts" or "occupying claimants laws," have not been entirely consistent but the holder of the paramount title is usually given the option of selling the land to the mistaken improver at its unimproved value, or of purchasing

27. 68 Miss. 161, 8 So. 332, 24 Am. St.Rep. 259 (1890).

28. Taylor v. Wallace, 20 Colo. 211, 37 P. 963 (1894); Taylor v. Allen, 131 Ga. 416, 62 S.E. 291 (1908).

29. See Madrid v. Spears, 250 F.2d 51 (10th Cir.1957) where the court noted: "It was these considerations [essential unfairness to the innocent improver] which undoubtedly led the Restatement to adopt the 'whichever is the least rule' to the effect that 'where the improver is permitted to recover for the improvements, he is entitled to the reasonable value of his labor and materials or to the amount which his improvements have added to the market value of the land, whichever is smaller.' Restatement of Restitution, s. 42, Comment on Subsection (1)."

the improvements from him at an amount equal to the value they add to the property.[30]

If the paramount title holder elects to keep the land, there will be difficult problems of proof as to the value added to the property. The City of Poplar Bluff v. Knox [31] casts some light on this problem. "The compensation to which a good faith occupant is entitled for improvements he makes on the land of another is generally held to be the amount by which the value of the land has been enhanced by the improvements and *not* the actual value of the improvements themselves or the amount the improvements cost the occupant."

The countless intricate problems which can (and do) arise when parties are forced into litigation over covenants for title demonstrate the vital importance of making sure that the title is merchantable before accepting delivery of a deed. Covenants for title do give additional assurance to the purchaser but they are no substitute for the other methods of title assurance discussed in succeeding sections of this chapter.

SECTION 4.   ESTOPPEL BY DEED (AFTER-ACQUIRED TITLE)

A conveys land he does not own to B by warranty deed. Later A acquires the title from C. Who now owns the land? Since A owned nothing at the time of the conveyance, nothing passed to B and A would appear to own Blackacre. If so, B can sue A on the covenants in the deed and recover the purchase price. To avoid this "circuity of action" the courts have long held that the title passed to B, thus giving him what he should have had all along and ending any suit on the covenants.[32] Suppose the deed to B had been quitclaim in form? If the avoidance of circuity of action is the sole basis for the doctrine of after-acquired title then A is the owner still, because B could not sue A on a quitclaim deed. However, the better and more modern view bases the doctrine on

---

30. Id. See also State Mutual Insurance Co. v. McJenkin Insurance & Realty Co., 86 Ga.App. 442, 71 S.E.2d 670 (1952) and Dobbs, Remedies s. 12.8 note 72 (1973).

31. 410 S.W.2d 100 (Mo.App.1966). The court held the act did not apply, however, in a case where a city sought to eject a defendant from a portion of the street purportedly conveyed to the

defendant years earlier. The defendant was allowed to remove her improvements from the street. See also ftn. 29 supra and the Restatement of Restitution quote.

32. Robben v. Obering, 279 F.2d 381 (7th Cir.1960). This case gives a good, general discussion of the doctrine and holds it applies to leases as well as to deeds.

estoppel, i.e., A is estopped to deny that the title passed to B since he *represented,* at the time of the original deed, that he owned Blackacre.[33] This estoppel would nearly always work when a warranty deed was involved,[34] hence we discuss it under covenants for title because it does give the grantee some further title assurance. It *might* also work with a quitclaim deed, however, providing the intent of the grantor, gathered from the deed, was to convey the full interest and not just release any possible claim he might have. Thus, the usual quitclaim deed would not carry after-acquired title but if there were recitals, such as "A, being seised of a fee simple absolute, conveys and quitclaims to B", this could form the basis of an estoppel by representation.[35] A number of the states have clarified the doctrine by statute.[36]

Although the point is in conflict, the better view is that the doctrine operates to "feed the estoppel", i.e., it transfers the title automatically to B, rather than furnishing him with an equitable defense if sued by A or his privies.[37] This is the better view because it allows the title examiner to rely on this after-acquired title as a link in the chain of title.[38] It can cause complications, however, if the grantee, B, does not want to accept this after-acquired title but prefers to sue on the covenants instead. Although the doctrine normally works *eo instante,* it would seem that in this last situation the grantee should have his option to accept the title or sue.[39]

33. Hagensick v. Castor, 53 Neb. 495, 73 N.W. 932 (1898).

34. Suppose, however, the language of the warranty deed states "I hereby warrant whatever title I may have at this time, if any." This would form no basis for estoppel. See Cunningham, Stoebuck and Whitman, The Law of Property 745 (1984).

35. See Stevens v. Stevens, 10 Wash. App. 493, 519 P.2d 269 (1974). (A quitclaim deed was involved but it contained an express conveyance of after-acquired title.)

36. See, for example, Ill.Rev.Stat. ch. 30, § 6 (1985). The Illinois statute reads as follows: "If any person shall sell and convey to another, by deed or conveyance, purporting to convey an estate in fee simple absolute, in any tract of land or real estate, lying and being in this state, not then being possessed of the legal estate or interest therein at the time of the sale and conveyance, but after such sale and conveyance the vendor shall become possessed of and con-

firmed in the legal estate to the land or real estate so sold and conveyed, it shall be taken and held to be in trust and for the use of the grantee or vendee; and the conveyance aforesaid shall be held and taken, and shall be as valid as if the grantor or vendor had the legal estate or interest, at the time of said sale or conveyance." See also 44 Ill.Bar J. 263 (1955). Note this statute does not turn on whether a warranty or quitclaim deed was used but rather on whether a grantor *purported* to convey an estate in fee simple absolute. Other states have statutes to a similar effect. See Colo.Rev.Stat. s. 38–30–104 (1973) and Miss.Code, s. 89–1–39 (1972).

37. Perkins v. Coleman, 90 Ky. 611, 14 S.W. 640 (1890).

38. For further discussion of chain of title problems and how they relate to estoppel by deed see p. 319 infra.

39. Resser v. Carney, 52 Minn. 397, 54 N.W. 89 (1893); 3 Am.L.Prop. s. 15.23 (1952).

Chapter 3

THE RECORDING SYSTEM (HEREIN OF TITLE EXAMINATION AND TITLE INSURANCE)

The previous section demonstrates that covenants for title leave much to be desired as a method of title assurance. Aside from their technical defects they require a lawsuit, unless the warrantor pays willingly, and if he is insolvent they are worthless. Moreover, even at best, they will not enable the purchaser to keep his land and he will have to settle for money damages. The buyer of land wants assurance that the vendor has a merchantable title which he can transfer to him. The recording system helps give him that assurance.

"Apart from the recording acts priority between deeds, mortgages, judgments and other liens or titles, is determined by the order in point of time in which they become effective. Where A conveys land by a valid deed to B, and conveys or mortgages the same land to C, nothing passes to C since A had nothing to convey to him, having already conveyed the same property to B. So, if A mortgages the land to B and later conveys or mortgages it to C, the right secured by C is subject to B's mortgage. This is true though C be a purchaser for value without notice of B's deed or mortgage. The doctrine that a purchaser for value without notice will be protected against prior claims applies only to cases where the legal title has passed to such purchaser and the prior claims are equitable and not legal rights. This doctrine is purely equitable, equity refusing to disturb the legal title by enforcing a prior equity where such title is held by a purchaser for value without notice. Apart from the statutes, therefore, a valid title or lien existing and enforceable at law is never cut off or affected by a subsequent deed or mortgage executed by the same vendor or owner to another person, whether a purchaser for value or not."[1]

There is logic in the "first in time, first in right" scheme of priority, but it is the logic of theory, not of practice. In a complex society purchasers have no way of checking on the status of title unless they can rely on some official record which shows all of the transactions in regard to the land in question. In the United States[2] the recording system has furnished the solution to the

1. 2 Walsh, Commentaries on the Law of Real Property 487, 488 (1947).

2. "Except as registration of title under a Torrens law obtains in the city

306

purchaser's dilemma by creating a permanent record which can be examined by anyone wishing to buy land or lend money on it as a security interest.   The net effect of the system is to introduce by statute the equitable concept of bona fide purchaser for value without notice so that the b.f.p. takes free of prior deeds, mortgages, leases, etc., if they are not recorded as required by the particular act.

The acts set forth the instruments which are authorized to be recorded, and while there is considerable variation they generally include deeds, mortgages, assignments of mortgages, leases, and executory contracts.   Some acts are broad enough to include virtually any document: "Deeds, mortgages, powers of attorney, and other instruments relating to or affecting the title to real estate."[3]   These instruments are copied (originally in a flowing script unknown today and now by photostatic means) into books kept in a public office in the local unit of government (usually a county) where the land is located.   Typically the instruments go into the record as tendered, without regard to the names of the parties or the location of the tracts being conveyed.   (Indeed in some areas little attention is paid to the instruments themselves and one wag tells of the county clerk who would put a menu on record if a fee were tendered.)   Since in many counties there will be hundreds of books and thousands of instruments, it is apparent that careful indexing is required if the recording system is to make any sense whatever.

There are two basic systems of indexing—the grantor-grantee system and the tract system.   The present trend is to reduce the number of indexes and use only one grantor-grantee index, but many states have a separate index for each type of instrument (mortgagor-mortgagee, mechanic's lien, index to miscellaneous documents, etc.).   For example, Idaho has twenty-four different indexes.[4]   Note how these indexes work in practice.

and county of London, and except lands affected by the registry acts for the counties of Middlesex and York, proof of title in England is to this day by possession of the property and by exhibition of the original title deeds. . . . But, with the exception first noted, there has never been any provision in England by which proof of title may be made from public and semi-public records alone, as is now so universally the case in this country." 1 Patton, Titles 8 (1957). England is now moving rapidly to the Torrens system. See pp. 330 to 332 infra.

3. Ill.Rev.Stat. ch. 30, § 27 (1985).

4. Idaho Code, § 31–2404 (1948) provides for the following indexes: Grantors, grantees, mortgagors of real property, mortgagors of personal property, mortgagees of real and personal property, releases of real property mortgages in the name of the mortgagor, releases of personal property mortgages in the name of the mortgagor, two similar indexes for releases in the name of the mortgagee, powers of attorney, lessors, lessees, marriage certificates in the name of the husband, same in the name of the wife, assignors (of mortgages and leases), assignees (of mortgages and leases), wills, official bonds, mechanics' liens, judgments, attachments, notices

"A title searcher tracing title by means of the public records employs an official index of names, called the Grantor–Grantee Index.[5] Suppose, for example, that the United States Government records show that the United States sold a particular tract of land to John Jones on March 15, 1840. The title searcher will turn to the Grantor Index, which is arranged alphabetically, and, beginning with the date March 15, 1840, he will look under the letter 'J' for any deeds or mortgages made since March 15, 1840, by John Jones. Naturally he would not expect to find any deeds or mortgages of that land made by Jones prior to March 15, 1840, because Jones did not acquire title until that date. Therefore, except in a few states, the law does not require him to look for any such deeds or mortgages prior to that date. Suppose he finds that John Jones conveyed the land to Joseph Smith by deed dated September 10, 1860, and recorded November 1, 1860. He will now look under the letter 'S' for any deeds or mortgages made by Smith on or after September 10, 1860, the date when Smith acquired title. This process is repeated until he has brought the title down to date. This process is called running the chain of title.

"Suppose, however, that Joseph Smith had made a mortgage on the land in question, dated September 5, 1860, and recorded September 6, 1860. Observe that both of these dates are prior to the date of the deed by which Smith acquired title, namely, September 10, 1860. A title searcher would not find this mortgage, since he would not look under the name 'Smith' for any deed or mortgage prior to September 10, 1860. Such a mortgage is not in the line of title. It is also said that the mortgage is not in the *chain of title.* The legal result is the same as though the mortgage had not been recorded at all. A person buying the land not knowing of the existence of this mortgage would get good title free and clear of the mortgage.

"In other words, the records show the ownership of land passing from one person to another, and the name of each successive owner must be searched during the period of his ownership to see what recorded deeds and mortgages he has signed. The person searching the name indexes must always have some point of time to mark the beginning of his search of a name that appears on the records, and as a rule, where the records show that Smith became the owner of the land, the searcher need not look for documents that may have been executed by Smith prior to the date on which

of actions (lis pendens), separate property of married women, possessory claims, homesteads, real property agreements, mining claims, water rights, and federal tax liens.

5. The following five paragraphs are quoted from Kratovil, Real Estate Law 94–95 (3d ed. 1958).

the records show Smith became the owner of the property. [However, in a few states, a warranty deed or mortgage executed and recorded by Smith, who does not *then* own the land, is, nevertheless, binding on all persons dealing with the land after the deed *to* Smith is recorded. Ayer v. Philadelphia Brick Co., 159 Mass. 84, 34 N.E. 177. This is a poor rule, for it requires searchers of the records to check a name for an indefinite time *prior* to the time such party acquired ownership of the land, merely to guard against the possibility of such 'wild' deeds and mortgages executed by him prior to his acquisition of ownership of the land. 2d ed. 1952.]

"In a few states, the name index (grantor-grantee index) has been superseded by a *tract index*. This index allocates a separate page in the index to each piece of property in the county, and if you are interested in a particular piece of property, you simply locate the proper page in the index, and there you will find listed all recorded deeds and other documents relating to this piece of property.

"In virtually all states, including those in which the only official index is the grantor-grantee index, abstract and title companies maintain their own private tract indexes."

SECTION 1.   GENERAL OPERATION OF THE SYSTEM

With minor exceptions, recording adds nothing to the validity of a legal document except as that document affects the rights of a b.f.p.[6] Title will pass from the grantor to the grantee as soon as the deed is delivered. Recording the deed simply assures the grantee that the world has constructive notice of the conveyance thus cutting off the grantor's power to defeat the former's interest by a new conveyance to a b.f.p. In the early days of the recording acts, the courts were somewhat bothered by the legal theory of the acts. If *A* conveyed the legal title to *B*, what did *A* have left to transfer to *C*, even if the latter was a b.f.p.?[7] The best answer

6. In Mountain States Telephone and Telegraph Co. v. Kelton, 79 Ariz. 126, 285 P.2d 168 (1955) the court held a contractor, owning no interest in the land, did not have a duty to search for recorded underground telephone line easements and thus was not negligent in damaging the lines, since he was unaware of their presence. "It is sometimes said that the record of a deed is constructive notice to all the world. That, it is evident, is too broad and unqualified an enunciation of the doctrine. *It is constructive notice only to those who are bound to search for it.*"

7. Earle v. Fiske, 103 Mass. 491 (1870) illustrates the remnants of this theoretical difficulty although the court decided correctly for the b.f.p.

seems to be that *A* has the apparent title, as disclosed by the records, even though *B* has the actual title. This apparent title does not give *A* a *right* to convey the land again but it does leave him with a *power* to do so until *B* records his deed.

Nor can recording give validity to a void deed or mortgage.[8] Recording places on file, in a public place, the written evidence of a conveyance; if that conveyance were void for want of delivery, forgery, lack of capacity in the grantor due to infancy or insanity, etc., it is void still. Some statutes do make recording conclusive evidence of delivery in favor of a b.f.p.,[9] but beyond that concession the title examiner takes the record as he finds it, subject to numerous possible defects that are not disclosed on its face.

The recording acts were drafted to apply to written or paper titles that depend for their proof on a connected chain of deeds, contracts, mortgages, leases, etc. This will cover the bulk of the ownership problems but, even today, there are good titles which do not depend on a written document. Adverse possession of land for the requisite statutory period (typically twenty years) will give a good title to the adverse possessor but its proof will depend entirely on physical acts, not written words. This sets the stage for conflict. *A* has record title; *B* has possessed adversely for twenty years, but has temporarily left the land so his current possession gives no constructive notice of his claim; *C*, a b.f.p., buys from *A* on the strength of the record. Who owns the land? Mugaas v. Smith [10] gave judgment for *B*, the adverse possessor, since the recording acts do not apply to this type of title and once *B* has perfected his ownership he need not keep his "flag flying forever" on the land in order to be protected. This clearly cuts into the effectiveness of the acts, but they could be amended to require the adverse possessor to, at least, file for record an affidavit of his claim in order to protect innocent parties. It is true, of course, that he could not record his title, since he has nothing in writing, unless he brings a quiet title suit to confirm his claim by a decree in equity.

Mistakes will inevitably occur in the administration of a recording system. In the early days, when the documents were copied by hand, it was easy to misdescribe the land and, while photostating largely eliminates that error, it is still possible to index a document improperly. An instrument mistakenly indexed or not indexed at all is worthless to the title searcher, but who must bear the loss? The recording party has done all required of him, he can scarcely be expected to supervise the work of the

8. Stone v. French, 37 Kan. 145, 14 P. 530, 1 Am.St.Rep. 237 (1887).

9. Mass.Gen.Laws Ann. ch. 183, § 5.

10. 33 Wash.2d 429, 206 P.2d 332, 9 A.L.R.2d 846 (1949).

recorder's office; the b.f.p. has relied on the records as they appear to him and has no possible way of discovering the error. The cases split on this tough issue and tend to turn on whether the particular act makes indexing an essential part of recording or whether it treats recording as complete in itself and covers indexing separately.[11]

Mortensen v. Lingo,[12] in a well-reasoned opinion, promoted the integrity of the recording system by holding for the b.f.p. Noted the United States District Court for Alaska: "A deed might as well be buried in the earth as in a mass of records without a clue to its whereabouts." However, in Gregor v. City of Fairbanks,[13] the Supreme Court of Alaska took a contrary view, without citing Mortensen v. Lingo. Said the court: "In reaching this conclusion we have implicitly rejected the line of cases which holds that where the record of a conveyance is either incorrectly or never transcribed by the actions of a careless recording officer, the grantee must suffer the consequences, regardless of the fact that she has done all she can do to ensure that the deed is properly recorded. These cases would remit the unfortunate recording grantee to a remedy against the recording officer or his sureties."[14] When one of two innocent parties must suffer, courts always have a difficult time in reconciling their decisions but note, in any case, that the losing party should have an action against the recorder on his official bond.

A nagging problem under the recording acts concerns the effect of a defective, but not void, instrument which fails to comply with certain statutory requirements. The most common defect is a faulty acknowledgment but others may be involved. If the statute requires acknowledgment or attestation and the deed is recorded without it, does the instrument give constructive notice of a conveyance? The general rule seems to be that it does not, since there has been a failure to follow the statute.[15] While this may be a good way to put teeth into the statute and force proper acknowledgment, etc., it seems unfair to allow a subsequent purchaser to ignore a recorded document just because of a technical error. He can scarcely claim that he had no constructive notice of the grantor's effort to make a valid conveyance. This view has led to some statutory changes which declare that the document in

11. 4 American Law of Property, § 17.25 (Casner ed. 1952).

12. 99 F.Supp. 585 (D.Alaska 1951).

13. 599 P.2d 743 (Alaska 1979).

14. To the same effect see King v. Stephens, 9 Mass.App.Ct. 919, 404 N.E.2d 115 (1980) and Maddox v. Astro Investments, 45 Ohio App.2d 203, 343 N.E.2d 133 (1975).

15. Nordman v. Rau, 86 Kan. 19, 119 P. 351 (1911); Messersmith v. Smith, 60 N.W.2d 276 (N.D.1953).

question shall be notice to subsequent purchasers and creditors even though not acknowledged.[16]

Up to this point the discussion has proceeded as if the recording acts were all of one piece. It is true that they all seek the same general end, but there are substantial differences in detail. Moreover, you have probably noticed that the acts are strictly construed and, at times, seem hypertechnical. This is because they are deemed to be in opposition to the common law, which followed the "first-in-time, first-in-right" system of priorities, and hence fall under the old canon of statutory interpretation that statutes in derogation of the common law must be strictly construed. This means that no case under the recording acts should be considered without first analyzing the statute in the particular jurisdiction, plus its judicial interpretation.

It would be pleasant if the recording acts were all based on a uniform statute and the problems could be mastered by an analysis of the basic pattern. But statutes never seem to be passed to give pleasure to students, and the acts are far from uniform. Fortunately, however, there are not fifty separate types. Many writers have classified the acts into four categories.

(1) *Pure race.* Under an act of this type the grantee who first places his deed on the proper records prevails over other conveyances from the common source of title. The first party to record is protected even though he took with notice of a prior unrecorded conveyance.[17] North Carolina and Louisiana seem to be the only states which have a pure race statute for conveyances generally, although a few other states use it for mortgages or oil and gas leases only. The pure race statute is easiest to apply and is an added incentive for prompt recording but it seems inherently unfair to protect the first recorder if he knows of a previous unrecorded conveyance, mortgage or other claim to the land in question. When certainty and fairness conflict nearly all states have opted for the latter value and this probably accounts for the unpopularity of the pure race model.

(2) *Period of grace.* This type of act was designed to protect the first conveyee for a set period of time whether or not he

---

16. See, for example, Ill.Rev.Stat. ch. 30, § 30 (1985). The extreme importance of specific statutes is illustrated by Flexter v. Woomer, 46 Ill.App.2d 456, 197 N.E.2d 161 (1964). Despite Illinois' liberal position in regard to acknowledgments, the court held that a recorded mortgage was not constructive notice to a subsequent b.f.p. when it did not state the maturity date or the amount of the note. The statute required the mortgage to recite the nature and amount of the indebtedness. Should not the defectively recorded mortgage at least put the purchaser on notice of a prior lien and force him to make inquiry as to the date and amount?

17. Dulin v. Williams, 239 N.C. 33, 79 S.E.2d 213 (1953); Simmons v. Quick–Stop Food Mart, Inc., 307 N.C. 33, 296 S.E.2d 275 (1982).

recorded. If he still had not recorded at the end of the period he lost the special protection. This type was common in an earlier day when it took some time to travel to the county seat and when such trips might be infrequent for the landowner. Delaware seems to have been the last state with such a statute and since it was repealed in 1968 this category is of historical interest only.[18]

(3) *Race-notice.* Acts of this type require that the subsequent purchaser be without notice at the time the conveyance is made and the consideration paid. In addition, the subsequent buyer without notice must record first.[19]

(4) *Notice.* Acts following this pattern protect the junior conveyee against a prior unrecorded conveyance if he has paid value and is without notice. They differ from race-notice acts, since the junior conveyee is protected even though the senior conveyee records after the grant to the junior and before the junior records, or even if the junior does not record at all.[20] In some states with acts which appear to be of the notice type, the race-notice principle prevails because of judicial interpretation.[21] Although notice acts originally were prevalent, at the present time notice and race-notice statutes appear to be about evenly divided. Acts of one type or the other are in force in most states.[22]

When a grantor conveys the same land twice he may be an utter rascal or he may simply have made a mistake due to carelessness on his part as where he owns large tracts of land, particularly if the land is heavily forested and the boundaries are not clearly defined. In either case, he should be liable to that grantee who pays consideration but gets no title to the land. Suppose a grantor conveys to A, who fails to record, and then

18. 56 Del.Laws, Ch. 318 (1968).

19. Cal.Civil Code s. 1214 (1980); Mich.Comp.Laws Ann. § 565.29 (1953).

20. Mass.Gen.Laws Ann. c. 183 § 4 (1977).

21. Simmons v. Stum, 101 Ill. 454 (1882). Professor Aigler, commenting on the Illinois case wrote: "It will be noticed that this statute in terms avoids the unrecorded instrument 'as to all such creditors and subsequent purchasers without notice.' The California statute contains, in essence, the same language, but with this significant addition—'whose conveyance is first duly recorded.' Thus, under the California legislation, and a considerable number of states have recording acts with similar provisions, the subsequent, innocent purchaser, etc., must beat the claimant under the earlier instrument to the record office. The Illinois court, however,

has interpreted their statute as leading to the same result. . . . Surely the Illinois court has read something into the statute." Aigler, Cases on Titles 848, n. 17 (3d ed.1942). Despite this criticism, Illinois continues to interpret its statute as the race-notice type. See Daughters v. Preston, 131 Ill.App.3d 723, 86 Ill.Dec. 944, 476 N.E.2d 445 (1985). In this case, the Third District Court of Appeals held that prior purchasers had superior title where they recorded their deeds one hour before a subsequent purchaser recorded his deed, even though the subsequent purchaser was a b.f.p. at the time he acquired his deed, which was before recordation by the prior purchasers.

22. For a detailed history and analysis of the recording acts see 4 American Law of Property, §§ 17.4–17.36 (Casner ed.1952).

conveys the same land to B, a b.f.p. who records first. B will get title to the land. (Note that in a pure race jurisdiction B would prevail even if he had notice of the prior conveyance to A.) A, in one sense, has only himself to blame since if he had recorded promptly B could not be a b.f.p. and B's only cause of action would be against the grantor. Should A's failure to record leave him without legal recourse? Note that the grantor still had apparent title and the power to cut off A's claim to the land until such time as A recorded or entered possession. But, while the grantor had the legal *power* to convey a second time he had no legal *right* to do so. Moreover, he has been paid twice and hence unjustly enriched at A's expense. If A's deed were a warranty deed, he might sue the grantor on the covenants for title (although even then the grantor could argue that he had good title at the time he conveyed to A and that the latter caused the problem by his own laches). If A's deed were a quitclaim deed, the plot thickens. Faced with this exact problem, the Supreme Court of North Carolina allowed A to recover from the grantor, even on a deed with no warranties.[23] Opined the court: "But to sustain this action it is not necessary for the plaintiff to maintain it as one in tort. If we wish to be technical about the forms of action . . . it may be regarded as an action of assumpsit, involving the principles of quasi contract, which are broad enough to include practically every instance where a defendant has received money which he is 'obliged by the ties of natural justice and equity to refund.'"

There are several possible variations on the theme of the previous paragraph but the important point is that the recording system was not designed to resolve all of the issues that may arise among the various parties in a controversy. Its purpose is to determine priorities as to title and provide a workable, albeit imperfect, system to protect those who invest in real property.

SECTION 2. PERSONS PROTECTED BY THE SYSTEM

The recording acts do not announce to the world, "*X* owns Blackacre"; they simply furnish a source of information on which the individual dealing with the land can, more or less, rely. The key to discovering who is protected by the acts lies in the word "rely." A donee, having parted with nothing of value, cannot be

---

23. Patterson v. Bryant, 216 N.C. 550, 5 S.E.2d 849 (1939). Since North Carolina is a pure race jurisdiction B was held to have priority even though he may have had notice of the prior conveyance to A.

said to have relied on the system.[24] A purchaser, who knows the truth about prior but unrecorded transactions, has not relied on the acts. However, the buyer need not actually have searched the records in order to be protected and he takes free of unrecorded claims even though he negligently failed to look for them. While this appears, initially, to negative reliance it is actually a compromise with practicality, making the test objective rather than subjective. If the individual fits into the protected class he gets the full benefit of the system. The basic test remains: is he a bona fide purchaser for value without notice? In the pure race jurisdictions a purchaser with notice who records first is protected too, but this is important in only a few states.[25]

The meaning of "for value" is the first hurdle. A valuable consideration is money or something that is worth money as opposed to a good consideration which refers to a relationship of blood or marriage. It is not necessary that the consideration be adequate and even though small or nominal it will suffice, in the absence of fraud.[26] Again, this view seems designed to make the system workable since an inquiry into the adequacy of consideration for each transfer would be intolerable. This is particularly true for past transactions in the chain which may well recite "for one dollar and other good and valuable consideration" even though a large sum was, in fact, paid. If the value paid was merely colorable or fraud was involved that is another matter. The authorities are split as to whether a grantee under a quit-claim deed is a protected party.[27] Good arguments can be made for either position since a quitclaim deed could be said to give notice on its face that the title may be defective and yet full value might well have been paid for the conveyance. Certainly, the position that "a purchaser for value by quitclaim deed is as much within the protection of the registry act as one who becomes a purchaser by a warranty deed",[28] is more in line with the spirit of the acts and is a major help to the examining attorney.

If a buyer has paid only a portion of the purchase price when he discovers a prior conveyance, mortgage, or valid lien, he makes

24. Colorado is the only state to reach a contrary position. Due to the peculiar wording of the Colorado statute, even a donee is protected in that jurisdiction. Eastwood v. Shedd, 166 Colo. 136, 442 P.2d 423 (1968).

25. See p. 312 supra.

26. Strong v. Whybark, 204 Mo. 341, 102 S.W. 968 (1907); 4 Am.Law Prop. § 17.10, at 558 (Casner ed. 1952).

27. Morris v. Wicks, 81 Kan. 790, 106 P. 1048 (1910). Despite the arguments made in Morris v. Wicks, most

modern jurisdictions protect a grantee under a quitclaim deed if he or she is otherwise a b.f.p. See Note, Deeds—Quitclaim Grantee as a Bona Fide Purchaser, 28 Or.L.Rev. 258 (1949) and Annot. 162 A.L.R. 556 (1946). See also Sabo v. Horvath, 559 P.2d 1038 (Alaska 1976) where the court said: "We further hold that Sabo may be a 'good faith purchaser' even though he takes by quitclaim deed."

28. Note 26, supra at 347 and 969.

further payments at his peril since he is entitled to protection only to the extent that he has been "hurt." This is called protection *pro tanto* and the rule is applied in various ways depending on the equities of the parties and the facts surrounding the transaction. "Some of the courts adopt that rule that allows the innocent purchaser to retain of the land purchased the proportion paid for. Some admit a lien in favor of the innocent purchaser upon the land for the amount of the purchase money paid. Other courts give to the innocent purchaser all the land, with a right in the real owner to recover from him the purchase money unpaid at the time of notice." [29]

Is a lessee a purchaser under the recording system? The answer is yes, according to Egbert v. Duck.[30] "Although a lessee is considered a purchaser, as a practical matter this means very little to the lessee, since he is protected only to the extent of rent paid prior to notice and must vacate the premises at the end of the period for which such rent was paid. This may result in a great hardship when the lessee has made expensive improvements or has otherwise substantially changed his position, as a lessee for a long term may well have done." [31]

Once the land comes into the hands of a b.f.p. it is, in effect, cleansed of its outstanding, but unrecorded, equities and even if it comes thereafter into the ownership of a purchaser with notice or a donee the title remains clear. This rule is essential to a proper functioning of the system since otherwise a b.f.p. would have less than full ownership of the land. If, however, the title comes back to one who was party to a fraudulent transfer or to a former owner who held subject to outstanding equities the defects revive and attach to the land in his hands. This prevents a holder of the title from using the b.f.p. as a "filter" to cleanse his defective ownership. He would scarcely be in good faith under these circumstances.[32]

The pre-existing debt, which is discharged as consideration for a conveyance of land, qualifies the grantee as a b.f.p. in some states but not in others. The crux of the matter lies in a change

---

29. Durst v. Daugherty, 81 Tex. 650, 654, 17 S.W. 388, 389 (1891).

In Alexander v. Andrews, 135 W.Va. 403, 64 S.E.2d 487 (1951) the court held that a purchaser who was paying the price in installments received notice of a prior unrecorded deed as soon as it was recorded. This places an intolerable burden on the buyer since he would have to examine the records immediately before paying each installment. It would seem preferable to require actual notice to the b.f.p. similar to that re-quired of a subsequent judgment creditor. See First Security Bank of Idaho v. Rogers, 91 Idaho 654, 429 P.2d 386 (1967).

30. 239 Iowa 646, 32 N.W.2d 404 (1948).

31. Johnson, Purpose and Scope of Recording Statutes, 47 Iowa L.Rev. 231, 235 (1962).

32. 3 Pomeroy, Equity Jurisprudence 55–57 (5th ed. 1941).

of position in reliance upon the acts. In Gabel v. Drewrys Limited, U.S.A., Inc.,[33] a mortgagee carefully searched the records, found the land free of prior liens, and then accepted the mortgagor's notes and mortgage. In fact, there was a prior mortgage, unrecorded, which was placed of record later. The mortgagee first mentioned had clearly relied upon the record but since no new consideration had passed to him—he simply took the mortgage to secure debts already due him—he was not entitled to priority and ended up with a second mortgage on the land. The court felt there had been no change in position and hence he was not entitled to protection. However, they said: "A definite extension of time for the payment of an existing debt, by a valid agreement, for any period however short, though it be for a day only, is a valuable consideration, and is sufficient to support a mortgage, or a conveyance, as a purchase for a valuable consideration." Since it is easy enough to draft an instrument which will meet this requirement, it makes the result turn on a very small point indeed. In the personal property field the matter has been resolved by legislation [34] and the pre-existing debt is sufficient to constitute value. Consistency and practicality call for the same result in real property.

A related question arises as to the role of the judgment creditor. *A* owns land that so far as the records disclose is free of all incumbrances. In fact, *B* has a valid mortgage on the land but has failed to record it. *C* obtains a judgment against *A* arising from some cause of action—the source is immaterial. The judgment normally becomes a lien against the land as soon as docketed. Who has priority? Once again, the cases are split with the results turning largely on the language of the particular statute.[35] The answer depends on whether the lien of the judgment extends to the actual title of the debtor or whether it reaches the apparent title as well. If it is the former, *A* has only a title subject to a mortgage; if it is the latter, he apparently owns it in fee simple absolute, free of all liens.[36] Note that, as in the case of the pre-existing debt, you can argue that the judgment creditor is not a b.f.p. because he has not parted with something new in reliance on the debtor's ownership of land. Conversely, you could claim that he would not have bothered to sue and reduce his claim to judgment but for the fact that he expected to have a first lien. While the weight of authority probably favors the view that the

---

33. 68 So.2d 372, 39 A.L.R.2d 1083 (Fla.1953).

34. Uniform Sales Act, § 76(1); Uniform Negotiable Instruments Act, § 25; Uniform Commercial Code, Section 1–204(44).

35. Holden v. Garrett, 23 Kan. 66 (1879).

36. Kartchner v. State Tax Commission, 4 Utah 2d 382, 294 P.2d 790 (1956).

judgment creditor is not a protected party, there is substantial authority and much logic to the contrary.[37]

The protected party must not only have paid value in reliance on the record but he must be *bona fide,* and without notice.[38] (This last phrase may be redundant since if he had notice of a prior claim he could not be *bona fide* in his actions.) It is clear that actual notice of a prior conveyance will disqualify the subsequent purchaser, but what about constructive notice? Recording itself is constructive notice and binds a party whether he looks at the record or not. Possession of the land by an apparent stranger to the title has the same effect in most jurisdictions, many of them going so far as to say "he must make inquiry as to the rights or title of the possessor, for possession is equivalent to registration [recording], in that it gives constructive notice of the possessor's rights." [39] This inquiry notice is normally held to bind the purchaser to anything which an investigation of the possessor's claim would have disclosed.[40] In some jurisdictions the purchaser seems to be bound only if he knew of the possession,[41] but even in those states a careful buyer should inspect the premises thoroughly

37. Some statutes give protection to the judgment creditor by express language. See, for example, Ill.Rev.Stat., ch. 30, s. 29 (1985). "All deeds, mortgages, or other instruments of writing, which are authorized to be recorded, shall take effect and be in force after the time of filing the same for record, and not before, as to *all creditors* and subsequent purchasers without notice; and all such deeds and title paper shall be *adjudged void* as to all *such creditors* and subsequent purchasers without notice, *until the same shall be filed for record."* (Emphasis added.)

See also Osin v. Johnson, 243 F.2d 653 (D.C.Cir.1957) where the court gave priority to a judgment creditor against prior unrecorded conveyances but refused to extend the priority as against a possible unrecorded constructive trust, unless the creditor could show actual reliance on the record title. The latter point is significant since there is nothing to record in a constructive trust because such a trust is merely an equitable remedy designed to "do justice" under the proper factual conditions. The equities between the person relying on a constructive trust theory and a judgment creditor who did not, in fact, rely on the records by making a search would appear to be rather evenly balanced as contrasted with a purchaser or mortgagee who failed to record.

38. A troublesome question arises as to the burden of proof when an issue of the purchaser's *bona fides* is involved. In Kindred v. Crosby, 251 Iowa 198, 100 N.W.2d 20 (1959), the court placed the burden on the alleged "purchaser" in a case where she looked suspiciously like a donee. Since she failed to prove her *bona fides,* she lost the case. Clearly, the burden of proof may decide many cases since, all too often, the evidence tends to be ambiguous and conflicting. The cases themselves are in conflict and reflect the diversity of opinion on the operation of the recording system. For a careful analysis of the problem see Johnson, Purpose and Scope of Recording Statutes, 47 Iowa L.Rev. 237–238 (1962). See also Nelson v. Hughes, 290 Or. 653, 625 P.2d 643 (1981) where the plaintiff alleged b.f.p. status but failed to prove it and hence lost the case.

39. Strong v. Strong, 128 Tex. 470, 474, 98 S.W.2d 346, 348, 109 A.L.R. 739 (1936). See also Wineberg v. Moore, 194 F.Supp. 12 (D.C.Cal.1961) for a discussion of what constitutes possession and its effect on the recording system.

40. Galley v. Ward, 60 N.H. 331 (1880).

41. Toupin v. Peabody, 162 Mass. 473, 39 N.E. 280 (1895).

before closing the transaction. Fortunately, a party is not bound by mere rumor as to claims against the land or by the general knowledge of people in the locality that someone has an unrecorded interest.[42] Nevertheless, even in this latter case, the facts may be sufficient to cast doubt on the *bona fides* of the buyer.

SECTION 3. THE CHAIN OF TITLE[43]

Documents affecting title may be recorded and still fail to bind a subsequent b.f.p. if they fall outside the chain of title. This paradox results from the use of a grantor-grantee system of indexing which can mean that a recorded instrument is, for all

42. Note 39, supra.

43. For a detailed analysis of the chain of title concept and some suggestions for reform see Cross, The Record "Chain of Title" Hypocrisy, 57 Col.L. Rev. 787 (1957). See also Sabo v. Horvath, 559 P.2d 1038 (Alaska 1976) for a thoughtful analysis of the problems involved. "The Horvaths' deed, recorded outside the chain of title, does not give constructive notice to the Sabos and is not 'duly recorded' under the . . . Act."

For the most extensive chain of title we have been able to discover, note the following story from a column in the Washington Post.

"This is a story about a lawyer—a New Orleans lawyer—who called at the Reconstruction Finance Corporation here to arrange a loan for his client. He was told the loan would be okayed if title to the property was good and sufficient so the lawyer returned home and sent a rather voluminous and accurate abstract of title by mail to the RFC office here. Soon afterward he received this letter: 'We received today your letter enclosing application for loan for your client, supported by abstract of title. Let us compliment you on the able manner in which you have prepared and presented the application. Your abstract clearly demonstrates that you are not without ample experience in this line of your profession. We have observed, however, that you have not chained the titles back of the year 1803 and, before final approval can be accorded the application, it will be necessary that title be chained back of that year.'

"The attorney read the letter and his blood pressure shot up. He called his secretary and dictated this letter:

'Gentlemen: Your letter regarding titles in Case No. 198156 received. I note you wish titles to extend further than I have presented them. I was unaware that any educated man in the world failed to know that Louisiana was purchased by the United States from France in 1803.

'The title to the land was acquired by France by right of conquest from Spain. The land came into the possession of Spain by right of a discovery made in 1492 by a Spanish–Portugese sailor named Christopher Columbus, who had been granted the privilege of seeking a new route to India by the then reigning monarch, Queen Isabella.

'The Good Queen, being a pious woman and careful about titles (almost as careful, I might say, as the RFC) took the precaution of securing the blessings of the Pope of Rome upon the voyage before she sold her jewels to help Columbus. Now, the Pope, as you know, is the emissary of Jesus Christ, who is the Son of God, and God, it is commonly accepted, made the world. Therefore, I believe it is safe to presume that he also made that part of the United States called Louisiana—and I hope to HELL you're satisfied.' "

practical purposes, lost in the vastness of the recorder's office.[44] If a tract system of indexing is used this problem evaporates.

The chain of title concept is illustrated by the following case. *A* leases to *B*, who neither records nor takes possession. *B* assigns the lease to *C* who records the assignment but does not enter into possession. *A* then gives a warranty deed to *D*, a b.f.p., who records. *D* will take free of the lease, even though its assignment was recorded, because it is outside the chain of title. In using the grantor-grantee index, *D* would find no prior conveyance indexed under the name of *A* as grantor. How could he ever discover the assignment since it would be indexed under names that are strangers to his chain of title? A contrary holding would make the system unworkable since no one could search every document in the recording office. Note that if a tract system were in use all instruments relating to that particular piece of property would be indexed in the same place and the assignment would then be discovered, giving notice of the prior unrecorded lease. If, under the above facts, *A*, prior to the warranty deed to *D*, had given an option to purchase (recorded) to *E* and that option had recited that it was subject to a prior lease to *B* that would have been sufficient to bind *D*. This is so, because the option is in the chain of title and the subsequent purchaser takes subject to all facts disclosed by the terms of the option, i.e., he is put on inquiry notice by the recital.[45]

There are many variations of the basic situation just discussed but it is safe to conclude that any time a document affecting title is left unrecorded, subsequent transactions based on that document will be out of the chain of title and hence will not give constructive notice to a subsequent b.f.p. from the original owner.[46] Of course, if the claimants under the unrecorded instrument enter into possession that will be constructive notice in itself.

Must a purchaser search the records for a conveyance recorded *after* a prior grantor in the chain parted with title? *A* conveys

---

44. The chain of title concept may also protect title insurance companies where the defect falls outside the chain. See Ryczkowski v. Chelsea Title and Guaranty Co., 85 Nev. 37, 449 P.2d 261 (1969). The issue is less likely to arise there, however, since most title insurance companies maintain their own system of tract indexes and would usually find the claim, if recorded.

45. Guerin v. Sunburst Oil and Gas Co., 68 Mont. 365, 218 P. 949 (1923). The reference to claims outside the chain, in recitals in documents inside the chain, has clouded many titles. This is particularly troublesome if the

reference is vague and gives no real clue as to the nature of the claim or the identity of the claimant. This problem has been dealt with by statutes in some states and the acts tend to protect the b.f.p. and promote merchantability of titles. See L.C. Stroh and Sons, Inc. v. Batavia Homes and Develop. Corp., 17 A.D.2d 385, 234 N.Y.S.2d 401 (1962).

46. Capper v. Poulsen, 321 Ill. 480, 152 N.E. 587 (1926), is another variation on the theme in which a recorded affidavit, which would have put the subsequent purchaser on notice, failed to have that effect because it was out of the chain of title.

to *B* but the latter does not record. *A* then conveys to *C* who promptly records but is not a protected party because he knew of the prior deed to *B*. *B* then records, but some time after the recorded conveyance to *C*. *C* then conveys to *D*, a b.f.p., who records. Who has priority? The better view would prefer *D*, since he is a b.f.p. and the deed to *B* is now out of the chain of title.[47] A contrary position, based on the fact that *B's* deed was recorded before the conveyance to *D*, has been adopted in some states.[48] The importance of the problem lies in the light it throws on the chain of title concept. It is impractical for a purchaser to search the grantor index for a period after the title has been conveyed because there would literally be no place to stop, short of the day when the purchaser's deed is recorded, and this would have to be done for every title holder in the chain, back to the patent deed from the government.

The converse of the situation discussed in the preceding paragraph is also interesting. Must a purchaser search the records for a conveyance recorded *before* a prior grantor in the chain acquired title? *A* conveys by warranty deed to *B*, who promptly records. Unfortunately, *A* has no title at the time since the land is really owned by *X*. Subsequently, *A* acquires *X's* interest and the deed is recorded. *A* then conveys to *C*, a b.f.p., who records. Who has priority? Again, the better view prefers *C* since he is a b.f.p. and the deed to *B* is out of the chain of title.[49] However, since this situation involves the doctrine of estoppel by deed it is possible to argue that the title acquired by *A* from *X* passed immediately to *B* under the warranties in the deed and hence left nothing for *C*. Several cases have so held [50] but this position has been vigorously attacked by Professor Walsh. "This obsolete doctrine of estoppel by deed has been applied . . . in obvious disregard of the recording acts and the necessary rule incident to their application that the recorded instrument must be in the chain of title. They have held that estoppel by deed binds all subsequent purchasers, though for value and without notice, and therefore the recording acts do not protect them—a shocking exhibition of technicality and ignorance of legal history. . . . Though the principle of legal estoppel is recognized, its application in these cases to defeat the recording acts by the fiction of relation is without any reasonable basis."[51] This latter view, which prefers *B*, would require the purchaser to search the grantor index for conveyances by the

47. Morse v. Curtis, 140 Mass. 112, 2 N.E. 929 (1885).

48. Woods v. Garnett, 72 Miss. 78, 16 So. 390 (1894).

49. Richardson v. Atlantic Coast Lumber Corporation, 93 S.C. 254, 75 S.E. 371 (1912).

50. Ayer v. Philadelphia and Boston Face Brick Co., 159 Mass. 84, 34 N.E. 177 (1893); Tefft v. Munson, 57 N.Y. 97 (1875).

51. Walsh, Commentaries on the Law of Real Property 511 (1947).

grantor clear back to the beginning—again, a hopeless task since it would have to be done for every grantor in the chain. Of course, a tract index would solve both of these knotty problems.

One final illustration should be sufficient to clarify the chain of title problem. *A* subdivides a tract of land into numerous lots, putting restrictive covenants (set back lines, limitations to residential use, etc.) in most of the deeds to his grantees. He fails to put any such covenants in a deed to *B,* a b.f.p., who is unaware of the restricted nature of the area. All of the prior deeds are recorded so that if they give constructive notice *B* is bound by the restrictions.[52] Once more the cases split, with some courts taking the position that the prior deeds are out of the chain of title since "subsequent purchaser" in the recording acts means purchaser of the same tract of land, *not* purchaser from the same grantor.[53] Other courts, claiming to represent the weight of authority, say that the "grantee is chargeable with notice of everything affecting his title which could be discovered by an examination of the records of the deeds or other muniments of title of his grantor." [54] Strict chain of title logic favors the former position, but the latter may be more practical since usually the restricted nature of the subdivision is apparent to the purchaser so that he may be put on inquiry notice as to the covenants.[55]

SECTION 4. EXAMINATION OF THE RECORDS OR OF AN ABSTRACT OF TITLE

The recording system was designed to protect a purchaser or a mortgagee of an interest in land.[56] That individual has constructive notice of all that appears in the records, and he would be most foolish to invest his money without a careful check at the appropriate offices in the county courthouse. He has constructive notice of matters other than those in the recorder's office; he must check the court records for judgments that may be liens against

---

52. See p. 380, infra, for a discussion of restrictive covenants and the theory by which *B* is bound if he has notice, actual or constructive.

53. Glorieux v. Lighthipe, 88 N.J.L. 199, 96 A. 94 (1915).

54. Finley v. Glenn, 303 Pa. 131, 136, 154 A. 299, 301 (1931).

55. For a more detailed analysis of this point see 4 Am.L.Prop. § 17.24, p. 602 (Casner ed. 1952).

Conveyances of subdivided land can cause other chain of title problems. For example, deeds using metes and bounds descriptions, after the land has been subdivided into numbered lots, may be outside the chain. See Baker v. Koch, 114 Ohio App. 519, 183 N.E.2d 434 (1960).

56. The following five paragraphs are reprinted from Cribbet and Johnson, Cases and Materials on Property 1513–1514 (5th ed. 1984).

the land, the probate records for proceedings in an intestate or a testate succession, the tax and special assessments records, etc. All of these have indexes, and since they are public records the purchaser himself could make the examination. Obviously this would be a waste of his time since, even if he found the relevant documents, he would have some difficulty in interpreting them. Therefore, the lawyer performs this service and renders his opinion as to the state of the title.

In some areas of the country the lawyer still makes the search, prepares his chain of title, and then gives his opinion. This is slow, detailed work, virtually impossible in large population centers because of the sheer bulk of the records. Private abstract companies have been developed to ease the lawyer's load (and make a good profit). These companies typically keep a duplicate set of records based on the tract index principle. They then prepare an abstract of the record for each piece of property, as the need develops, and the lawyer can examine this abstract in the privacy of his own office, then give his opinion of the title. The abstract company keeps its records up to date by a daily transfer from the various public records to the private set kept by the company. This is usually done by a "take-off man" who operates between the courthouse and the company office.

Once the initial abstract has been prepared, usually starting with the patent deed from the United States or the state, it is relatively easy to keep it up to date by a continuation each time the land is transferred. The abstracter need cover only the period from the last continuation down to date and add this to the constantly increasing bulk of the abstract. Needless to say, the abstract will become a valuable piece of personal property in its own right, frequently being worth several hundred dollars.

The examining attorney does not assume any responsibility for the correctness of the abstract but limits his opinion [57] to the

---

57. The opinion of title is usually a carefully worded legal document which strictly limits the area of the lawyer's responsibility and concludes that 0 is seized of a merchantable title in fee simple absolute (if this is the case) subject to stated incumbrances, liens, etc. The following opinion of a Texas lawyer is scarcely typical but it may lighten a somewhat dreary discussion.

A Slightly Imperfect Title

1214 Marcus Bldg.
Prewitt, Texas
January 4, 1928

Mr. Alex Deanton
Prewitt, Texas

Dear Sir:

In accordance with your order, I have examined abstract of title in seven parts covering the South 236½ acres out of the Edmundson Survey in _____ County, Texas, which you are preparing to buy and herewith render my opinion.

Don't buy the G_____ d_____ land. It has been my sorrow and burden to look over several horrible examples of a title examiner's nightmare, but this alleged title takes the cutglass flyswatter. It is my private belief that you couldn't cure the defects if you sued everybody from the Spanish Government (who started this mess) on down

title disclosed by the abstracted records. Any error in the abstract itself, such as the miscopying of a deed or the omission of a mortgage, is the fault of the company. Both the lawyer and the

to the present possessor of the land, who is in there by virtue of a peculiar instrument optimistically designated by the abstractor as a "General Warranty Deed."

In the first place, the field notes of the Spanish Grant do not close. I don't think it is possible to obtain a confirmation grant since the late unpleasantness in 1898. In the second place, there were nineteen heirs of the original grantee, and only three of them joined in the execution of the conveyance unto the next party in this very rusty chain of title, which is a major defect in the first place. We might rely on limitation here, except that I am reliably informed that nobody has succeeded in living on this land for a longer period than two years, before dying of malnutrition. Laches might help out, but anybody who undertakes to buy land under a title acquired by laches is (to paraphrase Mark Twain) setting out like the man who set out to carry the cat home by the tail—he is going to acquire experience that will be of great value to him and never grow dim or doubtful.

This land has been sold for taxes eight times in the last forty years. Nobody has ever redeemed one of these tax sales—glad to be rid of it, no doubt. The last purchaser sued the tax collector a month after he bought for cancellation of the sale for fraud and misrepresentation. He doubtless had grounds, but this incident will give you a rough idea of what kind of muzzle-loading smooth-bores have been fritzing this title.

On January 1, 1908, a gentleman who appears suddenly out of nowhere by the name of Ellis Gretzberg executes a quit-claim deed containing a general warranty of title to one Peter Perkinston. Perkinston, the prolific old billygoat, died, leaving two wives and seventeen children, the legitimacy of two of them being severely contested. I am not being funnier than the circumstances indicate; he actually left two wives, and it seems never to have been legally adjudicated who he done wrong by. Each one of these ladies passed away in the

fear of God and the hope of a glorious resurrection and left a will devising this land to their respective brats. A shooting match between the two sets of claimants seems to have assisted the title slightly by reducing the original number to six and substituting eleven sets of descendants. One of the most prevalent causes of defects in this title seems to be the amorous proclivities and utter disregard for consequences prevailing in this neighborhood.

Your prospective vendor derives title by virtue of an instrument concerning which I have previously remarked. It is executed by a fair majority of one set of the offspring of Peter ("Prolific") Perkinston, and is acknowledged in a manner sufficient to pass a County Clerk with his fee prepaid. Outside of the fact that it doesn't exactly describe the property under search, the habendum clause is to the grantors, the covenant of general warranty doesn't warrant a thing and it is acknowledged before it is dated, I suppose it is all right.

I might mention that this land was the subject of a trespass to try title suit between two parties who appear in the abstracts for the first time when the suit was filed, and one of them recovered judgment awarding title and possession. We may waive this as a minor defect, comparatively speaking.

I would advise you to keep the abstracts, if you can. They are a speaking testimonial to the result of notaries public drawing instruments, county clerks who would put a menu on record if a fee was tendered, and jacklegged jugheads posing as lawyers.

You can buy the land if you so desire. There are five hundred and seventy-three people who can give you as good a title as your prospective vendor has, not counting the heirs of the illegitimate son of Prather Linkon who died in the penitentiary in 1889 while serving a term for sodomy.

Yours very truly,

Kress L. Campel

P.S. You owe me two dollars more for headache powders I used.

abstracter may be liable to the client for any negligence in the areas of their respective responsibilities.[58]

As the term indicates, the abstract is not a reproduction of the original documents but consists of a condensed statement of the key facts in each transfer.[59] Normally the abstracter expresses no opinion as to the legal significance of the instruments but simply sets them forth for the lawyer's judgment.

The only way to clarify this method of title assurance is for you to look at some actual abstracts and try your hand at examining one of them. It would be worthwhile for you, at this point, to look at Mr. Flick's book on Abstract and Title Practice and study the short, but actual, abstract which he reprints there.[60]

It should be noted that while a title insurance company is normally liable only as an insurer and has no duty to search (it could write pure casualty insurance without any search of the records), it may be held to have such a duty and hence be liable for negligence in doing so.[61] This could mean liability in excess of the stated limits of the policy, if the company has overlooked a title defect causing the purchaser to suffer a loss.

There appears to be a trend toward ever-greater liability for abstract companies if they make mistakes in preparing opinions of title. Thus, in Ford v. Guarantee Abstract and Title Co., Inc.[62] the court allowed punitive damages against a company for "reckless

---

58. The abstract company may also be liable to third parties, who have relied on the accuracy of the abstract, on the principle of third party beneficiary contracts. Slate v. Boone County Abstract Co., 432 S.W.2d 305 (Mo.1968). In Chun v. Park, 51 Hawaii 501, 462 P.2d 905 (1969), the court held a title company liable to the buyers and a lending institution where the seller had ordered the title search. The title company was said to owe a duty to those parties, whose identity was known, to use reasonable care in making the search and preparing the certificate of title. The company, however, was liable only for those damages for which its negligence was the proximate cause of the loss. Loss of anticipated profits from resale of the premises and sums expended for plans and specifications for a new building on the land were thus held not to be recoverable. See also Williams v. Polgar, 391 Mich. 6, 215 N.W.2d 149 (1974).

59. If the contract is silent as to who must furnish the abstract (normally the contract provides that the vendor must

do so), who must bear the burden of preparing such a document? See Department of Public Works and Buildings v. Halls, 35 Ill.2d 283, 220 N.E.2d 167 (1966). "The option here was to buy certain property for $25,000. There was no reference therein to an abstract of title or a warranty deed, and it is clear that a seller is under no obligation to furnish an abstract (Turn Verein Eiche v. Kionka, 255 Ill. 392, 99 N.E. 684, 43 L.R.A., N.S. 44), or a warranty deed (Morris v. Goldthorp, 390 Ill. 186, 60 N.E.2d 857) in the absence of a specific agreement to do so."

60. 1 Flick, Abstract and Title Practice 22–40 (2d ed. 1958).

61. J.H. Trisdale, Inc. v. Shasta County Title Co., 146 Cal.App.2d 831, 304 P.2d 832 (1956). See also Note, Title Insurance: The Duty to Search, 71 Yale L.J. 1161 (1962) and Shotwell v. Transamerica Title Ins. Co., 16 Wash. App. 627, 558 P.2d 1359 (1976).

62. 220 Kan. 244, 553 P.2d 254 (1976).

indifference" towards the rights of the plaintiff and dictum in the case indicated that the company might be liable to all persons who purchased or invested in land relying on an abstract furnished for that purpose. However, the key to liability remains a legally justifiable reliance by the plaintiff on the abstracter's representations. For example, in Warrington v. Transamerica Title Insurance Co.[63] there was no liability to a plaintiff who was a stranger to the transaction for which the title report was prepared and where there was no evidence to suggest that the abstracter (a title insurance company) intended anyone to see the report other than the parties to whom copies were sent or that the company knew that any of the parties to whom copies were sent would supply the report to others.

This trend toward greater liability includes negligence for failure to refer to an original judgment where the docket entry was erroneous [64] and a holding that a plaintiff's knowledge, actual or constructive, of a prior mortgage was irrelevant if the plaintiff had, in fact, relied on the abstracter's representation that a prior mortgage did not exist.[65] Moreover, in White v. Western Title Ins. Co.[66] an abstracter (a title insurance company) was held liable for non-disclosure of water rights shown in public records even though such interests would not appear in records ordinarily searched by a title company. This was true even though coverage for such claims was excluded since the structure of the policy created an impression that coverage was provided for all claims of record. The trend reflects a belief that both abstracters and title insurance companies are engaged in a business affected with the public interest and should be held to a high standard of care and cannot, by a contract of adhesion, exculpate themselves from liability for negligence. This view is consistent with the growing protection for the consumer in most areas of the law.

SECTION 5. TITLE INSURANCE

Title insurance introduces no new principle into the law of property. It is based squarely on the recording system and involves a search of the records in the manner which we have just

63. 40 Or.App. 841, 596 P.2d 627 (1979).

64. Wichita Great Empire Broadcasting, Inc. v. Gingrich, 4 Kan.App.2d 223, 604 P.2d 281 (1979).

65. Tipton County Abstract Co., Inc. v. Heritage Federal Savings and Loan Association, 416 N.E.2d 850 (Ind.App. 1981).

66. 221 Cal.Rptr. 509, 710 P.2d 309 (1985).

discussed. Its principal advantage lies in title investigation by a group of specialists whose work is then insured by a financially stable institution. More will be said on this point in the critique of modern conveyancing, which follows our present exploration of methods of title assurance.

Title insurance usually covers defects in the title of record, hidden defects not disclosed by the record, and the costs of defending the title against attack. You will recall some of the hidden defects which no title examiner could discover from his search of the records: disability of a grantor in the chain of title; forgery of an instrument in the chain; fraudulent representation of marital status by a grantor; mistaken identity of a record titleholder and a grantor due to similar or identical names; errors in the record; errors in examination of the record; undisclosed heirs; exercise of a power of attorney after death of the creator of the power; and defects in conveyances in the chain due to lack of delivery.[67] There are also the difficulties in construction of a will, trust, etc., where capable attorneys will differ as to the correct result. Title insurance will, in effect, guarantee the interpretation decided upon by the insurance company. So, too, unjustifiable attacks may be made on the title which the owner can eventually defeat, but only after the expense and difficulty of a lawsuit. Title insurance companies will defend the title, as guaranteed, and thus bear this burden for the purchaser.

On the other hand, title insurance is no panacea and it has the inherent problems of all insurance, including the key one of coverage. The policy must be read carefully since the exceptions can be so broad that they destroy the protection. The companies are not above relying on technicalities to defeat liability,[68] and unless the purchaser has independent legal counsel to interpret the policy and point out areas of potential danger he still may end up without adequate protection. For example, most policies have exceptions for land use controls and the purchaser must ascertain zoning and subdivision control standards at his peril. In Hocking v. Title Insurance and Trust Co.[69] a purchaser bought two unimproved lots from a vendor who had merchantable title but the streets in the subdivision did not comply with the city ordinance and the purchaser was denied a building permit. Moreover, the subdivider had filed no bond on which he could be sued for failure to build the streets. The suit on the title insurance policy failed because of the exceptions in the policy. There is a difference between title to the land and the physical condition of the proper-

---

67. 2 Fitch, Abstracts and Titles to Real Property 445–446 (1954). (1939); Mayers v. Van Schaick, 268 N.Y. 320, 197 N.E. 296 (1935).

68. Beaullieu v. Atlantic Title and Trust Co., 60 Ga.App. 400, 4 S.E.2d 78

69. 37 Cal.2d 644, 234 P.2d 625 (1951).

ty and the adjacent streets. "One can hold perfect title to land that is valueless; or he can have marketable title to land while the land itself is unmarketable." [70]

Perhaps title insurance should not be expected to guarantee any particular land use status or guarantee against various physical infirmities in the land [71] but the purchaser should be aware of this fact and realize that title insurance will not resolve all of his potential problems.

As is true of abstract companies, there is a growing tendency to impose high standards on title insurance companies where the issue involved relates directly to title questions of record.[72] Thus the Court of Appeals of New York [73] held that an insured was under no duty to disclose to an insurer the facts as to a condemnation proceeding which were readily ascertainable from the public records. Even the insured's intentional failure to disclose a matter of public record did not result in the loss of protection. The court added: "Of course, an intentional failure by the insured to disclose material information not readily discernible from the public records will render the policy void." [74]

Title insurance is of two basic types—commercial and bar-related title insurance. The former operates much like any for profit corporation. The latter is essentially a lawyers' cooperative (also operating for profit) and was developed to maintain the lawyers' role in the title aspects of real estate transactions—a role which the bar was steadily losing as fewer individuals and firms relied on the lawyers' direct search of the records or on the examination of an abstract.[75]

70. See also Title and Trust Co. of Florida v. Barrows, 381 So.2d 1088 (Fla. App.1979) where a platted street was so flooded in the spring and fall that the plaintiff was denied vehicular access to his lot. The trial court awarded damages for breach of a title insurance policy but the decision was reversed on appeal, the court holding that the policy only insured against record defects and not against physical infirmities of the platted street.

71. Title insurance companies are designed to deal with record title problems but have no particular expertise in the complex areas of land use controls or of inspecting the land for numerous physical deficiencies such as soil conditions, water problems, etc. To assume these responsibilities would require a larger premium than is now charged for the normal *title* insurance policy.

72. Note that it is not always clear whether a company is being sued in its capacity as an abstracter or as a title insurer since the two activities are closely connected and, increasingly, abstract companies also issue title policies.

73. L. Smirlock Realty Corp. v. Title Guarantee Co., 52 N.Y.2d 179, 437 N.Y.S.2d 57, 418 N.E.2d 650 (1981).

74. For an example of this latter situation, in a title policy that had become a warrantor's policy after the sale of the land to a third party, see Stewart Title Guaranty Co. v. Lunt Land Corp., 162 Tex. 435, 347 S.W.2d 584 (1961).

75. For a good discussion of the latter type, by an admittedly biased advocate, see Rooney, Bar–Related Title Insurance: The Positive Perspective, 1980 S.Ill.U.L.J. 263.

Title insurance, in its various forms, is playing a growing role in modern real estate transactions. One writer correctly concludes that: "As long as we have a title system dependent upon searches in local recording offices rather than registered title, title insurance will play an increasing role. It insures risks which an attorney's opinion does not, both because of legal limitations on the attorney's liability and because of the economic stability and continuity of existence of the corporate insurer. This does not make title insurance the *sine qua non* of every real estate closing or, even when it is in order, the solution to all title problems, but it is a very limited vision which excludes it from the major title role in our ever burgeoning real estate market."[76]

76. Kuklin, Commercial Title Insurance and The Lawyer's Responsibility, 15 Real Property, Probate and Trust Journal 557 (1980).

Chapter 4

TITLE REGISTRATION—THE TORRENS SYSTEM

It is easy to confuse recording and registration because some of the terms are used interchangeably. However, they are entirely separate systems of title assurance, based on different theories and operating in distinct fashions. "The basic principle of this system is the registration of the *title* of land, instead of registering [recording], as the old system requires, the *evidence* of title. In the one case only the ultimate fact or conclusion that a certain named party has title to a particular tract of land is registered, and a certificate thereof is delivered to him. In the other the entire evidence, from which proposed purchasers must, at their peril, draw the conclusion, is registered [recorded]. Necessarily the initial registration of the title—that is, the conclusive establishment of a starting point binding upon all the world—must rest on judicial proceedings." [1]

The certificate of title to an automobile is the closest personal property analogy to title registration. It purports to show absolute ownership of the car and any liens against the title must appear on the face of the certificate in order to be binding on a b.f.p. Indeed, the concept of title registration was borrowed from personal property by an Australian, Sir Robert Torrens, whose name the system now bears. He had been associated with the shipping industry and saw how simply the title to huge vessels was transferred in contrast to the complexity of real property. He was appointed Registrar General of the Province of South Australia and demonstrated that the certificate system could work satisfactorily for land as well. He drafted the first law for title registration of land and from Australia the system has spread to many parts of the globe. It is not, however, widely used in United States and for that reason the discussion here will be quite limited.

Title is first registered, providing the necessary statutory authority for Torrens exists, by a judicial proceeding similar to a suit to quiet title. An abstract of the records to date is the basis of the registration and all possible claimants are made parties to the proceeding. Service by publication is provided for since this is an

1. State v. Westfall, 85 Minn. 437, 438, 89 N.W. 175 (1902).

330

in rem action. The resulting decree gives the owner a certificate showing the extent of his title and setting forth any exceptions to it. In the absence of fraud, mistake, or lack of jurisdiction, this certificate is conclusive as to title in the holder and any injured parties must look to an assurance fund, established from charges for registration, for reimbursement.

Transfers of title subsequent to the initial registration follow the same pattern of contract, escrow agreement, and deed already discussed, except that the final act is the cancellation of the vendor's title certificate, and the issuance of a new one to the purchaser. Until that has been done no title passes and the deed itself transfers only equitable title as between the parties until the registration is complete. Of course, the title search by the purchaser is quite simple since he need look only at the certificate; the memorial section will list incumbrances, liens, and similar interests in the land. The particular Torrens Act may make certain items (such as local tax liens) binding on the title even if not filed in the registrar's office, but usually these are held to a minimum.

In one classic case, the United States District Court in Minnesota (one of the strong Torrens' states) held that even the federal government was bound by the system and failure to memorialize a notice of a federal tax lien on a certificate of title allowed a b.f.p. to take free of the lien.[2] The lien had been filed with the *register of deeds* but not with the *registrar of titles* (they were two component parts of a single office). The District Court decision was a triumph for the Torrens system since the purchaser had relied on the certificate and did not know of the improperly filed lien. The triumph was short lived, however, because the case was reversed by the Eighth Circuit Court of Appeals[3] which held for the federal government without regard to the requirements of the state statute for memorializing all liens on the certificate. The Collector of Internal Revenue is a tough guy to beat even by the Torrens System!

The two cases illustrate the confusion caused by the two systems (recording and registration) when they exist in the same jurisdiction. Thus, a mortgage filed in the recorder's office gives constructive notice to subsequent purchasers of land under the recording system but would have no effect as to Torrens' land until filed with the registrar and placed on the memorial. The attorney must always be careful to discover which system applies to the land in question if the state has both systems.

2. United States v. Ryan, 124 F.Supp. 1 (D.Minn.1954).

3. United States v. Rasmuson, 253 F.2d 944 (8th Cir.1958).

No system is foolproof and nice questions of title arise under Torrens too. *A* entrusts his duplicate certificate of title (the original is kept in the registrar's office) to *B* during negotiations for sale. *B* forges a deed to himself and presents it to the registrar who issues a new certificate to *B*. *B* then transfers the title to *C*, a b.f.p. Who owns the land? Mr. Justice Holmes decided for *C*, in affirming a decision of the Illinois Supreme Court under the Illinois Torrens Act.[4] Since a forged deed could not convey good title under the recording acts, even if filed for record, the potency of the certificate of title becomes all the more apparent. If the forged deed had been presented to the registrar without the duplicate certificate, the result might well have been different [5] since Mr. Justice Holmes seemed to put the case on the basic principle, "As between two innocent persons one of whom must suffer the consequences of a breach of trust the one who made it possible by his act of confidence must bear the loss."

The relationship of "possession as notice" to title registration is a bit puzzling. Title cannot be obtained by adverse possession to Torrens land since the statutes of limitations do not run against such lands, but that does not solve the notice question. If a claimant is in possession prior to the initial registration and is not made a party to that proceeding his claim survives the suit. The court lacks jurisdiction over his person and failure to follow the statutory provisions would protect him.[6] Possession acquired subsequent to registration, even though based on a valid but unregistered claim, does not give *constructive* notice of the interest and the b.f.p. of the certificate is fully protected.[7] It has been held, however, that *actual* notice of an interest, such as a lease, even though not registered will bind the subsequent purchaser.[8] This leads to the conclusion that, even under Torrens, possession by an apparent stranger to the title may be material and is ignored at the purchaser's peril.[9]

4. Eliason v. Wilborn, 281 U.S. 457, 50 S.Ct. 382, 74 L.Ed. 962 (1930).

5. In fact, a later Illinois case held it *would* be different in a case where the original holder of a Torrens certificate had never parted with it and the whole series of transfers was a fraud on her. Hoffman v. Schroeder, 38 Ill.App.2d 20, 186 N.E.2d 381 (1962). This case is worth reading for the elaborate scam involved even under a supposedly foolproof system.

6. Follette v. Pacific Light and Power Corporation, 189 Cal. 193, 208 P. 295 (1922). In that case it was a public utility corporation which had a recorded easement and was using the right of way.

7. Abrahamson v. Sundman, 174 Minn. 22, 218 N.W. 246 (1928).

8. Killam v. March, 316 Mass. 646, 55 N.E.2d 945 (1944).

9. For further discussion of the Torrens system see p. 350 infra.

Chapter 5

STATUTES OF LIMITATION AND
RELATED LEGISLATION AS AIDS TO
TITLE ASSURANCE

At various points in the book we have referred to title by adverse possession, to prescriptive rights, and to the role of statutes of limitation.[1] However, we have not taken a detailed look at the operation of the statutes, and it is appropriate that we do so in this chapter, since the *principal* role of such legislation is to strengthen the title of the possessor of land. The interest obtained by the adverse possessor is frequently referred to as an original title—i.e., a new title obtained in opposition to the former record owner—as distinct from a derivative title, which is obtained by descent, devise, or purchase. It is possible to obtain an original title in this way, but it would be a rare case in which an individual would set out deliberately to acquire title by adverse possession. He may quite frequently, however, purchase what he thinks is a valid paper title only to find a major flaw in the chain. In this situation each year of possession adds to his claim and may thus be said to give him added title assurance. Mr. Justice Holmes, in a letter to William James, stated the "reason behind the rule" with his usual succinctness: "The true explanation of title by prescription seems to me to be that man, like a tree in a cleft of a rock, gradually shapes his roots to his surroundings, and when the roots have grown to a certain size, cannot be displaced without cutting at his life. The law used to look with disfavor on the Statute of Limitations, but I have been in the habit of saying it is one of the most sacred and indubitable principles that we have, which used to lead my predecessor Field to say that Holmes didn't value any title that was not based on fraud or force."[2]

The statutes are of many types and naturally vary from state to state. It is the purpose of this chapter to explore the principal varieties and to explain their operation. As usual, the roots must be traced to the English common law. From an early date numerous English statutes limited the time within which an action could be brought for a disseisin, but instead of stating a

1. The following three paragraphs are reprinted from Cribbet and Johnson, Cases and Materials on Property 1554 (5th ed. 1984).

2. Lerner, The Mind and Faith of Justice Holmes 417 (1953).

gross period they named a specific year beyond which the pleader could not go. For example, a statute enacted in 1275 barred the remedy by writ of right where the pleader relied upon the seisin of an ancestor before the first year of the reign of Richard I (1189). The modern method of measuring limitation was adopted in 1540, and in 1623 it was provided that no person should thereafter make any entry into any lands, tenements, or hereditaments but within twenty years next after his or their right or title accrued. While this act is the model for most of the statutes in the United States, it has been replaced in England by acts which bar any action to recover land after the statutory period has elapsed, without reference to the character of the defendant's possession. Many difficult questions plague the real estate lawyer in this country as he attempts to discern the character of the possession which the claimant must have for the statutory period in order to bar the rights of the original owner. It is clear that it must be adverse, but what does the term adverse mean?

The Statute of James adopted a gross period of twenty years after the cause of action accrued, and most states have used the same measuring stick, although a few require a greater or a lesser period. Many states have "short limitations" acts where the claimant is in possession under "color of title"; e.g., a judicial decree falsely purporting to vest title in him. Usually these acts require not only "color of title" but also payment of taxes for each year of possession.[3]

Since adverse possession for the statutory period can ripen into title because all other claimants to the land are deprived of a remedy, it might seem that the passage of time would make all possessory titles merchantable. There are, at least, six reasons why this is not so. First, it is not enough that the possession last for the requisite period; it must also be open, notorious, adverse, continuous, exclusive, and with a claim of right.[4] All of these elements must be established by the adverse possessor, who normally has the burden of proof, and while the title may be defensible so that he could defeat suits against him it is difficult to negative all possible claims when the parties are not before the court.[5] Second, most statutes do not run against non-possessory

3. See generally, Powell on Real Property, One–Volume Edition, s. 1015 (Powell and Rohan 1968).

4. See Marengo Cave Co. v. Ross, 212 Ind. 624, 10 N.E.2d 917 (1937) for a good discussion of several of these elements.

5. See Bartos v. Czerwinski, 323 Mich. 87, 34 N.W.2d 566 (1948). See also Escher v. Bender, 338 Mich. 1, 7, 61 N.W.2d 143, 147 (1953) where the court said: "Title established through adverse possession is free from encumbrance and of a character to assure quiet and peaceful enjoyment of the property by the owner, . . . but it is not a marketable title of record until there has been a judicial determination of such title."

interests. Therefore, A might occupy for twenty years adversely to B but if the latter had only a life estate the statute would not have run at all against C, the remainderman, and A would have only an estate *pur autre vie.*[6] Third, most statutes have disability provisions so that the interests of minors, insane persons, etc., may survive well beyond the basic period.[7] Fourth, typically the statutes do not run against the United States, the states or even local governments.[8] Fifth, the statutes do not run against co-owners unless it is made clear to the co-owner that the adverse possessor is repudiating the concurrent ownership and claiming the full interest in the land.[9] Sixth, if there has been a severance of title between the surface and the subsurface ownership, the statute may run against the surface but not against the subsurface if the latter estate has not been subject to adverse possession.[10]

Since it is difficult, if not impossible, to obtain the necessary information from the record, the purchaser's attorney must assume the worst and he puts little reliance on the statutory period for merchantability purposes.[11] If the time elapsed is so great as to negative all but the barest speculation as to possible claimants, then the court may rely on the statute of limitations and find the title merchantable.[12]

Fortunately, it is not necessary for the same individual to occupy the land throughout the statutory period. The law allows the tacking of successive possessors to make up the full period so long as there is privity of estate between the claimants. If the

6. Annot. 58 A.L.R.2d 299, 302–05 (1958).

7. "Some statutes provide that the duration of disability is not computed as a part of the statutory period. Other statutes provide for a designated time after the disability has been removed within which proceedings may be brought. Mindful of the fact that an exemption provision affects the marketability of land, courts have construed the exemption clause as applicable only to disabilities existing at the inception of adverse possession. In other words, only the disability, or disabilities, existing when the cause of action accrued will postpone the operative effect of the statute of limitations. Further, if land was held adversely when the owner died, a disability of the one succeeding to that interest will not interrupt the running of the statute. This is true even though the owner was under a disability at the time of his death. There is no tacking of disabilities, either with respect to disabilities in the same owner, or with respect to disabilities when the cause of action accrued, the disability of longest duration will control." Burby, Real Property 396–398 (2d ed. 1954).

8. Annot. 55 A.L.R.2d 554 (1957). There are exceptions to this rule and some statutes do bind governmental units so the individual statutes and court decisions would need to be consulted in specific cases.

9. See note 21 infra. This issue can be particularly frustrating since the question of adequate notice to a co-owner can be a close call on the facts and seldom will be disclosed from the records.

10. See note 15 infra.

11. Simis v. McElroy, 160 N.Y. 156, 54 N.E. 674 (1899).

12. Rehoboth Heights Development Co. v. Marshall, 15 Del.Ch. 314, 137 A. 83 (1927).

disseisins are unconnected, e.g., if A possesses for less than the period and then abandons and B comes in for the remainder, the seisin of the "true" owner revives in the interval and his rights are not barred. "To create such privity, there must have existed as between the different disseisors, in regard to the estate of which a title by disseisin is claimed, some such relation as that of ancestor and heir, grantor and grantee, or devisor and devisee. In such cases, the title acquired by disseisin passes by descent, deed, or devise." [13] The requirement of privity causes particular difficulty in boundary line disputes when tacking is necessary to make up the statutory period. This is because the deed usually describes only the basic tract and does not include the disputed area that is, in fact, being occupied. Although the cases are in conflict, the better view allows tacking under these circumstances on the theory that it is not the deed which creates the privity but the parol transfer of possession which accompanies the delivery of the deed.[14]

Tacking is clearly allowed on the disseisee side. A ousts B and, during the statutory period, B sells his interest to C, who dies leaving the land to his son D. At the end of the period, A owns the land even though he has occupied for less than the statutory period as against any one of the "true" owners. To put it another way, transfer of the "true" owner's interest does not interrupt the running of the statute, unless there is a termination of the disseisor's adverse possession.

As previously explained, the mere passage of time will not make all titles merchantable even though the claimant has been in possession for the statutory period. This is particularly true where there has been a severance in ownership between the surface and the subsurface. In Failoni v. Chicago and North Western Railway Co.,[15] the claimant had been in possession of the surface for more than forty years but earlier the mineral rights had been conveyed to another by a deed of record. While the claimant had title to the surface by adverse possession, she had no title to the subsurface. "To possess the mineral estate, one must undertake the actual removal thereof from the ground or do such other act as will apprise the community that such interest is in the exclusive use and enjoyment of the claiming party." Of course if there has been no severance, the possession of the surface will

13. Sawyer v. Kendall, 10 Cush. (Mass.) 241, 244 (1852).

14. Gregory v. Thorrez, 277 Mich. 197, 269 N.W. 142 (1936). See also Howard v. Kunto, 3 Wash.App. 393, 477 P.2d 210 (1970) for a good discussion of the meaning of privity and tacking.

15. 30 Ill.2d 258, 195 N.E.2d 619 (1964). See also Payne v. Williams, 91 Ill.App.3d 336, 46 Ill.Dec. 783, 414 N.E.2d 836 (1980) and Stoebuck, Adverse Possession of Severable Minerals, 68 W.Va.L.Rev. 274 (1966).

carry with it the possession of the entire land and adverse possession may ripen into title to the whole.

Statutes of limitation are of many kinds and obviously they will vary from state to state. They tend to fall into four categories: (1) the basic statute (typically fifteen to twenty years); (2) the short term statute (typically seven years); (3) the special purpose statutes designed to cure specific defects, such as stale mortgage claims, old restrictive covenants and conditions, etc.; and (4) the merchantability acts (typically forty years), passed to cure most defects of a certain age and to eliminate the disadvantages which have accumulated around the older, basic statutes. The latter two categories will be discussed in the following section which serves as a critique of modern methods of title assurance.[16] We must clarify here, however, the distinctions between the first two categories.

The basic or twenty-year statute does not require the adverse claimant to pay taxes in order to perfect his title. In fact, the "true" owner could pay the tax bill throughout the period and still lose his title. Nor does this statute require the possessor to have color of title; he could be a naked trespasser with no more business on the land than a thief and still attain a valid title by adverse possession. It is true that the courts say he must have a *claim* of right, but this means no more than that he must indicate that he holds the land as against the whole world, including the "true" owner. Most adverse possessors can be said to claim a fee simple so this is the estate usually obtained, but the claim does mark the extent of the title and if it is only for a life estate or a lesser interest that is the property right secured.[17]

On the other hand, the short term statutes usually require a union of possession, tax payment, and color of title in order to be effective. If these three factors coincide it is easy to see why legislative policy calls for earlier protection of the claimant. The short or seven-year statutes are normally subject to the same disadvantages as the basic statutes (problems of proving adverse possession, effective only against present, possessory interests, disability provisions etc.,) so that while they bolster merchantability of title they do not assure it. There is usually no difficulty in determining who has paid the taxes, but color of title can be troublesome. Obviously, color does not mean the same thing as a good or valid title or there would be no need for the statute. Nor is it synonymous with a mere claim of right, since the possessor who relies on a short term statute must have some basis for his

16. See pp. 356 to 360 infra.   O'Gara, 177 Mass. 139, 58 N.E. 275 (1900).
17. Ricard v. Williams, 20 U.S. (7 Wheat.) 59, 5 L.Ed. 398 (1822); Bond v.

actions. Color of title is that which has the appearance of title but is in fact none; normally, a written document is required and it should accurately describe the premises and purport to convey title. Frequently, color of title is supplied by a court proceeding or an official conveyance, such as a tax deed or a master's deed, which appears valid on its face but is void or voidable because of defective procedure. Even a forged deed can constitute color of title so long as it is regular on its face and a b.f.p. has relied on its validity.[18] However, where a father purported to convey his children's interest as "father and natural guardian of . . ." color of title was lacking because it was apparent on the face of the deed that he had no power to make such a transfer without following the prescribed judicial procedure.[19]

Color of title is also important in the constructive adverse possession cases, where the deed describes a large area but the claimant in fact occupies only a small proportion of the whole. Normally, the adverse possessor can claim title only to the *pedis possessio,* the portion of the land actually occupied. But if he claims under color of title and the larger area is accurately described in the deed, he may assert ownership to the whole on the basis that he has constructively possessed the described land and that the deed has served as requisite notice to the world.[20]

It is not too difficult to establish the adverseness of a claim against strangers. The very fact that *A* occupies land owned by *B,* with no apparent reason for doing so, tends to show adverseness. The situation is more complex if *A* is a tenant of *B,* a purchaser under a contract of sale, or a cotenant of *B.* In the first two situations, the possession, initially at least, was based on consent and *A* must show a repudiation of that relationship and a "hoisting of his own flag" before the statute of limitations will begin to run. The third situation is covered succinctly in Simpson v. Manson.[21] "The rule is well settled that the mere possession by one tenant in common [or any other cotenant] who receives all the rents and profits and pays the taxes assessed against the property, no matter for how long a period, cannot be set up as a bar against the cotenants. In such case the possession of one tenant in common is in contemplation of law the possession of all the tenants in common. Such possession, however, may become ad-

---

18. Bergesen v. Clauss, 15 Ill.2d 337, 155 N.E.2d 20 (1958).

19. Mercer v. Wayman, 9 Ill.2d 441, 137 N.E.2d 815 (1956). Comment, 1957 U.Ill.L.F. 120.

20. Note, 23 Harv.L.Rev. 56 (1909).

21. 345 Ill. 543, 551, 178 N.E. 250, 253 (1931). Cf. Nicholas v. Cousins, 1 Wash.App. 133, 459 P.2d 970 (1969).

See also Matter of Keamo, 3 Hawaii App. 360, 650 P.2d 1365 (1982) and Tremayne v. Taylor, 101 Idaho 792, 621 P.2d 408 (1980) where the court put it even more simply: "A cotenant (brothers and sisters were involved) who claims to have adversely possessed the interest of his cotenants must prove that the fact of adverse possession was 'brought home' to the cotenants."

verse if the tenant in common by acts and conduct disseizes his cotenants by repudiating their title and claiming adversely to them. . . . Before the possession of one tenant in common can be adverse to the cotenant there must be a disseizin or ouster by some outward act of ownership of an unequivocal character, overt and notorious, and of such nature as to impart information and notice to the cotenant that an adverse possession and disseizin are intended to be asserted by the tenant in possession. . . . Such notice need not, however, be formal in its nature and if one tenant in common holds exclusive possession, claiming the land to be his, and his conduct and possession are of such a character as to give notice to his cotenant that his possession is adverse, the statute of limitations will run."

Chapter 6

CRITIQUE OF MODERN METHODS OF TITLE ASSURANCE—SUGGESTIONS FOR CONVEYANCING REFORM

The previous five Chapters of Part Five should provide the student with a good over-view of the running gears of the methods of title assurance in use in the Anglo–American legal system. These methods are far from ideal but they do work and most of the professional energy has been devoted to strengthening and simplifying the system rather than in seeking radical reform. Before we leave this subject, it is important to survey the effectiveness of our modern methods of conveyancing and title assurance and provide a sense of direction for further improvements in this phase of property law.[1]

"For whom does land law exist? For the land owner and his neighbours, or for the conveyancer? Put in this way there can surely be only one answer to the question. Yet to the land owner, what is important is the substantive nature of his rights and duties; of those rights, the right to convey is merely one, and the technical method of exercising that right is to him of secondary importance and a matter which hitherto he has been content to leave in the hands of his technical advisers. If this be the true perspective, the time has surely long since passed when land law could be considered in the main as a secretion in the interstices of conveyancing.[2]

Professor Hargreaves, who in all of his scholarly writings has shown a rare instinct for the jugular, has asked the crucial question. "For whom does land law exist?" The omission of the word "land" leaves the query valid, but there is a peculiar relevancy for the property lawyer in this simple cross-examination. Discussions at bar association meetings, abstracters' conventions, title association gatherings, and some of the articles in law reviews and

1. This section, with considerable editing and some additional material, is based on an article by one of the authors of this text. See Cribbet, Conveyancing Reform, 35 N.Y.U.L.Rev. 1291 (1960). The article was part of a symposium on the reform of real property law and although it was written in 1960

it is still relevant in 1988. The mills of the Gods grind slow!

2. The quote is from the late Professor Hargreaves' (University of Birmingham) review of Potter, The Principles of Land Law Under the Land Registration Act (2d ed. 1948), in 12 Modern L.Rev. 139, 143 (1949).

such journals as Title News,[3] the official publication of the American Title Association, give the distinct impression that land law exists for the enrichment of the conveyancer and that the interest of the landowner is secondary. The relative merits of title examination by the lawyer, title insurance, and the Torrens system, as methods of title assurance for the landowner, are frequently lost to sight in the economic struggle for title business. Without preparing a brief for any "side," it seems clear that no useful social purpose is served by lawyers banding together for the sole purpose of preserving their historic monopoly in the face of encroaching title insurance, nor by insurance companies [4] competing in such a way that the landowner fails to receive the one thing he desires—a "good" title.

On the other side of the coin, any meaningful discussion of conveyancing reform must take into account the realities of modern methods of land transfer. It is useless to inveigh against the supposed "evils" inherent in title insurance if, in fact, the bulk of land transactions are to be handled by this device. It is equally futile to attack the admitted inefficiency of the laborious searching of the official records by a lonely, dust-covered attorney, wending his way back to a government patent, if this method is rapidly becoming passé.[5] What is wanted is a dispassionate analysis of our present methods of land transfer and a suggested program of reform, if one is called for,[6] that keeps in mind the key question posed by Professor Hargreaves.

SECTION 1. CHANGING NATURE OF THE LAW OF LAND

It is trite to remark that Anglo–American property law is balanced precariously on its feudalistic base, but one must start from this obvious fact. While feudalism was never a system to those who lived through its dominant period in history, it now appears as a way of life, law, and government which was adequate

---

3. See, e.g., Audrain, Report of Chairman of Judiciary Committee, 39 Title News 117, 119 (1960).

4. This is not a blanket indictment of title insurance, but there is real danger in the way the industry is developing in some areas. The responsible title insurance companies are just as concerned as anyone else. See Tarpley, The Future of Title Insurance, 38 Title News 2, 4 (1959).

5. For an attack of this type and a novel, if impractical, solution, see Comment, Enchancing the Marketability of Land: The Suit to Quiet Title, 68 Yale L.J. 1245 (1959).

6. It may be that conveyancing today represents the best of all possible worlds but many competent observers have felt otherwise. See, e.g., Payne, The Crisis in Conveyancing, 19 Mo.L. Rev. 214 (1954).

for the needs of its day.   Land was the central reality in the economy of feudalism and it is not surprising that a complex hierarchy of estates was spun from the concept of multiple interests in a single *res*.   Whether it was social security as exemplified by dower and curtesy, borrowing as illustrated by the lowly origin of the term of years, or national defense as reflected by the knight's fee, land was made to serve the needs of a crude society. Society lost some of its crudity, the needs changed, but the land law retained much of its early form.   As late as 1829, the English Real Property Commissioners still remarked that, "it [the land law] appears to come almost as near to perfection as can be expected in any human institutions." [7]   Most of this human institution had been adopted by the colonies in North America but not necessarily adapted to the nonfeudalistic society developing in the wilderness.

This vast superstructure of property law was supported on an antique conveyancing base that almost defies description.   For generations, livery of seisin, with its symbolic transfer of turf, twig, or rock, had sufficed to make graphic that change of possession which was conceived to be the major ingredient in change of ownership.   Even the charter of feoffment was but a memorial of the operative act and it took the Statute of Uses and the Statute of Frauds to make the conveyance a "paper" transaction.   The Statute of Enrollments could have given England a workable recording system but its clever evasion by secrecy minded clients and lawyers, through the deed of lease and release, left the conveyancing system in a chaotic state.   The principal reliance came to be on the original title deeds which passed with the land and were examined by each lawyer in turn.

By the end of the first World War, England was ready for real property reform and this readiness became a movement which culminated in the famous property legislation of 1925, designed to simplify the complicated structure.   The substantive changes wrought by the legislation are not within the scope of this text but the avowed purpose behind it is central to our discussion.   Professor Cheshire, then dean of the English property bar, wrote:

"[I]t will be as well to state at the outset the main idea which lay at the back of the legislation that resulted. *It was nothing more than a desire to render the sale of land as rapid and simple a matter as is the sale of goods or of shares. . . .*

"But the difference is inevitable, and the reason is that in the great majority of cases the possessor of personal goods is their absolute owner, and therefore able to pass a title which will confer upon their deliveree an equally full and unencumbered owner-

7. First Report, p. 6.

ship. . . . But for a purchaser of land to be content with the word of the vendor and with the appearance of ownership which flows from his possession would be an act of sheer folly." [8]

The reform legislation was designed to usher in a system of title registration which would replace the cumbersome examination of title deeds with a modern, workable method of title assurance. (It should be noted that England does not have title insurance in the American sense. Individual defects may be insured against, e.g., a dormant restrictive covenant that *may* cause difficulty, but no blanket title policy is available.) Since 1925, in contrast to the atrophy of the Torrens system in the United States, title registration has had a remarkable success in England and elsewhere in the common-law world.

Meanwhile, the land law had taken a different direction in the United States. Although starting with a common heritage, which fortunately gave the various state laws a thread of consistency, the American bar never developed a reliance on title deeds, but instead turned at an early date to recording acts as a basis of title security. "The earliest mention of the record of a deed in the United States is found in the records of Plymouth Colony in 1627, where a contract of a bargain and sale of land is apparently required to be written into the book of the colony, not as a copy, but as an original, and signed therein by the parties." [9] Without attempting a history of the recording acts,[10] it is safe to conclude that they came to be the central core of the real estate transaction in America and the strengths and weaknesses of our title system are reflected in them. Whatever the faults of the recording acts, they represented a big improvement over the examination of title deeds and did form a public record on which a bona fide purchaser could, more or less safely, rely. They reversed the tyranny of "first in time, first in right" as a rule for determining priority and cut off the claims of those who slumbered on their rights and failed to record. They have worked well enough so that, more than three hundred years after the record of Plymouth Colony, they still play the dominant role in title assurance. Title insurance relies on the records just as much as the lone lawyer-examiner or the abstracter-lawyer team; only title registration has kicked over the traces and tried a different method. The big change in the United States has come about, not through any major reform in the laws of fifty separate jurisdictions, but

8. Cheshire, The Modern Law of Real Property 5–6 (8th ed. 1958).

9. 4 American Law of Property § 17.4 at 527 (Casner ed. 1952).

10. For good historical studies of the system, see Beale, The Origin of the System of Recording Deeds in America, 19 Green Bag 335 (1907), and Haskins, The Beginnings of the Recording System in Massachusetts, 21 B.U.L.Rev. 281 (1941).

through the growth of title insurance companies [11] which add institutional security and an indemnity contract to the opinion of an individual examiner. Thus, it will be noted that conveyancing has changed its character far less in the United States than in England. The crucial question remains: Is there *need* for a radical change in this country?

What is important to the landowner is the substantive nature of his rights and duties, of which the right to convey is merely one. During the centuries the law of conveyancing has been changed as just indicated, but a much greater evolution has affected the substantive rights and duties of the man of property.

In Blackstone's day the law reflected society's emphasis on the *rights* of the owner of land. Blackstone's heavy emphasis on rights was overdrawn even for his day and later writers have put the matter in proper perspective. "The right of property is an exclusive right, but it has never been an absolute right. In so far as the right of property existed it was an exclusive right, that is, it excluded others; but it was not a right without limitations or qualifications. Notice the distinction between *exclusive* and *absolute*." [12] However, the fact remains that the earlier common law was more concerned with the rights of the landowner than with his duties to his neighbors and to society. If there are two sides to private property, the individual side and the social side, it was the former which was dominant in the land law of the nineteenth century and before.

The decades following World War I witnessed a major shift in emphasis so that today it is clear that the duties of the landowner are of great importance. Taxation has curtailed heavily the ability of the individual to transmit his property to later generations and makes restraints on alienation, the Rule Against Perpetuities, and similar "anti-dead hand" doctrines seem old hat as means of social control. During life, the landowner is hedged in by zoning, building restrictions, subdivision controls, etc., so that Blackstone's "sole and despotic dominion" seems to belong to another system of law entirely. Today's lawyer cannot serve his client simply by assuring him that his title is good; he must go another mile and tell him how Blackacre fits into the land use plan for his community. "While it [property law] is the field par excellence of certainty—for men and governments must arrange their affairs on the basis of expectations that will be honored—the

11. "There are approximately 160 title insurance corporations issuing their own policies in the United States. The majority of these are 'local' companies in the sense that they confine their insuring of titles to property within one state." Grimes, The Lawyer, His Client and Title Insurance, Student Law J., 4, 5 (1958).

12. 1 Ely, Property and Contract in Their Relations to the Distribution of Wealth 136 (1914).

law of property has proved over the centuries a marvelously flexible and supple instrument in accommodating new interests and wants." [13]   If the previous statement is true (and it is) in the field of land use, is it any less true in conveyancing? Must the procedural aspects of land transfer lag behind the other areas of land law?

SECTION 2. CHANGING NATURE OF LAND USE

Law seldom changes society; it only reflects and confirms changes that have already occurred. The shift from rights to duties as a focus of emphasis followed a major shift in land use from rural to urban. This shift, plus an exploding population which made land a scarce commodity in many areas, brought into play an old common law axiom, *sic utere tuo ut alienum non laedas,* and caused the ideas behind the court-developed law of nuisance to find new life in the legislature-centered law of zoning. These same changes in land use have great relevance for the law of conveyancing, even though that branch of the art has been slow to reflect them.

The principal change in land use of importance here is the relatively frequent ownership transfers which now occur for any given tract. We will take "textbook notice" [14] of the changing pattern of American life; not only is urbanization increasing apace but with it has come a high degree of personal mobility. When the family farm remained in a stable line for several generations (and even the city dweller often died in the house where he was born), title transfer by a search back to a government patent or some remote historical epoch was not unreasonable. Men made up their minds slowly and proceeded deliberately thereafter. It made sense to have a conveyancing system that operated at the same rate of speed. But today, when a big corporation moves a man from New York to California, he travels by jet and buys and sells land (or wants to) with split-second timing. Moreover, he doesn't deal in cash but in secured financing, and the lending institutions demand speed and accuracy before they make the kind of commitments required by present-day home buying. The simple truth is that land has become a

---

13. Haar, Land–Use Planning at viii (1959).

14. This is the equivalent of judicial notice and saves the trouble of citing voluminous statistics to prove a self-evident fact.

commodity that must move freely and easily in commerce. Does the law of conveyancing reflect this simple truth?

Of course, land cannot be equated with chattels, nor should it be. Land *is* unique, and its very immobility means that special laws are required for it and that its transfer will never be as simple as the purchase of a bag of apples at a supermarket. However, at this point we must remember that, in contemplation of law, property is composed of the legal relations among people in regard to a *res,* and not of the *res* itself. It would seem to follow that these legal relations can be so arranged by the law that even the most ponderous *res* may change ownership with relative ease. If this is what the changing nature of land use requires, then the law of conveyancing must provide it.

SECTION 3. BASIC PRINCIPLES OF CONVEYANCING REFORM

Real property reform is no sport for the uninitiated. It is relatively easy to reform the law of land; it is difficult to be sure that the change represents progress. The law is so intricate and so entwined in ancient history that the cutting of an old root frequently has unforeseen results. Two illustrations will suffice.

The destructibility of contingent remainders was obviously a relic of a bygone age. When a testator left land to "*A* for life, remainder to those children of *A* who survive him," he clearly meant for *A* to have no more than a life estate. Yet if *A* was also the heir of the testator he could obtain the fee and destroy the contingent remainder in his children by a simple conveyance to *X* and return.[15] Even if the reversion passed to some person other than *A,* the two parties could combine to defeat the children's interest. The statutes which abolished the doctrine of destructibility [16] were hailed as a major step in real property reform, and so they were, as devices for giving greater effect to the testator's or grantor's intent. However, they had a side effect which was not a step forward in the law of conveyancing. The doctrine of destructibility allowed the elimination of contingent remainders in at least one situation and thus made land more freely alienable by putting in someone's hands the power to convey a fee simple.

---

15. See Blocker v. Blocker, 103 Fla. 285, 137 So. 249 (1931).

16. For the present status of the doctrine, see 2 Powell, Real Property, § 314 (1950). See also ABO Petroleum Corporation v. Amstutz, 93 N.M. 332, 600 P.2d 278 (1979) where the court held the doctrine was never a part of the common law of New Mexico.

Since abolition of the doctrine, land is more likely to be tied up until the death of *A,* when his children's interests can finally vest. The ancient doctrine was not all bad; it defeated intent but it made land alienable at an earlier date.

Of course, defeating "legitimate" [17] interests in order to promote merchantability of titles seems unreasonable, but can't you have it both ways? Why not simply give the life tenant a power of sale, impress the proceeds with a trust, and let the parties have the same interests in the fund which they had in the land? This would protect the contingent remaindermen, carry out the intent of the testator (except that personalty rather than realty would pass to the children), and leave the land freely alienable. This is exactly what was done in the English property legislation of 1925, only on a much broader scale. The English abolished all legal estates in land except the fee simple absolute and the term of years, and, by creating a power of sale in the present owner of the freehold, made it possible for land to be more freely alienable while protecting the other diverse interests by giving them a share of the fund created by the sale.[18]

The Rule in Shelley's Case was even more barbarous than the doctrine of destructibility.[19] To hold that a grant to "*A* for life, remainder to his heirs" gave *A* a fee simple was absurd except as a lesson in feudal logic. But when the reformers abolished the rule and gave *A* a life estate, followed by contingent remainders in his heirs, they reduced alienability with the same stroke which resuscitated intent. The rule at least allowed *A* to convey a fee at once; its abolition tied up the land until his death.

These two illustrations are not intended to criticize the modernization of substantive rules of real property, but rather to show the complex character of those rules and plead for care in the field of conveyancing reform. What are the basic principles which should be observed if we are to improve modern methods of land transfer?

First, the system must give adequate *security* for land titles. Unless the purchaser or mortgagee can be assured that his investment is sound, the particular method fails, whatever other virtues it may possess. Second, it must provide *speed* in the determina-

---

17. A side issue: Are they legitimate?

18. For an excellent short account of the English law, see Hargreaves, Introduction to Land Law 128–37 (3d ed. 1952).

19. "That Rule is a relic, not of the horse and buggy days, but of the preceding stone cart and oxen days. . . . This Rule is only a trap and snare for the unwary, and should be repealed." Sybert v. Sybert, 125 Tex. 106, 110–11, 254 S.W.2d 999, 1001–02 (1953) (Griffin, J., concurring). The court nonetheless applied the rule! It has since been abolished in Texas but lives on in other jurisdictions. See Jones v. Stone, 52 N.C.App. 502, 279 S.E.2d 13 (1981) decided on the 400th anniversary of the Rule.

tion of title status so that the transaction can be closed with a minimum amount of cliff-hanging. Third, the method must be relatively *inexpensive* so that a disproportionate amount of the purchaser's dollar is not channeled into title service. Our present conveyancing practice should be scrutinized in the light of these principles and all changes analyzed for contribution to security, speed, and lack of expense.

SECTION 4. MODERN METHODS OF TITLE ASSURANCE—A CRITIQUE

There are essentially four modern methods of title assurance: personal covenants for title in a warranty deed, lawyer's title opinion based on the original records or an abstract therefrom, title registration (Torrens system), and title insurance. They are not mutually exclusive, since a warranty deed may be used in the latter three and a lawyer may, in effect, guarantee his own opinion, as in bar-related title insurance.[20]

A. PERSONAL COVENANTS FOR TITLE

As a method of title assurance the warranty deed can never be more than an auxiliary weapon in the conveyancer's arsenal. It is speedily delivered; it can be drafted for a nominal fee; but it secures nothing other than the personal promise of the grantor and is no better than his solvency and availability at some future date when suit may be necessary. Apart from this weakness inherent in all the warranty deeds, the covenants used today are still needlessly technical and hedged about with ancient dogma as to whether they will run with the land, when the breach occurs, the amount of damages due in case of breach, etc. Modern statutory short-form warranty deeds, with their covenants incorporated by shorthand use of a mystical word or words,[21] are a vast improvement over their prolix ancestors, but no well-advised purchaser would rely on such a deed as his sole title security. A careful re-evaluation of covenants for title is overdue and legisla-

20. See Rooney, Bar–Related Title Insurance: The Positive Perspective, 1980 S.Ill.U.L.J. 263.

21. See, e.g., Ill.Rev.Stat. ch. 30, § 8 (1985).

tion could improve their usefulness, but at best they are likely to remain a side show—the main attraction is in the big tent!

B. LAWYER'S TITLE OPINION

Professor McDougal wrote, nearly fifty years ago: "To a foreign anthropologist land transfer in the United States would probably look, as one of my former students forcefully put it, much like an aboriginal, ritualistic clambake. Like most other objects of 'property,' land is transferred by symbols, pieces of paper; but, unlike many of the other symbols, these particular symbols do not pass freely from hand to hand—their circulation is accompanied by much dilatory, costly, and extra-necessitous behavior of wise men." [22] The lawyer's opinion of title lends itself to parody about as well as any phase of the practice of law. The long search back to a government patent or to some remote period, the "fly-specking tendencies" of the conveyancing bar, the repetition of this process each time the land is transferred, etc., can be ridiculed with ease. Fortunately, unlike covenants for title, the system of using lawyers' opinions for title assurance is not beset with inherent defects, and with proper improvements such opinions can continue to fulfill the needs of large areas of the country.

The title opinion, if carefully done and as bolstered by statutes of limitations which protect even the unwary, does give adequate security for land titles. True, the lawyer does not guarantee the title and since he is liable only for negligence the client *may* suffer loss. In the main, however, the "horrible awfuls" do not occur, and the client can sleep soundly in his bed without fearing the dower-claiming spouse of a former owner if a competent lawyer has passed on his title. There is, of course, a lack of uniformity in lawyers' opinions and the big institutional lenders which operate on a nation-wide scale do prefer the title insurance scheme.

The lawyer's opinion is relatively inexpensive and indeed in many smaller communities it is doubtful whether the fee is high enough to cover the attorney's efforts on any realistic basis. The biggest defect of this method may be its slowness. In an effort to gain maximum security for the title and to prevent the next examiner from catching him in a technical error, the lawyer may spend an inordinate amount of time checking nonessentials. The

---

22. McDougal, Title Registration and Land Reform: A Reply, 8 U.Chi.L. Rev. 63, 65 (1940).

long period of search currently required in most jurisdictions adds to this difficulty.

In brief, the lawyer's opinion, as presently being handled, leaves much to be desired, but it is susceptible to reform and should have a vigorous future in some areas of the country.

C. TITLE REGISTRATION (TORRENS SYSTEM)

There is a strong temptation to overpraise the Torrens system. Theoretically, it is the best method of title assurance yet devised. In a law school property course, the student who brings a bright and inquiring mind, unhampered by the realities of the title world, to bear upon land transfer problems usually concludes that registration is the ideal system. It has been soundly praised by many impartial observers of the title parade. It has worked well in England and in the British Commonwealth countries and is considered to be the wave of the future in various parts of the world. It was the fair-haired child of property reformers in this country several decades ago when the legal literature rang with acclaim and denunciation.[23]

Even during the period when the greatest claims were being made for Torrens, some writers were already calling the system a failure.

"Explanations of this failure of registration to take hold are manifold. Much is to be attributed to inertia and ignorance, coupled with the fact that registration of land titles is entirely optional. Initial expense and time must have deterred some and insufficient assurance funds may have discouraged others. Title companies, which feel that they have only to lose by the adoption of the Torrens system, have done much to oppose stringent Torrens legislation, and by their refusal to extend loans on registered titles have prevented the successful operation of the system."[24]

---

23. The battle was joined when Professor Powell published a study critical of the Torrens system in New York. Powell, Registration of the Title to Land in the State of New York (1938). The champions of reform struck back in McDougal & Brabner–Smith, Land Title Transfer: A Regression, 48 Yale L.J. 1125 (1939), and in Fairchild & Springer, A Criticism of Professor Richard R. Powell's Book Entitled Registration of Title to Land in the State of New York, 24 Cornell L.Q. 557 (1939). The running battle continued with Bordwell, The Resurrection of Registration of Title, 7 U.Chi.L.Rev. 470 (1940), versus McDougal, Title Registration and Land Reform: A Reply, 8 U.Chi.L.Rev. 63 (1940). The more serious troubles abroad seemed to quell the domestic struggle as the forties wore on.

24. Handler, Cases on Vendor and Purchaser 674 (1933).

Torrens is not yet dead in the United States and it still provokes discussion in the law reviews.[25] But if burial is premature, rejoicing at a resurrection is equally out of place. The system exists to some extent in Colorado, Georgia, Hawaii, Illinois, Massachusetts, Minnesota, Nebraska, New York, North Carolina, Ohio, South Dakota, Tennessee, Utah, Virginia, and Washington.[26] In these jurisdictions three situations account for a substantial fraction of the registrations: first, it is a useful device for clearing a bad title; second, registration typically excludes adverse possession and is helpful where wild timber land and undeveloped mineral land might otherwise be lost by adverse possession; and third, registration of title in suburban developments has provided a relatively inexpensive evidence of title for purchasers.[27] Nowhere in the United States, however, has it become the dominant method of land transfer.

Professor Bade's succinct critique sums up the assets of Torrens. "Title registration is an obvious improvement over recorded titles. A registered title is a title that has been adjudicated in an officially directed and controlled proceeding in rem. The title is then kept clear by constant official supervision. There is no need thereafter to trace and examine the title from its origin. The present state of the title is normally represented on the face and obverse of an owner's certificate of title. When the title is transferred the former owner's certificate is cancelled and a new one is issued to the new owner. Subsisting encumbrances are carried forward to the new certificate. Those that have been eliminated by lapse of time, satisfaction, or other sufficient means, are not. Thus by examination of two sides of a certificate of title, in 99% of the cases, a competent lawyer should be able to examine a title in an hour or less. Furthermore, what appears on the certificate is not merely prima facie evidence of title, it is conclusive. If anyone is injured by errors of the Registrar of Titles, his recourse is not against the registered owner, but against a state administered assurance fund." [28]

25. See, e.g., Heinrich, The Case for Land Registration, 6 Mercer L.Rev. 320 (1955); Maher, Registered Lands Revisited, 8 W.Res.L.Rev. 162 (1957). The latter article concludes: "The registration of land in Ohio has largely been confined to the communities surrounding the larger cities, although a large minority of the counties have some registered titles. Whether additional land will be registered in the future is a matter of speculation, but it is not speculation that a practicing attorney must have a speaking acquaintance with the registered land statutes if he has much practice in real estate." Id. at 169.

26. 4 American Law of Property, § 17.39 (Casner ed. 1952). California repealed its title registration act in 1955. Cal.Gen.Laws Ann.Act 8589, § 1 (Deering Supp.1959).

27. Powell, Registration of the Title to Land in the State of New York (1938).

28. Bade, Cases on Real Property and Conveyancing 306 (1954).

One can agree wholeheartedly with the foregoing analysis and still conclude that Torrens has little or no future in the United States. If we were setting up a wholly new society in a virgin land we could forget the recording system and rely on registration. Its qualities are manifestly superior to the cumbersome system with which we are saddled. We *could* make the Torrens system work in the United States if we would pass legislation making registration compulsory for each parcel of land as soon as it is next transferred *inter vivos* to a new owner. This would have to be done in fifty states (if we wanted a nationally uniform system), over the combined opposition of most of the groups which make our present system operate, at a huge initial cost with state subsidy, and only after the personnel required for the new system had been adequately trained.[29] If we had no recording system and no title insurance, as in England, such a step would be required to keep pace with modern society. However, our title destiny lies in another direction, for it is impractical to expect a Torrens revolution short of an actual breakdown of the present machinery.

In brief, title registration provides maximum security, relative speed, and, after the initial charge, is not too expensive, but it remains too frail a reed to support modern conveyancing reform because other methods are so firmly embedded in our institutions of property.

D. TITLE INSURANCE

"Title insurance is available in nearly all parts of the United States. The insurable title is steadily increasing in favor as the most acceptable title and the one affording maximum protection and security to the insured. Life insurance companies, which are large investors in real estate mortgages all over the country, prefer title insurance to other forms of title evidence. In New York City, Chicago, Cleveland, and Los Angeles, and their suburban areas, title insurance predominates as a method of affording title protection.

"Title insurance is steadily growing in favor because it is a flexible form of title assurance, readily adaptable to the changing needs of lawyers and their clients in all types of transactions in real estate. It offers a degree of protection, security, and freedom from worry and expense no other kind of title evidence can match.

29. This last point is of major importance. The Torrens system cannot be efficiently operated with just anybody the political machine sees fit to appoint. Even England is proceeding slowly until personnel can be trained.

More and more lawyers have come to recognize that title insurance complements and does not displace their services to their clients in real estate deals." [30]   This quotation from Charles F. Grimes, formerly General Counsel and Secretary of the Chicago Title and Trust Company, one of the nation's leading title insurance companies, is an eloquent statement of the industry's claim to be the wave of the future.

Not all observers have seen title insurance through such rose-tinted glasses. Professor Bade would seem to damn it with faint praise. "Another device that is advocated by some as a remedy for the shortcomings of recorded title systems is 'Title Insurance.' In the first place the name of the thing is a misnomer. Titles are not insured. At most, named persons are insured against loss by reason of failure of title. But even in that aspect, it has its shortcomings. . . . It has been suggested that it insures only that the insurance company has made a careful examination of the title and has listed all serious defects in the exceptions from its coverage. . . . Generally, title insurance does not insure a marketable title. In addition to the limitations on coverage, they commonly require claim and suit to be brought under it within a short period of time. Insurance premiums are not low. The coverage is limited to those named or designated in the policy. Generally the policies are not assignable and do not pass with the land. New owners may have the policy endorsed in their favor, but must pay a further premium therefor. In contrast, title registration is permanent, and the benefit of it passes to each successive owner." [31]

It is possible to agree with Professor Bade's obvious preference for title registration, as a system, and still conclude that title insurance will be the dominant factor in the future of American conveyancing. The growth of title insurance has been phenomenal, particularly in the period since the end of World War II. Although title insurance has been spreading rapidly, it is still difficult to appraise its relative merits as a method of land transfer. Exact information about its operation is difficult to obtain, and most critiques have been prepared either by ardent enthusiasts with a vested interest in its propagation or by strong advocates of a rival system (lawyers' opinions or the Torrens system). Moreover, the title companies themselves vary so widely that generalizations are likely to be misleading. This last point is particularly important. Some of the companies are old, established corporations with highly professional staffs, concerned with the efficient operation of modern conveyancing and playing an important role in the development of the real property law of their

---

30. Grimes, supra note 11 at 24.   **31.** Bade, supra note 28, at 306.

particular state or states. In many metropolitan areas, title insurance has the principal role in land transfer and few lawyers would wish it otherwise. Such title insurance has met a need with the business-like efficiency that the situation demanded. Unfortunately, not all title insurance is of this type.[32]

Title insurance can give the necessary security (if the purchaser clearly understands the exclusions from coverage) and it operates with the requisite speed, but its Achilles' heel *may* be expense. Without making any present indictment, it is necessary to raise a warning flag. Both recording and registration operate as agencies of local government. This makes their cost to the purchaser of land low, and it does not seem unfair that the public should assume some of the cost of a system of land transfer. The lawyer's fee for examination of the records or of an abstract is based on a reasonable professional charge for service rendered and is kept within limits by the charges of his fellow practitioners. Thus far, title insurance has been forced to compete with at least one rival system, and in some areas two, so that charges have not been excessive. What will be the result if title insurance becomes a virtual monopoly? Land law exists for the benefit of the landowner and systems of conveyancing must serve him. Title insurance is a private business but it bases its services on public records and is affected with the public interest. If normal competition fails to keep the coverage adequate and the cost within bounds, it may be necessary for the state to regulate the industry like any other public utility. This could be the long range future of conveyancing in the United States—privately insured titles based on public records, with public control as to coverage and cost.

SECTION 5. SUGGESTED REFORMS

In a critique of conveyancing in Virginia, Professor Spies of the University of Virginia Law School concluded that no radical changes were necessary. He suggested that a system of tract indexes be substituted for the cumbersome grantor-grantee indexes, that title standards be adopted as authoritative guides to lend uniformity to title opinions, and that a marketable title statute be passed in the state to give reasonable scope to title search. To implement these proposals, he recommended the appointment of a

---

32. For the best impartial analysis of title insurance see Johnstone, Title Insurance, 66 Yale L.J. 492 (1957).

committee consisting of members of the bar and representatives of Virginia's four law schools.[33]

In contrast, an appraisal, nation-wide in scope, in the Yale Law Journal concludes: "In effect, this Comment has suggested that the objectives of the Torrens system be implemented within the framework of recordation." [34] This latter proposal envisages a series of periodic quiet title suits to cleanse the title chain of its accumulated debris. While this plan is far from revolutionary, it is more radical than the fence-patching suggestions of Professor Spies. The clarion call for sweeping reform has more impact on the printed page, but the laborious patchwork is, in this case at least, more likely to serve society's needs.

A. GENERAL SUGGESTIONS

Four broad points need to be made before we move into the area of specifics. First, there is no real need for a completely uniform system of conveyancing on a national scale. Symmetry can be a false god. Land remains a creature of the local jurisdiction and some variation in conveyancing procedure is probably inevitable, even desirable, since it leads to experimentation which may then be helpful elsewhere. It is true that the national lending agencies exert a powerful force for uniform procedures and that the trend is in that direction, but this need not become the focal point for national legislation. However, this primacy of local law does not rule out the need for model acts which can serve as the basis for local reform.[35]

Second, conveyancing reform is the responsibility of the state bar and each state should have active sections or committees working on the problems of the local jurisdiction, drafting legislation, preparing title standards, etc.

Third, some diversity in conveyancing method is desirable even in the same jurisdiction, i.e., there are situations where title insurance is called for, others where lawyers' opinions are preferable, and Torrens can always add a healthy leaven to the loaf. Moreover, so long as competitive methods are available the spectre of monopoly will be kept under control.

---

33. Spies, A Critique of Conveyancing, 38 Va.L.Rev. 245, 262–63 (1952).

34. Comment, Enhancing the Marketability of Land: The Suit to Quiet Title, 68 Yale L.J. 1245, 1315 (1959).

35. See, for example, the Uniform Land Transactions Act, the Uniform Simplification of Land Transfers Act, and the Uniform Condominium Act. (Official Texts 1978, West Publishing Co.)

Fourth, since the recording system is the heart of modern conveyancing, the recording acts should be strengthened so that both lawyers' opinions and title insurance can flourish at maximum effectiveness. Certainly, the recording system should not be allowed to become so complex that all title business is forced into the hands of the insurance companies by default.

B. SPECIFIC SUGGESTIONS

There are at least five varieties of reform by which our recording system may be restored to a reasonable degree of effectiveness. They are: (1) shortening the period of title search through merchantability of title acts or special statutes of limitation; (2) the elimination of purely technical objections by curative legislation; (3) making miscellaneous changes in the mechanical operation of the recording acts; (4) altering the substantive law of property so as to simplify title problems; and (5) the adoption by local bar groups of title standards or rules for the examination of abstracts. A brief look at each of these areas will point the way to a reasonable program of conveyancing reform.[36]

(1) MERCHANTABILITY OF TITLE ACTS [37]

The most hopeful device for bolstering the conveyancing system is a well drafted merchantability act which will restrict the period of search to a reasonable limit. A statute of limitations is an honored tool for giving stability in diverse areas of the law. Such statutes have for centuries—the first one goes back to 1275 in England—played a prominent role in real property law. As early as 1540, the modern method of measuring limitations was adopted and in 1623 the basic twenty-year period was established. Unfortunately, such statutes have never been of great help to the title examiner because they do not apply to claims of governmental units, contain exceptions for individuals under disability, do not run against future interests until such interests become pos-

---

36. For an excellent, detailed analysis of these five points see Basye, Clearing Land Titles (2d ed. 1970).

37. For a brief discussion of merchantability acts in the midwestern states, see Cribbet, A New Concept of Merchantability, 43 Ill.B.J. 778 (1955). See also Id. at 366–461.

sessory, and depend for their effectiveness on the proof of facts dehors the record, e.g., that the possession has been hostile, adverse, notorious, continuous, under claim of right, etc. What is needed is a statute which bars old claims solely because of the passage of time, unless there is a legitimate reason for keeping them alive. The various merchantability acts seek to fill this need.

When the recording acts were first passed, they had the effect of cutting off what would have been valid claims but for the failure of the claimant to follow the dictates of the statute. That is still the effect of the acts and no one contends that this makes them unconstitutional or unfair. The great social value in an effective recording system outweighs the occasional loss to the individual who fails to record. The principal defect of the recording system lies in its failure to be self-cleansing; once a claim is of record, it tends to remain valid indefinitely. In the early years of the recording system this was no defect but now the system is becoming more cumbersome each decade. Fortunately, there is no reason for this defect to continue in its present form.

The simplest way to cleanse the records would be to provide a gross period beyond which no claim of ownership could be enforced against the present owner. This method has in fact been used for certain interests, such as equitable servitudes,[38] possibilities of reverter and powers of termination,[39] and for foreclosure of mortgages.[40] In sustaining the constitutionality of the Illinois act limiting the duration of a possibility of reverter or power of termination to fifty (now forty) years, the court stated: "It has been said that the Reverter Act was passed in recognition of the operation of possibilities of reverter as 'clogs on title, withdrawing property thus encumbered from the commercial mortgage market long after the individual, social or economic reason for their creation had ceased, and at a time when the heirs from whom a release could be obtained would be so numerous as to be virtually impossible to locate.' . . . The statute reflects the General Assembly's appraisal of the actual economic significance of these interests, weighed against the inconvenience and expense caused by their continued existence for unlimited periods of time without regard to altered circumstances. As a result of that appraisal,

38. For legislation restricting the effectiveness of covenants, conditions, and restrictions to thirty years, see Mass. Gen.Laws Ann. ch. 184, § 23; Minn. Stat.Ann. § 500.20(2); R.I.Gen.Laws Ann. § 34–4–21 (1956).

39. Ill.Rev.Stat. ch. 30, § 37e (1985). The period was originally fifty years but was reduced to forty in 1959 to correspond with the forty-year period of the new merchantability act.

40. Ill.Rev.Stat. ch. 83, §§ 11b, 12 (1985), operates in twenty years from the due date where such date is determinable from the mortgage or in thirty years from the date of the instrument where the due date cannot be so ascertained.

their potential duration has been limited to fifty years. . . . We are unable to say that that method offends the constitutional provisions relied upon." [41] This succinct statement of the public policy in favor of merchantability highlights the usefulness of the gross period of limitation in clearing titles.

It would be unfair, however, to bar *all* claims more than forty years old since substantial estates or interests of record, not yet matured, would thereby be extinguished. But is there any reason why the holder of these old interests should not be required to re-record the claim within a reasonable period or lose it? Must such old claims cloud the title forever? The merchantability acts are based on the simple premise that unless the stale claim is kept alive by a new recording within a gross period (with a saving clause for old claims in existence at the passage of the act), it ceases to be enforceable. No attempt will be made here to analyze the various statutes of this type since they are not uniform in their operation and general statements can be misleading.[42] It should be noted, however, that Iowa has had a particularly rich development in this area and that the courts there have given full support to the legislative efforts to provide a self-cleansing recording system.

Thus the Iowa court held a title to be merchantable despite an alleged break in the title chain due to a misdescription in a 1907 deed. Relying squarely on the Iowa act, the court stated: "Iowa was the first of several states to pass a statute which bars all claims to real property arising prior to a stated date without regard to the nature of any legal condition on the part of a possible claimant. . . . It will thus be observed there is a growing tendency to effectively bar potential claims arising out of irregularities in a chain of title to real property where no claim is filed based on said irregularity by the date stated in a particular statute." [43]

If, in the material just discussed, the interests were "remotely expectant" [44] and of limited economic value, the same cannot be

---

41. Trustees of Schools of Tp. No. 1 v. Batdorf, 6 Ill.2d 486, 492, 130 N.E.2d 111, 114 (1955).

Note, however, that New York declared a similar statute unconstitutional on the grounds that it impaired the obligation of a contract and deprived an owner of his property without due process of law. Board of Education of Central School District No. 1 v. Miles, 15 N.Y.2d 364, 259 N.Y.S.2d 129, 207 N.E.2d 181 (1965).

42. For a detailed analysis see Basye, Clearing Land Titles 366–461 (2d ed. 1970).

43. Tesdell v. Hanes, 248 Iowa 742, 747, 82 N.W.2d 119, 121–22 (1957). See also Chicago and Northwestern Railway Company v. City of Osage, 176 N.W.2d 788 (Iowa 1970) and Presbytery of Southeast Iowa v. Harris, 226 N.W.2d 232 (Iowa 1975). The latter case contains an excellent analysis of legislative activity, not only in Iowa but elsewhere.

44. The language used in Trustees of Schools of Tp. No. 1 v. Batdorf, 6 Ill.2d 486, 130 N.E.2d 111 (1955).

said of the Indiana Mineral Lapse Act.[45] The avowed purpose of that Act was to reunite severed mineral interests with surface ownership after a period of twenty years where there had been no display of activity or interest by the owners of the mineral estate during such period.

The statute also contained a two-year grace period during which the owners of mineral interests could preserve their rights by filing a notice of claim. The Indiana Supreme Court held that the Act was constitutional as a value exercise of legislative power.[46] Said the court:

> Study of this Act reveals that its outstanding feature is its declaration that mineral interests are terminable. Whatever may be the exact legal dimensions of such interests, they are not greater than fee simple titles.
>
> . . .
>
> In limiting its incursion upon mineral rights to those which have been unused in the statutory sense for as long as twenty years, and in granting a two year period of grace after enactment of the statute to preserve interests, the Legislature adopted means which are rationally related to such objectives, and which themselves provide a reasonable time and a simple and inexpensive method, taking into consideration the nature of the case, for preserving such interests. We find that this act is within the police power of the states and does not unconstitutionally impair the obligation of contracts.[47]

Not surprisingly, Short v. Texaco was immediately appealed to the United States Supreme Court. The Court affirmed the judgment of the Indiana Court in a five to four decision with Mr. Justice Brennan filing a vigorous dissent.[48] He concluded that the two year period of grace, with no notice to the owners of mineral interests other than the passage of the Act, deprived the owners of their property without due process of law. Said he: "In my view, under the circumstances, the provision of no process simply cannot be deemed due process of law." [49]

Regardless of the merits of such legislation and the judicial reaction to its constitutionality, merchantability of title acts and their counsin, the Indiana Mineral Lapse Act, represent a changing concept of property rights. The acts go beyond the traditional statutes of limitation and cut off property interests even in the

45. Ind.Code §§ 32–5–11–1 through 32–5–11–8 (1979 & Supp.1985).

46. Short v. Texaco, Inc., 273 Ind. 518, 406 N.E.2d 625 (1980).

47. Id. at 524–26, 406 N.E.2d at 629–31.

48. Texaco, Inc. v. Short, 454 U.S. 516, 102 S.Ct. 781, 70 L.Ed.2d 738 (1982).

49. Id. at 554 (Brennan, J., dissenting).

absence of adverse possession (note as an example that the mineral interests in Short v. Texaco were not adversely possessed by the surface owners). Moreover, the acts affect a wide range of property interests. Although the law still recognizes such interests and allows parties to create them, they can be terminated under the police power if the state has sufficient social and economic reasons for doing so and provides a modicum of due process. These acts do not involve a "taking" by the state,[50] but they do represent a regulation of the various property rights in the sense that they can be terminated, without compensation, in the public interest. Another way of looking at it is that the state has allowed the creation of certain property rights and can determine how long they will endure as claims against the owner of a fee simple absolute, if those claims are not in active use or properly re-recorded. This strengthens the rights of the owners of the fee—at least some of the owners, since in Short v. Texaco the owners of the severed mineral rights also owned an estate in fee simple in the subsurface. Obviously, law cannot carve property rights into stone for all time and as long as the law changes, so will the contents of the "bundle of sticks." For our present purposes, the important point is that merchantability of title acts and related legislation point the way toward making the recording acts more effective (by requiring the re-recording of old claims) and thus shortening the period of title search.

Merchantability acts are relatively new and there may be some "wrinkles" in them, but these can be ironed out by amendment and, as the bar becomes familiar with their operation, they should do a great deal to improve the efficiency of the recording system. Forty years is probably too long a period for most claims and the length of time should be reduced as soon as feasible. Actually, the twenty-year limitation of the old English act seems long enough, particularly since an active interest can always be protected by a vigilant claimant. Most old clouds on title are not, in fact, active and should be dissipated as soon as practicable. Some of the impetus for reform should now be directed toward the further shortening of the period of title search.

---

(2) Curative Legislation

Nearly every title examination will disclose technical errors which tend to destroy merchantability but which could scarcely be

---

50. Short v. Texaco, Inc., 273 Ind. 518, 526, 406 N.E.2d 625, 631 (1980). "The State through this statute is not actually taking the mineral interest for its own use and benefit."

the basis of a serious lawsuit. Examiners object to these defects largely out of fear that a successor examiner will mention the ·error and make the first lawyer appear careless. These defects constitute one of the principal areas of "fly-specking." [51] A typical example is the omission of a private seal on a deed or mortgage. Many states periodically pass curative or validating acts to heal these relatively minor abrasions, e.g., "All deeds or mortgages heretofore irregularly executed by the omission of a seal are validated and made effective as though such omitted seal had been affixed." [52]

The history, scope, and constitutionality of curative legislation has been thoroughly explored in the legal literature.[53] Any state which wishes to avail itself of this valuable tool for the improvement of conveyancing can find detailed precedents to follow. The principal difficulty here is keeping the legislation up to date and covering all of the necessary points. It is grubby business, not unlike the daily polishing of brass on a ship, and unless an alert bar association committee keeps steadily on the job the technical defects will accumulate faster than they can be removed.

---

(3) CHANGES IN MECHANICAL OPERATION OF THE RECORDING ACTS

The recording acts originated in colonial times and were designed for a simpler society. While basically sound, they need to be examined in the light of today's needs. The major defect is faulty indexing. No record is worth much unless the examiner can find it quickly and accurately. There are two basic systems of indexing—the grantor-grantee and the tract. The present trend is to reduce the number of indexes and use only one grantor-grantee system, but many states have a separate index for each type of instrument (mortgagor-mortgagee, mechanic's lien, index to miscellaneous documents, etc.).[54] It is apparent that such a proliferation of indexes can lead only to delay and error. Moreover, since

---

51. Ward in his book, Illinois Law of Title Examination (2d ed. 1952), tells the story of the young examiner who objected because the President's wife had not joined in executing a patent from the government. Apocryphal but revealing!

52. Ill.Rev.Stat. ch. 30, § 34b (1985).

53. See, e.g., Basye, supra note 36, at §§ 201–364 (1970); Scurlock, Retroactive Legislation Affecting Interests in Land (1953); Day, Curative Acts and Limitations Acts Designed to Remedy Defects in Florida Land Titles (pts. 1–4), 8 U.Fla.L.Rev. 365 (1955), 9 id. at 145 (1956).

54. See, for example, Idaho Code Ann. § 31–2404 (1948).

the grantor-grantee index is usually held to be the official system, the chain of title concept has developed and instruments of record that are outside the chain have been held to give no notice.[55] The tract index is clearly superior and should be adopted whenever possible as the required, official system. This change plus a shorter period of search would go far toward restoring efficiency to the recording system.

Even when the indexing is adequate the acts may be defective in scope.[56] Since the acts reversed the common law scheme of priority, they are strictly construed and apply only to the instruments expressly described. This can mean that some legal documents which affect title to land do not have to be recorded and yet will be binding on a subsequent purchaser. Moreover, a title once obtained by adverse possession may survive to plague a subsequent purchaser even though the adverse possessor did not record any evidence of his claim and was not in possession at the time the alleged bona fide purchaser bought the land.[57]

The solution to this part of the recording act problem is simple to state but difficult to achieve. All claims, interests, liens, etc., affecting real property should be placed on record or be forever lost. This should include government liens since the state, of all groups, should never be above the principle of the law. It should also include claims of adverse possession since the purported owner can at least place an affidavit on record giving notice of his claim. Many records affecting land, e.g., probated wills, state tax liens, judgments, etc., must be found at offices separate from that of the recorder of deeds. These should be held to an absolute minimum and, where they are causing difficulty in the particular jurisdiction, should be required to be filed, by transcript, in the recorder's office. The Torrens system requires nearly all such records to be filed with the registrar on the memorial of title or fail as notice; the recording acts should copy this page from their sister system.

---

(4) Changes in Substantive Law of Property

Some of the conveyancing difficulties have little to do with the recording system; they spring instead from archaic rules of property law that have not been revised to keep pace with changing times. High on the list are such marital interests as dower (or

---

55. See pp. 319 to 322 supra.

56. Cf. 4 American Law of Property, § 17.8 (Casner ed. 1952).

57. See, e.g., Mugaas v. Smith, 33 Wash.2d 429, 206 P.2d 332 (1949).

curtesy) and homestead. Designed as a kind of feudal social security, in the case of dower, and as a mid-nineteenth century statutory exemption for debtors, in the case of homestead, they have survived largely as clogs on title and as levers to pry better financial settlements out of straying spouses. Where the husband (or wife) fails to sign a conveyance, even inadvertently, or where the record fails to disclose the marital status of a grantor, the title may be clouded for years. Moreover, this can be a peculiarly difficult defect to correct in a fluid society when the parties move freely from state to state. If these marital interests still play a useful social role they should be retained and legislation designed to remove the cloud as soon as possible.[58] However, many jurisdictions [59] have concluded that these interests should join livery of seisin and socage tenure in limbo, thereby freeing land from one more tentacle of the past.

The whole panorama of future interests should be viewed with a modern eye since such estates are a prolific source of title difficulty. That problem is beyond the scope of this text. It should be noted, however, that statutes limiting the existence of possibilities of reverter and powers of termination to a gross period [60] have a direct effect both on the law of future interests and conveyancing.

The foregoing examples demonstrate the types of substantive property law problems that need study in any full-scale conveyancing reform. These problems vary from state to state and generalizations on a national basis can be misleading, but the bar of each state should make an inventory of its principal "traps for the unwary" and then modify them by appropriate legislation.

---

(5) ADOPTION OF TITLE STANDARDS

All of the preceding suggestions require legislative intervention; title standards, however, can be adopted by the cooperative effort of the bar itself. In 1942, the Section on Real Estate Law of the Illinois State Bar Association adopted uniform rules for examination of abstracts. These rules do not purport to bind anyone but they serve as a guide for local bar associations and as a result have been influential with the title bar. The first rule sets the

---

58. For an example of how this can be done, see Ark.Stat.Ann. § 61–226 (1947).

59. Listed in 2 Powell, Real Property ¶ 217 (1950) plus supplements.

60. E.g., Ill.Rev.Stat. ch. 30, § 37e (1985).

tenor: "An attorney making an examination of title should raise objections only to such matters as are substantial defects in the abstract of title, and should be prepared to show by legal authority that the matter complained of is of such character as would substantially affect the merchantability of the title and would interfere with the ability of the owner to readily dispose of the same." [61]

Many of the rules simply state the existing law, either statutory or decisional, and to that extent are useful only as a method of calling details to the attention of the title examiner. Others go beyond "the law" and set up matters of custom which help to eliminate trivial objections.

Paradoxically, the strength of title standards (improvement in conveyancing without the necessity of legislative action) is also their weakness. As a cooperative venture of the bar they are a long stride forward, but, because the standards lack the sanction of law, they tend to disintegrate in the face of stubborn opposition. The Nebraska legislature has adopted as law the entire set of standards previously passed by the state bar association,[62] and the Connecticut bar association has expressed hope that all states will give such standards the force of law.[63] Nonetheless, the future of title standards lies in their voluntary approach to abstract examination rather than in legislative coercion. Once frozen into code form they become inflexible and call for overly frequent revision.[64]

SECTION 6.   THE LAWYERS' ROLE

Lawyers do not have the sole responsibility for the commercial transfer of real property. While the legal role is of great importance, many lay groups are involved in selling, financing, and title assuring. Since the economic stakes are unusually high, it is not surprising that conflicts have developed among the various interest groups serving the consuming public. All of the

---

61. Section on Real Estate Law, Ill. Bar Ass'n, Rules for Title Examinations, 31 Ill.B.J. 128 (1942). See also Recommended Uniform Rules for the Examination of Abstracts of Title, published by the Illinois Bar Association in 1977 with Commentary by Michael J. Rooney of the Illinois bar.

62. Neb.Rev.Stat. §§ 76–604 to 76–644 (1950).

63. Report of the Committee on Standards for Title Opinions, Proceed-

ings of the ABA Section of Real Property, Probate and Trust Law 130, 132 (1939).

64. However, see Staley v. Stephens, 404 N.E.2d 633 (Ind.App.1980) where the court held that title standards adopted by a county bar association had no legal effect unless a contract specifically incorporates them.

groups should remember that the goal is service to the public. This is particularly true of lawyers who are members of a learned profession and have been granted a kind of monopoly in the public interest. A desire to protect their own financial stake should not lead them into self-defeating attacks on real estate brokers, title insurance companies, and lending institutions, which may be able to provide adequate service at reasonable cost. Suits against real estate brokers and others for unauthorized practice of the law are probably doomed to failure in any case and only bring the bar into public disrepute.[65] It would seem the proper course for lawyers would be to concentrate on giving superior and more broadly based service and working out cooperative agreements with those other groups involved in commercial land transactions.[66]

65. See, for example, Chicago Bar Ass'n v. Quinlan and Tyson, Inc., 34 Ill. 2d 116, 214 N.E.2d 771 (1966) and State ex rel. Indiana State Bar Ass'n v. Indiana Real Estate Ass'n, Inc., 244 Ind. 214, 191 N.E.2d 711 (1963), noting particularly Judge Arterburn's concurring opinion in the latter case. The two cited cases limited the drafting of deeds to lawyers but allowed real estate brokers to "fill in the blanks" in contracts of sale and related documents. After the Arizona Supreme Court held with the bar in a suit against lay groups, the public reversed the decision by a constitutional amendment (which passed about 4 to 1), allowing laymen to practice law in a limited way.

66. See Foreman, The Illinois Real Estate Broker—Lawyer Accord, 55 Ill. B.J. 284 (1966) and Proceedings, Section of Real Property, Probate and Trust Law, Part II, Real Property Law Division 187–193 (1964).

*

Part Six

THE USE OF LAND

The use of land is often of great concern to persons other than owners of possessory estates. Some wish to use another's land in some manner, such as to cross it with utility lines. Others wish to have neighboring land restricted to compatible uses, such as residential uses in a residential area. The common law accommodates both of these types of concerns by (1) providing for acquisition of property interests to use another's land and to prevent uses of another's land, and also by (2) providing principles to guide courts in reconciling conflicting uses of neighboring lands when such property interests have not been acquired. In addition to these roles of the common law, an expanding body of legislation and administrative regulation regulates land use for protection of public interests. These three clusters of law are addressed here under the following headings: (1) rights in the land of another, which include easements, profits, licenses, real covenants, equitable servitudes and conditions; (2) natural rights, i.e., rights of use inherent in the ownership of the land such as the right to prevent a nuisance, the right to physical support of the soil, and the right to water on, under or adjacent to one's land; and (3) public regulation of land use, including planning, zoning, subdivision control, and environmental control.

Chapter 1

RIGHTS IN THE LAND OF ANOTHER

The types of property interests that courts, over centuries of litigation, have allowed in another's land are conceptually distinct, but they often serve similar or identical ends. This has resulted in confusion in terminology and, more important, in rationales of judicial decisions. To facilitate understanding, this subject is approached here in traditional fashion, which emphasizes historical concepts and terminology, but modern applications of traditional doctrines and contemporary problems are not neglected.

SECTION 1. EASEMENTS AND PROFITS

An easement is a property right in a person or group of persons to use the land of another for a special purpose not inconsistent with the general property right in the owner of the land.[1] It is best illustrated by rights of way across another's land, public utility telephone lines and pipelines, and flooding privileges, but it can include in modern times a wide variety of novel and interesting rights.[2] A profit a prendre (to use the technically correct terminology) is an easement plus, i.e., it is the right to use another's land by removing a portion of the soil or its products. An illustration is the right to go on the land of a seashore owner and collect seaweed for use as fertilizer on your own land. Much of the law of profits a prendre was developed in the old English seaweed cases but the right to remove gravel, minerals, and timber is more common today. There is no necessity for treating these two property interests separately since the same legal principles apply to both. In English law, there was a difference since

1. A more detailed and hence more accurate definition is found in Restatement, Property, § 450 (1944). "An easement is an interest in land in the possession of another which (a) entitles the owner of such interest to a limited use or enjoyment of the land in which the interest exists; (b) entitles him to protection as against third persons from interference in such use or enjoyment; (c) is not subject to the will of the possessor of the land; (d) is not a normal incident of the possession of any land possessed by the owner of the interest, and (e) is capable of creation by conveyance."

2. For a discussion of these novel easements see Drye v. Eagle Rock Ranch, Inc., 364 S.W.2d 196 (Tex.1962).

easements could exist only as appurtenant to other land owned by the holder of the easement while profits could be owned separately from any other land, i.e., in gross. While some remnants of this meaningless distinction haunt us in this country it has little practical significance because easements too may now be in gross.[3]

It may be useful to clarify a few terms. Easements may be classified in several ways: affirmative, allowing the holder to do acts on another's, or negative, allowing the holder to prevent the owner from doing acts on his own land; appurtenant, benefiting the other land owned by the holder; express, created by direct action of the parties, or implied, created by operation of law from the peculiar facts and circumstances involved; and several other categories, such as legal or equitable, of less importance. Easements are usually referred to in relation to dominant and servient tenements or tracts of land. The dominant tenement is the land benefited by the easement; the servient tenement is the land burdened by the easement. Thus, if A owns a tract north of B and has the right to cross B's land to reach a highway south of it, A's tract is the dominant tenement (benefited by the means of access) and B's tract is the servient tenement (burdened by having to allow A to cross his land). An easement is in gross when it burdens servient land but benefits no dominant land, e.g., telephone company wires.

A. CREATION

Easements can be created by express act of the parties, by implication, or by prescription.[4] At a very early date, even prior to the Statute of Uses when livery of seisin still ruled the roost for freehold estates, easements could be created by grant, an instrument under seal. Indeed, the old saw ran, those things which lie not in livery lie in grant. Today, "the formal requisites for the creation of an easement by conveyance inter vivos are (a) those required in a conveyance of an estate in land of like duration, and (b) subject to statutory modification, a written instrument under seal."[5] Therefore, one who wishes to buy an easement across the

3. Restatement, Property § 450, special note (1944).

4. Perhaps custom should be added to this list, since the Supreme Court of Oregon, in an historic and fascinating decision, relied on custom to protect the "dry-sand" area of the Oregon beaches from private exploitation. State ex rel. Thornton v. Hay, 254 Or. 584, 462 P.2d 671 (1969). The court, in effect, found an easement in the public, based on immemorial usage or custom, dating back to the Indians. The facts were unique, however, and the case finds little support in American precedent.

5. Restatement, Property § 467 (1944).

land of B may enter into a transaction not unlike that involved in purchasing a fee and take conveyance by means of a regular deed that describes the interest correctly. The parties must be careful to make their intent clear because there can be ambiguity as to whether a fee simple title to a strip of land or an easement only is being conveyed. Thus, "a strip of land for a right of way over and across Blackacre" may create a fee [6] or virtually the same language may create an easement.[7] The distinction becomes vital on abandonment of the way, as by a railroad, because if an easement only resulted the strip belongs to the servient owner when the use ceases. Failure to comply with formal requirements, such as a seal, may defeat the easement and give the grantee a mere license which can be revoked by the grantor.[8] However, if the grantee changes position in reliance on the grant, an easement still may result on the principle of estoppel.[9]

A grantor of the fee simple may attempt to create and retain an easement in the land conveyed. Typically, the retained interest is a right-of-way to serve retained land. This objective could be accomplished by contractually binding the grantee of the land to convey an easement back to the grantor. However, grantors usually resort to the simpler method of including in the deed of the land a "reservation" or "exception" of an easement. English courts, obsessed with conceptualism, did not allow this, but American courts do.[10] It usually makes no difference to American courts, ignoring historical distinctions, whether the deed refers to "reservation" or "exception" or even to some other words having the same general meaning.[11] But the careful drafter refers to "reservation" for this purpose. The word "exception" should be avoided here because it has other meanings. Typically it refers to retention by the grantor of fee simple ownership of a part of the tract being conveyed. It also might be used to refer to an existing easement owned by another, although the customary language for this purpose is "subject to."

Grantors of the fee simple also have attempted to reserve in the deed an easement for the benefit of a third party, usually an

6. Midland Valley Railroad Co. v. Arrow Industrial Manufacturing Co., 297 P.2d 410, 411 (Okl.1956).

7. Bernards v. Link, 199 Or. 579, 248 P.2d 341 (1952). See also Harvest Queen Mill and Elev. Co. v. Sanders, 189 Kan. 536, 370 P.2d 419 (1962).

8. Nelson v. American Tel. and Tel. Co., 270 Mass. 471, 170 N.E. 416 (1930). Note, however, that the need for a seal has been abolished in most jurisdictions by statute. Even where a seal is technically required at law, equity may en-

force a written grant which is unsealed, i.e., an equitable easement results. Baseball Publishing Co. v. Bruton, 302 Mass. 54, 18 N.E.2d 362, 119 A.L.R. 1518 (1938).

9. Stoner v. Zucker, 148 Cal. 516, 83 P. 808 (1906).

10. The "cobwebs of history" on this subject are explained in 3 Powell, Real Property ¶ 407 (1987 Rev.).

11. Mitchell v. Castellaw, 151 Tex. 56, 246 S.W.2d 163 (1952).

owner of adjoining land. Many American courts have joined the English courts in forbidding this—an unfortunate result.[12] While the better practice is to use separate deeds, the first to convey the easement to the neighbor and the second to convey the fee simple subject to that easement, no good reason exists to override the intent of the grantors who use one deed. While support for rejection of the traditional rule is growing,[13] that rule continues to have some steadfast adherents. As late as 1987, the New York Court of Appeals applied the traditional rule on the ground of "overriding considerations of the 'public policy favoring certainty in title to real property, both to protect bona fide purchasers and to avoid conflicts of ownership, which may engender needless litigation.' "[14] This reasoning is unpersuasive. If the recording system does not provide effective notice to bona fide purchasers of the existence of an easement reserved for a stranger, such purchasers should not be bound by such an easement, but it does not follow that the grantee of the fee simple and successors should not abide by the terms of the deed through which they claim.

Easements created by implication are of three basic types: (1) Easements implied from quasi-easements; (2) easements of ingress and egress implied from necessity; and (3) easements implied from representations relied upon by purchasers of land. One could argue that no easement should ever be implied because this allows the creation of an interest in land without the writing demanded by the Statute of Frauds. However, the courts have consistently treated such easements as exceptions to the legislative ban and have rationalized the result by interpreting the description of the land conveyed to include the easement as an appurtenance.[15]

An illustration of an easement implied from a quasi-easement follows. A owns Blackacre and has a house and farm dwellings on the north half, with a clearly defined road across the south half to a major highway. There is also a highway to the north so that A could have access by that route, but the highway itself is a poor one and the hilly, rocky terrain makes such a way difficult. A cannot be said to have an easement across the south half of A's own land, but A does have a quasi-easement and the north half is quasi-dominant land, the south half quasi-servient, i.e., the facts show an interest in the nature of an easement. If B buys the

12. See the discussion and citation of authorities in Willard v. First Church of Christ, Scientist, Pacifica, 7 Cal.3d 473, 102 Cal.Rptr. 739, 498 P.2d 987 (1972), which rejected the traditional position. However, the court declared in a footnote that an exception, unlike a reservation, "cannot vest an interest in the third party, and the excepted interest remains in the grantor."

No reason for this distinction was stated.

13. Id. Accord, Restatement of Property § 472 (1944).

14. Estate of Thomson v. Wade, 69 N.Y.2d 570, 574, 516 N.Y.S.2d 614, 615, 509 N.E.2d 309, 310 (1987).

15. 3 Tiffany, Real Property 254 (3d ed. 1939).

north half, B would undoubtedly expect to have the same access A had to the buildings. B should require A to make an express grant of such an easement across the retained half, but, if the parties fail to do so, a court will imply the easement by way of grant, unless the parties negate any intent to create such an interest. If B buys the south half of Blackacre rather than the north, the problem changes slightly. If any easement is implied, it must arise by way of reservation in A, since the quasi-servient land is being conveyed first. This would mean that A would be claiming an easement in derogation of the grant and, if a warranty deed were used, would be creating an incumbrance against the terms of his deed. For this reason, most courts are more reluctant to imply an easement in favor of a grantor (by way of reservation) than in favor of a grantee (by way of grant) and will do so only if it is strictly necessary to the enjoyment of the land.[16] Some courts do not make this distinction and will imply an easement whenever it is reasonably required for the enjoyment of the land, regardless of whether it is a reservation or a grant.[17]

Easements for ingress and egress may be implied by necessity, regardless of the prior use of the land. In the previous hypothetical case, if no highway had existed to the north an easement would have been implied in favor of either party to prevent the creation of a land-locked tract. The right of way would have been strictly necessary for the enjoyment of the north half of Blackacre and would have been implied even if no roadway across the south half had existed at the time of severance. The key here is strict necessity although a practical, as distinguished from an absolute, necessity will suffice.[18] Easements implied from necessity are said to be based upon the presumed intention of the parties; the implication will not be invoked unless both the dominant and servient tracts were once under a common ownership.[19] If, at one time, there had been unity of title, the way by necessity may lie dormant through many transfers of title and yet pass with each transfer as appurtenant to the dominant estate and be exercised at a much later date by the holder of the easement.[20] In spite of the emphasis on intent, it should be noted that public policy plays a large role and that full utilization of the land requires some sort of access to isolated tracts. Where this access can be furnished by a statute allowing eminent domain proceedings for land-locked owners, courts may cease to imply such easements.[21]

16. Mitchell v. Castellaw, 151 Tex. 56, 246 S.W.2d 163 (1952).

17. Walker v. Witt, 4 Ill.2d 16, 122 N.E.2d 175 (1954).

18. Flood v. Earle, 145 Me. 24, 71 A.2d 55 (1950); 19 Or.L.Rev. 362, 365 (1940).

19. Simonton, Ways By Necessity, 25 Col.L.Rev. 571, 575 (1925).

20. Finn v. Williams, 376 Ill. 95, 33 N.E.2d 226, 133 A.L.R. 1390 (1941).

21. Simonson v. McDonald, 131 Mont. 494, 311 P.2d 982 (1957).

If the easement was implied because of strict necessity, it will continue only so long as the necessity exists, whereas if it was implied from a quasi-easement it may continue indefinitely.[22] While most types of easements, including sewage disposal rights which can be very important,[23] may be created by implication, easements for light and air cannot arise in this country either by implication or prescription. They can be created only by express agreement.[24]

Easements may be implied from representations relied upon by purchasers of land. A common example is the implied easement in purchasers of lots to use streets shown on a plat.[25] Representations by vendors that purchasers will obtain recreational and similar interests in nearby land have been held to have that effect, despite the Statute of Frauds, unless the interests are so poorly defined as to make judicial enforcement extremely difficult or impossible. An Arizona case held that lot purchasers could require that land shown on brochures as a golf course continue to be so used.[26] An Idaho case similarly held that representations to purchasers that neighboring land owned by the vendor was subject to a "scenic easement" restricting it to existing uses were enforceable.[27] But a Texas case deemed too vague representations that lot purchasers would have "all the pleasure rights" in a 1,000–acre ranch shown on a plat.[28] Note that each of these three cases involved claims of rights to prevent most uses of the servient land by the owners of that land.

Many easements are created by prescription or adverse user. If adverse possession for a statutory period can ripen into a fee simple title, it ought to follow that adverse use of a right of way, drain, support wall, etc., should create an easement. Interestingly enough, the statutes of limitation were usually drafted to apply only to possession, not to use, so that incorporeal rights were not necessarily created by long continued use of land for purposes in the nature of an easement. Fortunately, the courts have filled

---

22. Martinelli v. Luis, 213 Cal. 183, 1 P.2d 980 (1931).

23. Wiesel v. Smira, 49 R.I. 246, 142 A. 148, 58 A.L.R. 818 (1928).

24. Maioriello v. Arlotta, 364 Pa. 557, 73 A.2d 374 (1950). England has a doctrine of ancient lights which does allow such easements to be created by prescription. The Pennsylvania court did not rule out all possibility of an implied easement but found no cases in which it had been allowed. A Georgia statute authorizes implied grants of easements for light and air. Goddard v. Irby, 255 Ga. 47, 335 S.E.2d 286 (1985).

25. Highway Holding Co. v. Yara Engineering Corp., 22 N.J. 119, 123 A.2d 511 (1956). Comment, 55 Mich.L. Rev. 885 (1957).

26. Shalimar Ass'n v. D.O.C. Enterprises, Ltd., 142 Ariz. 36, 688 P.2d 682 (App.1984).

27. Thomas v. Campbell, 107 Idaho 398, 690 P.2d 333 (1984).

28. Drye v. Eagle Rock Ranch, Inc., 364 S.W.2d 196 (Tex.1962).

this legislative gap and the period of the basic statute has been adopted by analogy as a basis for presuming a grant of an easement.[29] Having seized the statute of limitation analogy, the courts have tended to adopt its refinements as well, so that tacking by successive adverse users is allowed, if privity is present between them, disabilities toll the running of the period, etc.

Prescription means literally, "before written," and the common-law theory was that since the use had continued for so long (at one stage the phrase immemorial usage was much in vogue) it must have been based on a lost grant. This rationale made some sense in England, which had no recording system, but loses most of its appeal in this country, where the writing should have been recorded, if it existed. Of course, the lost grant was only a fiction anyway and the cases are full of learned discussions as to the kind of presumption of lost grant raised by the passage of time.[30]

If a prescription of lost grant is the true basis, then acquiescence of the fee owner in the use is material since it strengthens the fiction that at some time such a right was granted to the user. A letter of protest, forbidding the use to continue, written while the easement was still inchoate, would thus seem to be fatal to a prescriptive right since it negatives acquiescence. In fact, many cases so hold, thereby drawing a sharp distinction between prescription and adverse possession.[31] However, if the true basis is the adverseness of the use, the protest would seem to strengthen the case for the claimant and would not prevent the acquisition of the easement. Moreover, when a landowner remains silent in the face of use of the land by another, is that silence to be deemed acquiescence or consent?[32] The latter defeats claims of prescription as well as adverse possession. Some courts have wisely jettisoned the acquiescence requirement.[33]

Most courts agree that the adverse possession requirement of exclusiveness should not be applied to prescription, though some courts disagree.[34] It clearly is essential to a claim of a possessory estate to show that the claimant excluded others, but a claim of a non-possessory interest, such as a right to use a private road, is not inconsistent with uses by others, including the owner of the fee.

---

29. Parker and Edgarton v. Foote, 19 Wend. (N.Y.) 309 (1838).

30. O'Banion v. Borba, 32 Cal.2d 145, 195 P.2d 10 (1948).

31. Dartnell v. Bidwell, 115 Me. 227, 98 A. 743, 5 A.L.R. 1320 (1916).

32. Some courts surmount this impasse by invoking presumptions. Lunt v. Kitchens, 123 Utah 488, 260 P.2d 535 (1953).

33. Masid v. First State Bank, 213 Neb. 431, 329 N.W.2d 560 (1983).

34. Note, Exclusiveness in the Law of Prescription, 8 Cardozo L.Rev. 611 (1987).

B. TRANSFER

At this point, distinctions between easements appurtenant and in gross and profits a prendre become relevant. The easement appurtenant is a parasite attached to its host land, the dominant estate, and it has no life separate from that estate. When the dominant estate is transferred the easement follows along with it, even if not mentioned in the deed either specifically or under the catch all, "and other appurtenances." [35] If the grantor of the dominant estate wishes to prevent the transfer of the appurtenant easement to his grantee, this can be done by a proper provision in the deed, but this may extinguish the easement.[36] It will not normally change the easement into one in gross in the hands of the grantor.[37] Profits a prendre which are appurtenant to other land follow the same rules of transfer.

It is the right in gross which has caused difficulty. The profit in gross was an inheritable and assignable interest even in the early days.[38] As has been noted earlier, the English courts did not even recognize easements in gross, other than profits. This possibly was a manifestation of their pervasive antipathy for restraints on alienation of estates.[39] Easements, which of course impair alienability of the servient land, could be justified only if they benefited other land, according to the English judges. This view failed to recognize that some easements in gross confer enormous benefits to commercial enterprises and to the public, albeit not to other land. Two examples: easements for utility lines and for historic preservation. In England, some worthy, if not indispensable, easements in gross have been made possible by acts of Parliament.[40] While American courts recognize easements in gross, the reluctance by some of them to allow transfer of such easements may have been influenced by the English judicial rejection of easements in gross.

American courts, while sometimes expressing doubt about the transferability of any easement in gross, have approved the trans-

35. See Stockdale v. Yerden, 220 Mich. 444, 190 N.W. 225, 226 (1922).

36. Cadwalader v. Bailey, 17 R.I. 495, 23 A. 20, 14 L.R.A. 300 (1891).

37. "If the purpose of the provision is to change the easement appurtenant into an easement in gross, it will have this effect if, and only if, the manner or the terms of the creation of the easement permit such a change to be made." Restatement, Property, § 487, comment b (1944).

38. Post v. Pearsall, 22 Wend. (N.Y.) 425 (1839).

39. Sturley, Easements in Gross, 96 Law Q.Rev. 557 (1980).

40. Sturley, The "Land Obligation": An English Proposal for Reform, 55 S.Cal.L.Rev. 1417, 1422–1424 (1982) (referring to such easements as "statutory easements").

ferability of commercial easements in gross when faced with a decision.[41] But they typically declare or hold that non-commercial easements in gross are not transferable.[42] The rule of non-transferability of non-commercial easements in gross makes sense in those instances in which it was the understanding of the parties to the creation of the easements that they not be transferable.[43] An example would be a grant to "X, personally," to use a road on the grantor's adjoining land. If, however, the understanding was that the easement be transferable, is there any good reason for forbidding transfer? Certainly easements in gross for public interests, such as historic preservation easements, should be transferable, and they often are made transferable by statute. But there may be justifiable doubt about transferability of easements solely for personal benefit, such as a non-commercial right to fish in a neighbor's pond, even if granted expressly to the grantee, "his heirs and assigns." The pertinent issue in this instance is whether the permanent restraint on alienability is justified by the relatively unsubstantial interests served.[44]

<hr>

C. SCOPE

<hr>

Conflict between the holder of an easement and the owner of the servient land is built into this split of property rights. The easement may be indispensable to the owner of the dominant land and the pressure to increase the use may be irresistible as economic conditions change. The increase in benefit causes a corresponding increase in burden and a lawsuit develops.

Litigation over the scope of easements is usually a product of either (1) failure by the drafter of a grant of an easement to define the easement precisely or (2) inherent vagueness in implied and prescriptive easements. In such instances, courts typically apply a standard of reasonableness. Thus, a grant of a right of way that was silent as to its height was construed as limited to a reasonable height.[45] Also, a right of way acquired by adverse use by horse-drawn vehicles to benefit a farm probably would embrace use in

41. Miller v. Lutheran Conference and Camp Ass'n, 331 Pa. 241, 200 A. 646, 130 A.L.R. 1245 (1938); Note, The Easement in Gross Revisited: Transferability and Divisibility Since 1945, 39 Vand.L.Rev. 109 (1986).

42. Id.

43. Estate of Thomson v. Wade, 69 N.Y.2d 570, 516 N.Y.S.2d 614, 509 N.E.2d 309 (1987); Maw v. Weber Basin Water Conservancy Dist., 20 Utah 2d 195, 436 P.2d 230 (1968).

44. Restatement of Property § 491 (1944).

45. Sakansky v. Wein, 86 N.H. 337, 169 A. 1 (1933). See also State by Wash. Wildlife Preservation v. State, 329 N.W.2d 543 (Minn.1983).

later years by motor vehicles to benefit a new factory on the farm, in the absence of material increase in actual burden on the servient land.[46] But one should not ignore the California decision that a prescriptive right of way benefiting a farm could not be used to reach a nudist colony on the farm.[47]

It seems axiomatic that an easement appurtenant to one tract cannot be used for the benefit of another tract owned by the easement holder, even if use benefiting the latter does not increase the actual burden on the servient land. This position has general judicial support,[48] but one commentator has argued that uses on non-appurtenant land owned by the easement holder should be allowed so long as there is no actual unreasonable increase in burden.[49] The argument is that the reasonableness standard, that is applied to allow changes in uses of the servient and dominant estates, should also be applied in this context. One recent decision accepts this argument—at least as a basis for denying equitable relief sought by the servient owner.[50]

Separate conveyances by an easement holder to two or more grantees may create a surcharge. Suppose that a farmer who has an appurtenant easement to cross a neighbor's land subdivides the farm into hundreds of residential lots. Although this results in an increase in traffic, it will not necessarily be a surcharge. Whether it is such depends largely upon whether, at the time of creation of the right of way, it should have been contemplated that the farm would be subdivided into residential lots.[51] Conceptually, splitting of easements in gross is more likely to result in excessive use, since the needs of an appurtenant tract are not a limiting factor, but surcharge is not a necessary consequence, and division of the easement in gross may be allowed.[52] A sixteenth-century English case required that multiple grantees of a profit a prendre for mining exercise their interests in a single enterprise, such as a partnership—"one stock," as the court put it.[53] While this requirement for profits a prendre and other easements in gross has been stated in some American judicial opinions, it has rarely been applied.[54] It has

46. S.S. Kresge Co. v. Winkelman Realty Co., 260 Wis. 372, 50 N.W.2d 920 (1952).

47. Bartholomew v. Staheli, 86 Cal. App.2d 844, 195 P.2d 824 (1948).

48. S.S. Kresge Co. v. Winkleman Realty Co., 260 Wis. 372, 50 N.W.2d 920 (1952).

49. Kratovil, Easement Law and Service of Non–Dominant Tenements: Time for a Change, 24 Santa Clara L.Rev. 649 (1984).

50. Brown v. Voss, 105 Wash.2d 366, 715 P.2d 514 (1986).

51. Wood v. Ashby, 122 Utah 580, 253 P.2d 351 (1952); Restatement of Property § 488 (1944).

52. Miller v. Lutheran Conference & Camp Ass'n, 331 Pa. 241, 200 A. 646, 130 A.L.R. 1245 (1938).

53. Mountjoy's Case, 78 Eng.Rep. 11 (1583).

54. Note, The Easement in Gross Revisited: Transferability and Divisibility Since 1945, 39 Vand.L.Rev. 109 (1986). The requirement was misapplied in one case, Miller v. Lutheran Camp Ass'n, 331 Pa. 241, 200 A. 646, 130 A.L.R. 1245

also been criticized as obsolete.[55] In a period in history when commercial enterprises were relatively small, it may have been realistic to suppose that two companies would mine more ore than one, but one of today's corporate giants could easily out-produce a multitude of small entrepreneurs.

Division of easements in gross may be excessive for a reason having nothing to do with the nature or extent of physical usage, namely, competition by a grantee of a non-exclusive easement in gross with the servient owner in the sale of easements in gross.[56]

D.　TERMINATION

An easement may expire by its own terms. Like any other interest in land, it may be created for the life of the holder only or it may be designed for a particular purpose and end when the purpose is accomplished.[57] As previously noted, an easement implied from necessity will cease when the necessity ceases. Most easements, however, have a potentially unlimited duration and some specific action is required to terminate them. It is elementary that union of the dominant and servient estates in a single owner causes the easement to merge into the fee.[58] This is but another way of saying that one cannot have an easement in one's own land.[59]

Termination by estoppel, abandonment,[60] and prescription are all closely related. While non-use is not enough, if the servient owner thinks this means abandonment and makes substantial improvements, to the knowledge of the holder of the easement, the latter may be estopped to assert rights in the future.[61] Abandonment is the most frequent method of termination of the three just mentioned, but it requires a proof of intent to release all rights,

(1938), where the servient owner was not even a party.

55. Note, supra note 56.

56. Restatement of Property § 493, comment c (1944).

57. Griffin v. Dwyer, 181 Okl. 71, 72 P.2d 349 (1937).

58. Dimoff v. Laboroff, 296 Mich. 325, 296 N.W. 275 (1941).

59. Lake Bluff v. Dalitsch, 415 Ill. 476, 114 N.E.2d 654 (1953); Matteodo v. Ricci, 56 R.I. 208, 184 A. 573 (1936).

60. In Aggregate Supply Co. v. Sewell, 217 Ga. 407, 122 S.E.2d 580 (1961) the court held that a profit a prendre (in this case the right to remove sand and gravel from the land of another), being a corporeal interest, was not subject to termination by abandonment. This position conflicts with the Restatement of Property, § 450, Special Note, view that there are no significant distinctions in American law between easements and profits.

61. Trimble v. King, 131 Ky. 1, 114 S.W. 317 (1908).

and this can be a troublesome point.[62] Non-use is some evidence but overt physical acts by the holder, such as plowing the land formerly used to reach the easement or building a fence across the old way, are normally required. If non-use by the holder is coupled with an inconsistent use of the servient land for the statutory period by the servient owner, the easement will be extinguished by prescription.[63] Note that abandonment and estoppel do not require the passage of any particular period of time.

Destruction of the servient estate and failure to record an express easement may also lead to termination. The former type of extinguishment is most likely to arise in party wall situations or in easements of passage through a building subsequently destroyed by fire.[64] If a b.f.p. buys servient land subject to an unrecorded easement that is not apparent from physical evidence of its use, the easement will be extinguished. However, since the recording system does not apply to easements created by prescription or implication and since there is no written instrument to record in either case, the purchaser, even without notice, will take the land subject to these interests.[65]

SECTION 2.   LICENSES

The license is the least important of the rights in the land of another. A great deal has been written about this elusive interest but much of it turns out to be a lesson in semantics. Even that master of analysis, Professor Hohfeld, called it a "chameleon-hued term . . . a word of convenient and seductive obscurity."[66] It has been denied that it is an interest in land at all, but merely shields one from being a trespasser. It is not subject to the Statute of Frauds. Indeed, it has been stated that a licensee operating on the land of another is not entitled to legal protection from interference by third parties, but this seems incorrect on principle since even a trespasser receives some support against acts of a later trespasser.[67]

62. Lindsey v. Clark, 193 Va. 522, 69 S.E.2d 342 (1952).

63. Glatts v. Henson, 31 Cal.2d 368, 188 P.2d 745 (1948).

64. Shirley v. Crabb, 138 Ind. 200, 37 N.E. 130 (1894) held that no easement attached to a new building erected on the old site, but Douglas v. Coonley, 156 N.Y. 521, 51 N.E. 283 (1898) seemed to indicate the easement would be suspended and would attach to a new building if and when one was constructed.

65. McKeon v. Brammer, 238 Iowa 1113, 29 N.W.2d 518, 174 A.L.R. 1229 (1947).

66. Hohfeld, Faulty Analysis in Easement and License Cases, 27 Yale L.J. 66, 92 (1917).

67. See Note, 33 Yale L.J. 642 (1924).

Termination at the will of the licensor is the key to the distinction between a license and an easement.[68] Failure to comply with the technical requisites for creating an easement may result in a license, despite the obvious intent of the parties, but this is only another way of saying that the easement is unenforceable.[69] Conversely, some cases hold that a license may become irrevocable because of acts done in reliance on its continuance, but this can only mean that an easement has been created by estoppel.[70]

SECTION 3. REAL COVENANTS AND EQUITABLE SERVITUDES

Suppose that a recorded deed conveying part of the grantor's land contains covenants by the grantor and the grantee that neither the granted parcel nor the retained parcel will ever be used for a non-residential purpose. These promises are intended to bind and benefit not only the promisors and promisees, but also subsequent owners of both parcels. If the latter are bound and benefited, it is obvious that these promises have created interests in land very similar to easements. Most American courts would hold that, in the example given, subsequent owners are indeed bound and benefited, and accordingly have interests in each other's land. These interests commonly are referred to as real covenants (or by the longer term—covenants running with the land) or equitable servitudes. Not all promises by landowners create interests in land. To do so, promises must not only have been intended to run with the land, but also must satisfy certain judicial requirements, in addition to the Statute of Frauds. The meaning and justification of these requirements continue to this day to be uncertain and controversial. This short text can do no more than present the broad contours of this subject.

Assuming that promises will bind successors in ownership of the promisor's land and benefit successors in ownership of the promisee's land, does the promisor remain bound after transfer? The discussion of landlord-tenant law in this book shows that tenants are liable for rent that accrues after assignment of the leasehold. But covenants outside leases have been treated differ-

68. Baseball Publishing Co. v. Bruton, 302 Mass. 54, 18 N.E.2d 362, 119 A.L.R. 1518 (1938).

69. Nelson v. American Tel. and Tel. Co., 270 Mass. 471, 170 N.E. 416 (1930).

70. Stoner v. Zucker, 148 Cal. 516, 83 P. 808 (1906).

ently; promisors have been held not to be bound by defaults occurring after transfer.[71]   This divergence is explained on the ground that the probable intent of the contracting parties in the two instances is different.

A. PRIVITY OF ESTATE

The English courts, manifesting again their wariness of restraints on alienation of estates, flatly refused to allow the burden of covenants to run with the land,[72] except for covenants in leases,[73] which typically would not affect alienability of estates as severely as would covenants attached to the fee simple. In other words, each party to the covenant must have an interest in the affected land—privity of estate—and that privity must be the relationship of landlord and tenant. Of course, this blanket rule precluded the running of covenants the benefit of which would far outweigh their restraint on alienability of the fee. Even running covenants that would enhance alienability of the fee, such as the residential covenants mentioned above, would be prohibited. The English courts were unwilling to evaluate covenants on a case-by-case basis and were unable to devise general rules that would separate the good covenants from the bad ones. This unsatisfactory situation was vastly ameliorated, but not resolved, by the English Court of Chancery in Tulk v. Moxhay,[74] holding that one who acquired land with notice of a covenant restricting its use would be restrained by injunction from violating it. Thus was born the equitable servitude.

American courts are more tolerant than the English courts of attempts to create interests in land by promises. They do not confine the running of burdens of covenants to leases, but they require privity of estate of some kind. The prevailing view is that the privity of estate requirement is satisfied by the grantor-grantee relationship, as in the example mentioned at the beginning of this section.[75]   Another view finds the requisite privity of estate only where the covenant concerns an easement.[76]   But American courts stop short of allowing the relationship between owners of neighboring lands to qualify. Thus, promises by neigh-

---

71. Gallagher v. Bell, 69 Md.App. 199, 516 A.2d 1028 (1986); Goldberg v. Nicola, 319 Pa. 183, 178 A. 809 (1935).

72. Keppell v. Bailey, 39 Eng.Rep. 1042 (1834).

73. Spencer's Case, 77 Eng.Rep. 72 (K.B. 1583).

74. 41 Eng.Rep. 1143 (1848).

75. Wheeler v. Schad, 7 Nev. 204 (1871).

76. Morse v. Aldrich, 36 Mass. (19 Pick.) 449 (1837).

bors that their respective lands would never be used for non-residential purposes would bind only those parties—at law. However, successors with notice would be bound—in equity—by virtue of the general acceptance of Tulk v. Moxhay in this country.

There is an entirely different kind of privity of estate that should be distinguished from the relationship required between covenantor and covenantee, which has been called horizontal privity of estate. One who seeks to enforce a covenant, or one against whom enforcement is being sought, must have succeeded to ownership of the land benefitted or burdened by the covenant. This has been called vertical privity of estate. This requirement seems obvious and simple, but it is not. In an important case, it was contended that a home owners' association, owning no land, could not enforce covenants by lot owners to pay assessments for maintenance of common areas, but the association was permitted to sue as a representative of the lot owners, who also owned interests in the common areas.[77] A more difficult issue is whether succession must be to the very estate burdened or benefitted, or only to some interest in the land. For example, suppose that a purchaser of a lot covenants to pay assessments for maintenance and to make only residential use of the lot. The lot owner then leases the lot to a tenant for ten years. The tenant probably would not be required to pay the assessments, but would be bound by the residential use restrictions of which the tenant had notice. This issue was discussed earlier in this book in connection with the running of burdens in leases to sublessees. It may be generalized that in both contexts affirmative covenants run only with the estate burdened, but restrictions on the use of land will bind anyone with notice who takes any interest in the land, and even one who has succeeded to no interest, such as an adverse possessor.[78] This surely is the teaching of Tulk v. Moxhay, which grounds running of the obligation to one with notice on unconscionability. This generalization probably accords with the expectations of the covenanting parties in the example given. But one can imagine examples in which the affirmative-negative test might not effectuate the intent of the covenanting parties. One writer has suggested that an affirmative covenant by lot owners in a development to maintain front lawns should bind any occupier.[79] It may well be that an approach that seeks to effectuate the covenantors' intent would be preferable to the traditional affirmative-negative distinction. After all, the extension by American

77. Neponsit Property Owners' Ass'n v. Emigrant Industrial Savings Bank, 278 N.Y. 248, 15 N.E.2d 793, 118 A.L.R. 973 (1938).

78. The state of authority is discussed in French, Toward a Modern Law of Servitudes: Reweaving the Ancient Strands, 55 S.Cal.L.Rev. 1261, 1273–1275, 1278 (1982).

79. Reichman, Toward a Unified Concept of Servitudes, 55 S.Cal.L.Rev. 1179, 1249 (1982).

courts of Tulk v. Moxhay to enforcement in equity of affirmative covenants has substantially weakened the affirmative-negative dichotomy.

A relaxed position on vertical privity for the running of benefits has been taken. It is said that any lawful possessor may enforce covenants intended to benefit the lessee's land.[80] Thus, a lessee of a lot in a residentially restricted subdivision could have the owner of an adjoining lot restrained from making a commercial use of the land. This means that an adverse possessor cannot enforce, though there seems to be scant authority on the status of an adverse possessor.[81] One might question the fairness of denying enforcement by adverse possessors of the same restrictions to which they are bound in residential developments.

B. TOUCH AND CONCERN

Promises do not become real covenants or equitable servitudes unless they "touch and concern" the estates in land to which they are sought to be attached. The purpose of this requirement is said to be to prevent the serious restraint on alienability of land that might occur if landowners could impose upon subsequent owners obligations totally unrelated to the land of either party. If there were no touch and concern requirement, a grantor of land could, for example, aid the grantor's favorite charity by obtaining from the grantee a covenant expressly binding the grantee and the grantee's successors to contribute sums of money annually forever to that charity.

The discussion of landlord-tenant law elsewhere in this book also addresses this requirement, which applies to covenants in leases as well as to covenants between owners of fees. One might suppose that the touch and concern requirement would be applied more rigorously to covenants between fee owners than to lease covenants, in view of the typically longer duration of the former and the resulting greater restraint upon alienability of land. But discussion of the touch and concern requirement by courts and commentators usually assumes that it has the same meaning in both contexts.

As has been observed in the discussion of landlord-tenant law, there is no litmus test for determining which covenants touch and

80. Id. at 1253.

81. French, supra note 78, at 1275, n. 73.

concern the land involved. The word "touch" does not require physical contact with the land. An eminent jurist declared in a noted opinion that the pertinent question is: "Does the covenant impose, on the one hand, a burden upon an interest in land, which on the other hand increases the value of a different interest in the same or related land?" [82] He then added, however, that "whether a particular covenant is sufficiently connected with the use of land to run with the land, must be in many cases a question of degree." [83] An example of a covenant that clearly touches and concerns is the ubiquitous covenant restricting the use of a lot to residential uses for the benefit of other lots in a subdivision.

The traditional, and still prevailing, view is that both ends of a covenant must touch and concern their respective lands. Suppose that an owner of land abutting a public street promises for X and X's successors, for valuable consideration paid by the city, that no building will be erected within a strip of the promisor's land that the city plans to purchase later for street widening. According to the traditional view, this promise would not bind a purchaser of the land with notice.[84] That is, even though the burden of the covenant clearly touches and concerns the burdened land, the burden will not run because the covenant benefits the city and its inhabitants rather than any identifiable land. This is unfortunate. The apparent assumption of the both-ends-must-touch-and-concern rule that the only benefits sufficiently important to justify imposition of running burdens on land are benefits closely tied to other land is wrong. Its appeal may have been that it spared courts the difficult task of evaluating the worth of an infinite variety of benefits and interests that imaginative drafters might seek to advance through covenants burdening land. Consistency seems to require American courts, which (unlike English courts) allow easements in gross, to permit real covenants and equitable servitudes in gross as well.[85] Defeasible fees restricting land use for benefits in gross also are sanctioned.[86]

There seems to be no good reason for prohibiting in-gross real covenants and equitable servitudes. It has been argued, however, that real covenants and equitable servitudes typically are more burdensome than easements, since the latter typically are "clearly defined, limited interests, affecting only a portion of the servient

82. Lehman, J., in Neponsit Property Owners' Ass'n v. Emigrant Industrial Sav. Bank, 278 N.Y. 248, 257, 15 N.E.2d 793, 796, 118 A.L.R. 973, 979 (1938).

83. Id.

84. London County Council v. Allen, L.R. [1941] 3 K.B. 642, Ann.Cas. 1916C, 1932; Johnson v. State, 27 Or.App. 581, 556 P.2d 724 (1976).

85. Roberts, Promises Respecting Land Use—Can Benefits Be Held in Gross? 51 Mo.L.Rev. 933 (1986).

86. Jost, The Defeasible Fee and the Birth of the Modern Residential Subdivision, 49 Mo.L.Rev. 695 (1984).

land." [87] Some servitudes, such as conservation servitudes, forbid nearly all uses of the land. While many of these servitudes serve purposes generally regarded as laudable, such as preservation of threatened valuable natural environments, there is concern that the coupling of their sweeping scope and their permanence may make it extremely difficult or impossible to meet significant changing needs for land use. [88] Assuming that this is a serious concern, it should be addressed, not by deeming such servitudes barred by the touch and concern rule, but by allowing them subject to limitations in the public interest. [89] The problem is especially appropriate for legislation. Indeed, statutes authorizing conservation restrictions have been enacted by most state legislatures. [90] Interestingly, these statutes refer to such restrictions as "easements"—apparently for the purpose of obtaining favorable judicial responses to anticipated legal challenges. [91]

Unlike servitudes in gross, which clearly benefit no land, some servitudes confer benefits that raise a debatable issue of compliance with the touch and concern requirement. A covenant by a grantee of land not to compete with a business enterprise on the grantor's remaining land has been viewed by a few courts as benefitting the covenantee's business rather than land. The highest court of Massachusetts adhered to that view until 1979, when it overruled its prior decisions and adopted the realistic and overwhelming majority view that such a covenant enhances the value of the covenantee's land and that this benefit is sufficient to satisfy the touch and concern requirement. [92]

While the burden of a negative covenant restricting the use of the covenantor's land is uniformly deemed to touch and concern that land, the burden of an affirmative covenant to perform some act may, or may not, touch and concern the covenantor's land. Some affirmative covenants, such as a covenant to maintain a boundary wall or to pay a share of the cost of maintaining it, seem to be closely tied to the covenantor's land (although courts have had difficulty with such covenants). But a covenant to pay taxes assessed annually on a neighbor's land would not. Other examples are not so clear. In addition to the difficulty of resolving

87. Korngold, Privately Held Conservation Servitudes: A Policy Analysis in the Context of In–Gross Real Covenants and Easements, 63 Tex.L.Rev. 433, 477 (1984).

88. Id.

89. Id.

90. However, Korngold, supra note 89, maintains that most of these statutes inadequately protect public interests.

91. E.g., the Uniform Conservation Easement Act, 12 U.L.A. 51 (Supp. 1987), discussed by Katz, Conserving the Nation's Heritage Using the Uniform Conservation Easement Act, 43 Wash. & Lee L.Rev. 369 (1986).

92. Whitinsville Plaza, Inc. v. Kotseas, 378 Mass. 85, 390 N.E.2d 243 (1979).

close cases on the basis for their perceived relation to the covenantor's land, there is a traditional judicial hostility toward affirmative covenants, whatever their nature. The English courts flatly refused to allow affirmative covenants outside leases to run.[93] The Court of Appeals of New York initially adopted that position, but then proceeded to riddle it with exceptions.[94] Other courts have manifested a wariness of affirmative covenants, without erecting a barrier to their running. There is merit in the observation that "by the weight of authority and logic, . . . the distinction between 'affirmative' and 'negative' covenants is an anachronism which all too often precludes an analysis of the covenant itself. . . ."[95]

Covenants obligating owners of subdivision lots or condominium units to pay assessments for maintenance and improvement of common areas and facilities, such as streets, parks and golf courses, have been challenged frequently on the ground that they do not touch and concern the covenantors' interests in land. Most of these challenges have failed. It can usually be established that such assessments are for expenditures that enhance the value of the burdened lots or units. Moreover, the owners of lots and condominiums typically have an ownership interest (tenancy in common or easement) in the common areas or facilities maintained or improved. Some decisions have been put on the latter ground,[96] but that seems unnecessary.[97] Most courts,[98] but not all,[99] have been unpersuaded by the argument that covenants to pay for golf course maintenance do not touch and concern lots or units because some owners would not desire to play golf. Suppose that the governing rules allow only those owners admitted to membership in a club to use the golf course facilities, but require all owners to pay assessments for maintenance of those facilities. One court held that under those circumstances the covenant to pay assessments did not touch and concern the land.[1] Was this

93. The cases are reviewed and criticized in Bell, Tulk v. Moxhay Revisited, [1981] The Conveyancer and Property Lawyer 55 and Griffith, Tulk v. Moxhay Reclarified, [1983] The Conveyancer and Property Lawyer 29.

94. Neponsit Property Owners' Association v. Emigrant Industrial Sav. Bank, 278 N.Y. 248, 15 N.E.2d 793, 118 A.L.R. 973 (1938).

95. Petersen v. Beekmere, Inc., 117 N.J.Super. 155, 164, 283 A.2d 911, 916 (1971).

96. Neponsit Property Owners' Association v. Emigrant Industrial Sav. Bank, 278 N.Y. 248, 15 N.E.2d 793, 118 A.L.R. 973 (1938).

97. Except, possibly, in New York. Eagle Enterprises, Inc. v. Gross, 39 N.Y.2d 505, 384 N.Y.S.2d 717, 349 N.E.2d 816 (1976).

98. Streams Sports Club, Ltd. v. Richmond, 99 Ill.2d 182, 75 Ill.Dec. 667, 457 N.E.2d 1226 (1983).

99. Raintree Corp. v. Rowe, 38 N.C. App. 664, 248 S.E.2d 904 (1978). But cf. Four Seasons Homeowners Ass'n, Inc. v. Sellers, 62 N.C.App. 205, 302 S.E.2d 848 (1983).

1. Ebbe v. Senior Estates Golf and Country Club, 61 Or.App. 398, 657 P.2d 696 (1983).

court really objecting to the unfairness of the burden, rather than its relationship to land? Several baffling touch and concern cases have been explained by commentators on the ground that courts were actually guided by other unarticulated policies.[2]

C. IMPLIED COVENANTS

In view of judicial acceptance of implied easements, one would suppose that courts also would readily recognize implied covenants. Most do, but some, notably the highest court of Massachusetts, invoking the Statute of Frauds, do not.[3] The issue commonly arises when an owner of a large parcel of land subdivides it into lots suitable for residential development and inserts in most, but not all, deeds covenants restricting the land to residential use. Most courts conclude that such circumstances indicate that purchasers from the subdivider understood that all lots were intended to be restricted, and that understanding will be given effect. The Supreme Court of Michigan, in a leading opinion, characterized the implied interest, "[f]or want of a better description," "a reciprocal negative easement."[4] It is not clear why "implied covenant" or "implied servitude" would not have been sufficiently descriptive. This problem of deeds to some lots not containing express restrictions can easily be prevented from occurring by recording, prior to sale of any lot, a declaration of restrictions applicable to all lots.

Implied covenants may also come into existence as a result of representations relied upon by purchasers.[5] Easements, as has been observed earlier, may come into existence in the same way. Court opinions are inconsistent in terminology here. It should make no difference whether the implied interest is called an easement or a covenant (or servitude), but some opinions suggest that the characterization affects the decision as to whether the interest should be implied. A Texas opinion using easement terminology indicated that the court's decision not to imply was possibly affected by the English courts' refusal to recognize new types of easements.[6] Novelty would have been irrelevant to resolving a claim of implied covenant. An Arizona court, af-

2. French, Toward a Modern Law of Servitudes: Reweaving the Ancient Strands, 55 S.Cal.L.Rev. 1261, 1289–1292 (1982).

3. Sprague v. Kimball, 213 Mass. 380, 100 N.E. 622 (1913).

4. Sanborn v. McLean, 233 Mich. 227, 230, 206 N.W. 496, 497, 60 A.L.R. 1212, 1214 (1925).

5. Warren v. Detlefsen, 281 Ark. 196, 663 S.W.2d 710 (1984).

6. Drye v. Eagle Rock Ranch, Inc., 364 S.W.2d 196 (Tex.1962).

firming an injunction restraining a successor to ownership of a golf course from using it for other uses, reasoned that this land had been impliedly restricted by the developer's representations. This court distinguished a prior case on the ground that it involved an implied easement, while the instant case involved an implied covenant.[7] However, that court proceeded to minimize the difference in terminology by declaring: "We recognize that the rights we uphold here have been referred to as equitable easements, implied easements, equitable servitudes, implied equitable servitudes, implied grants, implied restrictive covenants, and rights arising by estoppel. The nomenclature used in the reported decisions is not consistent. Suffice it to say we are satisfied that 'implied restrictive covenant' sufficiently describes what exists here."[8]

There is another very important role played by implication. Even express covenants sometimes are silent or unclear as to the lands intended to be benefited. This gap must be filled by implication. Assume that a subdivider conveyed all lots in the subdivision with express covenants obligating the grantees and their successors to make only residential use of their lots. A narrow inference would be that the sole purpose of these restrictions was to benefit the subdivider in facilitating the sale of unsold lots. A somewhat broader inference would be that the subdivider was intended to have the power to enforce covenants on behalf of purchasers. Neither of these inferences would enable lot owners to sue in their own behalf—which would be the only effective assurance of enforcement. Most courts adopt the inference that all lot owners were intended to be benefited.[9] The commonly stated requirement that there must have been sufficient evidence of this intent when the first lot was sold seems insuperable in those instances where there was nothing more or little more than insertion of the residential restrictive covenant in the deed to the first lot. Most courts, however, including some that view the Statute of Frauds as a bar to implication of covenants, admit, as evidence of the existence of a residential development from the beginning, the uniformity revealed by restrictions in subsequent deeds by the subdivider to other lots.[10] But a few courts, invoking the parol evidence rule and the Statute of Frauds, exclude such evidence and other extrinsic evidence.[11] The unfortunate result in those jurisdictions is frustration of the residential development

---

7. Shalimar Ass'n v. D.O.C. Enterprises, Ltd., 142 Ariz. 36, 688 P.2d 682 (App.1984).

8. Id. at 43, 688 P.2d at 689.

9. Snow v. Van Dam, 291 Mass. 477, 197 N.E. 224 (1935).

10. Id.

11. Werner v. Graham, 181 Cal. 174, 183 P. 945 (1919). See also Riley v. Bear Creek Planning Committee, 17 Cal.3d 500, 131 Cal.Rptr. 381, 551 P.2d 1213 (1976).

plan. Of course, the careful subdivider avoids this problem by recording a properly drafted declaration of restrictions at the outset.

Even in instances in which it is established that residential restrictive covenants were intended for the benefit of all lot owners, there may be uncertainty as to the territorial extent of the subdivision. An owner of a large tract who subdivides parts of it over time intends either that each subdivision be separate or that it be part of a comprehensive development. If this intent is not clearly expressed in a declaration, a court must rely upon extrinsic evidence, if admissible in the jurisdiction.[12]

D.   ADAPTATION TO THE FUTURE

(1)   Construction

Drafters of real covenants and equitable servitudes, as well as other documents, often fail to address expressly events and circumstances that later occur. When this happens, courts must seek to ascertain the imperfectly manifested intent of the parties.

This process is influenced, when land use restrictions are involved, by a traditional constructional bias in favor of free use of land. Unfortunately, this bias in many instances may defeat the probable actual intent and significant policies other than free alienability of land. An example is the construction of a covenant forbidding "erecting" of non-residential structures as allowing non-residential use of existing residential structures.[13] The parties surely did not intend this result, which also threatens the policy of allowing landowners to establish and maintain exclusively residential neighborhoods. Many courts are now adopting the "modern viewpoint" rejecting the constructional bias against land use restrictions.[14]

Construction of covenants may also be influenced by policies other than anti-restriction bias. A recurring issue is whether restrictive residential covenants should be construed as allowing occupancy of a residence by a small number (four or five) of mentally handicapped persons and a supervisor. Treatment of such persons in a non-institutional environment is thought to be beneficial, but neighbors often object. Opposition has resulted in

12. Friedlander v. Hiram Ricker & Sons, Inc., 485 A.2d 965 (Me.1984).

13. Jones v. Park Lane for Convalescents, Inc., 384 Pa. 268, 270, 120 A.2d 535, 537 (1956).

14. Joslin v. Pine River Development Corp., 116 N.H. 814, 817, 367 A.2d 599, 601 (1976).

enactment of zoning ordinances by some local governments forbidding such group homes in residential areas. Some state legislatures have reacted by prohibiting such zoning. Such statutes usually do not forbid restrictive covenants excluding group homes from residential areas, but the policy of such statutes has been extended by at least one court to restrictive covenants.[15] It is apparent that this clash of attitudes toward group homes will have a bearing on construction of covenants where no statute is deemed applicable. Some courts construe the general terms "residential" or "single-family" as allowing group homes.[16] Others do not.[17]

(2) Modification

If all parties agree, they of course can modify covenants to accommodate new conditions. But this may be difficult to accomplish when there are many parties, as there are in the large subdivision or condominium. One dissenter can block change. Consequently, documents creating covenants often seek to authorize easier modification. One obvious approach is to allow modification upon approval by fewer than all of the parties. But even having to obtain approval by a simple majority of owners of lots might be unduly burdensome.

One approach sometimes taken to this problem is stipulation in the covenant document that the restrictions on any lot may be altered or annulled by agreement of that lot owner and the subdivider. Owners of other lots would have no voice in the matter, but would have to rely upon the judgment and good faith of the subdivider and successors. Some courts have held that the effect of this stipulation, even if never exercised, is that no restrictions enforceable by lot owners have been created.[18] The reasoning offered to support this unfortunate result is that retention of this power by the subdivider is decisive evidence that the covenants were intended for the sole benefit of the subdivider, despite other persuasive evidence to the contrary.[19] These courts may well have disliked this device because of its potential for abuse, but their remedy was too drastic. A better solution, which has judicial support, is to view the subdivider's retained amendment power as not precluding creation of an effectively restricted

15. McMillan v. Iserman, 120 Mich. App. 785, 327 N.W.2d 559 (1982).

16. Jackson v. Williams, 714 P.2d 1017 (Okl.1985).

17. Omega Corp. of Chesterfield v. Malloy, 228 Va. 12, 319 S.E.2d 728 (1984).

18. Suttle v. Bailey, 68 N.M. 283, 361 P.2d 325 (1961); Rosi v. McCoy, 79 N.C.App. 311, 338 S.E.2d 792 (1986),

aff'd on other grounds, 319 N.C. 589, 356 S.E.2d 568 (1987).

19. Compare Scott v. Rheudasil, 614 S.W.2d 626 (Tex.Civ.App.1981), holding that the circumstances may establish that lot owners in a residential subdivision were intended to have the right to enforce covenants despite express retention by the developer of the "exclusive" right to enforce.

residential development, but to require that the amendment power be exercised reasonably.[20] A court that does this is, of course, assuming the heavy responsibility of balancing the interests of all owners and making the final decision, without the benefit of standards—a decision possibly much different from that the lot owners would have made.

Another means of providing flexibility is to leave some matters to later decision. A common provision requires approval of building plans by an architectural review committee selected by lot owners, or by the subdivider if no committee is selected. The stated or implicit role of such committees is to approve only buildings deemed aesthetically harmonious with the neighborhood. One judicial view is that the vagueness of such a standard renders it unenforceable.[21] But even provisions authorizing committee approval without any express standard have been held valid and decisions approved if deemed reasonable.[22] The effect of the proposed building on the values of other lots has been considered significant. Committee decisions requiring, for protection of scenic views, building setbacks more stringent than those stated elsewhere in the restrictions have been held invalid on the ground that lot purchasers would not have been on notice that the committee would make such decisions.[23]

When the covenant documents have made inadequate provision for modification, should courts fill the void to relieve hardships? The traditional answer is that courts should not. One case involved a covenant provision limiting assessments for maintenance and improvement of certain facilities to "fifty-five cents (.55) per front foot." [24] When this became an unrealistic limit, threatening the continued viability of the residential development, a court was requested to modify it by allowing a majority of lot owners to change it, or by conforming the stated monetary limit to changing cost of living indices. These requests were denied. This judicial position differs from the willingness of courts to withhold equitable enforcement of covenants rendered obsolete by a change of conditions, discussed hereinafter in connection with termination

20. Moore v. Megginson, 416 So.2d 993 (Ala.1982). The subdivider's waiver power has been held to terminate after divestment of all interest in the subdivision. Armstrong v. Roberts, 254 Ga. 15, 325 S.E.2d 769 (1985).

21. See Seabreak Homeowners Ass'n, Inc. v. Gresser, 517 A.2d 263, 269 (Del.Ch.1986).

22. Rhue v. Cheyenne Homes, Inc., 168 Colo. 6, 449 P.2d 361 (1969).

23. Seabreak Homeowners Ass'n, Inc. v. Gresser, 517 A.2d 263 (Del.Ch.

1986); Davis v. Huey, 620 S.W.2d 561 (Tex.1981).

24. Lake Wauwanoka, Inc. v. Spain, 622 S.W.2d 309 (Mo.App.1981). But cf. Lake Tishomingo Prop. Owners Ass'n v. Cronin, 679 S.W.2d 852 (Mo.1984) (en banc), holding that after essential costs had been borne by a majority of owners, the "unique circumstances" of the case imposed an "equitable" obligation on others to share the costs.

of covenants.   Application of the change-of-conditions doctrine to requests for modification of covenants has been recommended.[25] Another approach to this problem is statutory authorization of modification of covenants by less than unanimous consent.[26]   This is less flexible than the suggested judicial approach, but does not burden courts with the difficult discretionary role of reshaping covenants to meet changing conditions.

C. TERMINATION

Restrictive covenants are sometimes drafted so that they will expire by their own terms, i.e., made binding for twenty, thirty, or forty years only.   This is a desirable practice because they tend to outlive their usefulness in about a generation and this builds in a device for the automatic clearing of the title with the passage of time.   In the bulk of the cases this is not done, however, and the covenants therefore have a potentially infinite duration as an interest in land.   Because of this fact, various statutes have been passed to eliminate stale restrictions after the passage of time. The legislation falls into four basic patterns: (1) The "substantial benefit" type, providing that if the restriction ceases to be of substantial benefit to the person for whom created, it is void; (2) the "fixed period of duration" type, terminating the restriction at the end of a gross period; (3) the "marketable title type," requiring a re-recording of the restrictions within a certain period in order for them to remain valid; and (4) the "inalienability type," prohibiting the transfer of the benefit.[27]   Many states have no such legislation and the parties will have to rely on non-statutory methods of extinguishment, such as release, merger, waiver, abandonment, and change in neighborhood conditions.

The party who has the right to enforce a covenant may release that right just as any other interest in land may be surrendered to the fee owner.   Merger occurs when the title to property subject to the covenant is acquired by the owner of property for whose benefit the restriction was imposed.   Resale of the previously burdened lots will not cause a resurrection of the

25. French, Toward a Modern Law of Servitudes: Reweaving the Ancient Strands, 55 S.Cal.L.Rev. 1261, 1317 (1982).

26. See Uniform Planned Community Act, 52–118, 74 U.L.A. § 2–118 (Supp.1981).

27. Simes, Elimination of Stale Restrictions on the Use of Land, A.B.A. Section of Real Property, Probate and Trust Law (1954).

covenant unless it is expressly created anew. A court of equity may refuse to enforce a covenant because of the acquiescence of the lot owners in such substantial violations as to amount to abandonment of the covenant or a waiver of the right to insist on compliance with its terms. Equity may also refuse to enforce the restriction because of such a change of conditions in the restricted area that it is impossible to secure, in any significant degree, the benefits sought to be realized by the covenant.[28]

This refusal by the chancellor to enforce the covenant is another example of equity's discretionary role and does not, in fact, terminate the covenant since it may still be possible to recover damages at law for the breach,[29] thus leaving the title in an unmerchantable state. Moreover, if the covenant is construed as a condition, creating a possibility of reverter or a power of termination, it is doubtful whether changed neighborhood conditions will affect the result.[30]

There is a serious question as to whether the changes must occur within the restricted area or whether the general alteration in the community outside the area, but in close proximity to it, will suffice.[31] Failure to require the changes to take place within the area can lead to destruction of the very plan for which the restrictions were created since once the buffer zone of border lots goes commercial, the pressures on the rest of the residential area become irresistible. But in some instances, border lots may become useless. Is it sufficient to say that this risk was assumed by purchasers of border lots? A compromise suggestion is that interior lot owners be entitled only to damages unless they compensate border lot owners for the consequences of an injunction.[32]

Covenants can be extinguished by condemnation of the burdened land, as where the city takes a tract in the heart of a residential area for municipal purposes. Since the taking permits a use inconsistent with the continuance of the covenant, it is no longer effective as to the condemned land, although the remaining land in the area may still be burdened. The courts are split on the issue of compensation for thus depriving the neighboring

28. Cowling v. Colligan, 158 Tex. 458, 312 S.W.2d 943 (1958). See also West Alameda Heights Homeowners Ass'n v. Board of Commissioners, 169 Colo. 491, 458 P.2d 253 (1969).

29. St. Lo Construction Co. v. Koenigsberger, 174 F.2d 25 (D.C.Cir. 1949); Pound, The Progress of the Law, 1918–1919, 33 Harv.L.Rev. 813, 820 (1920).

30. Goldstein, Rights of Entry and Possibilities of Reverter as Devices to Restrict the Use of Land, 54 Harv.L. Rev. 248 (1940). Changed neighborhood conditions will not result in the termination of an easement. Waldrop v. Town of Brevard, 233 N.C. 26, 62 S.E.2d 512 (1950).

31. Downs v. Kroeger, 200 Cal. 743, 254 P. 1101 (1927).

32. Comment, 31 UCLA L.Rev. 226, 250 (1983).

landowners of the benefit of their covenants.[33] Some courts indicate that the loss is damnum absque injuria because no property right in the strict sense is involved; others are more pragmatic and see the requirement of compensation as an unnecessary burden on the sovereign right of eminent domain. On principle, however, compensation should be paid since a covenant is analytically like an easement which is clearly a property right for this purpose. Moreover, compensation is not limited to tangible property interests but includes the right of use and enjoyment.

Although restrictive covenants can be extinguished by the power of the state, exercised through eminent domain, the police power, exercised through zoning regulations, does not ordinarily have this effect.[34] The private covenants may be more restrictive than the zoning and if so, they continue to control. If the zoning is more restrictive it will control. The development plan for the area, reflected in the zoning ordinances, may be used to show changing neighborhood conditions, however, and in that sense may lead to effective termination of the covenants.

E. REFORM AND UNIFICATION

The common law of easements, real covenants and equitable servitudes is plagued by inconsistency, confusing terminology and inadequate policy orientation. This body of law cries out for comprehensive clarification, reformulation and change.

Attempts to answer these cries were mounted during the decade of the 1980's. Several legal scholars addressed this problem in the law journals.[35] The American Law Institute undertook in 1987 to draft the Restatement of the Law, Third, Property—Servitudes. That project had not been completed when this book went to press.

There is much support for unification of both doctrine and terminology. Many scholars agree that there is no need for the separate concepts of easements, real covenants and equitable servitudes; all serve substantially the same function.[36] Why, for example, should courts allow easements in gross, but not cove-

---

33. Wells v. City of Dunbar, 142 W.Va. 332, 95 S.E.2d 457 (1956); Recent Decisions, 1957 U.Ill.L.F. 133.

34. See Berger, Conflicts Between Zoning Ordinances and Restrictive Covenants, 43 Neb.L.Rev. 449 (1964); Note, 24 Van.L.Rev. 1031 (1971).

35. Particularly significant are the symposium articles in 55 S.Cal.L.Rev. 1177 (1982).

36. The leading exponents: Reichman, Toward a Unified Concept of Servitudes, Id. (1982); French, Toward a Modern Law of Servitudes: Reweaving the Ancient Strands, Id. at 1261.

nants in gross? Other scholars, however, have expressed concern that unification could eliminate distinctions that ought to be preserved.[37] It is pointed out, for example, that easements, but neither real covenants nor equitable servitudes, may be acquired by prescription. Perhaps such objections to unification underestimate the capacity of formulators of new doctrine to accommodate some diversity within a single comprehensive concept.

The need for reform, of course, goes far beyond unification. Legal restraints on freedom of contract and conveyance should be recognized only to the extent that they are justified by contemporary policies. There clearly is no need for the horizontal privity of estate requirement. One may safely predict that it will not survive in The Restatement of the Law, Third, Property—Servitudes. Other restrictions also will fall. Professor Susan F. French, the Reporter (principal drafter) of that restatement, concluded in an article published prior to her appointment that "[o]nce the courts possess the means to terminate obsolete agreements, the parties should be free to make any agreements that suit their purpose." [38] She recommended replacing the touch and concern requirement with a broadened change of conditions doctrine reformulated to limit judicial enforcement of burdens on land use, whatever their traditional label, at any time when a court determines that they are unreasonable. Another scholar would go further, by limiting freedom to impose burdens on land only by requiring recordation.[39] These and similar proposals for almost unlimited freedom to burden the use of land can be expected to be received by some with skepticism that they adequately protect interests of successors in ownership of burdened land.

Legislation may be necessary to accomplish needed reforms. Even if (or especially if) the new restatement of servitudes substantially reorders its formulation of this body of law, judicial acceptance will require many years, and may never occur. Assuming judicial eagerness to embrace the new restatement, courts must wait for litigated cases raising the pertinent issues. When they come, the opportunity for reform may be blocked by *stare decisis*. Legislation would be much quicker, and arguably also better in other respects. One critic has asserted that the proposed judicial doctrine denying or qualifying enforcement of unreasonable burdens on land use would exacerbate the problem of uncer-

---

37. L. Berger, Unification of the Law of Servitudes, 55 S.Cal.L.Rev. 1339 (1982).

38. French, Toward a Modern Law of Servitudes: Reweaving the Ancient Strands, 55 S.Cal.L.Rev. 1261, 1306 (1982).

39. Epstein, Notice and Freedom of Contract in the Law of Servitudes, 55 S.Cal.L.Rev. 1353 (1982).

tainty in land titles.[40] One solution he prefers is a specific
statutory time limit on duration of land use burdens. But such
rigidity may defeat the reasonable expectations of those who
create burdens. Who can say how long residential restrictions
should be enforced—in all neighborhoods? Even a generous specific time limit for residential restrictions would not satisfy those
persons and organizations seeking to utilize conservation easements. This difficulty could be ameliorated to some extent by
statutory provision of several time periods for varying types of
burdens, but some undesirable inflexibility would remain. Even
relatively short time periods would not handle satisfactorily burdens that are unreasonable when first imposed upon a successor.
It appears that there will be roles for both courts and legislatures
in reforming this body of law.

Should unification be more comprehensive, embracing defeasible fees as well? This has been proposed.[41] The fee simple
determinable and the fee simple subject to condition subsequent
often serve the same goals as servitudes. Including them in
unification could facilitate their termination after they have outlived their usefulness.

40. Dunham, Statutory Reformation of Land Obligations, 55 S.Cal.L.Rev. 1345 (1982).

41. Korngold, For Unifying Servitudes and Defeasible Fees: Property Law's Functional Equivalents, 66 Tex.L. Rev. 533 (1988).

Chapter 2

NATURAL RIGHTS

The term "natural rights" refers to interests created by judicial doctrine in one parcel of land for the benefit of another. These interests, unlike interests created by conveyance or contract, are non-volitional. They are the result of judicial reconciliation of conflicting land uses. Over time, distinct bodies of law governing various types of land use conflicts have developed. The broadest of these is the law of nuisance. Others relate to lateral and subjacent support of land, water rights and air rights. Although these four bodies of law address essentially similar problems, they are inconsistent with each other in several respects.

SECTION 1. NUISANCE

The law of nuisance is summed up in an old Latin maxim, *sic utere tuo ut alienum non laedas*—use your own property in such a manner as not to injure that of another. This states the principle but solves no problems. In fact, it assumes the very point in issue, if quoted as an explanation of why a given court has decided to enjoin specific acts as a nuisance. What use injures the property of another and at what point does that use become unreasonable? Each case tends to be unique and no hard and fast rule can be established to cover all situations. "A nuisance may be merely a right thing in the wrong place, like a pig in the parlor instead of the barnyard." [1]

Most of the nuisance cases are decided in equity by a suit to enjoin, although money damages can be recovered at law in what would have been a common-law action of case. In the final analysis, most nuisance suits become a balancing of the equities, with the court trying to decide how much inconvenience and disturbance a land owner must endure as an incident of modern life. It is clear that the urban dweller cannot expect the peace and quiet of the countryside. Smoke, odors, pollution, etc., which

---

1. Village of Euclid v. Ambler Realty Co., 272 U.S. 365, 388, 47 S.Ct. 114, 118, 71 L.Ed. 303, 311 (1926).

would be enjoined in an isolated hamlet will not move the conscience of the chancellor if they occur in the industrial area of Buffalo, New York.[2] It may be relevant too that the complaining party has "moved to the nuisance" rather than vice versa.[3]

The balancing process is inexact. Judicial discretion is broad. The range of factors that might be deemed relevant and the weight to be accorded them are uncertain. In one case a defendant whose home was furnished electricity by a windmill argued, unsuccessfully, that the national interest in energy conservation should outweigh the plaintiff's interest in freedom from noise caused by the windmill.[4] Economists have been helpful in identifying a solution that is efficient, i.e., that produces the most wealth for all.[5] But even economists acknowledge that efficiency, albeit important, is not the only relevant consideration.

Flexibility in fashioning decrees in nuisance suits is possible. Two extreme cases make the point. A commercial enterprise found to be a nuisance and enjoined from further operation was nevertheless allowed to vacate the injunction upon payment of permanent damages.[6] A dissenting judge viewed this as tantamount to private eminent domain, and therefore improper. In another case, the court held that the plaintiff, who had developed a residential community near a cattle feedlot, would be entitled to an injunction only on condition that the plaintiff compensate the defendant for the resulting loss.[7]

Nuisances are classified as public, private, and mixed. The public nuisance affects an indefinite number of people, the public generally, and is normally abated by an officer, such as the state's attorney or attorney general, acting on behalf of the public. A private nuisance affects one or a small group of property owners in a manner different from its impact on the public generally and it is usually the subject of private litigation. Since the line of demarcation is hard to draw, many nuisances fall into the mixed category and may involve both public abatement and private suit for damages.[8] This classification makes more apparent the inherent weakness of the law of nuisance; it is really a kind of judicial

---

2. Bove v. Donner Hanna Coke Corporation, 236 App.Div. 37, 258 N.Y.S. 229 (1932).

3. East St. Johns Shingle Co. v. Portland, 195 Or. 505, 246 P.2d 554 (1952).

4. Rose v. Chaikin, 187 N.J.Super. 210, 453 A.2d 1378 (1982).

5. Ellickson, Alternatives to Zoning: Covenants, Nuisance Rules and Fines as Land Use Controls, 40 U.Chi.L.Rev. 681 (1973).

6. Boomer v. Atlantic Cement Co., 26 N.Y.2d 219, 309 N.Y.S.2d 312, 257 N.E.2d 870 (1970).

7. Spur Industries, Inc. v. Del E. Webb Development Co., 108 Ariz. 178, 494 P.2d 700 (1972).

8. Ozark Poultry Products, Inc. v. Garman, 251 Ark. 389, 472 S.W.2d 714 (1971).

zoning but carried out on a sporadic, hit-or-miss basis.[9] While the law of nuisance has had a distinguished past as a regulator of land use, in the days when life was less complex, it would appear to be of diminishing importance as legislative control by zoning takes over from the judiciary. It should be noted, however, that a land use allowed by zoning may still be a nuisance, if conducted in an improper fashion, and the old doctrines should not yet be consigned to the trash can.[10] The increased emphasis on environmental problems has caused a revitalized interest in the ancient law of nuisance. Although much of modern environmental law is found in statutes and administrative regulations, nuisance law plays a very significant role. An authority on environmental law has generalized that nuisance actions "have challenged virtually every major industrial and municipal activity which is today the subject of comprehensive environmental regulation. . . ." [11]

SECTION 2. LATERAL AND SUBJACENT SUPPORT

If private ownership means anything, surely *A* can dig holes on *A*'s own land (Blackacre) without consulting *A*'s neighbor prior to excavation. But *B*, owner of Whiteacre, may have a building close to the line and if it tumbles into *A*'s excavation that is scarcely consistent with *B*'s private rights, or is it? This is the stuff of the law of support. The owner of land has a right to the support of his soil in its natural state, both lateral, i.e., from adjoining land and subjacent, i.e., from the subsurface, so that the topsoil will not fall into a mine being operated by the owner of a mineral interest. The *extent* of this right to support is the heart of the matter.

Two closely related problems should be distinguished from the natural right to support. First, there is the question of negligence. If the excavator proceeds in a negligent fashion, so that adjoining property is damaged as the proximate result of poor engineering practice, then the liability is clear.[12] This matter is controlled by the law of torts and the excavator is liable just as the owner of an automobile must respond in damages for negligent driving. The law of natural support deals with absolute liability,

9. Beuscher and Morrison, Judicial Zoning Through Recent Nuisance Cases [1955] Wis.L.Rev. 440.

10. Comment, 54 Mich.L.Rev. 266 (1955); Comment, 34 Tex.L.Rev. 482 (1956).

11. Rodgers, Environmental Law 100 (1977).

12. Of course, it is far from clear just what constitutes negligent withdrawal of support. See Restatement, Torts, § 819 (1939).

i.e., the situations in which one landowner has an absolute duty to support the land of another and is liable, with or without negligence, if harm results. Second, there is the matter of an easement of support. Thus, even though *A* has no natural duty to support *B*'s land or only a limited duty, *B* can buy from *A* an easement of support which will require a certain standard of conduct. A party wall agreement is an example of this kind of easement. The natural right of support is not based on any such acquired easement, but is inherent in the ownership of the land. The converse of the above is also possible, i.e., the owner of the surface may sell the right of support to the subsurface owner so that the latter can mine at will with no concern for injury to the surface.[13]

The doctrine of lateral support, as applied in the majority of American jurisdictions, is limited to the right to have one's soil supported in its natural state by the land adjacent to it. Recovery will normally be granted only to the extent of injury to the land in its unimproved condition, i.e., without the weight of structures upon it.[14] This general principle seems to be based on the idea that to require the support of improved land would be an interference with the rights of the owner of unimproved land. Thus, if *A* built first, and *B* had an absolute duty to support both land and building, the development of *B*'s land might be frustrated. Therefore, *B* should be absolutely liable only for the land as it exists in a state of nature and the rest should be left to the law of negligence.[15]

This sounds simple but is not. Suppose *B* withdraws support in a careful and workmanlike manner but the surface of *A*'s land still subsides because it was resting on quicksand which flows into *B*'s excavation. *B* is liable according to the law of support. Now suppose further that *A* has a building on *A*'s land but the surface would have dropped even without the weight of the building. Is *B* liable just for the damage to the land or must *B* also pay for injury to the building? Here the cases are in conflict and precedent can be marshalled, together with good reasons, for either view.[16] Some courts call this situation a qualification of the general rule and state: ". . . a landowner by building upon his land has not

---

13. See Pennsylvania Coal Company v. Mahon, 260 U.S. 393, 43 S.Ct. 158, 67 L.Ed. 322 (1922) for an example of this type of property interest and the effect of a Pennsylvania statute regulating mining on the private right.

14. Comment, The Doctrine of Lateral Support in Illinois. 1956 U.Ill.L.F. 646.

15. It is frequently said that the "right to lateral support is limited to

land in its natural condition, and does not extend to filled ground." Jennemann v. Hertel, 264 S.W.2d 911 (Mo. App.1954). But in Bradley v. Valicenti, 185 Pa.Super. 403, 138 A.2d 238 (1958) the lapse of time (five years being deemed sufficient) was considered to convert filled land into "natural" land.

16. Prete v. Cray, 49 R.I. 209, 141 A. 609 (1928).

thereby lost his right to have his soil supported, and, when that right is invaded by his neighbor, and his land sinks, he is entitled to compensation for the direct results of such breach of duty, including any injury to buildings upon his land, when such injury is due to an interference with the lateral support of the soil, and cannot be ascribed to the weight and pressure of the buildings upon the land." [17] Of course, if the land would not have fallen but for the buildings there is no liability in the absence of negligence.

It is a tough question of fact as to whether the land would have fallen without the weight of the buildings and it is equally difficult to draw a fine line between absolute liability and negligence. While the analysis given in this section is theoretically accurate, there is reason to doubt its practical effect. One writer has concluded: "As a practical matter, the cases seem to substantiate the proposition that the naked right of lateral support is of little legal significance. On the other hand, it appears that the excavator's primary concern has been and will continue to be the problem of avoiding negligence, a more fertile field of litigation. In any event, notice should be given of the nature and extent of the excavation and the probability of injury to the adjacent owner. The excavation and construction should then proceed in accordance with professionally accepted engineering standards. Where possible, it would seem advisable to conclude an agreement beforehand with other interested parties as to the responsibility of each for any damages which might ensue." [18]

When supporting soil is removed and replaced by a retaining wall, the owner of the wall has an obligation to maintain it in an adequate state of repair. This duty devolves upon a successor in ownership of the land upon which the wall was built.[19] Buyer beware!

Landslides of unstable soil on steep slopes may be triggered by heavy rainfall. Typically, the resulting damage is to buildings downslope, but there could be damage to upslope lands deprived of support. The traditional rule is that a landowner is not liable for the consequences of natural conditions, but a few courts impose liability upon an owner who could prevent those consequences by taking reasonable action.[20]

Most of the preceding discussion has dealt with lateral support but the same legal principles apply to subjacent support. There are, of course, different practical problems of proof and the latter cases arise only where there has been a severance of the

17. Id at 213 and 612.

18. Note 14 supra at 650.

19. Noone v. Price, 298 S.E.2d 218 (W.Va.1982).

20. Sprecher v. Adamson Companies, 30 Cal.3d 358, 178 Cal.Rptr. 783, 636 P.2d 1121 (1981).

subsurface interest so that two or more parties own estates on different physical planes. An intriguing question arises as to the statute of limitations in these cases. If *A* mines without proper supports, the surface owned by *B*, will probably subside sometime, but it may remain unchanged for years. Does the statute begin to run when the subjacent support is withdrawn or does it wait until collapse occurs? A minority of courts follow a theoretical approach and hold that the cause of action arises when the support is withdrawn since the wrong consists in failure to maintain the natural state.[21] Others take a more practical view and, in effect, make harm to the surface a part of the cause of action so that the statute runs from the date of subsidence.[22]

One might suppose that the rule of strict liability for land subsidence due to withdrawal of subjacent support would be unaffected by the nature of the substance withdrawn. But where the substance is water, there is disagreement as to the appropriate rule. There is support for strict liability,[23] for non-liability [24] and also for a negligence standard.[25] This divergence stems from conflict between water rights and land support rights. In most instances, pumping of water from wells unavoidably causes some drainage of water from beneath nearby lands. Accordingly, mere drainage of water is not unlawful. Drainage that deprives a neighbor's well of water is also considered lawful, according to one water rights doctrine. [The topic of water rights is discussed in the following section.] If draining water from beneath a neighbor's land causes subsidence of land, this type of harm is viewed by some as indistinguishable from harm to a well, and it follows that a non-liability standard should apply here, too. But the two types of harm can be distinguished. Land subsidence due to pumping of water occurs only in a few localities, while water levels in wells are nearly always affected by pumping of nearby wells. Moreover, owners of harmed wells have the remedy of self-help. They can deepen or otherwise improve their wells. The negligence standard for land subsidence caused by pumping of water, occupying a middle ground between strict liability and non-liability, accommodates to the extent possible the interests of both parties.

21. Noonan v. Pardee, 200 Pa. 474, 50 A. 255 (1901).

22. Western Coal and Mining Co. v. Randolph, 191 Ark. 1115, 89 S.W.2d 741 (1936).

23. Restatement (Second) of Torts § 818 (1977).

24. Friendswood Development Co. v. Smith-Southwest Industries, Inc., 576 S.W.2d 21 (Tex.1978); Restatement of Torts § 818 (1939).

25. Finley v. Teeter Stone, Inc., 251 Md. 428, 248 A.2d 106 (1968); Friendswood Development Co. v. Smith-Southwest Industries, Inc., 576 S.W.2d 21 (Tex.1978) (prospective rule).

The common-law doctrine is sufficient to decide cases after the harm has been done, but it offers rather poor guidance to the property owner who is planning construction work requiring excavation on his own land. According to the leading case of Braun v. Hamack,[26] if a builder, seeing that a neighboring structure will topple into an excavation, goes on the adjacent land and shores it up, this is at the excavator's expense, even though the excavator had no duty to support the adjoining land plus building. It was argued that the builder should recover in quasi-contract for the benefit conferred but, while the dissenting judge thought this was a good position, it did not sway the majority. This leaves the builder in a greater quandary than ever. In an effort to alleviate some of the uncertainty, various ordinances and statutes have been passed. Some exonerate the excavator if he serves a statutory notice on his neighbor and is free from negligence; others add to the excavator's responsibility by imposing strict liability for structures as well as land; still others seek a middle ground by shifting the obligation between the parties depending on the depth of the excavation.[27] None of the legislative changes appear to be particularly satisfactory either to the engineers or the lawyers and a working agreement between the adjoining owners is probably the best solution.

SECTION 3. WATER RIGHTS

Some water rights are incidents of ownership of land. Others are not. Our concern here is primarily with those common law water rights that are included in the bundle of rights constituting land ownership. Speaking generally, a landowner has rights in, and sometimes obligations concerning, water that has physical contact with the land owned. This water may be in a watercourse (a stream or a lake) upon or along one's land. Rights in such water based upon land ownership are referred to as riparian rights. A landowner also has rights in water underground.

---

26. 206 Minn. 572, 289 N.W. 553 (1940).

27. See 5 Powell, Real Property, 702 (1956). For an interesting case involving a California land support statute see Holtz v. Superior Court of City and County of San Francisco, 3 Cal.3d 296, 90 Cal.Rptr. 345, 475 P.2d 441 (1970). The Supreme Court of California held the San Francisco Bay Area Rapid Transit District (Bart) strictly liable for damages to the plaintiffs' land and buildings injured in subway construction. (They were also liable for negligence if that could be proved.) The court used "inverse condemnation" principles and socialized the loss as a cost to the public of building public improvements. See Van Alstyne, Inverse Condemnation: Unintended Physical Damage, 20 Hastings L.J. 431 (1969).

These are referred to as groundwater rights. Finally, there is water that falls as rain or snow on one's land or flows onto it from neighboring land, but has not yet entered a watercourse. This water is referred to as diffused surface water. A landowner has rights in this type of water, too, but those most frequently litigated are rights to get rid of unwanted water and to be protected from similar efforts by others.

The scientist looks at water as a whole and speaks of the hydrologic cycle—the endless process of evaporation, transpiration, condensation, precipitation, and flowage to the sea. It follows from this physical fact that rights to water are usufructuary—rights to use water temporarily as it moves through the hydrologic cycle rather than to own the corpus of it, as one owns the fee simple in land. It also follows that every use of water has an effect, ranging from substantial to miniscule, upon other uses of water. The essential role of the law of water rights is to coordinate all water uses, with special attention to those uses substantially affecting others. Water rights thus tend to be relative and flexible, rather than absolute. The separate systems of water rights for water in watercourses, ground water, and diffused surface water defy the hydrologic cycle. This may be explained by the practical reality that conflicts in water uses typically do not cross those classes of water. But sometimes they do, and the existence of separate systems of water rights for water at stages of the hydrologic cycle then exacerbates the problem of coordination.

Water rights serve many diverse and sometimes conflicting needs. Some of these needs are consumptive, in the sense that they require removal of water from its natural source. Significant consumptive uses include drinking, cleaning, irrigation, and industrial process such as production of steam. Nonconsumptive uses include production of power by use of stream flow, navigation, recreational activities such as fishing and swimming, scenic enjoyment and habitat for wildlife. It is apparent that many of these uses may compete for the same water supply. Even when the water source is adequate for all consumptive uses, conflicts between consumptive and nonconsumptive uses may occur. An example is the frequent disparity in timing of releases from reservoirs needed for irrigation and production of hydroelectric power. Another example: the pollution of a source of drinking water by return flows from consumptive uses. Still another: the destruction of a wild and scenic river by construction of a dam or other structures for navigation and flood control.

The most significant water rights that do not originate as incidents to ownership of land are those based upon prior appropriation. As the term suggests, priority of actual use, rather than land ownership, is the origin of prior appropriation rights. The prior appropriation system is confined mainly to western states. In some of these, it is the sole system applicable to uses of water in watercourses. In other states, both riparian and prior appropriation rights have been recognized. Thus, the states fall into three groups with respect to consumptive uses of water in watercourses: (1) riparian; (2) prior appropriation; and (3) combined riparian and prior appropriation. In some states, the prior appropriation system has also been applied to groundwater.

The judicial doctrines of water rights have been altered substantially by statutes and administrative regulation. In many states, especially in the West, very little remains of the traditional judicial doctrines of riparian and prior appropriation rights. There is much variation among the contemporary water laws of the states. They will not be covered in detail here.

The water rights discussed to this point are private rights. There also are public rights in water that limit private rights. Perhaps the most significant of these are public rights in navigable waters. The public right to use such waters for navigation cannot be interfered with by a riparian use such as construction of a dam.

Navigation is not the only public right in navigable waters. It has been broadly declared that the states own their navigable watercourses as "trustee of a public trust for the benefit of the people." [28] These rights include, in addition to navigation, rights to fish, hunt, bathe and swim. The Supreme Court of California held in 1983 that the public trust included scenic and ecological interests of the public in Mono Lake, and that these interests required re-appraisal of certain private water rights.[29]

There are still other water rights that have characteristics of both private and public rights. Water that is part of the federal public domain has sometimes been reserved for the benefit of Indian reservations, forest preserves, national parks and national monuments.[30] These federal reserved rights usually have arisen from implication, based upon the anticipated needs of the beneficiaries, rather than from express language in treaties, acts of Congress and executive orders. As a consequence, there is often uncertainty, not only to the intent to reserve water, but also as to the authorized uses of water and the quantities of water reserved.[31] These uncertain rights to potentially huge amounts of water have priority over subsequently created private water rights

28. National Audubon Society v. Superior Court of Alpine County, 33 Cal. 3d 419, 434, 189 Cal.Rptr. 346, 355, 658 P.2d 709, 718 (1983).

29. Id.

30. E.g., Cappaert v. United States, 426 U.S. 128, 96 S.Ct. 2062, 48 L.Ed.2d 523 (1976).

31. United States v. New Mexico, 438 U.S. 696, 98 S.Ct. 3012, 57 L.Ed.2d 1052 (1978).

in the same source of supply, even though the implied federal reserved rights had not been asserted when the private rights were acquired, and the owners of private rights had been unaware of the existence or effect of the reserved rights.[32] To mitigate this destabilization of private rights, there have been efforts to quantify federal implied water rights.[33]

Finally, there are secondary water rights based upon contract or obligations of public utilities or governmental units or agencies. Nearly every resident of an urban dwelling has water rights of this sort. Large scale water users, such as industrial concerns, municipalities and irrigation enterprises, also may be dependent upon secondary water rights. The scope of these water rights is found in the terms of contracts, statutes and administrative regulations.

Water rights, as well as other property, are subject to regulatory and other powers of the states and the federal government. Due largely to the huge cost of many water development projects, such as dams, power plants, and levees, the broad powers of the federal government have been extensively used to address water problems. However, the magnitude of Congressional spending for water projects has declined drastically in recent years. To some extent, water rights and riparian lands are more vulnerable to regulation than are other property interests. Justice Rehnquist explained: "The navigational servitude, which exists by virtue of the Commerce Clause in navigable streams, gives rise to an authority in the Government to assure that such streams retain their capacity to serve as continuous highways for the purpose of navigation in interstate commerce. Thus, when the Government acquires fast lands to improve navigation, it is not required under the Eminent Domain Clause to compensate landowners for certain elements of damage attributable to riparian location, such as the land's value as a hydroelectric site . . . or a port site. . . ."[34]

---

32. Meyers, Tarlock, Corbridge & Getches, Water Resources Management 778 (1988).

33. Getches, Water Law in a Nutshell 314–330 (1984).

34. Kaiser Aetna v. United States, 444 U.S. 164, 177, 100 S.Ct. 383, 391, 62 L.Ed.2d 332, 344 (1979). But Congress has required compensation not required by the Eminent Domain Clause. Rivers and Harbors Act of 1970, Pub.L. No. 91–611, § 111, 84 Stat. 1818 (1970).

A. RIPARIAN RIGHTS

Courts have often declared that owners of land riparian to a watercourse have equal and correlative rights to use the water in the watercourse. This abstraction is of little help in resolving controversies between riparians whose uses interfere with each other. In 1827, in perhaps the first American case on the subject, Tyler v. Wilkinson,[35] Justice Story asserted that "no one has a right to diminish the quantity which will, according to the natural current, flow to a proprietor below, or to throw it back upon a proprietor above. This is the necessary result of the perfect equality of right among all the proprietors of that, which is common to all." Taken literally, this would deny riparians any substantial consumptive use. Story recognized this and hastened to modify that generalization. "When I speak of this common right, I do not mean to be understood, as holding the doctrine, that there can be no diminution whatsoever, and no obstruction or impediment whatsoever, by a riparian proprietor, in the use of the water as it flows; for that would be to deny any valuable use of it. There may be, and there must be allowed of that, which is common to all, a reasonable use." While there have been many references in court opinions and elsewhere to the "natural flow" theory of riparian rights,[36] the "reasonable use" theory has dominated the decisions.

The touchstone of "reasonable use" provides scant guidance in predicting the outcome of litigation, but years of adjudication have particularized this abstraction to some extent. The Restatement (Second) of Torts § 850A (1979) identifies nine relevant factors: purpose of the use; suitability of the use to the watercourse; economic value of the use; social value of the use; the extent and amount of the harm it causes; the practicality of avoiding the harm by adjusting the use or method of use of one proprietor or the other; the practicality of adjusting the quantity of water used by each proprietor; the protection of existing values of water uses, land, investments and enterprises; and the justice of requiring the user causing harm to bear the loss. None of these factors, alone, necessarily stamps the use in issue as "reasonable" and therefore entitled to protection.

Thus, priority of use does not necessarily confer priority of right, despite prior appropriation analogies in the common law, such as protection of prior possessors of land and chattels. This

35. 24 F.Cas. 472 (D.R.I.1827).

36. E.g., Restatement (Second) of Torts ch. 41, Introductory Note (1979).

means that existing users of water, who may have made substantial investments dependent upon those water uses, could be forced to reduce their usage to accommodate the reasonable needs of other riparians who subsequently initiate uses of water. It also means that, during periods of temporary shortage, the senior user's needs would not be entitled to satisfaction before those of the junior user. This policy would seem to discourage substantial investments in water-dependent enterprises, and thus to deter economic utilization of this basic resource. However, a survey of the cases prior to 1971 concluded that in fact courts usually protect existing water uses from interference by newcomers, despite the prevailing doctrine that first-in-time/first-in-right is not a riparian concept.[37]

In addition, an early riparian user possibly could acquire a prescriptive right, but this would require proof that the early use had been in excess of the riparian right, i.e., adverse, and that other requisites for prescription had been satisfied. This is difficult or impossible to establish. A riparian whose needs for water were not interfered with would have had no cause of action against a prior user, according to the prevailing view. It follows that a downstream user could never acquire a prescriptive water right against an upstream claimant; as it is commonly put, "prescription never runs upstream." If an upstream use is clearly without legal justification, such as use by a non-riparian, it has been held that this could be enjoined in a suit by a downstream riparian, who would be barred by prescription if no action were filed within the prescriptive period.[38] There is also contrary authority that even here a cause of action accrues only when actual harm occurs.[39] The latter view is more realistic and fair. Riparians whose water uses, if any, are not affected are usually unaware of, and unconcerned about, the legality of upstream uses. To impose upon them a duty to ascertain that information periodically would be unreasonable. To discover that water is being used on non-riparian land could require examination of land titles of upstream users, surveys of their lands and investigation of the locus of their water uses. Investigation would necessitate consent by the upstream user for entry upon lands of that user, or a court order so authorizing, which probably would be unobtainable.

The reasonableness standard requires a balancing of the merits of the competing uses. Preference is accorded "natural uses" over "artificial" uses. This preference was described by the Su-

37. Restatement (Second) of Torts § 850B, Associate Reporter's Note 113, 115 (Tent. Draft No. 17, 1971).

38. Pabst v. Finmand, 190 Cal. 124, 211 P. 11 (1922).

39. Stratton v. Mr. Hermon Boys' School, 216 Mass. 83, 103 N.E. 87 (1913); Restatement (Second) of Torts § 857(1) (1979).

preme Court of Illinois in the early case of Evans v. Merriweather as follows: [40]

> Now the question fairly arises, is that a reasonable use of running water by the upper proprietor, by which the fluid itself is entirely consumed? To answer this question satisfactorily, it is proper to consider the wants of man in regard to the element of water. These wants are either natural or artificial. Natural are such as are absolutely necessary to be supplied, in order to his existence. Artificial, such only, as by supplying them, his comfort and prosperity are increased. To quench thirst, and for household purposes, water is absolutely indispensable. In civilized life, water for cattle is also necessary. These wants must be supplied, or both man and beast will perish. The supply of man's artificial wants is not essential to his existence; it is not indispensable; he could live if water was not employed in irrigating lands, or in propelling his machinery. In countries differently situated from ours, with a hot and arid climate, water doubtless is absolutely indispensable to the cultivation of the soil, and in them, water for irrigation would be a natural want. Here it might increase the products of the soil, but it is by no means essential, and cannot therefore be considered a natural want of man. So of manufacturers, they promote the prosperity and comfort of mankind, but cannot be considered absolutely necessary to his existence; nor need the machinery which he employs be set in motion by steam.

This statement raises some questions. Is this preference confined to the modest needs of an individual or family? Or does it embrace large-scale uses, such as hotels, cattle feedlots, or municipal distribution of water to residents? Municipal domestic use has been held entitled to the preference over a manufacturing use,[41] but the reasonableness criterion probably would have produced the same result. The narrow view was adopted in a case declining to treat commercial cattle raising as preferred over irrigation.[42] In another case, the court equivocated, declaring initially that a resort hotel could be entitled to the domestic use preference, on the rationale that the hotel was merely the conduit for satisfying domestic needs of guests, but concluding later that competing "commercialized" domestic uses should be balanced to achieve a reasonable accommodation.[43] In another somewhat similar case, involving water for a boys' summer camp, the court

40. 4 Ill. 492, 495, 38 Am.Dec. 106, (1842).

41. City of Canton v. Shock, 66 Ohio St. 19, 63 N.E. 600 (1902).

42. Cowell v. Armstrong, 210 Cal. 218, 290 P. 1036 (1930).

43. Prather v. Hoberg, 24 Cal.2d 549, 150 P.2d 405 (1944).

observed that the boys were not riparians.[44] This also could be said of hotel guests and most residents of cities. The sensible view is to confine the preference to relatively insignificant amounts of water, if it is to be recognized at all.

Another intriguing question is whether the Merriweather dictum implied that an upper riparian natural use is entitled to satisfaction ahead of downstream natural uses. Statements according the preference of this meaning abound, but justification is elusive. Downstream domestic uses are no less deserving than upstream domestic uses, and it would be shocking if a court denied drinking water for downstream humans for the benefit of upstream livestock.

Finally, Merriweather suggests that irrigation might be deemed a natural use in arid regions. No American court has so held. The Supreme Court of Texas held to the contrary.[45] In view of the huge amounts of water consumed by irrigation, classification of this use as natural would have a devastating effect upon competing uses.

It is axiomatic that riparian rights belong only to owners of riparian land, but what is riparian land? Contiguity with a watercourse is an obvious criterion, but it may be difficult to apply to lands that sometimes abut fluctuating water levels and sometimes do not.[46] And contiguity is not the sole criterion.

Portions of a riparian tract that lie outside the watershed of a watercourse are deemed not riparian to that watercourse.[47] Downstream riparians are entitled to return flows from upstream uses, and this is unlikely to occur when water is transported beyond the watershed. However, water may be used on the portion of a riparian's tract beyond the watershed of the originating watercourse if this is within the watershed of another watercourse that joins the originating watercourse downstream, and the affected riparians are below the confluence of these watercourses.[48] Thus, the meaning of "watershed" for this purpose may be affected by the location of the parties, as well as by topography.

When an owner of riparian land enlarges the tract by acquiring adjoining land not theretofore riparian, does the newly acquired land become riparian? Conversely, when an owner of riparian land conveys a portion not abutting the watercourse, does the conveyed portion retain its riparian status? The relevant

44. McCord v. Big Brothers Movement, 120 N.J.Eq. 446, 185 A. 480 (1936).

45. Watkins Land Co. v. Clements, 98 Tex. 578, 86 S.W. 733 (1905).

46. Meyers, Tarlock, Corbridge & Getches, Water Resource Management 135 (3d ed. 1988).

47. Anaheim Union Water Co. v. Fuller, 150 Cal. 327, 88 P. 978 (1907).

48. Id.

decisions are conflicting. The opposing positions have been characterized as the "source of title" rule [49] and the "unity of title" rule.[50] The former is the more restrictive. It limits riparian land to the boundaries of the original grant from the sovereign, and terminates the riparian status of severed non-abutting portions of that land. The latter rule rejects both limitations. We suggest that this cleavage may be due to divergent concepts of the origin of riparian rights. They may be viewed as implied incidents of grants by the sovereign of land contiguous to watercourses owned by the sovereign—which tends to support the "source of title" rule. Or they may be viewed as originating in common-law doctrine applicable to land abutting watercourses. More significant than conceptual considerations are the policies served by the competing rules. The "source of title" rule may be favored in dual system states (recognizing both riparian and prior appropriation rights) because this rule tends to leave more water available for the "better" prior appropriation system.[51]

One other consequence of the notion that riparian rights originate as implied incidents of land grants from a sovereign should be mentioned. The Supreme Court of Texas concluded that lands abutting the Lower Rio Grande lacked irrigation rights because these lands were granted by Spanish and Mexican governments under laws and circumstances repelling the inference that such rights were impliedly granted.[52] A significant effect (also cause?) of this decision was the protection of major existing investments based upon prior appropriation rights from destruction by assertion of superior riparian rights for the irrigation of huge tracts of land never before irrigated.

It should not be assumed that the diversion of water from a watercourse for use on land not riparian to that watercourse is wrongful. Under the prevailing reasonable use theory of riparian rights, it would be reasonable in some circumstances for a riparian to use water on non-riparian land. This rationale is inapplicable to uses by non-riparians, who have no water rights, but if downstream riparians are not deprived by non-riparians of needed water, neither compensatory damages nor injunctive relief would be justified, and nominal damages would be justified only for the purpose of preventing prescription. And courts can remove the

49. Boehmer v. Big Rock Creek Irrigation Dist., 117 Cal. 19, 48 P. 908 (1897).

50. Jones v. Conn, 39 Or. 30, 64 P. 855 (1901); Restatement (Second) of Torts § 843, Comment c (1979).

51. There are also other policy implications. Farnham, The Permissible Extent of Riparian Land, 7 Land & Water L.Rev. 31 (1972); Levi & Schneeberger, The Chain and Unity Title Theories for Delineating Riparian Land: Economic Analysis As an Alternative to Case Precedent, 21 Buffalo L.Rev. 439 (1972).

52. Valmont Plantations v. State, 355 S.W.2d 502 (Tex.1962).

threat of prescription by holding that the prescriptive period begins to run only when actual interference with a riparian use occurs. This treatment of non-riparian uses is approved by the American Law Institute, which characterizes them as "privileged" and "to some extent legally protected interest."[53] Even though they have no water rights, non-riparians are protected against tortious intentional or negligent conduct of upstream riparians which harms economic interests of non-riparians.

B. PRIOR APPROPRIATION SYSTEM

The riparian system of allocation of water has been displaced in whole or in part in arid and semi-arid western states, and also (perhaps surprisingly) in humid Mississippi, by the prior appropriation system. This system bases rights to use water upon actual application of water to beneficial uses rather than upon ownership of riparian land. It thus allows water to be utilized on lands far removed from the originating watercourse. This is a vital distinction in states where irrigation is essential to successful production of farm crops. The most productive irrigable lands are not necessarily located on streams. The same is true of mines requiring large amounts of water.

The rejection of the riparian system in the West and adoption there of the prior appropriation system is a most remarkable instance of influence of climate upon development of law. The prior appropriation system is the sole system of water allocation in the most arid states—Arizona, Colorado, Idaho, Montana, Nevada, New Mexico, Utah and Wyoming. Combinations both riparian and prior appropriation systems exist in the tiers of less arid adjoining states east and west of the "pure" prior appropriation states. These are California, Oregon and Washington on the west and Texas, Oklahoma, Kansas, Nebraska, South Dakota and North Dakota on the east. Mississippi, in anticipation of severe water shortages even in humid areas, joined the "hybrid" states relatively recently.

There were also other factors responsible for the unique development of western water law. Many of the earliest water users were not owners of either the lands riparian to watercourses from which they diverted water or the lands upon which they applied water. They essentially were trespassers upon public lands of the United States Government, which acquiesced in such

53. Restatement (Second) of Torts § 856, Comment a (1979).

conduct, informally at first and formally later. Some of these water users were gold miners, who naturally extended the first-in-time mining concept to water. Another appealing aspect of prior appropriation, compared with riparianism, was its contribution to stability of investment in enterprises requiring substantial quantities of water in water-short regions. As previously noted, riparian doctrine renders existing riparian uses vulnerable to possible cutbacks to accommodate new riparian uses. And in times of shortage, all riparians, old and new, must share equally in the shortage. Senior appropriators, however, are entitled to full satisfaction of their water needs to the extent of their prior appropriations before junior appropriators are allowed to take water.

The Supreme Court of Colorado, in a noted opinion in 1882, justified its total rejection of riparian rights to water allocation as follows:

> It is contended by counsel for appellants that the common law principles of riparian proprietorship prevailed in Colorado until 1876, and that the doctrine of priority of right to water by priority of appropriation thereof was first recognized and adopted in the constitution. But we think the latter doctrine has existed from the date of the earliest appropriations of water within the boundaries of the state. The climate is dry, and the soil, when moistened only by the usual rainfall, is arid and unproductive; except in a few favored sections, artificial irrigation for agriculture is an absolute necessity. Water in the various streams thus acquires a value unknown in moister climates. Instead of being a mere incident to the soil, it rises, when appropriated, to the dignity of a distinct usufructuary estate, or right or property. It has always been the policy of the national, as well as the territorial and state governments, to encourage the diversion and use of water in this country for agriculture; and vast expenditures of time and money have been made in reclaiming and fertilizing by irrigation portions of our unproductive territory. Houses have been built, and permanent improvements made; the soil has been cultivated, and thousands of acres have been rendered immensely valuable, with the understanding that appropriations of water would be protected. Deny the doctrine of priority or superiority of right by priority of appropriation, and a great part of the value of all this property is at once destroyed.[54]

The earliest prior appropriation rights were established simply by self-help, but formalities were soon required. Among the earliest formalities were requirements of posting of notice at the

54. Coffin v. Left Hand Ditch Co., 6 Colo. 443, 446 (1882).

site of diversion and filing of claims in public records. Most prior appropriation states now require a permit from an administrative agency, which typically is empowered to deny applications for permits on stated grounds and to attach conditions to permits granted.

The prior appropriation system may be criticized for attaching too much significance to priority in time. The earliest appropriations may have devoted water to purposes less worthy than later efforts to appropriate would serve. Senior downstream diverters from streams suffering severe stream bed losses may demand that upstream junior appropriators leave sufficient water in the stream to satisfy senior needs after intervening stream bed losses. Senior appropriators also may claim that their priority entitles them to continue using inefficient methods of diversion (e.g., water wheels), transportation and application of water. Appropriators of water in fully-appropriated streams may habitually fail to use water to which they are entitled, while applications for permits are being denied.

Courts have attempted, without complete success, to remedy these problems.[55] In this they have been aided by the prior appropriation concept of reasonable beneficial use. In addition, prior appropriation rights, as other property interests, are subject to the police power and the power of eminent domain. Several statutes and administration programs are aimed at protecting public interests in water resources from the excesses of prior appropriation. Efficient practices may be mandated. Failure to use water for an extended period may result in partial or total forfeiture of water rights.[56] Obstacles to reliance upon the market to transfer water rights to more productive uses may be removed.

C. GROUNDWATER

Rights to water in underground streams or lakes are governed by the law applicable in the state to rights in surface watercourses. However, most water underground is not in a stream or lake, but is found in strata of sand, gravel or rocks.[57] This is called percolating groundwater. Courts apply a rebuttable pre-

55. E.g., Schodde v. Twin Falls Land & Water Co., 224 U.S. 107, 32 S.Ct. 470, 56 L.Ed. 686 (1912); State ex rel. Cary v. Cochran, 138 Neb. 163, 292 N.W. 239 (1940); State ex rel. Crowley v. District Court, 108 Mont. 89, 88 P.2d 23 (1939).

56. Such a statute was upheld in Texas Water Rights Commission v. Wright, 464 S.W.2d 642 (Tex.1971).

57. Thomas, Underground Sources of Water, in the Yearbook of Agriculture 63 (USDA 1955).

sumption that groundwater is percolating—a presumption very difficult to overcome.[58] Unless expressly qualified, the term groundwater should be understood to refer to percolating water.

There is widespread disagreement among courts as to rights in groundwater. The oldest common law doctrine in this country is the English rule of absolute ownership.[59] It attempts to give the landowner the same title to groundwater as to soil. The difficulty with this is that groundwater does not stay put.

Hydrologists tell us that most groundwater moves continuously through the hydrologic cycle, albeit sometimes very slowly. Water beneath Jones' land today may have been under Smith's land yesterday and destined to flow under White's land tomorrow. Pumping also affects the flow of groundwater. If Jones drills a well and commences pumping, water may be drained from beneath White's land into Jones' well. As White is the owner of the groundwater beneath White's land, it follows logically that Jones is not entitled to drain that water into a well on Jones' land. But if this were the law, groundwater could not be utilized without obtaining agreement of owners of all lands overlying the aquifer.

Courts applying the absolute ownership doctrine to groundwater have avoided this undesirable result by the simple expedient of ignoring logic and withholding remedies for drainage in the absence of malice.[60] This means that ownership of groundwater beneath one's land is qualified by a right of capture in others. While this avoids the monumental problem of obtaining consent of overlying landowners, it creates other problems. Owners of deep, large wells with powerful pumps can easily dry up neighbors' smaller wells. A homeowner's domestic well cannot compete with a municipal or industrial well. Although there may still be water remaining under the land of the homeowner, the increased cost of recovering it may render it unavailable. In addition, competition among well owners may result in withdrawals from an aquifer exceeding its capacity. An unqualified right of capture is an incentive to such excess because the costs of a pumper's lowering of a water level are not fully borne by that pumper.[61]

58. Maricopa County Municipal Water Conservation Dist. No. 1 v. Southwest Cotton Co., 39 Ariz. 65, 4 P.2d 369 (1931).

59. E.g., Houston & T.C. Ry. Co. v. East, 98 Tex. 146, 81 S.W. 279 (1904). This rule has been traced to Acton v. Blundell, 12 Mees & W. 324, 152 Eng. Rep. 1223 (1843). It has been substantially modified in England by legislation. Water Act of 1943, 8 & 9 Geo. 6, c. 42; 26 Hals. Laws of England 786 (2d ed. 1951).

60. City of Corpus Christi v. City of Pleasanton, 154 Tex. 289, 276 S.W.2d 798 (1955). This case allowed harmful drainage even though there was evidence that over half the water pumped was lost during transit in a stream bed to serve a city over 100 miles away.

61. The basic economics of groundwater use are explained in Hirshleifer, De Haven, & Milliman, Water Supply: Economics, Technology, and Policy 59 (1960).

The absolute ownership doctrine amounts to judicial abstention. Courts have candidly explained that too little is known about the characteristics of groundwater in any specific place to enable a court to devise a fair and feasible plan of allocation. The injured landowner is relegated to self-help, i.e., drilling a more powerful well. While this may have been a justifiable position at one time, the present state of scientific and technological capacity to ascertain the nature of aquifers enables courts to play a more active role. Most courts have abandoned or rejected the absolute ownership doctrine in favor of principles that entail greater judicial involvement.

One departure is referred to as the American reasonable use doctrine.[62] It, too, allows harmful drainage, but only if the water pumped is applied to some reasonable use on the overlying land. All uses on other land are branded unreasonable. The practical effect is protection of small wells from large wells serving distant cities or industries. Unlike the riparian doctrine, the American reasonable use doctrine of groundwater does not call for balancing of interests. It is irrelevant that distant uses may be of great economic value or that overlying uses may be of slight economic value.

The Supreme Court of California went further and restricted pumping by each landowner from an aquifer unable to meet total demand to a share based upon the size of one's tract in relation to the total size of overlying land.[63] This has been called the correlative rights doctrine. It has some following in other states. In California, this allocation formula has been modified by giving some recognition to prescription and by carving out a limited role for the prior appropriation doctrine.[64]

A genuine reasonable use doctrine has been proposed in the Restatement (Second) of Torts § 858. It imposes liability upon any pumper who "unreasonably causes harm" to others, including users of hydrologically related surface watercourses. The relevant criteria include the same long list in the Restatement for determining reasonableness of riparian uses. Liability is expressly provided for pumping in excess of one's reasonable share of groundwater. The Supreme Court of Texas declared that it will apply § 858 when the nature of the harm is land subsidence, but it has not departed from the absolute ownership doctrine rule of non-liability for harming access to groundwater.[65]

62. Forbell v. City of New York, 164 N.W. 522, 58 N.E. 644 (1900).

63. Katz v. Walkinshaw, 141 Cal. 116, 70 P. 663 (1902), 74 P. 766 (1903).

64. Los Angeles v. San Fernando, 14 Cal.3d 199, 123 Cal.Rptr. 1, 537 P.2d 1250 (1975).

65. Friendswood Development Co. v. Smith–Southwest Ind., Inc., 576 S.W.2d 21 (Tex.1978).

The prior appropriation doctrine has been applied to groundwater,[66] but usually in a substantially modified form. An unqualified prior appropriation doctrine for groundwater, entitling a senior appropriator to maintenance of the existing water level, excludes all subsequent pumpers or requires them to compensate the senior appropriator for the expense of reaching lowered levels caused by newcomers. Each new appropriator is required to compensate all seniors. The cumulative cost to new appropriators probably would halt new appropriations long before the limits of optimum utilization of the aquifer are reached. This situation calls for substantial modification of the traditional prior appropriation doctrine. One approach is to protect senior appropriators only in the maintenance of "reasonable pumping levels." [67] In some states, efforts are also made to coordinate prior appropriation rights in hydrologically related surface watercourses and groundwater.[68] One having an appropriative right in a stream may be permitted to exercise that right by pumping groundwater that would have entered the stream or had exited it.

The complexities of optimum utilization of groundwater, coupled with increasing reliance upon groundwater, are resulting in many states in expansion of administrative regulation of this resource. Water rights based upon judicial doctrine or statute are becoming less important than agency permits and orders. It is not enough to assure each claimant a fair share of an aquifer, though that alone is a formidable challenge. It may also be necessary to ascertain the maximum total rate of pumping that should be allowed from an aquifer. If the aquifer has substantial natural recharge, the probable goal is to limit total withdrawals to the rate of natural recharge—the "safe yield" of the aquifer.[69] If the aquifer has only minimum natural recharge, the aquifer must either be depleted or unused. The critical issue is to determine how long such an aquifer should be preserved.[70] Administrative programs for groundwater management also sometimes include artificial recharge of aquifers with water from other sources. These are some of the important aspects of modern programs of groundwater management.

---

66. Current Creek Irr. Co. v. Andrews, 9 Utah 2d 324, 344 P.2d 528 (1959).

67. Baker v. Ore–Ida Foods, Inc., 95 Idaho 575, 513 P.2d 627 (1973).

68. Langenegger v. Carlsbad Irr. Dist., 82 N.M. 416, 483 P.2d 297 (1971).

69. Ariz.Rev.Stat.Ann. § 45–562(A).

70. Mathers v. Texaco, Inc., 77 N.M. 239, 421 P.2d 771 (1966).

D. DIFFUSED SURFACE WATER

––––––––

Most water on the surface of land that is not in a watercourse is diffused surface water. Assertions of claims to use such water are rare, in view of the difficulty of capturing substantial amounts of it under commonly prevailing circumstances. The most frequently litigated issue concerning diffused surface water is drainage, i.e., the right of a landowner to divert that water onto the lands of others. Both use rights and drainage rights will be discussed briefly.

––––––––

(1) USE RIGHTS

––––––––

The landowner is traditionally viewed as owning (or having a right to capture) diffused surface water while it is on that owner's land.[71] This is analogous to the English absolute ownership doctrine of groundwater. Impoundment of diffused surface water behind small dams in ditches often may have no noticeable effect upon the availability of water in watercourses in the same watershed, but riparians and appropriators can be harmed by such impoundments, especially if they are numerous or in arid regions. To apply the absolute ownership doctrine in such instances is to deny the reality of the hydrologic cycle and to undermine riparian and appropriative rights. Some states address this problem by bringing diffused surface water into the prior appropriation system.[72] Another approach is to define "watercourse" in such a way that most earth depressions suitable for impoundment would constitute watercourses. In one such case, a ravine dry most of the time was held to be a watercourse because there was on occasion sufficient flow in it to support some irrigation.[73]

––––––––

71. Turner v. Big Lake Oil Co., 128 Tex. 155, 96 S.W.2d 221 (1936). Westview Irrig. Co., 96 Utah 403, 80 P.2d 458 (1938).

72. Nevius v. Smith, 86 Colo. 178, 279 P. 44 (1929); Richlands Irrig. Co. v. 73. Hoefs v. Short, 114 Tex. 501, 273 S.W. 785 (1925).

(2) DRAINAGE RIGHTS

Drainage rights are rights in land use. Development of land usually alters the existing drainage pattern. Most frequently, downslope lands of neighbors are affected. Typically, there are increases in the rate of flow caused by removal of vegetation, substitution of impervious surfaces (e.g., roofs and streets) or concentration of runoff by curbs and drainage pipes. Sometimes landowners protect themselves from drainage from up-slope lands by constructing barriers that push water back upon lands from which they flowed or divert it to lands of others.

Courts have taken three positions. The common enemy rule, in its most extreme form, imposes no liability for drainage harm caused to neighbors by land development. The sole remedy of harmed landowners is self-help. In defense of this judicial hands-off stance, one court declared that it was not "disposed to make drainage commissions of our already over-burdened trial courts."[74] A witty (?) critic might respond that it is most unlikely that courts would be "flooded" with drainage cases, regardless of the doctrine followed. Nor does it appear that the drainage cases, if approached as nuisance cases, would be any more difficult to resolve than other nuisance cases. The common enemy rule has been criticized, not only as unfair, but also as encouraging inefficient development by putting some development costs on others.[75]

At the opposite pole is the civil law rule, which, in its most extreme form, allows no harmful change in natural drainage. A court adhering to this rule has declared that "there can clearly be no other rule at once so equitable and so easy of application as that which enforces natural laws. There is no surprise in this, for each successive owner takes whatever advantages or inconveniences nature has stamped upon his land."[76] But, if strictly adhered to, this rule would preclude virtually all significant development of land, in the absence of acquisition of flowage easements in lands of affected owners.

Both the common enemy and the civil law rules have been modified. The modifications have tended to narrow the gap between the two rules. Some scholars have concluded that in fact, if not expressly, most modern appellate court opinions apply a

74. Argyelan v. Haviland, 435 N.E.2d 973, 977 (Ind.1982).

75. Armstrong v. Francis Corp., 20 N.J. 320, 330, 120 A.2d 4, 10 (1956).

76. Gormely v. Sanford, 52 Ill. 158, 162 (1869).

reasonable use rule, involving balancing of all relevant factors.[77] There certainly is a trend toward explicit adoption of the reasonable use rule.[78] But one still encounters modern appellate court opinions adhering to one of the old rules, with little or no modification.[79]

The ideal solution to drainage problems is development and application of a plan providing for the optimum drainage of an entire watershed. The practical obstacles to obtaining agreement of all landowners in a watershed to such a plan have led to imposition of drainage plans by government. Drainage districts have been created for some areas.[80] Municipal subdivision regulations commonly refuse approval of plats that do not conform to drainage requirements.[81] Despite these and other governmental interventions, courts continue to be called upon from time to time to settle drainage disputes.

SECTION 4. AIR RIGHTS

The traditional concept of land ownership is that it extends to an unlimited extent upward and downward. As explained heretofore, the downward reach of land ownership has been much modified judicially, as well as legislatively, regarding groundwater. The upward reach of land ownership has been modified to an even greater extent, for practical reasons that are quite apparent in the modern world of skyscrapers, aircraft, television and solar collectors.

Three issues have arisen: (1) To what extent may a landowner occupy airspace? (2) To what extent may a landowner exclude others from airspace? (3) To what extent may ownership of airspace be severed from ownership of the land? Each of these will be briefly discussed here.

---

77. Kinyon & McClure, Interferences with Surface Waters, 24 Minn.L. Rev. 891 (1940).

78. Note, 18 Val.U.L..Rev. 481, 490, (1984).

79. E.g., Argyelan v. Haviland, supra note 75.

80. E.g., Ill.Rev.Stat. ch. 42, Art. 1–12 (1973).

81. Extremely stringent drainage regulations may be invalid. Baker v. Planning Board of Framingham, 353 Mass. 141, 228 N.E.2d 831 (1967).

A. RIGHT TO OCCUPY

Regulation of the height of trees or buildings by zoning or other legislation is quite common and has been upheld.[82] In the absence of legislation, courts have disagreed as to whether mere height of a building that harms use of nearby land of another may be unlawful as a nuisance.

A Florida court held that the Eden Roc Hotel on Miami Beach was not entitled to an injunction restraining construction that would increase the height of the adjoining Fontainebleau Hotel to an extent that it would block direct sunlight from Eden Roc's swimming pool during the winter.[83] The court's simple rationale was that no landowner has a right to the free flow of light and air from adjoining land. The court seemingly believed that circumstances could never exist that would justify some limit upon a building that blocks sunlight from a neighbor's land. A more recent decision by the Supreme Court of Wisconsin, faulting this reasoning as conclusory, held that erection of a building that shades a neighbor's solar collector could be a nuisance if all relevant factors were balanced.[84] Prior to the Wisconsin decision, the Supreme Court of Illinois, indicating approval of the Fontainebleau opinion, held that interference with reception of television signals by construction of the 110–story Sears building in Chicago could not constitute a nuisance.[85] The source of the problem, as viewed by the court, was the inadequate height of the broadcasting antennas, a matter within control of the broadcasters. Perhaps this factor distinguishes the Sears decision from the sunlight cases.

While the Wisconsin court's reliance upon nuisance law as a possible restraint upon occupancy of airspace that deprives a neighbor of solar energy may seem appealing, legislative and administrative approaches to the problem are likely to be more satisfactory. Such approaches are now law in a number of states.[86] Indeed, at the time when the Wisconsin case arose, a statute in that state authorized local governments to enact solar

82. Welch v. Swasey, 214 U.S. 91, 29 S.Ct. 567, 53 L.Ed. 923 (1909); Rogers v. City of Cheyenne, 747 P.2d 1137 (Wyo. 1987).

83. Fontainebleau Hotel Corp. v. Forty–Five Twenty–Five, Inc., 114 So.2d 357 (Fla.App.1959), cert. denied 117 So. 2d 842 (Fla.1960).

84. Prah v. Maretti, 108 Wis.2d 223, 321 N.W.2d 182 (1982).

85. People ex rel. Hoogasian v. Sears, Roebuck & Co., 52 Ill.2d 301, 287 N.E.2d 677 (1972).

86. Sampson & Charo, Access to Sunlight: Resolving Legal Issues to Encourage the Use of Solar Energy, 11 Colum.J.Envtl.L. 417 (1986).

access ordinances. One judge in that case dissented on the ground that the legislative approach was preferable, that it made reliance upon nuisance law unnecessary, and that resort to nuisance law might undermine the legislative program. Similar views were expressed by a California appellate court that declined to follow the Wisconsin court's position applying nuisance law to solar access controversies.[87] Nuisance law is by its nature ad hoc. Each case requires a careful, time-consuming balancing of all relevant factors. This could be burdensome in communities with widespread use of solar collectors. Moreover, the cases usually come up after construction of a solar collector or offending building, when an ideal solution may be impossible.

The alternative solar access programs proposed or adopted will not be explored here. It is appropriate in this book on property principles, however, to note that one adopted approach is to create property rights in solar access. A New Mexico statute embracing this approach borrows from the law of prior appropriation of water.[88]

B. EXCLUSION OF OTHERS

Generally, one is entitled to exclude others from entry into airspace above one's land, as well as from entry upon the surface. One who so much as extends a hand over another's land without permission or privilege is a trespasser.[89] It would follow logically that overflights of aircraft, at any altitude, would also be trespasses, but that would stymie aviation. The problem called for a nation-wide solution, and Congress responded by declaring that any citizen of the United States has "a public right of freedom of transit through the navigable airspace of the United States," defined as airspace "above the minimum altitudes of flight" prescribed by authorized regulations, and also as "airspace needed to insure safety in take-off and landing of aircraft." [90] This declaration has not been held to constitute a taking of private property for a public use, for which compensation is constitutionally mandated.

87. Sher v. Leiderman, 181 Cal.App. 3d 867, 226 Cal.Rptr. 698 (1986).

88. Discussed in Gergacz, Solar Energy Law: Easements of Access to Sunlight, 10 N.M.L.Rev. 121 (1980).

89. Kenney v. Barna, 215 Neb. 863, 341 N.W.2d 901 (1983).

90. 49 U.S.C.A. §§ 1301(29), 1304 (Supp.1988). For the regulations, see Aeronautics and Space, 14 C.F.R. § 91.79 (1987).

While entries into navigable airspace do not now constitute trespasses, the Congressional declaration seemingly would not bar suits alleging that noise from flights within navigable airspace unreasonably impairs use of the land surface. However, Congress also has authorized a program of federal regulation of aircraft noise. This has been held to preempt the field of such regulation, precluding regulation by local governments [91] and, according to some courts, also nuisance suits by landowners.[92] This leaves only the remedy of inverse condemnation for aircraft noise. And this remedy is available only if the noise emanates from aircraft owned by government or from aircraft using an airport owned or operated by government. Courts have disagreed as to whether the inverse condemnation remedy is confined to noise from flights over the plaintiff's land or includes also noise from flights over nearby land. The notion that plaintiffs in these cases are suing for the taking of an avigation easement corridor over a plaintiff's land [93] suggests that only overflights could be takings.[94] But since plaintiffs in these inverse condemnation suits must establish that use of the land surface was impaired, it is obvious that it is surface use impairment that is the gravamen of the suit. It follows that inverse condemnation is a proper remedy for harm caused by nearby flights. The Supreme Court of Washington has so held.[95]

Aerial surveillance by law enforcement officers by law enforcement officers without search warrants has resulted in litigated claims that such conduct constitutes a search of private property in violation of the Fourth Amendment of the United States Constitution. In two 5–4 decisions in 1986, the United States Supreme Court held that there was no unconstitutional search in (1) visual observation of a residential yard and (2) photographing of an industrial plant from aircraft flying within navigable airspace as defined by Congress.[96] Subsequently that court, in another 5–4 decision, held that aerial surveillance from a helicopter flying below navigable airspace (though under circumstances au-

91. City of Burbank v. Lockheed Air Terminal, Inc., 411 U.S. 624, 93 S.Ct. 1854, 36 L.Ed.2d 547 (1973).

92. Bryski v. City of Chicago, 148 Ill. App.3d 556, 101 Ill.Dec. 795, 499 N.E.2d 162 (1986). Contra: Greater Westchester Homeowners Ass'n v. City of Los Angeles, 26 Cal.3d 86, 160 Cal.Rptr. 733, 603 P.2d 1329 (1979), cert. denied 446 U.S. 933, 100 S.Ct. 2149, 64 L.Ed.2d 786 (1980); Owen v. City of Atlanta, 157 Ga.App. 354, 277 S.E.2d 338 (1981), cert. denied, 456 U.S. 972, 102 S.Ct. 2235, 72 L.Ed.2d 846 (1982); Ursin v. New Orleans Aviation Board, 506 So.2d 947 (La. App.1987).

93. United States v. Causby, 328 U.S. 256, 66 S.Ct. 1062, 90 L.Ed. 1206 (1946).

94. Batten v. United States, 306 F.2d 580 (10th Cir.1962) cert. denied, 371 U.S. 955, 83 S.Ct. 506, 9 L.Ed.2d 502 (1963).

95. Martin v. Port of Seattle, 64 Wn. 2d 309, 391 P.2d 540 (1964), cert. denied, 379 U.S. 989, 85 S.Ct. 701, 13 L.Ed.2d 610 (1965).

96. California v. Ciraolo, 476 U.S. 207, 106 S.Ct. 1809, 90 L.Ed.2d 210 (1986); Dow Chemical Co. v. United States, 476 U.S. 227, 106 S.Ct. 1819, 90 L.Ed.2d 226 (1986).

thorized by Congress) constituted a constitutional search.[97] A California court had reached a contrary result in an essentially identical case; certiorari had been denied there.[98] This is not the place to delve into the complex law of unlawful search, but one may well question whether the Congressional declaration of citizen rights to use navigable airspace and prescription of safe practices for helicopter flights should be relevant in determining whether aerial surveillance is an unconstitutional search. A seemingly more relevant matter is whether the aerial surveillance would conflict with reasonable expectations of privacy under the circumstances.[99]

C. SEVERANCE

There are several modern instances in large cities of conveyance by landowners of the fee simple and other estates and interests in airspace. Buildings in separate ownership may be built on top of each other. The multi-story condominium severs ownership of portions of airspace from ownership of the surface. One might have supposed that these modern developments could have been accommodated easily by the courts. Landowners long have been permitted to sever ownership vertically and, as to the subsurface, horizontally. But severance of ownership of airspace was new and there was apprehension among lawyers that there might be legal obstacles to accomplishing it. Consequently, there has been widespread adoption of legislation authorizing separate ownership of airspace and addressing the consequences of severance. Several states have adopted the Model Airspace Act, sponsored by the American Bar Association.[1] It provides that airspace "may be divided or apportioned horizontally and vertically, and in any geometric shape or design," and that the severed units of airspace shall be subject to all laws applicable to real property, including taxation. Statutes addressing condominiums are ubiquitous.

Transfers of zoning development rights in airspace are permitted in some jurisdictions.[2] Instead of occupying all of the airspace

97. Florida v. Riley, 109 S.Ct. 693 (1989).

98. People v. Sabo, 185 Cal.App.3d 845, 230 Cal.Rptr. 170 (1986), cert. denied 107 S.Ct. 2200 (1987).

99. See the concurring opinion of O'Connor, J., and the dissenting opinions of Brennan, J. (joined by Marshall, J., and Stevens, J.) and Blackmun, J., in Florida v. Riley, 109 S.Ct. 693 (1989).

1. Wright, Final Draft of Model Airspace Act, 7 Real Prop., Prob. & Tr.J. 353 (1972). An appendix to this article contains the full text of the act.

2. The concept is described and recommended in Costonis, Space Adrift:

allowed by zoning ordinances, a landowner may transfer the unused portion of that allowance ("development right") to another landowner, who then is permitted to erect a higher or larger building than zoning would allow. This phenomenon is entirely different from the severance of airspace discussed in the above paragraph. Transfer of a zoning development right does not convey any right to occupy or use airspace in the land of the transferor. The effect simply is that permissible use of the transferor's airspace is now reduced and that of the transferee expanded. Cities may encourage owners of historic structures to preserve them by offering such owners the opportunity to transfer development rights to other lands owned by them. Achievement of other conservation and land use goals may also be aided by resort to TDR's. The mere availability of TDR's may save a stringent regulation from invalidation as a taking.[3]

Saving Urban Landmarks Through the Chicago Plan, (Univ. of Ill. Press, 1974). A less enthusiastic view is taken in Richards, Transferable Development Rights: Corrective, Catastrophe or Curiosity? 12 Real Estate L.J. 26 (1983).

3. Penn Central Transportation Co. v. City of New York, 438 U.S. 104, 98 S.Ct. 2646, 57 L.Ed.2d 631 (1978).

Chapter 3

PUBLIC REGULATION OF LAND USE

Legal restraints upon permissible uses of land are imposed not only by privately created servitudes and judicially created nuisance (and kindred) doctrines, but also by legislative and administrative regulation. Today, especially in urban areas, the latter—public regulation—is far more significant than the former. Most of this regulation is by local governments, but state governments and the federal government also are involved. Particularly important are state statutes authorizing local governments to regulate land use in certain ways. Except as qualified by home-rule powers of local governments in some states, state enabling legislation is essential. A common ground for challenges to local government regulations is that they are not authorized by enabling legislation. Some aspects of land use have been viewed as affecting national interests. Congress has established several programs regulating or affecting land use. Prominent among these are environmental protection laws and financial assistance for desired land development such as housing for low-income persons and urban renewal. Most Congressional programs involve cooperation with state and local governments.

There are many roles for lawyers in this field. Those who represent local governments are called upon to incorporate the community's land use goals into effective and valid ordinances, to give legal advice from day to day to administrators of programs established by such ordinances, and to defend those programs against attack in court and other forums. Lawyers who represent land developers must guide development proposals through the regulatory maze and seek to overcome legal obstacles. Lawyers who represent environmental groups and neighbors of proposed developments must seek to convince local officials that the proposals are unsound, illegal, or both. If their clients have standing, these attorneys may press their claims of illegality in court.

This chapter presents an overview of the field of land use regulation and focuses attention upon a few of the more significant issues.

SECTION 1. THE TRADITIONAL CONTROLS

———

A rather long list of regulatory approaches to guiding land use in the public interest has been generated over the years. Some of these serve unique purposes, but most of them are merely different techniques for reaching the same or similar goals. The major controls will be identified and described briefly here.

———

A. PROHIBITION OR REGULATION OF SPECIFIED USES

———

The most direct way to deal with unwanted land uses is simply to forbid them. Local governments have long used this approach to rid the community of such uses as houses of prostitution, rendering plants and other uses deemed serious threats to the public health, safety or morals. Such uses often have been labeled "nuisances" in the ordinance. Merely calling something a nuisance does not make it such. Courts have reserved the last word on this to themselves,[1] but courts usually have deferred to such legislative characterization of uses. According to most courts, the power to prohibit uses is not confined to nuisances, but also embraces uses "akin to nuisances," uses "likely to create nuisances," and any use the banning of which may be reasonably viewed as bearing a substantial relation to the public welfare.[2]

Legislative prohibition of specified uses is superior to reliance upon nuisance litigation. As already observed, it has a broader sweep than the law of nuisance. It is more likely to prevent nuisances from occurring than is vague nuisance doctrine. Substantial investment in a use not explicitly banned greatly complicates the court's task and may induce a court to allow the challenged use to continue. Unlike the costs of private nuisance suits, the costs of enforcement of ordinances (as well as public nuisances) are borne by the entire community. Another advantage of legislative banning is the availability of criminal sanctions.

———

1. Crossman v. City of Galveston, 112 Tex. 303, 247 S.W. 810 (1923).

2. Goldblatt v. Town of Hempstead, 369 U.S. 590, 82 S.Ct. 987, 8 L.Ed.2d 130 (1962).

B. BUILDING CODES AND DEVELOPMENT PERMITS

Building codes establish standards for construction of buildings to protect neighbors and occupants from fire, collapse, disease and other harms. These codes require governmental review of building plans and issuance of a building permit before construction may be commenced. The permit is issued only after officials are satisfied that the requirements of the building code—and other land use ordinances, including zoning—have been met.

The building permit is a significant regulatory device. It is more effective and less costly to prevent harmful uses from occurring than to terminate them. Development permits are relied upon for enforcement of many land use regulatory programs, in addition to building codes and zoning. A developer may need to obtain several permits from various agencies administering different laws.

There are other municipal codes besides building codes that regulate the condition of buildings. Among these are housing codes, fire codes, safety codes and health codes. These codes apply to existing buildings, as well as proposed ones. They frequently impose standards higher than those in force when some buildings were erected. This retroactive application has generally been upheld, even when the cost of compliance is substantial. The United States Supreme Court upheld required installation of automatic sprinklers costing $7,500 in a lodging house worth $25,000, even though the owner alleged that other fire safety features of the building, including an alarm system and constant watchman service, provided adequate protection.[3] The choice of methods of handling the threat of fire, so long as it is not arbitrary, lies with the legislative body, the court said. Moreover, it declared that all members of a class—lodging houses in this instance—may be subjected to identical requirements despite a showing that some members of the class could satisfy the purpose of the requirements in other ways.

Local codes usually follow closely model codes drafted by national organizations. They may be specification codes or performance codes. The former are criticized as being too rigid in some respects, as they may not take into account local conditions and may not keep pace with technological advances. Performance

---

3. Queenside Hills Realty Co. v. Saxl, 328 U.S. 80, 66 S.Ct. 850, 90 L.Ed. 1096 (1946).

codes may avoid those defects, but their administration requires more highly skilled enforcement personnel and equipment.

C. ZONING

Zoning is by far the most significant form of land use regulation. The traditional zoning ordinance restricts the use of nearly every parcel of land within the local community. Typically, each parcel is subjected to multiple zoning restrictions. Some of these restrictions seriously curtail permitted uses.

Zoning became common in the United States during the 1920's. Following conflicting opinions by state courts as to the constitutionality of the zoning device, the United States Supreme Court upheld it in 1926, in the landmark case of Village of Euclid v. Ambler Realty Co.[4] A few cities, the largest being Houston, Texas, have refused to adopt zoning, but some of these, including Houston, have other ordinances that serve many of the functions of zoning.[5]

Zoning divides the entire community into districts, within each of which appropriate and compatible land uses are allowed. Euclid's ordinance provided for three overlying sets of districts: use, height and area. There were six use districts, ranging from the most highly restricted to the least. Within each "lower" district, uses approved for "higher" districts were also allowed. The apparent dominant purpose of this scheme was protection of single-family residential neighborhoods from invasion by uses deemed incompatible. The highest use district allowed only single-family dwellings and a few specified non-residential uses, including parks. Duplexes and apartments were not allowed in that zone. Commercial and industrial uses were relegated to still lower districts. Height and area districts determined the extent to which land parcels, including their airspace, could be occupied by structures. Modern zoning ordinances are similar to the early prototypes, but have become more sophisticated. The list of districts is now longer. Some districts, such as watershed protection zones, address specific environmental protection concerns. Even residential uses may be excluded from industrial zones—a practice referred to as noncumulative zoning. Performance standards are beginning to be substituted for classification by building

---

4. 272 U.S. 365, 47 S.Ct. 114, 71 L.Ed. 303 (1926).

5. Comment, Municipal Enforcement of Private Restrictive Covenants:

An Innovation in Land–Use Control, 44 Tex.L.Rev. 741 (1966).

type and use.[6] Still other modern developments will be discussed subsequently.

The most obvious function of zoning is separation of incompatible uses, which may avert costly and possibly ineffective nuisance litigation, and also may exclude from some areas uses that are incompatible in those locations but would not constitute nuisances. But zoning also serves a broader and more significant function. Briefly stated, zoning is a means for shaping the physical development of the entire community. The declaration of purposes in the Standard State Enabling Act,[7] upon which most zoning ordinances are based, includes lessening of "congestion in the streets," "overcrowding of land," "undue concentration of populations," as well as "to provide adequate light and air," and to "facilitate the adequate provision of water, sewerage, schools, parks, and other public requirements"—all "in accordance with a comprehensive plan."

A municipality whose voters wish it to be primarily a residential community may seek that goal by zoning very little land for industrial use. Or, a municipality whose voters wish to attract industry may seek that goal by reserving for industrial use land most suited for that use, such as land near railroads, highways and waterways, by placing it in a non-cumulative industrial zone. Zoning may be utilized to encourage or discourage development of large outlying shopping centers. These suggested applications of zoning, far from exhaustive, demonstrate its powerful potential.

The classification scheme of Euclid's ordinance was challenged, unsuccessfully, as depriving landowners of constitutional guarantees of substantive due process and equal protection of the laws. The court declared that although zoning drastically reduces the value of some land parcels, excludes from some areas seemingly harmless uses, and presents difficult classification problems, it is not "clearly arbitrary and unreasonable, having no substantial relation to the public health, safety, morals or general welfare."

Euclid merely upheld zoning as a lawful technique. It acknowledged that specific applications of this technique could be invalid if found to be "clearly arbitrary and unreasonable." Two years later, in Nectow v. City of Cambridge,[8] the United States Supreme Court did just that. In that case, an owner of undeveloped land situated between a developed industrial area and a developed residential area contested the residential zoning of a narrow strip of his tract fronting a street opposite residences. The

6. Kendig, Performance Zoning (1980).

7. U.S. Department of Commerce, Standard State Zoning Enabling Act § 3 (1926), reprinted in Anderson, American Law of Zoning § 30.01 (2d ed. 1977).

8. 277 U.S. 183, 48 S.Ct. 447, 72 L.Ed. 842 (1928).

apparent purpose of this zoning was to protect established residences from expansion of industrial development. The court found that this zoning was "not indispensable to the general plan" and accepted a master's finding that "no practical use can be made of the land in question for residential purposes." The court's decision invalidated the portion of the zoning map (an ordinance separate from the zoning scheme ordinance) classifying this strip as residential, but left the balance of the map intact.

Was this decision sound? Arguably, residential zoning of this strip was reasonable, as it was merely a small portion of a tract that otherwise was unrestricted. The owner could have devoted more of his land than the narrow strip to residential use and then buffered it from nonresidential uses of the balance of the tract. It appears that Cambridge officials deemed it undesirable to draw the boundary in the middle of the street, which would have exposed existing residences to nonresidential uses across the street. The court's action left the zoning map in this state. It was left to Cambridge to fill this gap with some sort of nonresidential zoning. There surely is at least reasonable doubt about the proper drawing of this line. The highest court of Massachusetts had so concluded.[9]

Perhaps the United States Supreme Court was eager to demonstrate that its Euclid decision was not a carte blanche for city planners. But its refusal to pass upon another zoning case for almost forty decades showed that it was content to leave zoning review to the state courts in most instances. The multitude of state cases, even within a single jurisdiction, are difficult to reconcile. Some courts are much more inclined than others to invalidate specific zoning schemes or map boundaries.[10]

Due largely to concern about the constitutionality of zoning, zoning ordinances allowed existing uses not conforming to the zoning map to continue. However, nonconforming uses were viewed as threats to the effectiveness of zoning and devices for phasing them out over time were incorporated in zoning ordinances.[11] Expansion of such uses was forbidden. Improvement of structures accommodating nonconforming uses was restricted. If such a structure was substantially destroyed, it could not be rebuilt. Discontinuance or abandonment of a nonconforming use would terminate its privileged status. Modern ordinances often contain "amortization" provisions requiring termination of certain

9. Nectow v. City of Cambridge, 260 Mass. 441, 157 N.E. 618 (1927).

10. California and Illinois decisions are contrasted in Ellickson & Tarlock, Land–Use Controls 75 (1981).

11. Note, Nonconforming Uses: A Rationale and an Approach, 102 U.Pa. L.Rev. 91 (1953).

nonconforming uses, such as billboards and junk yards, within specified time periods.[12]

The policy of gradual elimination of nonconforming uses has enjoyed only limited success. Contrary to early expectations, nonconforming uses did not die on the vine; indeed, nourished by monopolistic advantages given them by zoning, they often enjoyed the best of health. Phasing-out provisions of ordinances have not been enforced vigorously. When courts have been called upon to apply such provisions, they have had difficulty with such issues as whether a nonconforming use existed,[13] what constitutes expansion of a nonconforming use,[14] and the relevance of intent to abandonment of a nonconforming use.[15] Some courts invalidate amortization provisions as unconstitutional takings.[16] Courts upholding this device have had difficulty determining whether the amortization period in question is sufficiently long to surmount the takings challenge.[17] Finally, there has been a change in the attitude of planners toward nonconforming uses; they no longer regard mixed uses within a neighborhood as necessarily bad.[18]

D. SUBDIVISION REGULATION

Owners of land who wish to divide it into lots for development, usually for construction of residences, are required by most local governments to obtain approval of their plats by local officials. Typically, these officials are members of citizen planning commissions that also administer the zoning ordinance. They are aided by local government employees, including planners and engineers, who assist developers in drafting plats and make recommendations to the commissions. The standards that must be met are set forth in a statement of subdivision regulations adopted by the local government pursuant to a state enabling act.

Because it comes at a critical point in the development process, subdivision regulation is a powerful device. It has been used

12. Note, Amortization of Property Uses Not Conforming to Zoning Regulations, 9 U.Chi.L.Rev. 477 (1942).

13. Helicopter Associates v. City of Stamford, 201 Conn. 700, 519 A.2d 49 (1986).

14. Id.

15. Anderson v. City of Paragould, 16 Ark.App. 10, 695 S.W.2d 851 (1985); Williams v. Salem Township, 92 Pa. Cmwlth. 634, 500 A.2d 933 (1985).

16. Ailes v. Decatur County Area Planning Commission, 448 N.E.2d 1057 (Ind.1983). Contra: City of Los Angeles v. Gage, 127 Cal.App.2d 442, 274 P.2d 34 (1954).

17. Murmur Corp. v. Board of Adjustment, 718 S.W.2d 790 (Tex.App.— Dallas 1986).

18. A.L.I., Model Land Development Code Art. 4, Commentary (1975).

to serve many goals. It complements and reinforces some aspects of zoning, particularly zoning requirements for the size and shape of lots. A prime function of subdivision control is coordination of streets on the proposed plat with existing and planned streets in the community. Another is coordination of utility facilities (such as the size of sewers) on the proposed plat with existing and planned utility facilities in the community. Assurance also is sought that streets and utility facilities within the proposed subdivision will be of sufficient quality, properly designed and completed prior to sale of lots. As development usually alters existing drainage of surface water, subdivision regulations seek to minimize harm from such alterations to lands within and without the subdivision. They also may seek to protect streams, lakes, and groundwater from runoff of wastes generated by the proposed development; they do this by controls such as preserving natural vegetation, maintaining low density of development, and requiring detention ponds. Subdivision regulations may even prohibit development of some lands, such as floodplains, where development would threaten safety or health, the natural environment or other public interests. Of course, prohibitions of development must be carefully drafted in order to survive challenges that they are unconstitutional takings of property. Another type of subdivision regulation that invites challenge is the requirement that subdividers compensate the local government for costs imposed upon the community by the development, such as costs for new schools, parks, water supplies and waste water treatment. The topics of takings and development exactions will be discussed subsequently.

There is much diversity as to the planning commission's discretion to deny approval of a plat or to attach conditions to approval. Subdivision regulations contain a multitude of specific standards, such as street width, lot size, etc. A developer whose plat meets all of the specific standards may take the position that the planning commission is obligated to approve the plat. Some courts, viewing the commission's role as ministerial, have agreed with that contention.[19] Other courts have concluded that the planning commission has discretion to deny approval of a plat that satisfies all of the specific standards but that poses a threat to public health, safety or welfare.[20] The breadth of the language of the enabling act and of the local regulations is likely to determine the resolution of this issue. Which role is supported by the better policy? Developers may suffer substantially if their plats, after the often costly process of conforming them to specific standards, are turned down for failure to comply with vague standards of

19. Kaufman v. Planning & Zoning Commission of the City of Fairmont, 298 S.E.2d 148 (W.Va.1982).

20. Durant v. Town of Dunbarton, 121 N.H. 352, 430 A.2d 140 (1981).

suitability. On the other hand, others (and even developers) may suffer substantially if bad projects are not nipped in the bud, before still more money is poured into them. The subdivision plat approval process may be the last realistic opportunity to stop or modify harmful developments.

Effective regulation of the subdivision of land requires that regulation embrace land outside municipal boundaries that will be annexed as the city grows. Cities commonly are authorized to give their subdivision regulations extraterritorial effect within a band several miles wide.[21] Authority for extraterritorial zoning, by contrast, is rare.

E. COMPREHENSIVE PLANS AND OFFICIAL MAPS

Regulation of land use by local governments presupposes that there is some sort of comprehensive plan for community development to be served by regulation. Indeed, the widely adopted Standard Zoning Enabling Act, promulgated by the U.S. Department of Commerce in 1928, provides that zoning regulations "shall be made in accordance with a comprehensive plan." This has been generally construed, however, as not requiring preparation and adoption of a comprehensive plan document.[22] It is sufficient to show that the zoning ordinance is a product of a rational process and substantially related to public interests. The zoning ordinance itself may constitute sufficient evidence of this. Many municipalities, especially small towns, have never prepared or adopted a separate comprehensive plan.

Several state legislatures have attempted to change this situation by making it clear that municipalities must adopt separate comprehensive plan documents. Some of these have even dictated the components of the mandated plan.[23]

If a local government has adopted a comprehensive plan, whether required to do so or not, must zoning and other land use regulations be consistent with it in order to be valid? In the absence of an explicit legislative mandate of consistency, nearly all courts have viewed the comprehensive plan merely as a general guide rather than as a legal constraint upon zoning or other regulations.[24] In other words, the comprehensive plan document

---

21. The Standard City Planning Enabling Act § 12 (1928) set the limit at five miles.

22. Kozesnik v. Township of Montgomery, 24 N.J. 154, 131 A.2d 1 (1957).

23. Cal.Gov.Code § 65302 (Supp. 1978).

24. Holmgren v. City of Lincoln, 199 Neb. 178, 256 N.W.2d 686 (1977). Contra: Baker v. City of Milwaukie, 271 Or.

does not regulate land use. This is not to say that glaring inconsistency between the comprehensive plan and zoning would not be persuasive evidence that challenged zoning was arbitrary.

The legal status of comprehensive plans may become an issue in another context. Suppose that a plan shows that a portion of X's land is designated as the site of a future public school, but that steps have not been taken to purchase this site or condemn it for public use and may never be taken. So long as this situation continues, the value of X's land for other uses is probably greatly diminished. Nevertheless, it is extremely unlikely that a court will invalidate the plan designation of the school site as an unconstitutional taking for lack of compensation.[25] The reasoning supporting this result is that the plan imposes no legal restraint on the use of X's land. A legal restraint will occur only when the landowner is prevented by zoning, subdivision regulation or some other regulation from developing the land. There is always the possibility that the school site designation on X's land will be altered or ignored by government officials. The landowner can force a decision by them by seeking regulatory approvals of proposed development that would devote the planned school site to some other use. If a landowner is dissuaded from such action by unequivocal official statements that approvals would be denied because public acquisition would occur soon, and then nothing toward that end is done by the city, that might constitute an invalid temporary taking.[26]

Unlike comprehensive plan maps, one type of plan—an "official" map for streets or other public uses—may alter the bundle of sticks constituting the fee simple. Official map ordinances not only require that subdivision plats conform to official maps, but also may prohibit building of structures within mapped street or other areas designated for public use. The purpose of this prohibition is to avoid compensation for buildings when the mapped lands are eventually purchased or condemned for the specified public uses. Such prohibition is a present restriction on the use of the mapped lands. It may or may not be invalid as a deprivation of substantive due process or as a taking without compensation. Official maps can protect significant public interests without seriously impairing private property. Placing a huge building in a mapped street could seriously impair the efficiency of the street plan and might not be necessary for profitable development of a

500, 533 P.2d 772 (1975). Consistency is statutorily required in some states. See Haines v. City of Phoenix, 151 Ariz. 286, 727 P.2d 339 (App.1986).

25. State National Bank of Connecticut v. Planning & Zoning Comm. of

The Town of Trumbull, 156 Conn. 99, 239 A.2d 528 (1968).

26. Suess Builders Co. v. City of Beaverton, 294 Or. 254, 656 P.2d 306 (1982).

private tract sufficiently large to accommodate the same building without encroaching on the mapped street. Well-drafted official map ordinances contain variance provisions designed to protect both public and private interests. These ordinances are likely to be upheld when challenged.[27] Also, when such provisions are available, resort to them is a prerequisite to a suit challenging the validity of the official map.[28] However, courts have demonstrated reluctance to uphold prohibitions of building in areas mapped for future public uses other than streets, such as parks.[29] The rationale for this distinction is uncertain, but may be based upon the long tradition of official street maps.

F. PUBLIC OWNERSHIP AND DEVELOPMENT OF LAND

A potentially effective method of obtaining uses of land in the public interest is acquisition of land by governmental units, by eminent domain if necessary. Resort to this approach is deterred not so much by its cost as by a widespread and strongly held view in this nation that private land ownership should be the norm and public land ownership the exception. Until this century, the dominant public land policy of the federal government was transfer of ownership of the public domain to private hands as rapidly as possible.[30] This policy of disposition finally gave way to a policy of retention of the remaining lands (about one-third of all lands in the nation) for conservation and management. Management of the remaining federal public lands raises many very significant issues of policy and law [31] but that topic is beyond the scope of this book. The focus here is upon governmental acquisition of land as an alternative to land use regulation.

The term "land banking" refers to acquisition by local governments of ownership of certain lands to prevent imminent undesirable development by private owners, the holding of such lands until such time as development is deemed desirable, and eventual transfer of such lands to private owners with restrictive covenants consistent with comprehensive community plans. Over time, land

27. State ex rel. Miller v. Manders, 2 Wis.2d 365, 86 N.W.2d 469 (1957).

28. Id.

29. Lomarch Corp. v. Mayor and Common Council of City of Englewood, 51 N.J. 108, 237 A.2d 881 (1968); Miller v. City of Beaver Falls, 368 Pa. 189, 82 A.2d 34 (1951).

30. Texas, which retained its public lands when it became a state, also pursued a disposition policy.

31. See Coggins and Wilkinson, Federal Public Land and Resources Law (1981).

banking would not necessarily require huge expenditures of public funds; indeed, net profits could be generated. This approach has been utilized to some extent in some foreign countries,[32] including Canada, but not in the United States. It has been advocated, however, by the American Law Institute in its Model Land Development Code 221 (1976). If a local government, duly authorized by state enabling legislation or home rule powers, were to embark upon a land banking program, including the necessary power of eminent domain, it almost certainly would be challenged as invalid for failure to satisfy the requirement of the Fifth Amendment of the United States Constitution that private land be condemned only for a "public use." Violation of similar provisions in state constitutions also would be alleged. This attack is based upon the possibly long periods of time when banked land would not be used at all and also upon the ultimate return to such land to private ownership and private use. To obtain a court decision upholding the land banking against this attack, it would be necessary to convince the court that significant public interests are served by this program. Courts have already held in cases involving analogous programs of condemnation for transfer to private ownership that the public use requirement is satisfied by establishing that significant public interests are advanced. A carefully drafted land banking program should survive the anticipated attacks based upon constitutional public use requirements.

The key case in the public development of land is Berman v. Parker,[33] decided by the Supreme Court of the United States in 1954. Congress had passed the District of Columbia Redevelopment Act of 1945 which empowered a redevelopment land agency to acquire and assemble, by eminent domain and otherwise, real property for "the redevelopment of blighted territory in the District of Columbia and the prevention, reduction, or elimination of blighting factors or causes of blight." The plaintiff sought to enjoin the taking of his property as unconstitutional since it would deprive him of his land without due process of law. The plaintiff's property was in a "blighted area", but was not slum property as such since it was, in fact, a department store. Furthermore, he contended no public purpose was involved since the leased land would be turned over to private owners to redevelop in line with a comprehensive land-use plan. The court held that this was a valid exercise of the governmental power and that the rights of the property owner were protected as long as he received that just compensation exacted by the Fifth Amendment as the price of

---

32. See Cribbet, Some Reflections on the Law of the Land—A View from Scandinavia, 62 N.W.U.L.Rev. 277 (1967).

33. 348 U.S. 26, 75 S.Ct. 98, 99 L.Ed. 27 (1954).

taking. The legislature can plan on a broad as well as a piecemeal basis and it was reasonable to clear all of the land in a given area to carry out the public purpose.

The court stated that in these cases the legislature rather than the judiciary is the principal guardian of public needs and that the role of the judiciary in determining whether the power is being exercised for a public purpose is an extremely narrow one. Moreover, Mr. Justice Douglas struck a blow for aesthetic values as a basis for redevelopment when he wrote: "It is within the power of the legislature to determine that the community should be beautiful as well as healthy, spacious as well as clean, well-balanced as well as carefully patrolled . . . If those who govern the District of Columbia decide that the Nation's Capital should be beautiful as well as sanitary, there is nothing in the Fifth Amendment that stands in the way." [34]

Berman v. Parker clarified the power to act under the Constitution of the United States but what about the state constitutions? The redevelopment laws of the several states, all depending on a heavy infusion of federal funds to make them more than pious expressions of intent, came under successive attacks. In some instances, the acts were struck down as authorizing a taking for a private purpose.[35] For example, in Edens v. City of Columbia [36] it was held that the law was valid to the extent that the condemned land would be used by the University of South Carolina, but invalid where it would be turned over to private developers to use for a light industrial area. The South Carolina Constitution allowed land to be taken for a public use only and the court felt that cases in states allowing a taking for a public purpose were not in point. Only an amendment of the constitution would allow this use of the power of eminent domain.

On the other hand, the majority of states followed the lead of the United States Supreme Court and sustained this extension of the power of eminent domain without much reference to the semantic distinction between public use and public purpose. They seemed to find sufficient justification for the power in the public interest served by the clearance of slum or blighted areas regardless of the ultimate use of the land, assuming, of course, that the use was in accordance with a valid comprehensive plan.[37] A series

34. Id. at 33, 102, and 38.

35. Adams v. Housing Authority of City of Daytona Beach, 60 So.2d 663 (Fla.1952); Housing Authority of Atlanta v. Johnson, 209 Ga. 560, 74 S.E.2d 891 (1953).

36. 228 S.C. 563, 91 S.E.2d 280 (1956).

37. See Mandelker, The Comprehensive Planning Requirement in Urban Renewal, 116 Pa.L.Rev. 25 (1967); Scheuer, Goldston and Sogg, Disposition of Urban Renewal Land—A Fundamental Problem in the Rebuilding of Our Cities, 62 Colum.L.Rev. 959 (1969).

of Illinois cases handled this theme as well as any in the nation and concluded that even private industrial development is consistent with this use of governmental power.[38]

The use of the power of eminent domain to prevent slums as well as to eliminate them was upheld in Gutknecht v. Chicago.[39] Mr. Justice Schaefer went to the heart of the matter. "It is also contended that the 'line of demarcation between a public and private use in the employment of eminent domain to eliminate slum areas . . . must be the elimination rather than the prevention of slums.' But we are aware of no constitutional principle which paralyzes the power of government to deal with an evil until it has reached its maximum development. Nor is there force in the argument that if the use of eminent domain in the prevention of slums is permitted 'every piece of property within the city or State can be condemned to prevent it from becoming a slum.' Legitimate use of governmental power is not prohibited because of the possibility that the power may be abused."

The United States Supreme Court again addressed the public use issue in its 1984 decision in Hawaii Housing Authority v. Midkiff.[40] This case concerned a program of the Hawaii Legislature to change a pattern of concentration of land ownership in a few owners. This situation was viewed by the legislature as preventing normal functioning of the residential land market, forcing persons to lease rather than to buy land for homes, and resulting in inflated land prices. Its approach to the problem was to authorize a state agency to purchase, by eminent domain if necessary, large tracts of land occupied by lessees and then sell such land to those lessees or others. The agency was not permitted to make a profit. The Court of Appeals for the Ninth Circuit invalidated this program on the ground that it authorized condemnation for private, not public, uses—a "naked attempt to take the private property of A and transfer it to B solely for B's private use and benefit." [41] Reversing that judgment, the United States Supreme Court, speaking through Justice O'Connor, declared: "The Hawaii Legislature enacted its Land Reform Act not to benefit a particular class of identifiable individuals but to attack certain perceived evils of concentrated property ownership in Hawaii—a legitimate public purpose." [42] Determinations of public purpose

38. Gutknecht v. City of Chicago, 414 Ill. 600, 111 N.E.2d 626 (1953); Gutknecht v. City of Chicago, 3 Ill.2d 539, 121 N.E.2d 791 (1954); People ex rel. Adamowski v. Chicago Land Clearance Commission, 14 Ill.2d 74, 150 N.E.2d 792 (1958). Comment, 1958 U.Ill.L.F. 477. See also Cannata v. City of New York, 11 N.Y.2d 210, 227 N.Y.S.2d 903, 182 N.E.2d 395 (1962).

39. 3 Ill.2d 539, 121 N.E.2d 791 (1954).

40. 467 U.S. 229, 104 S.Ct. 2321, 81 L.Ed.2d 186 (1984).

41. Midkiff v. Tom, 702 F.2d 788, 798 (9th Cir.1983).

42. 46 U.S. at 245, 104 S.Ct. at 2331.

by state legislatures are entitled to the same deference accorded Congressional determinations, the court said. The court also reiterated that "government does not itself have to use property to legitimate the taking; it is only the takings purpose, not its mechanics, that must pass scrutiny under the Public Use Clause." [43]

Among other things, the Supreme Court's decision in Midkiff established that it is not essential to a finding of public use that there be any governmental regulation of the use of land after it passes into private lands. The Supreme Court of Michigan, in Poletown Neighborhood Council v. City of Detroit,[44] similarly construed the essentially identical eminent domain provision in its state constitution. That case upheld condemnation of land to be transferred to General Motors Corporation for a plant site without any restrictions on its use. In one sense, this Michigan decision went beyond Midkiff, as well as Berman: it sanctioned taking of land that was not impacted by oligopoly, blight or any sort of harm. It was sufficient that the purpose of the Michigan program was alleviation of a socio-economic problem, in this instance unemployment.

SECTION 2. ADAPTATION OF REGULATION TO PLANS OF DEVELOPERS

Drafters of the earliest zoning ordinances realized that it was impossible to impose controls in advance on all land parcels in the community that would turn out to be workable and fair in every instance when concrete proposals emerged. The Standard State Zoning Enabling Act provided that zoning text and map ordinances may be amended. It also authorized municipalities to appoint a board of adjustment, authorized not only to hear appeals from decisions by zoning officials, but also to grant special exceptions and variances. These instruments of flexibility—ordinance amendment and administrative discretion—have played a far more important role than probably was anticipated, but even they proved to be grossly inadequate to accommodate the huge volume of developmental plans, many of them seemingly desirable, completely at odds with zoning or other regulations. Legislatures, local governments and courts have struggled for decades with a variety of techniques to allow "good" developments to go forward on an ad hoc basis without threatening the integrity of the

43. 467 U.S. at 244, 104 S.Ct. at 2331.

44. 410 Mich. 616, 304 N.W.2d 455 (1981).

community's land use program. The struggle continues. One scholar has concluded that zoning should be abandoned and replaced by avowedly case-by-case regulation.[45]

A. AMENDMENTS OF THE ZONING MAP ORDINANCE

One who wishes to devote land to a use prohibited by zoning may seek an amendment of the zoning map reclassifying that particular parcel. Typically, such a proposal is submitted to the city planning staff, then to the citizen planning commission and finally to the local legislative body. A public hearing is held by the commission and sometimes by the legislative body. Neighbors usually participate in such hearings in opposition to the proposed rezoning. Applications for zoning amendments are very numerous and consume much of the time of planning commissions. Some communities have deemed it necessary to divide the commission into subcommittees or to appoint hearing officers in order to handle the large volume of such requests.

Given the huge number of rezonings, the tiny land area usually involved in each, and the tendency of rezoning hearings to focus upon a particular development proposal rather than upon broader concerns, the zoning map soon appears to be a product of whim rather than plan.

Courts have reacted in various ways to piecemeal rezoning. If the rezoning allows uses greatly different from established and permitted uses in the neighborhood, courts are likely to invalidate the rezoning as "spot" zoning.[46] The prevailing judicial view, however, is that rezonings should be accorded the deference usually given legislation and upheld unless clearly not rationally related to public interests.[47] Consistent application of this approach would produce few invalidations. Other courts have been much more hostile toward rezonings. The most extreme view, with little support, is that a rezoning is valid only if there had been substantial change in land uses in the neighborhood or a mistake in the earlier classification.[48] Another severe, but more flexible, standard of judicial review is to view piecemeal rezonings as quasi-judicial, rather than legislative, acts; as such, they are not enti-

---

45. Krasnowiecki, Abolish Zoning, 31 Syracuse L.Rev. 719 (1980).

46. Fritts v. City of Ashland, 348 S.W.2d 712 (Ky.1961).

47. Bartram v. Zoning Commission of City of Bridgeport, 136 Conn. 89, 68 A.2d 308 (1949).

48. Wakefield v. Kraft, 202 Md. 136, 96 A.2d 27 (1953).

tled to a presumption of validity and must be supported by proof of a sufficient nexus with public interests.[49] Treating rezonings in this manner also requires compliance with procedural due process requirements for quasi-judicial proceedings. This is a heavy burden on local legislative bodies, which may be relieved to some extent by resort to hearing officers.

Whether piecemeal rezonings should be treated as quasi-judicial is much debated. The Supreme Court of Oregon, a strong advocate of this approach, has declared:[50]

"At this juncture we feel we would be ignoring reality to rigidly view all zoning decisions by local governing bodies as legislative acts to be accorded a full presumption of validity and shielded from less than constitutional scrutiny by the theory of separation of powers. Local and small decision groups are simply not the equivalent in all respects of state and national legislatures . . .

"Ordinances laying down general policies without regard to a specific piece of property are usually an exercise of legislative authority, are subject to limited review, and may only be attacked upon constitutional grounds for an arbitrary abuse of authority. On the other hand, a determination whether the permissible use of a specific piece of property should be changed is usually an exercise of judicial authority and its propriety is subject to an altogether different test."

If piecemeal rezonings are deemed quasi-judicial or administrative acts, the question then arises: what standards govern these acts? The Oregon court found the governing standard in the community's comprehensive plan. It thereby elevated comprehensive plans to a much higher status than they usually are accorded. Critics of the Oregon approach focus primarily upon its reliance upon the comprehensive plan as the standard, which they believe deprives the regulatory process of needed flexibility. These critics maintain an ad hoc decision-making process is more realistic and more likely to produce sound results than a planning process, and that the risk of arbitrary action inherent in the ad hoc approach is exaggerated and outweighed by its advantages.[51]

49. The leading case is Fasano v. Board of Commissioners of Washington County, 264 Or. 574, 507 P.2d 23 (1973).

50. Id., 264 Or. at 580, 507 P.2d at 26.

51. Rose, Planning and Dealing: Piecemeal Land Controls as a Problem of Local Legitimacy, 71 Cal.L.Rev. 839 (1983).

B. SPECIAL EXCEPTIONS AND VARIANCES

Zoning ordinances typically allow some specified uses in certain zones, not as a matter of right, but only after determination by the zoning board of adjustment that they are located and designed so as to be compatible with established uses and uses allowed as of right. For example, specified special exceptions in a single-family residential zone typically include water towers, college fraternities, libraries, fire stations, etc. Permits granted typically are made subject to conditions stipulated by the board. These are called special exceptions, but "conditional use" is often used as a synonym.

Ordinance standards governing the granting of special exceptions are often vague. A model ordinance proposed by the National Institute of Municipal Law Officers authorizes special exceptions in a single-family district "if adequate yard spaces and other safeguards to preserve the character of the neighborhood are provided, and in the judgment of the Board such buildings and uses are appropriately located and designed and will meet a community need without adversely affecting the neighborhood. . . ."[52] The broad discretion conferred by this language upon boards of adjustment creates difficulties for reviewing courts. Boards are required, at least by some courts, to state specific grounds for their decisions to grant or deny a special exception and to support those grounds by findings supported by substantial evidence.[53]

The Standard State Zoning Enabling Act empowers boards of adjustment to "authorize upon appeal in specific cases such variance from the terms of the ordinance as will not be contrary to the public interest, where, owing to special conditions, a literal enforcement of the provisions of the ordinance will result in unnecessary hardship, and so that the spirit of the ordinance shall be observed and substantial justice done." Unlike special exceptions, variances are not confined to specified uses, but they are declared to be available only to avoid "unnecessary hardship," and even then only if not "contrary to public interest" or "the spirit of the Ordinance." Judicial construction of these requirements has been strict. To establish "unnecessary hardship," one must show that a reasonable return cannot be had from any use allowed in that

52. Nimlo Model Zoning Ordinance § 11–212(a)(10), reprinted in Hagman, Public Planning & Control of Urban & Land Development 503 (2d ed. 1980).

53. Minnetonka Congregation of Jehovah's Witnesses, Inc. v. Svee, 303 Minn. 79, 226 N.W.2d 306 (1975).

zone.[54] The hardship also must be unique, the appropriate remedy for a hardship shared by others being amendment of the zoning map.[55] Some courts are reluctant to allow use variances (distinguished from area variances), as use variances are similar to amendments and therefore arguably not intended to be embraced in the variance procedure, and, according to a now discredited view, would be an invalid attempt to delegate legislative powers.[56] There is much diversity in judicial requirements for variances, due in part to departures in some states from the Standard State Zoning Enabling Act. Thus, in some states, the enabling act refers to "practical difficulties" either as an alternate to, or substitute for, "unnecessary hardship." A prominent treatise generalizes: "Here far more than elsewhere in America planning law, muddle reigns supreme." [57]

Despite the demanding stated requirements for obtaining variances, they are frequently granted—often, it has been shown, without insistence by boards upon compliance with the stated requirements [58] This situation is attributed to many factors, especially to the mismatch of zoning concepts and development realities.

Decisions by zoning boards of adjustment, often characterized as quasi-judicial, are generally subject to the same procedural requirements and judicial review as are other administrative agencies.[59] They traditionally are not accorded the presumption of validity enjoyed by legislation. However, the United States Court of Appeals for the Fifth Circuit takes the position that zoning variance decisions by boards of adjustment are properly characterized as legislative for the purpose of reviewing a claim that such a decision deprives one of property without substantive due process of law.[60] In other words, the granting or denying of variances will be given the presumption of validity accorded legislation and upheld if there is any possible rational basis, whatever the actual basis may have been. The court said: "That a state may choose to make a legislative decision by a process that

54. Otto v. Steinhilber, 282 N.Y. 71, 24 N.E.2d 851, 853 (1939).

55. Id.

56. Josephson v. Autrey, 96 So.2d 784 (Fla.1957); Lee v. Board of Adjustment, 226 N.C. 107, 37 S.E.2d 128 (1946). But compare Matthew v. Smith, 707 S.W.2d 411, 414 (Mo.1986) (en banc), recognizing a use variance, despite earlier Missouri cases viewed as establishing that use variances could not be obtained in that state.

57. Williams, 5 American Planning Law § 129.01 (1985).

58. Dukeminier & Stapleton, The Zoning Board of Adjustment: A Case Study in Misrule, 50 Ky.L.J. 273 (1962).

59. Topanaga Association for a Scenic Community v. County of Los Angeles, 11 Cal.3d 506, 522 P.2d 12, 113 Cal. Rptr. 836 (1974).

60. Shelton v. City of College Station, 780 F.2d 475 (5th Cir.1986).

resembles adjudication is not our immediate concern." [61]   The Fifth Circuit position that variances (and presumably special exceptions as well) are legislative contrasts sharply with the Oregon position at the opposite end of the spectrum that amendments are quasi-judicial.   The Fifth Circuit position perhaps can be explained as a manifestation of reluctance by a federal court to become involved in zoning controversies.[62]

C. INNOVATIVE FLEXIBILITY DEVICES

Piecemeal zoning map ordinance amendments and board of adjustment special exceptions and variances, though much used and abused, have not met the demands for flexibility in addressing concrete plans of developers.   Local governments have resorted to a variety of other measures as well.   One difficulty often encountered with these is lack of clear authorization in enabling acts. Another difficulty is the same as that encountered by the traditional flexibility devices: the risk of arbitrary action inherent in focussing upon particular development proposals rather than upon comprehensive planning.   The more commonly used flexibility devices will be discussed briefly.

Some local governmental legislative bodies have undertaken to make special exceptions (with or without conditions) instead of, or in addition to, delegating that function to the board of adjustment.   Unlike special exceptions by boards of adjustment, special exceptions by local governing bodies are not subject to standards or to procedural requirements for administrative agencies.   They are thus more vulnerable to abuse.   They have been judicially disapproved in Iowa,[63] but approved in Illinois.[64]

"Contract zoning" refers to piecemeal rezoning accompanied by restrictive covenants on the rezoned land.   Suppose that an owner of a mansion on a large lot in a residential zone seeks rezoning of the lot to a commercial zone in order to convert the

61. Id. at 481.   Four judges supported Judge Rubin's dissenting opinion, which declared: "There is no basis for the majority's claim that we should abdicate review of the quasi-judicial or administrative actions of a zoning board of adjustment by ignoring the record and cloaking its actions with a presumption of validity that is virtually irrefutable."   Id. at 490.

62. Another possible explanation is that the Fifth Circuit misunderstood

the function of the board of adjustment, which the court described as "deciding the best course for the community" rather than "adjudicating the rights of contending petitioners."   Id. at 480.

63. Depue v. City of Clinton, 160 N.W.2d 860 (Iowa 1968).

64. Kotrich v. County of Du Page, 19 Ill.2d 181, 166 N.E.2d 601 (1960).

mansion to a restaurant. Neighbors have been assured that the restaurant will be managed in a manner that will not affect them adversely, but they fear that the owner or a successor in ownership may change the use, possibly to some other use allowed in a commercial zone. The commercial zone allowing restaurant uses also allows bowling alleys, retail shops, gasoline service stations and many other uses. The owner of the mansion proposes to burden the lot with covenants running with the land that will allow no commercial use other than restaurant use, will allow no expansion of the building, will require continued maintenance of existing walls, will allow entry to the lot from only one designated street, and will allow only one small sign, which must meet detailed specifications. The neighbors are not pacified, the covenants are executed and the land is rezoned commercial. If the rezoning is conditioned upon execution of the covenants, the rezoning may be referred to as "conditional zoning."

Courts have reacted to contract (or conditional) zoning with wariness. Some courts have held it invalid,[65] but others have approved it.[66] One asserted objection to contract zoning is that it is an attempt by the local government to bargain away its legislative powers, but it is most doubtful that the local government is attempting any such thing, or could do so if it wished. Some courts, concerned that contract zoning may constitute invalid surrender of governmental power, nevertheless have manifested willingness to approve contract zoning if the agreement is between the owner seeking rezoning and owners of neighboring lots, rather than the city.[67] This approach unrealistically views the local government merely as a bystander reacting to an agreement by others.

There are some real concerns about contract zoning: it stimulates resort to piecemeal rezonings; it violates at least the spirit of the enabling act requirements that zoning regulations be uniform within districts; it may be vulnerable to favoritism; and it is enforced by private law remedies, which may not be as effective as remedies for ordinance violations. Even if valid, contract zoning probably should be eschewed by local governments in favor of other available flexibility techniques.[68]

One alternative to contract zoning is the floating zone. It is a special zone that is provided for in the zoning scheme ordinance,

65. Baylis v. City of Baltimore, 219 Md. 164, 148 A.2d 429 (1959); Allred v. City of Raleigh, 277 N.C. 530, 178 S.E.2d 432 (1971).

66. Sylvania Electric Products, Inc. v. City of Newton, 344 Mass. 428, 183 N.E.2d 118 (1962); Collard v. Incorporated Village of Flower Hill, 52 N.Y.2d 594, 439 N.Y.S.2d 326, 421 N.E.2d 818 (1981).

67. State ex rel. Zupancic v. Schimenz, 46 Wis.2d 22, 174 N.W.2d 533 (1970).

68. Mandelker, Land Use Law § 6.60 (2d ed. 1988).

but not applied to any land by the zoning map ordinance until requested by a landowner and approved by the local governing body. For example, one local government authorized a floating industrial park zone with detailed requirements for protection of neighboring lands, such as a minimum size of 25 acres, a single architectural scheme with appropriate common landscaping, off-street parking, location of all structures at least 200 feet from any street or property line, and restriction of buildings to 10% of each site. Any landowner anywhere in the community might apply to have this floating zone come to rest upon land meeting the ordinance requirements for the zone. Upon receiving such an application, the local governing body had discretion to anchor this zone as requested, possibly subject to additional conditions. The Supreme Court of Pennsylvania invalidated this floating zone ordinance on the ground that its reliance upon individual initiative was "the antithesis of zoning 'in accordance with a comprehensive plan,' " as required by the enabling act.[69] Most courts have upheld carefully drafted floating zone ordinances.[70]

Subsequently, the Supreme Court of Pennsylvania was much more tolerant of another flexibility device—the planned unit development (PUD), which the court upheld.[71] The borough of New Hope, without explicit enabling act authority, created a new type of zone, the PUD district, and applied this classification in re-mapping a large tract. The owner of land in a PUD zone was permitted by the ordinance to mix several types of land uses on lots of varied sizes and shapes, free from traditional requirements of yards and set-backs of buildings from streets and lot boundaries, so long as the developer's plan for the entire tract satisfied general requirements and was approved by the planning commission. A long list of uses allowed in a PUD included apartments as well as single-family residences, professional offices, theatres (but not a drive-in), hotels and motels, a municipal building, a school, churches, art galleries, restaurants and specified recreational facilities including golf courses. According to the court, the latter facilities were subject to a performance standard; they must "not produce noise, glare, odor, air pollution, etc. detrimental to existing or prospective adjacent structures." Overall density requirements were summarized by the court: "The PUD district may have a maximum of 80% of the land devoted to residential uses, a maximum of 20% for the permitted commercial uses and enclosed recreational facilities, and must have a minimum of 20% for open

69. Eves v. Zoning Board of Adjustment of Lower Gwynedd Township, 401 Pa. 211, 164 A.2d 7 (1960).

70. Huff v. Board of Zoning Appeals of Baltimore County, 214 Md. 48, 133 A.2d 83 (1957); Rodgers v. Village of Tarrytown, 302 N.Y. 115, 96 N.E.2d 731 (1951).

71. Cheney v. Village 2 at New Hope, Inc., 429 Pa. 626, 241 A.2d 81 (1968).

spaces. The residential density shall not exceed 10 units per acre, nor shall any such unit contain more than two bedrooms. All structures within the district must not exceed maximum height standards set out in the ordinance. Finally, although there are no traditional 'set back' and 'side yard' requirements, ordinance 160 does require that there be 24 feet between structures, and that no townhouse structure contain more than 12 dwelling units."

This decision is not easily reconciled with the court's decision in Eves. One might conclude that the court's attitude toward flexible zoning had changed. The court said:

"One of the most attractive features of Planned Unit Development is its flexibility; the chance for the builder and the municipality to sit down together and tailor a development to meet the specific needs of the community and the requirements of the land on which it is to be built. But all this would be lost if the Legislature let the planning cement set before any developer could happen upon the scene to scratch his own initials in the cement."

Other courts and legislatures in general have reacted favorably to the PUD, the details of which have departed from the New Hope version in many respects.[72] The PUD ordinance must be coordinated with the subdivision ordinance. The core feature of the PUD—site plan review—has not been confined to PUD's and subdivision plats, but has been applied also to shopping centers and other development proposals.[73] The standards governing site plan reviews increasingly tend to be performance standards.[74] When such standards are stated broadly, they increase the range of discretion of the reviewing body.

Euclidean zoning, i.e., the pre-set segregation of types of land use and structures into districts, has largely been replaced in fact, if not in form, by regulatory approaches that ignore district lines and focus upon specific development proposals. This trend toward ad hoc regulation tends to weaken the influence of comprehensive plans. Once referred to as "land use planning," this field of law is now more often referred to as "land use control." As land use regulation more and more resembles adjudication, the case for subjecting such regulation to procedural due process standards for adjudication grows stronger. Courts and legislatures are still engaged in addressing the difficult challenge posed by these forces. Possibly they will give us a new system of land use control that makes a clean break from tradition. Or, more likely, the process of gradualism will continue to evolve. Whichever direction is

72. Mandelker, Land Use Law §§ 9.20–9.26 (1988).

73. Ellickson & Tarlock, Land–Use Controls 268 (1981).

74. Experiences of a few cities with performance standards are discussed briefly in Porter, Flexible Zoning: How It Works, Urban Land 6 (April 1988).

taken, the major challenge will be to devise processes to assure (1) fair treatment of developers and their neighbors and (2) protection of public interests in community development.

SECTION 3. REGULATORY TAKINGS

Early challenges to the constitutionality of zoning were allegations of denial of substantive due process and equal protection of the laws. For fifty years, such challenges have had little likelihood of success in federal courts and most state courts. Absence of any rational basis for legislation must usually be established in order to have it invalidated on either of these grounds. A regulation is not regarded as unreasonable or arbitrary merely because it destroys much of the value of regulated land. Today, however, when landowners feel that regulations unreasonably burden their lands, they are more likely to rely upon the claim that such regulations violate the Fifth Amendment provision that "private property [shall not] be taken for public use, without just compensation." This has been construed as applicable not only to condemnation proceedings and physical appropriations, but also to regulation of property. The soundness of this extension has been debated,[75] but the extension is firmly entrenched.

Since all property is subject to proper exercises of the police power, even though property values are diminished, it is exceedingly difficult to determine the point where the police power ends and the obligation to compensate begins. The magnitude of diminution of the value of the land caused by the regulation is not the sole consideration. The nature and importance of the public interests served by the regulation also are material. The more vital the public interest at stake, the more likely the regulation will be upheld. The "question necessarily requires a weighing of private and public interests."[76]

Courts and commentators[77] agree that the dividing line between valid exercises of the police power and invalid regulatory

---

75. Bosselman, Callies & Banta, The Taking Issue (1973). See also Fred F. French Inv. Co. v. City of New York, 39 N.Y.2d 587, 385 N.Y.S.2d 5, 350 N.E.2d 381 (1976).

76. Penn Central Transportation Co. v. New York City, 438 U.S. 104, 124, 98 S.Ct. 2646, 57 L.Ed.2d 631 (1978).

77. A few of the many references: Mandelker, Land Use Law 6 §§ 2.01–

2.34 (2d ed. 1988); Johnson, Compensation for Invalid Land–Use Regulations, 15 Ga.L.Rev. 559 (1981); Michelman, Property, Utility, and Fairness: Comments on the Ethical Foundations of "Just Compensation" Law, 80 Harv.L. Rev. 1165 (1967); Sax, Takings and the Police Power, 74 Yale L.J. 36 (1964); Sax, Takings, Private Property and Public Rights, 81 Yale L.J. 149 (1971).

takings is unclear, despite their strenuous efforts to establish that line. Justice Brennan, speaking for the court in a 1978 case, acknowledged that "this Court, quite simply, has been unable to develop any 'set formula' for determining when 'justice and fairness' require that economic injuries caused by public action be compensated by the government, rather than remain disproportionately concentrated on a few persons." [78]

Three decisions by the United States Supreme Court in 1987 clarified some, but by no means all, aspects of taking law. This discussion will focus upon those cases.

The facts of Keystone Bituminous Coal Association v. DeBenedictis [79] are remarkably similar to those of the case in which the court, 65 years earlier, first applied the taking clause to a land use regulation, namely, Pennsylvania Coal Co. v. Mahon. [80] Both cases involved Pennsylvania statutes (but not the same statutes) forbidding the mining of coal that might cause subsidence of the overlying land. The statute in Mahon was struck down; that in Keystone was upheld. Both decisions were by divided courts. Holmes wrote for the court in Mahon; Brandeis submitted a dissenting opinion. Keystone was a 5–4 decision, Brennan speaking for the court and Rehnquist for the dissenters. Brennan found significant differences in the relevant factors in the two cases—differences said by Rehnquist to "verge on the trivial."

Whether these differences were indeed trivial or not, it is clear that the differences in the taking jurisprudence of the Brennan and Rehnquist opinions are significant. Brennan stressed that the statute in Keystone was enacted "to protect the public interest in health, the environment, and the fiscal integrity of the area." To Rehnquist, such a broad concept of the public interest is irrelevant to the taking issue. According to him, the public interest that is relevant is limited to the "nuisance exception," i.e., "where the government exercises its unquestioned authority to prevent a property owner from using his property to injure others without having to compensate the value of the forbidden use."

The majority and dissenting opinions also disagree as to the manner in which "property" is defined in applying the taking clause. Rehnquist found that the statute had totally destroyed the property of the mining companies in the coal which they were forbidden to mine and also had totally destroyed their estate in

78. Penn Central Transportation Co. v. New York City, 438 U.S. 104, 124, 98 S.Ct. 2646, 2659, 57 L.Ed.2d 631 (1978).

79. 480 U.S. 470, 107 S.Ct. 1232, 94 L.Ed.2d 472 (1987).

80. 260 U.S. 393, 43 S.Ct. 158, 67 L.Ed. 322 (1922).

land recognized by Pennsylvania law, namely, the "support estate," which entitles its owners to mine coal without liability for subsidence. Brennan perceived only a minimal effect of the statute on the property of the mining companies, which were required to leave less than 2% of their coal in place and had not shown that any of their mines had been rendered unprofitable. Brennan also rejected as unrealistic the view that the "support estate" is a "distinct segment of property for 'takings'" purposes. To him, it is merely "a part of the entire bundle of rights possessed by" the coal companies.

The outcome of most taking cases will be determined by whether the broad or the narrow views of "public interest" and "property" are adopted. Keystone adopts the broad view, but by the narrowest margin possible.

In Nollan v. California Coastal Commission,[81] the United States Supreme Court held (5–4) that a condition attached to a building permit for a residence on coastal land, requiring the owner to grant an easement allowing the public to pass along the beach, was a taking. The court, speaking through Justice Scalia, did not disapprove the common practice of requiring dedication of land or money as a condition for obtaining subdivision approval or other development permissions. The court acknowledged that, while government cannot demand transfer of private property to the public without compensation, it can withhold development permission in appropriate instances on condition that such transfer occurs. The court reasoned that if a permit can be denied outright, as it can if it is within the police power, it follows that dedication of property could be required as a condition for granting the permit so long as the condition "serves the same government purpose." The court accepted for purposes of discussion the contention that a sufficient nexus would have been established in this case if the easement had eased some public burden or need created by or contributed to by the proposed residence, but found no such relationship.

Justice Brennan, dissenting, viewed the facts as establishing a nexus satisfying both the traditional standard and the Court's "cramped" standard for judicial review of exercises of the police power. The replacement of a small dwelling with a much larger one "would both diminish visual access to the beach and move private development closer to the public tidelands," thereby threatening public access to the shore, he said. While the easement demanded by the commission would not affect visual access to the beach, it tends to offset the proposed building's impairment

81.   483 U.S. 825, 107 S.Ct. 3141, 97 L.Ed.2d 677 (1987).

of visual access by providing other access, he reasoned. This, said Brennan, was a rational response to the problem and entitled to judicial deference.

The separate dissenting opinions of Justices Brennan and Blackmun both stressed that the economic effect of the exacted easement on the landowner was minimal or non-existent. Scalia deemed this irrelevant in an instance, such as this, where the governmental action results in a permanent physical occupation of any part of the land by the government or others. As recently as 1982, the court held that a regulation of that type constituted a taking, regardless of its economic impact or the nature of public interests involved.[82] This was based on the conceptual rationale that a permanent physical occupation of any part of one's land, no matter how small, constitutes total destruction of an "essential" stick in the bundle of rights in the fee simple, namely, the right to exclude others. This is a departure from the usual approach of considering the economic impact of the regulation upon the total property interest rather than some segment of it. Brennan and Blackmun appear to be unconvinced that this departure is justified.[83]

Several state court cases have considered the validity of development exactions of various sorts. The most common and traditional exactions are dedication of streets and utility easements within a proposed subdivision as a condition for approval of the plat. This requirement is not likely to be challenged, as the subdivider is benefited by assumption by the local government of responsibility for maintenance of streets and easements. There also is no serious doubt about the validity of a requirement that the subdivider provide improvements that serve only the subdivision, such as paving of internal streets and installation of on-site utility facilities. Requiring the subdivider to dedicate a portion of land within the subdivision for a public park or school site, or alternatively pay a sum of money for development of a public park or school site elsewhere, has received mixed reviews by the courts. One court, invalidating such an exaction, declared that a developer can be required to assume only those costs that are "specifically and uniquely attributable to his activity and which would otherwise be cast upon the public." [84] Most, courts, however, approve such exactions if the subdivision would merely contribute to municipal growth, thereby generating needs for parks or school

82. Loretto v. Teleprompter Manhattan CATV Corp., 458 U.S. 419, 102 S.Ct. 3164, 73 L.Ed.2d 868 (1982).

83. The departure is criticized in Johnson, Compensation for Invalid Land–Use Regulations, 15 Ga.L.Rev. 559, 566–572 (1981).

84. Pioneer Trust and Savings Bank v. Village of Mount Prospect, 22 Ill.2d 375, 176 N.E.2d 799 (1961). But cf. Krughoff v. City of Naperville, 68 Ill.2d 352, 12 Ill.Dec. 185, 369 N.E.2d 892 (1977).

sites.[85] One court has also required assurance that money paid in lieu of dedication be earmarked for the benefit of the subdivision.[86]

In addition to mandated dedication of land or payment of in-lieu fees, some local governments have imposed "impact fees" for connections with utility systems or for building permits, to defray part of the cost of community facilities such as water plants.[87] Residential developers also have been required in some states and localities to set aside a portion of the project for housing affordable by persons with low or moderate incomes or make an in-lieu donation. These are referred to as "inclusionary zoning." One state court held such a program constitutes a taking,[88] but the highest court of New Jersey not only views such programs as lawful, but has ordered local governments under certain circumstances to adopt them.[89] Developers of offices have been required in some localities to pay "linkage fees" into a fund to be used to provide affordable housing, to balance displacement of such housing by the office project or creation by it of additional need for such housing.[90]

In its third "blockbuster" land-use decision in 1987, First English Evangelical Lutheran Church of Glendale v. County of Los Angeles,[91] the United States Supreme Court resolved the much debated question whether the taking clause mandates compensation for regulatory takings. It decided that when a court holds that a regulation is invalid because it denies a landowner all use of the land, the landowner is entitled to compensation for the period during which the land was burdened by the regulation. Chief Justice Rehnquist's opinion for the court equated a temporary regulatory taking with condemnation of leaseholds, for which compensation clearly is due. Justice Stevens, dissenting, argued that "regulatory takings and physical takings are very different in this, as well as other, respects." Even the slightest physical occupation constitutes a taking, but regulation is a taking only if it "goes too far." The economic impact upon land use of pending litigation culminating in a judicial decision that the regulation

85. E.g., Jordan v. Village of Menomonee Falls, 28 Wis.2d 608, 137 N.W.2d 442 (1965).

86. City of College Station v. Turtle Rock Corp., 680 S.W.2d 802 (Tex.1984).

87. E.g., Contractors & Bldrs. Ass'n of Pinellas County v. City of Dunedin, 329 So.2d 314 (Fla.1976).

88. Board of Supervisors of Fairfax County v. Degroff Enterprises, Inc., 214 Va. 235, 198 S.E.2d 600 (1973).

89. Southern Burlington County NAACP v. Township of Mount Laurel, 92 N.J. 158, 456 A.2d 390 (1983).

90. E.g., San Telmo Assoc. v. City of Seattle, 108 Wash.2d 20, 735 P.2d 673 (1987). See generally, Symposium on Exactions: A Controversial New Source for Municipal Funds, 50 Law & Contemp.Prob. 1 (1987); Bray, Caudill & Owen, New Wave Land Use Regulation: The Impact of Impact Fees on Texas Lenders, 19 St. Mary's L.J. 319 (1987).

91. 482 U.S. 304, 107 S.Ct. 2378, 96 L.Ed.2d 250 (1987).

was invalid as a taking is likely to be relatively small in comparison with the total value of the land. Rehnquist did not address that cogent argument, but did acknowledge that "normal delays in obtaining building permits, changes in zoning ordinances, variances and the like" would not constitute takings. Possibly, but not likely, compensation for regulatory takings is due only where the regulation has denied "all use" of the land. The procedural posture of First English when it reached the Supreme Court enabled the court to assume that the regulation there had that effect. If First English is so limited, in future cases when a regulation that does not deny all use of the land is held invalid as a taking, the court presumably would engage in balancing before deciding that a temporary taking has occurred.

Stevens also expressed concern that fear of liability, coupled with the uncertain state of taking law, would deter local governments from full exercise of their lawful powers. Rehnquist's short response was that "such consequences necessarily flow from any decision upholding a claim of constitutional right."

SECTION 4. EXCLUSION OF PEOPLE

Zoning segregates types of land uses and types of buildings and also sometimes excludes certain uses and buildings entirely from the community. Express segregation or exclusion of classes of people rarely occurs, but a consequence of zoning and other land use controls may be segregation or exclusion of people. This consequence is due primarily to failure to allow for housing that is affordable by persons having low or moderate incomes.

A. RACIAL EXCLUSION

Express racial segregation or exclusion is clearly invalid as a violation of the Fourteenth Amendment,[92] and also of the Fair Housing Act.[93] If racially neutral regulations do not allow sufficient affordable housing, and this has a disparate effect upon a racial minority, such regulations violate the Fourteenth Amendment only if racial discrimination was a motivation for their

92. Buchanan v. Warley, 245 U.S. 60, 38 S.Ct. 16, 62 L.Ed. 149 (1917).

93. Title VIII of the Civil Rights Act of 1968, 42 U.S.C. §§ 3601–3631 (1982 & Supp. III 1985).

existence, according to the latest decision by the United States Supreme Court on the subject.[94]

That court has not yet determined whether proof of discriminatory intent is essential to establishing violation of the Fair Housing Act. However, the Second Circuit of the United States Court of Appeals, in a case involving the Town of Huntington, New York, held that such proof is not required by that act,[95] and the Supreme Court affirmed its judgment per curiam.[96] Other circuits also have rejected the intent test.[97] The Second Circuit in the Huntington case stated that when land use controls of a local government are shown to have a disparate effect upon a racial minority, there is a *prima facie* violation of the act. The burden is then upon the local government to show that its actions "furthered, in theory and in practice, a legitimate, bona fide governmental interest and that no alternative would serve that interest with less discriminatory effect."

Applying these standards to Huntington's zoning, the Second Circuit concluded that the act had been violated. The town's zoning ordinance confined multifamily housing projects to a designated urban renewal area, where 52% of the residents were minority and where only one vacant land parcel zoned for multifamily housing existed. A sponsor of an integrated housing project for low-income families was denied rezoning to allow such housing in a residential neighborhood where 98% of the residents were white. Those and other facts were found to establish *prima facie* discriminatory impact, which was not rebutted by the town's assertion that its restriction of multifamily housing to an urban renewal area was for the purpose of encouraging restoration of that area. That purpose, the court observed, could be achieved as effectively by the less discriminatory means of tax incentives or abatements.

The *per curiam* opinion by the Supreme Court, reviewing the ordinance but not the refusal to rezone, declined to pass upon the appropriateness of the Second Circuit's disparate effect test, as the town had conceded that was the proper test for its zoning ordinance (but not for its refusal to rezone, which the town maintained should be judged by the discriminatory intent test). Assuming applicability of the disparate effect test, the Supreme

---

94. Village of Arlington Heights v. Metropolitan Housing Development Corp., 429 U.S. 252, 97 S.Ct. 555, 50 L.Ed.2d 450 (1977).

95. Huntington Branch, NAACP v. Town of Huntington, 844 F.2d 926 (2d Cir.1988).

96. 57 U.S.L.W. 3331 (Nov. 8, 1988).

97. Metropolitan Housing Development Corp. v. Village of Arlington Heights, 558 F.2d 1283 (7th Cir.1977), cert. denied, 434 U.S. 1025, 98 S.Ct. 752, 54 L.Ed.2d 772 (1978); United States v. City of Black Jack, 508 F.2d 1179 (8th Cir.1974), cert. denied, 422 U.S. 1042, 95 S.Ct. 2656, 45 L.Ed.2d 694 (1975).

Court stated that it was "satisfied on this record that disparate impact was shown, and that the sole justification proffered to rebut the *prima facie* case was inadequate." The Supreme Court thus remains uncommitted as to whether disparate impact or discriminatory intent is the proper test, but the Huntington case may generate anticipation that the Supreme Court will choose the disparate impact standard.

Which standard is applicable is a moot issue for litigants who cannot establish standing. The United States Supreme Court has adhered to standing requirements that are very difficult to meet.[98] In the Huntington dispute, that issue had been fought out at an earlier stage of the litigation.[99]

B. NON–RACIAL EXCLUSION

Equal protection and substantive due process attacks upon exclusionary zoning on non-racial grounds are subjected to more lenient judicial review. Such zoning will pass muster if it bears a rational relationship to a lawful objective, regardless of the importance of that goal or the availability of alternatives. Stricter judicial scrutiny would be called for in reviewing zoning impairing a fundamental constitutional right, but a majority of the United States Supreme Court has not yet recognized any such right in a non-racial land use regulation case.

Exclusion of apartments from duplex zoning districts was upheld in Euclid v. Ambler.[1] Much later, in Village of Belle Terre v. Boraas, the United States Supreme Court upheld a very narrow definition of "family" in a zoning ordinance restricting an entire small village to one-family dwellings.[2] This ordinance excluded from occupancy of any residence in the village three or more persons who were not related to each other by blood, adoption or marriage. It was violated in this case by occupancy of a residence by six college students. The court rejected an argument that the ordinance infringed a right to travel, as it was not "aimed at transients." Nor could the majority find that any fundamental constitutional right was impaired. In Justice Douglas' words, a "quiet place where yards are wide, people are few, and motor

98. Warth v. Seldin, 422 U.S. 490, 95 S.Ct. 2197, 45 L.Ed.2d 343 (1975).

99. Huntington Branch NAACP v. Town of Huntington, 689 F.2d 391 (2d Cir.1982), cert denied, 460 U.S. 1069, 103 S.Ct. 1523, 75 L.Ed.2d 947 (1983).

1. 272 U.S. 365, 47 S.Ct. 114, 71 L.Ed. 303 (1926).

2. 416 U.S. 1, 94 S.Ct. 1536, 39 L.Ed. 2d 797 (1974).

vehicles are restricted are legitimate guidelines in a land-use project addressed to family needs." Justice Marshall's dissenting opinion, not joined in by any other member of the court, expressed the view that the ordinance "unnecessarily burdens appellees' First Amendment freedom of association and their constitutionally guaranteed right to privacy." Three years later, in Moore v. City of East Cleveland,[3] the court encountered a definition of family it could not tolerate. It invalidated an ordinance defining "family" so as to make it a criminal offense for a woman to allow a 10–year–old grandson to live with her, but a majority of the court could not agree on a rationale.

In City of Cleburne v. Cleburne Living Center,[4] the United States Supreme Court held that denial of a special use permit, for operation of a group home for the mentally retarded in an apartment zoning district, was an unconstitutional denial of equal protection of the laws. The court could find no rational basis for distinguishing such group homes from apartments, sorority and fraternity houses, hospitals and other uses allowed in the apartment zone without the necessity of obtaining a special permit. The court added: "The short of it is that requiring the permit in this case appears to us to rest on an irrational prejudice against the mentally retarded." The court declined to arrive at its decision by viewing the mentally retarded as a quasi-suspect class, calling for a more exacting standard of judicial review than is normally accorded economic and social legislation, but not as exacting as the strict scrutiny of racial discrimination. The Court of Appeals had relied on such a middle-tier standard of review in invalidating Cleburne's ordinance. Justices Marshall, Brennan and Blackmun, declaring that Cleburne's ordinance "surely would be valid under the traditional rational-basis test," viewed the court's opinion as based upon an unarticulated stricter standard, which they advocated should be made explicit. The effect of this decision upon future equal protection challenges is unclear.

C. EXCLUSION IN THE STATE COURTS

Several state courts have manifested greater hostility toward exclusionary controls that has the United States Supreme Court. They have applied relaxed standing requirements and more demanding standards of judicial review. They have relied upon

3. 431 U.S. 494, 97 S.Ct. 1932, 52 L.Ed.2d 531 (1977).

4. 473 U.S. 432, 105 S.Ct. 3249, 87 L.Ed.2d 313 (1985).

state constitutional provisions similar to the Fourteenth Amendment.

There are decisions invalidating exclusion of apartments from the municipality,[5] segregation of mobile homes [6] and group homes,[7] and requirements that lots [8] and houses [9] be large. Of course, there also are contrary decisions. Following a much criticized 1952 New Jersey decision upholding a minimum house size ordinance,[10] several state courts exhibited increasing concern about the exclusionary effects of some types of zoning and other controls. Ironically, by far the most aggressive court in addressing this concern is the Supreme Court of New Jersey. Other courts in the vanguard of the assault upon exclusionary controls are California, Michigan, New York and Pennsylvania.[11]

The New Jersey Supreme Court launched a strong and comprehensive attack in its 1975 decision in Southern Burlington NAACP v. Township of Mount Laurel.[12] This suit, in the words of Justice Hall for the court, was a challenge to the entire "system of land use regulation" in the Township of Mount Laurel, "on the ground that low and moderate income families are thereby unlawfully excluded from the municipality." The court concluded that this attack was well-founded and directed Mount Laurel to correct deficiencies in its zoning ordinance noted by the court. Provisions singled out for criticism were: exclusion of all types of housing other than single-family residences (except for expensive PUD housing); excessive requirements for lot size, lot frontage and building size; and excessive zoning for industrial uses. The fact that Mount Laurel was a suburb in a region experiencing rapid growth exacerbated the harmful effects of exclusion. Mount Laurel was not assuming its "fair share" of the regional burden of accommodating the housing needs of the non-affluent. This obligation, grounded in state constitutional guarantees of due process and equal protection, is not merely negative, but requires affirmative action to make "proper provision for adequate housing" for

5. Appeal of Girsh, 437 Pa. 237, 263 A.2d 395 (1970).

6. Robinson Township v. Knoll, 410 Mich. 293, 302 N.W.2d 146 (1981).

7. Children's Home of Easton v. City of Easton, 53 Pa.Cmwlth. 216, 417 A.2d 830 (1980).

8. Appeal of Kit–Mar Builders, Inc., 439 Pa. 466, 268 A.2d 765 (1970).

9. Home Builders League of South Jersey, Inc. v. Township of Berlin, 81 N.J. 127, 405 A.2d 381 (1979).

10. Lionshead Lake, Inc. v. Wayne Township, 10 N.J. 165, 89 A.2d 693

(1952). Discussed in Haar, Zoning for Minimum Standards: the Wayne Township Case, 66 Harv.L.Rev. 1051 (1953); Nolan and Horack, How Small a House—Zoning for Minimum Space Requirements, 67 Harv.L.Rev. 967 (1954); Haar, Wayne Township: Zoning for Whom?—in Brief Reply, 67 Har.L.Rev. 968 (1954).

11. The relevant decisions in those states are reviewed concisely in Mandelker, Land Use Law 297–304 (2d ed. 1988).

12. 67 N.J. 151, 336 A.2d 713 (1975).

"all categories of people," housing being a "basic" human need. The court also sent a message to other "developing" municipalities. Most of them, said the court, also had failed to meet such regional obligations.

Justice Hall observed that there "cannot be the slightest doubt that the reason for this course of conduct has been to keep down local taxes on property (Mount Laurel is not a high tax municipality) and that the policy was carried out without regard for non-fiscal considerations with respect to people, either within or without its boundaries. . . . This policy of land use regulation for a fiscal end derives from New Jersey's tax structure, which has imposed on local real estate most of the cost of municipal and county government and of the primary and secondary education of the municipality's children. The latter expense is much the largest, so, basically, the fewer the school children, the lower the tax rate. Sizeable industrial and commercial ratables are eagerly sought and homes and the lots on which they are situate[d] are required to be large enough, through minimum lot sizes and minimum floor areas, to have substantial value in order to produce greater tax revenues to meet school costs. Large families who cannot afford to buy large houses and must live in cheaper rental accommodations are definitely not wanted, so we find drastic bedroom restrictions for, or complete prohibition of, multi-family or other feasible housing for those of lesser income." [13]

Eight years later, Mount Laurel's land use regulatory program, as altered in response to the remand, and programs of other municipalities challenged as exclusionary, came before the New Jersey Supreme Court.[14] It concluded that Mount Laurel "remains afflicted with a blatantly exclusionary ordinance" and that "there is widespread non-compliance with the constitutional mandate of our original opinion in this case." In this opinion, the court undertook to "put some steel" into its fair share doctrine.

It sought to clarify uncertainty as to which municipalities were subject to the doctrine by declaring that this class included every municipality, any portion of which is designated as a "growth area" by the State Development Guide Plan. The court announced that future "fair share" cases would be assigned to a few judges expected to develop expertise and consistency in such litigation. Trial courts were directed to retain jurisdiction following judgments adverse to the municipality, "order an immediate revision of the ordinance (including, if necessary, supervision of

13. Id., 336 A.2d at 723.

14. Southern Burlington County NAACP v. Township of Mount Laurel,

92 N.J. 158, 456 A.2d 390 (1983) (Mount Laurel II).

the revision through a court appointed master), and require the use of effective affirmative planning and zoning devices." The court authorized the "builder's remedy," entitling a developer-plaintiff to a court order allowing the project to be built, at least where the project includes a substantial amount of affordable housing, is well-designed (with due regard for environmental interests), and the developer has made a good faith effort to obtain relief without litigation. The "fair share" obligation, requires much more than a good faith attempt. It also requires more than "elimination of unnecessary cost-producing requirements and restrictions." Resort must be had to affirmative measures, "including lower-income density bonuses and mandatory set-asides." The local government "should cooperate with the developer's attempts to obtain federal subsidies." And mobile homes "may not be prohibited, unless there is solid proof that sound planning" so requires.

Responding to manifested concern that the Supreme Court of New Jersey had injected itself to an undesirable extent into regulation of land use, a concern expressed by the court itself, the New Jersey Legislature in 1985 enacted the Fair Housing Act, that shifted much of the supervision of "fair share" municipal obligations from the courts to a state administrative agency—the Council on Affordable Housing.[15] When the validity of this act came before the Supreme Court of New Jersey, the act was upheld and even applauded by the court.[16] Rejecting the contention that the act's mission was to "sabotage" the Mount Laurel decisions, the court expressed confidence that the newly formed council is a more appropriate instrument than the judiciary to accomplish the goals of those decisions. But the court warned that if the act "achieves nothing but delay, the judiciary will be forced to resume its appropriate role."

15. N.J.Stat.Ann. § 52:27D–301 et seq. (West 1986). See Franzese, Mt. Laurel III: The New Jersey Supreme Court's Judicious Retreat, 18 Seton Hall L.Rev. 30 (1988).

16. Hills Development Co. v. Township of Bernards, 103 N.J. 1, 510 A.2d 621 (1986).

Part Seven

CONCLUSION

The law of property is one of the most fundamental areas of jurisprudence to be found in any society. Property, as an institution, is a principal foundation of any stable civilization. Nowhere does the lawyer render greater service to society than in providing the professional skill necessary to the smooth functioning of our property system. Land reform has long been a first step in any revolution and widespread discontent with an existing property structure is a prime cause of social turmoil.

We, in the United States, are the inheritors of the most sophisticated, yet practical, system of property law developed in the world thus far. But nothing in life is static and Anglo–American law needs constant scrutiny lest its arteries harden and senility creep in. Balanced precariously on a feudal base, our land law, particularly, must slough off its archaic rules after they have served their purpose and we, as lawyers, must be alert to new social needs and aspirations. Change for the sake of change can produce chaos, but reasoned improvement of the law is more than a casual luxury, it is a prime necessity. In this sense, reform, far from being ivory tower, is of the essence of practicality.

Just as we must understand law before we can practice it successfully, so must we understand our property system before we try to reform it. Most legal principles are founded on reason, but it may be the reason of history, not the logic of the present. In property law, these reasons tend to run more deeply into the past than elsewhere and we must be careful not to disrupt a viable institution when we sever a particularly noxious root. Research and planning should precede reform so that all change is responsible change, paying respect to our great traditions of the past as we move into the future.

Property clearly has two sides—an individual side and a social side. The two are so intertwined that it is never possible to deal with one without affecting the other. Property rights, like all rights, are relative and just as the common law of nuisance once limited the fee simple owner of Blackacre in the activities on his own land, so today the law of zoning and its brothers limits the absoluteness of the fee. But this law that restricts also expands, and the right to run a filling station in a residential area, lost by

461

A, is restored to him in the right to live in a quiet suburb free from *B's* service station. Who, today, would want to live in New York, Chicago, or Los Angeles, subject only to the property law of Coke's time?

If we are Benthamites and agree that property is a creature of law,[1] then we are members of a profession which bears a heavy responsibility in maintaining the correct balance between the rights of the individual and the power of the state. What that correct balance may be will differ as our own consciences, beliefs, and motivations differ, but we must search for a consensus within the Western tradition of freedom and justice. This will require statesmen in the field of property and you must prepare to be one of them.

1. See p. 4 supra.

TABLE OF CASES

References are to Pages.

INDEX

†